Sunlight and Storm

By Alexander B. Adams

THOREAU'S GUIDE TO CAPE COD

(EDITOR)

FIRST WORLD CONFERENCE ON NATIONAL PARKS

(EDITOR)

JOHN JAMES AUDUBON: A BIOGRAPHY

ETERNAL QUEST: THE STORY OF THE GREAT NATURALISTS

ELEVENTH HOUR: A HARD LOOK AT CONSERVATION

GERONIMO: A BIOGRAPHY

SITTING BULL: AN EPIC OF THE PLAINS

*An account of the American Great Plains which comprise
portions of the States of Colorado, Kansas, Montana,
Nebraska, New Mexico, North Dakota, Oklahoma, South
Dakota, Texas, and Wyoming, from the appearance of the
first Europeans to the opening of the twentieth century.*

G. P. Putnam's Sons, New York

Sunlight and Storm

The Great American Plains

by Alexander B. Adams

SBN: 399-11563-3

Library of Congress Catalog Card Number: 75-15116

PRINTED IN THE UNITED STATES OF AMERICA

. . . look on plains half-sunlight and half-storm . . .

—Arthur Davison Ficke, 1914

A suitable dress for prairie traveling is of great import to health and comfort. Cotton or linen fabrics do not sufficiently protect the body against the direct rays of the sun at midday, nor against rains or sudden changes of temperatures.

—Captain Randolph B. Marcy,
The Prairie Traveler: A Handbook for Overland Expeditions, 1859

As I read over my husband's [General George Armstrong Custer's] magazine articles for the first time in many years, I find scarcely a reference to the scorching sun, the stinging cold, the bleak winds. His narrative reads like the story of men who marched always in sunshine. . . .

—Elizabeth Bacon Custer,
Tenting on the Plains, 1887

Contents

Part III
1848–1892
From the Gold Rush to the End of the Frontier

To
Arthur D. and Elizabeth Dyess

As a fragile live thing does, a book needs friends when it enters the world. I hope you will be this book's friends as you have been mine.

A Chronology of Events
Relating to the Great Plains
1528-1898

The reader may find this chronology helpful as he follows the events described in this book. Selected dates in general American history are included to serve as reference points.

By 1528 Columbus had completed his voyages, and the Spanish were the dominant European power in the Caribbean. On the mainland Balboa had crossed the Isthmus of Panama and discovered the Pacific Ocean. Ponce de León had landed twice in Florida. Cortés had established Spanish rule in what later became Mexico, and the remnants of Magellan's expedition had returned from their journey around the world. Pizarro had not yet started his brutal, although brilliant, conquest of Peru and was in Spain obtaining the titles of governor and captain general of the lands he might discover and the peoples he might subjugate.

By the Treaty of Tordesillas, the line of demarcation established by Pope Alexander VI had been moved westward, so that Brazil fell within the sphere allotted to Portugal; and Amerigo Vespucci, flying the Portuguese flag, had sailed along its coast. After the account of his voyage had been published, the geographer Martin Waldseemüller suggested that the New World be called America. At first the name was applied only to South America, but by the end of the century it had come to include the entire hemisphere.

The French had not been as active in the New World as the Spanish, but Verrazano had explored the northern coastline on their behalf. Several more years were to elapse, however, before the French attempted their first settlement.

John Cabot, a wealthy Italian merchant who had moved to England, had also explored part of the coast of North America on behalf of the British. Not obtaining the ready riches he had expected, his supporters lost interest, and neither the people nor the government were yet willing to finance further expeditions.

In spite of this activity, particularly on the part of the Spanish, no European had seen the Great Plains.

Part I
1528-1803

1528:   Núñez Cabeza de Vaca, treasurer of a Spanish expedition that planned to settle in Texas, was stranded on the coast. The location was probably present-day Galveston.

1534:   Jacques Cartier entered the Gulf of the St. Lawrence River, opening the way for the French fur traders who would drastically affect the culture of the Plains Indians.

1534–1536:   Núñez Cabeza de Vaca and several of his companions left the coast and journeyed across the continent, finally reaching Culiacán, Mexico. On the way, they traveled over the Great Plains, the first white men to do so.

1539–1543:   Hernando de Soto and Luís de Moscoso de Alvarado explored the lower Mississippi and some of the lands to the west. Although they did not reach the plains, they heard about the buffaloes. After de Soto's death on the banks of the Mississippi, de Moscoso led the expedition on to the Pánuco River in Mexico.

1540–1542:   Lured by rumors of gold, Francisco Vásquez de Coronado led an expedition through parts of Texas, Oklahoma, and Kansas.

1580:   Fray Agustín Rodríguez led an expedition to the pueblos of New Mexico. During their journey they ventured onto the Great Plains.

1584:   The British made an unsuccessful attempt to establish a settlement on Roanoke Island off the coast of North Carolina.

1593:   Francisco Leyval de Bonilla and Gutiérrez de Humaña led an unauthorized expedition that reached Kansas.

1598–1608:   Juan de Oñate secured the submission of New Mexico to Spain and explored as far east as Kansas.

1605:   Samuel de Champlain founded the first permanent French colony in North America at Port Royal, now Annapolis, Nova Scotia.

1607:   The British established the first permanent British settlement at Jamestown.

1610:   On behalf of British interests, Henry Hudson sailed through Hudson Strait and explored the eastern half of Hudsons Bay, thus laying the basis for the subsequent British fur trade.

1620: The Pilgrims arrived in Massachusetts.

1658–1659: Pierre Esprit Radisson and M. C. Groseillers expanded the western range of the French fur trade, which was now Canada's most important business, by exploring the far end of Lake Superior.

1670: A royal charter was granted to the Hudson's Bay Company by the British government, thus starting competition with the French fur traders.

1682: René-Robert Cavelier de la Salle reached the mouth of the Mississippi. In the name of France, he claimed the river's valley and all the lands through which the river's tributaries flowed. This included a large part of the Great Plains.

1689: King William's War (or the War of the League of Augsburg) broke out between the French and the British.

1690: Henry Kelsey on behalf of the Hudson's Bay Company made a journey to the Canadian plains and became the first representative of Great Britain to see them.

1697: The Treaty of Ryswick ended King William's War and brought peace to North America. Conquered territories were restored to the contestants.

1702: Queen Anne's War (or the War of the Spanish Succession) broke out between France and Great Britain.

1712: The Treaty of Utrecht, ending Queen Anne's War, recognized Great Britain's claim in the Hudsons Bay area and gave it possession of Newfoundland and Acadia.

1713: Louis Juchereau de St. Denis, contrary to Spanish law, attempted to open up trade between Louisiana and the Spanish colonies, thus increasing interest in a route across the southern Great Plains.

1717: Bernard de la Harpe pushed the French advance farther west by establishing a trading post at the site of present-day Texarkana and by making a trip to encourage the Indians in Oklahoma to trade with the French.

1720: Charles Claude du Tisné on behalf of the French explored the Missouri and Osage rivers, hoping to develop trade.

Pedro de Villasur, commanding a force of Spanish soldiers, was defeated on the Platte River in present-day Nebraska by Pawnees, who were friendly to the French.

1723: Étienne Veniard de Bourgmont established a French trading post on the Missouri River.

1724: De Bourgmont established trading arrangements with various Indians, including the Kansa tribe and probably the Comanches.

1733: Georgia, the last of the original American thirteen colonies, was founded.

1738:   Pierre Gaultier de Varennes, Sieur de la Vérendrye, a French fur trader, persuaded the Assiniboins, a tribe of Plains Indians, to take him to the Mandan villages on the Missouri. There he attempted to gather information that might lead to the discovery of a river that flowed west to the Pacific.

1739:   Pierre and Paul Mallet, French Canadians, crossed the Great Plains from the Illinois country to Santa Fé. Part of their route followed the Platte River.

1740:   The Mallets returned from Santa Fé, bringing news that the Spanish were interested in trading with the French. On this trip, the party separated; the Mallets went to New Orleans, following the Canadian and Arkansas rivers to the Mississippi. (Hence the name, Canadian River.)

1741:   The governor of Louisiana sent an expedition to follow the Mallets' route to Santa Fé. Although it failed to reach the Spanish city, it added to French knowledge of the country.

1742:   La Vérendrye's two sons, Louis and François, went back to the Mandan villages. From there they crossed the Great Plains in a southwesterly direction and returned to the Missouri.

1754:   Anthony Hendry, an employee of the Hudson's Bay Company, visited the Blackfeet Indians in Montana.

   The French and Indian War began.

1763:   In the Treaty of Paris, which ended the French and Indian War, France ceded to Great Britain its claims to Canada, Acadia, Cape Breton, and its lands east of the Mississippi.

   Great Britain issued the Proclamation of 1763. This prohibited the colonists from settling in the area between the crest of the Allegheny Mountains and the Mississippi River.

   Pierre Laclède selected the site of St. Louis as the center for his contemplated Missouri fur trade. Actual settlement was begun the following year.

1768–1775:   Plans were put into effect by the British colonists for the gradual and orderly establishment of settlements west of the Appalachians, starting a movement in the direction of the Great Plains.

1775:   The Battles of Lexington and Concord took place, and the American Revolution began.

1779:   The North West Company was established. This intensified competition among the British fur traders in Canada and led to further attempts to develop trade with the Indians of the Great Plains.

   The Continental Congress adopted a resolution that the lands owned by the colonies in the west would be disposed of for the common good of the United States and that they would eventually be converted into states.

1781:   New York gave up its claims to lands in the west. This was the beginning of the public domain.

Cornwallis surrendered to Washington at Yorktown.

1783:   Great Britain recognized the independence of the United States, which received the Mississippi as its western boundary and also the right to use the river for navigation.

1785:   The Land Ordinance, drafted by Thomas Jefferson, was enacted. This ordinance established the procedures for the survey and sale of the public domain, which had been enlarged when several additional states joined New York in relinquishing their western claims. The law affected the later disposal of the Great Plains.

1786:   Pedro Vial was employed by the Spanish government to map a route across the Great Plains from San Antonio to Santa Fé.

1787:   José Mares was employed by the governor of New Mexico to find a more direct route between his capital and San Antonio.

The Constitutional Convention met at Philadelphia.

The Northwest Ordinance was enacted, opening the Old Northwest Territory to settlement. It set the pattern of establishing territories that were later to be admitted as states, a pattern that was followed in the Great Plains.

1788:   Pedro Vial was again employed by the Spanish government, this time to lay out a route between Santa Fé and Natchitoches.

Captain John Meares from Canada discovered the bay of the Columbia River, although he did not discover the river itself.

New Hampshire became the ninth state to ratify the Constitution, thus putting it into effect.

1789:   Juan Meunier discovered the Ponca Indians on the Niobrara River in Nebraska.

George Washington was inaugurated as President, and Congress convened.

1790:   Jacques d'Eglise, a trader licensed by the Spanish, visited the Mandan villages on the Missouri River.

1792:   On behalf of the British, Captain George Vancouver explored the Pacific Coast and circumnavigated Vancouver Island.

Captain Robert Gray of Boston discovered the mouth of the Columbia River. This was the basis for the United States' claim to the Oregon country.

Vial was employed once more by the Spanish government. His assignment was to lay out a route between Santa Fé and St. Louis.

1793:   Alexander Mackenzie reached the Pacific Coast, having made the overland trip across Canada.

1794:   Jay's Treaty with Great Britain settled some of the differences between that country and the United States resulting from the Treaty of 1783.

The Missouri Company was formed. The Spanish hoped this would offer more effective competition to British fur traders. Jean Baptiste Trudeau went up the Missouri River on the company's behalf.

1795:   Pinckney's Treaty with Spain set the southern boundary of the United States and gave the United States the right to navigate the full length of the Mississippi and also the right to transship goods duty free at New Orleans.

The Missouri Company replaced Trudeau with James Mackay.

1796:   John Evans, an employee of the Missouri Company, evicted the British from the Mandan villages on the Missouri River.

1797:   John Adams inaugurated President and Thomas Jefferson Vice President.

1800:   By the Treaty of San Ildefonso, Spain returned Louisiana to France, which promised not to cede it to any other country.

1801:   Thomas Jefferson inaugurated President and Aaron Burr Vice President.

Mackenzie's journals were published in Great Britain.

1802:   Spain suddenly revoked the "right of deposit" at New Orleans, threatening the further development of the western portion of the United States.

1803:   The United States purchased Louisiana from France. Napoleon's problems in Europe and the defeat of his expeditionary army in Santo Domingo, which he had intended to use as a staging area for developing a western empire, led him to make the sale. The territory sold included the major part of the Great Plains. The actual transfer of Lower Louisiana took place that year. Upper Louisiana was transferred in 1804.

Part II
1804-1848

1804:   Lewis and Clark led a government-financed expedition to find a route to the Pacific and to explore the territory added to the United States by the Louisiana Purchase. This was to be an additional basis for American claims to the Oregon Country in the later dispute with the British.

Chouteau and Lisa were two chief rivals in the St. Louis-based fur trade. Chouteau, with the backing of the government, had the advantage.

1805:   Zebulon Pike explored the source of the Mississippi.

1806:   Pike's expedition to make peace with Indians and explore the Red and Arkansas rivers did not accomplish its objectives, but it added to the knowledge of the Great Plains.

Lewis and Clark returned from their expedition.

1807: Burr's trial for treason brought an end to his and Wilkinson's power but showed the new unity of the country.

Pike returned from his expedition to the Red and Arkansas rivers.

Robert Fulton's steamboat opened the possibility of practical upstream navigation on the western waterways.

Lisa started trading at the limits of the Louisiana Purchase and established Fort Raymond near the mouth of the Bighorn. John Colter, a member of Lisa's expedition, reported the thermal activity in the Yellowstone area.

1808: Lisa formed the St. Louis Missouri Fur Company to trade up the Missouri River.

John Jacob Astor incorporated the American Fur Company, although it remained for some years a paper organization only.

1809: James Madison became President.

1810: Fur trading in the rich Three Forks of the Missouri country proved difficult because of the hostility of the Blackfeet.

Astor set up the Pacific Fur Company and sent out two expeditions to establish a base on the Pacific Coast.

1811: Astor's trading post, Astoria, was established at the mouth of the Columbia River by the arrival of the *Tonquin*. This was to be the third basis for American claims to Oregon.

The Missouri Fur Company was set up by Lisa and his partners to replace the St. Louis Missouri Fur Company.

1812: Some of Astor's partners sold Astoria to the North West Company, leaving the Canadians with no American rivals in the Pacific Northwest.

Congress declared war on England. The war slowed the development of the Great Plains.

1813: Astoria was formally captured by a British naval force, greatly complicating Astor's subsequent claims.

The Americans almost entirely withdrew from the Great Plains.

1814: Lisa formed Manuel Lisa & Company with the assets of the old Missouri Fur Company.

The Treaty of Ghent ended the War of 1812, returning both sides to prewar conditions and settling almost nothing.

1815: Astor began to move into the fur trade between the Mississippi and Missouri valleys, and Lisa also returned to his trade, although general interest in the Great Plains was still low.

1818: The boundary between the American Great Plains and Canada was established at the 49th parallel, and Oregon was to be jointly occupied by the United States and Canada for ten years.

Long and Atkinson led the Yellowstone Expedition, which reached a site upstream from Omaha, Nebraska, but no farther. Its important contribution was the use of steamboats on the Missouri.

1819: The country was shaken by the Panic of 1819.

Missouri requested admission to the Union.

1820: Long led an expedition up the Platte to the Rocky Mountains in search of the sources of the Red and Arkansas rivers.

Although the Missouri River fur traders were trying to re-establish themselves, the fur market remained depressed until fall.

Congress adopted the Missouri Compromise. Missouri was admitted as a slave state, Maine as a free state. Further slavery west of the Mississippi was prohibited north of 36° 30′.

Pilcher succeeded Lisa as head of the Missouri Fur Company.

1821: The Hudson's Bay Company and the North West Company merged, permitting them to concentrate their energy on the development of business on the Pacific Coast.

Some of the able members of the North West Company, including Joseph Renville and Kenneth McKenzie, joined some Americans in forming the Columbia Fur Company, officially named Tilton & Company.

Mexico, now being independent of Spain, released the American traders it had previously made prisoner.

John McKnight and Thomas James in one party and William Becknell in another made the trip from Missouri to Santa Fé to trade.

Hugh Glenn, Jacob Fowler, and other Americans went to New Mexico to trap.

Stephen Austin, pursuant to an agreement made by his father, Moses, with the Mexican government, was scouting out lands for an American colony in Texas.

1822: William Ashley and Andrew Henry formed the Rocky Mountain Fur Company. Instead of building trading posts, they initiated the rendezvous at which the traders and trappers gathered.

William Becknell again went to Santa Fé, this time taking a better route. He also used wagons. Benjamin Cooper also led an expedition to Santa Fé.

John Jacob Astor opened an office in St. Louis. Until then he had been operating on the Missouri indirectly through connections with already established firms.

1823:   *May 31:* Michael Immell and Robert Jones, who were working for the Missouri Fur Company, were killed by the Blackfeet on the Yellowstone River. Their defeat severely damaged the Missouri Fur Company.

          June 2: Ashley was attacked by the Arikaras at their villages. He suffered heavy losses and was forced to turn back.

          August 9: Colonel Henry Leavenworth launched his punitive attack on the Arikara villages.

          Thomas James and Robert and John McKnight traded with the Comanches, buying horses from them.

1824:   The Arikaras returned to the village they had left following their battle with Leavenworth.

          Senator Thomas Hart Benton studied the need for military forts on the Missouri River.

          Ashley abandoned the Missouri River as the route to the mountains and instead followed the Platte.

1825:   General Atkinson led a peace mission up the Missouri River beyond the Yellowstone. Its military escort was the largest American military force to have advanced that far.

1826:   Henry Ashley sold the Rocky Mountain Fur Company to Jedediah Smith, David E. Jackson, and William L. Sublette.

1827:   Astor's American Fur Company bought out the Columbia Fur Company. Astor established the Upper Missouri Outfit within his Western Department and placed Kenneth McKenzie in charge of it.

1828:   Andrew Jackson defeated John Quincy Adams in the presidential campaign. The West regarded this as a victory for its interests.

          Indians attacked several caravans on the Santa Fé Trail.

1829:   Brevet Major Bennet Riley was assigned to escort a caravan to Santa Fé as far as the Mexican border. Riley's use of oxen proved that these animals could be employed on the Great Plains.

1830:   Jacob Berger persuaded the Blackfeet to trade with Kenneth McKenzie at Fort Union.

1831:   Hall J. Kelley formed the "American Society for encouraging the settlement of the Oregon territory."

          The *Yellow Stone,* a steamboat built for the American Fur Company, attempted the trip to Fort Union. Although it did not reach its destination, it went farther up the Missouri than any steamboat until that time.

1832:   Nathaniel Wyeth crossed the Great Plains, hoping to found a settlement in Oregon.

The steamboat *Yellow Stone* reached Fort Union.

George Catlin, the artist, made the trip to Fort Union on the *Yellow Stone* to continue his studies of American Indians.

Captain Benjamin Bonneville entered the fur trade. He was the first person to take wagons over South Pass.

The trappers and Blackfeet fought the Battle of Pierre's Hole.

1833:   Prince Maximilian went up the Missouri River. He was accompanied by the artist Charles Bodmer. His purpose was to write a book on North America.

About this time William and Charles Bent and Ceran St. Vrain built Bent's Old Fort.

The charter of the American Fur Company expired, and Astor sold out his interest in the business.

Jason and Daniel Lee answered the call of the Methodists for the missionaries to work among the Flatheads and left New York for Independence, Missouri.

The American Fur Company bought out the operation of Sublette and Campbell on the Missouri River and agreed not to compete with them in the Rocky Mountains.

1834:   Colonel Henry Dodge led an expedition into the Southwest to hold councils with the Comanches and Wichitas. George Catlin accompanied Dodge.

Nathaniel Wyeth made the second of his two transcontinental journeys to establish a business on the West Coast. Thomas Nuttall and John K. Townsend, American scientists, accompanied Wyeth on this journey. Jason and Daniel Lee also accompanied Wyeth's expedition.

William Sublette and Robert Campbell built Fort William, one of several forts that were to stand near the mouth of the Laramie River.

1834:   After the annual rendezvous in the Green River Valley, the partners of the Rocky Mountain Fur Company decided to dissolve their firm. Milton G. Sublette, Jim Bridger, and Thomas Fitzpatrick formed a new firm, but it did not play an important role in the fur trade.

1835:   Sublette, Bridger, and Fitzpatrick sold Fort William on the Laramie River and entered the employment of the American Fur Company.

Colonel Dodge made another tour through the southern Great Plains, treating with the Indians.

Samuel Parker and Dr. Marcus Whitman went to establish a mission in Oregon. Before reaching their destination, Whitman returned to recruit additional help.

1836:   Marcus Whitman took his bride, Narcissa, to Oregon. Also making the trip were the Reverend Henry Spaulding and his wife, Eliza. These were the first two white women to cross the American Great Plains on their way west.

            Texas declared its independence.

1837:   Alfred Jacob Miller went west with William Drummond Stewart, an aristocrat from Scotland. Miller's numerous pictures supplemented those of Bodmer and Catlin.

            A smallpox epidemic broke out on the Upper Missouri. Indian deaths reached a staggering toll, and many of the tribes never recovered.

            William A. Slacum, a purser in the United States Navy, made an official study of the Oregon territory.

            Jason Lee's mission attracted new recruits, including several women who came to Oregon by sea.

1838:   Jason Lee returned east. His talks on Oregon stirred up even greater interest in the Pacific Northwest.

1839:   The Mormons moved from Missouri to Nauvoo, Illinois.

            John Charles Frémont and Joseph Nicolas Nicollet surveyed an eastern portion of the northern Great Plains.

1840:   Father De Smet went to Pierre's Hole to visit the Flatheads and Nez Percés.

            John Marsh wrote to his friends in Independence, Missouri, describing the benefits of living in California. As a result a group organized to move to the West Coast.

1841:   A group of emigrants known as the Bidwell-Bartleson party crossed the Great Plains to California and Oregon. This is generally considered the first emigrant train.

            Father De Smet returned to Oregon to establish a Catholic mission.

            In an effort to alleviate its severe financial problems, the Republic of Texas attempted to open up commerce with Santa Fé. The expedition, however, was imprisoned by the Mexicans and served only to engender further ill will between the two countries.

1842:   Another group of emigrants went to Oregon. Among them was Lansford Hastings, who later wrote *The Emigrants' Guide to Oregon and California.*

            John Charles Frémont led a surveying expedition from Missouri to South Pass. This constituted official recognition of the needs of the emigrants.

1843:   Frémont made another expedition west, covering more ground and completing his survey of the Oregon Trail as well as examining parts of Oregon, California, and other places.

            John Deere was starting to manufacture his new plow.

Cyrus McCormick sold twenty-three of his new reapers.

1844:   Frémont returned to Missouri.

The Senate refused to ratify the treaty of annexation that Tyler had negotiated with Texas.

By this time, both white men and red had noticed a definite decrease in the buffalo herds.

1845:   Frémont led an expedition to California.

Lieutenant J. W. Abert explored northeastern New Mexico and northwestern Texas.

Colonel Stephen Watts Kearny led the First Dragoons on a march to South Pass and back to Missouri.

A joint resolution of the House and Senate (thus avoiding the necessity of obtaining a two-thirds majority in the Senate) approved the annexation of Texas.

1846:   Polk ordered General Zachary Taylor to the Río Grande; the Mexicans attacked; and on May 13 Congress declared war. Kearny's Army of the West marched across the southern Great Plains on its way to New Mexico and California.

Great Britain and the United States settle the boundary of Oregon.

1847:   General Winfield Scott landed at Vera Cruz and captured Mexico City.

1848:   By the Treaty of Guadalupe Hidalgo, Mexico ceded California and New Mexico to the United States, and recognized the Río Grande as the southern border of Texas.

Part III
1848-1892

1848:   James Wilson Marshall discovered gold on the south fork of the American River while working for John Sutter. In December Polk made glowing references to the goldfields in his annual message to Congress, and the fever for gold swept the country.

The Mormons continued to emigrate to the settlement Brigham Young had established the year before at the Great Salt Lake.

Fort Kearny was built on the Platte River to help protect the Oregon-

California Trail. This was a shift from the previous policy that had depended on infrequent patrols.

1849: The Gold Rush began, and the Oregon-California Trail was lined with emigrants going west.

The army purchased Fort Laramie and converted it into a base to protect the traffic.

A few businesses sprang up to serve the emigrants, such as a blacksmith's shop at Scotts Bluff.

Captain Randolph B. Marcy escorted a large number of California-bound emigrants from Fort Smith, Arkansas, to Santa Fé. In doing so, he opened up a new route to the West Coast.

1850: By the Compromise of 1850, California was admitted to the Union, and New Mexico and Utah became territories. The boundary between New Mexico and Texas was also established.

The government let a contract for regular mail service across the Great Plains from the Missouri to Salt Lake City, and private enterprise started regular stage service to Santa Fé.

The Chicago and Mobile Act initiated the practice of making grants from the public domain for the construction of railroads.

1851: In the Fort Laramie Treaty (also known as the Horse Creek or Fitzpatrick Treaty) the Plains Indians gave the Americans permission to build roads and posts on the Oregon-California Trail and guaranteed the safety of tavelers.

1852: Randolph Marcy explored the sources of the Red River.

1853: The government completed a double line of forts intended to protect the Texas frontier.

At Fort Atkinson, Kansas, the Comanches, Kiowas, and Kiowa-Apaches signed a treaty permitting the United States to build posts and roads in their territory and promising to refrain from further raids in both the United States and Mexico.

Congress provided an appropriation for the exploration of five possible routes for a continental railroad.

1854: The Kansas-Nebraska Act repealed the Missouri Compromise and established the territories of Kansas and Nebraska, both larger than the present states.

Second Lieutenant Grattan and his command were wiped out near Fort Laramie.

The trading post at present-day Pueblo, Colorado, was destroyed by the Indians, discouraging settlement on the western fringes of the Great Plains.

1855: Brevet Brigadier General William S. Harney led a punitive expedition against the Sioux and fought Little Thunder and the Brulés at Bluewater Creek (now Blue Creek) in western Nebraska.

1856:   General Harney held a council with the Sioux at Fort Pierre. They agreed to peace with the Americans, and he agreed to restore their annuities.

Short of funds, the Mormons began a series of migrations in which they carried their belongings in handcarts instead of wagons.

Minor skirmishes with the Cheyennes led to greater trouble.

1857:   In the Dred Scott Decision, the Supreme Court ruled the Missouri Compromise unconstitutional.

The government let out the first contract for through mail from the Mississippi to San Francisco.

1858:   The people of Kansas rejected the Lecompton Constitution prepared by the pro-slavery forces. The House of Representatives also rejected it, thus denying Kansas admission to the Union.

The first transcontinental stagecoaches successfully ran between Missouri and San Francisco.

Green Russell led a party of Georgians and Cherokees to Colorado in search of gold. A minor gold rush followed, and the city of Denver was laid out.

1859:   John H. Gregory located the first gold lode in Colorado, and the Colorado gold rush began in full strength.

The army experimentally used camels for transportation in Texas.

Horace Greeley, editor of the New York *Tribune* and proponent of western expansion, made the overland journey to California. His dispatches increased interest in the West.

1860:   The Pony Express commenced operations.

Congress provided a subsidy for the construction of a transcontinental telegraph line.

Major John Sedgwick and Captain Samuel D. Sturgis waged campaigns against the Comanches and Kiowas.

Lincoln was elected President.

1861:   The Civil War began.

The transcontinental telegraph line was completed.

The Pony Express ended its operation.

The central route was chosen for the transmission of mail, and the contract was given to John Butterfield's old company.

Confederate soldiers crossed the foot of the Great Plains and tried to capture New Mexico, but were repulsed.

1862:   The Homestead Act provided free land for settlers.

The Morrill Act provided financing for colleges teaching agricultural and mechanical arts.

Congress incorporated the Union Pacific and Central Pacific railroads.

1863:   Colonel Henry Sibley and General Alfred Sully carried the campaign against the Sioux into what is now North Dakota.

1864:   Congress issued a new charter for the Union Pacific Railroad, liberalizing its terms. Thomas C. Durant established the Credit Mobilier as the railroad's contractor.

Chivington attacked the Cheyennes at Sand Creek, in present-day Colorado.

Later the Indians attacked Julesburg, Colorado.

1865:   The Civil War ended.

Lincoln was assassinated.

General Patrick Connor waged a three-pronged campaign in the Powder River country.

1866:   General Grenville Dodge became the chief engineer of the Union Pacific and construction really got under way. Before the end of the year, the railroad had reached the junction of the North and the South Platte.

Congress revised the charter of the Central Pacific, giving it permission to come as far east as necessary to join the Union Pacific. This started the great race between the two roads.

Another council with the Indians was held at Laramie. Of particular concern was securing the safety of the Bozeman Trail to the Montana goldfields.

Colonel Henry Carrington built Forts Philip Kearny and C. F. Smith to protect the Bozeman Trail.

Captain William Fetterman and his men were wiped out by the Indians at Fort Philip Kearny.

1867:   General Winfield S. Hancock marched along the Arkansas, treating with the Indians and in one case destroying a Cheyenne village.

The Hayfield Fight took place at Fort C. F. Smith and the Wagon Box Fight at Fort Philip Kearny.

Still another commission tried to make peace with the Plains Indians.

John McCoy started shipping cattle east by railroad from Abilene, Kansas.

Farmers were beginning to settle in the eastern Great Plains.

1868:   The army abandoned Forts Philip Kearny and C. F. Smith on the Bozeman Trail.

Red Cloud agreed to make peace with the Americans.

A general uprising occurred among the Cheyennes, Comanches, and Kiowas.

Brevet Colonel George A. Forsyth fought the Battle of Bleecher's Island.

1869:   Custer continued Sheridan's winter campaign against the Cheyennes and Arapahoes.

On May 10, the tracks of the Union Pacific and the Central Pacific were joined in Utah. Ten days later through service commenced between Omaha and Sacramento.

Ned Buntline met Buffalo Bill Cody and wrote his first story about him.

1870:   The Washburn-Doane expedition explored the Yellowstone country.

1871:   Dr. F. V. Hayden led an expedition through the Yellowstone country as part of the U.S. Geological Survey of the Territories.

Ellsworth, Kansas, started cutting into the cattle shipping business developed by Abilene.

1872:   Yellowstone National Park was established.

A committee of the House made a study of the Indian question and the manner in which Indians were being treated.

More Indian delegations were taken to Washington to impress them with the power of the Americans.

A company was formed to establish Dodge City, Kansas, on the Atchison, Topeka and Santa Fe Railroad.

Wichita, Kansas, began shipping cattle over a newly built railroad that connected with the Santa Fe.

The advance of agriculture ended Abilene's days as a cowtown.

1873:   Joseph Farwell Glidden invented barbed wire.

Congress passed the Timber Culture Act.

A panic, caused by the failure of Jay Cooke's banking house, swept the country.

The price of cattle fell, causing great financial loss to many ranchers.

1874:   The Cheyennes and Arapahoes attacked the buffalo hunters at Adobe Walls.

Colonel Ranald Mackenzie defeated the Cheyennes in Palo Duro Canyon, Texas.

Custer led a government expedition into the Black Hills.

Charles Collins organized the first gold-seeking expedition to the Black Hills.

1875: Walter P. Jenney led another government expedition into the Black Hills to study their geology. The gold rush was on.

The government commenced negotiating with the Sioux for the purchase of the Black Hills.

1875: Refrigerated carloads of meat were sent east from St. Louis.

Charles Goodnight went into partnership with John Adair to form the JA Ranch, one of the first large cattle ranches.

A five-hundred-acre wheatfield in Kansas proved successful.

Colorado was admitted as a state.

1876: A major campaign began against the Indians on the northern plains. Crook fought the Battle of the Rosebud, and Custer was defeated at the Little Big-horn.

Crook made the Horsemeat March and fought the Battle of Slim Buttes.

Ranald Mackenzie fought the Cheyennes under Dull Knife.

1877: Crazy Horse surrendered to the Americans.

Sitting Bull retreated to Canada.

Congress passed the Desert Land Act.

Chief Joseph surrendered.

William Randolph Hearst bought the Homestake Mine in the Black Hills.

Crazy Horse was killed.

1879: The Cheyennes under Dull Knife, who had fled the reservation in Indian Ter-ritory to which they had been sent, unsuccessfully tried to escape from Fort Robinson.

1881: Sitting Bull surrendered.

1883: The Chicago syndicate that had built the Texas capitol established the XIT ranch.

The Transcontinental Traffic Association, formed by the railroads, tried to fix rates and apportion traffic.

The practice of large ranches enclosing the free range with barbed wire was becoming common.

1884:   Theodore Roosevelt bought his second ranch in Dakota and began raising cattle seriously.

1886:   A congressional report showed that large holdings of land on the Great Plains were owned by individual interests, sometimes foreign.

A serious drought hit the cattle industry, followed by a severe winter.

Homestead entries reached a new high.

1887:   Congress passed the Interstate Commerce Act in an attempt to control the railroads.

1889:   Montana and North and South Dakota admitted as states.

Part of Oklahoma was opened to settlement.

The Ghost Dance started.

1890:   Sitting Bull was killed.

Big Foot's band of Sioux were attacked at Wounded Knee Creek.

1892:   The Johnson County War was fought in the Powder River country.

The Great Plains

To those who love the nation, the United States presents a thousand faces: the mist-covered slopes of the Appalachians, the carved stone blocks that form the peaks of many of the Rockies, the Big Sur country, where California drops abruptly hundreds of feet into the Pacific, or the Georgia coast, where the land slips as slowly into the water as a child going swimming on a cold day. In southern Arizona the rivers are dry most of the year, empty gullies in the sun-baked soil, while in Maine they always run freely except when they are locked in ice. On Cape Cod the wind-stunted pines grow on the dunes, pygmies of their kind; yet on the coastal ranges of California stand the tallest trees of the continent.

With such variety, what is typically American? A New England village, looking like a Christmas card in a December snowstorm? A riverboat working its way upstream between the levees that contain the Mississippi? A forest, a desert, a lake? Each of these is typically American, but perhaps one place deserves the designation more than any other—the Great Plains.

That is the land where the cowboy loped into history, his rangy pony carrying him quickly into American literature, art, music, and tradition, until he became a primary symbol of our nation's free spirit and self-reliance. Once each year the Pilgrim Fathers emerge from obscurity in their stiff black clothing, and in a crisis, we may summon the ghosts of the Minutemen from behind the stone walls of Concord, but the resurrection of these and other folk figures is only occasional. The cowboys are with us in every season.

When we chose a mammal to put on our coins, we did not select a rabbit or a deer, two of our most common. We picked a representative of the vast herds of buffaloes that once roamed our land, some originally on eastern ranges but mostly on the Great Plains. When we think of Indians, those that followed trails through our eastern forests or floated in canoes down rapid-filled rivers rarely come first to mind. More often we conjure up romantic images on horseback, their magnificent warbonnets silhoutted against the sky. Those are the Indians of the Great Plains.

The Great Plains had no monopoly on violence and crime, and to walk Dodge City's streets on a dark night was far safer than wandering along the New York waterfront. Yet when we think of outlaws, we think of masked mounted men, riding down on a stagecoach, holding up a train, or herding stolen cattle through the sagebrush of a secluded ravine. The word "lawman" does not produce a mental picture of a dectective with his .38 police positive hidden discreetly underneath his jacket, but rather a man with a star pinned to his shirt and his Colt's revolver hanging conspicuously from his belt.

The westward movement in the United States was carried out by men and women on horseback, in canoes, and on foot, often cutting their way through deep forests, following the routes of turbulent streams, or climbing over mountain passes. But the scene that the two words "westward movement" most frequently bring to mind is a wagon train, lumbering across a

29

wide expanse of open space, fording a river, or drawn up in a circle, while attacking Indians gallop around it.

In each instance, these many images—all reflecting what we regard as the essence of America—come directly from the Great Plains. Something about the land—loved by many, hated by others—has gripped our imaginations; and even those who have never visited it or who have merely flown over it by plane, the grayish brown flatness flowing without detail in every direction beneath them, believe they know the Great Plains and can close their eyes and see the wagon trains, the herds of buffaloes, and the mounted Indians.

As with most of the modern world, the present topography of the Great Plains was formed during Cenozoic times, the last of the eras into which the earth's geological history has been divided. At the beginning of the era, mountains stood to the west; but rains and streams eroded them, filling their basins with debris, while other rivers flowed from the mountains and leveled the Great Plains area to the east. By the middle of the era, the combined actions of erosion and sedimentation had created a vast peneplain with an average altitude of between two and three thousand feet. Here and there a few monadnocks remained to testify to the previous existence of the mountains, but for the most part the region was a flat expanse of land in which the rivers wandered freely.

Then the troubled surface of the earth moved again, and a new time of uplift occurred during which the Rocky Mountains were formed. Flowing once more from higher altitudes, the river currents picked up the strength to scour out the old mountain basins and, clinging to their former courses, cut deep canyons through the new mountains. The Flaming Gorge of the Green River and the Royal Gorge of the Arkansas—its walls rise 1,400 feet above the surface of the water—are striking witnesses of the mountains' geological history. As the rivers left the new mountains to enter the Great Plains, they drastically carved out the earth for several miles eastward. But in southern Wyoming, the Great Plains still climb slowly toward the mountains, leaving a record of the past and the route followed by the Union Pacific Railroad.

During the early Cenozoic, the climate of the Great Plains area was remarkably unlike what it is today. Palm trees grew in the Dakotas, and alligators crawled beneath them. Those states then had much in common with present-day Louisiana and Florida, but the rising mountains began to intercept the rains, and the climate also became colder. Slowly the glaciers crept down over the northern portion of the Great Plains, blocking the northward drainage system that once emptied into the area of Hudsons Bay. Finding itself cut off from its former route by the glacial till, the Missouri River turned eastward toward the Mississippi. (If this change had not occurred, the British might have entered the Great Plains much earlier, and perhaps the area would not have become American territory.)

As the glaciers retreated, the winds and rivers continued cutting into the surface of the Great Plains, sometimes carving deep canyons, as did the Prairie Dog Village Fork of the Red River when it created Palo Duro Canyon near Amarillo, Texas. In other places, they eroded the soft material of the surrounding banks, converting them into the unreal-appearing badlands of the Yellowstone, White, and Missouri rivers. In yet others, the rivers flowed slowly across the surface of the Great Plains—the Platte in Nebraska, for example—scarcely ruffling it. Sometimes the water and winds found a core of stronger rock surrounded by weaker and left it exposed. Chimney Rock, which served as a landmark for the emigrants to Oregon, was one such monument to their work. At other times the forces of erosion were more gentle and left a peneplain. In the Llano Estacado, or Staked Plains, of Texas, the land looks almost as though it had been laid out by a mason with a level.

Adjoining the Great Plains to the east is the Central Lowland, a country that is better watered. The transition from one to the other is not always abrupt, although in places the edge of the Great Plains is marked by hills or an escarpment. But the real difference is caused by the rain shadow of the Rocky Mountains. On the Great Plains the land and air are dry, and the rainfall is irregular. This rain shadow starts at the edge of the mountains in New Mexico, Colorado, Wyoming, and Montana and extends east to cover part of western Texas, a small portion of Oklahoma, about half of Kansas, and most of Nebraska. In the Dakotas it runs roughly along the route of the Missouri River but somewhat to the east of it. (For a more precise, technical delineation of the Great Plains, see Appendix A.)

The paucity of rainfall, of course, affects the plant life of the region. Except along the riverbeds, there is rarely enough water to support trees; and grasses became the predominant plants, their large root structure and small leaf area making it possible for them to survive with relatively little moisture. These are not the high grasses of the Central Lowland to the east, but shorter species like the grama and buffalo grasses, which grow less thickly. Because the rainfall is insufficient to leach the minerals from the soil, they are nevertheless highly nutritious and provided ample food for large grazing animals like buffaloes and antelopes. (More accurately, these should be called bison and pronghorns, but the other names have been used so commonly they are more familiar.)

In addition to their grazing, these animals have two other traits in common: they are both large and swift of foot, characteristics typical of grassland animals around the world. Rodents are also common. Since the terrain offers them no protection, they can either run fast, as do the jackrabbits (a fleeing jackrabbit can sometimes reach a speed of forty-five miles an hour), or are able to burrow into the earth, as do the prairie dogs. Even the insects are affected by the climate, for the prevalence of grasses has made herbivores like locusts and grasshoppers common, which the early settlers sometimes learned to their sorrow.

Although the Great Plains are distinguished by their lack of rain, their climate boasts almost everything else except temperance. In summer, it is hot; in winter, cold. A range of 159 degrees in temperature has been recorded in the South Dakota Badlands, which ordinarily expect each year a total of almost thirteen days with the thermometer at a hundred or more and about eighteen when it stands at zero or less. Except for earthquakes and waterspouts, the Great Plains can offer almost every type of natural violence: hailstorms, tornadoes, heavy winds, dust storms, and blizzards. In a study covering a span of twelve years, the United States Office of Meteorological Operations learned that the three states with the largest number of severe storms were Texas, Kansas, and Oklahoma in that order. Parts of all three states are included in the Great Plains. (In fairness, the heaviest concentration of storms within those states was not necessarily in the Great Plains but at their margin. This does not, however, vitiate the Great Plains' reputation for unusual weather.)

Although the weather of the Great Plains can leap from extreme to extreme, it is also notable for its constancy. When the wind starts blowing, it may blow for days at almost the same velocity, beating steadily on the windows and bending the grasses so uniformly it is difficult to believe that curved stems are not natural to them. When the hot weather sets in, it remains the same for days on end, never relaxing its grip, and the cold does the same.

It is a stern, formidable land that invites no dalliance with the viewer, no light-hearted love affair with persons who visit or inhabit it. Yet for those who are willing to accept it on its own terms, to battle its storms and fight its droughts, it offers incredible beauty—buttes that turn purple in the fading twilight, pinnacles of rock as delicate as anything designed by a human architect, broad horizons that stretch as far as the limitations imposed by the earth's curvature, deep canyons and broad rivers, all covered by a sky unequaled for grandeur except on the ocean.

It was not just happenstance that such an area became so typically American. The men and women who first explored and settled it found it alien to their European backgrounds. Of the earlier arrivals, perhaps the Spanish were the best equipped to deal with this harsh and forbidding country. They were accustomed to aridity and knew how to herd cattle—one of the natural uses for grasslands. But they found themselves both confused and frightened by its alarming flatness and could find no way of making good use of it. But if they were unable to cope with such unfamiliar surroundings, the French and British who followed them—except for the fur traders—were initially even less able. Little in their previous experience suited them for life on the Great Plains, and they had to develop new customs and tools in order to live there. An Englishman, for example, could land on the Atlantic Coast and find that his plow worked just as it did at home and the materials for building an English-style house at hand. Not so on the Great Plains. There was little wood or rock—nothing with which to make even a fence— and an ordinary plow would not break the sod. Both the French and British were accustomed to plentiful rain. On the Great Plains this was lacking. Neither people had a tradition of cattle grazing, which was one of the industries that made settlement on the Great Plains possible. (In fact, before the rise of the cattle business at the end of the Civil War, the United States ate more pork than beef.) So when the Americans finally entered the Great Plains, they had to cast off much of their European heritage and become—Americans.

Here are just a few of the new tools, attitudes, and careers they had to develop: moldboard plows, combines, barbed wire, sod houses, windmills for pumping water (there were a few windmills elsewhere in the country, but nowhere else were they common machines), as well as cowboys and the whole tradition associated with them. Even the law had to be changed. Most American law was based on British jurisprudence, but in the arid West, riparian law had to be completely rewritten. The inability of the land to support a dense population also altered the Americans' social habits. On the Great Plains they could not build a multiplicity of urban centers or even have their farmhouses or ranches close to their neighbor's. (In many parts of the Great Plains today, a family farm may comprise a thousand acres, not because land is so abundant, but because a farmer needs a thousand acres just to support his dependents.) The Americans who lived on the Great Plains, therefore, had to be more self-reliant than their fellow countrymen to the east.

True, some of these unusual influences on the Americans prevailed to a lesser degree in other parts of the country too, but they were concentrated on the Great Plains. There in the blazing sunlight or darkening storm, often alone and besieged by problems and dangers, American men and women developed many of the qualities and traditions we now consider typically American. As a consequence, the Great Plains were the birthplace of much of the American spirit. Harsh and cruel as the area often was, it gave us the gift of being what we are.

Part I 1528-1803

From the Discovery of the Great Plains by
Europeans Through the Louisiana Purchase

Chapter 1

The Castaways' Remarkable Journey

Although ambition and love of action are common to all, . . . there are great inequalities of fortune, the result, not of conduct, but only accident. . . . Hence to one arises deeds more signal than he thought to achieve; to another the opposite in every way occurs, so that he can show no higher proof of purpose than his effort, and at times even this is so concealed that it cannot of itself appear.

—Álvar Núñez Cabeza de Vaca, 1555

Of all the many ships constructed by Europeans in the sixteenth century, these five were probably the crudest and most unseaworthy. About thirty-three feet long, their timbers were unshaped and unplaned. The caulking was made from the husks of palmettos, the ropes were twisted horsehair, and the sails had once been men's shirts. Yet the building of these clumsy craft represented a triumph of human ingenuity over adversity. For the shipyard was a Florida wilderness on the coast of Apalachee Bay, and the tools used by the workmen had been forged from their spurs, stirrups, and the ratchets of their crossbows, the only iron they had available.

None but the most desperate, like this group of Spanish adventurers, would have ventured to set out to sea in vessels such as these. But in the mist-drenched, swampy wilderness of Florida, they had left the great dreams they had nurtured in 1527 when they had boarded the ships that were to carry them to the New World. Then, standing at the quayside, nudging each other and exchanging jokes, they had imagined themselves returning to their homeland laden, as so many *conquistadores* had been, with gold, silver, pearls, and riches—

enough to last the lifetime of their youngest member. Now there was not a single precious gem in their leather pouches, and hardly a joke among them to make the hot day pass faster.

Their former hopes had been based on the piece of paper given by the crown to their leader, Pánfilo de Narváez. It contained a grant of land that ran from Florida to the Río Grande, encompassing half the coastline of the Gulf of Mexico and a hinterland that stretched into the vague, unknown distance. *Por Dios,* such a country must contain the wealth of another Aztec empire waiting to be seized from sullen natives.

No one could be certain of this, naturally, because most of the North American continent had never been explored by Europeans. The Spanish were entrenched in the West Indies, but on the mainland they had not pushed as far north as the present boundaries of Mexico. Juan Ponce de León had tried to establish a colony in Florida but had died in the attempt; the coast of the Gulf of Mexico had seen Spanish ships, but two attempts to form settlements in Texas had been failures. Farther north Giovanni da Verrazano and John Cabot had sailed along the shore, but Jacques Cartier, that intrepid Frenchman who opened the St. Lawrence River to his countrymen, had not yet put out from Saint-Malo, and Martin Frobisher had not won the support of Queen Elizabeth and the merchants of London. So to Europeans the North American continent was largely an unknown land mass, rising out of the ocean and creating a barrier between themselves and the kingdoms of the Orient. What it contained, no one knew. But after the experiences of Cortés . . . yes, it might contain anything.

The Spaniards under Pánfilo de Narváez had, of course, anticipated danger and hardship. They were not such fools as to have expected the natives to surrender their riches without a fight or at least a threat of force. For they had listened to the reports of those who had been in Florida or along the Gulf Coast, reports that told of the rigors of travel in that strange land, where often the sea and earth seem to merge in a hot cauldron of mosquito-infested swamps and where hostile Indians moved like phantoms in attack or flight. Even more dangerous, perhaps, was their fellow countryman, Hernán Cortés, who, like a mountain lion crouched on a limb overhanging a game trail, was ready to pounce on any intruder who encroached on the country near his domain. The royal grant in the hands of Pánfilo de Narváez might bear a monarch's signature and have the force of law, but there is another law that forms one of the keystones of western civilization. That is the right of prior possession as long as the prior possessor is neither red nor yellow nor black. Even Pope Alexander VI had been unable to prevail against it; and his Line of Demarcation, which had divided the New World between Spain and Portugal, could not withstand the claims of those who got there first.

Although Cortés had no legal rights to the lands given to Pánfilo de Narváez, he had a base on the mainland and had already demonstrated his determination to use it to his own advantage. The experiences of Francisco de Garay, former governor of Jamaica, testified to this. Parts of two expeditions Garay sent to Texas under royal authority were captured by Cortés. On his next attempt to establish a colony, Garay took personal command and himself ended up a prisoner of the experienced and ruthless campaigner. All this was known to Narváez and his followers, but since they numbered six hundred and were well armed and supplied, they were confident they could resist the Indians and defend themselves against Cortés.

In February, 1528, Narváez reached Florida. An Indian village stood near the bay where he came ashore. When the Spaniards first approached, the inhabitants seemed friendly; but during the night they fled in their canoes. The next day the Spaniards examined the empty settlement closely and found little of value except, lying among the fish nets, one small bit of gold, a lure for the greedy and unwary. Narváez's imagination, already fired by Cortés's successes, became enflamed; and tossing aside all discretion, he made an unwise and disastrous decision. Instead of remaining aboard ship until he found a safe anchorage that would serve as a base of operations and a point of rendezvous, he sent the vessels off by themselves, while he and approximately three hundred men, anxious to find the source of the gold without delay, remained ashore to explore inland.

Only one man raised his voice against this division of Narváez's forces. That was the treasurer, Álvar Núñez Cabeza de Vaca, the last three words of whose name meant "cow's head." The right to use this unusual designation, it was said, had been given to a maternal ancestor in honor of a signal service rendered to Spain. During the bloody fighting to expel the Moors, the ancestor had revealed a secret mountain pass that permitted the Spanish to outflank their enemy and win a notable victory. As a sign to point out the trail, he had used a cow's skull; hence the name his family treasured.

At first the Spaniards maintained friendly relations with the Indians they encountered and even obtained from them supplies of maize to augment their own meager rations. But their greed finally overcame them, and they forcibly seized one village—it was rumored to contain gold—and this caused open warfare between the red men and the whites. It was then the Spaniards discovered the capabilities of Indian warriors and learned that bows can be powerful weapons. Years later Cabeza de Vaca still had not lost his astonishment at their effectiveness.

"Some of our men," he wrote, "were wounded in this conflict, for whom the good armour they wore did not avail. There were those . . . who swore that they had seen two red oaks, each the thickness of the lower part of the leg, pierced through from side to side by arrows; and this is not so much to be wondered at, considering the power and skill with which the Indians are able to project them. I myself drew an arrow that had entered the butt of an elm to the depth of a span."

The triumphal march turned into a pitiful rout. The Indians made the utmost use of the terrain, hiding in the many lakes, where the Spaniards could not pursue them, and taking shelter behind trees, where the Spaniards could not see them. As they struggled back to the coast, Narváez's men ran short of provisions; some were killed, some wounded, and many fell ill.

"It was hideous and painful to witness our perplexity and distress," Cabeza de Vaca later wrote. Finally they reached the coast, but, he said, "we saw on our arrival how small were the means for advancing farther. There was not anywhere to go; and if there had been, the people were unable to move forward, the greater part being ill, and those were few who could be on duty."

All too late they realized the rashness of Narváez's decision to split his force without first agreeing on a rendezvous. The ships might be anywhere along the coast, or they might have run short of supplies and returned to Cuba. If the marooned explorers were ever to get out of the disastrous predicament into which they had impetuously plunged, they must build some boats. Yet they had no tools. One of the men volunteered to make a bellows out of wood and deerskin, which would enable them to forge their fancy spurs and stirrups into more useful objects. This done, they obtained maize from some more friendly Indians and, by butchering one of their remaining horses every three days, were able to sustain themselves until the boats were finished.

The voyage that followed was a nightmare of hardship and death. The vessels were so crowded they barely stayed afloat, and the men were unable to move about. The horsehide waterbags soon rotted; the small supply of food they had been able to take with them began to run out; and since none of the men was a seaman, they could not even use their crude boats to the best advantage.

Drifting westward along the coast, they came to the mouth of the Mississippi and found themselves floating on fresh water. This was a blessing, because at last they could quench their intense thirst; but the same current that forced the fresh water into the Gulf of Mexico also made it difficult for them to stay close to the land; and when a strong offshore wind suddenly reinforced the current, they were swept out to sea.

Several days passed before three of the boats again came in sight of each other. One of them was commanded by Narváez; and Cabeza de Vaca, calling across the water, suggested they get together. But Narváez, who was closer to land than the others, was unwilling to give up the advantage he had gained by good fortune and the muscles of his oarsmen. It was no time, he replied, for one man to stand above others. From now on it was each one for himself.

With those words, Narváez deserted both responsibility and honor. But the fates noted his cowardice and marked him for destruction. Several days later he fell into a fit of temper; and instead of remaining with his crew in their camp on shore, he decided to spend the night alone aboard his boat. While he was asleep, a vicious storm blew up and carried him out to sea, where he perished.

Narváez's destiny, however just, was no comfort to Cabeza de Vaca. Abandoned by his leader, he joined up with the third boat, and they traveled together until a storm separated them four days later. By this time the men in Cabeza de Vaca's boat were so weakened by hunger and thirst that only he and the ship's master were strong enough to steer.

Early one morning, while the others slept, Cabeza de Vaca and the master thought they heard the rumbling of surf, a welcome sound because it might mean the winds and currents had at last brought them near to shore. Heaving their improvised lead, they found they were in shallow water but did not dare risk a landing in the dark. Cabeza de Vaca rowed as best he could with a single oar, while the captain steered away from the shore. When the light broke in the east, they swung the vessel around and let the elements carry them toward land. Suddenly a gigantic wave struck the boat with such force that the entire crew was aroused from their unconsciousness. Seeing land a short distance ahead of them, they scrambled through the water on their hands and knees toward it.

After the tumbling, uncertain motion of waves, which had shaken them for days, the shipwrecked men welcomed the security of firm ground under their feet. But in the coming months they learned to curse the island on which they had landed, calling it Malhado, or Wretched, Island.

The exact spot where they came ashore cannot be positively identified, but it was somewhere in the vicinity of present-day Galveston. The land around them was almost as flat as the Gulf of Mexico on a calm day and barely rose above the level of the surrounding water, which lapped constantly at the beaches. Desolate as the country may have appeared to them, they soon learned it was inhabited by Indians, who welcomed and fed them; and in a short time, they were joined by some of their other companions, for another boat commanded by two captains, Andrés Dorantes and Alonso del Castillo, had landed only a short distance away.

The Indians were convinced that such strange-looking men must possess magical powers and compelled the Spaniards to treat their sick. Using a mixture of Christian and Indian rites, they did so, and fortunately the Indians considered the treatments successful and paid for them with food.

But the thought of escape was always uppermost in the Europeans' minds. At the beginning of their expedition, they had considered Cortés their enemy; now they looked on him as their last hope of salvation. If they could get word of their plight to the forces he had settled at the mouth of the Pánuco River to the south, they might be rescued. Since the boat commanded by Dorantes and Alonso del Castillo seemed to be in comparatively good condition, they decided to refit it and try to reach Cortés's outpost. But their confidence in the clumsy craft was ill-founded, for when they launched it, it sank to the bottom.

With this avenue of escape closed to them, they selected four Spaniards and one Indian on the basis of their strength and their ability to swim. These men were to travel down the coast, passing through country that was completely unknown to them, and try to obtain help. Months went by before the Spaniards remaining on Malhado Island became convinced the expedition had failed, and even longer before they learned that four of the men had died and the fifth had been taken a captive by Indians.

Shortly after the five men left for the south, winter set in. Even in the summer, the Indians had no great surplus of food, but with the cold weather they could no longer dig up roots or catch fish in their weirs, and were barely able to survive. For them, this hardship was a part of their way of life, but the Spaniards were not inured to it. One by one they began to die of starvation and exposure.

In their desperate effort to cling to life, some of them resorted to cannibalism. Of five who died together, the body of only one—the last— remained uneaten. At the sight of the mutilated corpses, the Indians became convinced the Spaniards were the incarnation of evil and the cause of an epidemic that was ravaging their settlements. To purge themselves, they considered killing the white intruders, but one Indian pointed out that if the Spaniards really possessed mystical powers, they would have been able to take care of themselves. "God our Lord," Cabeza de Vaca later wrote, "willed that the others should heed this opinion and counsel, and be hindered in their design."

When the horrible winter was finally over and spring returned to the Texas coast, only fifteen Spaniards remained alive out of the original group of approximately eighty men. Yet the weakened survivors had not lost their determination to leave the Indians and find their way south to their fellow countrymen. The captains, Dorantes and Castillo,

took the lead in organizing the attempt to regain their freedom. Cabeza de Vaca could play no part in their plans, for he had become seriously ill. Besides himself, two others were unfit to make the perilous journey, a man named Lope de Oviedo and a friend of his.

After the departure of the others, Cabeza de Vaca found his life increasingly difficult. Weary of supporting him, the Indians forced him to dig up roots to eat. "From this employment," he later wrote, "I had my fingers so worn that did a straw but touch them they would bleed." In order to improve his lot, he set himself up as a trader between the island Indians and those who lived on the mainland, exchanging shells and other products of the coast for flint, skins, and ochre. Although he still dreamed of reaching a Spanish settlement, one consideration held him back from trying. He did not want to desert Oviedo, whose companion had died. At least once each year he returned to the island where they had originally been shipwrecked and tried to persuade Oviedo to make the journey with him. But Oviedo, who was once one of the strongest of Cabeza de Vaca's men, was broken in spirit, and several years passed before he finally agreed to leave.

As a traveling companion, he proved more of a hindrance than a help, because he could not swim across the many streams and inlets that blocked their way. Finally they came to one so large that they could not walk around it. While they were deciding what to do next, they met a band of Indians who offered to ferry them over and who also told them that the Indians on the other side held three of their original party prisoners: Dorantes, Castillo, and Estavanico, a Christianized Moor who was Dorantes's slave. Oviedo suddenly took fright and returned north by himself, but Cabeza de Vaca, still determined to escape from this strange country, crossed to the other side and joined his friends.

From the reports of earlier explorers, the castaways had a general idea of the coastline's geography and knew that the shortest and most direct route to reach help was to follow the shore to the Pánuco River. Yet this presented certain hazards that could not be ignored. First, it would be necessary to cross many bodies of water; and second, the Indians were said to be warlike. After considering these factors, the men made an important decision. Instead of going south, they would go west and try to find the Spanish settlements in what is now Mexican Sonora. This would take them from the Gulf to present-day west Texas, across the foot of the Great Plains, through New Mexico, into Arizona, and then south. Where they planned to venture, no European had ever been before, and they had no idea what they would find.

But many months passed before they had an opportunity to escape. Of that period Cabeza de Vaca later wrote, "In this time I passed a hard life, caused as much by hunger as ill usage. Three times I was obliged to run from my masters, and each time they went in pursuit and endeavored to slay me; but God our Lord in his mercy chose to protect and preserve me; and when the season of prickly pears returned, we again came together in the same place."

After the long and frustrating delay, the four men were ready to start their long flight to freedom. Few men have ever undertaken a journey in less favorable circumstances. They had little in the way of clothing, no equipment, and no supplies. Their only knowledge of the land through which they would be traveling came from the Indians, whose descriptions were vague.

On the other hand, they had a few important assets. Having lived among the Indians, they had learned to endure hardship. They could find food where people of their upbringing would normally have said there was none, for they were now willing to eat lizards, frogs, and roots. They were also familiar with some of the Indian dialects and had become accustomed to dealing with strangers whose language was completely unfamiliar. Above all, they had courage. They had been lost in the Florida wilderness, attacked by Indians, adrift at sea, buffeted by storms, shipwrecked, and treated like slaves. This had hardened and toughened them, and they were ready to fight and struggle as long as they could breathe.

By good fortune they were able to slip from their captors unobserved and traveled as rapidly as possible to avoid recapture. At the end of the first day they came upon an Indian camp. So far they had been luckless men, but now for the first time in years their luck changed. Somehow a rumor of their supposed healing powers had spread, and like most rumors, the farther it went, the more exaggerated it became. When they arrived at the camp they were greeted as welcome guests and found themselves besieged with patients.

That night several Indians asked Castillo to cure them of the severe headaches from which they suffered. As Castillo could not refuse them without losing their goodwill, he made the sign of the Cross and commended them to the Christian God. The Indians claimed the pain immediately disappeared. They vanished and soon returned, bringing

with them prickly pears and a piece of venison. Soon others heard about the miracles the white men could perform and came with more requests for cures and more food, so much in fact that the four travelers hardly knew where to put it.

The news of their skill spread to other bands, and more Indians arrived at the camp. Castillo blessed them and once again commended them to God, while the other three Christians added their prayers to his, knowing that on the help of these Indians depended their own well-being. The willingness of God to effect these cures, as Cabeza de Vaca later remarked, was the only means they had of persuading the Indians to assist them.

Castillo, however, was worried. So far he had performed his rites with great success, but the memories of his past sins weighed on his mind. The mercy and forgiveness of God might not be endless, he thought, and He might withdraw the power of healing from such a sinner. Perhaps God would even punish him for being so presumptuous. Therefore, when he received an invitation to visit another village, he refused to go, and Cabeza de Vaca had to take his place. On his arrival Cabeza de Vaca learned that the principal patient had apparently died already, and his family were lamenting him. Nevertheless, he performed the healing ceremony and treated several more Indians, all of whom claimed complete recoveries. After he had returned to the original village, the rumor spread that even the dead Indian had come to life and talked with his friends. This, of course, greatly enhanced the prestige of the Spaniards.

The season for the prickly pears was now over, and since these plants would be the principal food on which the travelers would have to rely, they decided to remain where they were until the cacti again became ripe. During the winter even the Indians were in great want most of the time. They had no maize, acorns, or nuts and, of course, no fish. By day they went naked since they each possessed only a single deerskin with which they covered themselves at night. This was the existence shared by the three Spaniards and the Moor.

When eight months had gone by and the prickly pears had ripened again, Cabeza de Vaca and his three companions resumed their journey.

By now the fame of the Spaniards and the Moor as healers had gone ahead of them, and the reception given them at each village was almost overwhelming. The inhabitants had such great faith in the powers of the strangers that each one wanted to be the first to touch them. Waving rattles made from gourds, they pressed so close the travelers were almost afraid for their lives. When they started on their way again, the people of the entire village accompanied them to the next one.

There "began," Cabeza later wrote, "another novel custom, which is, that while the people received us very well, those who accompanied us began to use them so ill as to take their goods and ransack their houses, without leaving anything." The Spaniards were concerned over this practice, fearing it might create ill-will that would endanger their own lives. When their hosts noticed they were upset, they said not to worry. The joy of seeing the travelers and the benefits of their cures were well worth the cost. They did not add that their own losses made little difference, because they would recoup them from the next band when the time came for the men to move on.

The procession that wended its way across the unknown continent became stranger and stranger. The three Spaniards, their skin sunburned and cracked and their feet and hands thick with calluses, looked more like natives than cultivated Europeans. The Moor, handsome and flamboyant, was enjoying the attention in spite of the hardship. Around the four men flocked the Indians, whose numbers grew greater and greater, chanting and calling to one another in triumph and blessing the spirits who had sent these medicine men among them. Even if the travelers had wished to escape the hordes, they could not have done so, for the Indians would have pursued their guests.

Mile after mile they trudged across North America, their feet touching ground that had never before known the impress of a European foot. Each tree, each rock, each drinking hole at which they stopped to quench their thirst was a new sight to European eyes. The trails they followed and the places where they wearily threw themselves upon the ground to catch a night's sleep were familiar only to Indians and were absent from the maps drawn by the best of civilized cartographers. Rarely in history have men with so little equipment and knowledge ventured so far into the unknown. As they traveled, changes occurred in their own characters. Estavanico, the Moor, could forget he was a slave. The Indians did not know, and the white men no longer cared. What difference could there be between them when none had anything to give the other? Reduced to the primitive scale in which they all existed, they became equals. Estavanico rejoiced in this and reveled in the admiration of the Indians. He was now a man.

Cabeza de Vaca's mind took a different turn. Here in the wilderness nothing stood between him and death but his God, and God had proved merciful. Otherwise He would not have permitted them to effect the cures upon which their lives depended. Gradually the world he had known—the world of Spain and its culture—faded, and in its place came a detached mysticism. Even the Church he had attended from childhood could not wholly account for the miracles that were happening.

The geography of their discoveries—each day represented a discovery—concerned them little except as an obstacle that must be overcome if they were to reach the Spanish settlements. Step by weary step they walked onward. Food, water, rest at night, and safety from the Indians—these were all they asked, and these four elements of life occupied almost their entire attention.

Once they were diverted, however, by a present the Indians gave them—a large copper bell adorned by a picture of a face. Most of all the Spaniards wanted gold, but any metal interested them, particularly if it had been skillfully fabricated. That was evidence of civilization, and where there was civilization there might also be wealth. So they closely questioned the Indians, who told them that it had come from the north, where there was much copper. Cabeza de Vaca made a careful mental note of this information. If he ever reached Mexico City, this was news that would interest the viceroy.

At the beginning the travelers had become physicians only out of necessity, but their faith-healing had produced miracles. Castillo, after his conscience had started bothering him, never regained confidence in his own powers, but Cabeza de Vaca became more sure of himself. At one village the inhabitants brought to him a man who was bothered by an old arrow wound, for the head had remained embedded in the flesh. Somehow Cabeza de Vaca procured a knife and decided to risk an operation. Cutting open the patient's breast, he located and removed the arrowhead. Then with a needle made from deer bone he closed the gash with two stitches and cleaned the wound with the hair from a skin. Fortunately the operation was a success and added to the travelers' renown.

After a few more days of travel, they reached the most civilized community they had seen in years, which is believed to have been a pueblo on the Río Grande where the Río Conchos joins the larger river. In contrast to the poverty-stricken tribes with which the four men were now familiar, these people lived in permanent buildings, cultivated crops of beans, pumpkins, and maize, and had a good supply of buffalo meat and hides. In response to the Spaniards' questioning, they explained they had originally obtained the seed of the maize from communities farther to the west.

At this point in their journey the travelers were faced with a critical decision. Should they continue west toward the land of maize, or go north toward the land of the buffaloes? The Indians definitely advised doing the latter. If the four men went toward the setting sun, the Indians said, they would have to travel seventeen days through a land where food was extremely scarce. To prove this, they showed them a sample of the only edible plant they would probably find and demonstrated how to prepare it. It was so dry and pungent the Spaniards and the Moor could not eat it.

Nevertheless, they determined on the western route, as they feared the other would take them too far out of their way. This brought them across the foot of the Great Plains, which lay about them in every direction, carved and flattened by the winds and rains of thousands of years. No one from Europe, much less one with African origins like Estavanico, had ever seen this heartland of the continent with the prairie stretching out in every direction and the sky overhead so immense it dwarfed the land beneath it. No part of western Europe was vaguely similar to it, and few places in the world could match its majestic but frightening vastness.

Yet the beauty of it was lost on them. As they had been told, food was indeed scarce, but they carried with them some deer fat for this emergency, and every day they ate about a handful of it. On this meager diet, they continued their westward march, leaving the Great Plains and probably crossing southern New Mexico and part of Arizona. Then as they turned south and penetrated what is now the Mexican state of Sonora, conditions greatly improved. Once again they found permanent Indian settlements, well provided with food, luxuries, and even signs of wealth. The Indians gave the travelers pieces of turquoise and in one village presented Cabeza de Vaca with five arrowheads that he thought might have been carved out of emeralds, although the stones were more likely malachite.

The four men were also impressed by what they took to be the mineral riches of the land. "Throughout this region," Cabeza de Vaca later wrote, "wheresoever the mountains extend, we saw clear traces of gold and lead, iron, copper, and other metals." Then he added this sentence, which was enough to fire the imagination of any adventurous Spaniard: "The people of the fixed residences and those beyond, regard silver and gold with indifference, nor can they conceive of any use for them."

But of what use was the information they had collected about the country if they could not locate their fellow Spaniards? Since their escape from the coastal Indians they had traveled many miles, but the main purpose of their journey still eluded them, for they had seen no traces of their compatriots.

A few days after they had received the five green arrowheads, they were delayed for fifteen days in another town by a flooding river. While they waited for the water to subside, Castillo noticed an Indian was wearing a sword buckle around his neck and sewed to it was a horseshoe nail. Of course, he immediately asked how he had gotten it, and the Indian said it had come from heaven. Not satisfied with this vague answer, the travelers interrogated him further. Yes, indeed, the Indian avowed, some men, bearded like the travelers themselves and carrying lances and swords, had come on horseback from heaven to the river near the town. They had lanced two Indians and then had submerged themselves under the water and gone out to sea, meaning, of course, the Gulf of California.

Apparently the Spanish had visited the village, and if they had come from some settlement that was not too far away, the news was good. If, on the other hand, they were explorers who had arrived by boat, they might well be leaving soon, if they had not gone already. Haste in overtaking them was important. So as not to lose the confidence of the Indians, the four men said their purpose in looking for the Spanish was to prevent them from killing or enslaving any more natives.

What Cabeza de Vaca saw in the next days was enough to shake his faith in the humanity of his own kind. Often in the New World the Spanish were more exploiters than developers, coming not to create wealth with their own technology and work, but rather to seize what had already been created or could be produced by native labor. Both the church and the crown had tried to exercise a restraining influence. In his instructions to Narváez, for example, King Charles denounced the cruelty shown to the Indians by other explorers and settlers, and he expressly forbade Narváez to take slaves. But the court was a long way from the New World, the Spanish judicial process was slow and cumbersome, and punishment was uncertain. Many leaders and their men, therefore, flaunted the law, preferring to take the opportunity to gain immediate riches at the relatively slight risk of royal displeasure.

The countryside through which the travelers now passed bore the devastating marks of this attitude. "The sight," Cabeza de Vaca later wrote, "was one of infinite pain to us, a land very fertile and beautiful, abounding in springs and streams, the hamlets deserted and burned, the people thin and weak, all fleeing or in concealment. As they did not plant, they appeased their keen hunger by eating roots and the bark of trees. We bore a share in the famine along the whole way; for poorly could these unfortunates provide for us, themselves being so reduced they looked as though they would willingly die . . . and," he continued, "they related how the Christians, at other times had come through the land destroying and burning the towns, carrying away half the men, and all the women and the boys, while those who had been able to escape were wandering about fugitives. We found them so alarmed they dared not remain anywhere. They would not, nor could they till the earth; but preferred to die rather than live in dread of such cruel usage as they received."

With a small advance party, he finally located four of his compatriots. The Spaniards were so amazed at the motley band he was leading that at first they simply stared at him and would neither answer his hails nor come closer to find out who he was. Finally he identified himself and persuaded them to take him to their commander, an officer named Diego de Alcaraz.

Alcaraz was in a despondent mood. Contrary to the instructions issued by the king, he had been hunting for slaves; but since the Spaniards' reign of terror had made the Indians hide, he had been unable to take any prisoners or seize any Indian food. As soon as he learned that friendly Indians were following Cabeza de Vaca and attributing mystical powers to him and his companions, he sent guides to lead them to his camp.

The guides returned with Dorantes and Castillo, who brought with them not only their original escort but six hundred additional Indians they had recruited from nearby bands that Alcaraz had not found. Willingly these Indians shared their supplies of food with their erstwhile conquerors.

In the days that followed, Alcaraz revealed several traits that all too often reduced the effectiveness of Spanish colonization. Having been fed by the Indians, he now greedily wanted to make them prisoners, thus without any thought for the future plunging the countryside into desolation again. He also became jealous of the travelers for the reverence in which the Indians held them. With such control over the natives, he apparently thought, he could have seized slaves more quickly. But he hid his feelings, treated Cabeza de Vaca with courtesy, and gave him an escort to take him to Culiacán, the nearest Spanish settlement.

The last leg of their amazing journey should have been easy for the four travelers, but it was not. Their guides took them through a desert where no Indian lived and through thick woods in which they were lost for two days. They ran out of water, and seven of the escort died of thirst, but at last they reached a town inhabited by friendly Indians. There they rested while the commander of the escort went on to Culiacán to notify the *alcalde mayor*, Melchior Díaz, of their arrival. Surprised that men who had been lost on the east coast of Texas were in what is now western Mexico, Díaz did not wait for them to come to him but instead went to them. "He wept with us," Cabeza de Vaca later wrote, "giving praises to God our Lord for having extended over us so great care. He comforted and entertained us hospitably."

In this fashion in a small Indian village the three white men and the black Moor ended one of the most amazing journeys ever made. On foot and with no European supplies, they had walked more than a thousand miles through inhospitable and unknown country. Only later did they learn that the hardships of the final days had been unnecessary. Alcaraz had sent them to Culiacán by an out-of-the-way route, so they would see no Indians and hear no word of them. For as soon as they left, he made slaves of the followers who had guided and cared for them so faithfully.

Chapter 2

Death of a Dream

I remained twenty-five days in this province of Quivira, so as to see and explore the country and also to find out whether there was anything beyond which could be of service to Your Majesty. . . . And what I am sure of is that there is not any gold nor any other metal in all that country, and the other things of which they had told me are nothing but little villages. . . .

—Francisco Vásquez de Coronado, 1541

On his return to civilization, Cabeza de Vaca had much to relate—descriptions of the strange places he had seen, tales of hardships and danger, and accounts of the Indian tribes he had met. Almost every white man and woman in the New World was anxious to know more about the unexplored lands that surrounded them, hoping to learn they contained riches similar to those uncovered by Cortés and Pizarro. But unlike the ancient mariner, Cabeza de Vaca seemed to feel no great compulsion to hold his audience with a "glittering eye" and tell his story.

Anxious to return to Spain after his long absence, he chartered passage on a ship that was due to sail in October, 1536. But before he could embark, the ship capsized in a storm, and rather than risk crossing the Atlantic later in the year, he went to Mexico City, where he worked on the official report of the journey.

In their account the travelers could have told any stories they wanted, for no one could have contradicted them, but they used considerable restraint. Nevertheless, they did write about the emerald arrowheads, the bell made of copper, and the reports they had heard of large communities to the north and of numerous pearls on the Pacific Coast. These comments, vague as they were, were enough to kindle the imaginations of the Spaniards. And besides there were rumors that Cabeza de Vaca was not telling all he knew—at least in public.

The following year he returned to Spain, where he had an audience with the king, whom he unsuccessfully petitioned for a grant similar to Narváez's, and wrote his *Relación,* which described his adventures and was published in 1542. Subsequently he received an appointment in South America, where his professional career was brought to a close because of charges made against him by some of his associates.

Until then, except for the attempts to explore Florida and the Gulf Coast, most of the Spanish effort in the New World had been expended in Central and South America. Now interest in the north was increasing. Everywhere Spaniards gathered, in the New World and the Old, men and women were talking about the marvels reported by Cabeza de Vaca—or the marvels he might have reported, so they said, if he would only talk more freely.

In 1537, the year Cabeza de Vaca returned to Spain, the king appointed Hernando de Soto governor of Cuba and also gave him the rights to the mainland that had once been Narváez's. In his epic trek across the continent, Cabeza de Vaca had shown humanity, courage, and patience, surmounting each new obstacle with renewed faith in God. But Hernando de Soto was a veteran *conquistador,* who had served under Pizarro, was accustomed to commanding men, and possessed a ruthless determination that, perhaps in the king's opinion, Cabeza de Vaca lacked.

In the spring of 1539, de Soto left Havana at the head of an expedition consisting of almost six hundred men. Like Narváez before him, he landed on the coast of Florida and began to explore. By fall he had come to the site of Narváez's shipbuilding operation, which he recognized from the remains of the horses, since they were not native to America. A little later, as the weather was turning colder, he went into winter camp without yet having discovered the riches for which he was looking.

The next spring his search took him through present-day Georgia and South Carolina, but all he found were fresh-water pearls of poor quality. By summer his wanderings had brought him to present-day Alabama, where he got into a pitched battle with the Indians. Although the Spaniards claimed a victory, they suffered casualties they could ill afford. At this critical moment, word came to de Soto that his ships had reached the prearranged rendezvous on the coast, where he could reach them in a two-day march. Under those circumstances most lesser men would have abandoned the fruitless exploration, but de Soto's ambition was undulled. Physical safety awaited him in Cuba but so did the acknowledgment of failure. Once there, he could not deny how little he had accomplished and how barren the land was. So selfishly he kept the news from his men and sent the ships away.

His journey now led him through Mississippi and Tennessee; and continuing in a westerly direction, he reached a country covered with thick forests and dotted with ponds that made travel difficult. He was approaching the Mississippi, and soon he and his men were standing on its banks, gazing awe-stricken at the mighty volume of water passing before them as it flowed south.

The existence of this river had been known to the Europeans for a number of years, for its mouth had been discovered by the first Spaniards to cruise along the coast and had been named by them El Río del Espíritu Santo, or the River of the Holy Ghost. But no one had explored it, and so its size astonished de Soto's men, several of whom remarked that it was larger even than the Danube. While some of the men rested, he ordered the construction of four boats; and in these he ferried his expedition over to the western bank.

Pushing toward the setting sun, he led his force through present-day Arkansas and into what was to become Oklahoma. He was approaching the Great Plains and received reports that farther on there were so many wild cattle—which, of course, were buffaloes—that the inhabitants could not raise maize and lived almost entirely on meat. The Spanish could easily have supported themselves in that land, particularly since they had horses to use in hunting buffaloes. But even de Soto, tenacious and determined as he had been, was discouraged by the fruitless searching for riches and decided the time had come to return to Cuba.

Finding the Arkansas River, he followed it back to its mouth at the Mississippi, willing now to admit the defeat he had refused to acknowledge earlier. Instead of the vigorous man who left Cuba several years before, he was worn out and sick, destroyed by the land he had sought to conquer; and in May, 1542, he died in his camp at the edge of the Mississippi.

His second-in-command, Luís de Moscoso, tried to pursuade the skeptical Indians that, godlike, de Soto had gone on a magical journey and would return; but when they became suspicious of the loose sand around the grave, Moscoso dug up the body of his leader and dropped it into the river, where it would not be found. In this ignominious—but nevertheless practical—way, the remains of one of Spain's *conquistadores* and explorers were consigned to oblivion. His personal dreams had proved as illusionary as the images sometimes created by the fogs along the coast on which he had landed, but he had given Spain an empire, if Spain could hold on to it.

The ships had long since been sent back to Cuba, so Moscoso decided to lead his men to the Río Pánuco, which had also been Narváez's goal after his difficulties. First he attempted to go by land but, finding the terrain too rugged, returned to the Mississippi and built a fleet of boats. (After his original crossing of the Mississippi, de Soto had disassembled his ferries and prudently saved the nails.) With either better seamanship or better luck than Narváez, Moscoso reached the Río Pánuco in 1543.

Of all the countries in Europe, Spain now had the best claim to the Great Plains. Spaniards had traversed the foot of the vast area, others had approached it from the east; and, unknown to de Soto, another group of Spaniards had crossed it from the west.

After his conversations with Cabeza de Vaca and his companions, Antonio de Mendoza, the viceroy of New Spain, became determined to sponsor the exploration of the land to the north and chose as the leader of the expedition a young protégé, Francisco Vásquez de Coronado. A junior member of a family with an entailed estate, Coronado had few prospects except those derived from his association with the viceroy. These, however, had proved considerable, for he had been able to marry into a wealthy family and had received at least one important government appointment.

In effecting their conquests, the Spanish found the church was often as useful to them as the military. Appointed by the king or his delegates—and thus subservient to the crown—and driven by religious fervor, the men of the church were as willing to risk their lives and undergo hardship as many of the military; and sometimes their comparative gentleness accomplished feats that could not be accomplished by force of arms. Another substantial advantage in their use—at least in the eyes of the government—was the relatively low expense incurred, because it cost far less to send out a few priests than even a small detachment of armed soldiers.

Mendoza was not prepared to risk the large expenditure involved in sending Coronado north with troops without first scouting the country. For this assignment he decided to employ the church and chose as his representative an adventurous and courageous man, Fray Marcos de Niza. He had also obtained the services of the black Moor, Estavanico, who, of course, knew the country and the Indians' languages and could act as interpreter and guide. Several Indians from north of Culiacán, some additional Indians to carry the luggage, and another friar made up the scouting party. (The latter, however, soon became sick and so played a role of little importance.) Fray Marcos, according to the instructions given to him by Mendoza, was to explore the country generally, investigate the particulars of some of Cabeza de Vaca's reports, be alert to the possible proximity of both the Pacific and Atlantic oceans (the continent was still poorly defined on the maps of the time), and determine the nature of the people. On the basis of what Fray Marcos reported, Mendoza would decide whether to send Coronado with a second and larger expedition.

Under the watchful eye of Coronado, whom Mendoza had placed in overall charge of the project, Fray Marcos left Culiacán for the north in March, 1539, about two months before de Soto sailed from Havana. Of all the party, Estavanico was the one who most looked forward to the trip. He tied bells to his wrists and ankles and carried a medicine rattle he had picked up on his earlier

journey, while at his side walked two greyhounds. Life for a Moorish slave in the capital city could not compare with life as a respected medicine man among the Indians, especially since the only nearby white men would be so dependent upon him.

In his planning Mendoza had failed to take into account the differences in attitudes and opinions between the happy black and the gray-clad Fray Marcos and his companion friar. These differences soon brought about a rupture between Fray Marcos and Estavanico, for while the friar was attempting to spread the word of God, the Moor, according to the *conquistador,* Pedro de Casteñada, "took the women that were given him and collected turquoises, and got together a stock of everything. Besides," added Casteñada, "the Indians in those places through which they went got along with the Negro better, because they had seen him before."

To reduce the friction that was developing among his small band of travelers, Fray Marcos sent Estavanico ahead as an advance scout. If he learned the location of anything important, he was to go no farther but either return himself with the news or send a messenger. As a double-check on the messenger's veracity, Estavanico was to give him a cross, the size of which would indicate the importance of the discovery. So the Moor, glad to be free of the friar's direct supervision, went gaily ahead.

To Fray Marcos's surprise, a few days later messengers arrived, and they were carrying a cross as large as a man. A great country lay ahead of them, they assured the Spaniard, and thirty days of travel from the spot where Estavanico was resting would bring them to the first city. It was named Cíbola and was only one of seven.

Instead of hurrying forward immediately, Fray Marcos waited a while longer for the return of some messengers he had sent to the Pacific Coast. During this time, more messengers, carrying a cross as large as the first one, arrived from Estavanico.

Then began a strange will-o'-the-wisp chase through the wilderness. Although Fray Marcos had instructed Estavanico to wait for him, the Moor did not. As he passed from settlement to settlement, the friar found messengers and crosses waiting for him, but no trace of the Moor himself. Among the Indians, Estavanico was no longer a slave, but a leader to whom the natives brought food, women, and respect. Striding across the desert, his hawk's bells jingling and his greyhounds at his side, he was in ecstasy; and having escaped the restrictions of European society, he wished to continue avoiding them as long as possible. Nevertheless, he remained sufficiently loyal to Fray Marcos to advise the settlements of the friar's coming and to use his considerable powers to persuade the Indians to care for the cleric. Meanwhile he had attracted a personal following said to have numbered approximately three hundred Indians, a great caravan that contrasted dramatically with the handful of attendants that accompanied Fray Marcos.

Suddenly his gay and triumphant procession came abruptly to a tragic ending. Fray Marcos, who had still been unable to overtake him, encountered one of the Moor's Indian followers fleeing southward in terror. According to him, Estavanico had reached Cíbola (which was a Zuñi pueblo, or village) and had been received with outright hostility. Apparently the Indian's report was vague in its details, because Fray Marcos was able to prevent panic from spreading among his own followers and continued on his way. Two days later, however, he met two more Indians who had been with Estavanico. These, too, were fleeing southward, and their wounded bodies substantiated the story they told.

When Estavanico was approaching Cíbola, they said, he sent messengers ahead with his medicine rattle and the news that he was coming to make peace with the city's people. For some reason the rattle especially annoyed the Zuñis, who recognized it as belonging to aliens. They told the messengers to warn Estavanico he would be killed if he attempted to enter the pueblo. Estavanico merely laughed at this threat and boasted that the people of the village would never harm him.

But when he reached the community in the afternoon, the Zuñis would not let him enter. They gave him a place to stay in a building outside the pueblo, but they took away all his possessions and refused to provide him with anything to eat or drink. The details of what followed are not entirely clear, but apparently the Zuñis expressed doubt at everything Estavanico said. For example, how could he represent a race of men who were white when he himself was black? Estavanico did not help his cause with his arrogant manner and, instead of recognizing the danger he was in, seems to have followed his usual practice of demanding turquoises and women.

One morning when he left the house in which he was staying, armed men came pouring out of the pueblo. Too late he realized the deadly intent of the Zuñis. He and his followers turned to flee, but the Zuñis pursued them. As far as Fray Marcos could determine, the three Indians he met were the sole survivors among Estavanico's followers except for a few boys who were taken prisoner.

Although he knew from Estavanico's experience that the venture might result in death, he went on to Cíbola to see it for himself—or so he said—but was sensible enough not to attempt to enter the pueblo, merely viewing it at a distance. He later claimed he had not been afraid of being killed, for he had offered his life to God when he undertook the expedition, but his conscience demanded he remain alive to report to the authorities. So after a quick look, he hurried back to New Galicia to report his adventures to Coronado.

Fray Marcos was no neophyte as far as the New World was concerned. Before he had been given his current assignment, he had served in Santo Domingo, Guatemala, and then Peru, where he met Pizarro before returning to Guatemala. His letters to his bishop describing the cruelties practiced by the Spaniards in South America resulted in his being called to Mexico City to make a personal report. The bishop had been much impressed by his vigor and apparent honesty and so had Mendoza. Consequently they had chosen him to head this scouting expedition, but their confidence was entirely unwarranted.

Although Cabeza de Vaca's descriptions of what he had seen were restrained, several people later accused him of hinting he knew more than he would say. If his manner led some people astray, this was nothing compared with what Fray Marcos proceeded to do. Gullible, imaginative, and ambitious, he hoped to gain the attention of those in power by embellishing every favorable rumor he had heard; and when the rumors were not sufficiently dramatic, he resorted to invention, building fanciful towns where none stood, and populating Arizona and New Mexico with nonexistent civilizations. So warped did his mind become that he could no longer distinguish fact from his own fiction and began himself to believe the myths he had fabricated. From what he reported, people believed he had discovered another Peru.

To prevent this exciting news from spreading and thus creating a horde of applicants for a royal charter to explore the area, Mendoza prohibited anyone from leaving New Spain, but nevertheless word got to Havana and caused de Soto to hasten his preparations. Cortés, too, suddenly claimed an exclusive right to the lands. If Mendoza wanted to profit from his supposed discovery, he knew he would have to move fast.

First, as an act of caution, he sent Melchior Díaz—the official who had welcomed Cabeza de Vaca—north on a reconnoitering expedition to verify Fray Marcos's reports. But he did not think he could afford to wait until Díaz returned to start organizing his force. Finding volunteers was not difficult. Most of the people in New Spain had come there for the single purpose of getting rich, and they were ready to brave any danger to attain that objective. Money, however, was not so easy to obtain. The king never liked to spend his own, although he always took a percentage of the profits. Mendoza therefore had to raise the necessary funds himself, drawing on his own resources and persuading others to become investors.

Finally in February, 1540, everything was ready. After a high mass, Mendoza reviewed the expeditionary force he was sending north under Coronado. The little town in which they had gathered could not hold all the people, and some of them had had to camp outside. There were approximately three hundred Spaniards, so many that some malicious souls accused Coronado of depopulating the country. About two hundred and thirty of these men were mounted, many of them having more than one horse. Coronado, for example, as befitted the leader, had more than twenty. Their armaments were a miscellany. Some possessed coats of mail, others wore heavy leather jackets for protection; some had swords and pikes, others carried weapons of Indian origin. In addition to the Spaniards there were approximately eight hundred Indians, who were serving as allies. But this did not complete the group, because there also were grooms, herders, and personal servants as well as three women and several Franciscans, the latter headed, of course, by Fray Marcos. The three women were wives who were determined to follow their husbands on the long and dangerous journey. At the conclusion of Mendoza's review the men took an oath of fealty to the king and Coronado, and the following day they set forth.

Troubles began to beset them even before they reached Culiacán. While foraging for supplies, one of the principal officers was killed by Indians, and they met Melchior Díaz, who was returning from his reconnoitering mission with bad news. He had been gone for approximately four months, and although he had not reached Cíbola, he had gathered information from every other source available to him. Not possessing Fray Marcos's unbridled imagination, his findings controverted the friar's. The people of Cíbola, he said, were not as numerous as Fray Marcos had reported, and he could find no evidence they owned any precious metals. Furthermore, he had heard the Indians were in a hostile mood. But evil tidings are always difficult to accept, and at that point the momentum of the expedition could not be stemmed. Coronado,

therefore, attempted to keep as much of this news as possible from his men, and Fray Marcos assured them that what Díaz said was untrue. After all, he himself had been in the land of Cíbola and knew what was really there. Thus Díaz's words went unheeded, and the army continued north in pursuit of a myth.

Because Culiacán was the last Spanish outpost they would see in a long while, Coronado and his men rested there for about two weeks. During that time Coronado worried about the slow pace at which his army could march and pondered Díaz's warnings. If the country ahead was as inhospitable as Díaz had described it, it would be better to travel through it with a smaller, faster-moving body of men. Accordingly he selected about eighty horsemen and twenty-five infantrymen, as well as some Indians, to form a vanguard under his direct command. The remainder were to stay at Culiacán about twenty days and then move to the foot of the Sonora River Valley, where they were to camp near the present-day city of Ures and await further orders.

On his march, Coronado, unlike many of the other *conquistadores,* tried to treat the Indians equitably. Although he thus avoided warfare, and his journey was peaceful and uneventful, doubts began to creep into his mind whenever he looked at Fray Marcos, striding along in his Franciscan robes. No one could question the friar's fidelity to his God, but had he told the truth about the lands he had seen? When they came near one of the villages that Fray Marcos had described in particularly lavish terms, Coronado sent Melchior Díaz off to investigate it. Díaz reported the area was rather barren and instead of a village he had found only a few scattered Indian dwellings. Naturally this news spread dismay among the men. In addition, the road that Fray Marcos had said would be easy to travel turned out to be difficult and rocky. Only the Sonora Valley, green and well watered, lived up to their expectations and helped restore their confidence in Fray Marcos.

But their faith in the priest's word began to fade again, when more of his reports proved to be false, and the men began regarding him with ever-deepening mistrust and wished him ill for the untrustworthy information he had given them. The sight of the Zuñi pueblo of Cíbola did not restore their confidence, for it was a small, miserable-looking village with two or three hundred Indians gathered outside it, ready with bows and warclubs to defend it. Wanting to avoid warfare, Coronado sent emissaries ahead to tell the Indians that although they must submit to Spain they would be treated well. The Indians replied by attacking the advance command but failed to inflict serious casualties.

Even then, Coronado refused to give up hope he could establish friendly relations with the pueblo. His soldiers were angry and hungry and wanted to rush the town, but Coronado restrained them by telling them it was not fair to attack so small a group of men. Failing to understand the reason for the Spaniards' apparent hesitancy, the Indians thought their enemies were frightened and grew bolder and bolder, shooting arrows at them from closer and closer range. Finally Coronado's patience cracked.

At the order to charge, the Spaniards eagerly pushed forward, and the Indians quickly fell back, some of them retreating to the pueblo, while others sought safety in the surrounding countryside. These could have been easily killed, but Coronado saw no point in such a massacre and did not want to divert his soldiers' attention from their main objective, the pueblo. "As that was where the food was, of which we stood in such great need," he later said, "I assembled my whole force and divided them as seemed to me best for the attack on the city, and surrounded it. The hunger which we suffered would not permit any delay . . ."

At first the battle did not go well for the Spanish. Coronado ordered the musketeers and the crossbowmen to begin the attack, but the Spaniards and their equipment were in bad condition. The strings of the crossbows broke, and the musketeers were so weak as a result of the hardships they had endured they could hardly stand on their feet. Therefore they were unable to clear the outside walls of the Indians who were raining arrows down upon them.

Never a coward, Coronado attempted to scale one of the walls himself and was twice knocked down by the rocks the Indians hurled at the invaders. The second time, one of his officers, López de Cárdenas, dashed forward and threw himself on Coronado, protecting his commander's body with his own. This gallant act, according to Coronado, was all that saved his life. As it was, he had several small wounds in his face, an arrow in his foot, and many bruises on his arms and legs. Being unable to walk, he was carried from the battlefield by his men.

The others did not fare so badly. Coronado's glittering armor had attracted the Indians' attention, so they had focused their attack on him. But despite their efforts—and they fought bravely and well—they could not hold out against the Spaniards. Since the pueblo contained a good supply of maize, the soldiers for the first time in days had plenty to eat; and after they had satisfied their appetites, they took time to look around them.

So this was Cíbola, the fabulous city Fray Marcos had described in such extravagant terms, the object of their long march through the wilderness? As one soldier later said, "It is a little, unattractive village, looking as if it had been crumpled all up together." Fray Marcos's rapidly diminishing reputation for truthfulness was now completely destroyed. "Such were the curses," one soldier later said, "that some hurled at Fray Marcos that I pray God may protect him from them."

In August, 1540, Coronado prepared a long and unhappy report for Mendoza. One city, he wrote, "which the father provincial [Fray Marcos] praised so much, saying that it was something marvelous," contained only five or six houses. Another "kingdom" had proved to be only a single small city, and the Indians knew nothing about another "kingdom" that Fray Marcos had described. "God knows," he continued, "that I wish I had better news to write to Your Lordship but I must give you the truth . . ." He then selected messengers to carry the report to Mendoza and assigned Fray Marcos to go with them, probably as much for the friar's own safety as anything else, for there was hardly a man in the camp who could imagine a fate sufficiently dire to repay him for his lies.

While Coronado pondered his next step, two Indians came to the Spanish from a pueblo far to the east. One was a tall young man who wore a long moustache, which caused the soldiers to give him the nickname of Bigotes, the Spanish word for moustache. He told Coronado the people of his pueblo had heard about the white men and wanted them to visit. As a gesture of friendship, he and his companion had brought with them presents of tanned hides, shields, and headpieces. In response, Coronado gave them some glass dishes and some bells, which delighted the two Indians. The hides intrigued the Spanish, who could not recognize the animals from which they had been taken even after the Indians drew them a picture of one. Yet they suspected that these were the buffaloes about which Cabeza de Vaca had spoken. This reassured them, because it indicated that he was not a liar like Fray Marcos.

Coronado accepted the Indians' invitation and ordered one of his chief officers, Hernando de Alvarado, to take twenty men and accompany them back to their home. After several days of travel they came to one of the most spectacular pueblos in the Southwest, Ácoma, which sits perched on nearly inaccessible rocks. This was one of the cities about which Fray Marcos had woven his tales, but it was much smaller than the friar had described it. Nevertheless, the Spaniards were much impressed by its strength as a fortress, because the single trail leading up to it was so narrow, rough, and steep that a few men could have defended it against an army. But Ácoma lacked riches and therefore did not hold their attention long.

Continuing east, they came to a river they named Our Lady. This was the Río Grande, which they first saw near present-day Isleta, New Mexico. From there, they sent messengers, carrying the usual crosses as a sign of the Spaniards' desire for peace, to the neighboring pueblos. The response was gratifying, for in a short time a procession approached. It consisted of the people from twelve villages, each group led by its own chief to the sound of a pipe. They bore food, cloth, and hides as presents, and Alvarado gave them some of the trinkets he carried with him. As he reported to Coronado, these were not a warlike race, but more like laborers; and instead of preying on their neighbors, they raised crops of corn, beans, and melons.

Bigotes and his companion, Cacique, who was a pueblo leader, owned two slaves, one named Sopete and the other called by the Spaniards the "Turk," because, they said, he looked like one. These two Indians were captives from the Great Plains; and seeing in the Spaniards' avarice an opportunity to get home again, they began hinting about the wealth that might be discovered in the lands to the east. Since Alvarado had been ordered to explore in that direction, he immediately fell into the trap they had laid for him.

Traveling toward the rising sun, he and his soldiers became the second group of white men to enter the Great Plains, coming upon them in eastern New Mexico. What impressed the Spaniards most were the vast numbers of buffaloes. As one of them later said, "There is such a quantity of them that I do not know what to compare them with, except with the fish in the sea, because . . . many times when we . . . wanted to go through to the other side of them, we were not able to, because the country was covered with them."

Like the Indians, they found the buffaloes good eating, almost as good as the cattle of Castille, and a readily available source of food. When Alvarado and his men were tasting their first buffalo meat, probably about sixty million of the animals roamed the United States and Canada. Their range then was much greater than it later became, and they were found in such places as western Penn-

sylvania, northern Florida, and central Georgia. But their greatest concentrations were in the Central Plains and the Great Plains. Gregarious animals, they moved in herds, grazing lightly in one place for a few days and then moving five or ten miles to another location. Because they did not need to drink as frequently as domestic cattle, they could roam much farther from water. Usually they spread out as they fed, but occasionally the terrain would force them to walk in line. Then their hooves would cut trails into the ground, and the roadways they carved in some of the high riverbanks were later used by human tavelers.

Alvarado's men discovered from experience the dangers of hunting them and lost several horses while perfecting their skill. Under ordinary circumstances the buffaloes were not aggressive, but when they became aroused, they were fierce creatures, capable of killing men and horses. A charging buffalo (the bulls averaged eighteen hundred pounds) could knock down almost anything that stood in its way. The Spaniards soon learned how to ride safely among them and kill the ones they wanted with their pikes. The Indians at that time lacked the advantage of horses, but they knew how to approach the buffaloes on foot without alarming them and shot individuals with arrows, or sometimes they stampeded a herd over a cliff. The buffaloes were the source of life for many of the plains tribes, who ate their meat and used their hides, guts, and bones to make other necessities. Alvarado was looking for gold; the gold of the Indians was those herds of shaggy animals.

Alvarado's search for treasure probably took him along the course of the Pecos River and then east, where he picked up the Canadian River. The Turk, still anxious to get home, had been dropping hints about a land called Quivira, which he said was a wealthy kingdom. While they were going down the Canadian River, he insisted they should turn more to the north, but Alvarado refused. In the style of Fray Marcos, the Turk then began telling stories that played even more on Alvarado's imagination; but the time allotted for the mission was nearly over, and Alvarado was soon due back to report to Coronado. Becoming desperate, the Turk made a serious error. Like many liars past and present, he added one more detail to his story in order to make it more convincing and carelessly chose one that Alvarado could easily investigate. He said that when he had come from Quivira he had owned a golden bracelet, which he had given to Bigotes and Cacique.

A golden bracelet! Alvarado had seen nothing of the sort at the pueblo, but now that he had to turn back anyway, he could not wait to lay his hands on that piece of jewelry and offer it to Coronado as evidence that an expedition to the east would not be fruitless after all. So the poor Turk, who wanted so much to go in the other direction, found himself being hurried back to his captors. Realizing the mistake he had made and fearful of the consequences, he begged Alvarado not to tell Bigotes what he had said.

The Turk might as well have tried to stop a charging buffalo by throwing a pebble at it as to think he could stop Alvarado's search by pleading that his own life lay in the balance. As soon as Alvarado reached Bigotes's pueblo on the Pecos River, he demanded to see the bracelet. Since it was nonexistent, neither Bigotes nor Cacique could produce it. Up until now, Coronado's men had handled the Indians with some restraint. Conquerors though they were, demanding the submission of all the natives they encountered, they had not resorted to violence unless the Indians attacked them first or were otherwise hostile. But Alvarado, obsessed by the thought of that missing bracelet, was determined to find out the truth at any cost. Certainly the Turk might be lying, but then, too, so might Bigotes and Cacique. The only person who could judge between them was Coronado himself, so Alvarado invited them to come with him when he returned to the Río Grande to meet his commander.

The Indians were not fools. All three realized that what might be justice to the white men was not necessarily justice for them and refused to go. Losing his patience, Alvarado turned to treachery. He lured Cacique and Bigotes to his tent and took them prisoner. Naturally the Indians of the pueblo resented this high-handed treatment of their people. They charged Alvarado with violating their friendship, and arrows flew in the air before Alvarado could again restore calm.

In a day or two the Turk disappeared, and Alvarado was convinced that Bigotes and Cacique had engineered his escape, a logical conclusion since he was the star witness against them. Finally he agreed to release Cacique to hunt for the Turk. When the fugitive was finally located and returned to Alvarado's custody, the Spaniards promptly put Cacique in irons again, an act not calculated to increase the Indians' goodwill.

Then adopting a more conciliatory attitude, Alvarado joined the Indians of the pueblo on an abortive campaign against some of their neighbors, during which the Turk escaped once more. But again he was recaptured, and Alvarado marched westward, finally joining Coronado in the valley of the Río Grande, where the commander intended to spend the winter.

When the Spaniards had arrived in the valley of the Río Grande, they had been hospitably received by the Indians, particularly by the Tiwas, with whom they first stayed. But when Coronado's entire army began assembling among the pueblos, the Indians started to regret their earlier cordiality. This was a pattern that would be repeated over the North American continent for hundreds of years to come: first, the welcome to the white strangers; second, increasing friction as the whites' numbers and demands grew; and, third, open hostility. The Tiwas were not unique: they were merely among the original victims in the repetitive course of history.

As the winter wore on, they realized the Spaniards were asking for more and more of their scanty stock of supplies and that in spite of Coronado's strict orders, individual soldiers often harmed them. Resentment grew, and fighting broke out. After several battles—one of which ended only when the Spaniards literally smoked the Indians out of their pueblo—Coronado secured his position.

But the Spaniards' winter was not taken up entirely with fighting, because they had the Turk to listen to. Just as they had believed in what Fray Marcos told them even after Melchior Díaz's warning, so they took the Turk's words more seriously than the denials of Bigotes and Cacique. And the tales he told were wonderful. Compared to him, Fray Marcos was an unimaginative dullard. He told—and the Spaniards listened closely to every word—of a river in which there were fishes as big as horses, canoes so large they carried more than twenty rowers on each side and bore golden eagles fixed to their bows, and of a ruler who took his afternoon nap under a tree that was decorated with golden bells, the ringing of which helped to put him to sleep. The ordinary eating dishes in this land of marvels, according to the Turk, were made of plate silver, and the jugs and bowls of gold. Thus he described the kingdom of Quivira, lying somewhere to the northeast on those seemingly endless plains where he had guided Alvarado.

To test the Turk, the Spaniards brought him ornaments of gold, silver, and base metals, and he was able to distinguish the gold and silver from the others. Obviously he could have learned to do this merely by living among the Spaniards for a short time and noticing the care they took of anything made from the precious metals. But this did not apparently occur to the Spaniards, and since the Turk told them what they wanted to believe, they had faith in him. That winter, as the weather grew colder and the fighting continued, many a Spaniard comforted himself with the thought that spring might bring not only warmth and the resolution of combat, but the realization of their dreams of wealth.

The winter was a hard one. Far from home and surrounded by hostile Indians who had been subdued only by fierce fighting, the men of Coronado's army were sustained largely by their commander's leadership and by the hope that during the following summer they would hold in their hands the gold said to be at Quivira. As the soldiers sat around their fires exchanging gossip, some of them repeated the stories told by the Turk's guard. Once the Turk had asked him which Christians had been killed during a recent battle. For some reason, the guard said none had died; and the Turk, accusing him of being a liar, stated the correct number and the rank of one of the officers. Amazed, the guard wanted to know who had told him; and the Turk, taking the opportunity to claim occult powers, replied that no one had. He knew it without having to be told. After that, the guard watched him closely and once caught him speaking to the devil in a pitcher of water. Some of the less hardy shuddered at the thought of entrusting their lives to such a guide, but others would have followed Satan himself if he could have led them to gold.

Outside the shelter of the pueblo walls the wind blew down the valley of the Río Grande, and the river itself was frozen so solid the men could ride over it on horseback. Sometimes as the months dragged on, it seemed to the gossiping soldiers that spring would never come and allow them to continue their search for Quivira. But slowly the days lengthened, and the wind grew less cold. The river with resounding cracks freed itself of its burden of ice, and even on the upper slopes of the Sangre de Cristo Mountains the snow began to turn to water and run down the gullies and streambeds that lined the mountainsides. At last in April, 1541, Coronado assembled his men and started to Cicúye on the first leg of his journey to Quivira and, he hoped, fortune and fame.

Cicúye, which was situated near the modern pueblo of Pecos, New Mexico, was east of Santa Fé and the last of the pueblos before reaching the Great Plains. Well fortified and containing its own source of water, which made it less susceptible to siege, it was the focal point for trade between the Pueblo and Plains Indians. Here the two distinct cultures mingled, each selling to the other what it could best use.

Although Coronado had reason to worry about his reception at Cicúye, he found the pueblo, if not cordial, at least willing to provide the Spaniards with food. In a show of friendship Bigotes even gave Coronado the captive, Sopete, who was said to be a native of Quivira. To the Spaniards' pleasure, this young Indian substantiated what the Turk had been saying, although he warned that the gold and silver were not quite so plentiful as the Turk had suggested. This warning, however, did little to diminish the Spaniards' exuberance, because there would still be enough left to make Quivira a second Peru.

Since Cicúye was separated from the plains by high mountains to the east, Coronado did not attempt to march directly toward his objective but instead followed the course of the Pecos River in a southeasterly direction until he reached more level land. The Spaniards then stopped long enough to build a bridge across the river, which had been swollen by the melting of the winter's snows, and passed over to the other side. Although they were still in sight of mountains, which in several places jut out toward the east, they were now on the plains. The appearance of the land was overwhelming, not just because of its flatness and some of the strange geologic formations it contained, but also because of its incredible vastness. This was a point Coronado emphasized in a report he later wrote to the king. No matter where or how far they marched during their long journey, they never emerged from the plains or saw any end to them.

Neither the writings of Cabeza de Vaca nor the reports of Alvarado had prepared the Spaniards for the sight. Once covered by a great sea, the Great Plains still resembled one. On and on, they stretched into the distance, sometimes as flat as water that has been untouched by wind, sometimes rolling gently like an ocean swell and sometimes—particularly on their western edge—throwing themselves upward in strange formations against the mountains like waves breaking on a coast. The water and wind had chiseled and etched the land, leaving intricate canyons that were so large they were almost worlds in themselves. It was one of the few places in the world where much of the scenery was down rather than up, but even this generalization did not always hold true. In some instances the eroding forces had created an opposite effect by carving away the land that surrounded some more resistant rock, leaving a butte, a mesa, or some other pinnacle to stand high against the sky. The country was so different from anything they had ever seen, it filled the marching men with foreboding.

Next to the land itself, they were most amazed by the herds of buffaloes—or "cows" as they called them—which they found in such numbers that Coronado in his report to the king said he could not count them. Although the buffaloes were not distributed evenly over the plains, the Spaniards said they never passed a day without seeing at least one herd.

They learned the importance of these animals to the Indians when they came to a camp of Quecheros, as the Pueblo Indians called them. (They may have been Plains Apaches or Comanches, both of which could have been found in that area.) These Plains Indians subsisted almost entirely on the buffaloes and during the summer months were therefore constantly on the move, following the herds from one grazing ground to another. They ate the flesh of the buffaloes, drank their blood, and tanned the skins to make their clothes and "tents," as Coronado called their tipis. One observer traveling with Coronado noted even further uses the Indians made of the buffaloes. The sinews became thread; the bones, awls and other tools. The stomachs served as pitchers, and the buffalo dung, dried and hardened, took the place of wood when they made a fire.

Next to buffaloes, dogs were the most important animals in the Indians' way of life. When they moved, they made a travois by attaching two poles to a dog's back and letting the ends drag on the ground. On the primitive platform created by the poles, they placed their tipi and let the dog do the necessary hauling. They even constructed small pack saddles along the lines of those used for horses, which enabled them to employ dogs for carrying almost everything, including the provisions they took with them when they were off on a hunt.

Coronado asked the Quecheros about Quivira, and to his dismay learned they had never heard of it. But soon the Spaniards came to another band. This time the Turk took steps to have his story substantiated. Riding with the advance guard, he was able to talk to the Quecheros before Coronado; and when the commander arrived, they were ready to give him the sort of information he wanted to hear. Off to the east, they said, were many large settlements, located so close together that a man could travel for ninety days, and as soon as he left one he would enter another. This perhaps was the fabulous region for which the Spaniards were searching, and they hastened toward it, driven by their feverish imaginations.

Other bands of Indians, probably led on by the Turk and their own desire to please, confirmed the existence of the settlements; and when the Turk announced that the first town was only a two-day march ahead, Coronado sent out a scouting party of ten men under Captain Diego López.

Riding away from the camp, their armor flashing in the sun, they came upon a herd of buffaloes and decided to pursue it. Buffaloes panic easily, and this herd stampeded with the Spaniards galloping quickly behind it. In places the Great Plains are ribbed with ravines and canyons that cannot be seen until a man or animal is almost upon them. Such a gulf suddenly opened in front of the buffaloes. Unable to stop, the lead animals plunged into it, their massive bodies crashing to the bottom until the ravine was so filled with struggling animals that much of the remainder of the herd was able to cross over on their backs.

The Spaniards could not stop either but through some miracle suffered no casualties, although three of their horses completely disappeared in the mound of living animals. This was the only outcome of their scouting trip. They found no city, because there was no city to find.

The land itself was now becoming their greatest enemy. As one of them said, "The country is so level that men became lost when they went off half a league. One horseman was lost, who never reappeared, and also two horses, all saddled and bridled, which they never saw again. No track was left of where they went, and on this account it was necessary to mark the road by which they went with cow dung so as to be able to return, since there were no stones or anything else."

As Coronado himself said, the Great Plains had "no more landmarks than as if we had been swallowed up in the sea where they [the men], strayed about because there was not a stone, nor a bit of rising ground, nor a tree, nor a shrub, nor anything to go by." In the previous part of their long journey they had always been able to follow the lines of the mountains, but here there was nothing more to guide them than on the ocean. Only the sun and stars could tell them which way they were going when they were without a compass.

During this trying period the Turk kept up his cheerful comments, promising the Spaniards untold riches, but Sopete now took an opposite view. According to him, the Turk was trying to trick the

The Spanish were the first men of European descent to enter the Great Plains. Although they had conquered Mexico and Peru, this vast, flat area with no distinguishing landmarks frightened them. Often members of Spanish exploring parties became lost when they wandered away from the main body, and guns were fired at sundown to help guide the stragglers into camp. *Alexander B. Adams*

Rivers often cut deep canyons into the surface of the land, forming separate worlds that were invisible to the traveler until he reached the edge of the caprock. At Palo Duro Canyon in the Texas Panhandle, Coronado found an Indian village. Later the canyon served as a winter hideout for Indians being pursued by U.S. troops and then became the site of one of the first large cattle ranches. *Alexander B. Adams*

Spaniards, not lead them to great riches. As usual the voice of ill-tidings was unwelcome, and the men continued to believe in the Turk.

Coronado was now growing apprehensive. His food supply was diminishing, and, unlike the Indians, he could not live on the buffaloes alone. So far he had wandered pointlessly across the Llano Estacado—or Staked Plains of western Texas—and had neither found Quivira nor learned anything concrete about that supposed city. So rather than continue moving his entire army, he sent out another reconnoitering expedition under the command of Rodrigo Maldonado, one of his officers and a close friend.

After traveling four days, Maldonado came to a gorge, which may have been Tule Canyon in west Texas, and rode down to the river that lay below. There he found another camp of Plains Indians, who were called Teyas by the Pueblo Indians. They knew about Núñez Cabeza de Vaca and the miracles he had performed, so they were delighted to see the Spaniards. To show their pleasure, they set aside a tipi for the use of Maldonado and his men and gave him a large pile of furs and other possessions as a present.

To prevent the army from becoming lost, Maldonado had marked his trail with piles of stones and cow dung; now he also ordered guides to go back to Coronado and lead him to this spot where the Indians were so friendly. When the commander arrived and saw the pile of presents, he attempted to distribute them among his men in an orderly fashion. But because this was the only wealth they had come upon during their entire trip and because they were afraid it would not be divided evenly, the men fell upon it, each one grabbing for himself, and within an hour the pile was gone.

This disregard for his orders was not the greatest disappointment that Coronado received in that canyon. The Teyas knew about Quivira, but their descriptions of it differered greatly from the Turk's. The buildings, they said, were not multistoried and constructed of stone; they were made only of straw and skins. When the Turk was confronted with this information, he confessed he had lied about the buildings but claimed everything else he had said was true. The Teyas, however, also insisted there was no gold or silver in Quivira, only a small supply of maize. This news deeply disturbed Coronado. He was on what he called the "limitless plains," with no corn left and having difficulty, as many subsequent travelers did, in finding water. Now there was a strong possibility that he would not discover another Peru.

While Coronado was pondering what to do next, a violent storm swept over the canyon. The wind blew with the force of a tempest, and the hailstones that accompanied it were, in the words of one observer, "as big as bowls, or bigger, and fell as thick as raindrops." They ripped the Spaniards' tents, battered their helmets, and broke their crockery and gourds. This last was serious because the Spaniards could not replace them, since the Teyas neither made pots nor grew gourds. Even worse, the hailstones panicked the horses; and in spite of the men's efforts to restrain them, many stampeded up the sides of the canyon and were recovered only with difficulty. If the storm, one writer noted, had struck while they were on the plains and not surrounded by the walls of the canyon, they might have lost most of their mounts.

Once again Coronado could see no point in moving his full force when he did not know where he was going and instead sent out scouts. They came back with a report that another Teya village was located not far off in another canyon, so again the weary men packed their belongings and started marching. The second camp may have been in Palo Duro Canyon, a deep gorge slashed into the Great Plains by a fork of the Red River. Suddenly the traveler, who has seen nothing but the deadly evenness of the horizon, finds a different world lying at his feet. Descending into the canyon, which is not easy because of the sheer cliffs formed in the rimrock, he could believe himself transported hundreds of miles off into the distance instead of merely hundreds of feet down. There at the bottom is the river, flowing gently through the canyon with trees growing on its banks, in sharp contrast to the dry, unwooded land above the canyon's walls. A while before the traveler was enveloped in the sky. It hung over him like a great inverted bowl and touched the horizon at eye level in every direction. Now it is confined to the space immediately above the canyon, and the traveler can see earth and rocks even when he looks upward, just as though he were standing in the valley of some mountain range.

Because of his many worries, the grandeur of the scene was lost on Coronado. As he had approached this new camp, he had taken special precautions to prevent the Turk from talking to the Indians first and filling them with his stories, in this way hoping to learn the truth. Yes, the Indians replied to his questions, they knew about Quivira, but—and this was a thunderbolt—the Spaniards were traveling in the wrong direction. Like the water in an *olla* that has been carelessly left in the sun, Coronado's confidence in the Turk had been slowly evaporating. The earlier Indians had created serious doubts in his mind about the wealth of Quivira, and the Turk had finally admitted exaggerating. Now, it seemed, he was not even guiding them in the right direction.

Spanish society was marked by deference to rank and birth, but its armies by modern standards were remarkably democratic, and few commanders made major decisions without first consulting their officers. So Coronado called his staff together and laid the facts before them: they had run out of food and were existing only on buffalo meat; there was no place nearby where they could obtain supplies or even replace their pots; perhaps Quivira existed, but possibly it contained no wealth; certainly the Turk had lied to a considerable extent; and they were traveling in the wrong direction. Their predicament, he pointed out, was serious, and common sense would dictate they abandon the venture and retreat to the Río Grande.

But these were adventurous, hardy Spaniards, and there was a chance—although a slight one—that the Turk's descriptions of Quivira might be accurate after all. Furthermore, their rival, de Soto, was somewhere to the east, and he might get there first. At the conclusion of the conference the officers decided that Coronado should go ahead with thirty cavalrymen and half a dozen infantrymen, while the remainder returned to their base in New Mexico. They also agreed that Coronado should take the Turk with him in the event he had any information that might be useful, but they also agreed he should be clapped into chains and treated as a prisoner. Sopete, who had been jealous of the Turk and had warned the Spaniards against him, was to be the chief guide, and Coronado would rely on him to take them to the distant city.

When the army heard the decision, the men were dismayed. Return to the Río Grande without searching further for Quivira? Give up their remaining hope of finding a new Peru? No, they preferred to die with their commander. Their wish, however, was so impractical that Coronado refused to accede to it, but he did promise that if he found any hopeful signs of Quivira within eight days, he would send back messengers with orders for them to follow him.

After Coronado left, the rest of the army remained in camp, hoping the messengers would arrive with good news. While they waited, the men hunted buffaloes and dried the meat for their return journey. This was dangerous work, but it was the land itself that struck horror in their hearts—the

angry, hostile land whose flatness made east indistinguishable from west and obscured the difference between north and south. "Many fellows," wrote one soldier, "were lost at this time who went out hunting and did not get back to the army for two or three days, wandering about the country as if they were crazy, in one direction or another, not knowing how to get back where they started from, although this ravine extended in every direction so that they could find it. Every night they took a count of who was missing, fired guns and blew trumpets and beat drums and built great fires, but yet some of them went off so far and wandered about so much that all this did not give them any help, although it helped others. The only way was to go back where they had killed an animal and start from there in one direction and another until they struck the ravine or fell in with somebody who could put them on the right road. It is worth noting that the country there is so level that at midday, after one has wandered about in one direction and another in pursuit of game, the only thing to do is to stay near the game quietly until sunset, so as to see where it goes down, and even then they have to be men who are practiced to do it. Those who were not, had to trust themselves to others." The Indians were merciful to the Spaniards, giving them supplies and providing them with escorts, but the land was not.

Leading his small detachment, Coronado left the canyon with the Turk in chains and Sopete serving as the head guide. Some Teyas accompanied them to assist Sopete, but these quickly deserted, and Coronado had to send back to the canyon for replacements. The farther he ventured onto the plains, the greater became his chances of getting lost, for the knowledge of his Indian guides was necessarily limited to the areas through which they themselves had traveled. He had a compass—or "needle"—to give him the direction; and each day one poor wretch was assigned the task of counting his footsteps, so Coronado could tell how far they had traveled.

The Spaniards' route took them north and slightly east, thus staying on the high plains and avoiding the wild tangle of land in the escarpment directly to the east. Living entirely on the buffaloes they killed (they lost several horses, but no men, hunting these animals) and often having to go without water, they went up what is now the Texas Panhandle, over the western end of the Oklahoma Panhandle, and crossed the Arkansas River west of present-day Dodge City, Kansas. Sopete recognized the river as the one for which he had been looking, so they followed its downstream course, marching on its left bank. Quivira, whatever it might turn out to be, was close at hand.

Three days after crossing the Arkansas, they met a band of Indians from Quivira, who were out hunting buffaloes and came from a village that was about a three-day journey farther downstream. At the strange sight of these white men with their armor and horses advancing across the plains, the Indians took fright and started to flee; but Sopete called out to them in their own language, and they halted. Then Coronado wrote a message to the governor of Quivira, for among the many rumors circulating, one held that the governor was a Christian, perhaps a Spaniard who had been shipwrecked. Stranger things than that had occurred in the last half-century while Spain was opening up a new hemisphere. Taking the message with them, the Indians returned to their village, and the Spaniards followed after them.

Fortunately for the Spanish, the Quivirians received them peacefully, for they were so few in number and so far from their base they could have easily been destroyed. But their disappointment at the sight of the village was great. Here were no many-storied houses built of stone, which they had expected to find, only dwellings of straw. ". . . [T]he people of them," Coronado wrote in his sorrow, "are as barbarous as all those whom I have seen and passed before this; they do not have cloaks, nor cotton of which to make these, but used skins of the cattle they kill . . ."

The Indians gave Coronado a copper disk that one of them wore suspended around his neck. But this was all the metal they had, and Coronado suspected it had been carried to Quivira by one of his own soldiers, because he could figure no other way it might have gotten there. The poor appearance of the dwellings and the lack of gold and silver were not Coronado's only disillusionments. He had been told he could not travel through all the settlements in less than two months; all he found were twenty-five villages of straw huts.

They were now near present-day Lyons and Lindsborg, Kansas, a fertile country. Even though they were disappointed to find no gold or silver, the Spaniards took note of this, and Coronado judged it the best land he had seen on his journey. The soil was rich and well watered, and he thought it could produce all the crops grown in Spain. But agricultural possibilities were of little interest to the expedition. They had no seeds, no farming implements, and no market where they could sell their harvest.

Still not giving up hope of finding precious metals, Coronado summoned the "lord" who governed a settlement called Harahey. The "lord" arrived with about two hundred men, all of them nearly naked and armed with bows and arrows. Coronado later reported to the king that he had sent "captains and men in many directions to find out whether there was anything in this country which could be of service to Your Majesty. And although I have searched with all diligence I have not found or heard of anything, unless it be these provinces, which are a very small affair."

They had reached the end of their journey, and the golden dream had crumbled into the dust and dirt of the small fields that the Indians cultivated. Nothing remained for them to do except attempt a safe return to the main body of the army.

But first there was the Turk. He was at the root of their misfortunes, for it was his slippery tongue that had kept them on the road to failure. Why had he treated them so? Under questioning—and perhaps with the aid of torture—they made him confess that the people of Cicúye had asked him to lead them astray on the plains, hoping they would become so weakened by their wanderings and lack of food that they would either die or be easily destroyed. In addition the Spaniards became convinced he was trying to arouse the Quivirians against them. So one night, in the secrecy of a tent, they quietly garrotted him.

Maybe he really was an agent of Cicúye, although it is difficult to understand how he would have benefited. More likely, he was a simple-minded fool who enjoyed being the center of the Spaniards' attention and feeling superior to Sopete, not realizing where this course of action would inevitably carry him. At the last he paid for his lies with his life.

Without the Turk to guide them on the homeward journey, Coronado and his men took a more direct route, saving many miles of traveling. They returned as they had come, living off the land and relying on buffalo meat to sustain them, but they no longer had their hopes to urge them on. In Cicúye they found a detachment of soldiers waiting for them, which was fortunate, because the inhabitants of the pueblo had demonstrated outright hostility to the Europeans, a fact that reinforced the Spaniards' belief in the Turk's treachery. From there they went back to the valley of the Rio Grande and passed the winter.

Coronado's misfortunes, however, were not over. A broken saddle girth caused him to fall to the ground directly in front of a running horse, whose hooves struck him in the head. Although he finally recovered sufficiently to resume command, he never again was so forceful a person.

Once more spring came to the valley of the Río Grande, and the snow on the Sangre de Cristo Mountains began to melt and fill the streams with fresh running water. Many of the men wanted to continue searching for Quivira, but Coronado, now sick and weary, knew it was impractical to spend more time looking in the wilderness for what did not exist. But he did permit a few members of his expedition to remain behind. One of these was Fray Luís de Escalona, a lay brother who wished to work among the pueblos, using Cicúye as his headquarters. Another was an ordained priest, Fray Juan de Padilla, a man who combined courage and devotion to his Lord with a degree of bloodthirstiness. When the Hopis had attempted to resist the Spaniards, Padilla had urged the Spaniards to attack. Now, however, he wanted to return to Quivira and work for the salvation of that people. Coronado granted the requests of these men and perhaps allowed one other lay brother to remain, along with a small number of people who wished to stay with the friars. Then the army started the long march home.

Their arrival was not a joyous occasion. Friends welcomed friends, and wives were glad to be reunited with their husbands. But over the expedition hung the pall of disappointed hopes; and the viceroy, Mendoza, could hardly regard the copper disk secured in Quivira as an adequate return on the enormous sums he had invested.

In due time Coronado was called before the *residencia,* the almost routine inspection of the conduct of an important official. Because the *residencias* listened to all complaints, they provided opportunities for malcontents to voice their opinions and for the scurrilous to say their worst. But Coronado passed through this ordeal relatively unscathed. His poor health, however, lingered on,

and he never again played an outstanding role in the affairs of New Spain.

In terms of its objective—quick wealth—the expedition had indeed been a failure, but in terms of the future it had not. Coronado's journey across the plains and de Soto's explorations in the east had given Spain a claim to a vast area that would in time produce more wealth than that possessed by the Incas. But Coronado would never know the true value of what he had discovered.

None of the handful of people he left behind made a lasting impression on the country. Fray Luís was seen by some soldiers before the army departed from the Río Grande. They had driven a small flock of sheep to Cicúye as a present to him and had met him on the road, accompanied by a band of Indians and riding to some other pueblos to spread the Word of God. This they had taken as a good sign, but Fray Luís had told them many people were already deserting him and he was certain in the end they would kill him. His prophecy came true. Fray Juan had long ago pledged his life to God, and God took up the pledge. On the plains of Kansas, so unlike the mountains to which he was more accustomed, the friar was murdered.

There were, however, a few survivors among the remnants of the expedition that stayed behind. A Portuguese, who had accompanied Fray Juan, and several companions escaped from Quivira and made their way south to safety. Also an Indian woman, who was the companion of one of the Spanish soldiers, had run away and by chance met Moscoso on his return journey. Thus she alone took part in the two famous Spanish expeditions.

Out on the Great Plains, the hailstorms raged, and the winds blew, tossing the winter's snow or the summer's dust with equal impartiality. In the spring the Arkansas and Pecos rivers became full and then shrank as the season progressed, and the buffaloes came to their banks to drink. But no white men were there to see. At least temporarily the Great Plains had defeated them.

Chapter 3

The Struggle for an Empire

. . . the realm of France received on parchment a stupendous accession. The fertile plains of Texas; the vast basin of the Mississippi, from its frozen northern springs to the sultry borders of the Gulf; from the woody ridges of the Alleghanies to the bare peaks of the Rocky Mountains,—a region of savannas and forests, sun-cracked deserts, and grassy prairies, watered by a thousand rivers, ranged by a thousand warlike tribes, passed beneath the sceptre of the Sultan of Versailles; and all by virtue of a feeble human voice, inaudible at half a mile.
— Francis Parkman, 1869

Having been the first to discover the New World, the Spanish enjoyed an initial advantage in its subsequent conquest; and they made full use of it. The speed with which they established themselves in Hispañola and swept through thousands of miles of wilderness on the mainland was a miracle of the times. True, they were often cruel and treacherous, but the Indians were not above repaying them in kind. True, too, they had firearms and the Indians had only more primitive weapons; but the firearms themselves were primitive, and bows and arrows in the hands of experts were formidable. The Spaniards were also greatly outnumbered, and if the Indians had combined against them, they could have pushed the invaders back into the sea from which they had come. But the Spaniards exploited the differences between them, turning Indians against Indians to their own advantage and, with courage and aggressiveness that have rarely been equaled, spread their hegemony over two continents.

They could not, however, expect to maintain it without contest. With all his power, the king could not suppress the news of the discoveries being made, nor could he patrol the coasts of an entire hemisphere. Only a few years after Columbus's first arrival in the West Indies, John Cabot, acting on behalf of the British, ventured across the ocean.

Although his discoveries were not in themselves significant, his voyage laid a base for the later claims of the British. Other mariners also began sailing in seas that a few decades ago had been unexplored. French fishermen from Brittany and Normandy sailed the dangerous transatlantic crossing and dipped their nets into the fish-filled waters off Newfoundland. In 1534, the same year in which Cabeza de Vaca fled from the Indians and began his long journey, the French gave Jacques Cartier command of an expedition of two ships. The following year he made a return trip to the New World, this time exploring the St. Lawrence River, which was destined to become France's gateway to the West.

A small Indian boy, shooting with his toy bow and arrows, would have created no bigger dent in his father's war shield than these expeditions made on the Spanish empire. The important point, however, was that they were being made at all and in increasing numbers. Like a small nimbus cloud forming over the prairie on a summer's day, they presaged a storm to come.

In the last half of the sixteenth century, the future of Spain's control of the North American continent began to look less and less certain. John Hawkins, the British seaman, twice broke the

Spanish monopoly and sold slaves in Hispañola, although on his third attempt the Spanish put a stop to his efforts. The French established a fort on the St. John's River in Florida, which was a direct challenge to Spanish authority in that area. Spain destroyed it and then founded the settlement of St. Augustine. But these were delaying, rather than decisive, actions. In the meanwhile British ships were harassing Spain's, and Drake circumnavigated the world and claimed California for England.

It was not geography alone that prevented the Spanish from marching north, taking the Great Plains, and then fanning east and west to absorb the remainer of the continent. It was lack of resources and the need to concentrate the nation's men and energy on primary objectives. One of the most important of these was to produce enough ready riches to make the conquests immediately self-financing and also leave a surplus that could be applied to Spain's activities in Europe. As Coronado had clearly demonstrated, these riches could not be found in Quivira. So the Spanish in Mexico devoted much of their effort to expanding existing mines or developing new ones—they had learned that many minerals existed in that country—and on protecting the passage of the galleons.

Although no expedition had been launched in the direction of the Great Plains since Coronado's failure, there had been a slow movement north to the present state of Zacatecas, and miners were working at the settlement of Santa Bárbara near the boundary of the modern state of Chihuahua. From settlements such as this, the military made forays into the surrounding country, fighting hostile Indians and looking for sites of possible mines. During one of these trips the soldiers captured an Indian whom they brought back to Santa Bárbara. He told stories of a country to the north where the people wore clothes made of cloth, which the Spaniards took to be a sign of civilization and perhaps wealth.

When a friar named Agustín Rodríguez heard this news, he decided he wanted to lead an expedition of friars and soldiers to find these people and perhaps save their souls. Since the laws of Spain prohibited unofficial exploration, Fray Agustín journeyed to Mexico City to obtain the necessary government permit.

He arrived at the capital in November, 1580, and stated his case to the viceroy, who listened with interest. Since his authority was restricted—he, too, had to seek permission of the king before authorizing a major expedition—he allowed Fray Agustín to go but set a limit on the number of men who could accompany him.

On his return to Santa Bárbara, Fray Agustín looked for recruits and found two friars whose devotion to the cause of God was as great as his own. He also was able to recruit nine other Spaniards to serve as guards. They may have been partly inspired to make this journey from religious motives, but certainly in the back of their minds lurked thoughts of gold and silver. Each of the soldiers took with him an Indian servant, making a total of approximately twenty-five people. Where Coronado's army failed, this little band hoped to succeed.

Their way north was much less circuitous than that taken by Coronado. By following the Conchos River downstream, they reached the Río Grande, which led them into the pueblo country. The Indians, who had given Coronado so much trouble, could have easily wiped out this small band, only nine of whom bore arms. But instead they gave the travelers food and information in exchange for the hawk's bells and other trinkets the Spaniards brought with them. One of the three friars decided he should return to Mexico City with news of what they had found and, against the advice of his fellows, started on the long road back. Along the way he was attacked and killed by hostile Indians.

The others re-explored some of the country observed by Coronado's men. They also wanted to see the buffaloes, of which they had heard so much, and so they made a journey east of the Pecos River. They were not disappointed by what they found. The herds, they later reported, each contained from a hundred to two hundred buffaloes, which they rightly described as humpbacked, shaggy, and thickset. They also met a band of Plains Indians who were on a buffalo hunt. Just as Coronado's men had reported, these used dogs as pack animals, raising them especially for this purpose. Wanting to take advantage of the abundant supply of meat, the Spaniards killed forty buffaloes with their clumsy firearms, butchered the carcasses, and jerked the meat, cutting it into small pieces and drying it in the sun. The result was hard pieces of flesh that would not spoil; and although hardly an epicurean's delight, they could be made edible again by moistening them either in a pot of water or by holding the chunks in their mouths.

After their return to the pueblo country they intended to explore further, but the season was getting late, and a snowfall reminded them that winter was approaching. The time had come, therefore, to return home. The religious zeal often displayed by the Spanish was never better demonstrated than now. The two remaining friars had come to spread word of the Christian faith among the Indians, and they could not accomplish this by leaving with the others. So when the day of departure came, they stayed behind with the Indians they had brought as servants. As they watched their escort ride off into the distance, they must have known that a fate like Fray Juan de Padilla's probably awaited them. But they had faith in their God and believed death in His cause was better than an unfaithful life on earth.

As was the case with all Spanish expeditions, those who returned were required to make a report to the government of what they had seen and done, so several of the soldiers went before a notary and made depositions. Unlike Fray Marcos, they told no wild tales of gold and silver, but they did report they had seen a number of possible mine sites. (One man said he had observed as many as eleven.)

The viceroy, therefore, had two good reasons for sending out a second expedition: it could be charged both with rescuing the friars—an important consideration with the crown—and with examining the potential mines. A man named Antonio de Espejo offered to finance the expedition, since the crown and the Church rarely invested their own funds in exploration.

In November, 1852, the group started down the Conchos River toward the Río Grande and remained in the field almost a year, not returning to Santa Bárbara until September, 1853. During this time its members retraced many of the routes followed by Coronado, revisiting the pueblos in the area around the Río Grande. They confirmed the deaths of all three friars, but their force was not strong enough to mete out punishment. Because they did not attempt to take the trail to Quivira, they saw little of the plains. But on their return home they followed the Pecos River south, and Espejo named it El Río de las Vacas—the river of cows—because he saw so many buffaloes along its banks.

Although the Espejo expedition had penetrated into some areas previously unknown to the Spaniards, it did not greatly enlarge their knowledge of the land to the north. But Espejo had heard tales of people who wore gold bracelets and earrings, and he also had discovered some ores he thought were promising. This was enough to rekindle interest in the North American wilderness, but time was slipping away from Spain. The British, who had already tried with considerable success to disrupt Spain's ocean trade routes, were now trying to gain a permanent foothold on the western shores of

the Atlantic. In the year after the return of the Espejo expedition, British ships dropped anchor at Roanoke. Although the colony failed, the temporary presence of British settlers clearly indicated their nation's future intentions. As even the smallest of streams cuts at the rocks along its banks, events were slowly eroding the power of Spain.

During this period, the Spanish government, its resources strained, did nothing to encourage further exploration in the direction of the Great Plains. Individual Spaniards were still willing to undertake the physical and financial risks—Espejo himself unsuccessfully applied for a license to return—but Spain was involved in enough enterprises already, both in the New World and the Old. Because of Espejo's reports, however, more and more people wanted a license to conquer the pueblos, do battle in Quivira, and search for the straits that were supposed to link the two oceans that flanked the continent. Yielding to pressure, the king had a contract drawn up that would serve as a basis for such a license.

One of those who would not wait for legalities was Castaño de Sosa, who in 1590 led an expedition to the pueblos. He was arrested by the military and brought back. In 1593 two other men, Franciso Leyva de Bonilla and Antonio Gutierrez de Humaña, led another unauthorized expedition to the pueblos. After about a year they started in search for Quivira and found a large Indian settlement on the Arkansas River in eastern Kansas. Traveling twelve days more, they came to another river that may have been the Platte. During the journey Humaña murdered his partner, but he never profited from his violence, for later he was attacked and killed by Indians.

Among the many who took the legal course of formally applying for the right to colonize the northern country was Juan de Oñate, whose wife was a descendent of Cortés and whose father was the wealthy governor of Nueva Galicia. In spite of Oñate's prominence and influence, the king took a long time before deciding to award him the contract; and even then, Oñate had to go through the ordeal of several inspections before he was permitted to leave. Early in 1598 he had finally satisfied all the demands of the Spanish bureaucracy and began his expedition.

On arriving at the Río Grande, he held a celebration to take formal possession of the land in the name of Spain and then marched a relatively few miles upstream, crossing the river at El Paso—The Pass—where there was a ford. When he reached the pueblo country, he ordered the Indians to submit to Spain and proceeded to select one pueblo to use as his capital. As soon as he had established his base, he set about exploring the country, that being one of his contractual obligations. He himself went to the west, visiting the Zuñis and searching for the outcroppings of ore reported by Espejo.

At the same time, he ordered his nephew, Vincente de Zaldívar, to travel to the Great Plains and attempt to obtain some buffalo meat. With approximately sixty men and an Indian who had served with Humaña as a guide, Zaldívar entered the Great Plains. Unlike his predecessors, he did not immediately find any buffaloes, for the herds did not concentrate in a single spot but moved from place to place in search of grass. Wisely he made friends with the Indians whom he met, and they told him the direction in which the animals were then grazing. At last the Spaniards saw, not a herd of buffaloes, but a single old bull, which could hardly run. This caused much joking among the men, because each had dreamed of eventually rounding up no fewer than ten thousand of these "cattle," domesticating them, and becoming wealthy cattle owners.

After this disappointment, which they took in such good nature, they soon found about a thousand buffaloes and decided to capture them alive. If they could accomplish this and drive them back to the Río Grande, they would be able to provide the entire expedition with a source of fresh meat. But by the time they had finished building the necessary corral—it was a large structure, because it had to have long wings to funnel the animals into the enclosure—the buffaloes had moved away. Zaldívar went in pursuit of them with ten of his soldiers, but instead of buffaloes he found many Plains Indians, who had been trading with the Pueblo Indians. Their approach had frightened the animals and caused them to move even farther on.

Zaldívar was undoubtedly annoyed at the fruitlessness of his hunt, but this did not prevent him from carefully examining the Indians' tipis. The hides of which they were made were so well tanned they were waterproof; and when he cut away a small sample of the leather and soaked it in water, he discovered it remained soft and supple when it dried out instead of hardening, as leather often does. He was also astonished that a tent so large could weigh so little and bartered for one to take with him when he returned to the remainder of his men.

After a short holiday to rest his soldiers, he resumed his search for the buffaloes. This time he was more successful and killed a large number, but the soldiers still hoped to capture a substantial herd alive. To do this, they had to find another site suitable for a corral and also the wood to build it. Selecting a location by the side of a stream where enough cottonwoods were growing to supply the lumber, they spent the next three days building a corral that was so large it could have contained ten thousand animals.

When the construction work was finished, they set off on a buffalo round-up, not realizing that buffaloes were quite unlike the domestic cattle to which they were accustomed. The drive started in the traditional fashion, the Spaniards on horseback surrounding part of the herd and with shouts urging it slowly toward the corral. For a short time it seemed as though these first cowboys of the Great Plains would be successful. Everything was orderly, and the Spaniards dreamed of the great herds each of them would soon possess.

Then in a flash the buffaloes took fright. Turning around, they began moving toward their pursuers instead of away from them and gathered speed. Since the Spaniards were now in front of a stampeding herd, they had to get out of the way as quickly as possible. It was then that they began to realize that these "cows" were not the same as Spanish cows. If they pursued them too hard, the buffaloes ran away; if they stopped pursuing them, the buffaloes would also stop and, rolling in the dirt, take advantage of the chance for a slight rest. They also discovered that if they annoyed the buffaloes, the animals fought back, and that a charging buffalo was a dangerous enemy.

The Spaniards did not give up easily. These men were of a race that had marched against great odds through Mexico, had conquered Peru, and had created an empire that covered much of two continents. They had crossed mountains, forded rivers, and sailed on unknown oceans. But they had never before tried to round up buffaloes. They worked at it for several days, using every strategy they could devise, but although they could start a herd toward the corral, they could not make the animals enter it. Their failure was not caused by any lack of courage on their part. Three of their horses were killed and forty more badly wounded, and to ride a horse that is being gored by a buffalo is not an assignment for a timid man. But in the end the buffaloes did what the mountains and oceans and rivers had been unable to—they made the Spaniards give up. They might find silver mines, they might even, they still believed, find the golden city of Quivira, but it became clear to them that they were not going to be able to corral buffaloes.

If they could not capture the adults, at least, they thought, they could take some of the calves. But this effort, too, proved unsuccessful. They were able to catch a number of them without interference from the adults and either dragged them with ropes or carried them on horseback toward their camp. But the young animals struggled so hard that none of them reached the camp alive. Zaldívar finally concluded they should be taken earlier in the season and raised among domestic sheep and goats or crossed with some of the cattle from Spain.

While he was on the Great Plains, Zaldívar came across many bands of Indians who were also hunting buffaloes and was able to keep on good terms with them. The Indians were armed with large bows, flint-headed arrows, and lances. Instead of following the buffaloes on foot, which would have been slow and tiresome, they formed lines near their water holes, and when the animals came to drink, the Indians would shoot them. It took only a single shot to kill one, a further demonstration of the accuracy and power of a bow and arrow in the right hands.

Oñate did not wait for Zaldívar's return to start exploring. First he went a short distance to the southeast and then headed west toward the South Sea, or the Pacific Ocean. If his colonization was to be a success, he had to find some of those immediate riches for which the Spaniards continually searched. For, like so many Spanish expeditions, this one was badly undercapitalized, and much of the money had been provided by Oñate personally, either from his own purse or from borrowings. Since he alone could not supply everything that was needed, many of the individual settlers had used their own resources to equip themselves. From Oñate down, a number of them had overextended themselves, and they needed a quick return on their initial investment to remain solvent. If, as they hoped, they found pearls among the Indians of the South Sea, this would alleviate their problem.

When Oñate's western exploration failed to place the expedition on a self-liquidating basis, the members, seeing their slender resources dwindle, became increasingly disgruntled. Although Oñate had proved himself a man of vigorous action, he could not stem the rising tide of discontent and, frustrated, turned autocratic and harsh under conditions that called for tact and patience.

But if those two qualities were missing from his character, he had unusual courage and persistence. Many of the people under him were ready to give up and return to Mexico, but he insisted on clinging to hope. In 1601, nearly three years after his arrival in New Mexico, he determined on a desperate gamble to salvage his investment. He would go to Quivira, for there was always the chance that those who had made the journey before him might have overlooked something significant.

With about seventy of his best men and two friars, he started on the long journey. An Indian, Joseph, who had been with Humaña and also Zaldívar, served as a guide. To help assure the expedition's success, Oñate equipped it well, providing it with carts, cannon, servants, and more than seven hundred mules and horses.

After crossing the Pecos River, they entered the Great Plains. This country was no longer the unknown wilderness it had been when Coronado first approached it, and the men were not as frightened by it as some had been in the past. Nevertheless, four or five soldiers deserted, thus placing themselves at the mercy of any Indians they might encounter or any soldiers sent to capture them. If they considered this risky action the lesser of two evils, the sight of the Great Plains must have thrown them into a panic. On the other hand, in the official account of the expedition that Oñate later had prepared, the writer did not let the truth prevent him from placing the area in a favorable light. Oñate wanted no one in Mexico or Spain to lose heart, for he needed all the support he could get.

The weather, the writer declared, was pleasantly warm, although in truth it probably was unbearably hot. And Zaldívar would have laughed if he could have heard the description of the buffaloes. The report stated that their meat was good, which was true, but it also said they never became aroused like Spanish cattle and were never dangerous. The land, as the report described it, was also rich in fruits and fish.

The reality, however, was grim. The men were troubled by the flatness of the land and found it easy for individuals to get lost if they wandered any distance away from the main body. They also suffered from the violent weather of the plains. On some days it rained so hard they did not even attempt to break camp. So struggling against the elements and bewildered by their surroundings, this group of Spaniards moved into the heart of what later became the United States, following a route that took them along the Canadian River and then in the general direction of present-day Wichita, Kansas.

During the journey they met various bands of Indians. The first of these, they said, were Apaches, but they had no difficulties with them. Next they encountered a large encampment of a tribe they named Escanjaques, who at first prepared themselves to fight the strange white men who had come into their midst. But the Spaniards made signs of peace, and the Indians responded by inviting them to their village. They knew about the fate of Humaña's expedition and thought the Spaniards planned to avenge their countrymen's death. This, they believed, gave them an opportunity to use the Spaniards for their own purposes. Carefully placing the blame for Humaña's disaster on another nearby tribe with whom they were at war, they hoped to enlist the Spaniards as allies. Oñate saw the trap and delicately avoided making any commitments, for he could not afford to become involved in the Indians' intertribal wars. During their negotiations, the Spaniards noticed that, while these Indians had chiefs, they did not necessarily pay great attention to them, which was true of many tribes on the Great Plains. The personal prestige of the chief, rather than the office itself, determined whether the others followed his advice, making it a truly democratic form of government, so democratic that many white men never understood it.

The next day the Escanjaques, thinking they had deceived the Spaniards, insisted on traveling with them, placing Oñate in a difficult position. Nevertheless, when he approached the second tribe, he made signs of peace and was able to enter their village without hostilities, while the Escanjaques remained behind.

But the following morning the Escanjaques made warlike gestures against their enemies, threatening to attack them but without actually doing so. Fighting among the Plains Indians was often carried out in this manner, which was much like that of the ancient Greeks. Rather than engaging in pitched battles, both sides would line up facing each other and hurl taunts at one another. Then two individuals might engage in combat while the remainder of the Indians looked on. If an important chief or outstanding warrior was killed in this fashion, the losing side might retreat. But in this instance, the second band apparently did not let the Escanjaques lure them into a struggle.

When, as they always did, the Spaniards inquired about the country, the second band of Indians told them how they had attacked Humaña and his followers. Oñate had been quick in punishing rebellious pueblos but he was wise enough to realize that with about seventy men, far from his base, and in the open space of the Great Plains, he could not afford to engage in warfare. So he ignored the confession, continued toward the north, and shortly reached a river that was probably the Arkansas. There he found the first Quiviran village he had seen.

The place, however, was completely deserted.

The Spaniards wandered from one grass hut to another and found a plentiful supply of maize but no Indians. The inhabitants, learning of the Spaniards' approach, had fled to safety. Still anxious to maintain the government's support of his efforts to colonize New Mexico and the country to the east and north, Oñate later described the land as extremely fertile, which indeed it is, although his description of the Indians' cornfields was exaggerated. If he could not give the authorities gold, he could at least promise them a country rich in agriculture.

After a while some of the Indians returned, and the Spaniards asked them about the villages downstream. In an obvious attempt to frighten the white men away, one Indian said there were many settlements and their inhabitants were assembling to resist a Spanish advance. In spite of this warning, Oñate decided to explore a few miles of the river's bank. He was then probably near present-day Witchita or Hutchinson, Kansas. Prudence, however, won the day. His men may have petitioned him—the official account states they did—saying it was wiser to return with the news of this fertile country than to continue risking their lives. In his report Oñate made it clear it was not lack of personal courage that caused him to retreat and that he had agreed with the petitioners only reluctantly.

The trip back to New Mexico proved more difficult than the journey out, because one of the villages that had previously been friendly vigorously attacked the expedition. As the story was told and retold, the duration of the struggle and the number of Indian casualties grew in size, but in spite of the evident embellishments that came with time, the battle was fierce. A Spanish victory cleared the way to New Mexico, and the weary men recrossed the Great Plains and safely reached their base on the Río Grande.

The news awaiting them there was bad. Weary of trying to make a living in that inhospitable country, many of the settlers had taken advantage of Oñate's absence to desert. Oñate sent Zaldívar in pursuit, but the deserters reached Santa Bárbara before him and came under the protection of the viceroy.

For all practical purposes that was the end of Oñate's effort to colonize New Mexico. He hung on for several more years, continuing his explorations and trying to ingratiate himself with the Spanish authorities. But his glowing reports were blunted by the contradictory testimony of the deserters, and the government began to despair at the expense of maintaining such a colony, one that provided no income. In 1608 the Council of the Indies decided to abandon New Mexico. The only question was the future welfare of the converted Indians, but perhaps they could be taken to Mexico, by force if necessary. Late that year came reports that the converts were more numerous than had previously been supposed and also that samples of silver ore had been found. As a result, the colony was continued but on a more modest basis, and Oñate was replaced as governor and brought home to face an examination.

In relaxing their tentative and feeble grip on the Great Plains, the Spanish probably acted wisely, for they were faced with growing competition in the New World and needed to conserve their strength. While Oñate was struggling to maintain his precarious foothold in New Mexico, Henry Hudson, on behalf of his Dutch employers, had discovered the river that bears his name, the French had established their first colony in what is now Nova Scotia, and the British, after their failure at Roanoke Island, had landed at Jamestown. Of these three, only the French posed an immediate threat to the Spanish. The Dutch were soon dislodged, and the British stayed close to the coastline, but the French roamed far and wide, because they had discovered the equivalent of the Spaniards' treasure—a commodity that was light and thus easily portable and yet commanded a high price in the markets of Europe. That commodity was fur, particularly beaver fur.

The first Frenchmen had come to fish in the fertile waters off the northeastern coast but had found it more profitable to load their ships with furs purchased inexpensively from the Indians than to return home with a catch taken from the ocean. The fur trade, however, was not created instantly. Like the Spanish, the French were plagued with financial and administrative problems, and the Indians proved to be wily customers, quickly learning how to play one trader against another. The French overcame these difficulties, and in spite of the harsh winters of the northland, harassment by the Iroquois, and the vast, inhospitable wilderness, their traders and priests were steadily extending French control westward. Since the Spanish were working up the Pacific Coast, the Great Plains were becoming almost encircled by Europeans except in the north and the northwest, although no white man had been able to start a settlement in the area they embraced.

The Spanish strengthened their hold on Mexico by gradually settling the area along Oñate's route to Santa Fé, and they also explored to the east, becoming more familiar with Texas. In 1634 Alonso de Vaca made the journey to Quivira and probably reached the Arkansas River. But Spain's principal effort was concentrated on trying to consolidate its position in New Mexico and along the coast of the Gulf of Mexico.

If the Spanish were having trouble advancing into the wilderness, so, too, were the French, for they found themselves caught in a British vise. To the south, along the Atlantic Coast, were British colonies, well entrenched and determined to stay. Furthermore, the British had become friendly with the Five Nations, that group of Iroquois who were among the finest and fiercest Indian warriors in North America. Against them the Ottawas and the Hurons, who were the principal Indian allies of the French, were almost helpless. To the north, Henry Hudson had discovered Hudsons Bay, thus laying the basis for Great Britain's entry into the Canadian fur trade. Nevertheless, French traders and priests, a hardy and fearless band of men, were still penetrating westward. Two of them, Pierre Esprit Radisson, and his brother-in-law, Médard Chouart Groseilliers, both true adventurers, traveled as far as Lake Superior; and when they returned from their long journey, they brought back reports of the Mississippi River. No one, of course, knew either its length or its direction, but most men sensed its importance in giving access to the hinterland.

Although news of this great waterway stirred the spirits of the ambitious, it aroused no comparable enthusiasm among the officials who were then guiding the destinies of France. Like the monarch of Spain, Louis XIV could not immediately seize every opportunity offered him by the adventurers roaming through his overseas domain. Powerful as he was, his policies were restricted by his desire to retain firm control over his colonies and his colonists and his fear of overextending his military forces. Consequently he permitted no mad rush into the wilderness but instead commanded caution. Yet even the most powerful of rulers often cannot totally exercise his will. The intendant of Canada—the man charged with conducting its civil affairs as opposed to its diplomatic, military, and religious activities—was Jean Talon, whose sense of Canada's destiny was greater than Louis's. In spite of the king's admonitions, he was determined to solve the mystery of the Mississippi; and as leader of an exploratory expedition, he chose Louis Joliet.

A native-born Canadian, Joliet had been educated by the Jesuits but abandoned a career in the Church for one as a fur trader. In contrast to the many dramatic personalities that studded the era, he was quiet and unassuming, but he was a dependable man, knowledgeable in the ways of the Indians and a skilled woodsman. He was also familiar with the West, because he had made his trading headquarters at Sault Sainte Marie between Lake Huron and Lake Superior, which was then at the edge of French Canada's frontier.

In common with their fellow Catholics in Spain, the French combined proselytism with exploration, and the sword and the cross advanced side by side. The priest chosen to accompany Joliet was Jacques Marquette, a Jesuit devoted to the spiritual welfare of the Indians. As soon as he had arrived in the New World, he had begun to study the languages of his future charges and quickly became fluent in several of them. The more remote the mission, the more it appealed to Marquette; and having heard of the Mississippi, he longed to descend it and establish the Christian faith among the Illinois Indians.

Both geography and economics had a profound effect on the manner in which Spanish and French expeditions traveled. In the arid regions of New Spain, travel by water was, of course, impossible; but even when they explored parts of the country where canoes or other small boats might have been used, the Spanish generally preferred to ride horseback. For the quick return that they needed on their investment, they hoped for gold and silver or other immediate riches, and they could obtain these only by subjugating the peoples they met. In battle, their cavalry gave them a decided advantage over the enemy; and until the Indians became familiar with them, the very sight of horses often struck terror in their hearts. In Canada, on the other hand, horses were scarce. In summertime, they could not get through the tangles of the northern forests, while the numerous lakes and rivers provided a ready means of transportation; in winter, a man on snowshoes could move more rapidly than a horse floundering in the snow. So the French became adept canoemen, and when travel by water was not possible, they usually journeyed on foot. Also because the fur trade depended on gaining the Indians' cooperation, not conquering them, the French usually moved in smaller groups.

In sharp contrast to the expeditions of Coronado and Oñate, Joliet and Marquette had only five companions and made their trip by canoe. In the early summer of 1673—more than a month after they had started out—they paddled their canoes into the waters of the Mississippi near the present town of Prairie du Chien, Wisconsin. Of the many momentous events in the exploration of North America, this was one of the most significant. The Spanish

navigators had located the river's mouth in the Gulf of Mexico but did not know where it led. De Soto had crossed it upstream but had not followed its course. Yet control of this river and its great tributaries like the Ohio and the Missouri would for many years to come be a key factor in the development of the West. Like the veins in a leaf, the arms of the river's waterways stretched in every direction, creating a comprehensive transportation system in the wilderness. From the Appalachian Mountains to the Rockies, the Mississippi and its tributaries dictated where men would go.

Because theirs was an official exploring expedition, not a private fur-trading venture, Joliet and Marquette were more concerned with collecting information than collecting profits. They took soundings of the river's depth and made notes of what they observed along its banks, including herds of buffaloes. Moving through areas which no European had ever seen before, the tiny band of seven men came to the present site of St. Louis, where the waters of the Missouri, gathered from the western mountains and the Great Plains, joined those of the Mississippi to make their common run to the sea. The heavy influx of water made the Mississippi churn and indicated the size of the Missouri. By now Joliet and Marquette were almost certain the Mississippi emptied into the Gulf of Mexico, but they had not abandoned hope of finding a route to the Pacific. Perhaps the Missouri was the answer. From the Indians Marquette obtained as much information as possible about the river, put it in his notes, and expressed the desire to return someday and explore it. But their present assignment of determining the final destination of the Mississippi was enough to accomplish in one season.

Farther down the river, Joliet and Marquette came to the site of present-day Cairo, Illinois, where the Ohio joins the Mississippi. Without in any way realizing the full importance of what they had seen, they had now uncovered the secret of one of the world's great internal waterways. Without leaving the Ohio, Missouri, and Mississippi rivers, a man could travel from Canada to the Gulf of Mexico and from the western slopes of the Appalachians into the heart of the Great Plains.

Still moving with the current, they came to a village of Arkansa Indians. Once again they were received in a friendly manner, but their hosts warned them they would probably meet with hostility if they visited the tribes farther to the south. Joliet and Marquette could not risk being attacked, for they would have been unable to defend themselves, and their deaths would have accomplished nothing except to prevent the French from knowing what they had learned so far. On the other hand, they were sure they were near the Gulf of Mexico. Therefore they let prudence dictate their actions and turned north for the homeward journey.

The information brought back by Joliet and Marquette did not cause a sudden ferment of action in New France. In fact, many men were probably disappointed to learn the great river emptied into the Gulf of Mexico instead of providing a waterway to India, thus giving Canada easy access to that fabulous market. Nevertheless, there were in New France numerous adventurous souls to whom the unknown appealed and who dreamed of bringing new lands under the sway of the fleur-de-lis.

One of these was Réné-Robert Cavelier, Sieur de la Salle, whose name, la Salle, was taken from a property owned by his family and used, in accord with a common practice of the times, to differentiate between him and other members of the Cavelier family. Although his father was a wealthy merchant in France, la Salle, being a younger son in those days of primogeniture, had little money of his own and had come to Canada to seek his fortune. Of the many leaders who played a part in the development of France's western empire, he was perhaps the strangest personality, combining fortunate and unfortunate qualities to an unusual degree. He was well educated and extremely intelligent; he had a facility for dealing with Indians that was almost unequaled among his peers; he was both hardy and courageous; and his perseverance was outstanding. But he also had two great weaknesses. He was almost paranoiac in his obsession with those he regarded as "enemies"; and although he could inspire tremendous loyalty in some individuals, he was unpopular with many of those that served under him.

Shortly after his arrival in Canada, la Salle had secured some land at present-day La Chine, a few miles up the St. Lawrence from Montreal. During the following years he explored what was then considered the West and became a close ally of Louis de Buade, Comte de Frontenac, whom the king had appointed governor of Canada. With Frontenac's backing he received command of a new fort that had been constructed on Lake Ontario and a grant of lands surrounding it. La Salle's financial future was now virtually assured, because he was in a position to control an important part of the fur trade. But his restless, ambitious nature was still not satisfied, and he kept dreaming of the Mis-

sissippi and the lands to the west. Although Joliet and Marquette had proved the river did not flow to the west coast of the continent, la Salle understood its real significance. Whoever gained possession of the Mississippi, he realized, would be master of the fur trade from the Appalachian Mountains to the Rockies.

In 1677, with Frontenac's blessing, he returned to France and petitioned the king for a monopoly of the fur trade in the Mississippi watershed. His petition was granted, but the king was not generous; la Salle received permission to build as many forts as he wished, but he had to supply the funds and the men. Most persons would have thought such an undertaking beyond their capacity, but la Salle was not one of them, and even before returning to Canada, he started a successful money-raising campaign.

In 1679 he was ready to take physical possession of his new claim. As part of his plan, he built a ship on Lake Erie—the first commercial vessel to sail those waters—and took it to Green Bay, Wisconsin, where he loaded it with furs. The pilot was to return with the cargo to Montreal, where it would be sold and the proceeds used to pay some of la Salle's creditors. Meanwhile la Salle and his principal lieutenant, Henri de Tonty, an Italian who had joined la Salle in France, proceeded down the river. But the carefully planned program was undermined by a series of disasters. On its return voyage to Montreal, la Salle's ship and its cargo of furs were lost under mysterious circumstances. A fort he built was abandoned by his men, who deserted almost as soon as he had left them to continue his exploration. A scouting expedition he sent north on the Mississippi was captured by the Sioux, and la Salle and Tonty became separated in the wilderness and unable to locate each other. Because Tonty was one of the few persons la Salle completely trusted, this was a serious blow.

At the end of many long months of work and the assumption of enormous risk, la Salle's plan for the conquest of the West was shattered by the treachery of his men, the geography of the country, and the difficulty of the logistics. He had gambled for high stakes and had lost almost everything except his faith in himself. In spite of his devastating ill fortune, that faith continued high, and he immediately set about getting ready for a second attempt.

Although la Salle had difficulty in inspiring loyalty among his men when they were in the field, he seems to have been unusually persuasive elsewhere. For in a relatively short time he had raised enough money to finance another expedition. In December, 1681, he and Tonty, who had finally rejoined him, were again on their way south, following the Chicago River and the Illinois to the Mississippi.

At the beginning of the journey the men had battled against snow and ice, but with the passing days and their southward movement, they entered a springtime world. Although they passed beyond the range of the Indian dialects that la Salle could speak, his remarkable facility at dealing with the natives continued to stand them in good stead, and they moved safely from one village to another. As the days passed, they found themselves surrounded by the lush growth of Louisiana. On the banks stood magnificent live oaks, their branches festooned with gray moss that sometimes shone like silver in the sun. Then the trees became smaller and scarcer, and the explorers entered the flat, watery land of the Mississippi delta, where the sky runs down to the horizon on every side and only the position of the sun and the course of the river give the traveler a sense of direction. In April, 1682, they came at last to the river's mouth and saw ahead of them the Gulf of Mexico.

The small company had divided itself into three groups, each taking one of the "passes" into which the river splits as the fresh water enters the salt. They then reunited a short distance upstream and with considerable ceremony erected a column, bearing the arms of France and the name of Louis XIV. This done, la Salle laid claim in the name of France to the Mississippi River, its watershed, and the watersheds of its many tributaries. This was a vast area, perhaps larger than he realized, running from the Appalachian Mountains in the east to the Rockies in the west, and it included most of the Great Plains. The Spanish had crossed from New Mexico to Kansas before either the British or the French had been able to place a permanent settlement in North America, but now their claim to the Great Plains was threatened by an explorer standing with a small group and their Indian followers at the mouth of the Mississippi. Sitting in regal splendor in their various courts, the crowned heads of Europe were unaware of the portentous event; and the only witness was the great river itself, flowing silently by, its mystery at last uncovered.

By his elaborate ceremony—elaborate, that is, for men in a wilderness—la Salle had set in motion a series of events that in time would shake the capitals of Europe. Moving quietly by canoe through alien territory, he had at least on paper driven a wedge into the empire established by Spain through the explorations of men like de Soto and Coronado. La Salle was too realistic, however, to believe for one moment that Spain would respect his proclamation unless he and the French government had some physical means of protecting the claim.

On his return to Canada, therefore, he immediately took steps to establish himself more firmly in the territory he had opened up. In 1682, the same year he reached the mouth of the Mississippi, he began the construction of a permanent fort on the Illinois River. This was to be the first of several fortifications, but the ill fortune that had dogged him since the start of his ambitious enterprise persisted. His sponsor, Frontenac, had become entangled in a controversy with the ecclesiastical authorities in Canada and was recalled to France. His replacement was an unscrupulous, incompetent official, who plotted to enrich himself by preying on la Salle. La Salle's only recourse was to return personally to France and seek a reaffirmation of his privileges from the king himself.

Once again he demonstrated his extraordinary persuasiveness. Not only did he re-establish his position, he also convinced the court that a settlement at the mouth of the Mississippi would be in the best interests of France. So the government organized an expedition for this purpose and placed la Salle in command of the land operations; and in mid-summer of 1684, he sailed from France with four ships and approximately four hundred men.

When he entered the Gulf of Mexico, he faced two perplexing problems. Because of Spain's exclusionary policies, the French knew little about those waters and their currents, which made navigation difficult. Nor did la Salle know the exact location of the mouth of the Mississippi. When he had been there, he had taken its latitude but had been unable to determine its longitude, a common navigational problem of that era when accurate chronometers were rare. On many coasts this might have made little difference, because la Salle could have recognized outstanding landmarks. But much of the Gulf Coast looks the same, presenting to the seafarer only a long low line against the horizon. Even the Mississippi itself, mighty as it is, makes a furtive entrance into the Gulf, sneaking into the open water through a number of "passes" cut through the coastal wetlands. So la Salle's ill fate continued to pursue him like a wolf on the trail of a wounded buffalo, and he could not find the river for which he was searching. In desperation he finally landed his men in Texas, far from his objective, and sent the ships home.

Always willing to gamble, he took this dangerous risk rather than admit defeat. He soon learned the magnitude of his error when he led an initial scouting expedition and failed to find the river. He was, he realized, much farther from it than he had thought. Since the purpose of his venture was to establish a permanent settlement, he was encumbered with civilians, including some women. As he could not march with them through the wilderness, he began the construction of a temporary fort that, he hoped, would protect them from the Indians and any Spaniards who might chance to find them. The latter possibility frightened them as much as the first, for they knew they were in contested territory.

On one foray in search of the Mississippi, la Salle stayed at an Indian encampment where he was able to purchase some horses. Although he was pleased to have the animals to transport his supplies, he was unaware of the significance of their presence in the Indian village. When Cabeza de Vaca had been shipwrecked on the coast of Texas, there had been no horses in what was to become the American West. As the early Spanish explorers noted, the Indians had developed the *travois* for carrying loads, but the only pack animals they possessed were dogs. Gradually, however, the Spanisards had lost some of their horses, either as the result of Indian raids or because they strayed away. The rich grasslands of the plains were as ideal a habitat for them as they were for the buffaloes, and their numbers rapidly multiplied. The change for the Indians was almost as great as that created by the discovery of the wheel in other civilizations, since the absence of trees and mountains made the Great Plains ideally suited to the use of horses.

No longer did the Indians have to travel relatively slowly on foot. This affected their behavior in both war and peace. Mounted warriors were a far more formidable enemy than men on foot, and the Indians became as effective fighters as European cavalry. In peacetime, too, horses were becoming an integral part of the Indians' lives. A horseman was a far more efficient buffalo hunter than a man on foot, and since the buffaloes were the primary source of the Plains Indians' wealth, their riches rapidly increased. Furthermore, horses made it possible for the Indians to retain their wealth once they had accumulated it. With only dogs to carry their belongings, they had had to limit their posses-

sions, but the use of horses greatly expanded what they could take with them during their wanderings.

The animals that la Salle purchased had probably been stolen by the Comanches, who lived to the west, and then brought east for trading purposes. Among these Indians la Salle also noticed many other items that had been pilfered from the Spanish, including lamps, spoons, some old muskets, and clothing.

Aside from the stolen muskets, however, the Indians had no firearms or ammunition. The Spanish might be careless with their horses, but under no circumstances did their government permit them to trade guns or ammunition even with Indians whom they regarded as friends. Approaching the Indians as conquerors, they would not allow their adversaries the military advantage of European weapons. This policy, of course, was diametrically opposite to that of the French and British, who each regarded certain tribes as allies and therefore willingly armed them for both hunting and fighting. The two items—horses and guns—were changing the Plains Indians' way of life. La Salle was one of the first Europeans to see these influences entering the Indians' world.

He had little time, however, for speculation about the Indians' culture, for his entire thought and energy were concentrated on finding the river he knew better than any other European but was unable to locate. As he became more and more aware of the gravity of his position, he abandoned his original plan of founding a permanent settlement on the Mississippi and realized his only hope was to get outside help. The best way, he decided, was to lead a select group of men in search of the river and attempt to take his former upstream route back to Canada. He could then return and rescue those who remained behind at Fort St. Louis.

For years he had been making one desperate gamble after another, but none had been more desperate than this. Surrounded by Indians, many of whom were hostile, Fort St. Louis was an inadequate base. The morale of his followers, which had not been high when they landed, had grown steadily lower, as they, too, realized their predicament. Yet this courageous but arrogant, visionary but resourceful, leader was not ready to surrender to the fate that so far had disrupted his plans. Early in January, 1687, he left Fort St. Louis on the long journey that represented his last hope.

Chapter 4

Exploring an Unknown World

Then up ye River I with heavy heart
Did take my way & from all English part
To live amongst ye Natives of this place
If god permits me for one two years space
The Inland Country of Good report hath been
By Indians but by English yet not seen
                        —Henry Kelsey, 1692

The Texas coast lay as flat as the ocean floor it once had been. Only the sun and stars, the flow of the rivers toward the gulf, and occasionally glimpses of the gulf itself gave the travelers a sense of direction. Somewhere in the distant east, lying low in the land where earth and salt water met, was the river the French could use as a route to Canada and friends.

Although they had drawn heavily on the stock of supplies at Fort St. Louis, they were poorly equipped for the journey. Their clothing provided little protection against the cold, heat, or damp. The material was tattered and patched with animal skins and salvaged sailcloth. Their footwear was made of untanned buffalo hide, which stiffened like wooden boards unless they kept it constantly wet. They had brought five horses from Fort St. Louis. These carried their provisions, a supply of presents with which they hoped to purchase the amity of any Indians they met, and a crude bull-hide boat they used when crossing the countless streams in the coastal region.

Their common danger should have been a unifying force, binding them together for their common safety. But here la Salle failed as a leader. Instead of welding the group into a unit, he could not break

his lifetime habit of arrogance and aloofness. These disagreeable characteristics fanned dislike into hatred, and while part of the band remained loyal to him, a part blamed him for all their misfortunes and began to think of killing him.

Their opportunity came when they camped near a spot where la Salle on one of his previous scouting trips had hidden a cache of food. He ordered seven men to retrieve it. They found the contents had spoiled but, on the way back, saw some buffaloes and shot two of them. Immediately they made camp and sent word to la Salle that they needed horses to carry the meat. The next day, in response to their request, three men came with horses to help. Tempers were already short, and a bitter quarrel broke out between the new arrivals and the buffalo hunters over the disposition of part of the meat. Instead of relieving their pent-up emotions, the quarrel fanned them to a new heat; and during the night those in the camp who hated la Salle murdered those who were faithful to him. This dark deed set them on a course from which there was no turning back.

When the men did not reappear the next day, la Salle sensed something had gone wrong and himself went in search of them. The murderers were prepared for their leader. Two of them lay in ambush, while another served as a decoy and greeted la Salle with the sort of insolent language he could not tolerate. As la Salle approached, the man drew back, leading him toward his hidden companions. Then two shots rang out. In an instant the man who had dreamed of being governor of a vast territory was a motionless corpse, killed by his own men.

Although the law with its paraphernalia of officials and codes could not extend into the wilderness, the wilderness temporarily took its place, imposing an uncertain restraint upon the murderers. They could not flee, as they might otherwise have done, because there was no sanctuary in which they could take refuge, and they also needed the supplies and assistance of the remaining men. Therefore they spared the lives of a friar and an Indian who had accompanied la Salle and returned with them to the main camp. But even the wilderness could not continue to enforce the uneasy peace between the various factions into which the camp was dividing. Shortly, two of those involved in la Salle's murder were killed by their companions, and the band broke up, some choosing to stay among the Indians and others finally making their way back to Canada and France with news of the expedition's failure.

In 1689 the Spanish learned the exact location of la Salle's base and sent an expedition under Alonso de León against it. He reached the spot in the spring of the year but saw right away that the military precautions he had taken were unnecessary. Smallpox and Indians had devastated its inhabitants. Rubble and litter—the Indians had smashed boxes and barrels and scattered the books the expedition had brought—was all that remained of la Salle's vision of conquering an empire for his king. Off to the west and north, spring moved up the Great Plains, melting the winter snow and turning the grass green. The buffaloes, thin from their winter's fasting, began once again to fatten; and from the draws and other sheltered places where they had taken refuge during the winter, the Indians began to emerge, happy in spring's promise of good hunting. Many of them now had horses, and some of them had guns. The arrival of Europeans on the North American continent had so far only enriched the lives of the Great Plains Indians.

As for the Europeans, no matter what successes they had enjoyed elsewhere—in Mexico, along the Atlantic Coast, or in the cold forests of Canada— they had been thwarted by the Great Plains. More than a century and a half had passed since Cabeza de Vaca had crossed them, but the trails of men like Coronado and Oñate had vanished from the face of the plains, and la Salle's effort to take control of them had also ended in disaster.

Any concern Spain might have had that other Frenchmen would follow in la Salle's steps was not immediately justified. Several persons, including la Salle's brother and his old friend Tonty, applied for his grant, but Louis XIV was so embroiled in his European adventures that he was unwilling to make any further commitments in Louisiana. So while la Salle's body moldered and his creditors struggled over the partition of his few remaining assets, the battle between Spain and France for possession of the Mississippi watershed came to a momentary halt.

All this while, Great Britain, too, had been attempting to entrench itself in North America. Although its colonies along the seaboard were growing stronger and stronger and posed a potential threat to the French in Canada, the Appalachian Mountains limited their expansion to the west.

Compared to these flourishing settlements, full of vitality and attracting increasing numbers of immigrants, the holdings of the Hudson's Bay Company to the north might have appeared insignificant, but the geography of the bay made them strategically important. The tip of James Bay, which opens into Hudsons Bay from the south, is almost as close to Montreal as New York is. It is farther west, however, and no mountains bar the traveler who wishes to go in that direction. But in the north travel was not easy even with canoes and trustworthy Indian guides. As a consequence, the representatives of the Hudson's Bay Company were tempted to remain in the comparative comfort of their trading posts and wait for the Indians to come to them; but two considerations pushed them into the wilderness. One was national policy: the terms of its charter required the company to explore the country. Another reason was the desire to make bigger profits. Increasing the company's business demanded more of its representatives than establishing posts near Hudsons Bay and offering better goods at lower prices than the French. They had to persuade the Indians with whom they wanted to trade to cease fighting each other and concentrate on collecting furs. They also had to establish commercial relations with additional inland tribes and locate trade routes to them that would be safe from the French and their Indian allies.

Important as this work was to the future of the company, few men volunteered to undertake it. The hazards and discomfort were great, and the remuneration, either financially or in terms of personal renown, was small. No El Dorados or Quiviras were believed to exist in the cold wilderness to the west, and the profits from furs belonged to the company's owners. The company, however, was fortunate to have among its employees a few of those men who loved the wilderness for itself and preferred to sit beside a campfire than behind a desk or a trading counter.

One of these was a young man named Henry Kelsey, who had become an apprentice at the age of fourteen and delighted in the woods and the company of Indians. Traveling westward in 1690, he established a base at a place he called Deering's Point. This done, he continued farther west to carry out the main purpose of his undertaking—to make peace among the Indians who were warring on the plains and persuade them instead to trade with the British. Later he wrote an account of his experience, putting his thoughts in verse form and using the resulting rhymes as an introduction to his narrative describing the events of the following year. Among his observations, he noted that the balance of power had been seriously upset by the introduction of firearms. Those who owned them had a great advantage over the others, an advantage they used without mercy.

Guns enabled the Indians to gather more furs, but when the tribes used them to fight each othher, they disrupted the business of the Hudson's Bay Company. As the only British representative within hundreds of miles—in fact, as the only white man—Kelsey faced what many would have considered an impossible task in his role as peacemaker. Yet by September he had persuaded the Indians to stop fighting. The peace, however, was soon broken. Without Kelsey's knowledge, a group of Indians from the east attacked and killed a band of the Plains Indians. But this setback did not deter Kelsey from carrying on with his mission.

He returned to Deering's Point, where he spent the winter; and the following July, having received additional supplies from the Hudson's Bay Company, again went west. In particular, he was interested in talking to the "captain" of the "Mountain Poets," the word "poets" being used by the Hudson's Bay Company to designate certain tribes. While waiting for this Indian leader to appear, he had an opportunity to talk to other Indians and to observe some of their customs. Several times he watched them hunt buffaloes. Because they were farther north than the horses had yet spread, they still hunted on foot. When they saw a large herd, they tried to encircle it, closing in on all sides and shooting while they advanced. After a number of

animals had been killed, the remainder would become frightened, break through the circle, and stampede away. This method of hunting provided the Indians with the food they needed, but it did not give them the high standard of living they later attained with horses.

In time, the chief for whom Kelsey had especially sent came to see him, and the two men negotiated a trading pact. All the rest of the summer, Kelsey lived with the Indians, preaching peace and the benefit of trading with the British. As the days began to shorten and the air grow crisper, this extraordinary white man, who had ventured alone where no other European had ever gone before, returned to Deering's Point satisfied he had done his work well.

Like the French, the British had many Indian allies who had taken up the role of middleman, buying from the Indians in the west and selling to the British in the east. Again and again this practice caused the Europeans difficulties, for it led the natives to block their westward movement, not to protect their lands, but to safeguard the profitable monopoly they had established. Sometimes they reversed their tactics and attempted to prevent the western Indians going east to the source of trade goods. This happened during the winter Kelsey was at Deering's Point. The more easterly Indians killed two Indians belonging to a tribe Kelsey had persuaded to trade at York Fort. This struck fear into the others, who decided they would not accompany Kelsey back to Hudsons Bay, because they might not be able to return safely to their own country. Nevertheless, in the spring when he arrived at York Fort he "brought a good fleet of Indians downe with him," as the Hudson's Bay Company noted.

Henry Kelsey had not accomplished his original objective of establishing a comprehensive trading relationship between the Hudson's Bay Company and the Plains Indians. That would have been impossible, and it was unrealistic to think a single white man could change the Indians' flow of commerce and rearrange the pattern of their relationships. But he had secured for the company more trade than it had enjoyed before, and he had made Great Britain a contender with France and Spain for the Great Plains.

The Hudson's Bay Company could not immediately take advantage of Kelsey's exploration, however, for Louis XIV, engaged in war with Great Britain, used some of his resources to fight his enemy in the New World as well as in Europe. He reappointed Frontenac governor of Canada, encouraged his Indian allies and the Canadians to attack Great Britain's colonies, and supported the naval operations of Pierre le Moyne, Sieur d'Iberville, in Hudsons Bay. Although the British had become accustomed to fighting with the French along the shores of James Bay, the passage of French frigates through Hudson Strait added a new dimension to the conflict and tipped the balance in favor of the French.

In 1697 the Treaty of Ryswick brought an end to the fighting; and along the shores of Hudsons Bay, the guns of the traders were again aimed at game, not men. Although the Hudson's Bay Company had suffered heavy territorial losses during the war, the treaty restored all conquered possessions to their former owners, so the company emerged from the years of warfare relatively unscathed.

The coming of peace freed Louis XIV to concentrate more attention on Louisiana, and he reconsidered la Salle's original plan. In 1698 he selected Iberville, who had distinguished himself fighting the French in Canada, as governor of the colony la Salle had proposed. Once again the Spanish were haunted by the specter of the French slipping into the Gulf of Mexico and establishing a settlement in a land the Spanish considered their own. Nor could they ignore the English either, for there was talk in London that neither Spain nor France should be allowed uncontested domination of the area.

To defend what they regarded as their rights in the gulf the Spanish hastily sent ships to present-day Pensacola, Florida, and constructed a stockade. When Iberville arrived, they refused to let him enter the harbor, although they lacked the naval forces to pursue him and send him back to France.

Denied access to Pensacola, Iberville continued along the coast until he noticed the water becoming less salty, a phenomenon that made him suspect he had located the mouth of la Salle's river. He entered it and went upstream, but the flat delta with its low-lying vegetation did not appeal to him as a site for his settlement. Returning to the gulf, he went back to present-day Biloxi, Mississippi, where he built a stockade and then returned to France, leaving his brother, Jean le Moyne, Sieur de Bienville, in command at the fort.

When Iberville returned to France, he found the government more concerned than before that the British might attempt to take over the land claimed by la Salle, and he was ordered to lead reinforcements back to the settlement. This quickening of official interest was based more on fancy than on fact, as Iberville's instructions revealed. Among other projects, he was to domesticate buffaloes and

raise them for their wool—it was said to have special value—and look for pearls. The French were emulating the Spanish and hoping for El Dorados while overlooking the true value of what they might possess. He bred no buffaloes and found no pearls, but he built a stockade at the mouth of the Mississippi, explored the lower part of the river, and in 1702 moved his settlement to Mobile Bay, a stronger position, in case the Spanish decided to advance from Pensacola. The Spanish threat was no longer as great, however, for in the War of the Austrian Succession, which broke out that year (the British colonists called it Queen Anne's War), Spain and France were allies.

The danger to French Louisiana, which included the Mississippi watershed, now came from South Carolina, whose fur traders, being farther south, were able to flank the mountains that barred other British colonists from the west. But they did not come in sufficient numbers to prevent the French from tightening their hold on the interior of the continent. With the vigor they almost always showed when they were freed from the paternalism of the crown, the French, coming from Canada and from the Gulf of Mexico, were making themselves familiar with the Mississippi and the Missouri rivers. Long before Great Britain's colonies on the Atlantic dreamed of independence, the intrepid explorers of France had been through much of what is now the American heartland and a Sioux chieftain had been persuaded to visit Montreal.

The colony established by Iberville did not flourish. The government recruited additional colonists, including women whom it deemed suitable brides for those who manned its frontiers, but not in sufficient numbers to create bustling, prosperous communities. The few who did come could not make a living from the land, and instead of working indulged in the sort of intrigue that had so plagued Canada. In 1712 the government, grown desperate over the expense and difficulty of supporting a colony that was unable to support itself, offered a trading monopoly in Louisiana to anyone who agreed to pay the cost of colonizing the area. A wealthy merchant, Antoine Crozat, decided to take the gamble.

If the Spanish had known about the slim economic foundation on which Louisiana rested, they might have been less worried about French aggression from that direction. Even Antoine Crozat with all his wealth could not bear the endless expense and in 1717 successfully petitioned the throne to relieve him of his obligation. John Law, a Scotsman and a notorious speculator, had become well known in French financial circles. At the time, get-rich-quick plans were prevalent and popular in both Great Britain and France, but in magnitude and chimera only London's South Sea Company matched the company now established by John Law. He raised enough capital to obtain title to Louisiana and then issued banknotes secured by land. The short-run results were spectacular; the prospects for the Compagnie des Indes (as it became known) looked so bright that French investors drove up the price of a share 4,000 percent. In fulfillment of its obligations, the company induced several thousand settlers to come to Louisiana, but the emigrants—some of them late residents of French jails—often lacked the vitality to fend for themselves, much less wage war against the Spanish or extend the boundaries of France's holdings.

The French fur traders—whether they operated out of Montreal or New Orleans—were a different sort. Rarely has any group of frontiersmen showed such courage, determination, and imagination. They now firmly controlled the Mississippi River, which provided far better access to the interior of the continent than any route from New Mexico, were familiar with the Missouri River, and had ventured onto the Great Plains.

One of these enterprising men was Jean Baptiste Bernard de la Harpe, who in 1719 pushed the French advance farther west. Leaving Natchitoches, where he had served as second-in-command, he established a trading post at the site of the present city of Texarkana and traveled into what is now Oklahoma, encouraging the Indians to trade with the French. Another was Charles Claude du Tisné, who explored the Missouri and Osage rivers and visited the Osage Indians. From their lands he went even farther west, spreading French influence wherever he went.

News traveled quickly on the Great Plains. In their roamings, one band of nomadic Indians would encounter another, and, if they were at peace with each other, nothing came more naturally than an exchange of gossip. So the presence of the Frenchmen in Spanish territory soon reached the attention of the authorities; and in 1719 the viceroy ordered the governor of New Mexico, Antonio de Valverde, to proceed against the enemy.

Valverde's principal military responsibility was to protect New Mexico from the Utes and the Comanches, and he was not willing to enlarge it, but the viceroy's orders were explicit. Reluctantly he set out with approximately one hundred Spaniards and some Indian allies to locate the French and expel them. He failed to find any Frenchmen, but on his way back to Santa Fé, he met some friendly In-

dians who told him they had recently fought with the Kansa Indians. The Kansas, they said, had been armed with guns and supported by white men. Being a man of much imagination, Valverde let his fancy play, and the numbers of Frenchmen lurking somewhere on the plains grew accordingly. Soon he convinced himself that an army of several thousand men was approaching.

He tried to get the officials in Mexico City to share his conviction, but they were sufficiently familiar with the endemic nervousness of some frontier governors to discount his reports. Nevertheless, they realized there might be a factual basis underlying his exaggerations. So they devised a plan to protect New Mexico that included the construction of a fort as close to the Platte River as might be militarily feasible.

Sometimes a minor official makes a decision that affects the course of empire, and such was the case when Valverde received his instructions from Mexico City. Still fearful of those thousands of Frenchmen whose presence he believed real, he thought it impossible to carry out his orders and recommended the establishment of a post closer to Santa Fé. Although he lacked the qualities needed in a military commander, Valverde was a skillful bureaucrat. He knew his suggestion would cause a delay and this, in turn, might leave him open to a charge of being dilatory. To cover himself, he took a half-measure and sent out a reconnaissance party consisting of approximately forty Spanish soldiers and sixty Indians recruited from among the Pueblos.

The expedition, which was under the command of Pedro de Villasur, left Santa Fé in the early summer of 1720 and proceeded to the Great Plains by way of Taos. Villasur was a man of considerable courage to undertake such an assignment, for if Valverde had correctly estimated the enemy's strength, the little force under his command was entirely inadequate. Traveling under the hot skies of the Great Plains, he and his men ventured farther and farther from the security of their base at Santa Fé and finally reached the Platte. Since they encountered no French, they had reason to assume that Spain's sovereignty over the Great Plains remained intact except for one ominous portent: the Indians they met seemed unfriendly, which caused the Spanish to suspect they were under the influence of the French.

At the Platte River in present-day Nebraska, Villasur and his small force camped on the south bank opposite a Pawnee village. Since their overtures to the Indians were ignored, they rightly concluded the Pawnees were hostile and remained where they were without attempting to cross the river. Their advance having been halted in this fashion, they prudently decided to start back to Santa Fé the next morning. After all, theirs had been a mission of reconnaissance only.

As the sun dropped below the horizon and the soldiers finished their supper, many of them must have been relieved that their dangerous assignment was coming to an end. Soon with God's help they would be back with their friends at the capital. But their relief was premature. French adventurers like du Tisné had done much to stir up the Indians. During the night the Pawnees crossed the Platte; and early the following morning they attacked the Spanish. The Indian victory was almost complete. More than half of the Spaniards, including Villasur, died in the ensuing battle, and many of their Pueblo allies were also killed.

La Salle, proud, imperious, and now long dead, had asserted France's claim to the drainage basin of the Mississippi River. In 1720 on the banks of the Platte River in Nebraska, France's Indian friends, armed with French guns, had helped maintain that claim.

When Villasur's routed force straggled into Santa Fé, the news they brought shocked the tiny capital. It seemed that Valverde's dire predictions had materialized. The governor, now truly frightened, quickly notified the officials in Mexico City of the disaster and begged for reinforcements to defend New Mexico against what he imagined were the advancing French. This time the viceroy ordered him to build a fort on a site of his own choosing. He also instructed the Spaniards in other parts of the area under his administration to be more aggressive against the French. But before his program could be effected, improved relations between the two countries relaxed the tensions that had been mounting along their joint frontier, and the French stopped inciting the Indians against the Spanish.

With the defeat of Villasur, the French had won what might have been a decisive battle in the struggle to gain control of the Great Plains and a route from the northeast into New Mexico. But they were unable to capitalize on it. The year that Villasur fell mortally wounded on the banks of the Platte was the same year that France's economy collapsed. John Law was interested not only in his Louisiana venture but also in many other undertakings. In France, he had a monopoly on tobacco, was director of the national bank, and collected the government's taxes in return for having assumed the national debt. His policy of issuing banknotes

backed by Louisiana land had pushed the general price level up a hundred percent, while the failure of his company to show substantial profits had driven the price of its stock down. The result was economic disaster for many, and Frenchmen were in no mood to spend money on a concerted attempt to conquer the Great Plains and fortify that area.

Although many persons suffered grievously from the sharp decline in the stock of Law's company, the company itself did not go out of existence and continued to exercise the fur-trading monopoly that had been included in its original contract. To strengthen its grip on this trade and divert some of the commerce from Canada to New Orleans, it decided to erect a fort on the Missouri River and enter into alliances with several tribes to the west.

Among the Frenchmen in North America, there were numerous potential candidates to lead such an effort. The one chosen by the company was Étienne Veniard de Bourgmont, an unusually romantic figure who knew the ways of officialdom and its bureaucratic regulations but also understood the free-spirited attitudes of the traders who were not above breaking those regulations. Once he had been the commander at Detroit, but his love for an Indian girl had made him give up that high position and take to the field.

Bourgmont's task was complicated by the previous absence of any long-range policy. Skilled as they were in dealing with the Indians, the fur traders had been opportunists, giving little thought to anything beyond the conduct of this year's business. They had, for example, made friends with the Kansa Indians, but at the cost of providing a market for the slaves the Kansas captured from the Padoucas. (These were a plains tribe farther to the west who may have been Comanches.) Yet if the French were to reach New Mexico—trade with that Spanish colony was one of Bourgmont's objectives—they had to be on good terms with the Padoucas, who barred the way. On the other hand, if they discontinued buying the slaves, they might alienate the Kansas. Another complication faced by Bourgmont was the inability of the company properly to finance the undertaking. To gain control of the Great Plains, Bourgmont really needed an army, not a small number of traders.

But the history of the French in the New World was replete with instances of individuals overcoming the seemingly insurmountable, and Bourgmont followed that tradition. Late in the fall of 1723 he brought a small detachment of soldiers up the Missouri River and established a post that he called Fort Orléans near the mouth of Grand River in present-day Missouri. Early the following summer he was ready to start negotiations with the Kansa Indians and the Padoucas and try to persuade them to stop fighting each other. The Kansas were already familiar with European trade goods and, in common with most other tribes, wanted more of them. Therefore they listened while Bourgmont promised them friendship, threatened them with retaliation if they fought France's allies to the east, and pointed out the benefits of peace with the Padoucas. The lure of his trade goods led the Indians to agree at least superficially to his peace plans; and when he doled out the presents he had brought, the Kansas celebrated the event with great rejoicing.

In preparation for his dealings with the Padoucas, he next purchased from the Kansas five Padouca captives in the hope that the return of these people to their families would demonstrate the friendly intentions of the French. By the time Bourgmont had located the Padoucas and arranged a council with them, the winds blowing over the prairie carried with them the touch of October's chill. Once again Bourgmont gave out presents, including a French flag, and secured the promise of the Padoucas that they would help to enforce peace on the Great Plains. Bourgmont thought that another twelve days of travel would have brought him to Taos, but as the season was growing late and the snows might soon fall, he returned to Fort Orléans.

In 1725, he sailed for France, taking with him several Indians, including a "Missouri princess." The arrival of this party in the nation's capital created a flurry of interest in Louisiana. The Duke and Duchess of Bourbon helped sponsor a reception for the strangers from the New World, the king received them, and an audience came to watch them perform their dances at the opera.

Bourgmont's effort had extended France's control over the Great Plains. Whatever claim Spain had possessed over the area by virtue of Coronado's explorations and those of the Spaniards who followed him was being extinguished by the French. But France's sovereignty lacked a secure foundation and was based only on the exploits of a few hardy men. No soldiers were available to build the many needed forts and patrol the land, and no great supplies of presents were at hand to continue placating the Indians. Three years later the French abandoned Fort Orléans. The walls of its buildings started to rot in the sun and rain, and the power of France receded from the Great Plains.

If the French were having difficulty eking out a livelihood in Louisiana and if the Spanish were on the defensive in New Mexico, fearful of Apaches and Frenchmen alike, the Plains Indians were enjoying a prosperity they could not earlier have imagined. The rich grasslands of the plains were proving to be ideal for the horses stolen or escaped from the Spanish, and they were spreading rapidly. Their sale, theft, or capture had now become a major part of the Indians' life. The possession of swift, hardy horses led to success in war and on the hunt, so an Indian's position within his own group had become largely dependent on the quality of the animals he owned. The French—and to some extent the English—had sold them guns; and although they rarely had surplus ammunition for target practice, they were becoming adept in using European weapons. Never before had their existence been so easy or so good. Now when they hunted the buffaloes, they no longer trudged many weary miles on foot, but rode proudly on their horses; and when they located a herd, they could sweep down upon it with the ferocity of a plains tornado. They accumulated more meat than ever before for the long winter months and carried with them more hides. Even their methods of warfare were changing. The swift raid and the cavalry charge were now becoming common; and although bows and arrows still had advantages—for example, they could be fired more quickly than guns—firearms made the Indians more versatile and effective warriors. The Plains Indians, however, concentrated their energies on attacking each other, not the Frenchmen or the British, who were the bearers of trade goods.

In 1731 John Law's company, unable to make a profit, asked the crown to revoke its monopoly and Louisiana again became a royal colony. Individual traders, however, continued their explorations, following the Red River through eastern and northern Texas and the Arkansas River across what today is the eastern boundary of Oklahoma, and moved out from the Missouri in their dealings with the Kansa Indians and the Pawnees. But these were minor expeditions; and although the men who made them were courageous, they lacked the visionary character that had distinguished so many earlier French explorers.

This quality was revived in two brothers, Pierre and Paul Mallet, who dreamed as others had done before them of opening a route to Santa Fé and trading with the Spanish. Unlike the others, they decided to do something about it.

In 1739 they started up the Missouri but, realizing it was taking them too far north, returned to the Platte, which empties into the Missouri near Omaha, Nebraska, and forms a natural route across the Great Plains. They followed its course for some distance and then left it to go to the southwest, crossing the plains of Kansas and entering what is now southeastern Colorado.

There they met a band of Comanches, those warlike Indians who had been a barrier between Santa Fé and the East but who, because of the trade goods, had become friends of the French. Among them was an Indian who had once belonged to a Spaniard and had lived in Santa Fé. He agreed to serve the Mallets as their guide.

Toward the end of July, they arrived at the Spanish city. In view of Spain's traditional attitude toward Frenchmen who wandered into its domain, the brothers were not certain what sort of reception they would receive, but the inhabitants, including the governor, were delighted to see them and treated them well. The administrative centralization of the Spanish government, however, made it impossible for the governor to decide whether the Mallets could trade with his province. That question could be answered only by the viceroy in Mexico City. In a change of policy the viceroy said he was agreeable to having French traders enter the province and even invited the Mallets to explore some of the country to the west. They might have accepted this unusual invitation if they had not been anxious to return to their fellow countrymen and announce the extraordinary news that New Mexico was now open to French traders.

Leaving Santa Fé, they went east across the Great Plains to the Canadian River, which flows from the Texas Panhandle into the Arkansas River. Here half the expedition headed north to Canada, while the others looked for a practical route to New Orleans. Geographically that settlement was the logical focal point for trade with Santa Fé.

Traveling down the Arkansas River, they followed in the steps taken by de Soto as he had journeyed to his death so many years before. At the Mississippi, where de Soto had made his last camp, they turned south and arrived safely at New Orleans.

The town was soon buzzing with the news of the brothers' hospitable reception in New Mexico, and the governor, determined to use the concession won by the Mallets, organized another expedition the following year. One of its purposes was to make friends with the Indians along the way, thus assuring a safe passage for French traders in the future. The expedition, however, found the going difficult even though the Mallets, who had made the trip successfully, served as guides. Partway toward its destination, its leader, a man unequipped for such a venture, began vacillating between continuing the journey on horseback or by canoe until it was too late in the season to do either. Neverthe-

less, in succeeding years several Frenchmen made the journey across to Santa Fé, and France's claim to the Great Plains became more firmly established. La Salle's dream was brightening, while that of Coronado was growing dimmer.

"Un sauvage nommé Pako, le chef du Lac Nepigon [Lake Nipigon, north of Lake Superior], Lefoye et le Petit Jour son frére chefs Cris [Crees] me rapporterent avoir esté au delá de la hauteur des terres á une grande Riviére qui descend droit au Couchant du Soleil, et qui s'elargit toujours en descendant. . . ."

So wrote Pierre Gaultier de Varennes, Sieur de la Vérendrye and commander of the French trading post at Lake Nipigon.

"A savage named Pako, Chief of Lake Nipigon, Lefoye, and his brother, Petit Jour, Cree chiefs, reported to me that they had been beyond the height of the land and reached a great river that flows straight toward the setting sun and steadily widens as it descends," he wrote and, "that in this great river there are only two rapids, which are about a three-day journey from its source; and that according to their estimate, it flows through forests for only about two hundred leagues of its course.

"They speak highly of that country, saying it is extremely level, without mountains; the trees are hardwoods with here and there groves of oaks; there are many fruit trees and all sorts of wild animals; the savage tribes are numerous, always wandering and carrying their 'cabins' with them and camping together to form a village. They call these nations Assiniboin and Sioux, because they speak all the Sioux languages. The nations about three hundred leagues lower down are sedentary, raise crops, and for lack of wood make themselves mud huts. The forest comes to an end on the shore of a great lake . . . ; at the outlet of the lake, you come to a little river, the water of which looks red like vermillion, and is held in great esteem by the savages. On the same side of the river, but much lower down, there is a small mountain, the stones of which sparkle night and day."

France's explorers knew more about the plains that stretched to the foothills of the Rockies than any other Europeans, but the dream still persisted: somewhere there was a great river that flowed into the Western Sea. Joliet and Marquette had proved the Mississippi did not do this but ran south to the Gulf of Mexico. The travels of others had revealed no such river, but the French still continued to hope they could find a waterway across the continent. And la Vérendrye, stationed at the outer limits of the French domain in Canada, listened to anyone who could tell him more about the wilderness and the possibility of a yet undiscovered river that might link Canada to the wealth of the Indies.

The son of a former governor of Three Rivers, his family was well regarded, but not wealthy; and as one of ten children, la Vérendrye soon had to make his own living. He did so by joining the army and fighting the British in North America; in 1707 he went to France and secured a commission in the armed forces there. Finding the army held no future for a young man without money, he returned to Canada and eventually received permission to set up a small trading post near Three Rivers. Married and with a growing family, he could not support his dependents with the small trade he had developed, and so he successfully petitioned the governor for an appointment as commander of the trading post at Lake Nipigon.

Like almost every other Canadian, he knew the importance of finding a route across the continent. Therefore he listened avidly to the accounts related to him by the Indians and became convinced of the existence of a river that would permit the Canadians to reach the Western Sea by canoe. The evidence he collected was sufficient to persuade the government his idea deserved support but was insufficient to gain him financial backing. So although he received permission to explore the country and build posts, he was to pay his own expenses from any profits he might earn from the trading monopoly the government would give him.

A lesser man might have been daunted by these harsh and unfavorable terms, but la Vérendrye accepted them as the best he could obtain and, having little wealth himself, entered into a partnership with some of the rich merchants in Montreal. In the succeeding years and with the assistance of his four sons—one of whom was killed by the Sioux— la Vérendrye established several posts. One was at Lake of the Woods, which forms part of the northern boundary of present-day Minnesota, and another was at the mouth of the Red River, which flows north from the United States and forms the boundary between present-day Minnesota and North Dakota.

Although la Vérendrye was forced to devote much of his time to the conduct of his fur-trading business in order to support himself and repay his creditors, he still kept hoping he might find a river that ran into the Western Sea. As a consequence he closely questioned those Indians in whom he had confidence, trying to learn more about the geography of the country that surrounded him. Some of these Indians told him about another tribe, the Mandans, who lived on the Missouri River and seemed to have a culture superior to their neighbors. At least that is what la Vérendrye gathered from the reports he heard, and he was determined to talk to them.

In pursuit of this goal and also to enlarge the scope of his trading business, he built a new post, Fort La Reine, even farther west than the others. (Many of the privately owned trading posts were called "forts," because they were built like a fort and often served as one.) Fort La Reine was located near the present Canadian town of Portage-la-Prairie just north of North Dakota in the land of the Assiniboins, a tribe that was related to the Sioux but was less warlike. The difference in temperament had bred enmity between the two groups of Indians, and in the subsequent hostilities the Assiniboins were usually the losers, because they were scarcely a match for their fierce relatives.

La Vérendrye had two objectives in establishing the new post. Following the exploration of men like Henry Kelsey, the British had diverted some of the plains trade away from the French by persuading the Indians to make their purchases at Hudsons Bay. Part of la Vérendrye's purpose in building the fort was to regain this commerce. His other objective was to obtain an escort that would conduct him to the Mandans, for the Assiniboins had developed a lively trade with them and knew the route to their villages.

In 1738, the year before the Mallet brothers made their historic trip to Santa Fé, la Vérendrye was ready to set out. He had little difficulty persuading the Assiniboins to guide him and a few other Frenchmen to the Mandan villages, which were located on the Great Plains near the present-day city of Bismarck, North Dakota. Neither he nor any of his countrymen, however, could speak the Mandans' language, but he located a Cree who could. Since one of his own sons was fluent in Cree, the Indian could serve as an effective interpreter.

The Assiniboins who accompanied him comprised an entire village. Like other nomadic tribes on the Great Plains, they were accustomed to moving in large groups, especially at those times of year when the game was sufficient to support them. La Vérendrye carefully observed their method of travel. (It was one of the strengths of the French in the New World that many of them took pains to learn from the Indians.) The main body, he noted, moved in three columns with scouts in front, flankers on either side, and a rearguard. The warriors carried nothing but their weapons, so they could fight on a moment's notice; and the old men, who had passed their time and were useless in battle, stayed in the center, where they would be well pro-

Although the Great Plains are generally flat, the wind and water have eroded many areas into strange shapes. Here outcroppings from the past remain silhouetted against the level horizon. *Alexander B. Adams*

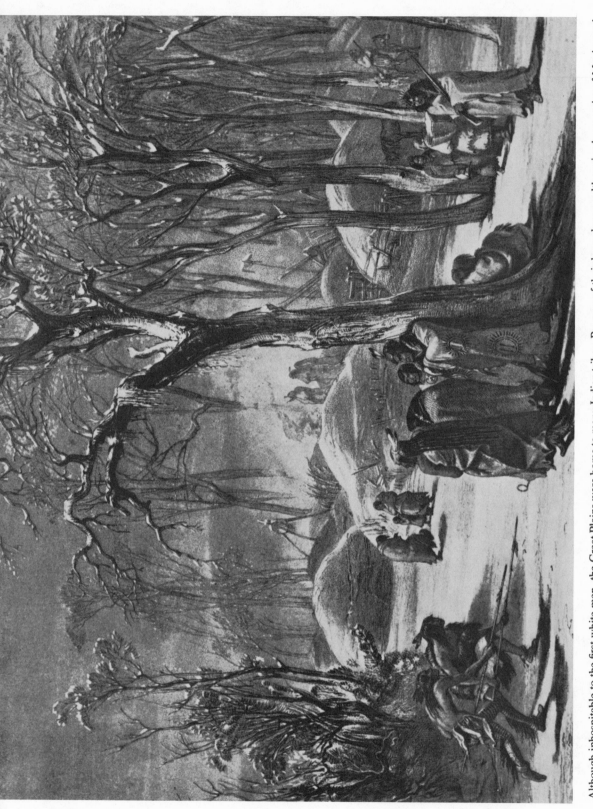

Although inhospitable to the first white men, the Great Plains were home to many Indian tribes. Rumors of their legendary wealth revived memories of Mexico and Peru and lured the Spaniards as far as Kansas. This picture of a Hidatsa village was painted by the Swiss artist Karl Bodmer in 1833–34. *National Archives*

tected. When the village stopped along the way to hunt buffaloes, a frequent occurrence, the vanguard marked out the campground for that night, and no one was allowed to proceed beyond that point. No band could move ahead of the others and find a herd of buffaloes they did not have to share with their fellows; nor could any band risk weakening the entire group by dividing it.

Before leaving on the journey, the Assiniboins had sent messengers ahead to tell the Mandans that la Vérendrye was coming and to fix a rendezvous from which they could take him to their villages. For more than a week they traveled toward this point, crossing the vast and almost woodless prairies. Like many travelers since the time of Cabeza de Vaca, la Vérendrye learned that their general flatness did not make the plains easy to traverse. Their surface, scarred by gullies and valleys that suddenly appeared before the traveler, made the trip difficult; and even the Indians, who knew the land well, could not find an easy way.

As they moved together toward the Mandan villages, the Assiniboins kept telling la Vérendrye about the people he soon would see. They were white, the Indians assured him, and were actually Frenchmen, descended from people like himself. These remarks excited la Vérendrye's imagination, and he was certain he was on the verge of a great discovery. If these people were as the Assiniboins described them, they would surely know about any river that flowed west. With a light heart, he rode toward the rendezvous.

The sight of the Mandan chief who came to greet him was a shock. The man wore nothing but a single garment made from a buffalo skin, not even a breechcloth. Theirs was not the superior culture la Vérendrye had been led to expect, and he noted wryly that hereafter he would always discount anything the Assiniboins told him.

In spite of their outward simplicity, the Mandans were among the shrewdest of tribes. Their chief immediately noted the number of Assiniboins accompanying la Vérendrye; and as tradition demanded that his village feed every guest, he quickly decided there were too many Assiniboins, all looking forward to free meals. After thanking them for bringing the Frenchmen, he gravely told them their arrival was timely. The Sioux were on the warpath, and the Mandans needed all the allies they could obtain. La Vérendrye, recalling the death of one of his sons at the hands of the Sioux, welcomed the opportunity to fight them, but the effect of the announcement on the Assiniboins was exactly the contrary. They almost panicked at the thought of meeting their enemies but finally decided in council that honor required them to continue escorting la Vérendrye. As a precaution, however, they left their women and children behind with a contingent of warriors to guard them. Thus the Mandans slyly accomplished their purpose, greatly reducing the number of mouths they would have to feed while still entertaining enough Assiniboins to do a brisk trading business.

Unlike the nomadic Assiniboins, the Mandans were a sedentary plains tribe that cultivated fields and lived in large permanent buildings constructed on the banks of the Missouri River. These were dome-shaped structures made of wood and dirt. Each had a covered entrance that kept out the elements. In summer they were cool, and in winter, warm. The leader of the Mandans took la Vérendrye and the Frenchmen to the one in which he lived. His fellow tribesmen, of course, were anxious to see their visitors and crowded into the lodge. Not wishing to miss the excitement, the Assiniboins also tried to get inside. Soon the large room was so filled with Indians that la Vérendrye asked that some of them be requested to leave, so there would be room for the Frenchmen and safety for their luggage. Unfortunately he did not act in time. In the confusion some Indian—either a Mandan or an Assiniboin, he never discovered which—stole a box; one containing the presents he had brought to repay the Mandans for their hospitality.

The loss, however, did not affect the attitude of the Mandans toward the French, for they were eager to trade directly with the Europeans instead of always dealing with Indian middlemen. While they made the French welcome, they also were conducting a profitable business with the Assiniboins. Being more skillful at dressing skins and at working with feathers and other forms of ornamentation, they had many articles the Assiniboins wanted. The Assiniboins, on the other hand, had guns and ammunition, metal kettles, and axes and other tools, which they had obtained from the British or French. As these were not otherwise available to the Mandans, the basis for a trading business existed between the two tribes. La Vérendrye noticed that the Mandans were the better traders and soon exhausted the Assiniboins' supply of goods.

From the Mandans' point of view, the time had now come to get rid of their visitors, because they were eating a large amount of the tribe's accumulated food. So they spread word that their hunters had seen the Sioux approaching, although they privately advised la Vérendrye of the nature of their ruse. Soon the Assiniboins had decamped and were on their way home.

As la Vérendrye quickly discovered, the Mandans had not one, but several villages, along the Missouri River, near where the Heart River flows into the Missouri from the west. Although the rainfall is slight and uncertain as it is everywhere on the Great Plains, the land is fertile; and the Mandans knew how to cultivate it, raising crops such as maize and pumpkins. Because the water has not cut as deeply into the earth as it has done in other parts of the Great Plains, the topography is gentle; and in the summer when la Vérendrye was there, the Missouri is not likely to be the raging, angry flood it often becomes in the spring. Although la Vérendrye was not insensitive to his surroundings, the enjoyment of the lonely grandeur of the Great Plains was not the object of his journey, and he concentrated his attention on learning everything he could about the Mandans and what they knew. He also asked his companions to examine the village in which they were staying and count the number of lodges—there were about a hundred and thirty of them—while he himself studied the palisade that surrounded the village and found it to be strong and well constructed.

When he questioned them, the Mandans told him about the people who lived downstream. Some, they said, lived much as they did, residing in earth lodges and cultivating crops. Beyond them was another, similar tribe. The principal difference between them was that the other two tribes had horses, while the Mandans had none.

Beyond those tribes were still another people who were white like the French and rode horses and wore armor. The way to kill one of these people, the Mandans explained, was first to kill his horse. Their armor protected them from guns and arrows, but it also prevented them from running fast once they were dismounted. The journey to where these white men lived required an entire summer, but the Mandans no longer made the trip, because they were forced to confront too many enemies along the way. From the Indians' description, these white men were clearly the Spanish, and probably the Mandans had visited them in the past.

With all his questions, however, la Vérendrye could find no indication that the Mandans knew of a west-flowing river that led to the ocean. Meanwhile the days were passing, and he was beginning to run short of supplies. He considered remaining with the Mandans for the winter but realized that in the spring the placid rivers would become roaring currents, making travel difficult, if not impossible. After consulting with his companions, he decided prudence demanded that they return to Fort La Reine before winter cloaked the Great Plains in snow and buffeted it with winds.

If the expedition had been financed by the government, it would have been considered a success, for it served several useful public services. It increased France's knowledge of the Great Plains, it revealed that the stories told about the Mandans were only myths, and it added to the white men's familiarity with the Plains Indians. But for a private citizen like la Vérendrye, trying to finance his own endeavor, the expedition had been a failure. All that summer he had not been making money; he had been spending it. In Montreal his creditors, who were more immediately interested in the returns on their capital than in the expansion of the French empire, grew restless. The discovery of a route to the Western Sea would have satisfied them because of its potential for profits, but since la Vérendrye had failed in this, they wanted canoes heavily laden with furs. La Vérendrye's were not.

His attempt to establish a business relationship with the Assiniboins had not offset the losses he had incurred on his trip to the Mandans, because the pattern of trade in North America was shifting. The Assiniboins had welcomed him and professed great pleasure at his coming, but they were no longer dependent solely on the French for their supplies. Explorers like Henry Kelsey had so expanded Britain's commerce that they had cracked France's monopoly of the western fur trade. The Assiniboins were glad of la Vérendry's presence, but it was clear they already had a market for their furs among the British at Hudsons Bay and regarded him only as an additional customer.

Many attributes set explorers apart from other men, and one of them is optimism; an explorer cannot exist without it. As la Vérendrye ended his report to the governor describing his journey, he wrote this wistful sentence: "I discovered a few days ago a river flowing west."

The hope that one of them would lead to the Western Sea was still alive. But as his commercial experience with the Assiniboins had shown, British influence had penetrated to the Great Plains; and all that France's adventurers had accomplished for their country was in danger of being lost.

Chapter 5

Changes in Ownership

He [Marbois] then took occasion to mention his sorrow that any cause of difference should exist between our two countries. The Consul [Napoleon] told him in reply, "Well, you have charge of the treasury; let them give you one hundred millions of francs, and pay their own claims, and take the whole country." . . . I now plainly saw the whole business: first, the Consul was disposed to sell. . . .

—Robert R. Livingston, 1803

Two factors conspired to check, even if they did not defeat, la Vérendrye: his creditors and the geography of western Canada. His creditors could not pay their own bills merely with the honor of supporting an extraordinary explorer. They needed and wanted cash, and their pressure forced him to turn from adventure and concentrate on business. Yet the monopoly he enjoyed was not sufficiently profitable to permit him to satisfy his creditors quickly and get back to the task of finding a route west. As he wrote to the governor of New France, all the rivers he had knowledge of—with the exception of the Missouri—flowed into Hudsons Bay, carrying the Indians directly into the arms of the British. On a map the bay may have seemed remote compared to Montreal on the St. Lawrence, but actually York Factory, the principal British trading post, stood at the end of a natural travel route for a people that used canoes. Henry Kelsey's trip west had therefore opened up a much larger market than the British had originally thought and given them a strong position among the Plains Indians of the north. La Vérendrye's monopoly was on paper only. And the topography did not permit any river to flow into the Pacific Ocean, as he hoped. The rising altitude toward the west forced even a river like the one he mentioned in his report to the governor to swing eventually in the direction of his hated competitors.

From his return to Fort La Reine in 1739 until 1742, la Vérendrye was almost entirely occupied with the demands of his creditors and his business, but at last he was able to afford another expedition. This time he did not lead it himself. Although his spirit remained strong, age and the rigors of wilderness living had drained his strength. An important diplomatic problem also demanded his presence in Canada. The Crees and Assiniboins were still hostile to the Sioux; and without his restraining influence, warfare might break out between them, disrupting the trade he had built up and perhaps blocking his access to Montreal. So he assigned the task of further exploration to two of his sons, while he remained behind to play the role of statesman.

The brothers and two other Frenchmen took the now familiar route back to the Mandan villages, where they awaited the expected arrival of another tribe called the Gens des Chevaux, who were more familiar with the country to the west. After a fruitless delay of more than two months, the brothers decided to wait no longer and go in search of the Gens des Chevaux. With two Mandans serving as guides, they walked for twenty days across the Great Plains in a south-southwesterly direction under the hot summer sun. No mountains or hills rose above the surface to guide them, as mile after mile passed beneath their feet. In every direction they

79

could gaze as far as the horizon, but although they could look such a distance, they did not see another person, white or red. Finally they met a tribe that could take them to the Gens des Chevaux, but when they reached the village they learned these Indians had never visited the coast. But they did know of yet another tribe, the Gens de l'Arc, who could tell the Frenchmen more about the unknown lands.

This experience was similar to that of many of the other early explorers. What they wanted—whether it was information or riches—always seemed to lie somewhere afar and never at hand. The more adventurous of them were distinguished not only by their courage and their willingness to travel in dangerous circumstance, but also by their spirit of optimism and their belief that the will-o'-the-wisp was real. The la Vérendrye brothers, like their father, shared this spirit.

Moving through country that was previously unknown to white men and helped by friendly Indians, they reached a village of the Gens de l'Arc and found them preparing to go to war. These Indians, too, had never been to the coast, but they knew of its existence from talking to prisoners taken by their enemies in the west. White men lived there, they said, and they spoke a few words of their language, which the brothers immediately recognized as Spanish. This disappointed them, for they had hoped to find unoccupied country. Nevertheless, they were still anxious to continue their exploration in the hope of discovering an overland route to the Pacific, if not a river running west.

The impending military campaign of the Gens de l'Arc presented a difficult problem for them. The French did not want to take sides in the Indians' internecine strife, but one or more of the Gens de l'Arc had participated in the fight against Villasur some twenty years earlier (one warrior described the battle to the la Vérendryes), and because of this they considered themselves allies of the French. To refuse to help the Gens de l'Arc now would anger them. So reluctantly they agreed on a compromise: to join the war party as advisers, but not active participants.

The warriors, one of the brothers later wrote, numbered about two thousand—a figure that was probably exaggerated—and they made a "considerable troop" as they rode together across the Great Plains. Every night they celebrated their expected victory with songs, and they looked forward with delight to the slaughter of their foes.

Their march brought them to some high, wooded mountains, which may have been the Bighorns.

Since this area was the homeland of their enemies, they sent out scouts to locate their village. In a while the scouts returned with disturbing news: the village was deserted. Panic overtook the Gens de l'Arc at this unexpected announcement. The rumor spread that their enemies had outflanked them and were about to attack their own women and children, whom they had left in a camp. What had been a self-confident advance now became a dismal rout. The warlike songs they had chanted around their campfires were forgotten, as each Indian raced toward the east and away from his enemies. In the confusion the French were left behind. Fortunately they had their guns, for the enemy, their ruse having worked, attacked the fleeing, disorganized Gens de l'Arc. The Frenchmen had been determined not to take an active part in the battle, but they could no longer maintain their neutrality. Attacked by approximately fifteen hostile Indians, they used their firearms effectively, drove off their enemies, and rejoined the main body of the Gens de l'Arc, who had by then reached safety.

Their lives had been spared, but the defeat of the Gens de l'Arc ended the brothers' hopes of going to the coast. Working their way east, they reached the Missouri River at a point that was probably near the present-day city of Pierre, South Dakota. Here they discovered a village of Indians—most likely they were Arikaras—who told the la Vérendryes that another Frenchman lived somewhere in the area. The explorers remained among the Arikaras in the hope he would appear; but after a long wait, they realized that this report, like so many others, was probably untrue. So they went up the Missouri River to the Mandan villages and from there returned to Fort La Reine.

Their journey had taken them into the present-day states of Montana, Wyoming, and both the Dakotas. By then Frenchmen had crossed the boundaries of every one of the modern states that compose the American Great Plains, knew many of the area's rivers and Indian tribes, and had visited the Rocky Mountains. They were more familiar with the region than any other European nation, but they were unable to establish a firm grip on it. In part this was because they had no systematic method of collating their information, and in part because the fur trade did not produce the profit needed to finance their efforts. Meanwhile the central government would not assume the costs and had been unable to devise a system that would encourage permanent settlement of individuals in large numbers.

Even the la Vérendrye family, which had shown such great initiative, could not maintain control of the vast area they had explored. Harassed by their creditors and impeded by the bureaucracy of the French government, they limited their further efforts to western Canada. Although they explored the Saskatchewan River and established a trading business on the Canadian Great Plains, they never again attempted to explore the land south of the present international boundary.

Although Spain and France were both giants among nations, they did nothing but glower at each other across the barrier formed by the Great Plains. Those miles of prairies, canyons, badlands, and broad rivers, which were sometimes flanked by quicksand, could be crossed only by those who, like the French explorers, were willing to travel light. Without enormous expense, no army could have been sufficiently well equipped to sustain itself during the long journey; and this consideration restrained the two countries. Individual Frenchmen might want to trade with Sante Fé, and Spaniards might be covetous of the profits reaped by the more successful fur merchants, but the Spanish outposts in New Mexico and the French settlements in the southern portion of Louisiana and in the Illinois country were not prosperous enough to warrant the cost of a properly outfitted army. So the geography of the Great Plains enforced the peace in what is now the western half of the United States.

In the years that followed the remarkable explorations of the la Vérendrye family, few travelers ventured far into the American Great Plains. Yet many Frenchmen continued to dream of developing trade with their distant neighbors in the west, and several of them actually made the journey.

In 1752, as Santa Fé lay enveloped in August's heat, its citizens were startled by the arrival of two Frenchmen, Jean Chapuis and Luis Feulli. They had come not from southern Louisiana, but from the Illinois country. This, however, is not what caused the excitement; it was the license they carried. It had been issued by the French authorities, thus making the expedition through Spanish territory official. The governor of New Mexico regarded this as both an affront and a threat. So he quickly made Chapuis and Feulli prisoners and sent them off to Mexico.

While Spain and France were stalemated in the southern Great Plains, the French were faring better with their northern competitors, the British. Thanks to the exploits of men like the la Vérendryes, France had succeeded in sealing off the Hudson's Bay Company from some of the most profitable trade. The Indians had become accus-tomed to selling their smaller and more valuable pelts to the French and trading their less valuable ones with the British. (The size of a skin affected its desirability; the smaller and lighter the skin, the easier it was to transport, an important consideration in the wilderness.) In fact, the Indians began buying the heavier European goods like pots and kettles from the British and selling them to the French at the more distant outposts, making it unnecessary for the traders to take the long trip to Montreal for bulky articles.

Such an arrangement was not at all acceptable to the British, who thought with justification that they were being used. Anthony Hendry, an employee of the Hudson's Bay Company, decided to do something about it. In an effort to outflank the French and divert the Indians' trade, he made a trip in 1754 to what is now Montana, where he visited the Blackfeet Indians. They were friendly to him but were already so well supplied with the goods they wanted they saw no reason for making the journey to York Factory. As an excuse for not doing so (they thought the truth might offend him) they said they could not leave their horses unattended, for these animals had now spread north and become an integral part of their way of life. As long as their horses were safe, they told Hendry, they never lacked buffalo meat.

In the Indians' possession were Spanish bits and bridles, which led Hendry into the mistake of believing he was relatively near Santa Fé. Actually he was seeing another effect of horses on the Indian culture. Many tribes on the Great Plains had traveled widely, covering hundreds of miles on foot. Now with a fast, easy means of transportation, they traveled even more than before, and the articles they used in trade circulated over a greater area.

Hendry was unsuccessful in persuading the Blackfeet to trade with the British, but the French were laying the groundwork for their own downfall by being too aggressive. Not content with the control of much of Canada, the Mississippi and Missouri rivers, part of the coast of the Gulf of Mexico, and much of the land in what is now the western United States, they began to probe up the Ohio and Allegheny rivers. La Salle's claim to the watershed of the Mississippi provided the legal basis for such a venture, but common sense would have dictated restraint. At mid-century, the population of France's colonies in Canada totaled about sixty thousand while the English colonies had a population of about one and a quarter million. David was challenging Goliath but without a slingshot.

The fighting that inevitably resulted first went against the British, but at last their superior strength changed the tide, and even an alliance between France and Spain could no longer stop their victories. The Peace of Paris, which ended the French and Indian War in 1763, dramatically realigned the political map of North America. The price exacted from France for its attempt to overexpand was enormous. Great Britain stripped it of all its mainland possessions, including Canada, and all the territory France claimed east of the Mississippi. Great Britain also demanded, and received, the Spanish Floridas. To compensate Spain for the losses it suffered for its unfortunate alliance, France had given it New Orleans and all of the Louisiana land west of the Mississippi. In this way the diplomats extinguished the claims made by la Salle so many years before and destroyed the hopes of French adventurers like the la Vérendryes. At the same time Spain gained title to the northern part of the American Great Plains, which, added to the possessions it already held, gave it control of the entire area. Coronado's trail, now grown faint in the prairie grass, once more passed through Spanish territory.

The Indians who had been allied with the French did not understand that the paper the white men had signed at Paris had ended the hostilities, and they still constituted a menace along the frontier. In order to gain time to solve this problem, the British government issued the Proclamation of 1763. Among other provisions, this prohibited the colonists from settling in the area that lay between the crest of the Allegheny Mountains and the Mississippi River. With a few pen strokes the government had obliterated the claims of several of the colonies to western lands and alienated many of the people who had contributed to its military successes. Although the proclamation was originally intended as a temporary measure, subsequent British governments failed to repeal it, adding one more grievance to the colonists' growing list. No regulation could stop the eventual westward movement of the colonists, but the Proclamation of 1763 prevented a sweep toward the Great Plains and gave Spain an opportunity to consolidate its hold on the area.

Spain needed that opportunity. In spite of its many years of experience in the New World, the Spanish government's methods of administration had remained relatively unchanged. It still looked for a quick return on its investments, it still was bureaucratic, and it had not fostered the aggressive spirit found among so many of the French and British traders. This lack of aggressiveness was reflected in the government itself. Instead of avidly seizing its new possession, Spain delayed in appointing a governor; and when Antonio de Ulloa did arrive to take charge, he relied so heavily on his French predecessor's guidance it was almost as if nothing had changed. French customs persisted, and French traders continued to dominate the commerce in furs.

Among these was Pierre Laclède Liguest (better known merely as Pierre Laclède) who with his partners had received a Spanish license to trade with the Indians on the Missouri. He recognized the importance of the juncture of the Missouri and Mississippi rivers and, foreseeing that it would be the gateway to both the north and the west, chose it as the base of his trading operations. In 1764 he and his partners began the actual settlement of St. Louis, which soon became a significant commercial center.

The Spanish government, however, was more interested in the Pacific Coast than in the forbidding Great Plains. Having established a firm base in Lower California, the Spanish moved northward and in a relatively short span of time established a system of *presidios* and missions at such places as San Diego, Monterey, Los Angeles, and San Francisco. At the same time, Spanish ships were pushing farther north along the Pacific Coast, reaching as far as the present-day state of Washington. Standing on the deck of their small ship as they piloted it through the rocky, fog-enshrouded waters, they saw the snow-capped peak of Mt. Olympus rising from the ocean. In a few years, they hoped, they could claim the coast as their own. And in Texas they were busy consolidating their hold by establishing *presidios,* not to protect themselves against the French, who were no longer an enemy, but against those Indians with whom they had been unable to make peace. Having nothing to fear now from New Orleans, they also moved into east Texas and in this way secured their grip on the southern approaches to the Great Plains. But that formidable land still repelled them. They did little to move north from their Texas base, and in the east they left the fur trade and further exploration largely to the French population. St. Louis flourished, and although Laclède did not share in its prosperity, he founded a fur-trading dynasty that was carried on by his stepson, Auguste Chouteau.

With the signing of the Peace of Paris, the British traders were quick to come down the rivers into the territory they had won. They found business profitable and soon were pressing against the borders of the land held by Spain. Their aggressive character would certainly have carried them westward and made a clash between the two powers inevitable. But the American Revolution soon absorbed Great Britain's attention, and it could not divert its resources for additional conquests in the New World.

The Americans, deep in a struggle with one of the world's greatest powers, might well have ignored the western lands. The Proclamation of 1763 had prohibited their settlement, and the Quebec Act of 1774 had attached the area west of the Allegheny Mountains and north of the Ohio River to Canada. Even if the Americans should win the war, which was far from a certainty, Great Britain might not recognize its former colony's claims to that distant area. Yet the question of those lands haunted the men who were drafting the Articles of Confederation.

Maryland, whose original charter gave it no rights in the west, was adamant in its refusal to ratify the articles unless colonies like Virginia, New York, and Connecticut agreed to surrender their western territorial claims. If the land should be wrested from Great Britain, Maryland's delegates argued, it would be accomplished by the common efforts of the thirteen colonies. Therefore the land should be held in common.

Two fears motivated Maryland to take this position. One was the fear that since it owned no lands itself it might be bankrupted when it came to pay the land bonuses issued as an inducement to military recruits. The second was its dread that the colonies with western claims would eventually become sufficiently big to overpower the others. This line of reasoning was so persuasive that New Jersey joined with Maryland, and the Continental Congress soon reached a deadlock.

In the fall of 1780 it finally adopted a resolution that the western lands were to be "disposed of for the common benefit of the United States." The resolution also provided that the lands should be eventually formed into states, "which shall become members of the Federal Union" and have the same rights as the original states. This was a historic measure. It not only showed a remarkable sense of unity among the colonies, it also introduced a revolutionary political concept, one quite contrary to European tradition. As America moved westward, there were to be no colonies, and every emigrant to the frontier could look forward to the day when he would have the same rights and political status as those who remained behind.

Neither Spain, France, nor Great Britain had created a political system that would eventually incorporate their newly settled lands into the nation as a whole, thus ensuring their inhabitants' continued loyalty to the central government. Instead the courts of the three countries were determined to keep their colonies in a subservient position, thereby making almost certain their future rebellion. But the delegates to the Continental Congress, who had so long been concerned with the philosophy of government, devised an unusual solution to a perplexing political problem. When New York ceded its western lands to the central government and Virginia promised to, Maryland ratified the Articles of Confederation, and at the same time the idea of a public domain became a reality. This had a profound effect on the growth of many areas of the United States, including the Great Plains.

Even while the war with the Americans raged on, British fur traders still looked covetously on the lands that the Spanish claimed but could not seem to exploit. In 1977 Benjamin and Joseph Frobisher and Simon McTavish became partners in the North West Company, entering into an agreement that was made more permanent a few years later. The territory assigned to it by the British government lay south of the Hudson's Bay Company's and ran from the Mandan villages to the Pacific, creating a potential conflict with the Hudson's Bay Company and the Spanish.

In October, 1781, the British surrendered at Yorktown, and the Americans again began to think of the lands beyond the Alleghenies. The emissaries who conducted the negotiations that led to the Peace of Paris of 1783, worked successfully to regain title to the area between the Great Lakes and the Ohio River, the territory that had earlier been attached to Quebec by the Quebec Act. Although it made this concession at the conference table, Great Britain, to protect its fur traders and the Indians who had been its allies, delayed abandoning its military posts south of the Great Lakes, creating a point of contention between the two countries that festered their relations.

Great Britain was tempted into taking this course because of the high profits in the fur trade. In fact, the profits were so enormous that John Jacob Astor, a young German who emigrated to the United States in the year the peace was signed, was immediately attracted by them. Previously he had been employed in his uncle's piano and flute factory in London and had come to New York to make his fortune. Hearing how much money could be made in furs, he quickly set himself up in that commerce and began building his fortune. He was not, however, a trader in the French tradition, going into the wilds, but preferred to remain in the marketplace and deal with the financial and administrative problems connected with his business empire.

While John Jacob Astor was grappling with the intricacies of the fur business and learning to become one of the most successful traders of all time, the Continental Congress was wrestling with an even more difficult problem. The public domain had now become a reality, and the poverty-stricken government looked to its disposal as a source of much needed revenue.

But how could the federal government survey such a large tract of land in a reasonable period of time? Until then the customary method of survey had been to select a starting point and describe it in relationship to some well-established physical feature. From this point, the surveyor began measuring the boundary lines, indicating the direction in which they went. Although this method had worked well for many centuries, some members of the Continental Congress realized it was an impractical way to survey the public domain. It gave a surveyor too great an opportunity to show favoritism by enclosing some especially desirable feature within a particular tract. It also required an on-the-ground survey of each piece of land and a cumbersome description that might be subject to misunderstanding and litigation.

The delegates from New England, who were accustomed to seeing land laid out in orderly townships, led the debate out of which emerged the Land Ordinance of 1785 and the rectangular system of survey. Stated simply, the surveyors were to lay out a meridian running north and south. Next they were to draw a baseline at right angles across the meridian, forming a giant cross on the map and dividing it into four large areas. These in turn were to be subdivided into townships, each boundary being six miles long and running either north-south or east-west. The townships were then again subdivided into thirty-six sections that contained 640 acres each. These in turn could be divided into quarter sections of a 160 acres. This system was a marvel of simplicity and clarity. Once the meridian and baseline had been laid out, the tracts within the four quadrants could be easily located and described. The principal weakness was the system's utter disregard of local physical features. A township boundary, for example, might fall ten feet short of a river, leaving it without access to water, while the neighboring township had more than an ample supply. This weakness sometimes caused problems and was inherent in the system. On the other hand, it is a tribute to its efficiency that it was used to survey the whole of the public domain, which eventually reached a total of almost a billion

and a half acres exclusive of Alaska, and was also adopted by Canada.

Two years later, in 1787, Congress passed the Northwest Ordinance to open up the Ohio territory to settlement. At one time, the Continental Congress, remembering the original concept that the land should not be carved into colonies, had believed new territories should be immediately admitted as states, but on second thought, this seemed impractical. The Northwest Ordinance provided for three stages of political development. In the first, a territory would be created, and its officials would all be appointees of the federal government. In the second, it would have its own elected legislature, but its governor would continue to be a presidential appointee. During this period its people would draft their own state constitution, decide on qualifications for voting and holding office, and set up the framework of their own government. It would then enter the third stage, which was admission to the union as an equal of all the other states. Although the law applied only to the Northwest Territory, it set a precedent for the admission of all future states. The Americans who had fought so hard against a colonial system were not going to establish one of their own.

While the Americans were preoccupied with opening the Northwest Territory and with their many financial and diplomatic problems, the Spanish, who for so long had been unable to establish themselves on the Great Plains, were trying to exploit the area west of the Mississippi. Like France, Spain wavered between developing the fur trade by monopolies or by free enterprise. Initially Spain left the traders to fend for themselves without government regulation. During this time a number of men expanded Spain's knowledge of its possession. Joseph Garreau, for example, a young Frenchman in his early twenties, went to the Arikaras to represent a trader. By then the Missouri River was well known to the white men, but they had been merely visitors to the area, exploring it, trading with the Indians, and then leaving it. Garreau, however, was one of those who prefer the wilderness to cities, natives to his own kind. He remained with the Arikaras, becoming probably the first permanent white resident in what is now the state of South Dakota.

Another adventurer was Pedro Vial. In spite of his Spanish first name, he was a Frenchman and had been christened Pierre. Not much is known about his early life, but he seems to have had the natural instinct of so many Frenchmen for dealing with the Indians. As a younger man, he had lived with several tribes—no one knew exactly which ones—and had traveled in distant places—no one knew precisely where. Rumors swirled around his past like the mist rising from the Missouri River on a cold October morning. Some said he had been a prisoner of the Comanches, that fierce tribe that blocked the way across the Great Plains, but had made friends with them and secured his own release. Others believed he had once been a renegade gunsmith, repairing the Indians' guns, which they sometimes later used for killing white men. Since Spanish policy discouraged the Indians' possession of firearms, the authorities could not look favorably on this aspect of Vial's life. Nevertheless, when they wanted a scout to explore a direct route from San Antonio to Santa Fé, they decided to utilize Vial's experience.

In 1786 he left San Antonio with instructions to keep a diary and make a map of his route, both of which he was to turn over to the Spanish authorities when he arrived at Santa Fé. Although Vial had been told to take the most direct way, he did not. Whether from ignorance of the country or a desire to visit tribes he already knew, he headed in a wandering, northerly direction from San Antonio. After only a few weeks, he became seriously ill but fortunately had reached the village of some friendly Indians, who took care of him for more than a month.

On resuming his journey, he came to another village whose inhabitants were distinctly hostile. One of their members had disappeared during a horse-stealing raid on San Antonio, and they wanted to know whether he had been taken captive or killed. Here Vial showed his skill in handling the natives. Before leaving San Antonio, he had been asked to identify the warrior's body, so he knew the man was dead. But instead of being defensive, he chastised the angry Indians who surrounded him for causing the Spaniards trouble and threatened them with retaliation if they did not behave in a more peaceful manner. This was a brave stance for a man who was traveling with a single companion. But his courage and directness impressed the Indians, and they promised to be more friendly in the future.

Later in his trip he also visited the Comanches. They too had raided the Spanish, suffered losses, and were in an unfriendly mood. Again Vial launched a psychological offensive and scolded them for having attacked the Spanish. His resolute manner so impressed them they gave him shelter for the rest of the winter.

In the spring of 1787 he continued on his journey and toward the end of May safely reached San-ta Fé. He had traveled more than a thousand miles and had been away from any white settlement for approximately seven and one half months. Going north to approximately the present-day border between Oklahoma and Texas, he had then turned west, crossing the Great Plains at the Texas Panhandle. Although much of the country through which he had traveled had been previously explored, he had once more pierced the barrier that the Great Plains imposed between east and west.

Now that the French no longer owned Louisiana, the Spanish were as anxious to promote travel between east and west as they had formerly been eager to discourage it. But the governor of New Mexico was not satisfied with Vial's route and wanted to discover a shorter one. So while Vial rested in Santa Fé, the governor employed a retired army corporal, José Mares, to try again.

In the middle of the summer Mares left the capital of New Mexico and headed east to Pecos, which had figured so largely in Coronado's eastern explorations. From there he crossed the Llano Estacado, whose flatness had so appalled the early Spaniards when they had first seen it. When he arrived in San Antonio that fall the governor realized that he had taken a roundabout route and was considerably annoyed. The viceroy, however, ordered him to provide Mares with supplies for the return journey.

In January, which was about the worst time of the year to make the trip, Mares set out for Santa Fé. On the way back he avoided the Indian villages he had detoured to visit when he was going to San Antonio and thus reduced the distance he covered. Although he encountered no particular difficulties, his trip took him longer, probably because of the season.

Clearly anxious to establish commerce with the settlements to the east, the governor of New Mexico assigned Vial a new task—laying out a route between Santa Fé and Natchitoches that would link these two Spanish settlements, one of them in New Mexico, the other in Louisiana. Furthermore, he was willing to spend money to equip Vial better than before and provided him with a military escort for part of the journey.

In June, 1788, Vial left Santa Fé for the East. With the French no longer a menace, the governor dreamed of a network of trails across the Great Plains that would lead to a profitable commerce between his impoverished settlement and Louisiana. The hour, however, was late. France's threat had faded, but a new one was rising farther east. For during the same month that the governor gave Vial his instructions in Santa Fé and saw him off, the legislature of New Hampshire met and ratified the new federal Constitution. Since it was the ninth state to do so, the Constitution, as Article VII provided, went into effect. The weak nation along the eastern seaboard was developing a stronger central government as well as an intense interest in the lands to the west. It, not France, was now the potential threat to the governor's ambitions.

Vial took an almost direct route to Natchitoches, leaving the mountains in New Mexico, entering the Great Plains, crossing the Texas Panhandle, and on to his destination. Natchitoches had been doing well. Its inhabitants numbered several thousand, and they lived and worked in wooden buildings, which were so well constructed they impressed the visitors from Santa Fé.

Particularly significant to the residents of Natchitoches was the relative ease with which Vial and his companions had made the trip. They had been able to find water along the way, there had been plenty of game, and the Indians had been peaceful. Even the Comanches, who had attacked the Spanish such a short time before, had been helpful. In the opinion of the commander at Natchitoches, Vial had proved that wagon trains could make the trip in forty days during the spring and fall without much difficulty. In his official report he also emphasized the friendly attitude of the Indians, pointing out that none of them were to be feared except the Osages. From his evaluation of the journey, it was clear that he, like the governor of New Mexico, foresaw regular trade between the two outposts.

When the governor of New Mexico had given Vial the assignment to go to Natchitoches, he had also instructed him to return to Santa Fé by way of San Antonio so as to link all three settlements. Therefore, after he and his men had rested, Vial set off for San Antonio. This trip, too, was relatively uneventful, but when they arrived at the settlement of Nacogdoches in what is now east Texas, most of the party except Vial came down with chills and fever, the symptoms of malaria. Their sickness held them up for more than forty-five days, making them lose most of the months of September and October and delaying their arrival at San Antonio until the middle of November. There, with the exception of Vial, they were taken ill once more, suffering probably from a recurrence of the same disease.

Since Vial had no official duties to perform in San Antonio until his men recovered, the governor sent him and another as emissaries to the Comanches. As the French had realized years ago, the friendship of this tribe was indispensable to those who wished to cross the Great Plains, and they had expended much effort in their successful attempt to placate them. The Spanish had taken up the same strategy, and the ease with which Vial had made the trip from Santa Fé to Natchitoches proved it was paying off.

So Vial, to whom miles of travel seemed to be nothing, set out again, taking with him a supply of gifts—"bribes" might be a more accurate word—that were intended to please the Comanches. These included seventy twists of tobacco, almost twenty yards of colored cloth, two pounds of vermilion, ten pounds of blue and white beads, two dozen knives, and, of all things, seven flags to appeal to the Indians' strong sense of pageantry. With the possible exception of the knives, nothing in the lot could be turned against the Spaniards, who were still adhering to their policy of not supplying the Indians with arms. If Vial had been able to handle the Comanches when he had nothing to give them, he was even better able to do so in the role of open-handed dispenser of presents and soon returned, bringing with him three Comanche leaders and their wives to talk with the governor.

By the end of June, 1789, Vial's men were sufficiently recovered to start on the journey back to Santa Fé. Four Comanches offered to serve as guides—a sign of the improved relations the Spanish had purchased from that tribe—and Vial arrived in the capital of New Mexico in August.

The importance of Vial's expeditions was not in the discovery of new land. Many of the places he visited had been seen before by white men. But he and his men had succeeded in finding direct and easy routes between Santa Fé, San Antonio, and Natchitoches, three important outposts in Spain's North American empire. They had also kept careful logs of their journeys, enabling others to follow in their steps. The alien renegade, who had once helped arm the Indians against the whites by repairing their guns, had served his adopted country well. For by breaking the barrier of the Great Plains he had given the Spanish a means of consolidating their holdings in New Mexico and Louisiana, making a single whole out of these two disparate areas.

The Spanish, however, were not concentrating their efforts on expanding in the interior of the continent, for they had never lost their ambition to possess the West Coast. The competition there was increasing. The British had sailed along the coast; the Russians had their eye on the profitable trade in sea otter pelts; and in 1788 Captain John Meares from Canada discovered the bay of the Columbia

River (although he did not discover the river itself) and established a trading post on Nootka Sound, an inlet on the Pacific coast of Vancouver Island. The Spanish, claiming prior discovery, seized several British ships in retaliation. But the show of strength produced only humiliating consequences. The following year Spain was compelled to pay reparations.

Spain's retreat from the firm stand it had taken at Nootka Sound revealed its principal weakness. In a crisis it could not rely on its chief ally, France. For France was now in the throes of the French Revolution. So Spain had to contend alone with its two aggressive neighbors in North America, the British and the Americans.

The British were in an expansionist mood, looking for new markets for their manufactured goods, and were glad to have their traders spill over the borders of Canada into Spanish territory. The British were also playing a cat-and-mouse game with the United States, holding out hopes of more cordial relations when war with Spain seemed imminent and withdrawing them when America's help was not needed. Meanwhile the possibility of a British invasion of Spanish territory seemed so great that George Washington was thinking about the appropriate American response to a possible British demand for permission to send troops through the old Northwest Territory.

To the Spanish, the United States also presented a potential threat. The new republic was not docile, and its interests ran contrary to Spain's. For one thing, sooner or later it would want control of the Mississippi River. Great Britain, might, therefore, be able to count on its assistance in the event that war with Spain broke out.

Although Spain could not send large military forces to protect its lands, it was not ready to abandon them. Instead it attempted to extend its influence up the Missouri River by issuing licenses to fur traders. Jean Baptiste Meunier, who discovered the Ponca Indians, was given permission to trade with them on the Niobrara River, which flows east through present-day Nebraska. Another Frenchman, Jacques d'Église, obtained a license from the Spanish and went up the Missouri River to the Mandan villages. There he learned from a compatriot who had lived with this tribe for several years that British traders came regularly from the north to do business with them.

But the outposts established by men like d'Église could not stem the pressures that were building up against Spain. No matter how enterprising they were, single individuals could not protect the far-flung Spanish claims. In 1792 George

Vancouver, an experienced British sea captain, arrived on the West Coast and began charting the shore the Spanish had been forced to evacuate after the Nootka Sound controversy. He explored Puget Sound and circumnavigated Vancouver Island, performing his work so well that today's maps carry many of the place names he originated.

Also ominous to Spain was the appearance on the coast of another power. Captain Robert Gray of Boston had discovered the enormous profits to be made in the sea otter trade. The skins were purchased from the Indians in what is now Oregon, Washington, and British Columbia and then taken to Canton, China, where they were exchanged for goods that could be sold at high prices in New England. In 1792, while he was making his second voyage in pursuit of this trade, he noticed along the coast of present-day Oregon a strong offshore current and, following its course, discovered the mouth of the Columbia River, which previous explorers, both Spanish and British, had missed. This discovery provided a basis for an American claim in the Northwest.

Whether or not the governor of New Mexico was aware of these developments along the borders of Spain's possessions, he optimistically continued with his plans to draw New Mexico and the East together. His next goal was a route between Santa Fé and St. Louis, and he showed his confidence in Vial by once more choosing him to establish one.

In 1792 with two young men as companions, Vial followed the now familiar road to Pecos and struck out across the Great Plains once again. Except for the illness that had disabled his men at Nacogdoches, his previous journeys had been relatively uneventful. This time, however, he was not so fortunate. While he was on the Llano Estacado, the weather became bad and forced him to remain in camp for several days. Then he fell sick and for more than a week could not continue the trip. Next came heavy rains, which turned the treacherous rivers—so often placid trickles meandering across the land—into violent torrents, which were dangerous to cross.

Toward the end of June he came upon some freshly slaughtered buffalo carcasses and, wishing to talk to the Indian hunters, searched for their camp. When he located it, he and his two companions fired shots to attract the Indians, who were on the opposite bank of a river. The first to cross the river identified themselves as Kansa Indians and were friendly. But their cordiality was only a ruse. As their number increased with new arrivals from the other side, they suddenly seized the travelers' horses and equipment and slashed their clothes with knives until the three men were entirely naked.

At this critical moment an argument broke out among the Indians. They had completely surrounded the travelers and were preparing to kill them. Some wanted to use their bows and guns; others warned they might wound the Indians on the opposite side of the circle. During the slight delay caused by this disagreement, an Indian whom Vial had known before recognized him and drew him up behind him on his horse. Another Indian also recognized him, and between them they saved Vial's life. The next day they reunited him with his two companions, who had also been spared because of the intercession of individual Indians.

For ten days they traveled with this band until they came to a river where they met a French trader. He procured their release and gave them some equipment and a boat to finish their trip to St. Louis, which they reached in October.

The lateness of the season with its threat of winter storms forced them to postpone their return journey until the following June. As they wanted to avoid the Osages, who were frequently hostile to the Spaniards, they went by boat up the Missouri River, fighting its current until they reached a point that was probably in the southeastern corner of present-day Nebraska. This was where traders usually met the Pawnee Indians, through whose territory Vial's instructions required him to return. After a wait of several weeks, a band of Pawnees arrived to take Vial to their main camp. Here the Indians held a council and declared their warm friendship for the Spaniards and their gratitude for the trade goods they brought into the country.

As his past experience indicated, Vial was by no means immune to danger from the Indians in spite of his skill at dealing with them. After he left the Pawnees, a group of Indians mistook him and his companions for Comanches, with whom they were at war. Another time, an Indian tried to steal one of their horses. But they safely made their way from the Missouri River, diagonally across Kansas, and through the panhandles of Oklahoma and Texas. At Tucumcari, New Mexico, they met a Comanche who had lost his clothing and weapons—Vial did not say how—and was dying from cold and hunger. Vial clothed and fed him, thus making one more Indian friend.

In the middle of November, 1793, the expedition arrived back in Santa Fé, its mission accomplished. Vial had charted two routes between the capital and St. Louis and had proved New Mexico could indeed be linked to the settlements on the Missouri and Mississippi and that trade could be maintained with the Indians in between. But in spite of this contribution to Spain, he did not receive the reward he wanted—a minor officership in the Spanish army.

His effort had come too late to help Spain, for its eastern settlements now had little time to trade with the West; they were too occupied keeping out the British. The problem of the Spanish was both military and economic. The continuing inability of the French government to come to their aid left them unable to oppose force with force; the declining profits from the fur trade made it equally impossible to attract enough civilian settlers to block the men slipping into Spanish territory from the north. The aggressive British, who were better supplied with goods, had diverted much of the Indians' trade. What was left for the Spanish near St. Louis was not enough to support the men engaged in the fur business.

To encourage expansion, the governor of Louisiana decreed that any Spaniard could trade on the Missouri River, provided only that he first obtained the permission of the lieutenant governor, Zenon Trudeau. But free trade—with the ruinous competition it engendered—aroused strong protests among the merchants of St. Louis. So in 1793 the governor revised his plan and drew up a set of regulations, which he submitted to them for their approval. This brought the merchants together and made them divide up the available trading areas. At the same time, it inspired several of them, under the leadership of one trader, Jacques Clamorgan, to consider forming a company for trading with the Missouri tribes living above the Poncas. The governor heartily approved of this idea, which was in line with his own, and not only gave the newly formed company exclusive rights to this trade, but also offered a monetary prize to any Spaniard who might reach the Pacific Ocean by following the Missouri River.

The company was named the "Commercial Company of the Missouri for Trade with the Tribes further up [the Missouri] than the Poncas" but became better known as the Missouri Company. It was the best answer to the encroachments of the British that the Spanish could summon.

The almost leisurely approach of the St. Louis merchants to the expansion of their trading grounds contrasted sharply with the activities of the Canadian traders, who were engaged in a violent competitive struggle between the rival North West and Hudson's Bay companies.

Alexander Mackenzie, a Scotch immigrant and a leader in the North West Company, was in many respects a spiritual heir of la Salle, a driver of men and a person of vast vision, although sometimes given to fits of profound depression. Among the many tasks he had performed for the North West Company, he had operated a post on Lake Athabasca, which cuts across the northern boundaries of Alberta and Saskatchewan. In 1789 he had made a historic journey from Lake Athabasca to the Arctic Ocean, following the Slave River to Great Slave Lake and then taking the course of the river that today bears his name. He accomplished this trip of approximately 1,500 miles through the wilderness in about one hundred days, which testifies to his own stamina and that of the handful of persons who accompanied him.

Yet he was not satisfied with his findings, for he realized he had an inadequate knowledge of surveying and insufficient instruments to produce the type of scientific report he desired. To remedy his deficiencies, he spent the winter of 1791 and 1792 in London. Although his unique understanding of the geography of the north would have made him welcome in scientific circles, he did little to call attention to what he had done. The man who had braved the wilderness and the Indians could not bring himself to risk possible scorn of his technical ignorance.

In 1792, the year he returned from England, Mackenzie began thinking about another journey, one that would be considerably shorter in total mileage than his trip to the Arctic Ocean but much more arduous—a "voyage" (he used the word) from the outposts of the North West Company to the Pacific Ocean.

Not knowing what difficulties he would encounter but realizing he must complete the trip in a single season or run the risk of becoming winterbound, he left Lake Athabasca in the fall of that year, going up the Peace River to the mouth of the Smoky River near the present town of Grimshaw, Alberta, where he established a temporary base. This put him several hundred miles on his way.

When the ice broke in the spring of 1793, he was ready to depart. Nine men had agreed to go with him, two of them Indians, and two of them men who had traveled with him to the Arctic Ocean and were willing to submit again to his driving leadership. He had a twenty-five-foot canoe that was large enough to hold the entire party and their equipment and yet light enough, he said, so two men could carry it three miles without resting. (Of course, those two men had to be like himself, strong and nimble.) His plan for the trip was simple and direct. He intended to follow the Peace River as far as it would take him into the moun-

tains, cross their crest on foot, find a west-flowing river, and let it carry him to the ocean.

The Peace River soon proved anything but peaceful, for they entered its canyon at the base of Portage Mountain, a spot where even the Indians dared not go. The current quickened, and the surface of the river foamed as it raced between the rocks. Progress forward was no longer possible, and the steep walls of the canyon seemed intended to prevent their escape. Feeling trapped and defeated, his men started talking about returning to their base camp, but Mackenzie would not listen to them. Instead he encouraged them into cutting a road up the wall of the canyon and carrying the boat to a point where the river again became navigable—a task that required several days of grueling work. In this determined fashion, the indomitable man pushed his way through the Canadian wilderness, leading his men toward their goal, the Pacific Ocean.

Finally they came to the juncture of the Parsnip and Finlay rivers, where they form the Peace. There he chose the Parsnip, planning to follow it to its source in the mountains. In order to reach the other side of the divide, they were finally forced to leave the river but found they could travel on a number of small streams and lakes, although the going was extremely difficult. At last they came to the Fraser, which runs south through British Columbia and then turns west to enter the Strait of Georgia just above the International Line. It would have taken Mackenzie quickly to his destination, the Pacific Ocean.

Mackenzie, however, was hesitant. Willing to run great risks for important causes, he nevertheless was a skilled woodsman and had a woodsman's caution. So he questioned the local Indians closely and from what they said decided to leave the riverways and proceed by land. This route proved relatively easy, for the Indians guided him along well-traveled trails to the Bella Cool River, which flows into Queen Charlotte Sound, just north of Vancouver Island.

On the morning of July 20, 1793, he and his men rose early, and at eight o'clock they entered the waters of the Pacific Ocean. Although the surrounding hills were covered with fog and the visibility was poor, they knew at once they had reached their goal—not just another of many lakes—for the tide was out.

During the next several days Mackenzie made observations, explored the coast, and traded for otter skins. The Indians had previously traded with white men who had come by ship and who had paid such high prices that Mackenzie—a true

Scotsman—commented on the improvidence of European traders. One of the Indians indicated he had been maltreated by a white man who, he claimed, had fired on him and his friends and had struck him on the back with the flat of his sword. To demonstrate these acts, he used Mackenzie's own weapons, causing the explorer considerable uneasiness. The attitude of this man and some of the other Indians conveyed an underlying sense of hostility; and when two canoes approached with a large group from an unfamiliar band, a friendly Indian advised Mackenzie it was time to flee. In a short while, he said, the others would attack him with bows and spears. Mackenzie, however, refused to leave immediately. While the Indians watched, he calmly took another observation, then mixed some vermilion with grease and used the compound to write an inscription in large letters on a rock. It read: "Alexander Mackenzie, from Canada, by land, the twenty-second of July, one thousand seven hundred and ninety-three."

The trip back was somewhat easier than the trip out. For one thing, they knew the way and did not have to struggle so much against the unexpected. For another, they traveled more lightly, because they had cached supplies against their return. But before they reached the Parsnip River, Mackenzie's feet and ankles had become so swollen he could barely walk; and his men, much to his disgust, had to carry him on the last portage to the Parsnip. From there, of course, their route took them downstream, and since it was late in the summer and the water low, they could canoe through some of the rapids and avoid the work of carrying their equipment around them.

Toward the end of August they saw ahead of them the base camp they had left that spring. In celebration they waved a flag they had carried with them and discharged their firearms. Then their paddles flashed in the air, and they covered the last few yards of their journey so quickly that the bow of their canoe touched shore before the two men they had left behind could come out and greet them.

This reunion of a handful of men on the banks of the Peace River brought to a conclusion a remarkable feat of exploration. With no government backing and only modest equipment and supplies, Mackenzie had led his party over hundreds of miles of wilderness and through lands that were inhabited by Indians who were sometimes unfriendly, and he had done so without losing a single one of his followers or ever firing a hostile shot. Others had crossed the North American continent before, but only from the Gulf of Mexico or the Caribbean, where the distance overland was much shorter. Mackenzie and those who went with him were the first to make the long journey from the Atlantic to the Pacific.

The backers of the Missouri Company, meeting in St. Louis, were so anxious to start doing business they did not wait to have their plan formally approved by the governor of Louisiana at New Orleans. As the leader of their first trading expedition, they chose Jean Baptiste Trudeau (he generally spelled it Truteau), a St. Louis schoolmaster who claimed experience with Indians and a distant relationship to the lieutenant governor, Zenon Trudeau.

Leaving St. Louis in June, 1794, Trudeau started up the Missouri River in a pirogue filled with supplies and trading goods. Laboring slowly against the current, he had almost reached the mouth of the Platte River when he was overtaken by Jacques d'Église, who was making another of his trips to the Upper Missouri. A much more experienced trader than Trudeau, d'Église was traveling in a smaller boat and with a lighter load, a combination that enabled him to move faster and perhaps pass the Indian villages lower down the Missouri undetected. These villages had a well-deserved reputation for harassing small traders, and Trudeau asked d'Église to join forces with him for their mutual protection. As the advantages of such an arrangement lay entirely on Trudeau's side, d'Église refused but did agree to take some of Trudeau's guns to the Arikaras' village. It was an inauspicious start for the Missouri Company's first expedition to have its leader depending on its principal rival.

Trudeau's lack of self-confidence produced his first mishap when he met a band of Yankton and Teton Sioux. Since he did not have the courage and resourcefulness of a Vial or a Mackenzie, they soon had the upper hand, playing on his fears and inducing him to sell them supplies at foolishly low prices. And what they wanted and did not buy at bargain prices, they stole.

By this time Trudeau was far behind his original schedule and, having failed to reach the Mandan villages before the end of autumn, was forced to establish a winter camp. There the Omahas descended on him and, using tactics similar to those of the Sioux, persuaded him to extend them credit, although they obviously had no intention of ever repaying their debts.

With the help of reinforcements and additional

supplies that the company sent him the next year, Trudeau was able to obtain some furs in return for the expenses the company had incurred. He also gained more knowledge of the geography of the Upper Missouri and established a trading relationship with the Cheyennes. But by the summer of 1795 the company's directors in St. Louis had decided to replace him with a Scotsman named James Mackay, who had been a trader in Canada, had visited the Mandan villages from the north, and had finally decided to switch his allegiance and join the Spanish.

It was time the directors took more vigorous action, for Spain's control of the fur trade—and therefore of the Great Plains—was being eroded. In the north, Canadian traders and explorers had outflanked the Spanish by their westward trips and also by moving south had become more familiar with the Mandan villages than the men licensed by Spain. In the East the fledgling United States was showing signs of maturing strength. While Trudeau was attempting to establish the Missouri Company among the Indians, John Jay was in England trying to settle the many serious differences that had arisen between Great Britain and the United States in the few short years since the two nations had made peace. He secured the promise that Great Britain would evacuate the posts it still retained on American soil and several other concessions, but the terms of the treaty he brought back so profoundly shocked the Americans that the Senate debated it in secret; and when its provisions became known, John Jay, and even George Washington, were publicly damned.

Nevertheless Spain interpreted the agreement as a sign of growing friendship between Great Britain and the United States and, fearful of the possible threat this might pose, decided to make overtures to the Americans. Spain's changed attitude resulted in Pinckney's Treaty, which settled the boundary of West Florida on American terms, opened up the Mississippi River to American navigation, and gave Americans the right to transship goods at New Orleans without paying duties. Paradoxically the price Spain was willing to pay for the Americans' friendship would help make the United States strong enough to become a potential enemy.

In their council chambers diplomats and politicians debated international boundaries, but other, less exalted persons were also affecting the course of history. These were the people on the spot, driven by their own political and economic aspirations. The church's influence had greatly lessened, and no one spent much time worrying about the Indi-

ans' souls, but the men and women on the frontier were concerned about the governmental system under which they lived and even more about the money they could earn.

James Mackay, as the Missouri Company's representative, had a good job—one that might possibly make him rich—and his objective was to get to work right away and start establishing a profitable trade with the Indians on behalf of his employers. He realized, as others had not, that this would require a firmer and more permanent base of operations. So he first built a trading post near the mouth of the Platte River among the Oto Indians, later explaining to the directors in St. Louis that the friendship of these Indians was necessary to the company and that it could not be gained by merely distributing a few gifts. What the Indians needed, he explained, was a source of trade goods that was non-British and a fort to protect them from their enemies. Clearly he did not intend to make furtive trips past the Indian villages on the Missouri, as Trudeau and d'Église had done. Rather he intended to set up a series of stations among friendly Indians. The experience he had gained in Canada was paying off, for this plan was more like that so successfully followed by the Hudson's Bay Company and the North West Company than like the haphazard pattern of Spanish trading.

Next he stopped among the Omahas, passing out presents, entering into a friendly relationship with one of their important chiefs, and constructing another post, which he called Fort Charles and where he spent the winter.

In the following year, 1796, he sent one of his lieutenants, John Evans, up the Missouri with instructions to go to the Pacific Coast. Evans never accomplished that—or even came close to it—but he did get as far as the Mandan villages. There he found the British not only active, but ensconced in a permanent post just as though that area of the Great Plains belonged to them.

Evans was in a delicate position. Far from his supporters in St. Louis and without enough men to use force, he chose the role of diplomat rather than policeman. Although he ordered the British out of Spanish territory, he was moderate and reasonable in his attitude and even permitted some of them to return later on a temporary basis. He also apparently made no effort to disturb their activities in the Red River Valley of North Dakota, where they were firmly established. This was just outside the Great Plains and also outside the territory claimed by Spain. Since the river originates south of the present international boundary, access to the valley was easier from the north, and Evans may have taken this into consideration. If the agents of the Hudson's Bay Company and the North West Company had come into armed conflict with Evans's men, they could have probably driven the Missouri Company back to St. Louis.

By that year, 1796, the Great Plains had lost much of their mystery. White men had traveled over most of the area, knew many of its major rivers, had traded with most of its Indian tribes, built posts along the Missouri, attempted to establish a mission in Kansas, and had laid out east-west routes across it with the thought of regular commerce between the two sections of the continent. Many parts of it remained to be explored, but it was no longer the forbidding barrier it had once been, its reality submerged in rumors of Quivira and remote civilizations rich in gold and jewels.

The effect of the white men's coming had been great. The Sioux, pushed from their woodland refuges to the east by their Indian enemies armed with white men's guns, had become increasingly dominant, often at the expense of earlier tribes, many of which were now on their way to extinction. Horses were spreading from south to north in ever greater numbers, changing the culture of the remaining Indians, not for the worse, but for the better. Guns were now commonplace. The sounds of thunder roaring and of the wind beating against the grasses were often coupled with the blast of gunfire, as Indians swept down on a herd of buffaloes or battled against each other. On the whole, the Indians welcomed the white men for what they brought and were becoming more and more reliant on them as a source of supply. If they had withdrawn, the Indians' standard of living would have plunged downward, a fact the Indians well knew.

The white men themselves had long since given up hope of finding precious metals already mined by the natives or lying close to the surface, where they could be easily extracted. These illusions had vanished, and the men in the field were no longer pursuing fantasies and dreaming of quickly obtainable wealth. But they did want possession of the Great Plains because of the fur trade. As long as the prices of pelts remained high in Europe, the Great Plains offered them potential wealth. But they did not want to remove the Indians, for they were as dependent on the Indians as the Indians were on them. The Indians and the few small garrisons were the principal markets for the white civilians along the frontier. And so they continued to struggle against the elements, the stern land, the vicissitudes of commerce, and, in many cases, against each other.

At this point, fate once again took the future of the Great Plains out of the hands of the men who knew the area best and gave it back to the diplomats. American foreign policy had become impaled on the word "forever," which was included in the military alliance it had made with France in 1778. Desperate to defeat Great Britain and overjoyed at the succor offered by France, the struggling country had enthusiastically envisioned a relationship that would last for all time. But now that it was at peace and profiting from trade with England, it was anxious not to become involved in the war between its former enemy and its former ally. By legalistic reasoning, it decided that the word "forever" did not mean what it seemed to mean, and by wise—albeit ungenerous and self-serving diplomacy—it had remained disengaged. Surprised at this treatment, France responded with a number of insulting moves that did nothing to further its cause and only helped to unify the Americans, making them a more formidable power in the New World and ultimately compelling France to become conciliatory.

The Spanish watched the growing strength of the United States with concern. With their grip on the Mississippi and their possession of New Orleans on the east bank of the river, they had a stranglehold on the new country but not the strength to use their advantage. This was an unenviable position; it annoyed and frightened the Americans but did not protect Louisiana.

In France Napoleon now headed the government, and under his leadership the country was again beginning to dream of a worldwide empire. The loss of its North American territories still rankled, and the purchase of Louisiana from Spain seemed a good way to start restoring its international position. The price Napoleon finally offered was high: the Italian kingdom of Tuscany or its equivalent. This, in Spanish eyes, was a good bargain. Louisiana had never been anything but a drain on the royal treasury, and as a buffer between Spain's possessions and the East, it was little more than a temptation to invasion. A secret agreement between Spain and France was concluded at San Ildefonso, Spain, in the fall of 1800, but the Spanish government soon decided—and probably with good reason—that Napoleon might withhold payment and therefore delayed the actual transfer of Louisiana.

Interest in the interior of the North American continent was quickened in 1801 by the publication of Mackenzie's journals in Great Britain. A copy was smuggled to France, where the government translated it and gave it to Jean Baptiste Bernadotte, the general and brother-in-law of Joseph Bonaparte, to study. Another reader was Thomas Jefferson, who wondered if Mackenzie's exploit of crossing the continent could not be duplicated by Americans.

The following year the history of the Great Plains rushed to a climax. Almost two and three-quarter centuries had passed since the waves of the Gulf of Mexico had tossed Cabeza de Vaca on the shores of Texas. During those years, explorers, coming from the south, east, and north, had criss-crossed the Great Plains, discovering many of its secrets; and in 1802 the process was still going on. A Canadian, Charles le Raye, and a companion were on a trapping expedition that took them to the Yellowstone, Powder, and Bighorn rivers. Title to the area had passed back and forth as freely as though it had been the real estate holding of a band of gamblers—which, in a way, it was—but no person and no nation had ever taken possession of it.

Of all those who attempted to do so, Napoleon was perhaps the best equipped. His enormous ambition, his expansive vision, and his extraordinary executive talent were perhaps a match for the area's forbidding greatness. But Napoleon's attempt to subdue the Great Plains in the name of France was even less effective than la Salle's. Planning first to re-establish French authority in Santo Domingo (now Haiti), in 1802 Napoleon sent to sea the largest expeditionary force that had ever left France. But in Santo Domingo it found only death and disgrace. Stricken by disease and bewildered by the guerrilla tactics of the inhabitants led by Toussaint l'Ouverture, the army crumbled; and as it did, it brought down with it Napoleon's dream of a western empire.

That same year the Spanish, in an unwise show of power, ignored the sense of Pinckney's Treaty and withdrew permission for Americans to trans-ship goods at New Orleans, thus cutting off the western part of the United States from access to the ocean. The act was senseless unless the Spanish had wished to provoke the United States into taking Louisiana, for it was an ominous portent of what might happen if Louisiana should be occupied by a stronger nation, such as France. And inevitably news of Napoleon's secret agreement had spread. Once France took actual possession of its purchase, the position of the United States could become precarious.

Even Thomas Jefferson, who preferred the French to the British and peace to war, realized drastic action must be taken. In a letter to the American envoy to France, Robert R. Livingston,

he stated the changing American attitude toward Louisiana. "Spain," he wrote, "might have retained it quietly for years. Her pacific dispositions, her feeble state, would enduce her to increase our facilities there, so that her possession of the place would be hardly felt by us, and it would not, perhaps, be very long before some circumstance might arise, which might make the cession of it to us the price of something of more worth to her. Not so can it ever be in the hands of France. . . ."

While Jefferson was trying to pry Louisiana—or at the very least New Orleans—from the hands of Napoleon, he was negotiating with the Spanish for the privilege of sending an exploring expedition across the continent to Oregon. Because of Gray's discovery of the mouth of the Columbia, the United States had a claim in that area, and Jefferson was interested in finding an overland route to it even if the route had to lead through Spanish territory.

Suddenly Napoleon reversed his previous position. The defeat of his army in Santo Domingo and the threat of renewed warfare in Europe made him realize he could no longer afford the diversion of North American adventures. During the evening of April 13, 1803, Barbé-Marbois, the French minister of finance, came to call on the American minister, Robert R. Livingston. The news he brought was so astonishing Livingston wrote his report that night rather than wait for morning. In short, Napoleon was now ready to sell not only New Orleans, but the whole of Louisiana.

As finally negotiated, the price came to slightly more than $11 million—to be paid for in six-percent bonds—and the assumption by the United States government of American shipowners' claims against the French for the seizure of their vessels and cargoes. The total cost was eventually slightly more than $23 million, for which the United States obtained 900,000 square miles at a cost of less than four cents an acre.

When the news of this transaction reached Spain, the Spanish government protested vigorously and with just cause. Fearful that such a transaction might occur, thus placing an aggressive neighbor close to Texas and New Mexico, Spain had insisted on a clause in its agreement with France specifically prohibiting a transfer of the title to any other country. Although the diplomatic correspondence was heavy, Spain was forced to accept what had happened or go to war. Sensibly it chose the first course.

Part II 1804-1848

From the Lewis and Clark Expedition
Through the Mexican War

Chapter 6

The Two Captains

The object of your mission is to explore the Missouri river, & such principal stream of it, as, by its course & communication with the waters of the Pacific Ocean, may offer the most direct & practicable water communication across this continent, for the purposes of commerce.

—Thomas Jefferson, 1803

Few men, not even la Vérendrye or Mackenzie, ever followed a trail more obscure or murky than the one taken by Thomas Jefferson when he purchased Louisiana from the French; and years later as an old man, he was still explaining his action and justifying it to himself and others.

When Napoleon made his startling offer, the nation was new, its institutions untested. With considerable reluctance and only out of necessity had the original colonies agreed to surrender their destinies to a central government, and they had jealously circumscribed its powers. Not a word in the Constitution—drafted and redrafted so carefully during the Philadelphia summer of 1787—even hinted at giving the President power to double the geographical size of the nation without consulting the people, and no delegate to the convention foresaw that such a question would arise in less than two decades.

Frightened by the awesomeness of the problem that Napoleon had laid before him, Jefferson would have preferred to submit the issue to the nation by asking for a constitutional amendment, but his advisers warned him that anyone who had changed his mind as quickly as Napoleon might change his mind again. So Jefferson, realizing the significance of the vast territory to the future of his small nation, ignored his constitutional misgivings, made the purchase, and rode out the subse-

quent diplomatic and political storms—the angry protests of Spain and the acid complaints of the New England Federalists.

Having completed the momentous international transaction, he pressed forward with his plan to explore the western country, a plan that took on much greater importance now that much of that land belonged to the United States. It would not be merely an attempt to find a route to the Pacific and determine the relationship of the United States to much of the rest of the continent but also to learn more about Jefferson's dramatic purchase—what it contained and what it promised. It was to be a nation's effort to discover itself.

Jefferson's private secretary at the time was a young army officer, Captain Meriwether Lewis of the 1st Infantry, whom Jefferson had selected for the post partly because of his knowledge of what was then the West, an area with which Jefferson was much less familiar than the eastern seaboard. Imaginative and intensely patriotic, Lewis—then in his late twenties—had served under General Anthony Wayne and therefore was acquainted with frontier life, although, like most Americans of that day, he knew little about the trans-Mississippi West. Sometimes he fell into periods of deep depression, but except for that one failing, Jefferson considered him ideally fitted to lead the expedition to the Pacific, particularly since he was thoroughly familiar with the President's thoughts on the subject.

As his second-in-command, Lewis chose an old friend and former commanding officer, William Clark, the youngest brother of George Rogers Clark, the Indian campaigner. In temperament Clark was Lewis's opposite. Red-headed and outgoing, he was less a thinker, more a man of practical action—an almost perfect complement to Lewis. One problem, however, had to be resolved. At the time he resigned from the army, Clark had been a lieutenant, Lewis an ensign. Since then Lewis had risen to a captaincy and outranked his former commander. The terms Lewis offered Clark—with Jefferson's concurrence—were unique and revealed his innate generosity, for Lewis proposed that Clark share equally with him in authority, responsibility, pay, and rank. But even with Jefferson's help, it turned out later, he could not obtain a captain's commission for him. The President who had just completed the Louisiana Purchase was unable to prevail against the army's bureaucratic rules. Somewhat reluctantly Clark accepted a lieutenancy, but Lewis always referred to him as "captain," lived up to the other promises he had made, and—most revealing of all—neither man ever gave a command to the other.

The heat of summer had gripped "Wilderness City"—as many called the nation's muddy, half-built capital—when Jefferson signed the written instructions he gave Lewis. They were long and detailed, because Jefferson wanted a thorough, fact-filled report, not a cursory review of the explorers' experiences and rumors of such places as Quivira. They were to take the latitude and longitude of every important point, such as the mouths of rivers; they were to observe and record every detail of the lives of the Indians they encountered. They were to note the soil, vegetation, and mineral deposits of the country through which they traveled and keep records of the weather, taking the temperature regularly and writing down the direction of the winds and the proportion of stormy days to clear ones.

Jefferson also instructed Lewis to remain on the friendliest possible terms with the Indians and, looking forward to a profitable fur trade, "confer with them on the points most convenient as mutual emporiums." Jefferson also hoped Lewis would determine whether it was practical to bring furs from the Pacific Coast eastward to the headwaters of the Missouri River. If it was, Americans would have overland access to the trade that had developed at Nootka Sound, an important advantage for a small nation competing with ones that were more powerful.

Although Albert Gallatin, Jefferson's Swiss-born Secretary of the Treasury, was practicing the economies dictated by his party's campaign promises, Jefferson was determined that the federal government would underwrite the entire expenses of the trip. Consequently he authorized Lewis to draw on the Secretary of War for all the supplies he needed, including boats and surgical instruments, presents for the Indians, and ten or twelve volunteers from the army.

Several features distinguished this expedition from those previously undertaken by the Spanish, British, and French. One of these was Jefferson's willingness to have the government pay the total expense without expecting any immediate financial return. Unlike Coronado, neither Lewis nor Clark had to raise any of the funds, nor were they responsible for coming back with a profit. Relieved of this enormous burden, they could devote their full attention to their primary purpose of gathering information. Britain, France, and Spain might haggle over the cost of exploring their domains, but the young nation had enough faith in its future to invest in itself.

Another distinguishing feature was Jefferson's peaceful intent. The men would carry arms, of course, if for no other purpose than to procure the game they needed for food, and also most of the personnel was drawn from the military. If an individual or a small party of enemies tried to stop them, Jefferson thought Lewis would have a sufficient number of persons under his command to proceed. But he was to avoid warfare, and under no circumstances was he to attack a superior force even if obedience to this order meant he had to retreat before reaching the coast. Further to ensure the peaceful accomplishment of the mission, Jefferson notified the Spanish, French, and British ministers in Washington of his plans and procured passports from the latter two. (Spain had relinquished title to the land, but he had not received a copy of the treaty with France, and the expedition would be passing through areas that might be disputed by Great Britain.) Jefferson wished to prevent any misunderstandings with overzealous local officials. The goal of the expedition was information, not the conquest of men, either red or white.

The third distinguishing feature was embodied in the philosophy stated in the Northwest Ordinance. Until they reached the Rockies, the unsettled lands through which Lewis and Clark would make their way were eventually to become not colonies, but states with rights equal to those of the original Thirteen Colonies. Although not expressly stated in Jefferson's letter of instructions, this philosophy gave a novel aspect to the expedition. Lewis and Clark were to be explorers of their own land, not the forerunners of colonizers.

In anticipation of the assignment, Lewis had already completed most of his preparations, selecting and ordering the necessary supplies and tutoring in certain subjects he needed to know, such as how to determine latitude and longitude. Shortly after receiving Jefferson's final instructions, therefore, he sent some money home to his sister, comforted his mother by assuring her that he would be as safe as if he had remained in Washington, and left for Pittsburgh.

That city, standing where the Allegheny and Monongahela rivers join to form the Ohio, provided the East with access to the great inland waterway discovered by Marquette and Joliet and thus was one of several American communities to earn the name "Gateway to the West." Here he was delayed—and greatly annoyed—by the boatbuilders on whom he was dependent for his means of transportation. Writing ahead to Clark, who was already down the river recruiting volunteers, he complained bitterly about the workers' inattention and drunkenness.

The fall that year was dry, and the Ohio River was lower than most people could remember it. This slowed his trip even further, but by the middle of October he had reached Louisville; and before the end of the month he and Clark—the two men were now together—started on the next leg of their journey, which took them down the Ohio to the Mississippi and up that river to St. Louis.

Although the American treaty with France had now been ratified, Spain had not formally transferred the territory to Napoleon's government, so the Spanish governor remained in office. Not anxious to encourage American exploration anywhere in the West, he told Lewis that he lacked authority to permit the expedition to ascend the Missouri and hoped that Lewis would wait until spring. By then, he was certain, he would have received clarifying instructions from his superiors. His dealings with Lewis were entirely amicable, and he even offered to find the explorer a winter residence in St. Louis. Lewis did not attempt to argue. The season was late, and he thought that by spring any obstacles to his passage would be removed. Therefore he went into winter camp at the mouth of Wood River opposite the mouth of the Missouri, diplomatically choosing a site on the eastern bank of the Mississippi and thus indisputably remaining inside American territory.

Once the initial work was done, the winter camp was like hundreds of others, a place of cold and boredom, broken only by a few bright moments. Christmas Day, 1803, brought a change in routine. Some of the men celebrated by getting drunk—a common pastime in isolated, frontier camps; others went hunting, shooting several turkeys; and one private returned to camp with a cheese and four pounds of butter, a welcome embellishment to the usual menu. New Year's Day brought a fresh snowfall, which was followed by mist, and more merrymaking. But the cheery, brief interludes of the holidays passed quickly, and the weeks resumed their accustomed slow measure. The best time the men had was when they practiced with their firearms, the prize for the highest score being an extra gill of whiskey.

Although Lewis had declined the Spanish governor's invitation to take up residence at St. Louis, he frequently visited the town to make additional preparations and to gather information for Thomas Jefferson. The President entertained the hope that the inhabitants could eventually be induced to move to the east side of the Mississippi, making space for the American government to move the eastern Indians west. Although he foresaw some problems, Lewis naïvely believed this exchange of populations could be effected within a few years. That men and women might be unwilling to leave their homes and businesses merely to satisfy the political strategy of a new government did not occur to him. His love for his country was so great he could not imagine that others might be unwilling to make considerable sacrifices on its behalf.

Because of this attitude, he found the reactions of the traders puzzling. Some like Auguste Chouteau were friendly. When Lewis decided he needed a larger force than the one originally suggested by Jefferson, Chouteau helped him recruit several civilians to assist him with the boats as far as the Mandan villages. On the other hand, some prominent traders like Manuel Lisa and his partner, Francis Marie Benoît, instead of making him feel welcome, convinced him of their underlying hostility.

Lisa and Benoît had reason to react as they did. Having broken through the virtual monopoly once enjoyed by the older St. Louis traders and having reached an understanding with the Spanish authorities, they now faced the prospect that everything they had gained might be lost in a flurry of new laws. Unlike Chouteau, who had the self-confidence of the well established, they were uncertain about the future; and the presence of the American government in the person of Lewis did not reassure them. His vigor and zeal, they thought, might reflect the vigor and zeal of the new officialdom. If so, the fur trade on the Missouri would never again be the same.

By the middle of May, almost eleven months after Jefferson had signed his letter of instructions, the diplomatic situation had been clarified, the river was again navigable, and the expedition was finally ready to set forth. Lewis had to make one more trip to St. Louis, but Clark agreed to take the expedition upriver to St. Charles, the last important settlement, where Lewis would join him, making the trip from St. Louis by land.

The party was now considerably larger than Jefferson had originally envisioned. Instead of the ten or twelve men the President had thought sufficient, there were almost thirty privates and noncommissioned officers, Clark's black servant, York, ten men who usually worked for the fur companies but who had agreed to help them get to the Mandan villages, and a detachment of seven soldiers who were to protect them as they passed some of the more hostile Indians along the lower reaches of the Missouri. In addition to the men, they also had a dog, a Newfoundland retriever named Scannon that belonged to Lewis, and two horses. These were to follow by land and serve primarily as pack animals for bringing in the game they killed along the way.

For transportation they had two pirogues, open boats which could be rowed upstream, and a fifty-five-foot keelboat, one of the many that plied the western waters in the infancy of the nation. The design of these boats evolved from the demands of such rivers as the Ohio, the Mississippi, and the Missouri. One of their common features was their slight draft, which enabled them to function in silted waterways. (The keelboat used by Lewis and Clark needed three feet of water, about a foot more than usual.) Aside from drifting with the current—and rivermen quickly learned to use the currents whenever they could—the boats generally had four means of propulsion, all but one of them drawing their power from the brawn of their crews. In relatively shallow water each man would grab a long pole, thrust it to the river bottom, and, pushing against it, walk astern in file along the footway that lined each gunwale. If the bottom was too deep for poling, they could row. If neither of these methods proved suitable for a particular part of the river, the men could tow their craft, heaving on the towline—or cordelle—from the banks or walking in the water if the banks were too high and steep. Many of the keelboats also carried a small square sail (Lewis and Clark's had a foresail, too) that could sometimes be used when the wind was blow-

ing in the right direction and the stretch of the river was fairly broad. The happy combination of these circumstances rarely occurred, but when they did, they provided a time for the crew to rejoice at the relief from their usual unremitting toil.

The middle of the boat used by Lewis and Clark was covered with lockers, which contained their supplies and could also be rearranged to form a breastwork in case of attack. In addition to their own supplies and instruments, the expedition carried medals, flags, and uniforms to give to the Indians, as well as other, less official gifts, such as tobacco and extra blankets. Among the unusual items they carried was a boat's iron framework, designed by Lewis. When assembled and covered with skins, it should provide them with transportation; unassembled, it would be easy and light to carry over the portages when they reached the mountains and had to abandon their other boats. Another unlikely item was a violin belonging to one of the enlisted men, Peter Cruzatte. In their lonely march across the continent, whenever they became bored, Cruzatte would be able to take out his instrument and entertain them with his music.

The skies over the Missouri River were gray and filled with rain on the morning of May 14, 1804, the day Clark had chosen for leaving Wood River. In the dampness the men set about the work of breaking camp and loading the last of their equipment and supplies aboard the boats.

Instead of tapering off at noon and giving the men a respite from the wet, the rain became even heavier later in the day and brought with it a gentle breeze. Many of the neighboring settlers left their work undone and assembled at the river's edge to watch the expedition embark, for this was not a private venture, shrouded in secrecy to prevent its discovery by competitors, but a public undertaking in which a whole nation shared. As the men pushed away from shore and into the turbulent stream, they carried with them the good wishes of the government and the entire people.

Because of their late start—the expedition did not leave Wood River until about four o'clock in the afternoon—they made only four miles that day, camping in the evening on an island. If Clark had not already been familiar with the hazards of navigating the shallow waters of the western rivers, he would have become so the following day. As a result of the melting snows and spring rains, the current of the Missouri was running strong and cutting away its banks, which tumbled into the river. Where these were wooded, the trees fell in also, their dirt-encrusted roots sinking to the bottom and serving as an anchor while their tops slanted upward to the surface, ready to block or pierce any boat that struck them. This phenomenon was so common that the rivermen had special names for the various types of snags: those whose tops bobbed up and down with the current were known as "sawyers"; those whose tops remained steady were called "planters." Three times during the day the keelboat was halted by such logs, and three times its crew worked hard to free it. Although the boat fortunately suffered no damage, Clark decided to shift the cargo further forward, because he thought the stern was riding too low.

Around noon of the third day, the party reached St. Charles, a small community with a single principal street running parallel to the river. Here Clark waited for Lewis to come from St. Louis and took steps to squelch the lack of discipline that had arisen among the soldiers. Three of them were court-martialed and sentenced to receive twenty-five lashes for being absent without leave, and one of the three was sentenced to an additional twenty-five lashes for insubordination. (Believing that this show of authority had taught the men a needed lesson, Clark later remitted the sentences of the two lesser offenders.)

On May 20, Lewis, who had finished his business at St. Louis, said goodbye to his host and hostess, the Pierre Chouteaus of the fur-trading family, and, traveling overland to St. Charles, arrived there about 6:30 in the evening.

The next morning the two captains procured a few final supplies at St. Charles, dined with acquaintances on shore, and were ready to set off at about 3:30 in the afternoon. As the boats moved out into the water, the men of St. Charles gave three husky cheers for them and their endeavor. The expedition was now truly underway.

Their start was not propitious. They had been on the river only a short time when a gathering storm broke, and strong winds lashed their faces and hands with heavy rain. The following day again introduced them to some of the dangers of river travel. They had been pulling the keelboat upstream with the cordelle when they ran on a sandbar. The swift, powerful current swung the boat around; the cordelle snapped under the sudden strain; and the boat, released from the restraining force of the rope, nearly capsized. All those on board jumped into the river and together tipped the boat away from its stranded side, permitting the current to wash the sand from underneath it. Now freed, the keelboat spun around again, struck one of the banks, and once more was lurching like a crazy thing on the wild waters of the Missouri.

Finally the crew attached a new cordelle to the boat's stern, and several men swam ashore with the free end. By heaving on the cordelle, they were able to regain control of the boat. But after all this hard, dangerous work, they found themselves back downstream at a point they had left a while before. Such was the progress of anyone attempting to ascend against the springtime current of the Missouri, and Lewis and Clark had been wise to employ experienced men to help them. The work required not only brute strength, but skill as well.

In spite of the need for many hands on board, a few of the party walked or rode on shore. This gave them a chance to stretch their legs, kill the game needed for food, and observe the country, which was otherwise often hidden from sight by the banks of the river. Because of the generally slow pace of the boats and the many bends that lengthened the distance they had to travel, those on shore had no difficulty keeping up with them and could even make fairly long excursions inland, thus enlarging their knowledge of the country through which they passed.

They had not yet entered the Great Plains, and the land was relatively kindly. Trees were still plentiful along the edges of the river, streams cut into the banks bringing fresh, unsilted water to the Missouri, and game was plentiful. This was country in which most of them could have farmed without changing their ways, for it had the natural attributes to which they were accustomed. But as they moved westward and then as the river took its turn to the north, the trees grew fewer, and to eastern eyes, the land became more barren and forbidding.

At this stage of their journey Lewis and Clark were surveyors and recorders of information rather than explorers, for their surroundings were already relatively well known. On May 31, for example, they met a Frenchman who was employed by the Chouteaus and who was coming down the river from the Osages, with whom he had been trading. Just a few days later, on June 5, they met two more Frenchmen, who had been trading with the Kansa Indians. At each such encounter, they stopped in the frontier fashion to exchange news, thus becoming familiar with events taking place at a considerable distance from the banks of the Missouri and carefully writing down everything they learned.

One of the most interesting traders they met was Pierre Dorion. A tough, courageous man, he had spent many years building up a trade with the Yankton Sioux. Although these were less warlike and fierce than the Teton Sioux, who lived to the west, he was one of the few St. Louis traders who could do business with them and make a profit.

Having lived with them for many years and being married to a Yankton wife, he had learned to speak their language and knew their customs. So Lewis and Clark persuaded Dorion to travel with them and help them deal with these Indians. They also hoped that later he would take some of their leaders to Washington, for Jefferson was convinced that the Indians would be favorably impressed by the Americans' strength and generosity if only they could see the nation's larger cities.

Under the hot June sun they continued to work their laborious way up the Missouri River. On those days when the sun disappeared behind the clouds, the temporary relief from the heat was often accompanied by the discomfort of violent rainstorms that drenched the men. At times the mosquitoes swirled in masses around their heads, and the grass at their campsites teemed with ticks. On June 29 discipline again broke down, for one of the soldiers, John Collins, opened a barrel of whiskey while he was on sentry duty and, instead of guarding the party, spent the early hours of the morning getting himself comfortably drunk. The warming fluid aroused his spirit of generosity, and in a convivial mood he shared the barrel's contents with another private. For this offense Collins was sentenced to receive a hundred lashes and his fellow fun-maker, fifty.

On the Fourth of July, when almost every American community—however small—was celebrating the anniversary of the nation's recent independence, Lewis and Clark joined the other celebrants by ordering their men to fire one of the swivel guns mounted on the bows of their boats. The sound was slight compared to the expanses surrounding them, but it expressed the young nation's challenge to the countryside it was taking over. That night they marked the occasion by firing the swivel gun once more and issuing an extra gill of whiskey to each member of the party.

July 12 found the two commanding officers holding yet another court-martial. This time the culprit, a private named Alexander Willard, was charged with two offenses: lying down while he was on sentry duty and then falling asleep. He pleaded guilty to the first, innocent to the second; but the court considered him guilty of both charges and, noting that his crimes were punishable by death under the rules of war, sentenced him to a hundred lashes.

Although they were gaining control of their men, Lewis and Clark could do nothing about the weather. Four days later another violent storm struck. The banks of the Missouri again caved in, and the riverbed on one side was filled with snags.

In consequence the keelboat clung to the opposite bank. As the storm's winds whipped across the river, they forced the keelboat toward a sandy island, where the waves and current would smash it to pieces. Some of the men leaped overboard to hold it back with the cable and anchor. For some forty minutes they battled the wind and water, dwarfed by the great black sky above them, pigmies fighting the Missouri River. But in the end they triumphed, swinging the boat away from the island and keeping it from going aground.

In spite of such adventures, they safely reached the mouth of the Platte River on July 21. Coming from the west through present-day Nebraska, its headwaters were high in the mountains; no one knew exactly where. Among the boatmen, who marked their progress by the river mouths they passed, it had some of the significance that the equator held for seafarers. To them, it marked the dividing line between the lower and upper Missouri (they had no idea how long the Missouri actually was), and they sometimes playfully initiated those who went by it for the first time.

With some difficulty, the men maneuvered their boats around the sandbar the Platte had created and went ashore. Since they knew that the Oto Indians had a village a short distance up the Platte, they made their own camp nearby, while the interpreter, George Drouillard (Lewis and Clark referred to him as Drewyer), and Peter Cruzatte, the private who played the violin, went off to see if they could find them. They returned shortly to report that although they had located the village, the Indians were away hunting buffaloes.

The expedition remained in camp a few more days, and during that time, Drouillard, on one of his hunting excursions, happened to meet a Missouri Indian. (Among his duties Drouillard helped keep the expedition supplied with meat.) The Missouri said he lived with a small band of Otos and that another, larger band was not much farther on.

Since they were supposed to treat with as many tribes as possible, explaining the change of government to them and hopefully winning their friendship, Lewis and Clark dispatched one of the French boatmen with the Missouri Indian to persuade the Otos to come to a council. (Since the Missouri had reported that a French trader lived among them, language would be no problem.) Just as the sun was dropping over the horizon on August 2, a band of Otos and Missouris, accompanied by the trader, appeared in response to the captains' invitation.

The night passed uneasily in the white men's camp. This was the expedition's first experience with a tribe of Indians, and no one was certain how it would go. Neither Lewis nor Clark had ever conducted official negotiations with Indians, and neither of them was familiar with those of the plains. Although they immediately gave their visitors some meat, flour, and meal and received some melons in return, they were not certain how much significance they could attach to this friendly exchange. Consequently they warned their men to be ready for anything, and the encampment of Indians next door was more effective in keeping the sentries awake than even the prospect of a hundred lashes. But their concern was unjustified, for the night passed peacefully.

In order to provide a setting for the council that took place the next day, Lewis and Clark ordered their men to fetch the mainsail from the keelboat and hang it up as an awning. Once this arrangement had been made, the soldiers put on a show by going through a few military exercises. After these were concluded, Lewis and Clark explained that the United States was now in control of this part of the country and that the Indians were to conduct themselves well and preserve the peace. The best of interpreters could not have given any real significance to the captains' words, because the Indians lacked the background for understanding them. They were accustomed to white men, having traded with them frequently, but knew nothing of governmental treaties, the Louisiana Purchase, or the number of white men who in time would advance against them. To them, this was merely another small band of alien visitors. Because it was small, it was weak and therefore could be expected to curry their favor with presents.

But if the Indians did not understand the white men, neither did Lewis and Clark understand the Indians. They had come provided with "medals" (actually medallions they could wear around their necks), to distribute among the leaders of the tribes they encountered. As these were of varying quality, it became imperative for the two captains to distinguish between the "chiefs" who appeared before them. Believing that they were dealing with a social structure at least as rigid as their own, they quickly ascertained to their own satisfaction that the principal chieftain was not present, so they gave the Indians one of their best medals to take to him. Then they gave second-grade medals to an Oto and a Missouri and third-grade medals to two more members of each tribe.

In selecting and rating the Indians' leaders, Lewis and Clark were assuming a function the Indians could not have performed for themselves. Their society was far too democratic to permit such

orderly rankings, and they had no "chiefs" in the way Lewis and Clark and many other white men supposed, only leaders who advised but did not command. These men, who had influence, although little authority, were chosen by an informal consensus of the band with whom they lived. The esteem in which they were held was based largely on two factors: their prowess in war and their generosity toward their fellow tribesmen. Public opinion being as fickle in the Indians' world as in the white men's, the standing of prominent warriors could shift faster than the white men could hold an election.

The captains also did not realize that no central government existed that had overall control of a tribe's actions and that while individual bands had many interests in common, each was independent of the other. An agreement made with one, therefore, did not bind any of the others. For Lewis and Clark to have reached an effective understanding with a tribe, they would have needed to gather together all its people—not merely a few individuals—and that was a task clearly outside their resources to perform.

Unaware of these quicksands of Indian diplomacy, in which many another negotiator would become mired, Lewis and Clark dispensed a few presents, including some gunpowder and a bottle of whiskey. The Indians expressed their pleasure at this generosity. The French, they explained, had never given them something for nothing, a statement that was probably untrue, since most traders sooner or later found themselves bullied into making a few gifts.

Satisfied that they had carried out their mission with the Otos and Missouris, Lewis and Clark gave the orders necessary for the expedition's departure. The men took down the mainsail that had protected them from the sun and carried it and their other belongings to the boats. Then the small group of white men were on their way again, leaving everything behind them just as it had been before.

As they ascended the river, Lewis and Clark were still having difficulty gaining the control over their men that they thought necessary. The French boatman they had originally sent to the Otos had not returned with the Indians; and a soldier, Moses B. Reed, said he had left his knife at one of their campsites but, having received permission to go back and get it, failed to rejoin them. Since the safety of the expedition largely depended upon the loyalty and reliability of its individual members, Lewis and Clark could not permit these desertions to pass unnoticed. They sent George Drouillard and three other men back to capture Reed and gave them orders to kill him if he resisted. They were also to go to the Otos' village and look for the French boatman. Meanwhile the expedition went into camp near the site of an Omaha Indian village.

Once strong and powerful, this tribe had been feared by Indians and whites alike, both of whom had suffered from its depredations. But the small-pox that had come with the white men's advance and had ravaged many groups of Indians had been particularly death-dealing among the Omahas. As Clark noted in his journal, they were now forced to endure "the insults of their weaker neighbors."

The Omahas were off hunting buffaloes, but the party that had searched for Reed came back with their prisoner and some more Otos, some of whom had missed the earlier council. They wanted to make peace with the Omahas, they said, using the good offices of Lewis and Clark. But even this chance to bring peace to two tribes did not prevent discipline from being the first order of business, and the captains immediately convened a court-martial to try Reed. (The search party had also captured the French boatman, but he had later escaped. Being a civilian, his offense, of course, was less serious.)

Reed pleaded guilty to the charges of stealing a gun and ammunition and deserting and threw himself on the mercy of the court. He was sentenced to run the gauntlet four times (each man was to have nine switches with which to hit him) and be dismissed as an official member of the expedition.

The Indians had been observing the white men's trial with interest, and such a sentence for such an offense ran contrary to their sense of justice, for their world lacked the tight discipline of the white men's. Among them, desertion could not be a crime, because membership in a war party depended entirely on the individual's own preference. So Reed suddenly had some unexpected advocates. Three of the warriors intervened on his behalf, pleading his cause with Lewis and Clark. But the two captains were not to be dissuaded, and the sentence was carried out.

To end the day, since it was Lewis's birthday, the captains issued an extra gill of whiskey to the men, Peter Cruzatte tuned his violin, and the men, choosing each other as partners, danced until eleven o'clock while their campfire flared in the prairie night.

The next morning the captains held a council for the benefit of those Otos who had not taken part in the previous meeting. Once again the mainsail was hung as an awning, Lewis delivered what was becoming his set speech, and the warriors listened with as little understanding as before.

Thinking that they may have ranked the Indians improperly the first time, Lewis and Clark now exchanged a small medal they had given out earlier for a larger one. Then trying to weave their way through the nuances of the Indians' social structure, they issued a small medal to a warrior who had not previously received one and five certificates of favor to five more warriors. The piece of paper seemed worthless to one of the recipients, who scornfully returned it. He was no more offended, however, than Lewis and Clark, who, as they said, "rebuked them [the Indians] severely for having in view mere traffic instead of peace. . . ."

Finally the Indians apologized, and the council ended, in the captains' words, "after a more substantial present of small articles and tobacco . . ."

Earlier on the trip Sergeant Charles Floyd, on whom both Lewis and Clark relied heavily, had been taken ill but appeared to have recovered. During the day of the council, however, he became seriously sick again and failed to respond to the treatment Lewis, who served as the expedition's doctor, could offer. Helplessly they watched his condition worsen in the night, and by the next morning he could retain no food. His pulse grew so weak that none of the men anxiously attending him could find it. Yet he did not lose consciousness, and died, as Clark noted in his journal, "with a great deal of composure."

They could not tarry to lament his death or call on a priest or minister to perform the final rites, but they named a nearby river in his memory, and buried his body with military honors on the top of one of the bluffs that towered above the Missouri. From this graveside the mourners could see in every direction the lands that Jefferson had purchased from France and know that the soil that covered him was the soil of his own country.

Because they paused so often to conduct geological studies—the fumes from one mineral analysis made Lewis sick for several days—draw maps, write down their notes, observe the fauna, and hold councils with the Indians, the expedition's progress up the river had been slow. Thoroughness, not haste, had been the burden of Jefferson's letter of instructions; and it was August 27 before they reached the mouth of the James River, which flows south through the present-day Dakotas. Having learned earlier from Dorion, the trader, that some Sioux Indians were camped upstream on the James, Lewis and Clark sent him to invite them to a council. Making peace with this tribe was one of the captains' most important missions.

Although the Sioux were relative newcomers to

the Great Plains—they had been pushed westward earlier by their better-armed neighbors to the east—they had quickly established for themselves a well-earned reputation for ferocity. Numerous in population and warlike by temperament and up-bringing, they were a scourge to their enemies, of whom they had many. Toward white men, their attitude was ambivalent, partly friendly, partly hostile. They wanted the supplies, especially the guns and ammunition, that the white men brought, but they were not subservient and preferred to take what they desired rather than trade for it. Between St. Louis and the Mandan villages they formed a barrier that could be penetrated by the traders only at the risk of their lives or by submitting to extortion. The Sioux were also known to be more friendly with the British in Canada than they were with the white men to the south, a state of affairs entirely contrary to American interest.

When Dorion reappeared with some seventy Yanktons, Lewis and Clark again went through the ceremonies and speeches that were now routine. After they finished, the Indians had much to say about the St. Louis traders, accusing them of charging high prices and being ungenerous in their dealings. They also made it clear that they regarded the presents Lewis and Clark offered them as scanty, although, of course, they accepted them. In return for these gifts, they agreed to keep peace with their neighbors, a promise they had no serious intention of fulfilling, because peace was not part of their way of life.

Lewis and Clark realized that they had spoken to only a few of many Yanktons and that Dorion was one of the rare traders who got along with them. So before starting up the river again, they gave him a small supply of presents to distribute to those who had been unable to come to the conference and promised to reward him well if he could persuade some of their chiefs to make the trip to Washington.

When they left the mouth of the James River near the present-day city of Yankton, South Dakota, they began to enter the Great Plains proper. Until then they had been skirting their eastern fringes, where the land was moister and the growth more luxuriant. They had talked with tribes of Great Plains Indians and felt the Great Plains' influence, which extended beyond their borders, but now the men came into the dry interior area of the United States. Day after day dashed itself in the early morning against the inverted hollow of the sky, flooding it with reds, yellows, and pinks, before it settled down to blue or gray or in stormy times a threatening coal black that seemed to menace the earth beneath it. The sun, no longer blanketed

from the world by a layer of moisture, burned hotter and brighter than it had before, a searing flame tracking its way across the sky; and on clear nights the stars and moon took on new luminescence.

They passed the shallow valley of the White River, which takes its name from the milky look it acquires from the mineral deposits in the Badlands, and the land around them became flatter and flatter with fewer and fewer trees they could use for fire or shelter. Thousands of acres lay empty on either hand, but none of the expedition expressed a desire to settle in this country, which was so alien to anything they had known before.

So far the captains' meetings with Indians had been uneventful and friendly, if rather meaningless, exchanges of words. The real test of their skill at dealing with them came on September 23 several weeks after leaving the Yanktons. The expedition had camped for the night on the eastern bank of the river when three Indian boys entered the water from the opposite side and swam over to visit them. The boys said that eighty lodges of Teton Sioux, who were more fierce than the Yanktons, were at the next stream upriver and sixty more were only a short distance away. This probably meant that several hundred warriors—more than Lewis and Clark might have wished to encounter at one time—were within a few miles of them. This was not a time for faint-heartedness; nothing would more quickly tempt the Sioux into attacking than the slightest sign of fear. So the captains gave the boys two carrots of tobacco (a carrot was a pear-shaped bundle of leaves) and instructed them to tell their leaders that they would hold a council with them the next day.

One of the pirogues led the upstream procession the following morning. Next came the keelboat and then the second pirogue. On board the captains laid out some clothes and medals to give the Indians. That was a preparation for peace, but they also looked to the men's arms and made ready for a possible attack. Peace or war—they did not know which the Sioux might want.

The Sioux's first response to their presence was neither one nor the other, but a minor harassment intended to probe their resolution without provoking them into flight on the one hand or a pitched battle on the other. John Colter, one of the most capable of the enlisted men, was on shore hunting. His luck was good and he killed four elk, but some Indians stole the horse on which he had intended to carry the meat back to the river. This was a direct challenge to the Americans and was in line with the Sioux's usual tactics with traders and other travelers.

Known for trying to bully any white men who

came their way, they first resorted to insults, threats, and relatively small thefts. If they met no opposition, they would escalate their offensive until they had stripped the white men of their most valuable possessions. Lewis and Clark, therefore, ran the risk of either losing their supplies or fighting a hundred and forty lodges of Sioux unless they could somehow temper the Indians' aggression.

Shortly after receiving the news about Colter's horse, they saw five Indians on the shore. Dropping their anchor at a safe distance from the land, they told the Indians to report the theft to their leaders and announced that they had come in peace but would not speak to the Indians until the horse was returned. That night two-thirds of the men slept on board while the remainder stayed on shore and served as a guard. Tension hung over the small expedition surrounded by potential enemies.

As a place to hold their council, the captains chose a sandbar at the mouth of what is now known as the Bad River. To lend an air of formality to the site, they erected a pole from which they flew an American flag and again hung their mainsail as an awning. But wisely not trusting the Sioux, they anchored the keelboat about seventy yards from the shore. In that position, the men on board could unobtrusively cover the meeting place with their guns and at the same time remain secure from sudden attack. Then the captains waited, hoping for the best and fearing the worst.

A little before noon about sixty warriors had assembled with two of their particularly important leaders. One of these, who was named Black Buffalo, was known as a fairly reasonable man; the other, called the Partisan, had quite a different reputation and was considered untrustworthy and unfriendly. Forgetting about the horse, Lewis started to deliver the speech he had now given so often. But Dorion, who spoke Sioux fluently, had remained with the Yanktons, and no one else was sufficiently conversant with the language to translate effectively Lewis's full text. Therefore, much to his and Clark's disgust, he had to abridge his remarks. When he had concluded, the men on shore paraded for the Indians, and Lewis and Clark gave out medals and other presents. The Indians' only reaction was to request more gifts.

As an additional gesture of cordiality, the captains invited the leading men aboard the keelboat, where they exhibited some of their equipment and gave them a quarter of a glass of whiskey. So fond of liquor had these Indians become that they sucked at the bottle even after it was dry, trying to extract an additional drop. Almost immediately the Partisan pretended to be drunk, using his faked condition, so Clark noted in his journal, as "a Cloake for his rascally intentions."

The captains next had to get these dangerous visitors back on shore. Finally persuading them to climb into one of the pirogues, Clark ferried them to the riverbank. As soon as the bow of the boat touched land, three of the young warriors standing there seized its cable and refused to let it go. At the same time the Partisan became increasingly insolent and directed his remarks at Clark personally. His meaning was so clear that Dorion's fluency with the language was not needed to interpret his words and gestures. The Americans' presents, he said, were insufficient and he would not permit the expedition to advance upstream.

This was one of those moments when a defensive, apologetic attitude would have been disastrous. As Pedro Vial and other experienced frontiersmen knew, appeasement at such a time would only encourage further outrages. Clark sensed this instinctively. His hand dropped to his sword hilt, and he drew his weapon from its scabbard while signaling to the men on the keelboat to prepare for action. Those with him on shore reacted as he did and readied their arms. Fortunately no one lost his head and fired, for the show of resistance was more valuable than resistance itself. At this demonstration of firmness, Black Buffalo, the more amenable of the two leaders, ordered the warriors to release the cable, but the crisis was not over.

The Indians had their bows strung and arrows out, and they still blocked the way between Clark and the pirogue. Since their threats were aimed at him, he decided not to force his way back to the water but ordered everyone except two interpreters to return to the keelboat and tell Lewis what was happening while he remained almost alone, facing the Partisan and his followers.

Lewis had already loaded the swivel gun, and as soon as the pirogue came alongside, he filled the boat with twelve well-armed men, whom he ordered back to shore to serve as a bodyguard for Clark. During this interval the Partisan continued to harangue Clark, berating him for the few presents he had brought and threatening to pursue the expedition and kill its members if they tried to proceed. Clark snapped back that he and Lewis were leading a band of men, not women, and were determined to fight if they had to. The arrival of the twelve reinforcements from the keelboat emphasized what Clark had said and brought an end to the loud, angry debate. The warriors withdrew out of earshot to confer among themselves while Clark got into the boat and pushed off. He had not gone far before the two chiefs and two other warriors waded into the water after him and asked permission to accompany him back to the keelboat. Knowing that four men presented little danger, he agreed to let them come on board.

That night was an anxious one. The Americans moved the keelboat a mile upstream and anchored it off an island with the two pirogues close by. Sentries stood guard on both the island and the boat, but the sun rose the next morning without bringing with it an Indian attack.

Time had cooled the Indians' temper and caused them to change their tactics. Many men and women gathered on the banks to look at the Americans, and the appearance of the women was a good sign, because the warriors usually hid their women and children when they were preparing for a battle. Since a more friendly atmosphere seemed to prevail, Lewis accepted an invitation to go ashore and took five men with him. After he had been away about three hours, Clark wondered if the Sioux might have played a trick on him. He sent a sergeant to find out, but the sergeant reported that Lewis was being well treated and that the Indians were planning to have a dance that night.

After Lewis returned, Clark went ashore. He, too, received a friendly welcome and was carried on a painted buffalo robe to what he called a "large Council house," where he was given a place of honor among the seventy men who had gathered there. A space in front of the chief had been cleared and covered with down. A peace pipe, mounted on sticks, was in the center. Other decorations consisted of two more peace pipes, the American flag that Lewis and Clark had given the Sioux, and—an ironic twist—two Spanish flags. (The ghost of Coronado still haunted the Great Plains.) Shortly afterward several warriors went to get Lewis, whom they carried to a place near Clark.

The evening was one of great ceremony. The Indians passed the peace pipe, offered the two captains such delicacies as cooked dog, which the Indians esteemed highly, and put on a concert with their native instruments. After the music had started, women appeared, all of them highly decorated and carrying the war trophies won by their husbands and other relatives. Gracefully they began a dance that lasted until midnight, when Lewis and Clark, pleading fatigue, returned to the keelboat.

During their visit on shore, Clark and Lewis learned that the Sioux had recently raided the Omahas, killing seventy-five men and taking almost fifty women and children prisoners. Indeed they had seen some of the captives, a sorry and de-

jected group. Already weakened by smallpox, the Omahas could not sustain such onslaughts much longer, and their former place on the plains was being occupied by the Sioux. In line with the government's policy of promoting peace, Lewis and Clark told the Sioux to send their prisoners to Dorion, who would see that they reached their native village. But they might just as well have ordered the Missouri River to reverse its current and flow upstream.

That night Clark slept fitfully, listening in the dark to every sound. Although the Indians had been friendly, their moods were like the weather on the Great Plains, moving swiftly from one extreme to the other. The belligerent attitude expressed by the Partisan had been quickly followed by gracious entertainment, but who knew when the second sudden change might occur? Furthermore, the concentration of Sioux was growing bigger, because new bands were constantly coming to join the others, placing the Americans at an ever greater numerical disadvantage.

After breakfast Lewis went ashore again. Nothing seemed to have changed from the previous day, and the Sioux were again friendly. That night the Indians put on another dance, which once more lasted until the two captains were sleepy. When it was over, the Partisan, in a mercurial shift of mood, said he and another Indian would like to spend the night on the keelboat. The two may have hoped for more presents, or they may have wanted to keep a watch on the expedition to prevent its escape. In either case, since their presence on board could not create a danger, Lewis and Clark agreed.

While Lewis remained on shore with a guard, the two Indians got into one of the pirogues with Clark, and the crew pushed off. The steersman was inexperienced and awkward. Instead of coming alongside the keelboat as he should have, he got above it and lost control. The strong current of the Missouri swung the pirogue around and carried it broadside toward the bow of the keelboat. Before it struck, it rode up on the anchor line, snapped it, and set the keelboat adrift. Seeing the great hulk swing free in the darkness, Clark shouted to the men on board to grab their oars before it went aground and was helpless.

The sound of his voice, combined with the bustle on the keelboat, startled the Indians, and one of them cried out that the Omahas were attacking. Within minutes two hundred armed warriors lined the banks. Since no further alarm arose in the next half-hour, the majority returned to their lodges, but sixty remained on guard during the night.

The Sioux's claim that they had thought the

Omahas were attacking did not reassure Lewis and Clark. It was much more likely, the two Americans believed, that the noise and confusion had convinced the Indians the expedition was leaving and that the quick assemblage of warriors had been intended to prevent its departure. This suspicion was reinforced by Peter Cruzatte, who could speak some Omaha and had talked with the Sioux's prisoners. They had told him the Sioux had no intention of letting the expedition go on.

Lewis and Clark's situation was considerably worsened by the loss of their anchor. With it, they could place the keelboat wherever they wished—in midstream, if that seemed the safest spot. Without it, they must cling to the shore. That night they stayed under a bank, where they were vulnerable to attack; and making their position even less secure, the bank itself was caving in.

So the next morning they gave high priority to the anchor's recovery, but the silt coming down the Missouri River had quickly covered it. The men knew its approximate location, but although they probed the bottom with poles and a boathook, they could not find it. They then strung a line between the two pirogues, weighted it with sinkers, and dragged the bottom. But the Missouri's mud, dark and deep, failed to reveal its secret, and they gave up the effort.

Most of the Indians had left the village and were standing at the river's edge watching the fruitless search. Many were armed and looked formidable, but in spite of this show of strength, Lewis and Clark were determined to leave. With some difficulty they persuaded the few Indians they had allowed on board again to go ashore and ordered the men to cast off. But two or three Indians, repeating the trick they had used before, grabbed the rope and held the boat fast. The Partisan, seeing an opportunity for more tribute, demanded another flag and some tobacco, but Lewis knew that a few last-minute gifts would only lead to more demands. Finally Clark tossed a carrot of tobacco to one of the more friendly leaders. He in turn gave it to the Indians holding onto the rope and jerked it from their hands.

Free at last, the boat moved upstream with a breeze filling its sail. Farther on, the expedition picked up one of the Sioux chiefs, who beckoned to them from the shore. (They first made certain he was alone.) Later they were joined by his son, whom they sent back to the encampment with a stern warning that they would fight if the Indians raced ahead and tried to stop them. As a further precaution, they paused long enough to collect some rocks they could use in place of their anchor.

The following day the Partisan and some of his friends appeared on the shore and asked to ride on the keelboat upriver to the next band of Sioux. But the captains were weary of this wily warrior's tricks and refused to have anything more to do with him. When they came to the band that the Partisan had mentioned, the Sioux called to them from the bank; but this time the Americans, their patience exhausted by dealing with this tribe, anchored the keelboat a hundred yards offshore. After briefly explaining their peaceful intentions and the new role of the United States on the Great Plains, they gave the Indians some carrots of tobacco and without wasting any more time proceeded on their way. These, they knew, were the last of the Sioux then living on the Missouri River, and they were glad to be rid of them.

When they had safely passed the Sioux, Lewis and Clark had overcome one of the major obstacles to the fulfillment of their mission. Their success had resulted not from having a superior force, but because they had made it evident to the Indians that the price they would have to pay to defeat the Americans would be higher than the possible spoils would be worth. In spite of their bravery, most Plains Indians were pragmatic about fighting and did not risk their lives foolishly. Unlike the supplies of goods in the boats of the fur traders, which were also generally less well guarded, the stores carried by Lewis and Clark represented a rather poor prize. Since the captains had made it clear they were willing to fight their way through, the Sioux, their bluff called, left them alone. But it had been an anxious time for the men and their leaders, and they all were glad to be underway again, forcing their boats against the Missouri's current.

Although they were far from St. Louis, they were not the only persons of European descent in that country. Near the mouth of the Cheyenne River they noticed a dwelling on the shore and called out to see if it was occupied. A small boy responded by putting off in a pirogue and paddling to the keelboat. The place, he said, was occupied by three Frenchmen who hoped to trade with some Sioux who, in turn, had gone to trade with the Arikaras. (This was another case of Indians developing a profitable business as middlemen.) One of the Frenchmen, Jean Vallé, was there and said that he had spent the winter on the Cheyenne River. He did not explain how he had passed the Sioux, who had caused such difficulties for Lewis and Clark, but he seems to have had a French fur trader's aptitude for handling Indians. Certainly his willingness to trade with the Arikaras through the Sioux indicated that he knew when to acquiesce to their customs.

By October 8, the Americans' expedition had reached the Grand River, which flows east just below the northern boundary of present-day South Dakota. The Arikaras, the next tribe they wished to visit, had their villages nearby and used a three-mile-long island at the river's mouth for planting their beans and corn. As the American boats appeared, the Arikaras swarmed out on the island to see them go by.

After the white men had found a suitable anchorage, Lewis went ashore for a preliminary visit while Clark stationed men to guard the boats. In a short time, Lewis reappeared, bringing with him two traders, Joseph Gravelines and Pierre-Antoine Tabeau, both of them employees of Régis Loisel of St. Louis. These men knew the Indians, their language, and the country and were willing to help Lewis by supplying him with information and serving as interpreters. Gravelines also agreed to accompany him to the Mandan villages.

That night it rained, the temperature dropped, and the wind blew. The unpleasant weather continued into the next day and forced Lewis and Clark to postpone their council. Many Indians, however, paddled out to see them in bullboats, those utilitarian craft made of a single buffalo hide stretched on a frame of cottonwood. So light that a woman could carry one by using a chest-strap, they were nevertheless remarkably seaworthy on the turbulent waters of the Missouri.

The principal attraction that drew the Indians was York, Clark's black servant. They had never seen a black man before, examined him from head to toe, and marveled at his strength and agility. York enjoyed the attention and, pretending that he had once been a wild man, jokingly made himself, as Clark noted, "more turribal than we wished him to doe."

Lewis and Clark held several councils with this tribe and visited their three villages. Following the general tenor of their previous remarks, they told the Indians about the sovereignty of the United States and preached peace. The Arikaras were a responsive audience. They had been thoroughly terrorized by the Sioux, and wanted an end to the fighting. But they expressed doubt that peace with the Sioux could ever be obtained. On the other hand, they were willing to send one of their leaders to treat with the Mandans.

Only one incident marred the captains' visit with the Arikaras. An enlisted man, John Newman, was court-martialed for "mutinous expression," as Clark called the offense, found guilty, and sentenced to seventy-five lashes. The Arikara chief who had agreed to accompany Lewis and Clark to the Mandans was horrified at the brutality of the punishment. He understood, he said, the need for setting an example, but his people never whipped anyone, not even their children. But the Indian's compassion did not deflect the white men's lash. Newman was flogged, stripped of his arms, dismissed from the army, and ordered to return to St. Louis on the first boat that went downriver. For the safety of the entire expedition, Lewis and Clark had to demand obedience and took the steps necessary to obtain it. Their treatment of Newman ended the problem, and that was the last instance during the journey that they sentenced any of their men to corporal punishment.

After leaving the Arikaras, the expedition passed the mouth of the Cannonball, another of the great rivers that fed the Missouri and served as landmarks by which travelers could gauge their progress. It flowed from the west just above the lower border of present-day North Dakota, and the bluffs near its mouth and the nearby shores contained many perfectly rounded stones that resembled cannonballs and left no doubt concerning its identity.

Near here the expedition met two French fur traders coming down the river. They were employees of Gravelines, who was still traveling with Lewis and Clark. Bitterly they complained about the Mandans, saying they had stolen some of their traps, furs, and other articles. But they were willing to turn around and go upstream again with their employer, apparently in the hope that the appearance of the expedition with its soldiers would awe the Mandans into either returning the goods or making other retribution.

On October 20 with a strong wind blowing from the east and northeast, the expedition came to the mouth of the Heart River, the site of the Mandan villages when la Vérendrye had visited them years before. The gentle slopes still rose gracefully to their left, the Heart still flowed slowly into the much wider Missouri, and the lands to their right stretched flat under the summer sun. But the place was deserted, for the Mandans, weakened by smallpox and the incessant attacks of the Sioux, had moved farther upstream. They could not, however, completely escape their enemies, because on the following day the expedition saw twelve Teton Sioux in war dress either going on, or coming from, a raid against the Mandans.

Although the villages in this area were now abandoned, the expedition soon came upon a band of six lodges of Mandans that composed a hunting party. Its leader greeted them in friendly fashion and made it clear that he welcomed the Arikara chief who had come to smoke the pipe of peace. Other Mandans came to greet the Americans—or to stare at them—as they worked their way through the maze of sandbars that impeded travel on this part of the river. (At one point they had great difficulty even locating the channel.) But finally on October 26 with the chill of autumn in the air they came to the first of the Mandan villages.

La Vérendrye's visit to the Mandans had been the disillusioning end of his search for a west-flowing river in that part of the country. From there he returned home encumbered with debt to face the demands of his creditors, knowing he had failed in the purpose of his trip. To Lewis and Clark, however, the Mandan villages represented not an end, but a beginning—the first and easiest part of their journey to the Pacific Ocean. With no financial concerns to worry them, they were free to concentrate on their objective of crossing the continent. And this, when the winter had passed, they were determined to do.

Chapter 7

Winter on the Plains

This day being Cold Several men returned a little frost bit. . . .
The weather is so cold we do not think it prudent to turn out to hunt in Such Cold weather. . . .
The Thermometer Stands this morning at 20° below 0, a fine day.

—William Clark, 1804

Winter sent advance signals of its approach from the north. The winds were no longer sultry with summer's heat, and the mud in the buffalo wallows that dotted the Great Plains began to harden with the freezes of fall; and like an old man, the tired sun, which had blazed so hot in July and August, rose later in the morning and sank to bed earlier in the evening.

After hiring a Frenchman, René Jessaume, to interpret for them, Lewis and Clark held their customary councils with the Mandans and the Hidatsa Indians, whose villages were upstream from those of the Mandans. Like the Arikaras and other tribes, the Mandans' population had been greatly reduced by smallpox, and they were fearful of the Sioux, who continually raided them. So they welcomed the Americans both as a source of supplies and a possible protection against their enemies. The Hidatsas, although more warlike and less cordial, raised no objections to the Americans' remaining in the vicinity. Therefore the explorers' plan to spend the winter months in that area was clearly feasible.

Axes sliced the brittle fibers of cottonwood trees as the men cut the logs needed to build the settlement that would serve as their winter quarters. Gradually two rows of small buildings, placed at an angle to each other, began to take shape. Both for protection against attack and to provide a slop-ing roof that would shed the winter's snow, the buildings were eighteen feet high on the outer side. Across the third side—the compound was shaped like a triangle—the men built a stout stockade. At the apex of the triangle stood a semicircular fortification that gave them a view of the outer walls of both rows of houses. Here a sentry stood duty every night. Named by Lewis and Clark Fort Mandan, the post was so sound and strong in their opinion it could almost have withstood cannonballs.

In addition to supervising the construction of Fort Mandan, the two captains had other business that needed attention. Those French boatmen who wished to return to St. Louis for the winter had to be released and seen off. Joseph Gravelines, the fur trader who had joined up with the expedition, was to spend the winter among the Arikaras, and arrangements had to be made for his departure. They also hired Touissant Charbonneau, a trader who spoke the language of the Hidatsas and had applied for the position of interpreter. Then, too, they had to put down the rumors that were flying among the Hidatsas. When la Vérendrye had visited the Mandans, he had remarked on their shrewdness and noticed that they did not let the truth interfere with their making a profit. On several occasions when he was there, they had conjured up an approaching Sioux war party to reduce the number of visitors they would have to feed. Now, to prevent the Hidatsas from trading directly with the Americans—the Mandans wanted to be the middlemen—they had fabricated a new story about the Sioux. The Americans, they said, had come to pass the winter there in order to join the Sioux in attacking the Hidatsas. The captains, of course, could not let such a lie stand uncontradicted, for it could have destroyed their relations with the Hidatsas. Lewis took upon himself the task of reassuring them.

On his way to their villages he met a representative of the North West Company, François-Antoine Larocque, who had led a party from Fort Assiniboin to trade with the Hidatsas and the Mandans. After a brief, although friendly, conversation, each went his own way, agreeing they would meet later. Lewis had no plans to interfere with the Canadian traders, but he wanted to be sure that they recognized the sovereignty of the United States.

Although Lewis talked to the Hidatsas and distributed presents among them, he did not entirely satisfy them. As a chief remarked to Charles Mackenzie, one of the Larocque's assistants, "had these Whites come amongst us with charitable views they would have loaded their 'Great Boat' with necessaries," and he complained that they did not even give the Hidatsas any ammunition. As an explorer with many miles of travel still ahead, Lewis could not carry the supplies of a trader, but the Indians were unable to distinguish the difference. Nevertheless, he succeeded in calming the Hidatsas' worst fears.

The Mandan and Hidatsa villages were no longer the remote, mysterious places they had been only a few years before, and competition for their fur trade was stiff. In addition to Larocque and his party, four men from the Hudson's Bay Company were also there. On their way to the villages they had been captured by the Assiniboin Indians—la Vérendrye's former guides—and held prisoner for about a week. Finally they had purchased their freedom, but the ransom took a large portion of their trade goods, leaving them undersupplied. Until the arrival of Larocque, they had expected to recoup their losses by paying lower prices than usual for the furs they bought. Now they had to meet Larocque's offers and were at a serious disadvantage. Nevertheless, because of their skill, they remained formidable competitors; and the representatives of the two companies spent much energy and thought outmaneuvering each other, racing to be the first to intercept homecoming hunting parties and following other such tactics.

As the official representative of the United States

government, Lewis—a relative newcomer—had to assert his nation's authority over these experienced men, who knew the land and the customs of its peoples better than he. In a talk with Larocque, Lewis set forth America's policy. In the first place, he said, under no circumstances were foreign representatives to give the Indians either medals or flags. These symbolized the authority of the government, and the United States reserved the prerogative of distributing them. On the other hand, any company could trade on American territory; there were to be no monopolies, for the young republic did not intend to follow the restrictive practices of the French and Spanish monarchies. The United States also had no intention of seeing the Indians abused. If the fur traders conspired to raise the price of European goods unreasonably high, the government would open its own trading posts and undersell them. In this way the excesses of free enterprise would be held in check.

As the official representatives of their government, Lewis and Clark were responsible for enforcing its laws and maintaining order even though they had only a small number of men and their stay at the villages, as everyone knew, was temporary. An additional complication lay in the diversity of the groups with whom they had to deal. Besides the two competing British fur companies, each trying to get ahead of the other, representatives of the St. Louis fur merchants were also active in the villages' trade. The Indians, too, were divided and had differing interests. The Mandans and Hidatsas were at peace, but they had varying temperaments and outlooks and also were in competition for the white men's business, while outside the villages were other Indian tribes, such as the Sioux, Arikaras, and Assiniboins, some of them openly hostile, others covertly so, and each also having different aims and goals.

Obviously the two captains could not impose themselves and their wishes on such a complex society, so they adopted a more diplomatic course. They were adamant about the right of the United States alone to issue flags and other formal tokens of nationality. As this was largely a question of protocol and did not affect the traders' profits, no one objected, although at least one trader muttered that Lewis took himself and his country a little too seriously. In everything else the captains tried to cooperate with those who seemed friendly.

When Larocque, for example, wished to make use of Charbonneau's services, Lewis readily agreed to give the interpreter a temporary release to help the Canadian. And when word came that a large party of Sioux had attacked five Mandan

The Spaniards brought the first horses to North America. As these strayed or were stolen, they quickly spread across the Plains and revolutionized the Indian way of life. Buffaloes became easier to hunt; and the nomadic tribes, with this improved means of transportation, could carry more belongings on their long treks. *National Archives*

At the junction of the Heart and Missouri rivers, where Lewis and Clark spent their first winter, the state of North Dakota has reconstructed a Mandan village. These houses were warm in winter, cool in summer. As the Mandans were a sedentary tribe, living behind palisaded walls, they could afford to build permanent homes.

Alexander B. Adams

hunters, killing one, wounding two, and stealing nine horses, Lewis and Clark sprang to the Mandans' defense. Anticipating a possible attack on the village itself, Clark quickly mustered twenty-three men, dashed across the Missouri, and drew his soldiers up in battle formation. Since he had not had time to notify the Mandans of his intentions, the Indians were startled by this sudden military invasion and thought the Americans were about to destroy them. But when they learned the reason for his action, they were pleased by his readiness to help them. As the Sioux did not attack and as the snow was far too deep to permit a scouting expedition, he soon returned to Fort Mandan, his men exhausted from fighting their way through the heavy drifts.

The cold lay over the Great Plains like a nailed-down coffin lid. The thermometer dropped to 20 degrees below zero, and the mighty Missouri ceased its restless rushing, its frozen surface glaring white in the sunlight. Several men suffered the agonies of frostbite, and the two captains agreed they should discontinue hunting until the men became more accustomed to the cold.

The bitter weather, however, did not stop more experienced travelers. Hugh Heney, an associate of Loisel, the St. Louis fur trader, had visited Fort Assiniboin and brought the captains a letter from the man in charge of the fur company's post. In it he pledged to cooperate fully with the expedition, so the captains needed to have no fear of interference. Because the traders were not above resorting to violence if they thought their business was threatened, the letter was reassuring.

Heney was an intelligent man who knew the country well, and the captains took the opportunity to question him closely about the land between the Mississippi and Missouri and about the Indians, particularly the Sioux. Outside the snug walls of Fort Mandan, the wolves hunted for the old and infirm among the buffaloes in the cold winter air, and the thermometer plunged to 42 degrees below zero while Lewis and Clark quizzed Heney. They wanted to know about the tribes, the land, the route west, and especially whether any great rivers flowed into the Missouri from the north. La Salle had defined Louisiana as the watershed of the Mississippi. If the United States could reaffirm this definition and if such a northern river did exist, the United States might be able to push its boundary above the 49th parallel. Not only would this increase its territory, but it might also provide a direct route into the heart of the rich Canadian fur country.

So the weeks passed, and the notes of Lewis and Clark became more and more voluminous. At dawn on Christmas Day they again fired the swivel guns in celebration, and each of the men discharged one round from his rifle. The officers issued some rum, and they all feasted on the best of their provisions. Some of them went hunting, and others danced, the gaiety lasting until nine o'clock in the evening. (They were not bothered by visiting Indians, having told their neighbors that this was a great "medicine day" during which they wished to be left alone.)

New Year's Day came to Fort Mandan with the sound of the swivel guns again being fired. Instead of withdrawing as they had done on Christmas, several of the men went to the nearest Mandan village and put on a white man's dance, much to the Indians' delight. They particularly enjoyed watching York and marveled that a man so strong could move so lightly. The temperature soared to 34 degrees above zero, and at sunset a few drops of rain fell. But this respite did not last long, as the rain quickly turned into a snowstorm that continued the greater part of the night.

The Mandans, too, celebrated the turn of the year by performing their Buffalo Dance. The old men of the village gathered in a circle and smoked a pipe. Then each young man, accompanied by his wife clad only in a buffalo robe, would approach one of the old men and, in a begging voice, plead with him to take the woman and gratify himself. The woman would then lead the man to some appropriate place to perform the act. If she failed to gratify him—and some of the men were so aged they could barely walk—her husband would offer her to another, whining all the while that he did not want himself and his wife despised. The purpose of the dance was to bring the buffalo nearer, so they could be more easily killed. As younger white men could fill the same role as the old Indians, Lewis and Clark permitted one soldier to take part in the ceremony. Before the dance was over he had substituted for four men whose vitality had faded.

From the Hidatsas, who habitually raided to the west, the captains learned of the existence of the Shoshone Indians, who lived at the edge of the Rockies. As they pieced together the crumbs of information they had collected, they decided that the geographical location of the Shoshones made them the logical tribe to supply them with the horses they needed for the portage over the Continental Divide. Therefore the friendship of these Indians would be critical to the expedition's success.

At least one Hidatsa leader raided the Shoshones every summer, and Lewis and Clark tried to dissuade him from following his usual practice that year. A demoralized, frightened tribe would be less likely to help them. They also put a higher value on Charbonneau's services. Originally they had considered him only as an interpreter who could assist them with the Hidatsas. But in addition to speaking that language, he had married a young Shoshone, Sacajawea, who had been taken prisoner during a raid and brought to the Missouri. To Lewis and Clark, her presence was a godsend, because she personally knew that part of the country and the people who inhabited it. They therefore immediately took steps to hire Charbonneau for the entire journey, not just for their stay on the Missouri. Consequently on Sacajawea's frail and youthful shoulders fell the burden of being the expedition's guide and ambassador when they reached the Rockies.

The keelboat and pirogues, which Lewis and Clark had failed to haul out in the fall, were now locked in the ice, and the two captains decided they must be pulled up on shore before they were damaged. Armed with axes the men started chopping, and the crystal white chips flew in the air. When they finally broke through to running water, they discovered the hulls were gripped by several layers of ice as the result of successive freezings. The spaces between the layers were filled not with air, but the cold water of the Missouri. While the men could cut the top layer standing in relative comfort on its dry surface, cutting the underwater layers proved impossible.

Next they hoped to free the boats by filling their hulls with water in which they intended to immerse hot stones, thus raising its temperature. This would have warmed the hulls and perhaps melted the surrounding ice; but that effort was also unsuccessful, because they could not find any rocks that would not shatter when they placed them in the fire. So the windlass they had built on the bank stood motionless, the rope they had created out of elkhide remained coiled, and the ice retained its grip on the boats.

The Mandans' Buffalo Dance failed of its purpose that winter, and few of the animals came near the villages or the fort. The expedition's supply of meat ran low, so Clark took sixteen soldiers and two Frenchmen on a hunting expedition, determined not to return empty-handed.

At five o'clock one afternoon while he was away, Sacajawea felt the first pangs of childbirth. Once again Lewis had to assume the role of the expedition's physician. By now he had even performed an operation for frostbite, but the part of midwife was new to him. Sacajawea's labor was long and painful—this was her first child—and the men watched anxiously, wishing they could relieve her. Jessaume, the French fur trader, had witnessed some childbirths and told Lewis he thought the rattle from a rattlesnake might be helpful. Lewis had one among his possessions and gave it to him. As the winter sun dropped in the bleak sky, replacing the cold day with an even colder night, Jessaume took two sections of the rattle, pulverized them with his fingers, and dropped the resulting powder into a small amount of water. With the gentleness of a nurse he administered this weird potion to the pain-ridden Indian girl. Whether or not the rattle was the cause Lewis could not decide, but ten minutes after drinking this strange draught Sacajawea gave birth to a fine boy.

Clark's hunting trip was successful, but he returned exhausted, having walked thirty miles through snow that was knee-deep. Several men set out with sleighs to recover the meat. On the snow-covered plains they encountered a band of more than a hundred Sioux, who had not heeded Lewis's admonition to remain peaceful. Since the Indians greatly outnumbered the white men, they decided to terrorize them. They dashed up to the sleighs, cut the horses loose, and also tried to steal the weapons of two of the men. However startled they may have been by this sudden onslaught, the Americans were not willing to allow themselves to be robbed in this fashion. When the Sioux saw they were going to resist, they left but took with them two horses and much of the meat.

Angry at this treatment of his men and disturbed by the loss of the much needed food, Lewis led a detachment of soldiers in pursuit. Fighting his way through the snow, he came to the spot where the encounter had taken place, but the Sioux by that time were too far ahead for him to overtake them. He did, however, recover part of the meat that the Indians had not found and also brought back some additional game he was able to shoot along the way.

The arrival of this supply of food was a good omen and so were the lengthening days, which were now warm enough to permit the men to sun their clothes occasionally, and which sufficiently softened the Missouri's ice so that by repeated exertions they were finally able to free the keelboat and the pirogues and pull them ashore. With the hesitant approach of spring the people on the Great Plains began to move about more freely. Gravelines arrived from the Arikara villages, where he had spent the winter, with news that the Sioux were threatening to attack the Mandan and Hidatsa villages in the summer and put to death any white man they found there. The peacemaking efforts of Lewis and Clark had failed to influence that fierce tribe. Larocque, who had made a quick journey to Fort Assiniboin, also returned with news of importance. The XY Company, founded by Alexander Mackenzie, had merged with the North West Company, reducing competition among the British fur traders and allowing them to concentrate more of their energy on developing trade along the West Coast.

The approach of spring also made more outdoor activity possible. In preparation for continuing their journey, Lewis and Clark put the men to work making additional pirogues, because upstream the river would soon become too shallow for the keelboat. On the other hand, the change in seasons brought out the worst in Charbonneau. He became unreasonable and set ridiculous terms for his services, saying he would do no physical work on the journey, would not stand guard, and reserved the right to leave the expedition anytime he chose. The captains wanted him, not for himself, but for Sacajawea, but they could not accept his exalted opinion of his worth. Finally he became more amenable, and that obstacle to the journey was overcome.

By the end of March the men were all in high spirits and spent almost every evening dancing with each other to the sound of Cruzatte's violin. They were getting along well and were generally healthy except, as Clark noted, for their "Venerials Complaints which is verry Common amongst the natives and the men Catch it from them."

On April 7, 1805, those who were to return to St. Louis boarded the keelboat, taking with them the notes of Lewis and Clark and the specimens and other articles they had so far collected. Gravelines was also returning downriver to carry out his assignment of persuading one of the Arikara chiefs to go to Washington, a task he was certain he could perform.

On the afternoon of the same day, Lewis and Clark and their men loaded the two pirogues they had retained from their upstream journey and the six smaller ones they had built that spring. The swivel gun boomed in defiance to the wilderness, and as its iron voice echoed across the Great Plains, the eight boats moved against the Missouri's current and in the direction of the Pacific Ocean.

The year 1805 was a time of fear, distrust, and maneuvering for power in the West. At St. Louis,

whether in the merchants' counting houses or along the busy riverfront where the boatmen moored their clumsy craft, everyone knew about the struggle between the Chouteaus and Lisa.

For the time being at least the Chouteau family appeared to be ahead. With the change of government, Lisa had lost his monopoly of the Osage trade (this had not proved as profitable as might have been expected, since the Chouteaus had lured many of the Osages away), and Pierre Chouteau had now been appointed the Americans' Indian agent to that tribe. The balance of power in St. Louis, which Lisa had tried so hard to upset, seemed to be gradually returning to its former equilibrium like a floating log that rights itself after being moved from its natural position.

In order to acquire capital for new ventures and to renew his struggle with the established merchants, Lisa began a series of lawsuits—some twenty in all—to collect sums that he thought were due him. At the same time he became closer with Jacques Clamorgan, discussing with him the possibility of entering the Santa Fé trade. If he could, Lisa intended to make a place for himself in the business circles of St. Louis.

But the intrigues of the fur traders as they tried to outmaneuver each other were nothing compared to the intrigues whirling around the office of the governor of Upper Louisiana, James Wilkinson. Since he was a favorite of Thomas Jefferson and also the commanding officer of the army, he had considerable power, which he used for no one's good but his own. Money and position were all that mattered to him, and he had long since placed himself on the block ready to be auctioned to the highest bidder; and by his code, no sales were final, and the auction was perpetual. Having earlier taken pay as a secret agent of the Spanish, he was now involving himself in Aaron Burr's shadowy plan for the possible conquest of his former employers. In the back of his restless mind he also had thoughts of sponsoring additional exploration in Upper Louisiana. The public reaction to Lewis and Clark's journey demonstrated the popularity of such missions.

The goal Wilkinson selected was the source of the Mississippi River, which had not yet been located, and he appointed as leader of the expedition Lieutenant Zebulon Pike, a young man of courage and ambition. Although he provided Pike with about twenty soldiers and a keelboat, he did not allow him the extensive time Lewis and Clark had had for preparations and sent him off at the wrong season of the year, early August, thus assuring him of a winter in the wilderness. Pike and his men consequently endured severe hardships. They also missed by a short distance the exact source of the Mississippi. But they returned with extensive notes on the territory east of the Great Plains and added significantly to the Americans' geographical knowledge of their country.

All this activity caused uneasiness in Santa Fé, Chihuahua, and Mexico City. The reports the Spanish officials received from the United States—some were false, some true—made them believe that such influence as they still retained on the Great Plains was in jeopardy and perhaps even the survival of their northern provinces. Of particular concern to them was their relationship with the Indians. According to their information, which had been considerably distorted during its transmission, Lewis and Clark were giving away large amounts of presents and forming firm alliances with many of the most powerful tribes.

So in 1805 they called on Pedro Vial, who had served them so well before, to make a trip to the Missouri, visiting particularly the Pawnees, the Omahas, the Otos, and other tribes. But even with his courage and resourcefulness, the old veteran could no more turn the flow of events than he could have prevented the north wind from sweeping the Great Plains during the winter. Lewis and Clark might not be having the triumphs the Spanish imagined, but their footsteps on the Great Plains were making that land truly America's own.

Chapter 8

A Journey West

Our vessels consisted of six small canoes, and two large pirogues. This little fleet altho' not quite so rispectable as those of Columbus or Capt. Cook, were still viewed by us with as much pleasure as those deservedly famed adventurers ever beheld theirs; and I dare say with quite as much anxiety for their safety and preservation. We were now about to penetrate a country at least two thousands miles in width . . . the good or evil it had in store for us was for experiment yet to determine, and these little vessels contained every article by which we were to expect to subsist or defend ourselves.

—Meriwether Lewis, 1805

Spring sent out its ancient call of hope, faint and delicate in the warming air, and the brant heard it and unfolded their wings for the flight north. Lewis and Clark and the other men in the eight pirogues saw them as they passed in flocks over the Missouri River. Along the riverbanks spring nudged the cottonwoods back into life, and their buds began to swell in the sunlight. Fresh sprouts of green grass appeared among the dry, dead stalks left from the previous year, and the geese circled and came down to feed.

As they had done before when traveling up the river, Lewis and Clark and several others of the party walked on shore to hunt and observe the country. At night the two captains slept in an Indian tipi, which they shared with the two interpreters, George Drouillard and Charbonneau, and Sacajawea and her baby son. Sometimes the wind blew in their favor, filling their sails and permitting the men to rest; sometimes it blew head on, making their forward progress difficult, if not impossible; and once it nearly capsized the pirogue in which they had stowed their instruments and records and in which Sacajawea and her child were riding.

Toward the end of April they could see in the distance the bluffs that once formed the margin of the wandering Missouri's riverbed and came to the mouth of the Little Muddy near present-day Williston, North Dakota. Recalling Jefferson's instructions to look for a river that might rise north of the 49th parallel, they mistakingly thought the Little Muddy perhaps fitted into this category. But they did not have time to explore it, for they had to cross the mountains while it was still summer and the passes were free of snow.

When they approached the Yellowstone River, Lewis went ahead on foot, reaching it about two miles above its mouth and then walking downstream to rejoin Clark. This river, it was rumored, might flow from New Mexico and therefore offer a route to the Spanish settlements. But the captains agreed that they should not tarry to investigate the possibility.

They had now entered the eastern range of the grizzly bears, one of the most dangerous of all North American mammals. Sometimes weighing fifteen hundred pounds or more and measuring nine feet from the tips of their noses to the ends of their small tails, the grizzlies were nevertheless agile and quick. (They have been known to run as fast as thirty miles an hour.) Lewis saw one and fired at it. His bullet struck the beast but failed to kill it. Wounded and angry, the bear charged forward to attack its tormenter, and Lewis fled. Fortunately the bear's wound was sufficiently serious to hamper its movements, and after running seventy or eighty yards, Lewis was able to reload his gun and fire a fatal shot.

Clark and Drouillard were the next to hunt a grizzly. They fired one shot after another, hitting it five times in the lungs and five times in other parts of its body, but it would not die. Luckily it did not pursue them but used its waning strength to swim halfway across the river to a sandbar. There it roared for twenty minutes before it fell motionless. When the members of the expedition examined the animal closely and saw how huge it was and at the same time realized how difficult it had been to kill, they gained a rightful respect for these animals. Several who had been anxious to shoot a grizzly themselves were now willing to leave that sport to others.

May 14 was a day of near disasters for the expedition. Toward evening the men in the two last boats saw a grizzly, and six of them who were experienced hunters went ashore to kill it. Taking advantage of a rise in the ground, they got within forty yards of their prey without being seen. By preagreement four of the men shot almost simultaneously, and two held their fire, so they could cover the others while they reloaded. All four bullets struck the bear but did not wound him mortally. With a roar he started toward the men. The two whose guns were still loaded then fired. One bullet did little damage; the other hit the bear's shoulder, but this checked the animal only momentarily. In a second the bear charged again, and the men, all their guns empty, raced to the river's edge. Two leapt into a boat and pushed off. The other four separated and hid among the willows.

For the moment they were safe, but the wounded bear remained in the area. Peering from the willows they could see him still angry and dangerous; and not wishing to be pinned down for the night, they fired again from their hiding places. Several of their shots hit their target but only infuriated the bear more and showed him the whereabouts of his enemies. On he came in renewed fury. Two of the men dashed in the direction of the river with the bear so close behind that in order to run faster they threw away their guns and pouches. At this point the banks of the Missouri formed a cliff about twenty feet high. A second's hesitation would have meant instant death, so the men never paused. Over the cliff they went, diving into the river.

But the bear dove, too, landing within a few feet of one of the men and still enraged. By this time a man on shore had reloaded his gun. Seeing the predicament of his fellow hunter, he fired another shot, aiming carefully. The bullet sped through the air and entered the bear's head. That finally was the end.

During those fateful moments Lewis and Clark had been farther upstream walking together, something they rarely did, because one of them usually stayed with the boats. Charbonneau, who was a poor boatman, was at the helm of one of the pirogues, and Peter Cruzatte was serving as the bowman. The boat also carried Sacajawea and her baby, two men who could not swim, and the expedition's most important possessions—instruments, books, medicine, and presents for any Indians they might meet.

Suddenly a squall struck with such violence that it tore the brace from the hands of the man holding it. Instead of running with the wind, Charbonneau tried to luff his clumsy rig, which with its square sail it could not do. Over went the boat on its side, and it would have gone bottom up if the pressure of the sail against the water had not checked it. Standing on the shore, Lewis and Clark both fired their guns to attract the men's attention and shouted instructions to cut the halyards and lower the sail, but they were too far away to be heard.

For about half a minute the pirogue lay on its side, its precious contents exposed to the clutching currents of the Missouri and its crew frozen into immobility by their fright. Then they regained control of themselves, freed the sail, and righted the boat. The craft floated, but only sluggishly, because it was filled with water up to an inch of its gunwales.

Watching helplessly from the shore, Lewis was tempted to swim to the boat and take charge. He had thrown aside his gun and pouch and was actually unbuttoning his coat when he realized his foolhardiness. The boat was three hundred yards away, the current swift, the water cold, and the waves high. He could easily have lost his life; yet the cargo in the pirogue was essential to the expedition's success.

Charbonneau, who as steersman should have been commander, had now become hysterical and was calling on his Lord to deliver him from danger. Cruzatte, unable to make him use his head, finally threatened to shoot him, and his words and exasperated tone at last penetrated the mental fog caused by the Frenchman's emotions.

All the while Sacajawea remained calm. Having assured herself of her baby's safety, she took up the task of retrieving various light objects that had been washed overboard and were in danger of floating away, scooping them up in her hands and returning them to the boat. Cruzatte now took charge. Fortunately there were two kettles on board, and he put men to work bailing while he and two other men rowed the boat to shore.

The whole cargo had to be unpacked, inventoried, and dried. To Lewis's pleasure, the losses were surprisingly light. Many of their medical supplies, some garden seeds, and a small quantity of gunpowder were either destroyed or gone, but everything else was all right. Between them, Cruzatte and Sacajawea had saved the expedition from a serious loss. Lewis, although sometimes critical of Sacajawea, was lavish in his praise of both of them.

The expedition's course up the Missouri carried them through present-day Montana and past the mouth of the Musselshell River. Sometimes they sailed, sometimes they rowed, but more often they towed their boats, for generally that was more practical. Except for the excitement of traveling in a new country, most of their days were uneventful and filled only with drudgery and hard work.

One night, however, they were roused from their sleep by the anxious cry of their sentinel. Each man grabbed his gun and jumped to his feet, looking into the surrounding darkness for the cause of danger. A bull buffalo had crossed the river, and as he had climbed ashore, he had stepped into one of the pirogues. The unfamiliar footing frightened him, and he dashed up the bank into the camp, his hooves coming within a foot and a half of the heads of some of the sleeping men before the sentinel could make him swerve. When he changed direction, he ran between the embers of four campfires, nearly trampled another row of sleeping men, and started directly toward the tipi of Lewis and Clark. But Lewis's Newfoundland saved the day. It barked and snarled at the buffalo, frightening the animal into shifting course once more. It missed the tipi and vanished into the darkness.

Another day as they were going up the river a terrible odor filled the air. Under a cliff lay the mangled, stinking remains of at least a hundred buffaloes. They had been driven to their deaths by Indians, who found this method of hunting more productive than shooting them one by one. Unfortunately, as Lewis noted in his journal, they often killed more buffaloes than they could use, destroying an entire herd and leaving the surplus to rot.

Because of the geographical information Lewis and Clark had collected during their stay in the Mandan villages, they had a reasonably accurate picture of the course of the Missouri River to the edge of the Rocky Mountains. As they went along, they checked off the major tributaries they expected to find, but they had mistaken one river for another, throwing out their calculations. Thus they were unprepared for the confluence of the Marias River and the Missouri and did not know which was which.

The mouth of the Marias was less wide than the Missouri, but the channel was deeper. Its current, however, was not as swift. On the other hand, it carried with it the whitish-brown sediment they had come to regard as characteristic of the Missouri, while the Missouri itself ran clear and exhibited none of its usual turbulence.

Their quandary was deep. If they took the wrong turn, the river might lead them miles away from their destination, causing them to lose a season of travel and perhaps frustrating the whole purpose of their journey. Although they were in the minority, Lewis and Clark correctly believed that the river to their left was the Missouri; but even they were not certain. Perplexed and disturbed, they made camp on the point formed by the two rivers.

The feet of some of the men were in terrible condition, having been cut and bruised by the rocks over which they had struggled when they hauled on the towlines. They could not walk—or even stand—without suffering excruciating pain and for several days had been unable to wear their moccasins. These men remained in camp dressing skins that would be used for clothing, while two groups of the more able-bodied made one-day reconnaissance trips up each of the rivers.

Since the report of neither group was satisfactory, Lewis and Clark decided they themselves would lead two missions, going as far and as long as necessary to make sure which river was the Missouri. Clark followed the actual Missouri and within a few days was able to identify it by its course and the rapidity of its current. Lewis took a little longer to convince himself that the Marias was not the river they wanted.

To facilitate their return, he had his men build some rafts, thinking the current would carry them back in the direction of the camp. But they soon learned they had made the rafts too small and too narrow to float safely on the river and had to abandon them.

On both sides of the Marias the Great Plains were ribboned by deep ravines that made an overland route impractical. For a while the men tried walking along the top of the bluffs, but a drenching rain had made the clay treacherously slippery. With the river some ninety feet below him, Lewis's feet suddenly slid from underneath him, and the motion carried him to the edge of the cliff. He had with him a spontoon, a half-pike or short staff hooked at one end. With its help he stopped his deadly slide and then was able to work his way back to surer footing.

No sooner had he done so than he heard a horrible cry behind him. Looking back, he saw one of his soldiers lying on the ground with his right arm and leg over the edge of the precipice and clinging precariously with his left arm and leg. Trying to reflect a confidence that he did not feel, Lewis told him he was in no danger and instructed him to take his knife and with his right hand dig a hole for his right foot. This the soldier did, enabling him to rise to his knees. Then Lewis called to him to take off his moccasins, which were slippery, and crawl back to safety.

Although no one lost his life, these two instances—one coming immediately after the other—proved this method of travel too dangerous, so as soon as they could, the men moved back to the river itself. Sometimes they forced their way across the bottomlands, which the rain had turned into sloughs; at others the banks pressed so close to the water's edge that they had to wade, often up to their breasts. And if the water became too deep, they proceeded by cutting footholds into the faces of the banks. In this dismal fashion they went downstream and finally reached the mouth of the Marias River, where they found Clark worrying about their late return.

Combining the information they had obtained during their two trips, Clark plotted the courses of both rivers. After studying his sketch, the two captains were more certain than ever that the river to the left was the Missouri, which indeed it was. Lewis named the other Maria's River after one of his cousins with whom he was much taken.

Because the current had now become so swift, the two captains decided it was pointless to take one of the large pirogues any farther, so they cached it and some of their heavier supplies against their return. As these included their blacksmith's bellows and tools, this was their last chance to repair their firearms. Working hastily, they fixed their guns, but the busy day passed in good humor, and that evening Peter Cruzatte, the expedition's principal entertainer, played on his violin while the men danced and made merry around their campfire.

Because of their original doubts about the river, the two captains decided that while Clark brought up the boats, Lewis should go ahead by land, that being the faster way to travel, and see if he could find the Falls of the Missouri. The Indians had told

them about that famous landmark, and its presence would be certain proof that they were heading in the right direction.

Although he was not feeling well, Lewis set out briskly at eight o'clock on the morning of June 11, 1805; but before the day was over, he was stricken with such pain that he could no longer walk and was forced to make camp. In addition to the agony in his intestines, he had a high fever, but he had brought no medicine with him. Nevertheless, he told his men how to prepare a concoction from native berries; and after several doses of the black, bitter liquid, his fever lessened, and he spent a comfortable night on his bed of willows.

After first taking a day off to recuperate, Lewis left the river and led his men in a southwesterly direction, hoping to save time by shortcutting one of the river's great bends. Their way took them through country that was more rolling than the land they had traversed the day before and brought them to an overlook from which they could see a beautiful, level plain that extended into the distance for some fifty or sixty miles. On its surface grazed more buffaloes than Lewis had ever before observed in one place. Always glad of an opportunity to obtain fresh meat, he instructed his men to fan out, shoot some of the buffaloes, and rejoin him at the river.

Left to himself, he walked approximately two miles when suddenly he heard an awe-inspiring sound. It was the voice of the Falls of the Missouri, a distant roar that told of snow-capped mountains, deep forests, vast treeless plains, of storms that blackened the sky and turned noondays into midnights, and of clear heavens in which the stars sparkled like crystals and the sun burned like the branding irons used by the Spanish. Not a tinkling soprano accompanied by the castanets of lightly jostled stones, but a solid, booming bass befitting one of the world's greatest rivers as it poured its gallons of water over the several rock ledges that impudently tried to block its way to the ocean.

When Lewis approached a little closer, he saw a cloud of spray rise above the level of the plains from the invisible canyon and hang in the air, a sunlit cloud to be dispersed by the wind and replaced by another and another.

As enraptured as any tourist seeing for the first time a long-sought marvel, Lewis sat on a rock and watched the plunging waters, the churning foam, and the maelstroms dancing at his feet like demons performing a devil's rite, and enjoyed the refreshingly cool and damp air, which was a welcome relief after the hot, dry days he had spent on the plains. In a space of about twelve miles, as he learned, the Missouri River dropped several hundred feet. This change in altitude was divided among several falls, leaving none of them able to compete in height with wonders such as Niagara, but the volume of water that flowed over them gave them a unique character. The topography upstream permitted the river to wander freely, extending its banks this way and that with little constraint. Suddenly it found itself forced into a narrow waterway much less broad than those it had made for itself earlier. In angry response its waters quickened their flow and raged between the narrow banks over the falls, roaring in their fury as they plunged downward.

Picking up his journal, Lewis tried to write a verbal description of what he was seeing in the hope that he could give his fellow Americans an impression of the grandeur that was theirs. But he could not find the words to match the scene and started to cross out what he had written as being inadequate. Then he changed his mind again as he realized that perhaps he could do no better.

The next day, while waiting for Clark, Lewis explored the other falls and rapids. Having so much to observe, he thought that perhaps he might not want to return to his camp in the evening and, seeing enough sticks around to make a fire, decided to shoot one buffalo out of a nearby herd in order to have meat for his supper. After firing, he waited to watch the buffalo fall without reloading his gun—an unpardonable, amateurish mistake for an experienced hunter. Intent upon his own prey, he did not realize he was playing a similar role for another carnivore until he noticed that a grizzly bear was approaching him and was only twenty paces away. He raised his gun to his shoulder, but of course it was empty. The nearest tree was three hundred yards away (grizzlies rarely climb trees; their claws lack the curvature to make good hooks for grabbing the bark), and not a single bush or rock offered him shelter while he reloaded.

Not wishing to excite the bear, he walked, rather than ran, toward the tree, but the bear was not fooled by this ploy and began to charge. Lewis dashed to the Missouri and plunged into the water up to his waist. Since grizzlies are at home in the water, the river offered a poor defense, but it was the best Lewis had in sight. He then whirled around and raised the spontoon that had saved him from falling off the cliff. The grizzly charged to the water's edge, and since these bears are a notoriously aggressive species, Lewis thought his fate was sealed. But inexplicably the bear stopped and, equally inexplicably, ran away.

Back on shore Lewis reloaded his gun and wrung out his clothes. He then noticed an animal that he thought was a wolf, but on drawing closer to it, decided it was more catlike. Then it crouched as though determined to spring on him, but he fired his gun, and the animal disappeared into its burrow. As he noted later in his journal, "It now seemed to me that all the beasts of the neighborhood had made a league to distroy [sic] me, or that some fortune was disposed to amuse herself at my expence [sic] . . ."

And perhaps he was right. For no sooner had he repulsed the bear and driven the catlike animal into its burrow than three buffalo bulls separated themselves from a herd that was grazing about a half-mile away and began charging toward him. Since he could not kill all three with a single shot, he walked toward them resolutely, hoping this show of defiance would check their advance. The buffaloes came within a hundred yards, stopped, looked at him, and ran back to their herd.

Although not normally superstitious, Lewis half believed that some sort of enchantment must lie over the place or time and that it would be inadvisable to spend the night alone. On his way back to camp it seemed to him he was living in a dream; but occasionally the thorns of a prickly pear cactus would pierce his feet and restore him to reality.

Even without the large pirogue they had left at the Marias, Clark had difficulty bringing up the boats. Many of the men were exhausted and in poor physical condition. Two suffered the nagging pain of toothaches, three had tumors—one of them accompanied by a fever—and Sacajawea was seriously ill. None of Clark's ministrations seemed to take effect, and the presence of the invalid woman in their midst hindered them. As the current was far too strong either to row or sail the boat, the men had to wade in the water, pulling on their towlines. Their footing was insecure, being largely composed of rocks that were sharp and cut their feet or stones that the river had polished to a slippery surface. More than once they stumbled and fell as they heaved against the current.

When after several days of grueling work Clark rejoined Lewis, the two captains immediately set about making plans for the portage that lay ahead. Since the boats were heavy and the distance about sixteen miles, they decided to leave the second of the two large pirogues behind and build axles and wheels on which they could mount the others. This was more easily said than accomplished because of the scarcity of trees. Six men formed a detail to search for building material and fortunately found a cottonwood sufficiently large to make wheels with a diameter of twenty-two inches. This was a stroke of luck, because, as Lewis commented, there probably was not another tree of such size within twenty miles. Since they were leaving behind the second of the two large pirogues, they cut its masts in two and made a pair of axles. This was the only lumber they had that was not cottonwood, which being brittle and weak was not suited to their purpose.

Lewis now took over the care of Sacajawea; and the miserable Indian girl, her baby still with her, began to mend. In addition to medicine made of bark and doses of laudanum, Lewis had her drink from the remarkable sulfur spring whose waters flowed into the Missouri at the falls. Except for one relapse when Charbonneau let her overeat, she soon regained her health.

After looking over the terrain and consulting with each other, the captains decided that the southern side of the Missouri offered the better route around the falls. Clark went ahead and selected a site to serve as the end of the portage. It was opposite a spot they named White Bear Island because of a grizzly who contested their claim to it. One of the men had gone to pick up a load of meat when the bear saw him and chased him to within forty yards of the camp. Clark was there with another man, and the bear, deciding that odds of three to one were too great, ambled off in another direction. But one of the soldiers, James Colter, was in the area toward which the bear was headed, so Clark collected three other men and went to his rescue. It was lucky for Colter that he did, for when they arrived, they found the bear had chased Colter into the river and was still threatening him.

In spite of all the activity, a nervous sense of uncertainty dominated both camps. Since leaving the villages of the Hidatsas they had not seen any Indians. Therefore they wondered what sort of reception awaited them ahead—friendly or hostile? Earlier they had intended to send some of their men back from the Falls of the Missouri to St. Louis and had reported this plan in their dispatches to Jefferson. Now they reconsidered the idea and came to the conclusion that they should not weaken their small force in case the Indians proved unfriendly.

The "wagon," if the axles and wheels could be called that, was now completed, and the hard work began. Approximately eighteen long, hard miles separated the two points, and the men trudged over them with ever-increasing weariness and pain. They heaved, they pulled, they swore as the wheels caught in the many furrows carved in the dirt by the passing hooves of numberless ancient

buffalo herds. Axles broke, wagon tongues splintered, and replacements had to be cut and fitted. The mats of cacti covering the ground thrust their pain-bearing spines through the tough leather of the men's moccasins and into the flesh of their feet. They were a hardy lot, tough, sunburned, and inured to discomfort, but many grew faint as they pulled and pushed, yanked and levered, strained, and damned their heavy loads across the plains.

On June 24 the temperamental weather blew up a following wind, sending it hustling through the skies in the direction they were going. The men jokingly hoisted the sail on the boat they were then moving. It filled, and the wagon rattled forward with the sail doing, as one soldier remarked, the work of four men. On June 27 the weather turned harsh and pelted them with hailstones. On June 29 it assaulted them with uncontrolled fury.

Early in the morning a slight rain fell, but then the clouds rolled back, and the sky became clear. Clark had spent the night at the halfway camp they had established between the foot of the falls and the camp near White Bear Island. Finding that the ground was too wet to continue the second half of the portage, he sent some of the men back to their base to bring up some of the luggage; and he himself went off with York, Charbonneau, Sacajawea, and one soldier to re-examine the falls. Barely had they reached that wonderful site than they noticed a large black cloud that threatened to drench them with rain. About a quarter of a mile upstream a deep ravine cut its way into the Missouri. Along its side were shelving rocks under which they sought protection and nearby was another dry spot where they could put their guns and compass.

The rain was gentle at first, although accompanied by a violent wind. But this was just the overture to the storm, the first low snarl of a wolf about to attack. Suddenly the heavens were torn by a spasm of rain and hailstones—Clark said he had never seen anything like it before—and the creek at the bottom of the ravine, collecting the run-off, swelled into a monster that rushed toward them with a force so great it carried everything before it, including large rocks.

Charbonneau seized the hand of Sacajawea, who was clutching her baby, and tried to pull her up the side of the ravine, but he was so frightened and the earth so slippery that it seemed to Clark he hardly moved forward. Clark grabbed his gun and pouch in one hand and with the other pushed Sacajawea from behind. The water swirled around Clark's waist, wetting his watch, before he could free himself of its deadly grip. When they reached the top, they looked back and saw that the surface of the current was fifteen feet above the spot where they had taken shelter.

Back at their camp they met the men who had gone to get the luggage at the foot of the falls. The hailstones that had accompanied the storm had struck them with such ferocity they had cut and bruised the heads of those who were not wearing hats, and one man had been knocked down three times as they dropped their loads and ran for cover. Lewis, who was at the camp near White Bear Island, measured some of the hailstones and found they had a circumference of seven inches.

Even though he was unaware of all the difficulties that lay ahead—he still thought the mountain ranges were less broad than they actually were—Lewis was growing impatient with their slow pace. Almost three months had elapsed since their departure from Fort Mandan, and it was now the end of June. The hope he had once entertained that they might be able to return to Fort Mandan that season was gone. But he was well pleased with his iron boat. He had put together the metal framework and covered it with buffalo skins. ". . . She lay like a perfect cork on the water," he wrote, and was so light that even assembled five men could easily carry it. Clark had brought up the remainder of the luggage, so they loaded the pirogues and the iron boat and were ready to continue their journey.

Before they could leave, a violent wind blew up, forcing them to unload the pirogues to prevent their swamping. The wind kept whipping the surface of the Missouri, churning it into waves that tossed the iron boat and broke against its sides. Gradually the water loosened the "composition" with which Lewis had covered the skins, washing it away and removing the protective coating from the seams. These gradually opened up, the water seeped inside, and soon the boat was leaking badly.

After examining it, even Lewis admitted he could not repair it with the materials at hand, although he still stubbornly maintained that with some fresh skins and pitch he might have done so. Since these were not available, he set about recovering the skins he had used by first sinking the boat entirely to soften them. As he watched the men remove them and disassemble his invention, the pieces lying on the ground in front of him, he felt a deep sense of mortification. He had carried the contraption all the way down the Ohio and up the Missouri, and it had turned out to be nothing but junk.

Clark had always been a little skeptical about his

friend's boat but had tactfully kept his opinions to himself. And now, he knew, was not the time for jokes or other comments. Instead, sensitive to Lewis's feelings, he gathered a group of men and quietly went off to start building the two extra pirogues they would need.

On July 15, 1805, they were finally ready to leave the Falls of the Missouri, which had proved to be the most difficult stretch of the river they had encountered and which also represented the outer limits of the Hidatsas' detailed geographical knowledge. Beyond stood the snow-crested mountains, and over them hung the black question—where were the passes by which this barrier might be penetrated?

From the middle of July to the middle of November the two captains pushed into the unknown country. Battling wearily against the Missouri's ever-quickening current, they passed through the canyon in western Montana that Lewis named the Gates of the Rocky Mountains. The steep rock cliffs on either side were far too high to use towropes, and the bottom too deep for poles to touch. Fortunately at this point the river flowed slowly enough to let them row against it.

It took them along the western flank of the Big Belt Mountains and on to the Three Forks of the Missouri, where the Madison, Gallatin, and Jefferson rivers join. Here they faced two perplexities: The three streams looked so much alike that it was difficult to decide which one to follow, and they still had seen nothing of Sacajawea's people, from whom they had hoped to obtain horses and information. After reconnoitering, they selected as their route the Jefferson; but although Sacajawea recognized some landmarks, they saw no Indians until August.

After tortuous negotiations with this band, in which Sacajawea played a leading role (the leader turned out to be her brother), the captains finally procured horses and two guides, an Indian whom they dubbed Old Toby and his son.

After caching their boats and some of their supplies, they followed a course that brought them over the Beaverhead Mountains, whose crest forms the boundary between present-day Idaho and Montana, down the valley of the Lemhi River and by various streams and rivers to Lolo Pass in the Bitterroot Mountains. The high altitudes rolled back the season, and the men trudged over ground whitened by snow. They ran short of food in the game-scarce peaks; hunger and fatigue were their daily companions and shared their blankets at night; and dysentery sapped their strength. Yet they found a route through the tangle of mountains and reached the site of the modern city of Lewiston, Idaho.

The Clearwater River, down which they floated in the dugouts they had built on the mountains' western slopes, soon joined the Snake. After carrying them at such a speed that they sometimes covered forty miles in a day and after nearly destroying one of their boats by dashing it against a rock, the Snake brought them safely to the Columbia. Since it had carved a route for itself through the Cascade Range, it offered them passage through the mountains to their goal, the ocean, which they reached on a rainy day in the second week of November, 1805.

Others had crossed the continent before them—Cabeza de Vaca, fleeing from the coastal Indians and trusting in a God who encouraged him to perform miracles and never deserted him, and Alexander Mackenzie, the Scots fur trader with dreams of a mercantile empire and a will of iron; and others like la Vérendrye were already familiar with much of the Missouri River and the Great Plains. But these men were the first to carry with them the American flag. It was a young flag, its canton and bars only newly designed, and the blue field contained a mere handful of stars, seventeen in all. But there was room for more within the confines of that rectangle, and Lewis and Clark had done much toward placing them there.

Chapter 9

The Way Home

The Indians believed that these traders were the most powerful persons in the nation; nor did they doubt their ability to withhold merchandise from themselves; but the thirst displayed by the traders for the possession of their peltries and furs, added to the belief that they were compelled to continue their traffic, was considered by the Indians a sufficient guarantee for the continuance of their intercourse. The Indians, therefore, felt themselves at liberty to practice aggressions on the traders with impunity.

—Meriwether Lewis, unfinished
manuscript, c. 1807

Although the black star of Zebulon Pike's fortune had caused him to miss the precise source of the Mississippi River, thus depriving him of the fame of its discovery, he looked forward to several months of well-deserved leave on his return to St. Louis in 1806. Ill-planned and ill-equipped, the expedition had suffered many hardships during the northern winter months, and its leader had certainly earned a rest. But General James Wilkinson, commander of the American forces and governor of Upper Louisiana, had further plans for his youthful protégé.

In his murky, devious manner, Wilkinson rarely made his purposes clear. When he gave Pike command of a new exploratory expedition, he may have secretly instructed the lieutenant to spy on the military defenses of the Spanish in preparation for helping Aaron Burr attack them. On the surface, however, his directive to Pike, although detailed, revealed only peaceful intentions.

One of Wilkinson's avowed objectives was to stop the constant warfare between the Osage and Kansa Indians. But that was not all. As soon as Pike had finished this formidable task—and Wilkinson seemed to have no doubts that he would succeed—he was to proceed west and persuade the warlike Comanches to make peace with their neighbors, too. In the course of these endeavors and almost as a sideline, Pike might also, Wilkinson thought, explore the Red and Arkansas rivers, locate their headwaters, and help define more clearly the boundary between America's newly purchased territory and that of its neighbor, Spain.

Much as he would have liked to have remained a while with his family, recuperating from the rigors of the previous winter and enjoying the comforts of home life as contrasted with his harsh northland existence, Pike in the long tradition of soldiers, answered the call of unreasonable duty.

On July 15, 1806, he left Belle Fontaine, a settlement near St. Louis and the place where his wife and children were living. In addition to some Indian captives whom the government had ransomed from other tribes as a gesture of goodwill, he was accompanied by General Wilkinson's son, Lieutenant James B. Wilkinson, a surgeon, three noncommissioned officers, sixteen privates, and one interpreter; and for transportation he had two boats.

After about two weeks of the usual hardships endured by river travelers—snapped towlines, hidden snags, and inclement weather, all complicated by the presence of so many Indians—the expedition reached the mouth of the Osage River.

More days of travel, more days of discomfort, close calls with rattlesnakes (Pike spared the life of one, because it had spared his; he had nearly stepped on it, but it had not struck his leg), rain and more rain, delays while they dried out their gear and supplies, more delays while they searched for men who became lost when they walked on shore—such were the dangers and annoyances encountered by the expedition as it moved up the Osage River past the ruins of Auguste Chouteau's old trading post and on to a meeting with White Hair, the principal Osage chief.

Instead of arriving with a handful of followers, as Pike had expected, White Hair appeared with 186 men, all of whom had to be fed. This forced Pike to serve a repast that sorely strained the expedition's resources. After a return visit to White Hair's village, which was known as the Grand Osage, Pike also went to the other of the two Osage villages, the Little Osage.

Then he called the customary council during which he attempted to explain the change in government and how the Americans expected the Indians to behave peacefully. The youthful officer—he was twenty-seven—spoke gravely on behalf of the nation that was only a few years older than himself, but while the Indians listened attentively, the words as usual meant little. They had heard other white men speak, and these phrases about alien governments and their laws and expectations were less real than the sound of winds and flowing rivers.

The Osage River had taken Pike to the west; his route to his next destination, the Pawnees, carried him roughly to the northwest. Once more the expedition faced periods of bad weather and, unable to move at all one day, Pike passed the time in his tent reading the Bible and Alexander Pope's essays. The Osage guides that accompanied him proved unreliable—two of them plotted to desert—and Pike regarded them as "a faithless set of poltrons [sic]" with some possible exceptions whom he had not yet found.

He also learned from a passing Pawnee hunter the startling news that only recently a large Spanish military expedition had been in the vicinity. This was a force of one hundred regulars and five hundred New Mexican militia under the command of Lieutenant Don Facundo Malgares, who had been ordered to go down the Red River, intercept Pike, and patrol the area between the Kansas and Platte rivers. If Lewis and Clark's expedition had evoked concern among the Spanish, the news that

Pike was traversing the country farther to the south produced a more dramatic response. The Spanish government had no intention of sitting idly by while the United States nibbled at its borders and subverted the Indians.

Since Malgares had already gone on, the Spaniard's mission did not deter Pike from visiting the Pawnees. But in spite of a friendly beginning to his dealings with that tribe, the council that he subsequently held with them was far from satisfactory. Years before, they had routed Villasur and had driven the Spanish back from the north. But Malgares had struck them favorably. Each of his soldiers had been mounted on a white horse, while Malgares himself and his two leading officers rode pure black mounts. With them, of course, they had brought ample presents, including Spanish flags; and one of these was unfurled to decorate the village on the day of the council.

Some four hundred warriors gathered to hear Pike speak. Again, he futilely tried to explain the change in government—a topic that seemed more abstract than real to the Indians—and outlined the new position of the United States. All the while, he kept eyeing that Spanish flag that was so prominently displayed on American territory. If he was to impress on them the sovereignty of his country, he thought he could not ignore it. So in stern tones he told them that they must take it down, bring it to him, and replace it with one of the American flags he had given them. His tiny band of travel-weary men compared poorly with Malgares' magnificent host. So when the Pawnees responded to various points made in Pike's speech, they failed to say or do anything about the flag.

Pike, therefore, brought up the subject anew. At his insistence, they did what he ordered, but he noticed that every face at the council grew dark with anger. Perhaps he had carried "the pride of nation a little too far," as he put it in his journal, especially as he had such an inferior body of troops. So retreating from his original position, he praised them for acknowledging the American government and returned the flag to them, saying he did not want them to be embarrassed should the Spanish happen to come back. But he ordered them not to fly it again while he was in the village.

The replacement of the Spanish flag with the American ensign that now hung at the doorway of the chief's lodge did not, however, signify any material change of heart on the part of the Pawnees. In a conversation with Pike the chief kept urging him to turn back and then, when his pleas failed, admitted that he had promised Malgares that he would not permit the Americans to advance any farther. If force was necessary to check them, he had agreed to use it.

When the time came for Pike's departure, many of the young warriors had gotten out their guns and lances and had strung their bows. Milling around in a threatening manner, they appeared eager for an excuse to fight. Calmly Pike kept his men in compact order and maneuvered them around the village in such a way that the Pawnees could not fire from the shelter of their lodges but would have to remain in the open. Later Pike estimated that if the Indians had attacked, his small band could have killed about a hundred before being themselves exterminated. This was too high a price for carrying out Malgares's request, so they let the Americans head off toward the west to fulfill the remainder of Wilkinson's directive.

On the West Coast during the winter of 1805–1806 the gray fingers of the Pacific fogs probed the shore, and the warm ocean winds, pressing against the cooler land, turned to rain that soaked the forest and dripped through the chinking of the two wooden buildings that Lewis and Clark had built as their winter quarters. Having failed to find a trading ship that could carry them back to civilization (this had once been their hope) the men of the expedition resigned themselves to the cold, soggy months until the sun opened their route home by melting the snows in the mountain passes. The time seemed interminable. No man waiting to meet his lover ever found the days longer or the nights filled with more vacant hours; but on March 23, 1806, they at last started on their return journey.

No one regretted the day. Even Lewis and Clark, usually so enthusiastic, had become weary of the weather and irritated by the Indians. At the beginning of their trip, they had been scrupulous and idealistic in their dealings with the natives, but their travels had taught them an important truth: that tribes and individuals were not all alike. Some were honest, straightforward, and brave; others could be the contrary. On the West Coast the Indians had committed many acts of petty thievery and had practiced commercial prostitution as wanton as that of a madam hawking her girls in the roughest district of a riverfront town. These were not people whom they hated to leave.

On their way back they battled the currents of the Columbia River, made the necessary portages, and reached the Nez Percé Indians, who during the winter had cared for the horses that had carried the expedition over the mountains the year before. Although a few of the horses had been overworked, the majority were in good condition, and the Nez Percés provided the travelers with more.

But the expedition could not proceed immediately. Ahead of them lay the mountains, and May's sun, the Indians warned, was not warm enough to open the snow-choked passes. So the men spent their time hunting, treating their own sick and those of the Indians, and expounding the aims and policies of the United States. Fortunately the Nez Percés were generous and considerate—so much so that the captains later praised them highly and compared their kindness with that of the most civilized nations. Therefore the expedition was well equipped with food and horses, and its men healthy and rested when it started out again on June 10, 1806.

The Indians had told Lewis and Clark that in spite of the weeks they had spent waiting, it might still be too early to cross the Bitterroot Mountains, and indeed it was. In places the ground was covered by eighteen feet of snow, food for the horses was scarce, and the best frontiersmen among them had difficulty finding signs of the trail. About a week after leaving the Nez Percés, the two captains decided it was pointless to flounder in that white wilderness. Sadly retracing their steps—Clark noted in his journal that it was the first time they had been forced to retreat—they withdrew to a campsite where there was enough grass and game to support them while they tried to obtain guides. With the help of several Nez Percés, who caught up with them and showed them the way, they finally crossed the Bitterroots; and the first days of July found them at Travelers Rest just inside the western boundary of present-day Montana.

On their journey west one of the captains' objectives had been to get over the mountains before they might be caught by snowstorms. This urgency had prevented them from exploring as thoroughly as they would have liked the western portions of the Great Plains and the eastern entrances into the mountains. On the return journey time was not so important, and they had therefore decided to expand their knowledge of the country's geography.

Their plan was rather complicated. Lewis was to go north on the Bitterroot River and pick up the Blackfoot River, which flowed into it from the east. This, they thought, might be a shorter route to the plains than the one they had taken the previous year. He was then to go to the Falls of the Missouri and leave there three men to uncover the cache they had hidden the year before. These men were to wait at that point for the appearance of some of Clark's men, while Lewis again went north and explored the Marias River. Lewis's earlier reconnaissance up it had failed to show whether or not its source lay in the Canadian fur country.

Clark was to lead the remainder of the men back to the point where they had left the last of their boats on the westward journey. He was then to travel by water to the juncture of the Jefferson and Missouri rivers, where he was to divide his men. One group would continue down the Missouri to the falls and join Lewis's men. Meanwhile he himself would strike overland to the Yellowstone and follow it downstream. All three parties would meet again at its mouth.

This was a dangerous decision, as both captains knew. It would be the first time they had ever let the expedition split up; and the way they had now planned it, there would be a period when their small party would be divided into as many as four groups, none of them representing a force of any size. Yet they believed the risk was necessary if they were to bring back the information that Jefferson and their countrymen wanted.

Shadows of somber thoughts played across Lewis's mind on the morning of July 3, 1806. For more than a year the two captains had been inseparable, working in the closest unity and sharing each other's thoughts. Now they were going different ways, and Lewis hoped, as he noted in his journal, that "this separation was only momentary."

After seeing his good friend depart for the north, Clark mustered the remaining men and Sacajawea and headed south toward the cached boats. Using Sacajawea's knowledge of the country, they took a slightly different route than on their way west and reached the cache on July 8. The men rushed to unsaddle their horses and recover the goods they had hidden the previous August, for among them was one item that many of them craved—tobacco. It took them only a day to reassemble their belongings and repair a hole in one of the boats. Then they were on their way again, some of the men riding downstream in the boats while others followed along the shore with the horses.

At the three forks that form the Missouri proper, Clark took ten men and Sacajawea to make the overland trip to the Yellowstone while the others continued downstream to start the portage around the Falls of the Missouri. Sacajawea's knowledge of the country again proved useful, and she guided Clark by the best route to the Yellowstone, which they reached near present-day Livingston, Montana.

The hooves of the unshod horses were worn nearly to the quick, and Clark had hoped that when they reached the river they could build a boat and proceed by water. But they were back on the plains where timber was difficult to find. So with green buffalo hides the men improvised a sort of moccasin that served as a shoe and enabled the horses to limp along. At last they came to a grove of trees, none of which was sufficiently tall to make a large pirogue; but after scouting around and failing to find any that were taller, Clark decided to construct two smaller boats and lash them together to prevent their capsizing.

Off in the distance they had several times noticed smoke, which, they thought, indicated the presence of Indians. This conjecture was verified when they woke one morning to find that twenty-four out of their fifty horses had disappeared during the night. Clearly they had not wandered by themselves from the lusher grazing in the river bottom to the sparser grass on the uplands, where the hard surface made it difficult to track them. Then, too, not far from camp one of the men found a piece of a robe and a moccasin that was still wet. Pursuit of the thieves, who were undoubtedly Crows, was out of the question, but Clark resolved to send the remaining horses directly to the Mandan villages as soon as possible. Since he had finished the construction of the two small pirogues, he no longer needed them for transportation, but he could trade them for supplies.

The distraction caused by the stolen horses did not prevent Clark from faithfully keeping a record of each phenomenon he observed, including the weather. In the meteorological record for that day, he noted one of the recurring horrors of the Great Plains—an invasion of locusts. Over large areas along the river and for some distance from its banks, the winged host, swirling out of the sky, had destroyed every species of grass, leaving the earth barren.

As the men floated down the river, they noticed a remarkable rock about two hundred and fifty paces from the bank. It was some two hundred feet high and accessible from only one side, the others being sheer cliffs. Clark climbed to the top to look at the view and then named the rock Pompey's Tower (now Pompey's Pillar) after Sacajawea's child, to whom he had given the affectionate nickname "Pomp." Before leaving, he scratched his name and the date on the stone surface.

The following morning, when they left their camp at the mouth of the Bighorn River, they had their last view of the mountains, that barrier of upturned rocks, steep slopes, and fast-flowing streams that divided the continent. They had first sighted it from the west almost three months ago, and its disappearance behind the curvature of the earth was a welcome indication that they were approaching home. The Yellowstone now broadened, and its course was dotted with islands and sandbars. This and the tendency of its banks to cave in reminded Clark of the Missouri, but he remarked that the islands were more numerous, the current faster, and the water clearer.

On August 3, 1806, the river carried them to its mouth, where it emptied into the Missouri. Here they were to wait for Lewis's appearance, but the campground soon became uninhabitable. On their way down the Yellowstone—and earlier on their trip up the Missouri—they had frequently complained of the mosquitoes, which buzzed around them and covered their bodies with welts. But they were never so numerous as at the mouth of the Yellowstone that August. The men could neither hunt nor work around the camp, and their only escape was to move out onto the sandbars in the river. But as soon as the breeze stopped blowing, the mosquitoes attacked them even in that sanctuary.

Weary after a sleepless night of torment and driven wild by the incessant itching, the men rejoiced when Clark decided in desperation to go a little farther down the Missouri. He wrote a note to Lewis telling him what he was doing and tied it to a pole that he stuck in the ground. But the change of location produced no relief. If anything, the mosquitoes were even worse at the second campsite. So he kept moving slowly, trying unsuccessfully to escape the insects and hoping that Lewis would soon overtake him.

As he slowly floated down the Missouri, Clark was surprised to see a boat ahead of him close to the shore. He immediately landed and was delighted to find that it contained two fur traders, Joseph Dickson and Forest Hancock, the first white men that any member of the expedition had seen in more than a year.

Naturally Clark was anxious to hear what news they might have. Dickson and Hancock had met the boat that Lewis and Clark had sent to St. Louis from the Mandan villages, and they also knew that Gravelines had carried out the captains' instructions to take one of the Arikara chiefs to Washington. But all their news was not good. In their patriotic innocence Lewis and Clark thought they had really persuaded the Indians not to war on one another and little realized that their gifts and speeches would have small impact on the habits of years. During their absence, Clark learned, the Hidatsas and the Mandans had joined forces against the Arikaras, killing at least two of them, and the Assiniboins had gone to war against both the Hidatsas and the Mandans and had also killed two

employees of the North West Company. Yet even as he stood on the banks of the Missouri River and received these dismal tidings of war and bloodshed, Clark deeply hoped that he and his absent friend, once they were reunited, could create a stable and lasting peace on the Great Plains.

After Lewis had said goodbye to Clark, the Nez Percés guided him down the Bitterroot River toward the present-day city of Missoula, Montana. That afternoon when they made camp, the mosquitoes were thick and so tormented the horses that Lewis thought they might stampede. To prevent this, he had the men kindle large fires and tether the animals in the smoke. This was the last camp that the Nez Percés and the white men were to share. Fearful of their enemies to the east, the Indians refused to go any farther, but they willingly and accurately described the route to the Missouri. The river that they were now on would lead the Americans to the Big Blackfoot River, which in turn would take them to the Continental Divide. There they would have a choice of two passes, those now known as Cadotte's and Lewis and Clark's. Their recommendation was to take the one that now bears the explorers' names. Once on the Great Plains, the Sun River would lead them to the Falls of the Missouri.

By following these directions, Lewis reached his old camp opposite White Bear Island, where the grizzlies had caused so much trouble the year before. The men dug up the caches and found that the wagon wheels were still in good condition, but to Lewis's deep regret, many of his plant specimens had been destroyed.

The danger from the grizzly bears remained as great as it had been before. Without seeing it, one soldier rode within ten feet of a grizzly hidden in some brush. The scent frightened his horse, which, suddenly shying, threw him in front of the bear. Powerful and enormous, the monster rose on its hindlegs before attacking. The moment's delay caused by this maneuver gave the soldier time to pick himself up; and grabbing his gun by the barrel, he clubbed the grizzly so hard that he broke the gun in two. Surprised and slightly stunned by this attack, the bear dropped to the ground and began to scratch its head. In a flash the soldier raced to a nearby willow tree and climbed it. The bear, however, waited at the foot of the willow until late in the evening. Then at last it left, and the man came down, captured his horse, which had wandered two miles away, and returned to camp.

Although not as dangerous as the bears, the mosquitoes continued to be a problem. Lewis's dog howled with the torture of their bites, and they were so numerous that the men frequently sucked them into their throats when they breathed. Notwithstanding such hardships as well as the loss of seven of his seventeen horses, which had been stolen by Indians a few days earlier, Lewis was determined to carry out his and Clark's original plan of exploring the Marias River and discovering conclusively whether or not it provided the United States entry to the Canadian fur country.

After making two drawings of the falls—the water was much lower than it had been the year previous, but they still presented a magnificent sight—Lewis started off toward the Marias River with George Drouillard, the interpreter, and two enlisted men, Joseph and Reuben Fields. The plains over which they rode did not contain a single tree or bush and were broken only by oceanlike swells that gave the earth's surface a semblance of motion. The absence of any cover was a source of uneasiness, for by all reports the Indians in this area were skilled horse thieves and natural warriors. So Lewis was relieved when they located a woods on the far side of the Teton River and, finding no Indian signs nearby, bedded down for the night where they could not be easily seen.

The following day they reached the Marias but at a point higher than that to which Lewis had ascended the year before. Fearful that he might have missed a major branch leading to the northland, Lewis dispatched two men downstream while he made an observation of the sun and noted down the data.

When the men returned with a report that no such branch existed, Lewis started upstream, traveling wherever the terrain permitted along the northern bank so that a tributary from that direction would not escape his attention. From the general slope of the land, he wrongly deduced that some of its drainage must flow into Canada's Saskatchewan River; and so he was still hopeful of finding an important northern tributary when he came to the Forks of the Marias and took the one that leads in the direction of the present-day city of Cut Bank, Montana. He was quickly disillusioned, however, when he followed the course of Cut Bank Creek, a tributary of the Marias, and could see where it descended from the mountains far short of the fifty degrees of latitude that he had hoped it would reach.

For several days he remained in camp trying to ascertain his exact position, but cloudy weather interfered with the necessary sightings of the sun, and for some inexplicable reason his chronometer temporarily stopped. Therefore he could never find out his longitude, and when he prepared for the trip back to the Missouri, he bitterly called the spot where he had stayed Camp Disappointment.

On the return trip Lewis decided to take a more direct route back to the Missouri by leaving Cut Bank Creek and picking up some of the more southern tributaries of the Marias. On July 26 he was following one of these downstream. While George Drouillard, the interpreter, rode down the river valley to hunt, Lewis and Joseph and Reuben Fields climbed the hills that rose above it. Suddenly Lewis noticed ahead about thirty horses standing together. Taking out his spyglass, he examined them more closely and saw that almost half of the horses were saddled. On a rise above them, several Indians had gathered and were looking down into the river valley, probably at Drouillard.

This was precisely the type of encounter Lewis had wanted to avoid, for he and his men were badly outnumbered. Yet if they turned and fled, the Indians could easily overtake them, since their horses were in better condition. Furthermore, flight would have meant abandoning Drouillard, a step Lewis had no intention of taking.

Since the only alternative was to appear friendly and self-confident, Lewis unfurled a flag that he carried for ceremonial occasions and, followed by his two men, rode toward the Indians. At first the Indians' attention was so concentrated on Drouillard that they did not notice Lewis; but when they did, they appeared greatly disconcerted and some of them rushed to round up their horses, which they drove within gunshot of the rise, where they could protect them against a possible raid. Then one of the Indians rode out to meet Lewis, but in spite of Lewis's gestures of friendship, he would not come close and suddenly wheeled his horse and dashed back to his friends. Then the whole band rode down from the rise together. Although there were only eight of them, Lewis, judging by the number of horses, suspected there might be many more hidden nearby.

Rather than lose his carefully collected papers and his instruments, Lewis was prepared to fight and told Joseph and Reuben Fields to be ready for a battle. But when the Indians had come within a hundred yards, one of them advanced alone while the others remained where they were. Telling the Fields brothers to stay still, Lewis went forward and shook the Indian's hand. He then continued on and greeted the other seven in a similar fashion. In response the leader of the band greeted the two Fieldses.

An uneasy armistice having been established, the Indians expressed a desire to smoke with Lewis. But the safety of Drouillard, who was alone in the river valley and probably unaware of the Indians' presence, was uppermost in Lewis's mind. So he told the Indians that Drouillard had the pipe and they must find him first. When a young warrior volunteered to help Reuben Fields search for the interpreter, Lewis was relieved, and he was even more so when they returned with him.

The Indians identified themselves as Piegans, a division of the war-loving Blackfeet. To seal the peace he was apparently making with them, Lewis gave the three leaders an American flag, a medal, and a handkerchief and then proposed that they camp together near the river, a proposal they accepted. Since no other Indians had appeared, he now felt certain he was dealing with only eight and thus the odds against him were less than he had originally feared.

The Indians erected a large semicircular tent made of buffalo skins and asked the white men to share it. Drouillard and Lewis accepted, but the two Fields brothers preferred to sleep near the fire outside. With the help of Drouillard, who was adept at sign language, Lewis had a long talk with the Piegans, who told him they were part of a larger band that was out hunting. They also said it was an easy six-day journey to the British trading post on the Saskatchewan, where they sold all their furs.

Lewis, in turn, described his efforts to make peace among the Indian tribes and invited the Piegans to come with him to the mouth of the Marias River and meet the rest of his party. In the future, he told them, they might want to trade with the Americans. Since the Indians liked tobacco, Lewis smoked with them until late that night, hoping both to keep them in a friendly mood and to tire them out. As soon as the last of them had fallen asleep, he woke Reuben Fields and ordered him to stand watch. If any of the Indians left the tent—which would probably signify they intended to steal the horses—he was to arouse Lewis.

The night wore on, and the only sounds were those made by some man rolling over in his bedding or by a nocturnal animal or bird. After he had done his share of sentry duty, Reuben awakened his brother, Joseph, and fell asleep himself. Gradually the night noises gave way to those of daytime, and the eastern sky felt the first bright touch of dawn. Lewis, Drouillard, and Reuben Fields slumbered on, oblivious to the brightening world around them. Joseph Fields, still on watch, remained near the fire, his gun on the ground behind him close to the sleeping form of his brother.

The Indians were the first to stir. In friendly fashion they gathered around the fire that Joseph Fields had been feeding during the early hours of the morning. The peace made the night before and confirmed by clouds of tobacco smoke lay quietly over the camp.

Then, like a cloudburst, the Indians shattered it. The one to whom Lewis had given the medal the day before slipped behind Joseph Fields, snatched up his gun and that of his brother, and ran off with them, while two other Indians grabbed the guns belonging to Lewis and Drouillard.

Joseph Fields shouted to his brother, who leaped from his bedding, and the two men pursued the fleeing thief. Within a short distance they overtook him and began struggling to regain their weapons. During the fight Reuben's knife blade glistened in the air and then turned red with blood as he plunged it deep into the Indian's body. The man ran a few paces and fell dead. Again in possession of their guns, the two brothers raced back to camp.

Drouillard opened his eyes in time to see the Indian who was taking his gun. Cursing loudly he leaped to his feet and seized the thief. The noise of their struggle awakened Lewis, who instinctively reached for his own gun. Finding it gone, he drew his pistol from its holster and ran after the Indian who had taken it. He had caught up with him and was threatening him with his pistol when the Fields brothers returned. They wanted to shoot the Piegan, but Lewis refused to let them, since the Indian appeared ready to release the gun. Seeing himself surrounded now by three angry, armed white men, he did so, insolently dropping it on the ground and slowly walking away. By then Drouillard had recovered his gun also; and still furious he, too, wanted blood. But because the Indian showed no sign of resistance, Lewis forbade his death.

Since the Americans were now awake and had their guns, they were safe from attack; but their horses, which had grazed with the Indians' during the night, remained unprotected. Six of the Piegans started to drive the main part of the herd—the Americans' horses included—up the river. Lewis shouted to his men to shoot if gunfire was needed to stop them; and he himself raced after two other Indians—one was the man who had tried to steal his gun—who were driving off some other horses that had become separated from the rest of the herd.

He moved so quickly that the Indians did not have time to round up twelve of their own animals, which they therefore left behind. Panting and almost completely out of breath from running, he saw the Indians drive the horses into a niche in the river bluffs. There was one American horse among them, and he called out to the two Indians to release it, or he would shoot.

Instead of doing what he asked, one of the Indians jumped behind a rock and spoke to the other, who stopped and turned around. Lewis pulled his trigger, the gun went off, and the bullet entered the Indian's stomach. The man fell to his knees and rested on his right elbow. Partly raising himself, he fired at Lewis, who felt the wind of the bullet as it whistled harmlessly close to his head. As he had not had time to pick up his pouch, he could not reload, so he returned slowly toward the camp, catching his breath as he went.

Having heard the exchange of shots, Drouillard left the Fields brothers and came back to see if Lewis needed help. Lewis, still panting, told Drouillard to call to the Fields brothers to return. With the twelve Indian horses they had already captured, they had more than enough. But the soldiers were too far away to hear him.

There was no time to lose. The night before, Lewis had told the Piegans that his destination was the mouth of the Marias River, so they knew exactly where he was going. If they should get reinforcements from the larger hunting band they had mentioned, they might cut him off. So he and Drouillard did not wait for the Fields brothers before starting to gather the horses and getting ready to leave.

When the two soldiers rejoined Lewis and Drouillard, they brought with them four American horses they had recovered. The Indians had therefore lost more horses through their treachery than they had won, and they had also left their other belongings behind. Lewis threw several bows, arrows, and shields onto the fire, although he kept a gun he found. (It was one of two that the band had possessed.) He also retrieved the American flag he had given them such a short time before. But he left the medal around the neck of the dead Piegan as a reminder not to attack Americans.

As the fire's flames licked at the Indians' weapons, the four Americans jumped on their horses and, herding the loose stock, began their race to the mouth of the Marias River. Their own safety was not their only concern; they were also afraid the Indians might get there before them and ambush the men who were coming down from the falls. Pushing their horses as hard as they could, they rode for approximately sixty miles before halting to rest for an hour and a half. Fortunately the plains were smooth and flat, and recent rains had filled the otherwise dry water holes, making the fast trip somewhat easier. After their brief stop, they remounted and took off again. By dark they

had covered approximately seventeen more miles and halted again, this time for about two hours, during which they shot a buffalo and took a small quantity of its meat.

By two o'clock in the morning Lewis figured they had come an additional twenty miles and it was safe to stop again. Gladly the men unsaddled their horses, set their mounts free to graze, and lay down on the ground. In the short time since daybreak, they had fought the Indians and ridden nearly a hundred miles. Sleep came easily to them.

Lewis awoke at dawn the following morning. Every muscle in his body ached from the previous day's ride, and he could barely stand up. When he roused the other three men, they, too, were stiff and sore, but they could afford no more time for resting. Some wanted to go directly to the Missouri, cross it, and travel down the other side, putting the river between themselves and the Piegans. Lewis insisted this would cause too great a delay. Their obligation to the men descending from the falls demanded that they reach the mouth of the Marias River as quickly as possible to prevent an ambush.

They had ridden about twelve miles more and were nearing the Missouri when they heard a sound that resembled a gunshot, but it was too far off for them to be certain. About eight miles farther on, they heard the sound repeated several times. Unmistakably it was gunfire. Racing to the river, they found the men they had left at the falls and the contingent Clark had sent to help with the portage. After a joyous reunion, the Americans continued down the river together. In spite of the disappointment of finding that water had destroyed the contents of another of their caches and in spite of the rains that kept drenching them, they moved quickly and easily without seeing the Piegans again.

On August 7, they reached the mouth of the Yellowstone, where they had expected to meet Clark. But he had already gone; and although Clark's stake was still standing, only a fragment of his note remained. Sergeant Pryor had come down the Yellowstone separately by bullboat and, thinking that Lewis had already passed by, had taken the note with him. The remnants of another note remained attached to a pair of elkhorns; and from this Lewis learned that the mosquitoes had been bad and the game scarce, but he received the mistaken impression that Clark was camped only a few miles away. Consequently, he set out again that same afternoon, thinking he would overtake his friend before nightfall. But in this hope he was, of course, disappointed.

After traveling a few more days, Lewis conclud-

At the junction of the Missouri and Yellowstone rivers, Lewis and Clark hoped to rendezvous on their return journey. Mosquitoes drove Clark away before his friend's arrival. The site later became the location of an important fur trading post. The flatness of the land has permitted the rivers to shift their channels. *Alexander B. Adams*

Although they were relative newcomers to the Great Plains, the Sioux soon became a dominant tribe. In the early days of the fur trade, they often demanded tribute from the white men going up the Missouri. They later became one of the last tribes to resist the Americans. Normally the Sioux could gather in large villages only for short periods because of the lack of forage and game. *National Archives*

ed that he might not overtake Clark and prepared to make the trip back to the Mandan villages alone. As they approached the spot that Lewis believed was the Missouri's most northern point, he decided to determine its longitude. In order to get a noonday observation of the sun without having to stay over until twelve o'clock the following morning, he pushed ahead of the others, some of whom were hunting. Unfortunately he arrived twenty minutes after the hour. Therefore instead of taking out his sextant while he waited for the others, he crossed the river and with Peter Cruzatte hunted some elk they had seen on a willow-covered sandbar.

Both fired, and Lewis killed an elk, while Cruzatte wounded another. They then reloaded, and each began a separate search for game in the willow thicket. Lewis was just about to fire again when he heard a gun go off and felt the impact of a bullet that struck him in the rear, entering his left thigh, missing the bones, emerging on the other side, and tearing a gash across the back of his right thigh.

As he was wearing brown leather clothing and Cruzatte had only one eye, he immediately assumed that Cruzatte had mistaken him for an elk. He called out as loudly as he could, but there was no answer. Peering in the direction from which the shot had come, he looked in vain for Cruzatte and kept on shouting. Since he was certain the gun had been fired not more than forty yards away, he was also sure that the shooter was within range of his voice. Cruzatte's failure to reply left only one reasonable possibility: the person who had fired the shot must be an Indian. Not knowing how many Indians there might be, he ran back to the river for help, calling a warning to Cruzatte as he went.

The men waiting in the pirogue leaped to their arms at the sound of his voice and joined him in an attempt to rescue Cruzatte from the Indians in the thicket. But after a hundred paces Lewis's wound became so painful he could not continue walking. Telling his men to retreat in good order should they find themselves outnumbered, he limped back to the pirogue and prepared to defend both it and himself.

In about twenty minutes the men reappeared, having found Cruzatte unharmed but seeing no trace of any Indians. Cruzatte claimed he had only shot an elk and denied hearing Lewis call to him. But the ball that Lewis recovered from his britches matched those used by Cruzatte. At first Lewis had dark thoughts that Cruzatte might have shot him on purpose, revenging himself for some imagined injustice Lewis had committed. But then his better sense took hold, and he realized the soldier was so chagrined he could not bring himself to admit what he had done.

Although the wound was painful and bloody, the bullet had not touched any bones or cut an artery. With the help of one of the sergeants, Lewis dressed it as well as he could and sent men to recover the elk. Since the position of his wound would make it extremely painful to take the observation he wanted, he decided not to stay over until the next noon.

The day, however, was not entirely marked by misfortune, for about four o'clock they passed the campsite that Clark had left only that morning. By then Pryor had overtaken Clark and told him about his having picked up the note at the Yellowstone, so Clark had written another, explaining what had happened and where he was. The following day Lewis met Dickson and Hancock and learned they had seen Clark only a short time before, and at one o'clock he finally overtook his friend. The two were overjoyed to see each other and know that the dangerous period of separation was safely over. Lewis had an additional, personal reason for pleasure; Clark could do all the journal-keeping. Lewis's wound made it difficult for him to sit down and write.

The swift current of the Missouri—it carried them as far as eighty-six miles in a single day—quickly brought them to the Indian villages of the Upper Missouri, which they had left more than a year before and where they had lived during the winter months of 1804–1805. Here was a site they knew well and faces that they recognized, but time had not stood still during their absence, and much of what had happened was not to the captains' liking.

Naïvely proud of their country and innocently unaware of its weakness in a warring world—British frigates stopped its vessels with impunity, and British gangs routinely impressed its citizens—the captains believed its wishes would be respected even on the distant frontier. But now they confirmed at firsthand what Dickson and Hancock had told Clark. As soon as the explorers had left for the Shoshones, fighting had broken out between the Arikaras and Sioux, on the one hand, and the villages on the other (the villages claimed they had been attacked first), and the Mandans had fought with the Pawnees. To the captains' bitter disappointment, their speeches and distribution of flags and medals had changed nothing.

In his letter of instructions Jefferson had told Lewis to persuade some of the Indian chiefs to come to Washington. So far this had been one of the least successful aspects of the expedition. Gravelines had taken an Arikara chief on the long journey, but he was the only one to have accepted the government's invitation. Now Lewis and Clark tried to enlist the interest of the Hidatsas in making the trip, but for all their outward expressions of friendship, this tribe actually looked on the Americans with contempt and had given the flags and other tokens they had received to those whom they disliked, considering them tokens of evil. Rather than openly offend Lewis and Clark by flatly refusing to go, they pleaded their fear of passing through the territory of the Sioux.

With the Mandans, Lewis and Clark were more successful. Although their first efforts came to nothing, the fur trader René Jessaume agreed to persuade one of their chiefs to go to Washington in return for passage for himself, his wife, and his child to St. Louis. Whatever argument he used was successful, and one chief agreed to accompany them down the river.

Its principal objective—the trek to the Pacific—now accomplished, the expedition began breaking up. Charbonneau's services were no longer required, so they paid him off. Clark, who had grown fond of the interpreter's young son, offered to take the family to St. Louis and perhaps act as their sponsor; but Charbonneau knew enough to refuse. He had lived too long among the Indians to resume the ways of his own kind.

Dickson and Hancock, who had returned to the villages, proposed taking the enlisted man John Colter into partnership. Colter, who had been stalked by the grizzly at White Bear Island, had acquitted himself well during the journey, and Lewis and Clark agreed to release him provided nobody else asked for the same privilege. With the best wishes of the members of the expedition, Colter received his discharge from the United States Army and entered on a career as a fur trapper.

As they came nearer and nearer to St. Louis, many of the white men they met were surprised to see them, for it was generally accepted that after so long a time they had all been lost, especially since no one had returned from the Falls of the Missouri as they had originally planned. But young and relatively inexperienced as they were, the two captains had carried out Jefferson's instructions; and at noon on September 23, 1806, they permitted their men to fire a salute to St. Louis, which lay just before them.

The arrival of Lewis and Clark was a cause for rejoicing among their friends, but their mission, at least for the time being, had left the Great Plains

materially unchanged. The pattern of the Indians' relations among themselves and with the white men was little affected. The old alliances held firm, as did the old enmities. Except among the Mandans, the stature of the United States had not been much improved. The meager gifts brought by the two captains were no better, and perhaps even a little worse, than those the Indians had come to expect from traders who wished to curry their favor; and the official nature of the presents of flags and medals was outside their understanding.

The bullet and knife that had struck the Piegans, however, were not. The blood that had poured from the wounds of their two tribesmen onto the soil of the Great Plains had been real blood. Overlooking their own responsibility for what had occurred, they remembered the Americans only with hostility.

The fur traders, too, were disinclined to change their habits merely because a small expedition of Americans had passed through the country. When requested, they had submitted their papers for inspection and had solemnly received instructions that they must not compete with the American government by giving out the insignia of another power. But once the Americans had gone, they shrugged their shoulders and continued doing business just as they had before.

Even the scores of specimens and stocks of information that resulted from the captains' journey had little direct influence on the immediate future of the Great Plains. Years were to elapse before the full official account of their travels was drawn ink-wet from the press and thus made available to the public. Even then much of the information from those pages so meticulously kept in rain, snow, and sunshine and treasured against the ravages of water and wind did not become known. For some of it disappeared in the intellectual debris that cluttered the study of the scholar assigned to edit them.

But the emergence of the captains from the mysterious void into which they had disappeared for so long sent a spring breeze blowing across the continent, nourishing the spirit that had been dampened by the nation's humiliations on the high seas.

The achievement did not belong to the captains alone but also to the country that had financed and organized the expedition. No detractors could lessen the sense of accomplishment, and a critic wrote in vain when he told Lewis that Alexander Mackenzie "with a party consisting of about one fourth part of the number under your command, with means which will not bear a comparison with those furnished you, and without the *authority*, the *flag*, or *medal* of his government, crossed the Rocky mountains . . . and for the *first time* penetrated to the Pacific Ocean.'' Such thoughts were summer dew on the prairie grass, quickly evaporated by the pervading warmth that swept the nation.

No one could deprive Americans of their tri-umph or cast a shadow on it. Furthermore, although Lewis and Clark's way had been long, where Americans had once been, Americans could go again. The marks left by the explorers might disappear from the earth's surface in a season, but not the marks they left on the minds of Americans.

Chapter 10

The Traders Follow

. . . it is not to be expected that they [the Indians] . . . should appreciate the character of the whites in general in any other manner than as expressed in the prevailing sentiment on this subject among several nations on the Missouri, to wit: "The white men are like dogs; the more you beat them and plunder them, the more goods they will bring you, and the cheaper they will sell them."

—Meriwether Lewis, unfinished
manuscript, c. 1807

The sun sank at night, spraying the sky with burnished silver and gold, and climbed in the morning, hot and red, over the rim of the plains. As the summer of 1806 faded into autumn, and autumn in turn fell back before the advancing days of early winter, the rising sun lost its heat, the setting one, its brilliance. Contemplating the shortening days, Manuel Lisa must have felt a sense of frustration over the events of the past season. Daring and innovative, he had cracked the closed society of St. Louis, forcing a place for himself as one of its prominent, although not respected, merchants. But, as he had feared, the change of government had reversed his fortune, and the year had seen the Chouteaus and their allies regain their former positions of influence.

Wilkinson, too, was experiencing a reversal of fortune. With Burr's arrest, he turned informer and in flamboyant terms denounced his former associate while portraying himself as the nation's savior. This rash act drew him quickly into the vortex of Burr's trial. But even before the grand jury had completed its hearings, Wilkinson appeared more like a suspect than a star prosecution witness, and the evidence aroused suspicions about his conduct that he could never again quiet.

His patron's imminent downfall was unknown

to Pike when he maneuvered his troops past the Pawnee village in battle formation. But he had been told of Lewis and Clark's safe return by two French traders who had come to purchase horses from the Indians. The news was received with "general joy through our party," Pike noted in his journal. Not only did the men share in the nation's general pleasure over the safe completion of the captains' journey to the Pacific Coast, they also felt that if others had succeeded, they could, too.

Taking a route over the Great Plains that led them south, they reached the Arkansas River in the vicinity of present-day Larned, Kansas. As he started upstream, Pike came upon a large herd of wild horses. These animals, running loose and belonging to no man, either red or white, were free for the taking. So he ordered his best shots to crease one or two by stunning them with a bullet so they could be captured without permanently damaging them. But this required better marksmanship than any of his men possessed.

Next he chose six of his best riders and gave each one a rope noose to drop over the neck of a wild horse. The results were ludicrous. The men knew nothing about throwing a rope, so they had to get alongside their quarry and close enough to hand the rope over its head. The wild horses, unencumbered by saddles or riders, were far too quick. Tossing their manes and dodging this way and that, they easily eluded the soldiers, whose own mounts began sweating from the futile chase. Pike finally acknowledged to himself that the riches of the country were not as easy to gather as he had at first thought, and the faint echo of laughter pealing down the centuries might have been Zaldívar's, as his ghost recalled his Spanish soldiers' attempts to capture buffaloes.

The amount of game in the country was impressive—enormous herds of deer, elk, and buffaloes. (One herd of buffaloes stretched out across the plains as far as the men could see.) Although meat was plentiful, as the expedition moved closer and closer to the mountains, it entered deeper into the rain shadow cast by their summits. As a result, the rainfall was less, the grass became sparse, and the horses, weak. The men cut branches from the cottonwoods that grew along the river to provide the animals with browse, but this was not enough to keep them strong. Several had to be left behind, crippling the expedition. Meanwhile winter had already threatened the men with the first of the season's snows.

On November 15, 1806, Pike was ahead with Dr. John H. Robinson, a physician who was accompanying the expedition as a volunteer. At two o'clock that afternoon he thought he "could distinguish a mountain to our right, which appeared like a small blue cloud," as he remarked in his journal. Taking out his spyglass, he was even more certain that he was within visual range of the Rocky Mountains; but fearing to arouse false hopes among his men, he told no one except Dr. Robinson about his discovery.

In half an hour, however, there was no further need for secrecy. The mountains stood out clearly against the sky, their snow-covered flanks glistening in the sun. At the sight the men, thinking they were nearing the end of one phase of their journey, gave three cheers for the "Mexican mountains." Unaware that the dry air of the Great Plains greatly extends visibility, making distant objects seem close to the uninitiated, Pike believed he was much nearer to them than he actually was, for in his journal he marked their resemblance to the much lower Alleghenies. During the following days, his error became apparent to him, for he had to travel many more miles before he reached their foothills, which rise abruptly from the flat plains.

A few days later the expedition reached the site of the present-day city of Pueblo, Colorado, where they constructed a breastwork to serve as a headquarters for the main body of the party, while Pike,

Dr. Robinson, and two enlisted men explored the mountains in the direction of the peak that today bears his name. Once again the excellent visibility caused by the dry air distorted his estimate of the distance, and instead of reaching the base of the mountains in a short day's march, he found it took him two long ones.

Looking at the slope that now finally stood directly in front of them, Pike was again misled by the visibility. Instead of reaching the summit and returning to the base that night, as he had planned, the setting sun found them only partway up, and they were forced to spend the night in a cave without any blankets, food, or water.

They awoke in the morning, hungry as well as lame from lying on rocks all night, but the view made up for their hardships. "The unbounded prairie," Pike wrote in his journal, "was overhung with clouds, which appeared like the ocean in a storm; wave piled on wave and foaming, whilst the sky was perfectly clear where we were."

An hour's climb brought them to the summit, but when they gazed out at Grand Peak, as he named the mountain that is now known as Pikes Peak, they realized it was much higher than the one on which they were standing and that they were separated from it by a large valley.

Wilkinson had not given Pike time to prepare properly for the expedition, so he had brought only cotton clothing for himself and his men. This deficiency in equipment made itself terribly apparent as he and the others stood waist deep in snow looking at Pikes Peak. The hungry, shivering men agreed they could go no farther. Besides, from what he could see of the mountain, Pike thought it unclimbable even if they could reach its base.

Rejoining the main body of men at the breastwork, they once more started up the Arkansas River. Cold weather and a new snowstorm added to the difficulties of travel. The horses were in poor condition, underfed and covered with sores. The men, lightly clad, suffered from the cold. Three froze their feet, one while looking for a horse that had escaped, the others while fording a river. After considerable hardship the expedition finally reached the vicinity of present-day Cañon, Colorado, where the Arkansas emerges from the mountains through the Royal Gorge.

Pike camped there and sent out scouting parties in an effort to determine which of several streams was the Arkansas. The unlucky star that had misled him when he was looking for the source of the Mississippi again rose high in the sky. He chose a tributary instead of the main river and, finding that it soon dwindled to a little stream, erroneously assumed that he had located the Arkansas's headwaters.

His next objective was to discover the origin of the Red River of the South, which cuts across the face of the Texas Panhandle and forms the boundary between present-day Oklahoma and Texas. To accomplish this, he should have headed south and slightly east, but apparent logic led him astray. He had looked for and found traces of the trail left by the Spanish soldiers under Malgares. Since Malgares was known to have come from Santa Fé and to be returning there, Pike correctly assumed that his trail would provide a route through the mountains. But at this point he mistook an Indian trail for the one followed by the Spaniards and started north.

Struggling through the mountains, he finally came to a large river, but to his surprise it flowed northeast. Obviously it was not the Red River for which he had been searching, and he correctly surmised that it must be part of the Platte, whose southern fork flows many miles through the Rockies and emerges onto the plains near today's Denver, Colorado.

The days that followed took on a nightmare quality. The men suffered terribly from the cold, the horses were failing, and many of the guns on which they depended for both protection and food burst or were otherwise damaged. Game was scarce, and they often marched on meager rations if they had any rations at all. At night some of the men no longer had blankets with which to cover themselves, since they had had to cut them up to make crude replacements for their worn-out shoes.

When the discovery of the Platte made them realize their original error, they had changed direction southward and at last came upon a river they were certain was the Red. Although still cold and hungry, they gained renewed spirit from this discovery. Overcoming the obstacles placed in their way by nature—snow, ice, boulders, freezing temperatures, and lack of game—they descended the river toward the plains, confident that they had found the Red and could fulfill their mission by following it to the east and home.

January 5, 1807, was Pike's twenty-eighth birthday. It was not a happy day for him. In the morning he wounded several deer but was surprised to find he had killed none of them. Examining his gun, he saw that it was bent. Probably it had struck some ice or a rock during one of his many falls. Shortly after that he stumbled again, and this time the gun broke at the breach. He felt the despair that only a hunter can feel when his favorite firearm has failed him; and in this case, he could neither repair nor replace it. But worse was still to come. At ten o'clock he reached a summit that gave him a view of the plains below.

Only a short time before, when he had climbed toward the mountain he called Grand Peak, he had marveled at the sight of the plains rolling off into the distance. The clouds, he had written in his exultation, had "appeared like the ocean in a storm, wave piled on wave and foaming. . . ." This time the sight made his spirits fall into the blackest of abysses and what remained of poetry in his soul sicken. From where he stood, he could clearly see the river they were following leave the mountains and enter the plains. He recognized it immediately; it was the Arkansas again.

For almost a month they had been traveling through the mountains and enduring the hardships imposed by the weather and the terrain, and now after all that suffering they were back at the point from which they had started. As he closed his journal entry, Pike commented on his birthday and added, "most fervently did I hope never to pass another so miserably."

Pike pondered his next step. His horses were so worn-out they were useless in their present condition; and as he now knew, winter in the Rocky Mountains was a deadly adversary. Yet he was determined to continue his search.

Before going on, he built a small fortification at his campsite in the vicinity of modern Cañon, Colorado, to protect the two men he planned to leave behind and who would serve as guards for the horses and part of the luggage. He himself would lead the others through the mountains; and when he found a suitable trail, he would send back for them, hoping that by that time both horses and men would be restored.

The horrors of the last months were magnified in the next weeks. The mountains, which at their first sighting had roused the men into giving three cheers, became a cruel labyrinth of narrow valleys, small passes, and streambeds that led them a distance and then mockingly dwindled into nothing. When the sun was out, the slopes glared blinding white, hateful and disdaining of the men's puny efforts to free themselves of their grip. When the sun disappeared, they turned into amorphous monsters, looming upward and disappearing in the gray nothing.

Game was again scarce; and once when they had marched four days without food, Pike became so weak and dizzy he wondered whether he could go on. He was out hunting, and as he looked at the blank waste around him that contained no sign of

Many Americans believed that peace would come when the Indians finally comprehended the size and might of the United States. Consequently they encouraged sending Indian delegations to Washington. Here a group of Indians rests on the White House lawn. *National Archives*

The Pawnees, shown here in front of one of their lodges, were at first hostile to the Americans but later became their allies. The Pawnee scouts fought valiantly with the army against their Indian enemies, including the Sioux. *National Archives*

game, dread seized him at the prospect of again returning to camp empty-handed and seeing the disappointment in the hungry, suffering eyes of his men. Rather than that, he thought, he might lie down in the woods alone and let the snow engulf him and its cold put an end to his own misery. Fortunately at that moment he saw game. His reactions quickened, he threw off his despairing lethargy, and a successful hunt ended his thoughts of self-destruction.

But the fresh supply of meat only temporarily relieved the desperate condition of the expedition. Two of the men could walk only with the aid of staffs and were unable to carry their packs; their loads had to be distributed among the others. Two others could not walk at all on their badly frozen feet. To carry them through the mountains was impossible, so sadly Pike gave them some ammunition and most of the expedition's remaining meat and left them with the desperate promise that he would return to their rescue.

The cold remained intense, and the game again vanished. Pike shared every discomfort with his men except the terror of his doubts. His clothes were no warmer, his load was no lighter, and he assumed additional duties that he did not ask of them. He made himself the expedition's principal hunter, walking the extra miles that this task imposed, and busied himself at every camp with the many jobs that needed doing. His example helped keep up the spirits of the others, who followed him for mile after mile. But finally one man lost hope. Pike overheard him complaining bitterly in a way that threatened to spread disaffection throughout the entire group. Discipline was the thread that held the expedition together, and its disintegration could be more disastrous than a blizzard. Looking at his tired, famished men, Pike thought this was no time for harsh words and wisely held his tongue. But shortly after, when they had found game again and the men's stomachs were filled with meat, he severely reprimanded the offender in front of the others, reminding him that a court-martial could sentence him to death for his mutinous remarks. This warning took effect, and he never again had to threaten his men in order to maintain his authority.

By dint of superhuman perseverance he brought his expedition to the San Luís Valley of Colorado and the banks of the Río Grande. He thought he had found the Red River and started downstream. Below today's city of Alamosa, Colorado, he came to the mouth of the Conejos River, and five miles up it, he built another fortification to use as a base.

Although he later denied knowing it, Pike was well inside the Spanish border. He and Robinson now agreed that the doctor should go to Santa Fé under the pretext of collecting a debt that had been turned over to Pike before leaving for the West. "Our views," he wrote in his journal, "were to gain a knowledge of the country, the prospect of trade, force, &c. . . ." By treaty American citizens had the right to seek the recovery of debts, so Robinson might escape being arrested as a spy.

At the same time, Pike sent men back for those he had been forced to leave behind in various places. Two of them, when they were discovered, were still unable to walk and sent Pike pieces of bone taken from their frozen feet along with their prayers that he not allow them to perish "far from the civilized world." Another detachment returned to the Arkansas River to bring up the men who had remained there with the horses.

While he waited to regroup his small force, time was working against him, and the Spanish inevitably discovered his whereabouts. To the troops that came out to escort him to Santa Fé, he expressed great surprise on hearing that he was camped beside a tributary of the Río Grande, not the Red River, and claimed he had merely intended to follow the Red River back to Natchitoches.

Notwithstanding these professions of innocence, he was interrogated at Santa Fé and then escorted to Chihuahua for further questioning by higher authorities. (The commander of his escort was Malgares, whose trail he had attempted to follow; the two men became good friends.) Convinced that the American government had had ulterior motives in sending Pike to trespass in their territory but not wishing to exacerbate relations with the United States, Spain lodged a strongly worded protest against Pike's infringement of its borders, but it agreed to return him and those of his men who were still with him. (Others later straggled back by themselves; some never saw their native country again.)

On July 1, 1807, Pike reached Natchitoches and was safe again on American soil. He had been promoted to captain during his absence, but he did not receive the glorious welcome that he might have expected. Burr's trial had damaged Wilkinson's reputation by revealing some of his intrigues. Since Pike's close association with the general was well known, many people thought that he, too, had been involved in the conspiracy. Therefore he found himself under attack from a number of quarters, a sad reception for one who had suffered such hardships for so long.

He still had with him, however, many maps,

navigational observations, and other information. Concerning much of the Great Plains, he reported that "here a barren soil, parched and dried up for eight months in the year, presents neither moisture nor nutrition sufficient, to nourish the timber. These vast plains of the western hemisphere, may become in time equally celebrated as the sandy deserts of Africa . . ."

In addition, although forbidden to do so by the Spanish authorities, he had secretly kept notes of all that he had seen and learned while traveling through their lands. He might be regarded by some as a potential traitor through his nebulous relationship with Wilkinson's conspiracy, but he gave his nation a voluminous store of geographical information about its own territory and that of its neighbor and a stirring example of heroism and perseverance in the face of unending obstacles.

Commodore James Barron was in command of the United States frigate *Chesapeake* when it left Norfolk Roads on June 22, 1807, and headed down Chesapeake Bay toward the open ocean. Although relations between the United States and Great Britain were strained, the two nations were at peace, and therefore Barron saw nothing unusual in the approach of the British frigate *Leopard,* which hoisted the signal that meant "dispatches." But when the *Leopard*'s boarding party climbed onto the deck, it had with it no mail, only an order from the admiral commanding the British squadron to search the *Chesapeake* for deserters from the Royal Navy.

The British had been gravely concerned by the attrition caused by their seamen jumping ship and were particularly anxious to capture one named Jenkin Ratford, who was reputed to be a ringleader in helping others. Having received information that he might be on board the *Chesapeake,* the British government had protested to the United States, but the Navy Department could not discover the man on its rolls. Trusting their own information more than the Americans' denials, the British had decided to make a search.

Regardless of any provocations they might have suffered—and there was reason to believe that Americans encouraged the desertions and also supplied false citizenship papers on occasion—the British action was both arrogant and without basis in international law. Quite properly Barron refused to permit the search, and the boarding party left.

As soon as the British reached the safety of their own vessel, the *Leopard* fired a broadside at the *Chesapeake*. The salvo caught Barron unprepared, for having just refitted, his deck was still in disor-

der, many of his guns not even mounted. The *Leopard* fired two more broadsides, to which Barron could reply with only a single shot. Added to the confusion were the piles of fallen rigging cut loose by the broadside, and some twenty Americans were already dead or wounded. Rather than let the slaughter continue, Barron lowered his flag.

The British came on board again, located Ratford, seized three Americans who had previously been pressed into the British navy, and with a slight show of decency refused to accept Barron's sword, which he offered them in surrender.

Few greater insults could have been hurled at the American public. The brief action had not taken place in British waters but only about ten miles off the Virginia coast. The *Chesapeake* was not a merchant ship owned by private interests, but an American frigate. Yet there was little the American government could do in retaliation.

Two days after the *Leopard*'s guns had humiliated the American navy, the grand jury filed back into the House of Delegates in Virginia's capitol. (The courthouse had proved too small for the large number of people attending.) The foreman handed a document to the clerk of the court; it contained the indictment of Aaron Burr for treason. The prisoner was quickly arraigned and pleaded innocent, and the trial was set for August 3.

In the short space of two days the republic had suffered two blows so severe that many older nations might not have survived them: the surrender of a major naval vessel at a time when the country was not at war, and the indictment for treason of its former Vice President. Both events threatened the republic's very foundations, for they made it appear that the United States was so weak it might easily succumb to the many predatory nations ringed around it, all of them anxious—or at least willing—to see the new nation restricted or divided. But they could take no satisfaction in the Americans' reaction.

The *Leopard*'s attack caused a wave of anger to sweep over every part of the country. North, South, East, and West had found a common cause that submerged their sectional differences. The Burr indictment, too, proved that there was an underlying strength that tied the nation together. Only a few years ago, the Louisiana Purchase had integrated the Mississippi River into the United States, and the threat that the great waterway might be closed to commerce no longer offered the Westerners a temptation to secede. Few serious thinkers believed that, even if he had wanted to, Burr and his handful of followers possessed the power to separate the West from the rest of the country.

Over the land hung an atmosphere of growing self-confidence. This fresh spirit was justified not so much by what was taking place along the perimeters of the nation, but by what was happening in the interior. Robert Fulton, the artist who turned inventor, had almost completed the first practical steamboat, the *Clermont.* Years ago Marquette and Joliet, using their canoeists' skills to travel down the Mississippi, had uncovered the great interior waterway in what would be part of the United States. Ever since then men had been making use of it; and plying the streams were rafts, keelboats, and flatboats, craft that could carry heavier cargoes than the light vessels built by the Indians. But going upstream—except on those rare occasions when sails could be profitably employed—the propulsion power depended on the sweat and brawn of the crew. Fulton was now preparing to change that; and although he was momentarily diverted by a futile effort to interest the American government in his torpedoes as a means of counterbalancing Great Britain's naval strength, he was on the verge of revolutionizing river navigation, thus giving his country an efficient and practical means of interior transportation.

The future was rushing toward America with the speed of a herd of stampeding buffaloes; but Manuel Lisa, the St. Louis fur trader, was not one to wait for its arrival. The return of Lewis and Clark and the reports they gave of the country beyond the Hidatsa villages set his imagination racing, for with brilliant astuteness he foresaw that the day of the small fur traders was coming to an end. Their resources were inadequate to cope with the problems of doing business at a long distance from their bases or to control the Indians. Yet an organization large enough and strong enough to penetrate to the limits of the Louisiana Purchase and beyond would be tapping a rich and virgin area, and the men connected with it might make fortunes.

In his enthusiasm over the prospects that he envisioned, he formed a new partnership with Pierre Menard and William Morrison, both well-known traders in the Illinois country. Since Lisa was the only partner who actually planned to make the trip, the other two employed George Drouillard, the interpreter who had served Lewis and Clark so well, to act as their representative. By April, 1807, Lisa had recruited some forty men, many of them veterans of the Lewis and Clark expedition, and started up the Missouri.

"This trading expedition," as one contemporary of Lisa's remarked, "was very different from a journey of discovery. The difficulties would necessarily be much greater. A party of men well armed and equipped, and under proper submission to their officers, with presents to bestow to the different tribes, and not encumbered with goods and effects, might, with prudence, pass through with much less difficulty. The case is different where the trader has unruly hands to manage, who think themselves perfectly at liberty when once out of the reach of law: without discipline, badly armed, and coming to the nations, not for the purpose of making presents, but of trade."

The truth in this remark was evident even before the expedition left St. Louis. Among Lisa's *engagés,* as the employees who bore the brunt of the heavy labor were known, was a man named Bouché, who had fallen in debt to a St. Louis tavernkeeper. Knowing that he would not otherwise see his money again, the tavernkeeper filed charges against Bouché, detaining him in St. Louis and delaying Lisa's departure until the debt was settled. Lisa, of course, could have let Bouché stay in jail, but to have done so would have cost him the advance wages he had already given his *engagé.* So reluctantly he counted out the amount needed to secure the man's release, entered it against his account, and was ready to begin the upriver journey with his full complement of employees. When Lewis and Clark faced such problems, they could fall back on formal army procedure, hold a court-martial, and mete out sentences ranging from floggings to death. The fur traders, on the other hand, had few legal weapons with which to enforce discipline, although their need was just as great.

The next personnel problem occurred about four weeks later when the expedition had reached the mouth of the Osage River. Another man, Antoine Bissonet, disappeared, an obvious deserter. If too many followed his example and returned to St. Louis, the trip would be a complete failure. So Lisa instructed Drouillard to hunt him down and bring him back dead or alive. Accustomed to army discipline after his long service with Lewis and Clark, Drouillard did not question the propriety of the order and shortly reappeared with Bissonet, whom he had seriously wounded. Since the *engagé* was in no condition to proceed, Lisa sent him back to the nearest town. The wound, however, was severe, and the man died before reaching civilization.

At the mouth of the Platte River, Lisa met John Colter, who had left the Lewis and Clark expedition at the Mandan villages the year before to go trapping and trading. The partnership he had joined was now dissolved, and he was heading back to St. Louis; but Lisa, always alert to seize every opportunity that came his way, persuaded him to join the group, thus adding to his roster one of the men most knowledgeable about the Upper Missouri.

It was fortunate he did, because game was scarce. Even with such expert hunters as Drouillard and Colter, rations were slim; and Bouché, who had already caused trouble with his debt to the St. Louis saloonkeeper, was caught stealing meat from the general supply. Lewis and Clark would have court-martialed the offender, but Lisa could only express his anger and hope that the other men would support him in trying to prevent such stealing.

But discipline and the shortage of food were not the most serious problems facing him on this stretch of the river. The Arikara chief whom Lewis and Clark had sent to Washington had died during the journey; and the tribe, being certain that the Americans had killed him, were angry and hostile. When Lisa approached their village, several hundred warriors lined the bank and by firing their guns indicated exactly where he was to land. Realizing that once he touched shore he could be easily overrun, he made it clear that the Indians were not to approach his boats. His resolute action calmed the crowd, and the women, who were the traders, came to the river's edge with bags of corn and offered to start bartering. But one warrior dashed forward and with his knife split the bags.

A show of weakness would have been an invitation to attack. Lisa, however, ordered his men to take up their arms and aim the swivel guns at the crowd. This sign of determination made the Indians fall back, and one chief stepped forward and offered to smoke with him. The test of wills having been decided in Lisa's favor, the Arikaras let him proceed.

At the Mandan villages he passed out the usual trader's presents and all went well, but the Hidatsas demanded more than he was willing to give. Dealing with the Indians took cool nerves, an acute sense of timing, and sensitivity to their moods. A harsh word or an aggressive move at the wrong moment might prod them into seizing their arms and fighting, but so also might too soft a word or too defensive an action if they read it as a sign of fear or weakness. Somewhere between the two was the proper balance; striking it was the mark of a good trader or negotiator. Lisa knew that additional presents would indicate weakness to the Hidatsas and open up a floodgate of demands. So he remained quietly firm and, without provoking them, convinced them they would get no more if they killed him.

Lisa's next crisis occurred when he reached the land controlled by the Assiniboins. This tribe, too, was determined to exact tribute, and they arrived in such numbers that it seemed to Lisa that the plains were "red with them." He could not afford to get into a battle with such a host, but neither could he afford to let himself be bullied. Swinging his boats in their direction, he came within a hundred yards of the bank. Then all at once he fired his swivel guns and ordered his men to discharge their firearms, not with the intention of killing any Indians, but merely to frighten them with the sudden burst of sound. The effect was just what he desired. Startled by the aggressive, although harmless, display of strength, most of the Indians fled, and Lisa won this test of wills, too.

Behind Lisa on the Missouri River was Nathaniel Pryor, Lewis and Clark's former sergeant who had now been promoted to ensign and given command of a detachment to escort home Shahaka, the Mandan chief whom Lewis and Clark had persuaded to visit Washington. In addition to approximately a dozen soldiers, Pryor was accompanied by Pierre Chouteau, Jr., who was leading a company of traders and trappers up the river. When Pryor reached the Arikaras, that tribe gathered as usual for the purpose of frightening the white men, collecting as many presents as they could, and preventing them from proceeding farther. But Pryor lacked Lisa's skill and was unable to gain an ascendancy over them. Emboldened by the success of their tactics, the Indians became more insulting and more demanding; and soon the war of psychological maneuvering turned into a war of physical conflict. The Arikaras drove Pryor back, killing three of his men and seriously wounding several others, and sent him retreating to St. Louis.

Fortunately Shahaka escaped unhurt. Otherwise the Mandans might have joined the Arikaras in their hatred of the Americans. With the Sioux also unfriendly and the Hidatsas' position uncertain, the Missouri could have been closed to the United States for years to come, and the gains of the Louisiana Purchase and Lewis and Clark's explorations lost during the period.

If that had occurred, Lisa's route home would have been blocked and his expedition probably ruined. Happily for him, he was unaware of this potential threat; he already had enough to concern him as he turned his boats from the Missouri and entered the Yellowstone, which the members of the Lewis and Clark expedition had described as having more plentiful beavers. Selecting a site at the mouth of the Bighorn, he hastily began construction of winter quarters, for it was November and the winds were blowing cold.

In order to do business with the Indians, he first had to let them know he was there, and he assigned this task to Colter, who filled his pack and set off into the wilderness. Strong, self-reliant, and skilled at adapting to both the woods and the plains, he covered many miles during the next months, visiting the Crow Indians, engaging in one fight with the Blackfeet when that tribe attacked some Indians with whom he was traveling, and observing some of the thermal activity that has since made the Yellowstone National Park so famous. Few believed he was telling the truth, and most thought that his descriptions of the wonders he had seen were figments of his imagination and derisively called the area "Colter's Hell." Drouillard, too, being one of the most experienced men Lisa had, went out on a similar mission, going somewhat farther to the south.

The others remained closer to the mouth of the Bighorn, where Lisa had plenty of work for them all to do. Like some of the other farsighted explorers and traders in the past, he realized that the white men could gain no permanency without bases of their own. Therefore he constructed one, which he named Fort Raymond after his son, although he himself usually spelled it "Remon."

Most of the men recognized his leadership, but a few did not take kindly to following his orders. Bouché, the troublemaker, was caught stealing food, refused to put out his traps in the spring, and tried to undermine morale by spreading the rumor that the gunpowder Lisa issued was inferior in quality. Another man, one in whom Lisa had placed particular trust, followed Bouché's example in raiding the common larder and, when Lisa threatened him with a knife, deserted and went to live with the Indians. But in the spring of 1808, as they looked at the piles of pelts that they had trapped or bought and that were ready for shipment to St. Louis, the majority realized they had been wise when they had thrown their lot in with Lisa.

For all the success he had had so far, Lisa nearly lost everything at the last moment because of a misunderstanding with one of his men. A mulatto named Edward Rose, who had been a trader among the Osages, had taken a supply of goods and gone to spend the winter with the Crows. While he was there, he had learned that the Crows—in common with a number of other tribes—most admired those of their people who gave things away and that the prestige of the donor rose in direct proportion to the munificence of his gifts. Caring more for his personal standing than for Lisa's profits, Rose had been extremely openhanded with Lisa's goods and had given them

away instead of trading them for pelts and horses. When Lisa upbraided him for his conduct, Rose did what no member of a military expedition could have done. He started to manhandle Lisa. Fortunately, John Potts, another veteran of Lewis and Clark's expedition, grabbed him, giving Lisa a chance to leap into the boat that was waiting to take him to St. Louis.

Before the boat was out of gunshot distance, Rose broke free of Potts and, still raging with anger, raced to one of the loaded swivel guns, aimed it at the departing boat, and touched it off with his pipe. That a man was walking in front of the gun at the very moment did not deter him. The cannister of bullets passed between the man's legs, leaving him emotionally shocked but otherwise unharmed, and crashed into the boat's cargo box without hurting either Lisa or any of the crew. With the noise of the swivel gun resounding in his ears, Lisa started back to St. Louis. He carried with him a fine cargo of furs, enough to make any trader jealous, and also the knowledge that he and Drouillard might stand charged with murder in the death of Antoine Bissonet.

Soon after their leader's departure, the gray mist of misfortune descended on the party Lisa left behind. Beaver became scarce and hard to obtain either by trapping or trading, and the Blackfeet lived up to their reputation for fierceness by attacking any Americans they met.

Even John Colter, that experienced frontiersman, ran into difficulty. Along with John Potts, who had saved Lisa from the swivel gun, he had returned to the Three Forks of the Missouri, which all the members of the Lewis and Clark expedition had noted as good beaver country. Early one morning they were out in their boat examining the traps they had set in a tributary of the Jefferson. Suddenly the sound of trampling hooves broke the quiet. The banks were sheer and blocked their vision, but Colter was certain that the noise was caused by Indians' horses and advised a cautious retreat. Potts, however, was of a different mind. Accusing Colter of cowardliness, he said the sound was caused by nothing more than a herd of buffaloes.

His disregard of Colter's warning was a mistake, for a few minutes later several hundred Indians appeared on both sides of the creek. Retreat was no longer possible, so Colter headed their boat toward shore exactly as the Indians directed him to do. No sooner did it touch land than one Indian seized Potts's gun. Colter, a man of great strength, leaped to his companion's aid and retrieved the weapon, but Potts had now lost his head. Although there was no place to flee, he pushed the boat back into midstream, leaving Colter ashore. Almost immediately an arrow flew through the air and struck him. Colter, still remaining calm, called to him to come back, but instead Potts aimed his gun at one of the Indians, fired, and watched him fall dead. The Indians' retaliation was quick. Arrows flew through the air, and Potts's short but intensive life of exploration and adventure was over.

Angered by Potts's rash action, the Indians gave Colter no opportunity to parlay with them but seized him, stripped him naked, and argued about the best method of killing him. They considered using him as a live target until one of the leaders asked him if he could run fast. Colter was sufficiently familiar with their customs to know what they intended. They would give him a slight headstart and then enjoy the sport of hunting him down. Wisely he told the chief that, although the Americans considered him swift, he was actually a slow runner.

To prolong the game, the chief led him out on the plains about three or four hundred yards, while the remainder of the band stayed where they were. Then he told Colter to run and save himself if he could. A whoop went up from the Indians, and the death race began. Colter headed directly to the Jefferson River about six miles away. The ground was covered with prickly pear cacti, and their spines plunged deep into his bare feet, but when he had gone half the distance, he looked over his shoulder and saw that he had gained on every Indian but one. That one Indian carried a spear and was within a hundred yards of him. For the first time Colter thought he had a slight chance of escaping.

He ran even faster, but his strength was giving out. Blood gushed from his nose and covered his chest, and yet he still had a mile to go to reach the river, where he hoped to find cover. Looking back over his shoulder once again, he saw that the lone pursuer was still gaining on him and was now only twenty yards away. Colter stopped abruptly, turned to face his enemy, and spread out his arms. The Indian tried to stop, too, but fell forward in the act of throwing his spear. It stuck in the ground, and the shaft broke in his hand. Colter immediately grabbed the pointed end, thrust it into the Indian's body, and started running again.

He had won more than a victory over this single Indian; he had also won a victory over time. For when the other Indians discovered the body of their dead tribesman, they paused long enough to examine it and to set up an angry, loud lament. Those few seconds of delay gave Colter a chance to reach the river.

The western waterways were notorious for the large number of floating and half-floating logs they contained. When these did not take the form of sawyers or planters—those serious hazards to navigation—they often became entangled to create what were called "rafts." These could be of various sizes, sometimes small, sometimes so large they completely blocked passage up or down a river. As Colter reached the bank of the Jefferson, he noticed one such raft—a relatively small one—at the upstream end of an island just a short distance away. No other cover offered itself, so making do with what he had, he raced into the water and worked his way underneath the raft until he found a spot where the chinks in the branches allowed him to raise his head and breathe unseen. The Indians arrived too late to observe their quarry disappear.

All day long Colter clung to the security of the jumble of dead trees. From time to time he could hear the Indians climb onto the raft and examine it closely, looking for a possible hiding place among the massed trunks and limbs. The horrible thought occurred to him that they might set fire to it, turning it into a giant funeral pyre from which escape would be impossible. But luckily for him this idea did not strike them, and with the fall of darkness, they gave up their hunt. Protected by the night's blackness, Colter slipped away from his refuge and silently swam downstream until he was sure that he was out of his enemies' sight and hearing. Then he went ashore and struck out in the direction of Fort Raymond.

In spite of his recent escape, his predicament remained desperate. Alone, without clothing or any means of killing game, his feet pincushions of prickly pear thorns, he had many miles to go before he would see the wooden walls of the fort. For seven days the sun burned his naked body, and he subsisted solely on roots he wrested from the ground with his bare hands. But so great was his physical strength and so firm his determination that he reached the fort and was able to resume his life as a trapper and trader.

Colter's adversaries were Indians who preferred fighting the Americans to trading with them; Lisa's were more civilized, but none the less formidable—investors and the law courts. On his arrival in St. Louis, he and Drouillard faced murder charges for the death of Bissonet; and one of his first acts was to retain counsel and post a bond of $5,000 to secure the temporary freedom of himself and his associate.

The court came to order on September 23, 1808,

and all St. Louis watched the proceedings with interest. Not only were Lisa and Drouillard well known in the community, which would alone have stirred excitement, the issue was also one that affected every fur trader and his *engagés*. The relationship between the two classes of people had not been clearly defined in the United States. (In Canada tradition answered many of the questions that arose.) The commercial contracts the two entered into had little practical effect during the period they were away from civilization, because no court could enforce their terms. What, then, were the rights of a man like Lisa to prevent desertions, thefts, or refusals to work—all acts that could not only undermine the financial success of an expedition, but also physically endanger its participants?

Lisa had been certain of his position until he found himself facing a prosecuter and a jury. When he had ordered Drouillard to bring back Bissonet dead or alive, he had thought himself acting only for the general good of everyone connected with his enterprise. Even now, in his mind, the issue was legal, not moral. Drouillard was more intimately involved in Bissonet's death, for it was his finger that had pulled the trigger. As he listened to the prosecution and the defense present their sides of the case, he began to see his act in a different light and, with a sense of guilt that he had not felt before, blamed it on "a lack of reflection in this unhappy moment." The jury did not share his misgivings. With only fifteen minutes of deliberation, it returned a verdict of not guilty.

Having disposed of the criminal action against himself and Drouillard, Lisa now concentrated on building the bigger organization that he realized would be needed to carry out the venture he envisioned. Previously he had gone outside St. Louis to obtain capital. His disregard for the established order had alienated the city's merchants, and his willingness to take risks frightened them. But his profits from one season had been sufficient to attract the attention even of the cautious, and the closed circles of St. Louis could always widen to admit a man with a proven ability to make money. By the time he had finished forming the St. Louis Missouri Fur Company (it was a partnership, not a corporation) its investors included practically every important trader in St. Louis in addition to Lisa's two partners of the year before.

The year 1808 was marking a change in the fur trade in the western United States. Not only was Lisa forming a company with a far broader foundation than any St. Louis had seen before, the federal government was beginning to move up the Missouri River. That fall at a site some three hundred miles beyond St. Louis it established Fort Osage, which not only housed a garrison but also contained a government trading post—or "factory"—where the Indians could obtain supplies at reasonable prices. (Such factories were intended to control the rapacity of the traders and formed a part of the federal government's Indian program.) The intrusion of government into the Indian trade was distasteful to some; on the other hand, any white man who now dealt with the Kansa and Osage Indians knew that, if trouble occurred, American troops were close at hand.

Yet the merchants of St. Louis, although they had combined as they had never done before and although the government was moving to protect commerce on the Missouri River, could not look forward to monopolizing the commerce they had done so much to develop. John Jacob Astor, who had come to the United States in 1784 to sell his flutes and make his fortune, had never forgotten what he had heard about the profits in furs. He had traveled over New York, buying pelts from farmers and from Indians and reinvesting his earnings in the development of his business. With one brilliant stroke after another, he had constantly become wealthier and more powerful and expanded his interests at every opportunity. Like Lisa, he, too, had commercial dreams that surpassed in scope those of most of his associates and competitors; and also like Lisa, he realized that the day of the small fur trader was passing.

At his request the New York State Legislature in 1808 passed an act incorporating the American Fur Company with capital not to exceed $1 million during the first two years of its existence, after which time it could be doubled. His past success had led him to believe that he could challenge the giant fur companies of Canada, but to do it, he needed a strong company of his own.

He had also been considering the information brought back by Lewis and Clark; and although Lisa might take an almost proprietary attitude toward the Upper Missouri, Astor saw no reason why he, too, should not eventually obtain some of the wealth that lay in the area explored by Lewis and Clark. The advance of the frontier was, at least for the time being, slipping from the hands of explorers, soldiers, and small trappers into the province of big business.

Chapter 11

The Lure of Riches

This grand commercial scheme [Astor's], appearing now plain and practical, at least to men of sanguine disposition, gave much satisfaction to the American public, who, from the results contemplated, became deeply interested in its success; for all the rich cargoes of furs and peltries thus to be collected annually over the vast expanse were to be shipped in American vessels for the great China mart, there to be sold, and the proceeds invested in a return cargo of teas, silks, beads, and nankeens, and other articles of high demand in the United States; which would not only prevent to some extent the American specia going out of the Union for such articles, but also turn the barren wilds of the north and far west into a source of national wealth.

—Alexander Ross, 1849

The Indians of the Great Plains had led Coronado onward with their tales of Quivira and a great river on which a king floated in a golden canoe, and the *conquistador* had risked his life and fortune in pursuit of a myth. Hard facts, not myths, stirred Manuel Lisa into action. The Three Forks area of the Missouri was incredibly rich in beavers—that had been confirmed by every reliable source—and their skins in the world's marketplaces would be worth fortunes. There was no question about the existence of the wealth; the only question was how to obtain it.

With his astute intelligence, Lisa realized that the methods used for so many years by the old trading organizations would not apply in this case. In the first place, he would have to contend with the Blackfeet, and that tribe could be controlled only by the presence of considerable numbers of men with a well-fortified base into which they could withdraw when attacked.

In the second, he foresaw a new role for the Indians, no matter what their tribe. Depending on them as the primary source of furs had many disadvantages. They were moody and sometimes

trapped and sometimes did not. The prices they demanded varied, depending on their needs of the moment and whether or not they could terrorize the white men into paying more. The traders, therefore, were at their mercy. As Lisa saw the problem, more dependence should be placed on white trappers working on shares. They would have one purpose—obtaining beaver skins—and thus were likely to work harder and longer at that single task.

He did not, however, overlook the part that might be played by the Indian traders. They could still more than justify their existence by the number of pelts they bought. He also saw for them an additional role: keepers of the peace. A tribe that had its own trader—particularly if the trader had a permanent post that was difficult to attack—was more likely to be friendly than one that did not. He did not intend to pay exorbitant tribute to any tribe, but he was willing to operate a trading post at somewhat less than the usual return if that post also served a tactical purpose and helped protect his line of communications.

To carry out his ideas, however, Lisa needed capital and manpower on a scale unprecedented among the conservative St. Louis merchants. Consequently he had made no attempt to be selective but, using the lure of his past season's profits, enlisted support wherever he could find it. Several years before, he had expressed his dislike of Lewis and Clark, who, it had seemed to him, were merely officious representatives of an unwanted government. Since his business demanded that he now forgo the luxury of such dislikes, he set his prejudices aside. William Clark, now the government's Indian agent for the territory, was a member of the partnership; and Reuben Lewis, the younger brother of Meriwether Lewis whom Jefferson had appointed governor of Upper Louisiana, was both an investor and one of the active managers in the field. Other investors included representatives of most of the leading families in St. Louis, people whom he had long regarded as adversaries.

Although discipline and experience were keystones in the conduct of a successful expedition, Lisa, in order to increase the manpower of his party, also was willing to provide an opportunity for untrained, but adventurous, spirits to test their luck in the fur business. Among those who grabbed this chance were a group of Americans (not the usual Frenchmen who made up the majority of trading and trapping personnel). About twenty-five of these were in a barge commanded by Reuben Lewis and steered by a settler named Thomas James, who knew as little about the Missouri River and the fur trade as the rest did.

The expedition was further strengthened by the presence of a military escort employed to protect the Mandan chief, Shahaka. Nathaniel Pryor's failure to return him to his village had become a source of embarrassment and deep concern to Washington. Of all the tribes along the Upper Missouri River, the Mandans seemed to be the most favorably disposed toward the United States, and the location of their villages made them an important base for exploration on up the river. What could happen when a tribe believed itself betrayed by the loss of a chief had been demonstrated by the angry reaction of the Arikaras. Conscious of this problem, Lewis saw in Lisa's expedition a heaven-sent chance to get Shahaka safely home. With the addition of some more men and some extra guns, the group would be so large that even the embittered Arikaras would hesitate to attack it.

So Lewis entered into a contract with the partners whereby the government would pay them $7,000, and in turn they would raise 120 men to serve in the territorial militia and act as Shahaka's bodyguard and escort. The partners were also bound to supply guns and ammunition and to place the temporary soldiers under the command of Pierre Chouteau.

By the time the rolls were filled, 350 men, according to one estimate, were engaged with the expedition in one way or another, making it by far the largest that had ever left St. Louis. Its departure, however, did not take the form of a mass exodus, because some went ahead of the others, planning to rendezvous later on. In Lisa's case, the press of business, including the settlement of a dispute with Jacques Clamorgan, kept him in St. Louis until June, 1809.

As the last contingent moved up the river, the difference between the veteran Frenchmen and the inexperienced Americans almost immediately became apparent. The Frenchmen knew how to handle their boats and were accustomed to the usual discipline of a fur-trading trip; the Americans were not. When the Americans raced the Frenchmen—which they sometimes did as a diversion—they could beat them at sprints, but they found the day-to-day work grueling and distasteful.

Although the hot June sun beat down upon them, Lisa knew the season was already late, for they had many miles to travel and much work to do before the first snows fell. Consequently he pushed the men hard. His French boatmen responded in their usual willing fashion, but the Americans continually lagged behind, arriving late at each night's camp and grumbling that they saw no need to stick so close together.

By the time they reached Fort Osage, where the militia were to receive their final inspection, the various contingents had met up with each other, but some of the Americans had already started to desert. With a smaller company of men and the assistance of George Drouillard, Lisa had been a stern disciplinarian. But circumstances were now different. He had had one experience standing trial, and perhaps another jury might take a different view. His partners, too, were now men of position who might not condone such action, thinking it would tarnish their reputations.

Furthermore, the number of malcontents was so great they could have met force with force, leading to a battle between those faithful to the expedition's leadership and those who were not. That was a chance Lisa could not risk taking, for it would have meant the end of the entire venture. All he could do was curse and write off the money he had advanced each deserter and the cost of the supplies he had stolen before leaving. Neither patience nor forgiveness was natural to his temperament, and he found the need for restraint trying.

Unfortunately his unaccustomed behavior

seemed to accomplish little. The French boatmen worked hard as always, but the others seemed just as discontented as ever; and after passing the Platte, the Americans in the boat steered by James became openly rebellious. They had not properly rationed their food and were now living solely on boiled corn. When they stopped one day at lunchtime, a crew member named James Cheek rolled out a barrel of pork that belonged not to the boat's supplies, but to the expedition's general stock. Jumping astride it and brandishing a tomahawk, he asked only a word from James to break it open.

Lisa's temper was already worn thin by these men who endangered his project by straggling up the river and sometimes deserting. At the report of Cheek's action, it snapped. Grabbing his pistols, he dashed to James's boat, ready to kill Cheek if he had to.

But the sight that awaited him was completely unexpected. He had thought he would find Cheek and perhaps two or three others standing alone. Instead the entire crew had loaded their guns and, taking Cheek's side, were lined up prepared to fight. Against more than twenty rifles, Lisa's pistols were useless. Cursing the fools who were so unaware of the need for conserving their supplies, Lisa reluctantly gave them permission to open the barrel. But at the first opportunity, he saw that such supplies were unloaded from their boat and placed on board another well out of their reach.

In spite of the desertions that had afflicted it, the expedition was still sufficiently large to impress the Teton Sioux, whom they first encountered at the mouth of the James River. While these Indians had been glad to harass Lewis and Clark's small party, they were more respectful and diplomatic with Lisa's larger force, and the white men safely passed by.

Since he was never overconfident when dealing with Indians, Lisa did not permit this psychological victory to lessen the precautions he thought necessary on approaching the Arikaras' village. (As Pryor could attest, this tribe now surpassed the Teton Sioux in their unfriendliness toward white travelers, and Lisa wanted to earn the $7,000 for the safe return of Shahaka.) Under the command of Pierre Chouteau, some of the militia landed below the village and approached it in military formation. The sight of their advance, coupled with the threat of the expedition's cannon aimed at the village, had a dampening effect on the Arikaras' bellicosity; and this time, instead of waging a battle, they agreed to hold a brief council, during which Pierre Chouteau severely chastised them for their conduct during the previous year. Their promises of better

behavior in the future meant nothing, but they let the expedition pass without opposition.

As the boats finally reached the Mandan villages, the wind blew strong and churned the surface of the Missouri. Nevertheless, the Indians put out in their bullboats to greet their visitors. The waves were so great that the bullboats often disappeared from view in their troughs, but the Mandans were neither frightened nor discouraged by the storm and kept coming. When they saw that the boats carried Shahaka safely home again after his long journey to Washington, their delight was boundless; and in their subsequent celebration, they all but forgot the white men. Some of the Americans were irritated by this, thinking it showed lack of due respect, but such petty concerns did not worry Lisa. Shahaka in the Mandans' village was worth $7,000 to the partners, and he had earned it for them.

Of more moment to him than whether the Mandans provided a free feast was the report he received from Benito Vasquez, the man he had left in charge at Fort Raymond during the winter and who, according to their plan, was waiting for him at the villages. The furs he brought with him numbered far less than Lisa had expected, and the Blackfeet had proved as hostile as ever, attacking the trappers in the Three Forks area whenever the opportunity offered. Every party had been driven back except one, and it, Vasquez believed, had crossed the mountains to spend the winter with more friendly Indians to the west. Another group of Lisa's trappers was with the Crows, and from everything that Vasquez knew, it was doing all right. Yet another was trapping farther to the south. But no definite word had been received from any of them.

At this point in many businesses a man of Lisa's intelligence might have decided to cut his losses by liquidating at least part of his current undertaking. In the fur trade, however, that was not possible. The partnership could probably have been legally dissolved without much difficulty, because its members were for the most part men of affairs who understood such questions. But the partners in turn were bound by contracts to each of the other participants, and these contracts were not uniform. To have untangled them before they were fulfilled would have meant risking more than a hundred lawsuits.

In addition, the Upper Missouri River offered no ready market for the expedition's tangible assets. Sets of traps and other supplies had almost no monetary value except ultimately in terms of furs; and if there were no furs, they could be exchanged for nothing else that was salable in St. Louis. Lisa, like a man who has pushed his pirogue into the current of a swift-flowing rapids, could not, once he had started, turn back.

Just above the Hidatsas, he selected a site for the construction of a fort and trading post. When completed, it consisted of a square blockhouse, the ground floor of which served as a trading room and storage area for furs while the top floor contained living quarters for the man in charge and some of the trappers. There were a few small outhouses, and all the buildings were surrounded by a palisade that was about fifteen feet high. Like most frontier trading posts, it was designed to serve both as a place of business and a fortification.

The hard, long trip up the river in the summer heat and the dangers shared when they passed the Arikaras and the Assiniboins had done nothing to unite the men. Those with experience and those without it still regarded each other more as adversaries than as co-workers; and ever since the mutiny over the barrel of pork, hostility had smoldered between Lisa and the men in the boat James had steered. Now it broke into the open in a dispute over the supplies the men were to receive as independent trappers and became so bitter that years later James said that "we found ourselves taken in, cheated, chiseled, gulled, and swindled . . ." and called Lisa "the most active, the meanest and most rascally of the whole." James and two companions finally obtained the supplies they thought they required to go off trapping on their own, but their departure did little to relieve the tension at the new fort.

Cheek, who defied the partners whenever possible, had lost none of his rancor. In front of Lisa, he remarked that if he ever caught Chouteau a hundred yards from camp, he would shoot him. When Lisa remonstrated, he remarked that many of the men, himself included, felt the same way about Lisa, and if Lisa went to the Three Forks, he would not return alive. Such talk was not all idle boast. Men like Cheek were the tough products of the frontier, accustomed to fighting if not to the hardships of traveling on the Missouri River. Lisa had no legal means of retaliation, and he could not afford the luxury of personal vendettas with any of the individuals making up the expedition. So he swallowed his pride—a difficult thing for him to do—and, joined by Pierre Chouteau, returned to St. Louis to attend to the partners' business there.

Discouraged and apprehensive about the future, Manuel Lisa disembarked at St. Louis in November, 1809, and found the community buzzing with the latest sad news. Meriwether Lewis, explorer, governor, and patriot, had met his death. On his way to Washington, where his official duties were calling him, he had taken shelter one night with an impoverished and ignorant frontier family. Sometime in the darkness he had died a violent death. The woman of the household insisted that he had been in a nervous state of mind on his arrival and that his death was the result of suicide; others thought this most unlikely in spite of Lewis's tendency to melancholia and suspected that he had been murdered.

Whatever Lisa's past feelings toward Lewis might have been, he could only regard the governor's death as a serious blow to the partners. Lewis, as evidenced by his brother's active participation in the company's affairs, had taken a lively interest in its success. More than any other person in authority—with the exception of William Clark—he had recognized the potential of the area in which Lisa intended to plant the American flag. With him in office, the partners could always count on an official voice that would speak in their behalf. The death of Lewis, while not immediately critical to their undertaking, was another in the series of misfortunes that seemed to pursue them.

Of less importance, but also unpleasant, were the rumors being circulated by two fur traders, Ramsay Crooks and Robert McClellan. These men, who had been attempting to establish their own business on the Missouri, had met Lisa on his upstream trip and had later tried to follow in the same direction. They had, however, met the Sioux and, not having mustered sufficient force to impress those warriors, found themselves subjected to the Sioux's usual bullying tactics and effectively blocked from proceeding farther. On their return to St. Louis they had blamed their failure to get up the river not on their own inadequacy, but on some presumed machinations of Lisa, forgetting that he could not have influenced that tribe into doing his bidding even if he had wanted to.

Nothing could be done about the death of Lewis, and the rumors spread by Crooks and McClellan, although damaging to Lisa personally, could not be materially harmful to a company with partners of such standing as Pierre Chouteau. So Lisa wasted little time before concentrating all his attention on preparations for the next season.

The items most preferred by the Indians were usually of British manufacture, an advantage that helped the Canadian traders. Over the years Lisa had developed good connections with merchants across the border at Detroit, so he went there to purchase the trading supplies he would need the coming year. The Canadian merchants offered to outfit him at what he considered generous terms; but although the Embargo Act had been repealed the previous winter, it had been replaced with the Non-Intercourse Act, and trade with Britain was still forbidden. Guards were posted along the boundary to make certain that no goods crossed it.

From Detroit he went to Montreal, where he met with no greater success, and then as a last resort journeyed to Philadelphia. There he was received coolly. Goods were in short supply, and the results of his past year's operation, in the opinion of the merchants, did not justify the extension of credit. The Three Forks area might contain as many riches as he claimed, but to the Philadelphians in their counting houses it seemed as distant and unreal as Quivira. Even in the older East, capital was scarce, and there seemed better ways to invest it than to risk it among the Sioux, Arikaras, and Blackfeet. When he returned to St. Louis, he brought with him the bleak outlook of a spring season in which the expedition could not be fully re-equipped. This meant that the men on the Missouri and the Yellowstone would have to stretch their supplies over two seasons instead of one.

Fortunately this gloomy word could not reach them, for they were already besieged with difficulties. After Lisa's departure, Andrew Henry, one of the most capable members of the expedition, went overland to Fort Raymond, while Pierre Menard, one of the partners, took the longer water route with the boats. As Lisa had foreseen when he urged the men to hurry up the Missouri, winter was close at hand, and Menard had to struggle against both snowstorms and ice as he worked his way up the Yellowstone to the mouth of the Bighorn.

The problems he encountered, however, were relatively minor to those that James soon faced. With the overconfidence of tenderfeet he and his two companions had jauntily set out, glad to be free of the men who, they thought, had "cheated, chiseled, gulled, and swindled" them. The icy weather that troubled Menard soon brought them to a stop, but they had expected it to be cold and built a small cabin in which they intended to spend the winter before going on to the Three Forks in the spring. Since game was plentiful and the cabin, banked with earth, was warm, they planned to pass the next few months in comfort. Whenever a storm raged across the Great Plains, blowing the snow in misty columns and then dropping it in heavy drifts, they had only to retire to their own fire and wait for it to pass. But on Christmas Day James stayed out too long and froze his feet so badly he was unable to walk. They had caught a few beavers after leav-

ing the fort, so they decided that James's two companions would take the skins back and trade them for additional ammunition.

Sitting alone in the cabin with his aching feet, James counted the days against his friends' return. But nothing broke the monotony of swirling snow and gusting winds, and he looked in vain across the snow for the reappearance of his friends. His rations had started to run out when a band of friendly Indians visited the cabin and fortunately were willing to trade food for some tobacco and other minor goods from James's supply.

The next visitors to emerge from the white wasteland that surrounded him were three men carrying messages to Fort Raymond from the fort near the Hidatsas. They told him that his two companions had reached the fort safely but did not intend to go up the river in the spring and seemed, in fact, in no hurry to return to the cabin. James took pride in the independence of the Americans as opposed to what he considered the subservience of the experienced Canadian trappers, and he had sided with them in every disagreement with the partners, whom he regarded as contemptible disciplinarians without proper concern for the rights of free men. The point he had not understood—and that Lisa did—was that only a fine line divided independence from irresponsibility. Now he himself had almost become the victim of the free spirit he so much admired.

Because he could not remain where he was, he decided to accompany the three messengers to Fort Raymond, particularly since they had horses and promised him the use of one until his feet became better. This promise, however, was more easily made than fulfilled. The horses were in such poor condition that they could not carry the extra load, and James was after all compelled to walk. The torture from his feet was at first great, and the crust on the snow made traveling difficult. Gradually, however, his feet seemed to get better, and in a few days he found he could walk less painfully than before.

All went well until they reached the mouth of the Little Missouri. Here they met some Indians who advised them to go up the Little Missouri for two days and then turn northward. A half-day's travel, the Indians said, would then bring them to a tributary of the Yellowstone.

Thinking they would save many miles of travel in the bitter cold of the Great Plains, they took the Indians' advice; but, as James later figured it out, they did not travel as fast as the Indians and therefore left the Little Missouri much too soon. Shortly afterward they realized their mistake and began suffering its horrible consequences. In summer men could lose their way on the Great Plains, as the Spanish had discovered early; in winter it became even easier. The wind-blown snow leveled their surface, filling up the gullies and smoothing out the ridges, and many of the few landmarks that might have guided a traveler were extinguished. The world became a bleak, almost unchanging white, devoid of form and like something conjured from the brain of a madman.

"For five days," James later recalled, "we kept our course to the north in an open plain, and in the heart of winter. The cold was intense, and the wind from the mountains most piercing. The snow blew directly in our faces and ice was formed on our lips and eyebrows. In this high latitude and in the open prairies in the vicinity of the mountains, where we then were, the winters are very cold. On the first night we were covered where we lay to the depth of three feet by the snow. No game was to be seen and we were destitute of provisions. For five days we tasted not a morsel of food, and had not even the means of making a fire. We saw not a mound or hill, tree or shrub, not a beast nor a bird, until the fifth day when we descried far off a high mound. We were destitute, alone in the vast, desolate, and to us limitless, expanse of drifting snow, which the wind drove into our faces and heaped around our steps.

"Snow," he continued, "was our only food and drink, and snow made our covering at night. We suffered dreadfully from hunger. On the first and second days after leaving the Little Missouri for the desert we were now traversing, our appetites were sharper and the pangs of hunger more intense than afterwards. A languor and faintness succeeded, which made traveling most laborious and painful. On the fifth day we had lost so much strength and felt such weakness for want of food that the most terrible of deaths, a death by famine, stared us in the face."

The three men who had kindly rescued James from the solitary prison of his cabin had made for him moccasins of buffalo hide, which he wore with the hair inside. On that fifth day his feet had become much worse, and as he later said, he could feel "the blood gurgling and bubbling" inside these moccasins at every step.

So desperate did the men become that they decided to kill one of their horses, abandoning its pack to the wind and snow. Before they did so, they climbed a mound they had seen and, looking out in the evening light, saw some trees and buffaloes. Here at last were the means to obtain both food and fire.

They killed some buffaloes and made camp that night in the shelter of the woods. Like many starving men, they found that the first taste of food stimulated their pent-up appetites, and without waiting to cook the meat, they gobbled much of it raw. Their greed exacted its toll. When they awoke the next morning, their bodies were bloated, and they were so sick they could not travel again until a day later.

Finally they struck the Yellowstone well below Fort Raymond and followed the river upstream. The river's ice-covered surface was treacherous, sometimes solid and firm, sometimes nothing more than a thin sheeting over an air space large enough to engulf either a man or a horse. The winds continued to blow, and the cold remained intense, but woods, which provided them with fire and shelter, skirted the river, and buffalo herds wandered along its banks. Struggling mile after terrible mile, they finally saw the wooden walls of Fort Raymond rising dark against the surrounding whiteness; and as they later stood before its warming fires, they knew the joy in being alive that only those can feel who have walked with death leering at their sides.

Although the men at Fort Raymond differed greatly in their points of view, they almost all shared one common opinion: the wealth of the area centered around the Three Forks. The members of Lewis and Clark's expedition had reported this, and the few men who had dared to return to that country dominated by the dangerous Blackfeet had confirmed it. Menard, therefore, had little difficulty getting recruits when he started to carry out Lisa's plan to take a relatively large group to the confluence of the rivers and construct a fort, for the men who went with him could image themselves soon rich.

They set out in the bitter cold of March, 1810, with Colter as their guide. Some of them suffered the excruciating pain of snow-blindness—a pain so great that one man wanted to commit suicide—and floundered in snow so deep that even their horses could not beat a passage through it. But at last they reached their destination, and Menard lost no time in putting the men to work building a fort. Since the entire party was not needed for this task, James and three other men almost immediately went off trapping. A few days later another group of eighteen men, including Cheek, the former mutineer, went up the Jefferson River and made camp about forty miles away. Cheek and two other men were busy about the campground, and the others had gone off hunting nearby, when they saw twenty or thirty Indians approaching, some mounted and some on foot. One of the hunters rushed back to camp to warn Cheek and the other two men. But Cheek, to whom obstinacy was a way of life, was no more prepared to yield to the Indians than he had been to the partners' rules. Instead of fleeing, he determined to remain and fight it out. Before he went down firing his rifle and his pistols, he killed at least one Indian, whose body the trappers later found close to his own. One other trapper, who did not share Cheek's stubbornness but who was too frightened to run, remained with him, and he, too, died. The rest of the party were widely scattered, and when they regained the safety of the fort and counted their numbers, three more were discovered missing.

Menard, who had meanwhile recalled James and his companions, sent out a band of well-armed men to pursue the Indians. They tracked them for a distance, but Menard, who feared being lured into an encounter with an even larger body of the enemy, refused to let his men continue the search. So they returned to the fort, where they remained for some days in a state of virtual siege, hardly daring to venture outside.

Jim Colter, who had now been attacked three times by the Blackfeet, decided that there was perhaps a limit to his luck. He might find wealth in the Three Forks country, or he might find death. Preferring to stay alive, even if poor, he made up his mind to return to St. Louis and take up a career as a farmer.

With him he carried reports from Menard and Reuben Lewis, both of whom were beginning to entertain doubts about the practicality of Lisa's vision. The problem, of course, was the Blackfeet. Menard hoped he could form alliances with some of their enemies, take some Blackfeet prisoners, and then negotiate a peace with them. Lewis was not so sanguine. In fact, he went so far as to consider whether or not the Lewis family and William Clark should not sell out their interest in the company.

In the meanwhile Menard could only continue with the spring hunt, hoping to salvage at least some part of the partners' investment. Since the Indians did not reappear, the men moved out cautiously, setting their traps as far away as four miles from the fort. Their newest enemies were the grizzly bears that were common in the region. Like Lewis and Clark's men, they found these animals intelligent and aggressive and a dangerous foe. Several trappers had narrow escapes, and one was severely mangled by a bear.

Although he was not at all certain that the company could maintain a permanent post at the Three Forks, Menard strengthened the building he had already constructed, so the Indians would not dare attack it. Above the fort flew the American flag, a proud symbol of their country fluttering in the Rocky Mountain winds. Several times the men saw Indians and carefully tried to approach them in an effort to negotiate an agreement, but the Indians always fled. As a result of this apparent timidity the nightmare memory of the attack grew dimmer, and in a gesture of defiance the men hoisted the scalp of the Indian Cheek had killed in place of their banner.

As their confidence returned the men began to go farther off and in small groups. George Drouillard, who had served Lewis and Clark so well and now Manuel Lisa, discovered he could trap more effectively by himself than in the company of others. In response to a warning against this practice, he replied, "I am too much of an Indian to be caught by Indians."

The calm was only temporary. The Indians, like ghosts rising from the wilderness, struck again. They killed two men who had gone hunting, and they also killed George Drouillard and mutilated his body by cutting off his head, tearing out his entrails, and hacking the rest of his corpse into pieces. Judging from the tracks on the ground, he had put up a vigorous fight, but one man could not defeat an entire band.

By this time even the bravest realized that they could not remain at the Three Forks, although some were willing to go with Andrew Henry farther west, where they would be dealing with more friendly Indians.

Menard returned to St. Louis, where he reported to Lisa on the season's operations. The Blackfeet had made it impossible to hunt and trap at the Three Forks; eight men had been lost to the Indians; the Hidatsas had broken into a company cache on the Yellowstone, taking the most valuable supplies and equipment; and a number of the men, including James, were prepared to sue the company for breach of contract. On the other hand, in spite of these misfortunes, they had secured enough furs to keep the company in the black. Lisa had not realized his dream, but he had not been defeated.

His quest for additional credit having failed, Lisa could not justify the expense of a trip up the river in a relatively empty boat. So he spent the hot, muggy months of the summer of 1810 in St. Louis trying to collect various sums that were due him and handling lawsuits brought by some of those who thought themselves maltreated in their dealings with the company. Without adequate funds, he was unable to expand his operation any further and could only hope that a turn of fortune would bring him the money he needed.

In contrast to Lisa, John Jacob Astor was not handicapped by any lack of resources. He was now one of the wealthiest men in the United States, and his business interests had expanded far beyond the fur trade to include real estate and the China trade. His imagination, too, had been fired by the reports of Lewis and Clark, but his attention centered not so much on the Upper Missouri and the Three Forks, as on the Pacific Northwest; and he was already making plans to establish himself in the void that existed along the Pacific Coast both above and below the present-day international boundary.

He had incorporated the American Fur Company with a charter issued by the New York State Legislature and had then created a partnership that he named the Pacific Fur Company. As partners, he had attracted Ramsay Crooks and Robert McClellan, the two traders who had been slandering Lisa in St. Louis's mercantile circles; a man named Wilson Price Hunt, in whom he placed considerable confidence; and several members of the North West Company, whose experience he thought would be helpful.

To these men he offered an unusual opportunity, for he agreed to put up the necessary capital and to assume all the losses for the first five years. But Astor rarely gave anything away without expecting something in return. In this case he retained complete control of the management and the right to merge the partnership into the American Fur Company. By giving the men an interest in the projected operation, he hoped to assure their loyalty and their hard work. Then if it was successful, he would make it part of his company. If not, he could write it off and try something else. He gambled with his money, they with their time and perhaps their lives.

As Astor drew up his plans, he decided to make his first foray into the Northwest from two different directions, one party going by land and the other by sea. The overland group was to be led by Wilson Price Hunt, who went to Canada early in 1810 to recruit experienced personnel. Although he understood the fur business, Hunt was not accustomed to dealing personally with the frontiersmen on whom it was dependent. In Montreal he had great difficulty attracting the people he needed, and it took the assistance of one of the more experienced partners to do so. By that time, however, it was the middle of August and too late in the year for completing a long trip. Nevertheless, he and his men set out on the first leg, following

the inland waterway that Marquette and Joliet had explored to St. Louis.

Although Reuben Lewis had earlier suggested to his brother that an investment in Astor's company might be worthwhile, the merchants of St. Louis did not welcome this new competitor. Whenever they could, they discouraged the sale of supplies to Hunt and tried to dissuade men from joining his ranks. As a result of the delays they caused, coupled with those that had plagued him in Canada, he would not be able to reach the Pacific before the rivers were blocked with ice and the mountain passes covered with deep drifts of snow.

To remain at St. Louis, however, was clearly impractical. Surrounded by the temptations offered by the tavernkeepers, many of the men would have either deserted before spring or accumulated debts that Hunt could not afford to pay off; and in view of the unfriendly attitude of the merchants, he also would undoubtedly have to pay high prices for his food. Therefore he went up the Missouri and made a winter camp just above the present-day city of St. Joseph, Missouri.

In the late summer of the same year the seaborne half of the expedition began to assemble in New York. Astor had recruited many of its members in Canada, and they arrived at the city in a large birchbark canoe, having portaged it by wagon and finally launching it in the Hudson River.

To transport them to the Pacific Coast, Astor was providing a ship named the *Tonquin*, whose captain was Jonathan Thorn, a veteran of the wars with Tripoli and on leave from the navy. As he looked over the men he had assembled, Astor had certain misgivings. Although he had taken many risks in his lifetime, his character was marked by a broad streak of caution, and he wondered if these exuberant Canadians understood the dificulties they might face. But he overestimated the loyalty of his Canadian partners. Several of them were sailing on the *Tonquin;* and learning that the British minister to the United States was in New York, they called on him, divulged all of Astor's plans, and received his assurance that they would not be jeopardizing their British citizenship by working for Astor. Their concern for their personal standing was comprehensible. What was heinous was their divulgence of Astor's plans, for they knew that everything they told the British minister would be reported to the North West Company, Astor's principal competitor in attempting to trade on the Columbia.

Since he was not going with them, Astor wrote out detailed instructions for the partners, explaining just what they should do when they reached the

Pacific Coast, and another set to guide Thorn in his handling of the ship. "I must recommend you," he warned Thorn in closing, "to be particularly careful on the coast, and not to rely too much on the friendly disposition of the natives. All accidents which have as yet happened there arose from too much confidence in the Indians."

Under Astor's watchful eye, the *Tonquin* set out to sea in September, 1810. The calm of the voyage was soon broken by dissension reminiscent of la Salle's last voyage so many years before. As commander of his expedition's land forces, la Salle had soon become involved in a bitter dispute with the naval commander, and such was the case on board the *Tonquin*. The partners felt themselves superior to Thorn, and Thorn believed himself superior to the partners. By the time the *Tonquin* left the Hawaiian Islands, where it stopped to purchase fresh supplies, Thorn was so overwrought that he seriously believed the partners might try to seize control of his ship. Fortunately for Astor, each side restrained itself so that open fighting did not break out, and the *Tonquin* reached the mouth of the Columbia River in March, 1811.

The dangerous sandbar that guarded its mouth took eight lives before they landed and began unloading their ship. But no members of the North West Company were there ahead of them. Astor had won the race, and his company was the first to establish a base at the mouth of the Columbia River.

Between Hunt's winter camp and Astoria, as the new post was named, lay the Great Plains, formidable and dangerous in themselves and haunted by tribes like the Sioux who had little respect for the lives of white men. The way across them was now known, thanks to the reports of Lewis and Clark, but they still presented a serious obstacle to travelers. Familiarity had not tamed the Missouri River, cleared its waters of planters and sawyers, or subdued the Sioux. For this reason Hunt had enlisted additional recruits at St. Louis; and now as March approached, he was ready to start on the journey that he hoped would take him to the Pacific Ocean.

Before leaving, he made a quick trip to St. Louis on business. While he was there, he met two scientists, John Bradbury, who had been employed by the Botanical Society of Liverpool to collect American plant specimens, and Thomas Nuttall, another Englishman, who had come to the United States as a printer but who soon became a leading authority on the country's plant life. The exploration of the continent was opening up a treasure trove of new species, and to many men their discovery was as important as the discovery of a new river or mountain pass. Bradbury and Nuttall, therefore, were delighted to accept an invitation from Hunt to accompany him as far as the Mandan villages. On the same trip to St. Louis, Hunt also hired as an interpreter, Pierre Dorion, Jr., the halfbreed son of the man who had so ably helped Lewis and Clark in their dealings with the Yankton Sioux. Dorion, Jr., although he lacked his father's strength of character, had formerly worked for Lisa.

When Lisa learned that Dorion had hired out to Hunt, he was furious. Dorion, who possessed a strong taste for liquor, had wanted more than the usual allotment of whiskey on Lisa's last trip. Lisa had given it to him but had charged his account for the excess. Since the trip had been unprofitable, Dorion had not had the means to pay his debt, and furthermore he claimed that Lisa had overcharged him. By the prevailing code, Dorion should have settled the dispute in court, paid his bill, or have considered himself bound to work for Lisa until his account was settled. Instead he had taken a job with one of Lisa's potential competitors.

Lisa reacted as most fur traders would have done. He immediately swore out a warrant to detain Dorion, and a man went up the river to serve it. When Bradbury and Nuttall, who had remained in town to collect their mail, heard what Lisa had done, they left St. Louis at two o'clock in the morning to warn Hunt, who had started up the river.

Dorion, duly advised, avoided the process server. Hunt's boats a few days later came near the place where Jim Colter now owned a farm. Bradbury was anxious to talk to him, because he had heard that somewhere along the Missouri the members of the Lewis and Clark expedition had found the skeleton of a forty-foot-long fish. If anyone knew the exact location of this oddity, that person would be Colter. Although he could not provide the information Bradbury wanted, Colter walked some distance with the boats, easily slipping back into his old ways and thinking of the wilderness that lay ahead. "He seemed," Bradbury noted in his journal, "to have a strong inclination to accompany the expedition; but having been lately married, he reluctantly took leave of us."

The man whose eyes had seen parts of the United States unknown to any other white man, whose feet had outraced the fiercest Indians, and whose trigger finger had been responsible for the death of many dangerous grizzlies walked slowly back to his farm, where his most distant horizon was at the end of his longest furrow.

The approach of spring had brought Lisa some slight hope. His partners were reluctant to invest much more money in a venture that had produced so little return. Yet they wanted to salvage what they could and also relieve Andrew Henry, who had spent the winter in the mountains. Largely at Lisa's urging, they put together enough money to purchase one barge and a small amount of supplies with the understanding that Lisa himself would take the cargo up the river. A lawyer, Henry Marie Brackenridge, happened to be in St. Louis, pursuing his interests in geography and natural history. He, too, wanted to go to the Mandan villages, and Lisa agreed to take him as a passenger.

Brackenridge appreciated the better aspects of Lisa's character and also the difficult position in which circumstances had placed him. "A person better qualified for this arduous undertaking," Brackenridge later wrote, "could not have been chosen. Mr. Lisa is not surpassed by anyone, in the requisite experience in Indian trade and manners, and has few equals in perseverance and indefatigable industry. Ardent, bold and enterprising, when any undertaking is begun, no dangers, or sufferings are sufficient to overcome his mind. I believe there are few men so completely master of that secret of doing much in a short space of time, which arises, from turning every moment to advantage. . . ." Yet Brackenridge realistically noted that "the majority of the members of the company have not the confidence in Mr. Lisa, which he so highly merits," but added that "on this occasion, he was intrusted with the sole direction of their affairs, in some degree, from necessity, as the most proper person to conduct an expedition, which appeared little short of desperate."

Because of his lack of funds, Lisa had with him only about twenty men compared to the approximately eighty who were with Hunt. If he could join Hunt before he reached the territory of the Sioux, his chances of a safe passage would be enhanced by the presence of the larger group. Although Hunt had a big lead, Lisa thought he might be able to overtake him and drove his crew toward setting a new record for a speedy trip. Increasingly concerned about the difficulty of passing the Sioux, he sent a messenger to Hunt from Floyd's Bluff, which he had now reached, requesting him to wait at the village of the Poncas.

His worries were confirmed by one of the company's employees, whom they met coming down-

stream from the Mandan villages. He reported that Andrew Henry, who had remained in the Rocky Mountains over the winter, was in difficulties and that all along the Missouri River the Indians were in an ugly mood. The Sioux in particular had become openly hostile, killing several white men. Only the night before, his own boat had been fired upon, and he strongly suspected that the attackers had been Sioux.

Lisa's messenger overtook Hunt at the Poncas' village, but Hunt's mind was already poisoned against him. Ramsay Crooks and Robert McClellan, who had already spread stories about Lisa, were with Hunt, and they convinced him that Lisa had been the source of their trouble with the Sioux the year before. He was also influenced by his own experience in having Lisa attempt to detain Dorion. Lisa's only reason for asking him to wait, he thought, was to cause him trouble. So although he sent back word that he would stop at the village, he moved on, hoping to leave Lisa behind.

The first Teton Sioux Hunt encountered were three warriors, who sat and smoked with him. The meeting was strained, because one of Hunt's men had been with an Arikara war party the previous summer and had killed a Sioux more by luck than anything else. (He had fired across the river at a point where it was a half-mile wide.) After they finished smoking, Hunt gave the Indians a few presents, and they quietly went on their way.

Two more Sioux then appeared, and Hunt gave them additional gifts; but in surly tones they expressed contempt for the presents and demanded more. Hunt was not going to let them think he was frightened by their bullying, so he told them that if they or any of their tribe again followed the expedition, he would treat them as enemies. The Sioux left, but their angry reaction to Hunt's scolding made the expedition aware that they should proceed with caution.

High banks soon flanked the Missouri River on either side, making visibility difficult and increasing the opportunity for an ambush. Hunt wisely arranged to have the keelboat stay close to the right bank, while the three smaller boats hugged the other side. In this way each of the two parties could get a better view of the bank above the other. If one or the other saw Indians, they were to fire two shots in quick succession as a warning.

Suddenly the men in the small boats saw with horror that the keelboat had entered what seemed to be a trap. Clinging to the bluffs, it had passed between a sandbar and the shore, but the water ahead proved to be too shallow, and it had to turn back. Meanwhile at least a hundred warriors had gathered on the bluff at the lower end of the sandbar and would be waiting when the keelboat returned.

There was not enough time for the small boats to cross over to help Hunt, but a surprising thing then occurred. The keelboat passed close to the Indians without being molested, and the Indians threw down their weapons. Some of them even jumped into the river and swam over to greet the three smaller boats.

They were not Sioux after all, but a war party of Mandans, Arikaras, and Hidatsas, who had been planning to attack the Sioux. On seeing the white men, they assumed that the boats were going to the Arikaras' villages and would be giving away arms and ammunition. That being the case, they decided to return to the villages to get their share and then resume their attack better armed. For some reason that even the wisest frontiersmen could not explain, Hunt's party had passed through the territory of the Sioux without being stopped.

Lisa's luck in getting by the Sioux was almost as great as Hunt's. On June 1 a band of twelve or thirteen Sioux appeared on the bank, fired one or two guns, and displayed an American flag, perhaps one of those given out by Lewis and Clark. Since the flag was regarded by the Indians more as a trophy than as a national emblem, its display meant nothing. Lisa knew that the slightest show of cowardice would encourage the Indians' natural aggressiveness, and so when they beckoned him to shore, he boldly ordered his boat in that direction. Upon landing he and Brackenridge leaped out of the boat and shook hands with the waiting warriors, although they believed that a larger group probably lurked in hiding somewhere nearby.

Lisa had no interpreter, but he was well versed in sign language and was able to make the Sioux understand him. He acknowledged that he was a trader but said that he had fallen on hard times and was now a poor man. The purpose of his present trip, he explained, was to rescue the men whom he had left behind and who had been ill-treated by the Indians farther up the river. In conclusion he added that he hoped to return in three months and establish a trading post that would be convenient for the Sioux and asked them to give this news to other members of their tribe. The plea of poverty and the promise of future services, combined with a handsome gift, seemed to satisfy them. For the next Indians Lisa saw were a band of Arikara warriors, who had come from their village to help assure Lisa's safe arrival.

After all the reports he had received of the Sioux's angry mood, he had difficulty explaining to himself why they had not stopped either Hunt or himself. He could think only that they had not attacked Hunt because his party was too large, and had not interfered with his own journey because he had come up the river so quickly they had not expected him so soon.

Since he had overtaken Hunt, the two parties were at last united physically, but suspicion created a breach between them. Lisa's outward friendliness, Hunt was convinced, only concealed a mind that was plotting to do them harm among the Arikaras, and Lisa did not improve Hunt's opinion of him by the way in which he handled his dispute with Dorion. Dorion's desertion—and desertion is what Lisa considered it—rankled deeply. He needed every cent he could collect, and here was Dorion, owing him money and yet helping a possible competitor instead of working off his debt. In fact, Dorion's behavior was a threat to the structure of personnel relations in the fur trade. If a man could accept credit from one trader—and they all did— and then work for another, there would be no end to the credit demands on the traders, who were already stretched thin.

Instead of immediately starting an argument with Dorion, Lisa first tried diplomacy. He invited Dorion to his boat, gave him some whiskey, which he knew Dorion liked, and then tried to persuade him to leave Hunt's employ. This was a tactical error. If Hunt learned about it, he might think Lisa was trying to subvert his men. In spite of the whiskey—or perhaps because of it—the meeting on Lisa's keelboat did not go well. Dorion once again accused Lisa of overcharging for his liquor, and after bitter words, Dorion angrily departed.

That evening Lisa visited Hunt's camp to borrow a towline. When Dorion, who was in his tent, saw Lisa, he came out, hurled some insults at his former employer, and struck him several times. Livid with rage, Lisa yelled that he was going to get his knife and ran toward his boat. His threat caused Dorion to get his pistols.

Having less far to go, he returned before Lisa and told his new employers how Lisa had tried to hire him away, not mentioning, of course, Lisa's reasons. On hearing what Lisa had done, Crooks and McClellan became so angry that Hunt had to restrain them from personally entering the quarrel.

The situation was not improved by Lisa's reappearance with a knife stuck in his belt. In the course of cursing out Dorion, Lisa unwisely expanded his remarks to include Hunt himself on the ground that Hunt had stolen Dorion's services. Up until then Hunt had been something of a moderating influence, having persuaded Crooks and McClellan to keep calm. But at Lisa's words, his temper flared, too, and he told Lisa to get his pistols. The two leaders between them would settle the argument there and then.

The shadow of death hung over the campground and played in the light cast by the flickering fire. Bradbury and Brackenridge, who shared many interests and had become good friends, realized that the dispute had gone too far and that saner heads must take control. Since they belonged to neither partnership and were respected by the heads of both groups, they became intermediaries and finally restored peace and order, although they did so, Brackenridge noted, "with the greatest difficulty."

If the Arikaras had been in their former hostile mood, the antagonisms between the white men would have made them easy victims. But acting as unpredictably as the Indians often did, the Arikaras had changed their attitude since the time they had defeated Sergeant Pryor. Probably they had decided that the Sioux were the greater enemies and that the Americans might provide arms against them. So they had sent out their warriors to escort Lisa; and when the boats of the two expeditions reached their village, they invited Lisa and Hunt to a council.

After their argument over Dorion, the leaders of the two parties were not on speaking terms, and they crossed the river to the village in separate boats, while Crooks muttered that he planned to shoot Lisa if Lisa tried to race over first in order to make a treacherous bargain with the Arikaras.

In response to the chief's welcome at the council, Lisa spoke first, explaining that he hoped to trade with the Arikaras provided the prices they asked for their buffalo hides and beaver skins were not too high. Before he closed, he stated flatly that Hunt and his party were his friends and that he would join them in retaliation for any insults or injuries that they might receive. In saying this, he was completely sincere. He might quarrel angrily with Hunt, but he knew that in front of the Indians anything but unity could be disastrous. His open support of Hunt did much to remove the suspicion that had been hanging over him.

When it came Hunt's turn to speak, he explained that he himself was not a trader but was on his way to the Pacific Ocean to see the Americans who were already there. Therefore he would not establish a post nearby, but he did want to purchase some horses.

While coming up the river he had discussed the problem presented by the Blackfeet with some of the more experienced frontiersmen and had begun to question whether it would be safer to follow Lewis and Clark's route or to cross the Great Plains farther south, traveling through the lands of the Cheyennes. Finally deciding to take the southern route, he had to abandon his boats for horses and told the assembled Indians he would pay good prices for any animals they wished to sell.

The purchase of the horses was a slow business. Each one, of course, had to be examined separately and a price agreed upon with its owner. As soon as the men completed a transaction, they cropped the horse's tail as a means of identifying it when it was again turned loose to graze.

While this commerce was going on, Bradbury was free to wander through the village and observe the Indians. He carefully studied the contents of a medicine man's deerskin bag, making notes on the plants it contained, and he also visited the lodge of a warrior whose acquaintance he had made earlier. The Indian gave him a painted buffalo robe, and in return Bradbury gave the Indian a pair of silver bracelets and some other jewelry that he had brought for such purposes. The gifts so delighted the young man that he invited Bradbury to spend the night, offering him both a bed to sleep on and his sister to sleep with.

The Arikaras' sexual habits, as Bradbury later noted, were loose. Every evening the warriors would flock to the boats with their wives, sisters, and daughters to market their relatives' services for the night. Vermilion and beads were the currency usually employed in these exchanges, and Hunt was kept busy doling out these commodities and charging them to the men's accounts. On one evening Bradbury estimated that at least eighty women had been brought from the village to take part in this trade. Yet the Indians he noticed were not completely callous, for in several instances he saw a warrior consult his wife about the price before delivering her.

Although their sexual practices might seem debased to those with a European background, the qualifications the Arikaras demanded of their leaders were outstanding. "It is utterly impossible to be a great man amongst them," Brackenridge wrote in his journal, "without being a distinguished warrior, though respect is paid to birth, but this must be accompanied by other merits, to procure much influence." And Bradbury noted that ". . . generosity, or rather an indifference for self, forms here a necessary qualification in a chief. The desire to acquire and possess more than others, is thought a passion too ignoble for a *brave man;* it often happens, therefore, that a chief is the poorest man in the community."

Since Hunt no longer had any use for his boats, he was glad to sell them to Lisa; and Lisa, anxious for any supplies or cash he could pick up, agreed to sell Hunt some of the horses he had at the fort above the Hidatsas' villages. Some of the men, therefore, had to make a flying trip up the river, and both Bradbury and Brackenridge, wanting to collect more information, went with them.

After this trip had been successfully completed, the men reassembled at the Arikaras' village. From there Brackenridge and Bradbury returned in one of Lisa's boats to St. Louis and civilization to write up their accounts. (Nuttall did not go with them, having decided to remain with Lisa a while long-er.) Hunt with about eighty horses—they were fewer than he wished, but all he could buy—struck out for the West, hoping to avoid the Blackfeet and reinforce the men at Astoria.

Bradbury, Brackenridge, and Nuttall expected intellectual recognition when their writings eventually appeared; Hunt and his men expected to find wealth on the West Coast. Only Lisa knew his own prospects were dim. But he intended to stay on the Missouri and—if fate and labor made it possible—salvage something from the company he had worked so hard to create. But it was a question whether fate and labor would.

Chapter 12

The Frontier Retreats

. . . [T]he trade with the several Indian tribes of North America, has, for many years past been almost exclusively carried on by the merchants of Canada; who, having formed powerful and extensive associations for that purpose, being aided by British capital, and being encouraged by the favor and protection of the British government, could not be opposed, with any prospect of success, by individuals of the United States.

. . . [B]y means of the above trade, thus systematically pursued, not only the inhabitants of the United States have been deprived of commercial profits and advantages to which they appear to have just and natural pretensions, but a great and dangerous influence has been established over the Indian tribes, difficult to be counteracted, and capable of being exerted at critical periods, to the great injury and annoyance of our frontier settlement.

—John Jacob Astor, 1812

Brackenridge's journal, which was published in 1814, and his *Views of Louisiana,* which appeared with it, gave him his reputation as a public man and a chronicler of his times. Bradbury was delayed returning to England, and someone else classified many of the specimens he had sent ahead, depriving him of the deserved honor of their discovery. Yet much of his collection remained to be catalogued, and his journal, too, gained wide readership when it was published in 1817.

Thomas Nuttall, the third of the three intellectuals on the trip, decided to remain with Lisa a while longer. For some reason—perhaps because of his relative youthfulness—he had not become close to the other two, although they had much in common; and among the traders and boatmen, he was thought to be crazy, because as soon as they reached a new location, he dashed ashore and avidly collected plants, completely unmindful of Indians or other hazards. His purpose became apparent in 1818 when his book, *Genera of North American Plants,* appeared. It was the most comprehensive

publication of its kind up until that time, and among the plants he described in it were those he collected during his trip up the Missouri River.

Bradbury, Brackenridge, and Nuttall found fame, if not fortune, but Hunt fared less well. Lewis and Clark had headed west from the Mandan villages during the first week of April; Hunt failed to make his departure from the Missouri until the middle of July, thereby virtually assuring himself trouble with the winter snows of the Rocky Mountains. Furthermore, although everyone agreed that the Blackfeet were vicious toward Americans, no one was certain that the tribes Hunt would encounter farther south would be friendly. A more experienced man would have demurred at undertaking such a journey so ill prepared and so late in the season, and in fact, some of Hunt's men did. Just before leaving the Missouri, they stole a barrel of gunpowder and some weapons to enable them to desert, but fortunately for Hunt one of his more trustworthy employees revealed the plot.

Although the sun burned hot overhead, the gradually shortening days should have warned Hunt

159

that the solstice had passed and the season for travel was slipping away from him. But his initial progress along the Platte River was slow. Several of the men were not well, and Ramsay Crooks was so sick he had to be carried on a litter with a canopy of boughs to protect him from the sun. Hunt also had been unable to obtain all the horses he wanted, so most of them were used as pack animals and only the partners were mounted. This slowed their progress even further. Then Hunt, who should have been aware of the need for haste, permitted his men to camp leisurely and spend a prolonged amount of time hunting buffaloes. Meat was a necessity, but time, too, was a valuable commodity, and Hunt was wasting it.

Although he was unconcerned about winter's approach, he was uneasy about his interpreter, Edward Rose, whom he had hired to help him deal with the Crows. As they drew nearer to the land occupied by those Indians, Hunt began to suspect that Rose, who knew the Crows well, was planning to desert the expedition and remain with the tribe, perhaps taking some of the other men with him. Since his services would be of little use farther west, Hunt offered to pay him off as soon as they reached the Crows. This made loyalty more valuable than disloyalty and, since Rose accepted, ended Hunt's worries about his apparent schemings.

When they finally reached the foothills of the Rockies, two Crow Indians cautiously approached, riding their horses carefully through the rocks that surrounded Hunt's camp, ready to take cover at the first sign of danger. Since they were Crows, Hunt told Edward Rose to invite them to the camp. The Indians were friendly, and Hunt entertained them as well as he could before they left to return to their band. The following day a larger group of Indians galloped up and with good nature invited Hunt and his entire expedition to come for a visit. Hunt accepted, the men broke camp, and the Indians provided them with an escort.

The reception at the Crows' village was cordial, and Hunt passed out presents to the principal leader and the warriors. But since the Crows had the reputation of being thieves—they were noted among the Indians for their skill at stealing horses—Hunt was careful to stay on the alert.

Trading started the next day. Hunt wanted to buy some buffalo robes and, most of all, additional horses and replacements for those that were now unfit for further travel. Everything went pleasantly until Hunt's wants were satisfied and he would buy no more. Thereupon the Crows' attitude changed abruptly. Displeased, they became insolent and

menacing. Like a flash of lightning crashing through the skies of the Great Plains, Hunt's old suspicions of Edward Rose's motives rose anew, and he thought the Indians' change in manner might have been instigated by the interpreter. McClellan, Crooks's companion in the slandering of Lisa, swore that in the case of an Indian outbreak he would shoot Rose first.

Not wishing to remain any longer than necessary among people whom he did not trust, Hunt departed from the Crows early the next morning. After saying goodbye to the Indians—and also to Rose, whom he was glad to dismiss—he led his men south along the foot of the mountains in search of a valley or canyon that would provide a route west. The mountains, however, presented an unbroken front, and after traveling fifteen miles, Hunt went into camp still at their base. Having failed to locate a pass, he next decided to assault the mountains directly but soon found his way blocked by cliffs and rocks. Reassembling his men, he again went into camp and pondered his next step.

The following morning he had a new cause for worry, because Rose suddenly arrived accompanied by several Crow warriors. Immediately Hunt believed that his fears of Rose's treachery had been confirmed, although he nervously let the interpreter and the warriors approach. But Rose explained that when the Crows' chief had learned that Hunt was hopelessly lost, he had asked Rose to show him the way into the mountains. Since his own efforts had proved so unrewarding, Hunt uneasily accepted this offer of help. To Hunt's great concern, however, they soon joined the main band of Crows, who were going in the same direction. The route was rough, and Hunt with his heavily burdened horses could not keep up with the Indians' pace, but he was glad to lag behind, for having at last found the trail, he wanted to be rid of the Crows.

Before leaving the Missouri River, Hunt had wisely employed some men who had trapped with Andrew Henry; and with their assistance, he safely crossed the Continental Divide. There in accordance with his instructions, he left two groups of trappers, who were to spend the winter in the mountains.

So far luck had been with him. Although unaccustomed to the Great Plains, and to the life led by the frontiersmen, he had brought his party safely up the Platte and well into the mountains without losing any of his men or having to fight any Indians. But when he reached the Snake River, luck abandoned him. The Canadians, who were more accustomed to boats than to horses, wanted to descend the waterway in canoes, and Hunt agreed to this.

The results were disastrous. The river soon became impassable even to the skillful Canadians. One canoe was torn apart, and one man drowned. Finding that they could go no farther by water, they cached their supplies and began an overland journey to the Pacific that quickly became a nightmare.

Unfamiliar with the route, lacking sufficient supplies, and caught by the bitter winter, they struggled desperately toward their goal. Several times the group became separated; one man vanished; three more preferred to live with the Indians than to continue the bitter struggle; Dorion's Indian wife gave birth to a child, who died in just a few days; one man became so ill they had to leave him with some Indians; and all of them suffered a horrible existence of hunger, cold, pain, and illness. The survivors who finally struggled into Astoria were a sorry lot and bore no resemblance to the group Astor had intended to send to his Pacific post. The dream of quick wealth that Hunt had entertained when he left the Missouri had long since disappeared, and he thought himself fortunate merely to be alive.

Lisa did not suffer physical hardships such as those endured by Hunt and his men, but the remaining months of the year brought with them some successes but no triumphs sufficient to restore the confidence of his partners.

One of his men, Jean Baptiste Champlain, returned from a trip to the Arapaho Indians, who lived far up the Platte River. He did not bring back many furs, but he had heard that the Spanish came once a year to trade with that tribe. Lisa's imagination was stirred by this report. If it was true, the possibility existed of using this route to trade with New Mexico; and this could give the St. Louis Missouri Fur Company new life. As soon as he could spare enough men, Lisa intended to explore this potential opportunity.

When Andrew Henry arrived from his winter's trapping in the mountains, he carried with him enough skins to insure the company a modest profit. But, he reported, the Three Forks of the Missouri were still unsafe for Americans. A large band of Blackfeet had attacked his trappers, and one man had been killed before they could retreat to their fort. Then the Crows had demonstrated their skill as horse thieves, running off with a number of animals along with the packs they were carrying. The winter, which they had spent on a tributary of the Snake River, had been extremely cold,

and the scarcity of game had forced them to dig for roots in order to survive. The obvious conclusion seemed to be that only a large, well-financed company could provide the protection necessary to make the area secure.

To add to Lisa's worries, Tecumseh, the son of a Shawnee warrior, was stirring up the Indians east of the Mississippi and was welding the tribes of the region into a unit to oppose any further American advance. Word of his accomplishments was beginning to spread across the Mississippi, and the Indians on the Missouri River were becoming sullen and resentful. Lisa, like many others along the frontier, thought the British were encouraging this change in attitude. If the Indians, he reasoned, could be persuaded to resist the movement north from St. Louis, the Canadian companies would soon enjoy a monopoly over their trade. That was cause enough for the British to involve themselves.

This consideration among others discouraged Lisa's partners. The year's operations had not been sufficiently profitable to warrant the risks they were taking; and as the cold winds of January blew down the streets of St. Louis, driving the town's citizens to the warmth of their firesides, the partners met and dissolved the St. Louis Missouri Fur Company. Shortly thereafter they established a new partnership to be known simply as the Missouri Fur Company. They deeply hoped that it would do better than its predecessor.

John Jacob Astor had accomplished the nearly impossible: within the space of a few years he had built a great commercial empire and had established himself in shipping, real estate, and the fur trade. His plan to start a trading post in the Pacific Northwest, however, was one to test even his vast wealth and great acumen, and he needed luck as well as expert management to make a success of this enterprise. David Thompson's fear of the Piegans was part of Astor's good fortune. Thompson, who was regarded as the North West Company's leading geographer, was given the responsibility of beating Astor to the Pacific Coast. In every respect he was equal to the assignment except that he went to such lengths to avoid an encounter with the Piegans that the resulting delay permitted the *Tonquin* to arrive at the mouth of the Columbia before the Canadians did.

But Thompson's slowness exhausted Astor's luck in the Northwest. In spite of the detailed instructions Astor had given him, Captain Thorn of the *Tonquin* quickly forgot his employer's warning to be cautious in his dealings with the Indians. After leaving the men and supplies at Astoria, he sailed north, as he had been ordered to do, to trade with the Indians. Putting into a harbor on Vancouver Island, he permitted the Indians to loiter on the ship's deck, where he had laid out a display of his trade goods. Honest and bluff, he failed to understand the nuances of Indian bargaining and, once having set the price he would pay for a sea otter pelt, refused to change it. This led the Indians to make jokes about his miserliness, which so angered Thorn that he began kicking the piles of skins, scattering them in every direction. Insulted and irate, the Indians went on shore.

The next day they were back, and Thorn again allowed them on board. When a large number of them had collected on the ship, they dropped their pretensions of friendship and turned on the crew, overwhelming the white men in bitter hand-to-hand fighting. Soon only five members of the *Tonquin*'s original complement were left alive, and they were barricaded below decks. Four of them escaped only to be killed later. The fifth, who was wounded and unable to leave with them, lighted some gunpowder. The reverberation of the explosion echoed above the waves beating along the coast, and pieces of timber and bodies of Indians flew in the air. Revenge, even if it meant suicide, the wounded man believed, was better than death at the hands of the Indians. The arrival of Hunt and his party during the winter helped bring Astoria up to proper strength in manpower, but the loss of Hunt's supplies and those on board the *Tonquin* greatly crippled the post's trading potential.

Equipping Astoria was not Astor's only concern. The election that had made James Madison President had also changed the composition of Congress, which now contained many members who were anxious to go to war with Great Britain. These were not the representatives of the maritime states, which were directly affected by the issues of impressment and freedom of the seas, but Westerners, who believed that the British were stirring up the Indians and who in their desire for more land anticipated an easy conquest of Canada. When the British minister delivered a communication from his government indicating that the restrictive Orders in Council would not be rescinded, Madison recommended war, and Congress voted its declaration on June 18, 1812.

This act sealed the fate of Astor's Northwest venture. The arrival of another supply ship, several good catches of beaver, and the journey of his employee, Robert Stuart, from Astoria to the Missouri River by way of the North Platte did not alter the effect of the hostilities. Astor had been pleased

when he had hired away employees of the North West Company, but in doing so, he had permeated his organization with incipient disloyalty. The North West Company had more men and closer ties to the Indians than the Pacific Fur Company. Nevertheless, the Pacific Fur Company might have retained Astoria if it had not been for the Canadian sympathies of some of Astor's partners and employees and the rumored approach of a British frigate. As Astor waited anxiously in New York for news of his trading post, one of his partners negotiated its sale at an unrealistically low price to the North West Company, which immediately hoisted the British flag and renamed it Fort George.

When Astor later learned what had happened, he was understandably furious. "Had our place and our property," he complained, "been fairly captured, I should have preferred it. I should not feel as if I were disgraced." He was a financial giant, but, for the time being in the Northwest, a helpless one.

The warhawks had wanted nothing more than open hostilities with Great Britain and a chance to invade Canada, but they had done little to prepare their country to meet its enemy. The nation's population was large compared to Canada's, but its army was relatively small, and the wave of patriotism that swept the country after the declaration of war did not produce a proportionate number of enlistments. America's first attempts to invade Canada were disasters and persuaded Tecumseh to join the British. At sea the Americans did better. Their frigates won several outstanding victories that heartened the country after the failures it had met on land. But its navy was not sufficiently strong to wrest control of the oceans from the British, and soon its best ships were either defeated or blockaded in port.

By absorbing America's energies and throwing open its northern frontier, these wartime events slowed down the further exploration and development of the Great Plains. Astor's Northwest base had fallen into the hands of the enemy, and he was not one to send good money spinning after bad. Once he had envisioned the possibility of establishing a chain of trading posts across the country, but the terminal point was now gone. So in New York he fumed at his partners' betrayal of his interests and set to work enlarging his fortune by other means, including overseas trade. By virtue of his political connections, extraordinary luck, and his usual wily foresight, Astor was destined to emerge from the war wealthier than before.

Lisa's lack of capital prevented him from diversifying his investments as Astor did. All the money he had and all that he could borrow or otherwise raise was sunk in the Missouri Fur Company and in his hopes for the Upper Missouri fur trade and a possible connection with Santa Fé. Astor had his eggs in several baskets; Lisa had barely enough eggs to fill one.

As he laid his plans during the winter and spring of 1813, Lisa found that the newly reorganized company did not win ready investor confidence and suppliers were reluctant to extend it credit. A further disappointment was the arrival in St. Louis of two traders, Robert McKnight and James Baird, who hoped to open up commerce with Santa Fé using a southern route. If they should be successful, they would make Lisa's projected route through the country of the Arapahos pointless. Yet the outlook for the Missouri Fur Company was not entirely bleak. It had established trading posts with several tribes, including the Sioux and the Arikaras, and still owned the permanent post above the Hidatsas. Any of these or any of the bands of trappers who were still out might have had a successful winter, and even with the depressed fur prices resulting from the war, it was possible the company would earn the cash it so desperately needed.

With a speculator's perpetual optimism, Lisa started up the river again, for although his partners now questioned his fundamental concept, they still regarded him as the person best suited to supervise the field operations. The first news he received, however, as his crew pushed against the current was disheartening. One of his men brought word from Fort Osage that McKnight and Baird had been able to purchase the supplies they had needed and were on their way to Santa Fé by a shorter route than the one he hoped to use. He next met one of his boats coming down from the Arikara villages with the skins the company had procured at that post during the winter. There were so few of them that Lisa did not think the men were justified in the expense of continuing to St. Louis and ordered them to turn back until they could obtain a larger cargo.

The Sioux, pleased with the arrangement that Lisa had made the previous year for trading with them, greeted him with friendliness, but they explained that the winter had been poor and they had little or nothing to trade. Most traders would have merely given them a few presents and proceeded on their way. But Lisa believed in establishing posts not only for the profits they might bring but also to secure his line of communications. A strong post with an able man in charge and supplies on hand when the Indians wanted them, he was convinced, helped ensure peace. So he set up another post for the Sioux's benefit, stocked it with goods, and left one of his abler men, Louis Bijou, to run it.

When he reached the Arikaras, he found the Indians agitated at his arrival and unfriendly. Only one chief instead of the three he had expected attended his initial council, evidence that the other two for some reason were offended. In the early afternoon the warriors sent their women and children away from the boats and back to the villages, an ominous sign, since they usually removed their women and children only before fighting. Lisa was so greatly outnumbered that he and his men could easily have been massacred if the Indians decided to attack. Demonstrating his usual cool courage, he took the initiative and marched with a dozen well-armed men to the village, where he demanded the presence of the chiefs at a council to explain their conduct. To his relief, all three appeared, which indicated that they were not yet prepared for an open break with him.

In part their hostile attitude had resulted from an earlier mistake in the distribution of presents, one chief complaining that he had not received his due. But the underlying reason for their attitude was the result of their year's hunting. They had obtained few skins to trade and were therefore afraid he would close his post and move it farther up the river. Lisa told them that this was exactly his intention and that he planned to carry it out; but he and the Arikaras finally agreed on a site about twelve miles away near the mouth of the Grand River.

After work had commenced on the new post, which Lisa called Fort Manuel, he went to see the Hidatsas, who, he learned, had stolen some of the company's horses and attacked several hunters. The Hidatsas traded furs with him but refused to surrender the horses, a sign that they had lost some of their respect and friendship for him. Obviously the British had been encouraging them to be more independent in their dealings with the Americans. This was a possibility foreseen by the cautious businessmen who had refused Lisa credit.

As he appraised the company's circumstances, Lisa's thoughts again turned to New Mexico. Not having heard from Jean Baptiste Champlain, whom he had sent in the direction of Santa Fé, he dispatched another man, Charles Sanguinet, in search of him. To Sanguinet, he also gave a letter of introduction to any Spaniards he might meet, inviting them to trade with the Missouri Fur Company. He still had substantial hopes that he could salvage the business by developing trade with Santa Fé. Then he organized his trappers into groups, placing Reuben Lewis in charge of the largest one, and sent them out into the field.

For all his vitality and intelligence, Lisa was the victim of conditions that he could not alter. He completely understood that to maintain the peace he needed for a successful operation he should establish a post for each important tribe and that the posts should be well manned and supplied. Only in this way could he offset the influence of the British. His post for the benefit of the Sioux seemed to be accomplishing its purpose, but this was only one of several his plan required. Yet his limited resources were stretched as far as they would go. Now he could only await the outcome of Sanguinet's trip in the direction of Santa Fé and the efforts of his trappers to secure skins.

In December, 1812, the directors of the Missouri Fur Company met in St. Louis to discuss the results Lisa had achieved so far. He himself was not present, but he had sent a boat from Fort Manuel. Instead of being heavily laden with furs, however, its cargo had been discouragingly light. Their confidence severely shaken, they voted to remove Lisa as a director and replace him with Pierre Chouteau, who was much more conservative.

Shortly after his demotion, Lisa received a message from Sanguinet. Because of the hostility of the Indians, Champlain had failed to reach Santa Fé, his group had been broken up, and several members of it had been killed. The fate of Champlain's expedition clearly demonstrated that the Missouri Fur Company could not hope to reach Santa Fé by the route Lisa had proposed and therefore could expect no revenues from that source. Then word came that the Sioux had killed Bijou and raided the company's trading post. Disaster seemed to be following disaster.

One small ray of hope brightened the otherwise dark picture. Reports from the trappers he had sent out indicated they had collected quite a number of furs, and a possibility still existed that the company might have a profitable year. Then Bijou sent word to Lisa at Fort Manuel that the earlier rumors were false; he was still completely in control of the post and, moreover, had been doing a brisker business than expected.

Among Lisa's employees was Charbonneau, Lewis and Clark's interpreter, who lived at Fort Manuel and made occasional trips upriver to trade with the Hidatsas and other Indians. Sacajawea had become a familiar figure around the post. Qui-

et and unassuming, she had helped the white men cross the continent, but they could not offer her much assistance in the cold December days of 1813 when she was stricken by a fever. They did what little they could with their slim knowledge of medicine and the supplies they had on hand, but the indomitable spirit that had led her to scoop the expedition's instruments out of the river when the boat swamped and that had supported her during the long journey through the unknown could carry her no farther, and she died at Fort Manuel on December 20.

As she lay on her deathbed, the Indians outside the fort were growing increasingly hostile and dangerous. With British encouragement, they seemed to be preparing to drive the Americans out, and Lisa did not have enough men to force them into line or enough presents to buy their allegiance. His own men knew this, and inside Fort Manuel a sense of uneasiness was beginning to grow. The stout walls of the fort offered protection, but no one knew what lurked beyond them on the windswept, snow-covered plains.

During the short days and long nights of December and January, several men refused to carry out assignments that Lisa gave them. If this had been an army expedition like Lewis and Clark's, he could have court-martialed them and had them flogged, but his own experience in the courts had taught him that private traders could not impose military discipline on their employees. In January, to quell the rising spirit of mutiny, he finally took the drastic step of discharging four men. Since they had no means of repaying the company for the credit they had received, this act caused a considerable financial loss for an organization that was already tottering on the brink of insolvency. But Lisa thought the expense worthwhile to rid himself of men whose bad examples might influence others.

During that bleak winter Charbonneau made another trip to the Hidatsas. Although he knew those Indians well, they had not been eager to trade with him, and it was clear that the British were increasingly successful in their efforts to turn the tribe against the Americans. Soon this source of furs would be closed to the company, and even worse, the river itself might be made impassable as a route to the West.

Outside Fort Manuel other tribes continued to camp in large numbers, and their mood was sullen and threatening. Even Lisa began to have doubts about the security of his position. Should the Indians decide to attack the fort—and that seemed a strong possibility—they could overrun it; and since the United States was involved in war with Great Britain, he could not expect to receive help from either the army or the Canadian traders. Realizing that his position was rapidly becoming untenable, he decided to drop down the river to Bijou's post among the Sioux.

He had not yet heard from Reuben Lewis and the trappers under his supervision. Perhaps they had had a successful season and would bring in enough skins to rescue the company. But after waiting several weeks, he decided he could not risk any further delay. Sending messengers to warn them of the growing danger from the Indians, he loaded his boats with what skins he had been able to obtain and returned to St. Louis.

Considering the circumstances under which he had labored, Lisa had done remarkably well. He had a considerable number of skins but not enough to convince the directors it was worth their while to continue to take the enormous risks they had been running. Lisa had lost about fifteen men in all, including one who had been slain near Fort Manuel, and the Indians' hostility was rising, not falling. Another expedition would probably be cut to pieces. Originally the partners had joined together in high hopes, with Lisa's vision pointing the way, but the company could not succeed under the conditions that now prevailed on the Great Plains. In September, 1813, the partners met once more, not to plan a new enterprise, but to go through the process of dissolution.

The warhawks, who had been so anxious to test America's strength against the British and put them in their place, had practically lost the Great Plains. Lisa was the one person in St. Louis with the courage and imagination to follow in Lewis and Clark's steps toward the west, and when he failed, no one else was prepared to succeed him.

Astor, too, was having additional difficulties with his Northwest post. He had already lost Astoria to his competition by sale. The loss was now confirmed by military conquest, making it twice as unlikely that he would ever get it back. A British naval vessel had landed at the mouth of the Columbia River and taken over the area in the name of the British government. Astoria not only belonged to the North West Company, it now stood on British soil as well. The Americans' claims in Oregon, based on Robert Gray's sailing up the river's mouth so many years before, were in jeopardy, and farther east the boundaries that Jefferson had enlarged with his brilliant coup were shrinking. For all practical purposes, the northern Great Plains no longer belonged to the United States, whose citizens could not venture far from St. Louis. No great armies had marched across those lands, but their conquest by the British and Indians was just as real as if they had.

Chapter 13

The Slow Return

Two leading objects of commercial gain have given birth to wide and daring enterprise in the early history of the Americas: the precious metals of the south, and the rich peltries of the north. While the fiery and magnificent Spaniard, inflamed with the mania for gold, has extended his discoveries and conquests over those brilliant countries scorched by the ardent sun of the tropics, the adroit and buoyant Frenchman, and the cool and calculating Briton, have pursued the less splendid, but no less lucrative, traffic in furs. . . .

These two pursuits have thus in a manner been the pioneers and precursors of civilization. Without pausing on the borders, they have penetrated at once, in defiance of difficulties and dangers, to the heart of savage countries: laying open the hidden secrets of the wilderness; leading the way to remote regions of beauty and fertility that might have remained unexplored for ages, and beckoning after them the slow and pausing steps of agriculture and civilization.

—Washington Irving, 1836

The winter winds blew the snow across the Great Plains, and the drifts grew deep wherever an obstruction slowed their pace and caused them to drop their white burden. Small shrubs disappeared, then bigger ones; rocks lost their shapes, ravines their depths; the roaring Missouri became sluggish, and ice outlined its tremendous falls, glistening like silver lacework when the sun broke through the clouds. The buffaloes, sheltered in willow groves from the wind's sharp teeth or shoveling with their heads where the snow lay thin to find the browse hidden beneath it, were gaunt, and the outline of their ribs showed through their heavy coats.

In the Mandan villages the Indians gathered in their sacred lodge while the young women dressed themselves in buffalo robes and prepared to use their bodies to bribe the gods that controlled the hunting. Their husbands and brothers brought them out and offered them to the old men. Pair after pair slipped from the lodge, but this time no vi-rile young American soldier replaced the men too old to recapture their youthful powers during those few nights.

No Americans were anywhere on the Great Plains. The smoke curled lazily from the lodges of the Sioux, but the warriors did not watch the river for passing American traders they could threaten or cajole into giving them ammunition and other presents. If they wanted supplies, they had to turn to the North West or Hudson's Bay companies, whose representatives had the Upper Missouri to themselves.

The Hidatsas, having stolen Lisa's horses and refused to trade pelts with his representative, Charbonneau, could now travel a few miles up the river and watch the fort he had built crumble away. The grass had recaptured its garden, and the beetles and other insects had been busy turning its log walls into dirt. No busy trader supervised the unloading of supplies, piling them where he could reach them easily when he purchased skins from an Indian.

166

On the Yellowstone River, down which Clark had come with hopeful thoughts of his expanding nation, Fort Raymond no longer bustled with activity. Only the wind whistled through its empty rooms, and the surface of the white snow that piled against the fort's walls was unbroken by American footprints. It was almost as though Lisa's men had never come that way. Quickly the wilderness was reclaiming its own.

When spring came back, the geese, too, returned, following the edge of the retreating cold. At times they circled, strong and purposeful against the blue sky, and landed on a springtime pool of water, just as they had done when Lewis and Clark had left the Mandan villages to start the journey that would take them across the continent. But no American officer was there to watch them or to bring down one or two with carefully aimed shots to relieve the steady diet of buffalo meat. History seemed to be running backward, carrying the Great Plains into the past. The only white men who traveled across them came from the north, just as they had done many years ago, and merchants from American cities like St. Louis were unknown.

The young nation, beset by the powerful army and navy of Great Britain, found itself barely equal to the task of defending its centers of population and had no resources left over for reconquering the wilderness. In chagrin it watched its soldiers defeated, its militia prove themselves nearly worthless, and the official buildings of its new capital burned by an invading army. Yet the British were not satisfied with the progress of the hostilities. They might defeat the Americans here and there, their experienced troops driving back the untrained militia. But the war dragged on without the decisive victories that would have brought the Americans to the conference table in a conciliatory mood. British soldiers could land almost anywhere on the American coast—only Fort McHenry repelled them, giving the Americans their national anthem—and then march inland, but they could not secure the permanent foothold that would have made these forays worthwhile. Fighting the Americans was like putting out a brush fire on a windy day; the sparks might be crushed out in one place, but they would blaze up again in another.

As the war ground on, John Jacob Astor fretted and fumed in New York about the loss of Astoria. By then he was so enormously wealthy he could afford the financial cost it had entailed, but his pride was badly hurt. He who considered himself so much smarter at trade than his contemporaries

had been outwitted by the North West Company. Without firing a single shot they had taken over his post and its entire stock—both the trade goods it contained and the pelts that had already been purchased on his account—and paid him in compensation a trifling sum. Astor liked bargains, but he liked them the other way around. When the war was over, he planned to reclaim Astoria and renew his effort to establish a string of posts across the continent, ending on the Columbia River; it would be a commercial undertaking such as the United States had never seen. Meanwhile, with the prices of furs depressed because of the war and the risks in obtaining them ever higher, he bided his time and watched for other ways of adding to his enormous fortune.

Lisa, too, felt the impact of the falling prices for the one commodity in which he knew how to deal; but stubborn as always, he would not give up. Furs were his life, and no matter how great the odds against him, he would continue in that trade. In 1814, although the prospects of peace seemed dim—in fact, Napoleon's surrender that year freed British troops for service in North America—he took in another partner, Theodore Hunt, and formed a new organization, Manual Lisa & Company, which assumed the assets and liabilities of the Missouri Fur Company.

In August, 1814, he was again at the banks of the Missouri River, supervising the loading of a boat and preparing for another season of trading with the Indians. He could go only as far as Council Bluffs, not today's city, but a point in Nebraska about twenty-five miles above modern Omaha. This was a long distance from the Rocky Mountains, where most of the furs were, but he was still in business.

Early that year the British government, weary of a war it could not easily win, had invited the United States to send delegates to Ghent to discuss possible peace terms. But the negotiations quickly became deadlocked. When the veterans of the Napoleonic Wars began to land in North America, Great Britain became less anxious for peace. With fresh troops gathering in Canada, the British envisioned an invasion of the United States, one that would finish the war and end the impudence of the former colony.

But events soon proved that the British would have as much difficulty invading the United States as the United States had had when it had tried to send troops against its northern neighbor. Sir George Provost with ten or eleven thousand seasoned troops pushed the Americans backward and expected soon to overrun the fort of Plattsburg, New York, where only fifteen hundred regular American troops and a few thousand militia held the line. But before doing so, he wanted control of Lake Champlain. The naval battle that followed, fought within sight of farmland, was bloody. The ships, being small, lacked bulwarks behind which the men could take protection, and their crews fought in a most unnaval fashion, anchoring along-side each other and shooting at each other with pistols. The casualties were high, but the American commodore, Thomas Macdonough, bested his adversaries; and Provost retreated, leaving the fortifications at Plattsburg securely in American hands.

The failure of this plan induced the British to be more reasonable at the negotiating table. Almost a year had elapsed since Britain had first asked President Madison to discuss possible terms of peace; but at last in December, 1814, the delegates from both countries signed the Treaty of Ghent; and the war came to a close.

Considering how many lives had been lost and how much treasure had been expended, the Treaty of Ghent was a strange document. For it settled none of the issues over which the war had presumably been fought. The British did not surrender their rights to impressment; the Americans did not give up their rights to the Newfoundland or Labrador fisheries or provide the British with access to the Mississippi. Even the question of the boundary between the United States and Canada, one of the most hotly contested issues, was not settled, although provisions were made for setting up commissions to examine the question later.

In spite of the inconclusive nature of the peace, the Americans had obtained certain national gains, both tangible and intangible. In addition to the Battle of Plattsburg, where the Americans had acquitted themselves well, Andrew Jackson's defeat of the Creek Indians, although tragic for the tribe, removed them as a serious threat to the American South, and his victory at New Orleans, although it occurred after the treaty was signed and therefore did not affect the war's outcome, added immeasurably to American prestige. For it showed the world that Americans, when properly led, could rout European troops and European generals.

Until the War of 1812, the British had regarded the United States as a wayward offspring, not to be taken seriously, a derogatory attitude that was shared by other nationalities. After the last cannon had sounded, however, their opinion perceptibly changed. The British looked on the Americans with considerably more respect, and other European powers began to realize that the country had come of age and was ready to take a place among the community of nations.

But the end of the hostilities did not bring about a sudden upsurge of renewed interest in the Great Plains. The recovery of the fur market was slow, the Indians still aggressive, and the land itself as forbidding as ever. Optimistic and undeterred by all the disappointments that had befallen him and the hardships he had endured, Lisa spent the winter of 1814–1815 on the Missouri River at Council Bluffs. He would have preferred to be heading a larger organization with bases much farther upriver, but since he could not raise the capital for such a venture, he contented himself with developing a brisk trade with the Omahas and keeping their sentiments pro-American. As he had long observed, sound commercial relations generally resulted in friendship.

He had the satisfaction, too, of seeing himself and his skill at handling the Indians become more widely recognized in St. Louis. Once feared as an alien and revolutionary, he was now regarded by the merchants of the city as an expert; and William Clark appointed him a subagent. He could hardly have done better, for Lisa knew as much about the Indians of the Missouri as any man.

In his official capacity, Lisa called a council of the Sioux at the mouth of the James River in the spring of 1815. His relationship with the tribe and his earlier establishment of a post to serve their needs stood him in good stead. As usual he distributed gifts and received in return pledges of everlasting friendship. But in Lisa's case the pledges had more significance than usual. The Sioux promised to—and did—wage war against some of the tribes to the east who had proved themselves allies of the British and enemies of the Americans.

Lisa also persuaded some of the Sioux's leaders to come to St. Louis and meet Clark. Among them was the Partisan, that wily, untrustworthy warrior who had caused Lewis and Clark so much trouble. But that was some years before. He was not as vigorous now, and he wanted the attention and gifts he thought he would gain by making the trip.

This undertaking of Lisa's almost turned into a disaster, for on the journey back to their homes, five Sioux and one Omaha, who had also gone to St. Louis, caught the white man's scourge, small-pox, and died of the dread disease. When the Arikaras had lost a chief on one of these ceremonial visits, their angry reaction had halted traffic on the river. But Lisa understood the Indians and arranged for the most elaborate burial he could provide, thus showing respect for the dead and demonstrating his concern to the living. The Indians accepted his act in the spirit he intended, and he forestalled a crisis in his relations with them.

After the Treaty of Ghent, Astor, although still smarting from his setback in Oregon, was determined to return to the fur trade. Like a campaigning general, he considered his plans and decided to concentrate the first of his renewed efforts around the Great Lakes and the Mississippi Valley rather than farther west. Ramsay Crooks and Robert Stuart, who had proved their loyalty and ability during the Astoria venture, took charge of rebuilding the war-disrupted business.

Astor next turned his attention to the future of his South West Company. The original articles were shortly to expire, but he was not yet ready to enter into competition with the North Westers, so he renewed his agreement with his Canadian partners. Then with the deviousness that was second nature to him, he encouraged the American government to prohibit foreigners from entering the fur trade on United States soil. His influence in Washington had not waned, and largely as a result of his lobbying, Congress enacted the legislation he desired. Then he expressed his regrets to his Canadian partners that such a thing could have happened, enjoying all the while the thought that they were now at his mercy.

Once he had secured the blanket prohibition against foreigners, he began persuading the government to make exceptions. As Lisa had learned when he took James and the other Americans up the river, Canadians, particularly Canadian boatmen, were essential to the successful conduct of the fur business. Only they would do the hard, back-breaking work without constantly complaining, and only they had the patience to endure the days of dull, monotonous labor. So Astor began to use his connections to secure licenses for a limited number of Canadians, including the boatmen he needed and the partners he trusted. He was not against aliens doing business on American soil; he simply wanted to be able to select the right ones.

While he was going through these maneuvers to resuscitate the South West Company and gain control of it, he had not forgotten Astoria. The loss of his post still rankled, but in attempting to solve this problem his usual magic touch failed him. Although he made appeal after appeal to the government for assistance, his highly placed friends could not help him. By the Treaty of Ghent each nation was to restore to the other any territory it had taken, thus returning their boundaries to their original status until the various boundary commissions could conduct their negotiations. That provision of the treaty made Astor's claim look good. But the sale of Astoria had been consummated before, not after, the military takeover. If the British naval forces had arrived a little earlier and had assisted the North West Company, the case would have been clear, and Astor would have received Astoria back. But the final ruling termed the sale a valid transaction. Therefore the soil on which Astoria stood became American soil, and the American flag flew over the fort. But the fort itself and the business conducted there belonged to the North West Company by virtue of its purchase. Astor received nothing in addition to the small sum the company had already paid him.

Yet he did not lose his hope of sharing in the profits of the fur trade west of the Mississippi, and as soon as he had his plans for the future of the South West Company in order, he turned his attention to St. Louis, thinking he might start there and, using it as his base, move west. This was a reversal of his prewar program, but under the circumstances he thought it might prove more practical.

Astor had always cast his nets wide, taking care not to miss an opportunity to make an acquaintance who might later be useful to him. Before the War of 1812 broke out, he had already had some slight dealings with the St. Louis merchants and had lent one of them, Charles Gratiot, some money and had purchased some deerskins through him. If he needed anything in St. Louis, he could always write to Gratiot. Another trader there, John P. Cabanne, had also become an acquaintance, and Astor had sold him some supplies, thus gaining another informant on conditions in St. Louis.

By 1816 Astor was ready to move more openly and instructed Ramsay Crooks and Robert Stuart to go to St. Louis in person. At the same time he asked Gratiot to assist his two representatives in making connections with some St. Louis firms. Since Astor was generally detested in St. Louis because of his reputation as a brutal competitor, Crooks and Stuart could not expect a warm reception. With help from Gratiot, however, they negotiated agreements with both Berthold & Chouteau and Cabanne & Company by which the two firms would deal only with Astor and he, in turn, would not send any of his men to trade on the Missouri. These arrangements gave Astor a toehold in the western trade without the risk and trouble of direct involvement. (As soon as the agreements were completed, he told Gratiot that in view of his new connections he could no longer do business with him. Some of the hatred Astor attracted was well deserved.)

A sense of caution colored the country's attitude toward the Great Plains. In the wake of the Louisiana Purchase and Lewis and Clark's expedition, enthusiasm had swept the nation, and men like Lisa and Astor had planned great enterprises while lesser men looked on with approval even if they would not dig deep enough into their pockets to provide all the capital that someone like Lisa needed. But the War of 1812 had blunted much of the nation's zest for its new land. Most of the traders in St. Louis, still shuddering from the experience of seeing the plains closed to them and friendly Indians turned into enemies, were now exercising more restraint. Lisa could find no one interested in his old idea of tapping the wealth of the Rocky Mountains; and even Astor, who liked to do things on a grand scale, was moving into the Missouri River business slowly and carefully.

The St. Louis waterfront was still lined with boats, their crews sweating as they loaded or unloaded them and filling the air with expletives in English, French, and Spanish. Merchants still watched the prices being paid for furs with the same intensity that a Southern planter kept tabs on the price of cotton, but the boats going upriver to the Indians were fewer, their cargoes lighter, and the dreams of the men who manned them smaller.

But interest was far from dead. Astor took steps to reorganize his operation by first dissolving the South West Company and incorporating it into the American Fur Company, the organization originally chartered by the New York State Legislature. Up until now it had been largely a company on paper only, but Astor had foreseen the time when he would merge his fur interests under the one name. All the business he had previously developed to the east formed the company's Northern Department; its other business, which he hoped to develop, was placed in its Western Department.

He then had his representatives apply to Clark for a license to trade on the Mississippi. He was not yet ready to enter the Missouri trade on his own account, but he was moving west, creeping across the country instead of trying to take it with one vast assault as he had done before. But those who had known him as a competitor did not believe he would be easier to deal with.

One of the issues left unsettled by the Treaty of Ghent was the boundary between the United States and Canada, several sections of which were in dispute. In 1818 the commission established in accord with the treaty decided that westward from the Lake of the Woods the line would follow the 49th parallel as far as the Rocky Mountains. Oregon, which then included the present state as well as Washington and the lands to the east, posed greater difficulties, because both nations had good claims to it. Finally the commissioners agreed their two nations should occupy it jointly for ten years, thus postponing the final settlement. At least the northern boundary of the Louisiana Purchase, and thus the northern boundary of the American Great Plains, was now defined.

The commissioners' decision had no immediate practical effect on the United States. No Americans were trading in Oregon, and no Americans were approaching the new boundary, although Crooks was complaining to Astor that he thought they should get into the Missouri trade directly instead of working through other firms, and Lisa was busy organizing another company—a constant occupation of his—hoping to create one large enough and strong enough to return to the Rockies.

Although the traders had still not penetrated into the wilderness as far as they had before the war drove them back, the nation as a whole had not lost the interest in the Great Plains that Lewis and Clark had aroused. Pike had described the area as uninhabitable except by nomads, and his opinion was spreading among those who had read his reports. On the other hand, the traders had already demonstrated that parts of it were rich in furs, which made it a valuable asset. The truth was that only a tiny group of Americans had first-hand knowledge of it, and many of those were not sufficiently trained to evaluate the land.

Congress, therefore, decided to launch another expedition, but one better equipped and staffed than ever before. Its purposes were to explore as far as the Yellowstone (hence it became known as the Yellowstone Expedition), impress the Indians with the power of the United States, and encourage the fur trade. To accomplish these ends, it was divided into two parts: a military branch under Colonel Henry Atkinson and a scientific branch under Major Stephen H. Long, a young officer with experience as an explorer and engineer.

John C. Calhoun, who was then secretary of war, was particularly interested in the scientific aspects of the expedition and saw an opportunity to increase the prestige of the United States among intellectuals abroad. He therefore instructed Long to assemble a scientific staff. Among those who agreed to accompany him were an artist, a physician and botanist, a geologist, Titian Ramsey Peale, son of Charles Willson Peale and later manager of the family museum, and Thomas Say, who had already published the first volume of his *American Entomology*.

Lewis and Clark's men had poled and rowed and towed their boats against the Missouri's current in the laborious manner of the fur traders. Long, however, had suggested that he conduct his explorations by steamboat. When he made this suggestion, no one had as yet used steamboats on the Missouri, which was shallower and more difficult to navigate than the Ohio or the Mississippi, but the idea seemed such a good one that the military arm of the expedition was also instructed to travel the same way.

Long helped design the boat that he himself was to use and had it built in Pittsburgh. Christened the *Western Engineer,* its appearance was calculated to create awe in the hearts of the Indians—or reduce the skeptical to gales of laughter. Attached to the bow and extending beyond the deck was a bowsprit manufactured of sheet iron. It was shaped and painted to resemble the head of a snake or dragon. A pipe from the boiler permitted steam to escape from its mouth, making it, according to the hopes of its designer, look like a fire-eating monster. To add to the effect, the jaws were hinged. Therefore the engineer, by regulating the amount and frequency of the steam he released, could make the jaws clank open and shut. Being a sternwheeler, it stirred up the waters directly behind it. This, its admirers believed, added to the illusion of its being a gigantic water snake with a boat on its back. (The Indians, being sensible people, did not believe this even when they were told so, but all the white men who saw it thought it a wondrous invention. The true illusion was their belief that they had created an illusion.)

Since Long had never built a boat before, he underestimated the time it would take and was behind schedule when he left Pittsburgh; and with practically every passing week, he got further behind. The boat did not have the speed Long had expected, and the engines developed a wide variety of ailments that required frequent treatment.

With one delay after another, it took Long about a month to reach the mouth of the Ohio, and that was all downstream. When the *Western Engineer* began to breast the Mississippi's current in order to reach St. Louis, its former speed seemed fantastic. Nor did the Missouri treat it kindly. Sawyers, planters, sandbars, and the current all worked against its forward progress. (Once it stood still in the river when its engines were running full-steam

ahead.) But finally in September it reached Fort Lisa, one of the posts that Lisa operated, at Council Bluffs above the mouth of the Platte.

The military arm of the expedition did not fare much better than the scientists, for steamboats were not yet well enough developed for efficient service on the Missouri. Also, the soldiers were undisciplined and did not like leaving their more comfortable quarters to make the journey. Desertions were so common that one officer took drastic inhuman steps to stop them. He sentenced four would-be deserters to twenty-five lashes a day on four consecutive days. As this punishment was intended to be an example to the others, he had the deserters flogged at mealtime and ordered everyone else, including civilians, to come and watch. When this punishment was completed, he ordered his surgeon to take a scalpel and cut off the deserters' ears. (One of them committed suicide rather than run the whole course of the officer's tortures.)

Finally the two arms of the expedition began the construction of their separate winter camps at the edge of the Great Plains near Fort Lisa, but a long way from their destination, the Yellowstone. Calhoun had instructed Long to study with particular care the northernmost point on the Missouri, where Lewis had been prevented from making observations by Peter Cruzatte's erroneously aimed bullet. But at the rate he was progressing, it looked as though it would be a while before he got that far.

The year 1819 was a period of restlessness and change in the United States, marked by one important acquisition of land: the purchase of Florida from Spain. At the same time Spain ceded to the United States what claims it had to Oregon, claims based on the early discoveries of its intrepid mariners, and agreed on the boundary between Mexico and the United States.

But in spite of these accomplishments, the era of political goodwill that had followed the War of 1812 was coming to a close, and the nation was racked by economic troubles resulting from the speculative spirit that had prevailed across the land. The government, anxious to sell its public domain, had offered acreage on terms that tempted purchasers into buying more than they could afford. Rising prices had also lured farmers into overextending their holdings; optimistic creditors had been careless in their lending; the banks, including the Second Bank of the United States, which should have been a restraining influence, acted imprudently; and many persons found themselves with debts they could not pay or with safes crammed with worthless notes and mortgages. The

Panic of 1819 touched every segment of society from the frontiersmen and the small farmers to the bankers and merchants anxiously tallying their losses.

To all who would listen, the economy signaled caution, but Lisa's ears were deaf to that word, thrown at him so often by so many different partners and creditors. Deep in the Rockies, he knew, was untold wealth for the man able to collect it, and he was still determined to be that man. Landowners and merchants could worry about mortgages and banknotes; before his eyes danced the vision of a chain of forts up the Missouri and into the mountains and a flotilla of keelboats laden with furs returning to St. Louis at the end of each season.

In 1819 he reorganized his company once more, selecting as partners several St. Louis businessmen. One of these, a former hatter from Nashville, Tennessee, was Joshua Pilcher, a man much like Lisa in temperament. He had moved to St. Louis in 1814 and had quickly earned for himself both a place in the city's business circles and a reputation for a violent temper. Once he got into a quarrel with Stephen F. Austin, then a resident of St. Louis; and when an exchange of letters failed to settle their dispute, Pilcher severely damaged one of Austin's eyes. On another occasion, when his fellow directors of the Bank of St. Louis refused to employ a more conservative cashier, he led a crowd that took physical possession of the building. His willingness to use force was in line with Lisa's way of doing things.

Although Pilcher had had no experience with the Indians, he had learned about furs as a hatter, and he had also been a partner in a St. Louis auction house that handled skins. Being vigorous and considerably younger, Lisa thought he could take over some of the field operations that Lisa had so long managed himself.

If the panic had little effect on Lisa's perpetual optimism, it was changing the government's attitude toward the Yellowstone Expedition, which so far had not lived up to the expectations of Calhoun and the public. When Long left the expedition in camp and returned to Washington that winter to report to Calhoun, he discovered that the atmosphere at the nation's capital was considerably chillier than when he had last been there. The expedition had spent a large amount of money with few results, and Congress was unenthusiastic about appropriating more funds. Long offered several less costly proposals, and these, too, were rejected by a money-conscious government. Finally he suggest-

ed that he leave his steamboat and with a smaller group of men explore the Platte, Arkansas, and Red rivers the following summer. This was not the grand endeavor that he and his fellow countrymen had once thought the Yellowstone Expedition would be—one newspaper had likened it to Napoleon's scientific expedition to Egypt—but for a nation that was down on its luck and counting its pennies, it seemed enough.

On June 1, 1820, Long issued his orders and made his assignments. The crew of the *Western Engineer* was to take the boat back down the Missouri; the remainder of the men, accompanied by a military escort of six soldiers, were to go west by land. Although much of the country through which they would be traveling had been explored before, Long had a sense of danger. "The duties of the expedition," he wrote in his order, "being arduous, and the objectives in view difficult of attainment, the hardships and exposures to be encountered, requiring zealous and obstinate perseverance, it is confidently expected, that all embarked in the enterprize [sic] will contribute every aid in their power, tending to a successful and speedy termination of the contemplated tour." These words were still ringing in their ears when, on June 6, they left their winter camp, some twenty men in all.

As they came to the edge of the Great Plains, a violent thunderstorm broke. To replace the physician and botanist, who had died earlier, the War Department had assigned a doctor, Edwin James, to the expedition. He had also had training as a botanist and was given the additional duties of geologist and official chronicler. Describing the storm, he said, "The plain about us, for a great distance, was destitute of timber, and so level that our party formed the most prominent object in an extent of several miles. It is not surprising that, in this situation, we were a little startled at seeing the lightning strike upon the ground, at the distance of two hundred yards from us. We could not have been deceived, in relation to this appearance, as we distinctly saw the water and mud thrown several feet into the air by the shock."

Continuing along the Platte, their route took them to the villages of the Pawnees, who, in their customary fashion, tried to discourage them from proceeding farther by telling them of the hardships they would have to endure and the dangers they would face. But Long and his men were not to be turned back by words, and the Pawnees did not threaten to attack them, as they had done to Pike.

At the first of the three villages, Long and James attempted to interest the Indians in being vaccinated against smallpox. For this purpose, they had a small quantity of vaccine, which had been sent to them by messenger after their departure from the Missouri. Unfortunately the boat that had brought it up the river had been wrecked, and the vaccine itself immersed in water and ruined. Nevertheless, they lectured the Indians on the efficacy of vaccinations, and James gave a demonstration by vaccinating three men, including Long. But none of the Pawnees asked to be treated in a similar fashion. Secretly James was relieved, because he thought the water-soaked vaccine would not have given them immunity.

As they traveled along the river, James noted that "in the scenery of the Platte, there is the utmost uniformity: a broad plain, unvaried by any object on which the eye can rest, lies extended before us; on our right are the low and distant hills which bound the valley; and on our left the broad Platte, studded with numerous small, but verdant, islands. On these islands is usually a little timber, which is not met in other situations."

Sometimes the sun beat down on them, sometimes the rain drenched them, soaking their baggage and making the air hideous with peals of thunder and the skies bright with flashes of lightning. At times they could not find wood to use as tent poles; once a single log floating down the Platte made them rejoice, because it gave them fuel other than buffalo chips with which to cook their food. And, as other travelers, they marveled at the herds of buffaloes, which roamed the Great Plains in such numbers. When they came to the juncture of the North and South Forks of the Platte, they kept to the South Fork, and the land became more broken as they approached the Rockies.

On June 30 they saw shapes rising from the horizon to the west. "For some time," James wrote, "we were unable to decide whether what we saw were mountains, or banks of cumulous clouds skirting the horizon, and glittering in the reflected rays of the sun. It was only by watching the bright parts, and observing that their form and position remained unaltered, that we were able to satisfy ourselves, they were indeed mountains. They were visible from the lowest parts of the plain, and their summits were, when first discovered, several degrees above our horizon."

The men were cheered by the sight of their goal but soon learned, as Pike had done, that the clear air made distances deceptive. They did not arrive at the mountains the next day or the next or the next. They then took comfort in the thought they would reach them on July 4 and have a double cause for celebration. But although they received

an issue of whiskey and some extra food on the anniversary of the nation's birth, the Rockies were still a distance away. On the fifth of July they were certain the mountains were not more than five miles off, so Long, Peale, and two enlisted men went ahead of the others to explore the route. After riding for eight miles, they turned back, realizing they were not going to reach the Rockies on that day either. But on the sixth they finally arrived at the base of the elusive mountains, which for a week had risen in front of them, apparently close at hand and yet for so long unattainable.

The illusion of the *Western Engineer* was not nearly as effective as the illusion created by the Rocky Mountains. At a distance they had duped Long, as well as Pike and others, into believing they were near. Even close at hand, they continued to confuse their spectators. "From our camp," James wrote, "we had expected to be able to ascend the most distant summits then in sight, and return the same evening, but night overtook us and we found ourselves scarcely arrived at the base of the mountain." Like Hunt leading the men to Astoria, Long could not find a pass that would take them into the Rockies, so they turned south toward Pikes Peak.

One of their objectives was to climb that mountain, and Long assigned four men to James, two to guard his horses and maintain his base camp and two to accompany him on the actual ascent. Their way was rough and steep, and the first night out they could not find a level place to sleep and had to build a barricade to prevent themselves from rolling into a nearby brook.

They awoke the next morning, however, in good spirits and expected to reach the summit that day. Climbing at a more favorable season of the year than Pike, they made rapid progress upward, but when they halted at two o'clock in the afternoon to rest, they realized they could not make the trip up and back during the daylight hours. Nevertheless, they agreed to continue on and risk the chance of a supperless night.

At four they stood on the top of Pikes Peak and looked at the world below them. The weather was calm and clear, although their thermometer registered only 42 degrees in the middle of July. "From the summit of the Peak," James wrote, "the view towards the north, west, and southwest, is diversified with innumerable mountains, all white with snow. . . . To the east lay the great plain, rising as it receded, until in the distant horizon, it appeared to mingle with the sky."

In spite of the beauty extending on every side

beneath them, they could remain on the summit for only half an hour. The temperature was falling, and the sun slipping slowly toward the mountains in the west. Darkness overtook them before they could find the place where they had camped the previous night, so they went to sleep without food. The next day as they continued their descent, they saw below them a forest fire whose flames were licking at several acres of trees and realized it must have been started by their campfire of three nights ago. In that great woodland, where there were more trees than anyone could then cut, the loss of the timber did not disturb them, but they were alarmed that Indians might notice the smoke from afar and come to investigate it. This fear remained unrealized, but they discovered that the flames had burned their cache, destroying most of their equipment and provisions and leaving them only a scanty breakfast. But they got safely back to their horses and soon were again with Long.

Having accomplished the objective of climbing Pikes Peak, Long took his expedition south to the Arkansas; and after exploring as far west as the site of present-day Cañon City, Colorado, where Pike had previously camped, he started on the journey home. Since his original orders called for him to explore both the Arkansas and Red rivers, Long now divided his party. James, Peale, and seven men were to go with him in search of the Red; the remainder were to follow the Arkansas under the command of Captain John R. Bell.

On July 24, 1820, Long's group forded the Arkansas while Bell watched them. When they reached the other side, they turned around and gave three cheers, then marched off toward the south. That same morning Bell started down the Arkansas. His trip was marked by the usual hardships encountered when traveling across the Great Plains—mosquitoes, violent storms, blazing heat, and strayed horses. A thunderstorm that broke on the first day was, Bell said, the worst of the entire trip, and the men could see the lightning strike the plain not far from where they stood holding their horses and trying to keep the animals from panicking.

One of Thomas Say's particular responsibilities was collecting information about the Indians, so he welcomed every encounter with them, and Bell delayed as long as he could with each band while Say took notes on their costumes, customs, and behavior. His task was greatly complicated by the many unfamiliar languages of the tribes they met. Sometimes the process of interpretation became so cumbersome and involved as to approach the ludicrous. Long or Bell would speak in English,

explaining why they had so few presents to give away or asking questions about the land and its inhabitants. Another man would pick up their words and translate them into French, so they could again be translated into an Indian language understandable to one of their visitors. He in turn would repeat them in another Indian language known to more of the gathering, after which they might again be translated to reach an even broader audience. Under such circumstances, as Bell wryly remarked, misunderstandings were inevitable, and yet Say was able to obtain a considerable amount of information that he transcribed into his notes.

By August 30 they had reached the edge of the Great Plains. Men and horses were tired, and they were looking forward to the end of their long journey. The trail, well worn by the Indians, had been obscured in places by a recent fire; and during the day they had noticed fresh signs that Indians had been traveling that way. This did not particularly concern them, as they had met several bands during their trip back from the Rockies, and none had been hostile. But they were determined to keep careful watch throughout the night.

Say finished his records for the day and placed them in his saddlebags, where he stored the five notebooks that contained the information he had collected. A lieutenant, William Henry Swift, did the same with the journal in which he had kept detailed topographical records since the expedition had left the Missouri. As was their custom, they then piled the saddlebags with the knapsacks in which they kept their extra clothing. Since these were both carried on the pack animals, they were placed with the other packs for the night.

As darkness fell and their campfire began to flicker, the weary men started to get into their blankets. Bell assigned the men who were to stand watch during the night, not only to guard those who were sleeping but to keep an eye on the horses and packs in case any thieving Indians should happen to have noticed their camp. With everything in order, those not on duty dropped off to their well-earned rest.

At the first daylight when the camp began to stir, someone gave the alarm. Three men were missing, all of them assigned that past night to sentinel duty. With them they had taken the three best horses, two rifles, all the clothing that was not marked as belonging to the government and, worse yet, all the saddlebags, which they thought contained the leaders' valuable articles.

Bell followed the rascals—he called them worse than that—for their trail showed clear in the dew-wet grass. Apparently they were planning to retrace their way along the Indian trail they had ridden the night before. But as the grass dried, the tracks they left became less clear, and there was little point in continuing the chase. They had stolen the three best horses; those that remained, Bell remarked, could not be whipped into a faster pace than a walk.

The theft was a serious and disheartening blow to the expedition. The loss of their clothing and some of their equipment increased the hardship of the remainder of their journey, but at least they could be replaced once they reached civilization. But no one could rewrite from memory all the details in Say's and Swift's notebooks. Making the loss even more bitter was the knowledge that the deserters had taken the saddlebags thinking they contained items of more tangible worth. On finding the notebooks, they would discard them, tossing them to the winds and rains.

After Long's men had forded the Arkansas and paused to give the three cheers for the contingent under Bell, they headed south until they picked up a river that Long was certain was the Red. Following its course downstream, he and his men also suffered many hardships. Their tent was not large enough to shelter more than half their number, but as they were determined to share and share alike, each man slept with his head and shoulders under its protection, and left the rest of his body exposed to the elements. At one time they were pelted so ferociously by hailstones that the horses refused to move in any direction except with the wind. Rather than go off their course, the men dismounted and waited until the hail stopped. Then they moved on, soaking wet in the rain, until dark when, being unable to find wood for a fire, they went to sleep supperless under their tent in, as James noted, "the most sociable manner imaginable."

Obtaining sufficient food and water was a frequent problem. On August 3 James wrote that "little delay was occasioned by our preparation for breakfast. The fourth part of a biscuit, which had been issued to each man on the preceding evening, and which was to furnish both supper and breakfast, would have required little time had all of it remained to be eaten, which was not the case. We were becoming somewhat impatient on account of thirst, having met with no water which we could drink, for near twenty-four hours. . . . We had travelled [the] greater part of the day enveloped in a burning atmosphere, sometimes letting fall upon us the scorching particles of sand which had been raised by the wind, sometimes almost suffocating by its entire stagnation, when we had the good fortune to meet with a pool of stagnant water, which though muddy and brackish, was not entirely impotable . . . Here also was a little wood, and our badger [which they had killed the day before], with the addition of a young owl, which we had the good fortune to take, was very hastily cooked and eaten."

Such days were common as they persevered against the unfriendly land, following the river and making notes of all they had experienced and seen. On September 10 they came to a juncture with another, much larger, river, which they immediately recognized. It was the Arkansas.

During all those weary days of travel, they had been pursued by the same ill-luck as Pike, for they had been following not the elusive Red River, but the Canadian, whose course had guided the Mallet brothers so many years before when they had come from the north to explore the plains. "Our disappointment and chagrin," James wrote, "at discovering the mistake we had so long laboured under, was little alleviated by the consciousness that the season was so far advanced, our horses and means so far exhausted, as to place it beyond our powers to return and attempt the discovery of the sources of the Red river."

Long's two expeditions, which Calhoun had originally sponsored with such high hopes, had fallen far short of their purposes. The Yellowstone Expedition, aborted even as its members waited in their winter camp near Fort Lisa, had added little to Americans' knowledge of their country. The less pretentious second expedition had taken routes that were already known, and the theft of the saddlebags with their bulging notebooks resulted in the loss of much of the carefully gathered information. Nevertheless, Long's reports to the government and the publication of James's record of the journey gave Americans new insight into their own country.

The explorers also reaffirmed Pike's evaluation of the Great Plains. "In regard to this extensive section of the country," Long reported, "we do not hesitate in giving the opinion, that it is almost wholly unfit for cultivation, and of course uninhabitable by a people depending upon agriculture for their subsistence. Although tracts of fertile land, considerably extensive, are occasionally to be met with, yet the scarcity of wood and water, almost uniformly prevalent, will prove an insuperable obstacle in the way of settling the country. . . .

"This region, however, viewed as a frontier, may prove of infinite importance to the United

States, inasmuch as it is calculated to serve as a barrier to prevent too great an extension of our population westward, and secure us against the machinations or incursions of an enemy, that might otherwise be disposed to annoy us in that quarter.''

Such was the opinion of Long and the learned scientists who accompanied him. To them the Great Plains were useful only as a no-man's-land between the more populated part of the United States and an enemy attack from the west. But Lisa, less well educated but more familiar with the frontier, thought differently. He continued to see the Great Plains as an area that could produce wealth in itself and also provide access to the even greater riches of the Rockies.

Others might cling to St. Louis, but in the fall of 1819, he had gone upriver again to Fort Lisa, taking with him his new partner, Joshua Pilcher. He was now forty-seven, and almost every year of his life had been a difficult one, its days spent struggling with men of less vision, fighting the elements, maneuvering against the Indians, disciplining his crews, and arguing with creditors, debtors, and government officials. During the winter of 1819–1820, he let Pilcher carry the heaviest burden of the work and travel across the snow-covered plains to barter with the Indians while he stayed close to the fort. In the spring of 1820, his health no longer what it had been, but his confidence in his new partner great, he left Fort Lisa for St. Louis.

His doctor was unable to determine what was wrong with him, but his illness had no effect on his temper. On August 1 he got into an argument with another man and beat him severely with his fists and an iron bar. This outburst was his last. Shortly afterward he went to a nearby sulfur springs in an attempt to find a cure. But the remedy was ineffective, and on August 12 he died.

The man who had done so much to open up the northern Great Plains and who had led the fainthearted where they otherwise would not have ventured was dead, but his dream was not. The day before his death he prepared his will, and in it he expressly stated that he wanted the company to continue. Furthermore, he instructed his executors, if necessary, to mortgage his property to finance it.

Chapter 14

The Road and the River

If we compared the present condition of our Union with its actual state at the close of our Revolution, the history of the world furnishes no example of a progress in improvement in all the important circumstances which constitute the happiness of a nation which bears any resemblance to it. . . . At the first epoch half the territory within our acknowledged limits was uninhabited and a wilderness. Since then new territory has been acquired of vast extent. . . . Over this territory our population has expanded in every direction and new States have been established almost equal in number to those which formed the first bond of our Union.

—James Monroe, 1823

Slavery's dark cloud shaded the land, chilling the spirit of nationalism and pitting Northerner against Southerner. For a time the issue had been quieted by the delicate balance between the slave states and the free states. As new states were admitted, following the principles set down in the Northwest Ordinance of 1797, the balance was maintained, and the Mason-Dixon line in the east and the Ohio River in the west served as boundaries between the two categories.

The purchase of Louisiana, however, upset this balance. Because both France and Spain, the territory's former owners, had permitted slavery, the institution lived on in the ceded land. The admission of the southernmost part of the territory as the State of Louisiana had raised no problems, for it was within the general geographical zone of the slave states. But in 1819 Missouri also requested admission and assumed that it, too, would be a slave state. When the question came up in Congress, many Northerners took alarm. Although no boundary—tacit or otherwise—limited slavery's expansion west of the Mississippi, they had assumed it would remain south of the same general latitude. Now it appeared to them that all of the Louisiana Purchase might be carved into slave states, leaving the North outvoted in the Senate and perhaps in the House. Sectionalist feelings flared, and Congress went home without having resolved the problem.

Before it again met, discussion moved from the legislative chambers to the streets and became more and more heated. As some saw it, the interests of the industrial and commercial North, so different from those of the largely agricultural South, might be completely submerged in the eventual flood of slave states. Responding to the wave of feeling that had swept the country, Congress in 1820 hammered out the Missouri Compromise. Missouri was to be a slave state, whose influence in Congress would be offset by Maine, newly separated from Massachusetts and admitted as a free state. Thus for the present the numbers would remain equal. For the future, slavery would be prohibited in the rest of the Louisiana Purchase north of 36° 30′, a line that runs through modern Oklahoma. By this decision all but a tiny portion of the Great Plains then owned by the United States would be free.

To many people in Missouri, the outcome of the issue had been a matter of economic life or death. In the ebullient period following the War of 1812,

177

many slaveowners had moved west to farm the rich lands along the lower Missouri River. The loss of their slaves would have been a devastating blow. To men like Joshua Pilcher, however, the resolution of the issue made little personal difference, because slaves were of no particular use in the fur trade. Besides, he had many other pressing problems to concern him in 1820. He had to track down a thief who had stolen some of the company's beaver skins and bring him into court; he was having trouble dissolving a previous partnership in which he had been involved; and the price of pelts dropped to a frightening low. It was not a good time for a man new to the fur trade to be entering it, but Pilcher had Lisa's faith in the future and confidence in his own ability.

Older and more experienced in the fur business, Pierre Chouteau, Jr., and B. Berthold were beginning to entertain doubts about the ability of small firms to survive and thought of tightening their ties with Astor, but they had difficulty working out an agreement with him. On the other hand, another important firm, Stone, Bostwick & Company, had opened a St. Louis office. It had formerly competed with Astor's Northern Department and wanted nothing more to do with him. So it had sided with Lisa's forces and sold supplies to his company. In fact, it was debts to that partnership that had most concerned Lisa on his deathbed when he authorized his executors to mortgage his property. The battle lines were being drawn between the fur traders in the fall of 1820 when Pilcher, taking Lisa's place as the operating head of the Missouri Fur Company, started up the Missouri.

Because of the poor fur market, he was not able to buy as many supplies as he would have liked, but he had recruited almost two hundred men. Under the supervision of two of the company's best leaders, Robert Jones and Michael Immel, he sent some of them to build a post, Fort Benton, on the Yellowstone near the mouth of the Bighorn. Ultimately he wanted them to go back to the Three Forks of the Missouri, in the country of the Blackfeet, but he instructed them at first to trap and trade in the land of the Crows.

He himself, Pilcher decided, would spend the winter at Fort Lisa near the spot where Long's scientists had made their camp in 1819–1820. This would give his principal partner at St. Louis time to wait for a better fur market and perhaps persuade Stone, Bostwick, & Company to equip him more generously. But, like Lisa, he had no taste for idleness and, while he waited, set his men to work constructing a new fort on an island near the mouth of the White River.

The collapse of the military branch of the Yellowstone Expedition had upset his plans. Originally the army had expected to establish a fort at the mouth of the Yellowstone, using it as a base from which to protect any Americans in the area. Since this was no longer an immediate possibility and since Pilcher was unwilling to wait until the army organized another expedition, he decided to provide his own protection by constructing a string of trading posts.

As he watched spring come, the Missouri freeing itself from the ice and the brant again flying overhead, the market for beaver skins greatly improved, placing the company in a far sounder position and enabling Pilcher's St. Louis partner to order more supplies. But that year goods were short in St. Louis, and he could not place his hands on what they needed. The buds on the cottonwoods had burst and the yellow green of spring had turned to the darker green of summer before he was able to gather enough to load a keelboat and start it on its way. But the boat broke loose from its mooring—the line either snapped or someone cut it—and the Missouri's current grabbed it and carried it downstream. Fortunately his employees were able to locate it. Its hull was undamaged and its contents safe, so with towlines, poles, and oars, its crew began the journey upriver to Fort Lisa. On the night of August 13, when the men had made their camp and the boat lay anchored in the dark river, it sank, perhaps as the result of sabotage by a disgruntled employee or an unscrupulous competitor.

With the rise in the fur market, the company's credit was good enough to load another boat, but the season was now late; and about two miles below Fort Lisa, the blocks of ice coming down the Missouri made it impossible for the men to move the new boat farther. There it lay, trapped by the elements, its cargo useless for Pilcher's purposes.

Astor, too, was having his troubles. For years he had had an extraordinary relationship with the members of the North West Company, sometimes as their partner, sometimes as their competitor. He had enticed them into giving up much of their trade south of the border by setting up the South West Company and letting them participate in it. He had then sponsored legislation making their participation illegal and had gradually squeezed them out. He had lured away some of their best men to help him win the race to Oregon, conscious that he was bribing them to turn against their former employers. But the victories had not all been one-sided. The Canadians, accustomed to the rough-and-tumble aspects of the business, had snatched Astoria away from him. But in this commercial battle between giants, Astor enjoyed a singular advantage over the North West Company: all his other competitors were the relatively weak American firms while the North West Company had to battle with the mammoth Hudson's Bay Company. In 1821, however, this changed. In one of the biggest commercial transactions that had taken place in either Canada or the United States up to that time, the two Canadian companies announced their merger. No longer would each be distracted by competition with the other.

In addition to creating one strong company where there had been two, the merger had another effect unfavorable to Astor. An employee of the Hudson's Bay Company, Joseph Renville, decided to engage in the fur trade of the Upper Missouri and formed the Columbia Fur Company. (Its formal name was Tilton & Company after William P. Tilton, one of the two American partners whom he took in so he could trade legally on American soil.) Renville was an experienced, aggressive trader, and he brought with him outstanding men like Kenneth McKenzie, a veteran of six years' service with the North West Company. Renville lacked Astor's capital and his connections with the federal government, but he and his associates were a formidable entry into the Missouri fur trade. Earlier, Crooks had urged Astor to stop being so cautious and enter the trade directly. Now it looked as though he had been right. Competition on the northern Great Plains was increasing.

Except for Long's expedition, little had occurred in the southern Great Plains since the War of 1812. The Indians incited by the British were not active that far from the Canadian border, but no inducements lured travelers across the lands that both Pike and Long had characterized as so barren. The prospects for furs were not as good as in the north, and the Spanish had made it clear that they not only did not welcome trade with the Americans, they were likely to put would-be merchants in jail. That is exactly what they had done with James Baird and Robert McKnight, the two men who had so worried Lisa in 1812. Just as Lisa had thought he might salvage his company's prospects by discovering a route to the New Mexican capital from the north, Baird and McKnight had arrived in St. Louis, purchased a supply of goods, and started off for Sante Fé through the southern plains. Their reception, however, had been similar to that accorded other alien visitors, and they became more familiar with the iron of Spanish prison bars than the silver of Spanish pesos.

But after so many centuries, Spain's grasp on the New World was weakening. Revolt after revolt had shaken its Latin American colonies, and Mexico, too, had caught the fever. Now it had won its independence, and although its people were uncertain what form of government they wanted—the conservatives favored a monarchy; the liberals a federal republic—a new sentiment prevailed in the country, and many of the old Spanish restrictions were set aside. This led to the release after all these years of Baird and McKnight. Although McKnight remained in Mexico, Baird and other members of the party returned to the United States with the news.

Moses Austin, father of Stephen Austin, with whom Pilcher had fought, also profited from the changing spirit of the newly freed Mexicans. A victim of the Panic of 1819, he was searching for a way to recoup his fortune and thought he might be able to do this by establishing an American colony in Mexico. Skillful with people and sensitive to the feelings of others, he had observed every Mexican regulation and formality during a visit to the official in charge of the eastern provinces. As a consequence of his diplomatic approach, he had won approval for a plan to bring three hundred American families to Texas as settlers, provided they agreed to obey the law, swear allegiance to the government, and become members of the Catholic Church. On the way home, he caught pneumonia and died, but Stephen had carried on with his father's work and in 1821 was scouting out the specific lands that would be best suited to the settlers' needs.

John McKnight, Robert McKnight's brother, was living in St. Louis when the erstwhile traders returned from Santa Fé. Not having seen Robert since 1812 and knowing that it was now safe to visit Santa Fé, he persuaded Thomas James to organize a trading expedition that he could accompany to the New Mexican capital. After his experience with Lisa, when he had suffered so from the cold and had learned that independence may be nothing but irresponsibility, James had opened a store in a small community south of St. Louis.

In 1818 he purchased a large stock of merchandise in the East, much of it on credit, and carried it to Pittsburgh in wagons. Since the river was too low to operate a keelboat, he left it there to be shipped when the Ohio had risen. The timing could not have been worse. When the spring of 1819 pushed the dogwoods into bloom and the Ohio threatened to overflow its banks, prices had dropped, and the panic made even the brave cautious. Like other frontier merchants James was a victim of the long time lag that sometimes occurred between the purchase of merchandise and its display on a merchant's shelves. In 1821 he was still looking for a way to retrieve his fortunes and agreed to go with John McKnight to Santa Fé.

Their route took them along the Arkansas—the river that had deluded both Pike and Long and caused them so much difficulty—past Fort Smith on the western border of present-day Arkansas, and from there beyond the mouth of the Cimarron River. The month was August and the water so low they could proceed no farther by boat, so James sent three men to a nearby Osage village to tell the Indians he would like to buy some horses. In a few days the men returned with about forty Indians and a white man who lived among them. He was Nathaniel Pryor, who had served Lewis and Clark as sergeant and who had been attacked by the Arikaras. With the end of the War of 1812, the army offered him no future, and being untrained for much else, he had gone to live with the Indians.

At the Osages' village, James found several other Americans, including Hugh Glenn from Ohio and Jacob Fowler from Kentucky. They, too, hoped to exploit the Mexicans' new cordiality, but they preferred to travel alone and refused James's invitation to join their expedition to his when he set out again mounted on the horses he purchased.

The party had reached northwestern Oklahoma when it was intercepted by a band of Comanches, who behaved in a hostile manner. James's interpreter warned him that it was a war party and he should placate the Indians with gifts. James responded generously, giving away a large portion of the trade items he was taking to Santa Fé.

Among the Comanches were two chiefs, one who seemed friendly and one named One-Eye, who appeared the opposite. James thought that One-Eye intended to kill them, but instead he soon left. Whereupon the friendly chief demanded more presents on the ground that he had interceded with One-Eye on James's behalf. In the ambivalent spirit often shown by Indians, the friendly chief invited James to visit their village, while some of the other Comanches, noticing that the white men were riding the horses they had bought from the Osages, accused them of being spies for that tribe.

James decided to take the advice of the friendly chief and not continue up the Arkansas. (He later learned the advice had been good; One-Eye had planned to ambush him there.) Instead he accepted the invitation of the friendly chief to visit his village, which was a considerable distance away.

After several days of travel—they were now in the northern part of the Texas Panhandle—they noticed a band of Comanches appear over a rise in the ground in front of them. At their head was the friendly chief, who rode up and, embracing James, welcomed him. Just at that moment an Indian grabbed a brass kettle and dashed off with it. This gave James pause, and he asked the chief whether he could guarantee the safety of their belongings. When the chief replied no, James said he would make his own camp and asked for an Indian guard, which the chief provided.

The next morning they forded the river and went two miles up the other side, where they found the Comanches' village. One of the principal chiefs greeted them, but with little warmth, although James unloaded his goods in front of the man's lodge. Since their first unlucky encounter with the Comanches, this moment had been inevitable, for in that country, which the Comanches knew so well, they could not have escaped. It was better to have accepted the invitation and assumed friendship than be tracked down as fugitives.

After James had handed out presents of vermilion, calico, lead, powder, and other goods, he thought he had been sufficiently generous, but the Comanches demanded more and began to tear apart his bales of cottons and woolens, which he had intended to sell in Santa Fé. Finally their leading chief, Big Star, appeared and told them they had taken enough. James then smoked with the principal men, while the other Indians ripped the cloth they had stolen into blanket sizes or made handkerchiefs, which they tied to their hair.

James was now ready to leave, having paid his tribute to this fierce tribe, who for so long had dominated the route to Santa Fé, but the Indians told him he would have to spend the night. The next day they announced the arrival of a new band and demanded additional presents. Once again they began to break into James's supplies while their chiefs looked on indifferently.

By the time they appeared to have satisfied themselves, James had taken a considerable loss. He had been prepared to distribute gifts along the route to Santa Fé, but the price of peace with the Comanches had come much higher than he had expected. He was certain, however, that they would soon release him.

But on the following morning One-Eye, James's enemy, appeared with a band of armed warriors painted black. Through Big Star, he demanded cloth, powder, vermilion, lead, knives, beads, and a sword he had noticed among James's possessions when they had met on the Cimarron. James was running out of many of the items One-Eye demanded, and he had already given the sword to Big Star. One-Eye said he would be content with cloth instead of the other goods he had demanded, and Big Star returned the sword, so James could give it to his tormentor. Even then the Indians would not allow the Americans to leave immediately but said they could go the next day.

"We had the horses brought up," James later wrote, "and prepared that evening for an early start in the morning. One-half kept guard while the rest of our party endeavored to sleep. But there was no rest for any of us on that most dismal night. This was the third sleepless night which we had passed with these ferocious savages, and we were nearly worn down by fatigue, anxiety, and watching."

In spite of the Americans' guard, the Comanches stole six of their horses during the night, and a group of small boys climbed a rise at the rear of their camp and pelted them with stones until the friendly chief finally chased them away. When morning came, the friendly chief appeared and warned James to keep his men together or otherwise they would be killed. Instead of letting the expedition pass on, as they had promised, the Comanches were preparing to attack them.

"Sometime after sunrise," James wrote, "I perceived about fifty of the chiefs and other Indians going up onto the mound above us, in our rear, followed by a multitude of young warriors and boys. An old man turned and drove them back: the two friendly chiefs did not go up. Arrived at the top, this company formed the circle, sat down, and smoked. Then one of their number commenced what seemed to us, from his gestures, to be a violent harangue designed to inflame their passions. I told my company that this council would decide our fate."

While the council was going on, other Indians were breaking camp, taking down the lodges and rounding up their horses. As they started to move off, James and his men noticed that the women and children were leaving too, while those who remained were only armed warriors, a sign that fighting might take place.

When the friendly chief and Big Star approached the white men to say goodbye, James asked them to stay, but they shook their heads and walked away. James and his men had drawn themselves up in a circle with their goods and saddles piled in a heap in the center. Each man's rifle was loaded and primed, and they had their fingers on their triggers, ready to fire at an instant's notice.

One man who did not have a gun grabbed an ax and swore that he would hack to pieces as many Indians as he could before dying. Nearly half an hour passed after these preparations while the two groups glared at each other.

Then an Indian dressed in a bear's skin and holding his lance rode through the crowd. Five paces from James, he stopped his horse. Since he could not reach the American with his lance, he took out his pistol, examined it carefully, and reprimed it. All the while James covered him with his rifle, ready to shoot him if he raised the pistol to fire.

The tension became almost unbearable. McKnight urged James to start fighting. The suspense was worse than death, he said. James tried to calm him, for once fighting started, there could be no turning back. But he did agree that at the first shot, the Americans must charge forward and take as many Indian lives as possible. Suddenly one American's nerve cracked under the strain. Raising his gun over his head in surrender, he walked away from his friends and into the crowd.

Almost immediately the Americans heard a cry of "white men, white men" in Comanche. It started in the distance and then spread through the assembled Indians. At first James thought it had something to do with the surrender of the one American, but then he saw six horsemen galloping across the plain toward them and calling out, "Save them, save them," in Spanish. They were six Mexican soldiers, and the officer in charge rode through the crowd until he reached James. Pulling up his horse, he dismounted and embraced the surprised, but happy, trader.

In reply to the officer's questions, the Comanches said that the Spanish governor at Santa Fé had told them to prevent any Americans from reaching the city. The officer explained to them that Mexico was now independent and the rules of Spain no longer applied. The policy of Mexico, he said, was to be friends with the Americans.

"As we approached the [Mexicans'] camp," James later wrote, "there came out to meet us a tall Indian of about seventy years of age, dressed in the complete regimentals of an American colonel, with blue coat, red sash, white pantaloons, epaulets, and sword. He advanced with an erect, military air and saluted us with great dignity and address."

This surprising figure, suddenly appearing on the Texas Panhandle, was a Comanche named Cordaro. Previously he had visited the American post at Natchitoches on the Red River, and the Indian agent there had given him a letter recommending him to all Americans and had issued him the uniform. As James soon learned, Cordaro had not forgotten his promise to the agent to be friends with all Americans thereafter.

The soldiers and some Comanches who were with them had been on a raid against the Navajos. After finishing their military assignment, they had come to the Great Plains to hunt buffaloes and had met some members of the group that were holding James. The younger Comanches rushed to get their share of the prospective plunder, but Cordaro had dashed back to camp and persuaded the Mexicans to race to James's rescue.

Through an interpreter who was with the Mexicans, James learned why the other Comanches had treated him so harshly. They had mistaken him for a Frenchman who had fought and defeated them the previous year. Since they thought this Frenchman was allied with their enemies, the Osages, the horses James had bought had confirmed them in their mistake.

Following the Canadian River, James continued across the Texas Panhandle but with a Mexican from Santa Fé to guide him. On every side were the Great Plains, hot and threatening in the summer sun. From the Canadian, they crossed over to the Pecos River. This brought them to the town of San Miguel, a community with about a hundred houses and a large church. But James noted that in spite of the wooded slopes nearby and a source of potential waterpower, the Mexicans had done little to develop the area.

Taking the road followed by the Spanish for hundreds of years, they reached the Indian pueblo of Pecos, where Alvarado had placed the Turk in chains for lying to him about the golden bracelet. Then the Indians had been sullenly suspicious of the strange white men; now they had become fully accustomed to them, and the Spaniards had built a fort in their midst. Looking at the buildings that composed the old pueblo, James was impressed by the high degree of civilization the Indians had achieved before the appearance of the first Europeans.

In December, 1821, James arrived in Sante Fé and had no difficulty securing permission to sell the goods he had brought. Nor was John McKnight, whose interest was principally in his family, prevented from traveling to Durango, Mexico, where his brother, Robert, had been living since his release from prison. Hugh Glenn, one of the Americans whom James had met on the way to Santa Fé, had reached Taos to the north and then come to the capital to obtain a license to trap along the upper

Río Grande. He, too, had no problems with the authorities.

But the desire of the Mexicans to be friendly toward the Americans did not automatically ensure the success of James's venture, for they were poor and therefore bought little. As his wares remained unsold, the goodwill James had felt when the Mexicans rescued him from the Comanches gradually eroded. Malgares, who had led the troops to the Pawnees and had encouraged them to stop Pike, was now governor, and James developed a particular dislike for him, finding him officious and pompous. But he also considered Mexicans generally as having a "disposition of treachery," and he compared their women unfavorably with the women of at least one Indian tribe.

True to a promise he had made, Cordaro came to Santa Fé to check on James's safety and held a council with him. During the course of their talk, he invited James to trade with the Comanches, promising that they would not again maltreat him, and asked him to plead with the American government to stop selling guns and ammunition to their enemies, the Osages.

As spring came up the Río Grande, James looked with disconsolation at his still large stock of goods. Malgares would not permit anyone to guide him to Sonora, where he had been told there was silver and gold; and few in Santa Fé would buy his articles, and fewer still, pay when they did. Finally he disposed of what was left at its original cost and, having suffered serious financial loss, started back for St. Louis.

This time he took a more northern route to the Arkansas, going from Santa Fé up the valley of the Río Grande to Taos, then over the mountains to the Great Plains, and again picking up the Arkansas. Hugh Glenn, whom James had met on the way out, traveled with them, although James had taken a strong dislike for him. (James, a fiery-tempered man, had many dislikes.)

On their way they met a party of Americans from Boone's Lick, Missouri, led by Benjamin Cooper, who was accompanied by his two nephews, Braxton and Stephen. The year before, a resident of that community, William Becknell, had gone west to trade with the Indians. On learning about the new policy toward Americans from a patrol of Mexican soldiers, he, too, had gone on to Santa Fé. Although his supply of goods had been small and his visit there much shorter than James's, he had made a good profit and was returning with his goods loaded in three carts instead of using pack animals. (Years ago Pedro Vial had said the trail could be followed with wagons, and

Becknell was proving him correct.) Word of his success had spread among his neighbors, so Cooper was setting out in 1822 to try his own luck with the Mexicans.

After stopping in St. Louis, where the expedition disbanded, James returned to his home in Illinois. His losses had been staggering for a man of moderate resources, and much of what he owned was attached by the sheriff to pay off his debts. For him the Santa Fé trade had been both physically hazardous and financially unprofitable. Becknell, on the other hand, had made some money from the trade with the Mexicans. Santa Fé was not as rich in gold and silver as earlier dreamers had supposed, but the longtime vision of commerce between Missouri and New Mexico was at last turning into a reality.

In the early years of the 1820s traders had opened the road to Santa Fé, and other traders and trappers were going up the Missouri and thinking not merely of posts near St. Louis but of forts along the river's length. The West had recovered from the shock of the War of 1812, and its citizens were once again moving across the Great Plains from which they had largely withdrawn almost a decade ago.

Of all Lisa's trappers, one of the most vigorous and able had been Andrew Henry. When the Blackfeet had made it obvious that only an army would be able to stay in their country, the others had turned back toward St. Louis, but Henry had spent the winter in the Rockies. The months had been long and hard, and he was later attacked by the Crows, who had stolen horses and furs from him. Nevertheless, the profits from the pelts he had brought back had done much to keep Lisa in business.

With the advent of the War of 1812, however, he had decided that the future in the fur trade was too limited and had gone into lead mining at Potosi, Missouri. (The Missouri lead mines were productive and well known.) There he had become a friend of William Henry Ashley, a Virginian who had discovered a deposit of potassium nitrate. From this he extracted saltpeter, which he used for manufacturing gunpowder in a small factory that he owned. In addition to his business interests, he entered politics and became Missouri's first lieutenant governor on its admission to statehood.

As the fur market gradually recovered and the possibility of making money in the trade increased, Andrew Henry began to think of returning to it. He knew it well, and he had never forgotten the potential riches to be garnered in the mountains. He discussed his plans with Ashley, who, although intelligent and prominent, had not found the gunpowder plant lucrative. As a result of their talks, the two men decided to become partners.

Lisa had been an innovator in the business, and it was his vision that had helped the Americans drive to the edge of the Louisiana Purchase and beyond; but Henry thought he saw a fallacy in Lisa's strategy. Lisa had intended to build a line of posts up the Missouri River that would serve two purposes: protect his communications with St. Louis and, since the Indians would trade with each post, provide a source of furs. In addition he employed *engagés* and individual contractors to obtain even more furs either by trapping themselves or by trading with the Indians who did not come to the posts.

As he had demonstrated, this strategy would work, but it also required a large amount of capital. Each post had to be constructed at considerable expense and, whether the season was a good one or not, maintained, stocked, and manned. This entailed overhead in bad years as well as good. Yet Henry knew that his own winter in the Rockies had produced a profit for Lisa even though he had had no post and even though he had lost a large amount of furs to the Crows. His plan with Ashley, therefore, was to eliminate permanent posts. Instead they would underwrite the expenses of individual contractors and then once a year meet them at some rendezvous, buy their furs, and re-equip those who still wanted to stay out. The plan involved great risks because of Indian attacks, but the amount of money invested would be less. Although this system had in part been used successfully by the Hudson's Bay Company, it represented a fundamental change, but one, Ashley and Henry agreed, worth trying.

So another competitor was entering the field; but Astor, under Crooks's prodding and guided by his own sense of timing, was beginning to move; and he instructed Crooks to establish an office of the American Fur Company in St. Louis. Everyone knew that Astor had been tied in with Berthold and Chouteau and that his men had been trapping and trading between the Missouri and the Mississippi, but they now understood that his interest in the Missouri was not casual. He intended to be in the business permanently.

Although Astor could barely tolerate competition, he was not a man to look for a fight if one could be avoided at reasonable expense. He was therefore likely first to try to buy out his competitors. In these transactions his reputation stood him in good stead, not a reputation for always offering the best of terms to the seller, but his reputation for treating brutally those who refused him. Vicious price cutting was the least of the weapons he stored in his arsenal, for he was not above bribing officials or taking similar actions to secure an advantage for himself. Stone, Bostwick & Company had already felt the weight of Astor's hand when it had competed with his Northern Department, so when his representatives approached the partners in St. Louis they quickly agreed to sell out to him. In a period of a few months, the American Fur Company not only had an office in St. Louis, it had a functioning business.

Although Pilcher's keelboat had been stopped the year before by the Missouri's ice, he had rescued the supplies it carried and had taken them to Fort Lisa. During the winter of 1821–1822, he had distributed them overland to the men he had in the field—no mean task in the cold weather of the Great Plains—so they would be ready to continue work when spring came. Meanwhile the company had enjoyed a profitable season, which meant that he entered the summer of 1822 with a good standing among those on whom he might have to call for credit. Noticing all the activity at the Missouri Fur Company, Ramsay Crooks offered to buy the firm on Astor's behalf, but Pilcher refused.

That year was more like old times on the Missouri, as the traders again began moving up it in force. Ashley and Henry had had no difficulty recruiting men. The lure of quick profits was back in the fur business once more, and those who wanted to make their fortunes thought this might be the way to do it. The partners had trouble, however, with their first keelboat. It overturned, and they lost their cargo and equipment. Ashley, who had remained at St. Louis, was able to load another, which he accompanied personally.

Pilcher followed. After spending the summer about twelve miles above the Knife River, where he supervised the construction of Fort Vanderburgh, with which he planned to secure the trade of the Mandans and the Hidatsas, he went down the river again, but not before he had sent out trappers under his two best men, Robert Jones and Michael Immel. They were to spend the winter at Fort Benton and then go west once again to trap near the Three Forks of the Missouri in the country of the Blackfeet. Although in a dangerous area, the rich beaver ponds were a constant lure, and Andrew Henry was planning to trap there, too.

In spite of the treachery of the Arikaras, who tried to ambush Pilcher on his way downstream from the Mandans' villages, the company had a successful year. Its profits, although not enormous, were sufficient to give it a good credit standing in St. Louis and provide for the further expansion of the organization.

Michael Immel was a former army officer, fearless, strong, and a man accustomed to leading others. Robert Jones had already earned Pilcher's trust, and the pair were considered by Pilcher as one of the company's greatest assets. If any men could handle the Blackfeet, they were the two. As soon as the ice began to melt, they left the fort on the Yellowstone and headed for the Three Forks of the Missouri. Their expectations were high, but the results of their trapping proved they had not been too high. In a short period of working the streams, they obtained a fine collection of skins, enough to give the company a handsome profit and put it in the forefront of St. Louis firms. And the Blackfeet had not appeared.

On their way back to the Yellowstone with their rich loads of furs, they met a band of almost forty of these Indians. But instead of attacking the white men, the leader produced a letter written by a Canadian that attested to his good character. Although unsigned, it was headed "God Save the King" and said that the Indian was a principal chief of his tribe and friendly toward white men. Immel and Jones were not thrown off their guard by this credential, but they agreed to camp with the Indians for the night. To have done otherwise might have looked like an insult.

The next morning they were up early and on their way, putting as much distance as possible between themselves and the band, not knowing if the Indians had been impressed by the white men and particularly by Immel's strength—his contemporaries said that in a fight he was a host in himself—or only by the valuable packs of skins they carried.

On May 31, 1823, they had safely reached the Yellowstone and were near Pryors Creek, named for the officer whom James had found living among the Osages. (His part in the Lewis and Clark expedition had earned for him a name on the map but little else.) They were now in the country of the Crows, with the Blackfeet about two weeks behind them and their own fort not far ahead.

A steep bluff at the edge of the river would have blocked their progress except for a trail that the buffalo herds had cut in its face. So narrow that they had to ride single file, it nevertheless guided them surely through a tangle of rocks and trees. Suddenly several hundred Blackfeet attacked. Immel and Jones died almost immediately. Five other trappers fell dead trying to fight their way out of the trap, and four more were wounded. The remaining men scrambled to the river and escaped by crossing the Yellowstone on an improvised raft, but they left behind them all their furs, horses, traps, and other equipment.

It was a staggering loss for Pilcher. The theft of the furs and equipment cut deeply into the company's slender resources, but the loss of Immel and Jones was an even greater blow. Beside his natural humane feelings, Pilcher lamented, "The flower of my business is gone, my mountaineers have been defeated, and chiefs of the party both slain."

Pilcher might curse his luck, but Ashley and Henry were having a difficult time that year, too. Henry had also gone to the Three Forks region in search of beaver skins, but all he found were the Blackfeet. They killed several of his men and forced him to retreat to the Yellowstone.

Even more serious troubles plagued Ashley: After leaving Hunt, he had returned to St. Louis, where he recruited more men, including Edward Rose, the interpreter whom Hunt had so suspected. With two keelboats, he started up the river in March, 1823, and reached the Arikara villages during the end of May. According to the information he had received, the Arikaras had attacked a party of Pilcher's men, because they were accompanied by some Sioux with whom the Arikaras were at war. In the fighting the Arikaras had lost two of their warriors. Infuriated by this defeat, they had determined to attack any white men who came their way.

With justifiable concern, Ashley anchored his two boats below the village in midstream, where they could be neither attacked nor plundered. With only two men he went ashore, presenting a rather poor prize should the Arikaras decide to fight. But when he met a band of Arikara warriors, he thought that his fears had been ill-founded, for they greeted him cordially and invited him to unload some of his goods and trade with them. This invitation suited his own needs, for a message had recently arrived from Henry, asking for a supply of horses, since the Assiniboins had recently raided the company's herd.

The Indians wanted Ashley to take his goods to their village, but this he refused to do. In spite of their smiles and professions of friendship, Ashley insisted that all trading be done at the edge of the river, where he and his men would be better protected. The trading went smoothly, and he soon had all the horses he wanted. This meant he could be on his way again the following morning, which pleased him.

In the afternoon an Arikara chief named the Bear asked him to come to his lodge. Ashley ac-

cepted the invitation and was reassured by the chief's friendly attitude. Nevertheless, he posted his men carefully that night. The two keelboats were anchored about ninety feet from the riverbank. Approximately fifty men remained on board them. Another forty were posted on shore to watch the horses, making their camp at a point between the two boats where they could be covered by the rifles of the men in the river.

Night gripped the land in its black glove, and the Missouri lapped against the sides of the boats, gently swinging them with its current. On shore the men lay rolled in their blankets, and occasionally one of the horses snorted in the night. In the darkness Rose and several other men apparently woke and slipped into the village—the Arikaras were notorious for their sexual laxity—a quarrel ensued, and one man was killed. Ashley was awakened by the report of what had happened and the news that the Indians intended to attack the Americans at daybreak.

The battle began as soon as it was light enough for the Indians to see their gunsights. A murderous fire rained down on the men occupying the camp on shore, for they were the nearest and the least protected. Outnumbered, they suffered the additional disadvantage of fighting Indians who could take cover in their village. Ashley first hoped to move the horses to a sandbar in the middle of the river, where the water was only a few feet deep. But as soon as the animals and the men with them entered the water, they were completely exposed. The surface of the Missouri, spouting little sprays, showed the murderous effect of the Indians' arrows and bullets. Men and animals could not live through such fire.

Ashley next tried to reinforce the shore party, but the men on the boats were unwilling to leave their safe position to rescue their companions on land. Ashley was the leader of a divided force of which one half would not help the other. But at last a few brave men volunteered to go ashore with two skiffs in which they would be able to evacuate twenty or thirty of the forty men. On the keelboats, safety had divided the men; on the riverbank, danger had unified them. Only a few men—some of them already wounded—were willing to leave their friends.

Their admirable courage only added to Ashley's command problems. First the cowards had mutinied; now the brave refused to do what he asked. Confusion and defeat were inevitable. Never tempering their attack, the Indians continued to rake the men on shore until almost half of them were wounded or killed. Retreat offered the only hope of survival for those who remained. Since none of the skiffs could make the trip back to the bank, the men must either jump into the river and swim or die. Some of them made it through the ninety feet of water that separated them from safety; some did not.

When the keelboats had collected the survivors and dropped downstream, Ashley counted the casualties they had suffered in the brief battle. Of approximately ninety men, thirteen were dead, and some ten or eleven wounded. All the horses were dead or lost to the Indians.

Ashley was still determined to continue up the river, staying in the keelboats while they maneuvered past the Arikaras, but most of his men had had enough fighting and wanted reinforcements before they came near the village again. This forced Ashley to change his approach. Instead of pressing forward, he sent word to Henry to bring as many men as he could and dispatched one of his keelboats to Fort Atkinson, which was more than four hundred miles down the river near where Long had spent the winter. With the boat went a letter from Ashley requesting the army's help. Then he went into camp and waited.

The keelboat arrived at Fort Atkinson at about the same time as a messenger bringing news of the deaths of Immel and Jones. Two Indian attacks in such rapid succession and with such serious consequences prompted Colonel Henry Leavenworth, who was in command, to take action. The Blackfeet in the mountains of present-day Montana were obviously beyond his reach, but he could certainly punish the Arikaras for closing the river to the traders. Pilcher with sixty men and two keelboats was on his way upstream, and he volunteered to join his forces with the army's. The traders might compete vigorously among themselves, but they made a common cause of keeping the river open.

On June 22, 1823, the punitive expedition set out. Leavenworth had two hundred and fifty men, some of whom went by land and some on the three keelboats he had secured. (One of them was Ashley's.) Pilcher followed with his boats and a five-and-one-half-inch howitzer and, when one of the army's boats sank, took on board some eleven barrels of military provisions it had been carrying.

Along with the management of the Missouri Fur Company, Pilcher had inherited from Lisa the company's good relations with the Sioux. So he was able to recruit a number of Sioux warriors whom they encountered and who were delighted at the prospect of having the Americans fight with them against their old enemies, the Arikaras. When they reached Ashley's camp, they found that

he had already been reinforced by Henry, who had sent every man he could spare. The current had carried them quickly from the Yellowstone, and they had passed the Arikaras' village safely by refusing the Indians' invitation to come ashore and trade.

Pilcher and others who knew the Indians well had warned Leavenworth that he must punish the entire tribe, not just a few individuals. Otherwise the Indians would not take their defeat seriously and would soon return to their hostile ways. With the combined forces now under his command, Leavenworth had the strength to do it.

On August 9 he launched his attack. The Sioux with Pilcher led the way, engaging the Arikaras outside their village. The fighting was intense, and a number of Arikaras were killed, but there were so many of them that Pilcher sent for reinforcements. Leavenworth then brought up his entire force. At the sight of his soldiers and the other white men supporting the Sioux, the Arikaras darted from the small trenches in which they had hidden and raced back to their village, permitting Leavenworth to advance to within three or four hundred yards of the village.

There he halted to await the keelboat that was carrying his artillery while the Sioux dismembered the bodies of their slain enemies. Since the boat did not arrive until almost sundown, Leavenworth decided to postpone his attack until the tenth.

He opened it with artillery fire. One gun, however, was placed on an elevation that was so high the men could not depress the barrel sufficiently to hit the village. At the same time Leavenworth marched forward with his infantry, who fired a volley at the village. The attack produced no results. Leavenworth made a closer study of the Arikaras' village before ordering a charge. But to maintain the offensive, he instructed Ashley and his men to fire on the smaller of the two villages.

At this point Leavenworth came to the conclusion that a charge would be unsuccessful unless the Sioux joined it. But the Sioux, who had so far borne the brunt of the fighting, were enjoying the fruits of their attack and were raiding the Arikaras' cornfields. So Leavenworth abandoned his proposed charge and warned the Sioux that his slackening of the offensive would make it dangerous for them to remain where they were. His lack of resolution shook the Sioux's confidence in his leadership. As they wanted to fight only on the winning side, they began to withdraw.

At the time of his landing Leavenworth had held all the advantages, but he had been frittering them away. Now he was frightened by the prospect of a prolonged battle, so when he noticed a Sioux parleying with an Arikara, he asked the Sioux to say that he was willing to hold a council with the enemy. The Arikaras welcomed this overture, for at least it would give them a temporary respite.

When ten or twelve Indians appeared to start the initial negotiations, Leavenworth delivered a speech about the power of the United States and the necessity of obeying its government. He also demanded the return of the goods and horses stolen from Ashley. The Arikaras replied that they could not return the horses, because most of them had been killed. Before the meeting broke up, Leavenworth smoked with the Indians. Pilcher, who had told the colonel to treat the Arikaras harshly, was disgusted by his willingness to compromise, and when he received the pipe, he at first refused to puff on it. When he finally agreed to, he sucked on it only with conspicuous reluctance. This disturbed the Arikaras, because Pilcher's interpreter had loyally told them that Pilcher was the most important of the Americans. The council ended with both sides unsatisfied but agreeing to meet the following day.

The Sioux were annoyed by the whole business. Their enemies had been at their mercy, but the white men would not fight. During the night the last of them vanished, taking with them a few of the Americans' horses, which they loaded with some of the Arikaras' corn. The desertion of these allies shook Leavenworth's confidence and left him in a still weaker bargaining position.

Dissension now split the Americans. Leavenworth was willing to treat with the Arikaras; Pilcher wanted to punish them severely; and the others took positions between the two. The Arikaras finally agreed to return Ashley's horses; but as Pilcher had expected, they did not return them all. Since Pilcher was an Indian subagent, Leavenworth asked him to draft a treaty, but he refused. If Leavenworth proposed to make peace on easy terms, he could write the treaty himself.

As the negotiations dragged on, many of Leavenworth's men grew impatient and wanted to attack the village, but the colonel held them in check. Several days had passed since the first landing, and still no agreement existed between the Arikaras and the Americans. On August 13, Leavenworth decided to renew his offensive the following morning, but when day broke, the Arikaras' village was empty. In the darkness they had eluded Leavenworth's patrols.

When his scouts failed to locate the Indians after a day's search, Leavenworth gave up the campaign. He and his men went downstream. Several of Pilcher's men, however, remained behind and, after Leavenworth had left and against his orders, burned the village.

The results of the campaign were mostly negative. Ashley had lost men and supplies, and Leavenworth had tarnished his reputation. But the greatest loss of all was the respect of the Sioux. Lisa and then Pilcher had spent much time and money gaining their friendship. Leavenworth's dilatory tactics had disgusted them, and it would be difficult ever to secure their allegiance again.

A battle of words followed the battle of bullets. Leavenworth praised Ashley for his cooperation and condemned Pilcher, charging him with having provoked the Arikaras into attacking Ashley and the Sioux into deserting. Pilcher, whose temper was as short as Lisa's, returned a verbal barrage of his own. His language was excessive, and some of his countercharges as exaggerated as Leavenworth's worst. But he struck close to the truth when he told Leavenworth, "You came to restore peace and tranquility to the country and to leave an impression which would insure its continuance. Your operations have been such as to produce the contrary effect and to impress the different Indian tribes with the greatest possible contempt for the American character. You came (to use your own language) to 'open and make good this great road,' instead of which you have by the imbecility of your conduct and operations created and left impassable barriers."

Chapter 15

New Goals in the West

So far from being to the benefit of persons engaged in the fur trade, to have hostilities with the Indians, the very existence of such a trade depends on their pacific disposition; and both the interest and safety of persons engaged in that business, require, that they should not only preserve a friendly understanding with the Indians themselves, but, so far as possible, to keep the different Indian tribes at peace with each other, in order that their property and men may not be exposed to roving war parties, who, particularly amongst those remote wandering tribes, are always, disposed to mischief, when on such excursions.

—Joshua Pilcher, 1824

The smoke curled lazily from the remains of the Arikaras' lodges. Here and there a flame, fanned by a breeze, leapt into life and then subsided again into the charred blackness. Notwithstanding Leavenworth's firm orders to leave the village unharmed, Pilcher's men had done their work thoroughly, placing their fire against this bit of tinder and that, until the hungry flames had rushed from structure to structure, and then, sated, had fallen back. The site where a prosperous village had stood yesterday, its cornfields ripe for picking, was today a gutted black spot on the face of the prairie, devoid of Indian life, the sound of horses neighing, babies crying, and the humdrum bustle of daily existence. Even if the Arikaras returned, and the seed again sprouted in the fields, the old days could not be recreated. For change was coming to the Great Plains, subtly like the first chill wind on a September day, a touch only of the cold of winter, merely a whisper of the future, but its being real and its warning significant.

When Pilcher instructed his men to remain behind and set fire to the village, he was inflicting the punishment that Leavenworth would not. In exercising restraint, the colonel was not motivated by purely humanitarian considerations. He had al-

ready revealed his cautiousness, and probably he wished to avoid a prolonged war that he had no authority to initiate. Pilcher, on the other hand, better understood the Indians and knew that the Arikaras would soon return and resume their former ways unless they were thoroughly chastised. Peace, whether bought with presents or enforced by fire, was a necessity to the traders. Without it, they would again be stopped by the warriors and the "great road," as Leavenworth had called the Missouri, would be closed to those who could not force their way past the village or buy the Arikaras' favors with expensive gifts, either burden too great for businessmen like Pilcher.

Yet his willingness to destroy the villages was in itself the signal of a change, for he and the other traders did not care whether the Arikaras ever returned. In fact, they would probably have agreed that their trade would benefit from the Arikaras' remaining away forever, disappearing into the wilderness or, for that matter, from the earth. They were a tribe that was no longer needed, precursors of many others whose roles would switch from needed allies to annoying impediments.

When the Spanish marched across the land some of them had been wanton destroyers, burning, pillaging, and killing. But their objective, except against the most aggressive tribes, was subjugation, not elimination, of the Indians. Even the slave-hunters who had so upset Cabeza de Vaca when he emerged from the wilderness at the end of his long journey were not interested in killing for killing's sake. They slew only to break down resistance, and the true success of their missions was measured in the numbers of Indians brought back alive, not the numbers left dead on the battlefield. For the economic basis on which Spanish exploration and colonization were laid demanded the presence of Indians. Without them—or without a substitute labor force imported from some other land—the Spanish system would have collapsed, the galleons sailing to Spain empty and the coffers of the kings standing unfilled.

When the French pushed up the St. Lawrence River and on to the Great Lakes or explored the Mississippi and the Ohio, they, too, did not slaughter Indians except those who sided with the British in their frequent wars or were ancient enemies of those tribes they called allies. Rather than fight Indians, they preferred to be friends with them, and their peacemaking efforts were extensive. Indians who were not at war were more likely to make up the packs of beaver skins that commanded such high prices on the other side of the Atlantic. Quebec, proud on its heights above the river, and Montreal, closer to the center of the later fur trade, produced the *voyageurs*, the *engagés*, the traders, and the missionaries, but their populations were too meager to produce the trappers. For this work, the French depended largely on the Indians.

When the British entered Canada, using Hudsons Bay as their gateway to the interior, and later when they assumed control of the whole colony, they adopted the French methods and relied largely on those Indians whom they could attract as allies. When young Henry Kelsey went to the edge of the plains, he took with him no great force of men. Whatever furs he brought back would have to be trapped by Indians, and the purpose of his journey was to persuade the natives—not Frenchmen or Englishmen—to work in the interests of the Hudson's Bay Company. If by some chance there had been no Indians in the area he visited and none could have been persuaded to go there, he would not have made his lonely journey west.

This dependence on Indian labor had been characteristic also of the traders originally operating out of St. Louis. Lisa's first struggle with the established elite had not been to obtain the privilege of trapping but of trading. And when he finally secured Chouteau's former monopoly, Chouteau countered by persuading some of the Osages to move to a new area. It was not the place that counted; it was the service of the Indians.

As the trade had expanded and more Americans moved west, this had changed. When Lisa attempted to enter the land of the Blackfeet, he had not expected that warlike tribe to reverse its ways and exchange furs for the goods he had brought; he had counted on his own people to trap the furs. Hence Lisa's willingness to take inexperienced and undisciplined men like Thomas James. Now white hands, not red, were to force open the jaws of the trap, fasten its chain, and bait it with castor. He still traded with the Indians, he still built posts, but he had derived more profit from Andrew Henry's winter in the Rockies than from the tribes along the Missouri River.

The Americans' reliance on the Indians was fading. Ashley stopped to trade with the Arikaras because he suddenly had a need for horses and they owned some, not because he thought they could be an important source of furs. He did not even need their corn, a food that earlier travelers had often purchased from the tribes they visited. Nor could they guide him anywhere. The Indians had supplied la Vérendrye with information about the land and had taken him to the Mandan villages. But many of Ashley's men knew as much—perhaps even more—than the Arikaras about the country through which they planned to travel.

Joshua Pilcher wanted even less from them than Ashley. He had no need for horses, knew the land well, and had brought his own food. All he desired was peace, so he could pursue his business. Whether or not the Arikaras ever reoccupied their villages was to him a matter of no moment. Hence he could burn their community with an obliterating fire, knowing that no trader would suffer in the future from the Arikaras' absence, whether temporary or permanent. That was the ominous sign carried to the skies by those wisps of gray smoke rising in the air. Any Indian looking at them might have shuddered at their meaning; when night fell over the remains of the village, its darkness was the darkness that comes with the end of a civilization.

Among those who failed to recognize the change and therefore became its victim was Thomas James. On his return from Santa Fé, he brought with him the invitation of Cordaro to return to trade with the Comanches. With his creditors pressing him and faced with lawsuits that threatened to strip him of everything he owned, James decided to avail himself of Cordaro's friendship. In the old days, when the white men had been dependent on the Indians for furs, such an invitation from a leading chief would have been a roadway to fortune, and it still might prove valuable.

Faith rode high on the western frontier; and the foot of the rainbow, like the Rockies approached from the plains, always seemed near. Therefore, impoverished as he was, James could find those who were willing to supply him with capital, not a large amount of money, for even inveterate gamblers might be shaken by James's singular lack of success, but enough to provide him with a small supply of goods.

His former associates, John and Robert McKnight, joined him in this new venture, and early in 1823 they built a temporary trading post on the North Fork of the Canadian, while John McKnight left to seek the Comanches. When he failed to reappear after more than a week, James became concerned for his safety. Then two of the men who had gone with him showed up. They had left the Comanche village after—not before—McKnight and were surprised not to find him waiting for them. Their interpreter, they explained, had proved less fluent than expected and had had difficulty making himself understood. Finally the Comanches gave McKnight permission to go for his brother, Robert, who spoke Spanish, a language they understood. Looking back, they remembered that shortly after his departure, the Comanches had mentioned having a battle with some Osages. It was now clear that the battle had not been with the Osages, but with McKnight. Some of the Comanches had obviously followed and killed him.

Tragedy constantly stalked the lives of the fur traders. Dealing with the mercurial Indians, who might be amicable one day, hostile the next, they became inured to the loss of friends and relatives and regarded death as one of the prices of their business. Those who wished the luxury of mourning followed other pursuits.

Robert McKnight, therefore, resumed negotiations with the Comanches, but the Indians insisted on dealing with the Americans only at their own village. Since James's enemy, One-Eye, was in the camp, the prospect was not pleasant. On the other hand, the Comanches produced some horses that James thought would bring a hundred dollars each at St. Louis. But when he had purchased seventeen of the finest animals, the Indians began offering him inferior stock. Since he could not afford to waste his borrowed assets on such horses, he refused to buy any more. Immediately the Comanches became sullen. Although James then reluctantly bought some buffalo and beaver skins he

did not want, the Comanches were not satisfied and asked him to leave their country. Seventeen horses were not enough to pay for his expedition, so James would not go.

By holding another council with some of the leading chiefs and by distributing more presents to them, he finally obtained permission to stay for a while longer, but the crisis was not over. That afternoon one of his men came to him with a gun barrel. One-Eye, who had not previously appeared, had approached the man in the village, thrown the barrel at his feet, and told him to carry it to James. No threat could have been more explicit.

Realizing that the success of his trip—as well as his own life—depended on peace, James decided to make one more effort to placate One-Eye. He searched him out, shook hands with him, and took him to the lodge where he was staying. There he smoked a pipe with his enemy and made him a present of a silver breastplate and four silver armbands, all of which he placed on One-Eye's body himself. The two again smoked a pipe together, after which One-Eye departed without saying a word. James was in complete ignorance as to One-Eye's reaction to his overtures, for the smoking of a pipe might be conclusive evidence of friendship, or it might not. Many Americans had been killed by Indians with whom they had smoked only a short time before.

In the evening after he had talked to One-Eye, the warrior came to him and, much to his surprise, asked him to visit his lodge. If the Comanches failed to trust James, he understandably failed to trust them. Being alone with One-Eye was not his idea of a comfortable and safe evening, so he refused, but the chief was insistent; and noticing that he was completely unarmed, James finally agreed to accept the unwanted invitation.

On entering One-Eye's lodge, James carefully noted where the Indian kept his weapons and seated himself so he could shoot One-Eye if he reached for them. But One-Eye merely lighted a pipe, and they smoked together until his wife brought in a meal of buffalo meat, apologizing for having had no marrow in which to cook it. Everything was more friendly than James had expected, and after the meal he and One-Eye smoked again.

Then One-Eye began an astonishing confession. Yes, he admitted, he had originally intended to kill James, being restrained from doing so only by the chief, Big Star. Before their first meeting, he went on, he had been on a raid against the Osages. During a battle with them his brother had been killed. He had then returned to his village and organized a war party to avenge his brother's death. He was starting on this mission when he first met James, and the sight of the Osage horses James had bought made him think James was an ally of his enemies. He decided he need go no farther to do his dead brother justice.

While he talked, he knocked the ashes from the pipe into his hand. He now placed them on the ground and covered them with dirt, which he tamped down three times with his hand. Weeping violently, he added two more handfuls of dirt while James watched uneasily. But his meaning soon became clear. When he had finished patting and smoothing the third handful of dirt, One-Eye's expression changed. He had buried one brother, he said, and now he had found another. With those words, he embraced James. From then on One-Eye's sponsorship was the only protection James needed. None dared offend that warrior.

For hundreds of years the Comanches had held a reputation as fine horsemen and important horse dealers. The horses that la Salle, searching desperately for the mouth of the Mississippi, had purchased from the Gulf Coast Indians had been brought east by the Comanches. In those days, they stole most of their livestock, sweeping down on a Mexican town or an army detachment and stampeding the animals (the word "stampede" itself came from the Spanish *estampida*), or they quietly slipped in at night and took a few of the best.

Although they had not given up stealing, theft was not now their only source. Horses had become common on the southern Great Plains; and the Comanches, adopting the ways of the Spanish, had become expert at catching and breaking them. While he was in their village James had an opportunity to watch them do this. "A small party of less than a hundred well-mounted Indians were in ambush," he wrote, "while a multitude scattered themselves over the prairie in all directions and drove the wild horses to the place where the others were concealed, which was a deep ravine. As soon as the wild drove was sufficiently near, these last rushed among them and every Indian secured his horse with his lasso [another word derived from the Spanish] or noosed rope, which he threw around the neck of an animal and by a sudden turn brought him to the ground and there tied his heels together. This was the work of a few minutes, during which both horses and men were intermingled together in apparently inextricable confusion. . . .

"The Indians," James continued, "use their fleetest horses for catching the wild ones, and throw the lasso with great dexterity over their heads, when by turning quickly around and sometimes entangling their feet in the rope they throw them on the ground and then tie their legs together two and two . . .''

When Pike had found that his men could not crease the horses, he had sent them out with nooses, hoping that they could drop them over the necks of the wild animals. Later when he traveled in Mexico, he observed how the Spanish lassoed them. It was an eye-opening experience, and he reported it in some detail. Now James was seeing how skillfully the Indians had adopted the Spaniards' techniques and were harvesting the riches of the plains.

The Spanish had looked for gold, silver, and jewels; the French, British, and later the Americans sought furs. James purchased a few furs to keep the Indians happy, but his emphasis had been on livestock. When he headed back to St. Louis, he took with him a herd of 323 horses and mules.

On his journey home he was pursued by the misfortune that seemed to haunt all his enterprises. In one way or another, he lost most of the animals with the result that he returned to Missouri still impoverished. But the significance of his journey was the herd he had purchased. Like the smoke curling above the Arikaras' village, it signaled a change. He had needed no Indian guides, no Indian supplies, no Indian furs; rather he wanted to buy only their horses. If the Americans could become as adept with the lasso as the Comanches, they could go out on the Great Plains and capture their own.

On December 2, 1823, James Monroe delivered his annual report to Congress. The rebellions in the Western Hemisphere against the Spanish government had set the eyes of European diplomats gleaming at the opportunities that offered themselves. Threatened by the diplomatic spider web being woven in the capitals of Europe, Monroe had consulted some of America's ablest statesmen, both retired and active. For he believed it necessary to make some sort of response to the maneuvering of the European governments. Largely influenced by his Secretary of State, John Quincy Adams, he used his annual report to enunciate certain principles.

"The American continents," he said, "by the free and independent condition which they have assumed and maintain, are henceforth not to be considered as subjects for future colonization by any European powers." He also voiced this warning: "We should consider any attempt on their [the European powers'] part to extend their system to any portion of this hemisphere as dangerous to our peace and safety.'' Critics might say the statement of policy was meaningless, because the President had no constitutional authority to declare war and because the immediate crisis was past. Nevertheless, the United States, only recently unable to win the War of 1812 against a single European power, was now speaking forcibly to them all. Monroe and those who advised him were reflecting a national self-confidence which may not have been justified but which was real.

This was the same spirit felt by the people in St. Louis and similar communities along the edge of the Great Plains. They had been driven back by the War of 1812 and shocked into a state of paralysis by the Indians' hostility and the depression of the fur market. But the balm of time had quieted their uncertainties and soothed their self-doubts. These were now gone, and the West was like a young buffalo bull in the springtime, flexing its awkward muscles in the sun and bursting with undirected energy.

Pilcher and the Missouri Fur Company were among the few exceptions to the generally optimistic spirit. The defeat of Immel and Jones and the loss of approximately $16,000 worth of furs and equipment to the Blackfeet were too great a blow for an underfinanced concern. Pilcher could only curse his luck and Leavenworth, cling to the shrinking line of Lisa's forts, and hope that in some way the gray storm clouds would brighten.

Ashley, on the other hand, had suffered no such losses, the blows he had received from the Arikaras being small by comparison. While he returned to St. Louis to look after his company's business there and to promote his own political future—he wanted to be governor—Henry headed back toward the Yellowstone.

Among the fur traders' greatest assets were the men they attracted. The St. Louis waterfront was crowded with toughs, glad to sign a contract for the advance that came with it but equally glad to accumulate debts with the tavernkeepers and then either desert or shirk whatever work was required of them. The currents of their own irresponsibilities had carried them west, but the frontier possessed no magic quality that transformed them. What they had been at home, wherever their home was, they remained, useless both to society and themselves.

A few came because of the challenge and opportunities the frontier offered. These were the vigorous, the ambitious, the men who believed that with hard work and determination they could make a place for themselves in the shifting and rapidly expanding world of the West. Ashley and his partner, Henry, had the ability to pick these out of the crowd of applicants who hoped to make their fortunes.

Jedediah Strong Smith was one of them, a New Yorker by birth, young, extraordinarily brave, and physically and mentally energetic. In a society noted more for its blasphemies than its prayers, he was extremely religious and throughout his life retained a faith in his Protestant God as enduring as Cabeza de Vaca's in his Catholic one. The four Sublette brothers also joined up with Ashley and Henry, the most prominent in later years being William L., light-haired, blue-eyed, and standing over six feet. James Bridger was another member of Ashley's group. Born in Virginia, where his father had operated a tavern in Richmond, he had come west as a young boy and had been apprenticed to a blacksmith. But shoeing horses and making ironware had not appealed to him as much as those distant plains and mountains of which every St. Louis youth had heard; and when he was eighteen, he, too, joined Ashley.

Although many of these persons, with the notable exception of Henry, were inexperienced at the fur trade, they were willing workers, quick learners, and undaunted investigators of the unknown. With Henry to lead them, they quickly expanded the fur trade in the area beyond the Great Plains. Until then most traders had stayed relatively close to the Missouri or the Yellowstone except when they tried to penetrate the lands controlled by the Blackfeet. But these men in a remarkable outburst of energy went farther in their pursuit of skins. They discovered the rich fur country of the Green River, which rises in northwestern Colorado and flows into Utah; they located South Pass at the southern foot of Wyoming's Wind River Range, a practical way to cross the Continental Divide for those going west; and Jedediah Smith penetrated the wilderness to the Snake River, met some men working for the Hudson's Bay Company, and with considerable skill and diplomacy persuaded them to sell their skins to the Rocky Mountain Fur Company instead. Astor, who so often was in the lead, was still trying to wear down the Missouri River traders closer to St. Louis while these wild spirits were suddenly opening up a whole new world beyond the Great Plains. At the same time, they proved in the season of 1823–1824 that the original business concept of Ashley and Henry would work, for they brought the Rocky Mountain Fur Company a good profit.

NEW GOALS IN THE WEST 193

The renewed activity in St. Louis and the West's increasing political importance caused the federal government to take another look at that part of the Louisiana Purchase that included the Great Plains. In spite of Pike and Long's assertions that it was uninhabitable except by Indians and useful only as a buffer against an attack from the west, Americans were crossing it with growing frequency in search of furs, livestock, and the Santa Fé trade. Under pressure from men like Senator Thomas Hart Benton of Missouri, the War Department in particular was being asked to provide new services for these American citizens to help ensure their safety and permit them to make more effective use of the resources that lay in the West.

As a preliminary step, the Senate Committee on Indian Affairs directed questions to a number of informed persons; and when they asked Pilcher if the traders needed an American fort beyond the Mandan villages, his answer was an emphatic yes. The Blackfeet were the obstacle to entering the Three Forks area, and those Indians had long dealt with the British, from whom they always obtained the arms and ammunition they needed to attack Americans. For the time being at least, the American traders, in his opinion, should be "protected in extending their business into those remote regions, until such time as they acquire an influence sufficient to counteract that of the British trading companies." A fort, he argued, should be located at the mouth of the Yellowstone or even farther up the Missouri, but it was the only one on the river that needed to be large. Smaller ones at the site of Fort Atkinson, the Great Bend of the Missouri, and near the Mandan villages would be sufficient to protect the rest of the river. As far as the Blackfeet and other hostile Indians in the area were concerned, Pilcher said, "If all trade, and intercourse, between those tribes and British traders, can be cut off, and the American trade introduced, it would very soon protect itself. Most Indians, who have long been accustomed to intercourse with whites, become dependent on them for the supply of particular articles, without which they cannot well live, once having acquired a knowledge of their use."

Always conscious of his constituents' needs, Senator Benton did not limit himself to alerting the War Department to the need for protecting American interests in the northern Great Plains but also investigated the trade with Santa Fé and the help that should be afforded those engaged in it. Franklin, Missouri, upriver from St. Louis and therefore farther west, was becoming the originating point

for this commerce, and for information Benton turned to W. Augustus Storrs, a resident of the community and one who had already made the trip to the New Mexican capital.

Although new, Storrs reported, the commerce was burgeoning at an extraordinary rate. The first entrepreneurs had gone with small supplies of goods carried on pack animals. Then Becknell had ventured forth with three wagons, unknowingly testing Vial's theory that they could make the trip. In 1824, only a few years later, Storrs had helped organize a veritable caravan, consisting of eighty-one men with 156 horses and mules and carrying their merchandise in four-wheeled wagons. To protect themselves against the Indians or others who might attempt to hold them up, they also took along one piece of field artillery.

Storrs tried to estimate the value of this trade and decided it must come to $180,000 for 1824 alone, and that figure did not include the profits from an expedition that had set out in the fall of the year with $18,000 worth of trade goods but had not yet returned. This sizable business was not all that made the route across the Great Plains so important to the American economy. Hugh Glenn, whom James had met, had come with his companions to New Mexico, not to trade, but to trap, and now others were following suit. The center of their activities was Taos, upstream on the Rió Grande from Santa Fé and with ready access to the mountains. This area was rich in beavers, which the New Mexicans did not trap to any great extent, and it was easy for Americans to make a profit. According to Storrs, the returns so far totaled $10,044 "by actual sales." Although dwarfed by comparison with the direct trade, this, too, was important business. Many a St. Louis firm, including Pilcher's Missouri Fur Company, would have welcomed that much revenue.

The goods carried in wagon trains like Storrs's were various, but the most popular items were mostly cloth—cotton goods, calicoes, a few woolen goods, some silk shawls, as well as light cutlery, looking glasses, and other articles. New Mexico's problems, Storrs said, were severalfold. The Spanish colonies had too long depended on mining precious metals, and this, "by enabling them to live without resorting to manual employment, has destroyed the energy of her national character." Furthermore, he went on, "The policy of the mother country has strongly co-operated with these causes to degrade the political condition of Mexico and to discourage her manufactures." After pointing out that New Mexico had only one newspaper and few books, Storrs added, "Maternal jealousy and ecclesiastical influence have removed from the people every means of information, and prevented their improvement in every art and every science."

As a consequence they produced almost none of the manufactured or processed articles they needed. Ore was abundant, but iron was expensive and almost lacking in their farm tools; they had extensive flocks of sheep but not enough woolen goods for their own use. "These particulars," Storrs continued, "are in themselves, too trifling for enumeration, but, when considered in relation to the late administration of the government, and the condition of the people, and the practical consequences to be deduced by statesmen, they become more important. From them, also, may be inferred the variety and extent of supplies demanded by that market."

The province, however, was not destitute. It exported copper, sheep, tobacco, and buffalo robes, the last two purchased from the Indians, and received in return wines, brandy, and specie. Therefore they could pay for American goods with Spanish dollars and bullion, supplemented by mules and horses. Since Santa Fé was far removed, Americans could compete successfully with the traders from Chihuahua and other cities that also supplied the provincial capital.

To make this market even more promising, the reaction of the New Mexicans, relieved to have an additional and competing source of imports, was cordial. "Their professions of respect for our national character," Storrs said, "and of attachment to our principles, are universal; and their actions are a sufficient proof of sincerity. The door of hospitality is opened with a cheerful welcome, and every office of friendship and kindness, which might be expected from intimate acquaintance, is voluntarily proffered by a stranger. In all their principal towns the arrival of the Americans is a source of pleasure, and the evening is dedicated to festivity and dancing."

He told Benton he did not believe that another fort located farther upstream on the Arkansas would serve any useful purpose unless it were located at the point where the traders left that river to cross over to the Cimarron. But there the climate was arid, and the soldiers would not be able to supply themselves with the necessary garden produce. Furthermore, their presence would be likely to frighten away the buffalo herds, and this would engender more ill-will among the Indians than the protection of the soldiers' guns would be worth. He did think, however, it would be helpful to have the government survey the route, marking out the

best fords across the creeks and erecting dirt mounds to guide the travelers along their way.

The government of the United States had already taken some slight official notice of the importance of the Santa Fé trade. At its center in Franklin, Missouri, the Public Land Office, which was charged with selling parcels of the public domain, accepted Spanish dollars at full value according to their weight. This was an important service, because the milling of many Spanish coins was faulty, and therefore they were usually discounted. But this single service, rendered by the local Land Office on its own initiative, was not what Benton envisioned for his constituents. They needed a road to Santa Fé and protection from the Indians on the Upper Missouri. If he could get this for them, he would; and the growing economic and political importance of the West was rapidly improving his chances.

As Ashley and Henry reviewed their operations, they realized they were spending much time and money ascending the Missouri. Yet the area they were opening up with such profitable results lay considerably to the south of the Great Falls. The Platte offered them a more direct route, and the mystery had long since been stripped from it by frontiersmen, such as those who had followed its course back from Astoria, and by Long, who had used it and its South Fork as a guide to the Rockies. Now that South Pass was also familiar to the Rocky Mountain Fur Company, it seemed unnecessary to be bound by the route of Lewis and Clark and the tradition of previous traders.

In November, 1824, Ashley left Fort Atkinson, where the military arm of the Yellowstone Expedition had wintered. Because the Platte was so shallow, they had abandoned the traditional transportation system in which keelboats played the major role and horses the lesser. Instead the twenty-five men of the Rocky Mountain Fur Company had fifty pack animals but no boats.

The ground was already covered with about two feet of snow, which the wind picked up and blew with such violence that it was difficult to make headway. The cold was deadly, and progress so difficult that the pack train made only ten or twelve miles in about two weeks. By this time, however, they had reached the Platte, where they were fortunate to find plenty of game.

From there on the traveling became easier. The hunters were able to keep the expedition well supplied with game, and the many islands in the Platte provided grazing for the horses and firewood for the men. Several times young Pawnee warriors visited the party, and although they were not war-

From a distance the Great Plains appeared deceptively even, but the view from Scotts Bluff on the Oregon Trail shows the land to be crisscrossed by steep ravines through which the wagon trains were forced to thread their way. *Alexander B. Adams*

To pioneers crossing the Great Plains, the mountains offered a welcome sight. Although the Rockies presented hazards of their own, they signaled that at least part of the long journey was over. Because of the visibility resulting from the dry air, the frontal range seems nearer than it actually is. *Alexander B. Adams*

like, they made themselves nuisances by their petty thieving. Consequently when Ashley met the main body of Pawnees on their way to their usual winter quarters on the Arkansas, he was pleased to find them friendly and willing to order the young men to return the items they had taken.

Although Ashley's route was now relatively familiar to the Americans, he was the first to attempt to traverse it during the middle of winter with a pack train, and so he did not know what to expect. The Indians warned him that once he passed the Forks of the Platte his going would become much more difficult, since he would have trouble finding both wood and game. If he tried to advance farther before spring, they said, he and his men might lose their lives. This was discouraging news, for if he delayed at the forks, he would not reach his trappers on schedule in the spring. The seasons were imperious, inflexible dictators to those engaged in the fur trade.

When Pike had visited the Pawnees before the War of 1812, he had found them divided into two major groups. Ashley now met a band of the second group, who were on their way to the Forks of the Platte, to spend the winter. As they were both going in the same direction, he joined this band.

The bitter cold persisted, his men suffered from it, and many of his horses died. But he hoped that when the Pawnees assembled, they might supply him with both meat and horses to enable him to complete the remainder of his trip. Although Indians were no longer as essential to the traders as they had formerly been, they could still occasionally help.

At the forks, where the second group of Pawnees were gathering, the chiefs and leading warriors held a council with him. The winter had treated them harshly, too, and many of their own horses had died, but they were willing to spare the twenty-five he wanted and also sell him meat during the time he remained at their camp.

As Pike had learned, the South Fork of the Platte entered deep into the heart of the Rocky Mountains far to the south of Ashley's destination, but the Pawnees advised him not to take the North Fork, which would have been the shorter route. It was, they said, almost devoid of firewood and food for the horses. In the middle of winter, it would be wiser, if he insisted on continuing, to go along the South Fork even if it led him out of his way.

Along the South Fork of the Platte, Ashley was pleased to find the valley filled with buffalo herds and the weather fine. But suddenly, as often occurred on the Great Plains, the weather changed. The temperature dropped, the winds began to

howl, and the snow fell. When the men awoke one morning, they discovered that four of their horses were so numb with cold they could not stand. After considerable exertion the men got them to their feet, but they were in no condition to move forward. Each animal was valuable to Ashley, and he would have no chance from here on to procure replacements. But he decided that to remain in camp where they were would cost all their lives and reluctantly gave the word to break camp, move on, and leave the weak horses behind.

If anything, the weather became worse. The snow was now so deep the horses would have floundered except that they followed the trails broken by the many buffalo herds that ranged along the river. And where they had cleared the snow to graze, pushing it aside with their great shaggy heads, the horses grazed also, eating what little dried grass was left. Otherwise they would have starved.

Around the first of January, Ashley saw to his relief a grove of trees ahead. Pushing toward it, he found it was a cottonwood-covered island. This pleased him, because the site would be relatively easy to defend, and he planned to rest there until both men and horses had recovered.

When the horses had eaten all the cottonwood branches that were nourishing, the time had come to push on. Both men and animals were rested, but the weather remained cold. Each day the men were able to collect a small supply of driftwood and willow brush with which to make the fires that kept them warm, but they could not find enough food for the horses, which grew thinner and thinner.

Before the horses gave out, they came to another small island, which contained enough cottonwoods to last them for two days while they again rested. From there they could see the Rocky Mountains rising in the west. Ashley was wise enough to realize that they represented, not the end of the challenges facing him, but the beginning. The Indians had told him he could not cross them at this time of year, but his business did not permit him the leisure of waiting until spring had unlocked their passes and cleared the snow from the slowly greening browse. Yet he knew it would be foolish to hurl himself and his men against their flank, in hope that luck would bring him to an opening in the formidable wall they presented.

Consequently he moved his men and horses to their foothills, where he made a base camp from which he could scout the land ahead. In choosing to follow the Platte in the dead of winter, he had taken an enormous gamble. If he won, he would sharply reduce the time and money spent reaching the rendezvous; if he lost, he might just as well have stayed in Missouri manufacturing gunpowder for a small profit. This was the critical moment. Somewhere in that bold, rising bulk of rock and trees and snows there might be a crevice through which men and horses, dwarfed by the peaks above them, could make their way to the greater heights behind.

Ashley, the genial politician and former candidate, hardly seemed the person to find it. With the bleak white plains to the north, east, and south and the mountains looming to the west, he was a lonely figure of a man hurling himself, his followers, and his fortune against the gigantic forces of ancient geology and contemporary weather.

But when he mustered his men and the packs were loaded again on the tired backs of the animals, he headed in the right direction—up the Cache la Poudre Canyon near present-day Fort Collins, Colorado. Its boulder-littered streambed, camouflaged and made treacherous by the drifting snow, and its high canyon walls, spired by strange formations of rock now encrusted with snow and ice that sparkled when the sun struck them, may have looked at times like a death trap, but the way was clear and the grade relatively slight compared to the altitude that had to be climbed. Ashley's route then carried him between the Medicine Bow Range and the isolated height later known as Elk Mountain. From there he reached Pass Creek, which flows into the North Platte after it has looped north from Colorado's North Park. By now he had arrived in the general area in which his trappers were working and had done so before the advent of spring. It was a remarkable achievement, especially for one so new to the fur trade.

For all his growing influence in the Senate, Benton could not submit a report, snap his fingers, and have the government erect forts wherever he wanted them. But he did succeed in persuading the War Department in 1825 to send a peace commission up the Missouri to make treaties with the Indians and report its findings. Both General Henry Atkinson, Leavenworth's superior, and Major Benjamin O'Fallon, the Indian agent, were members, and they were accompanied by an army escort of 476 men. No military force of this size had ever ascended the river, and yet, like Lewis and Clark's expedition, the emphasis was to be on peace, not war. The expedition was a harbinger of the Indians' future. Unlike the Spanish, whose armies when they crossed the Great Plains were explorers, this army was following, not preceding, its citizens; and a nation that could thrust this many armed men into the wilderness to ensure the safety of its people was a nation that intended to stay.

As they moved up the river, the commissioners called the Indians to councils, exchanged speeches with them, gave them presents, received their assurances of friendship, and went on to the next tribe. Even the Arikaras, who had now returned to the site of their former villages, made a favorable impression on Atkinson. In his official report he said, "Their late outrages, committed on the whites, are well known . . . and it should be remarked that they have, for many years before, been treacherous and insolent to strangers. It is believed, however," he added hopefully and unrealistically, "that the offensive operation against them, by our troops, conducted by Colonel Leavenworth, has brought them to a full sense of their misconduct, and that they feel humbled and chastened; this, with our late visit to them, on which occasion a good understanding has been established, and all former difficulties removed, we have no doubt they will remain friendly." The army, still smarting from the criticism of Pilcher and his friends, was trying to justify Leavenworth's conduct of the battle. At the same time, the Arikaras, impressed by the appearance of 476 armed Americans, were on their best behavior.

In spite of the superficiality of their councils with the Indians—Atkinson and O'Fallon could not explain to their audiences in understandable terms what they were trying to do and what their mission would eventually mean—they visited many tribes, including even the Hunkpapas, one of the smaller and more remote divisions of the Sioux, whom the commissioners reported as "friendly to the whites."

After passing the Mandan villages the commissioners went to the mouth of the Yellowstone, hoping they would meet some of the Blackfeet and Assiniboins. With an escort such as that under Atkinson's command, the Blackfeet were not likely to attack them. But when the commission learned that those enemies of the Americans were at the Forks of the Missouri, they realized they could not reach them that season.

In his final recommendations to the War Department, Atkinson described the problem of providing adequate protection to the traders. What was really needed, he wrote, was a fort at the Three Forks of the Missouri in the heart of the beaver and Blackfoot country. But he realized such a post would not be practical. ". . . This is a point so remote," he said, "that a garrison could not be sustained there without vast expense, for it would be highly imprudent to depend on the game of the country for subsistence . . . and besides the expense, it would be difficult to send up supplies from the interior.'' What he suggested instead was dispatching three or four hundred soldiers into the area once every three or four years. Lisa could have told him the tactic would not work, for the Blackfeet would have faded as they always did before a superior force only to return when it had gone. But the general was correct in realizing that the government could not assume the expense of a fort on behalf of so few citizens, regardless of the lucrative fur trade that might have resulted.

With the Indians not daring to defy such a large military force, the trip was rather uneventful. The one really momentous occasion occurred on August 19, 1825. They were still camped at the mouth of the Yellowstone when Henry Ashley, who had entered the Rocky Mountains months before through the canyon of Cache la Poudre River, reappeared down the Yellowstone with a flotilla of skin-covered canoes. His trappers had roamed far and wide during the season of 1824–1825, and the rendezvous—his substitute for fixed posts—had been highly successful. Although he had been at-

tacked twice in the last few weeks, first by the Blackfeet, who had wounded one of his men and stolen many of his horses, and then again by the Crows, he still had beaver skins and hoped that Atkinson would carry him and them back to St. Louis. When the men loaded them on the keelboats, they counted a hundred packs, each pack weighing the full one hundred pounds that was the standard measure. A half-ton of beaver skins represented a small fortune.

Ashley's new approach to the fur trade had paid off, and the country he and his men had opened to American trappers had proven itself as rich as anything about which Lisa had dreamed. If the Indians with whom Atkinson had counciled had thought the presence of the Americans was only temporary, an understanding of those bundles of furs would have dispelled the notion. With wealth such as that lying within their grasp, nothing would make the Americans give up their assault on the wilderness. From then on they would be crossing the Great Plains in ever greater numbers, for that was the road to riches.

Chapter 16

Questions of Protection

Of the measures necessary to the safe and successful prosecution of this [fur] trade, the Committee conceive that they resolve themselves into two classes: first, for protecting the lives of our citizens; secondly, for ameliorating the condition of the trade itself.

At the head of the measures in the first of these classes, would come a provision for excluding all British traders from our territories; but as these traders now enter by virtue of a treaty stipulation, which it is in the power of the Executive government only to terminate, the Committee can do no more than express their opinion, that this right of entry ought to be terminated; that the project of a joint occupancy by the British and Americans, of the country west of the Rocky Mountains, ought to be abandoned; a line of demarcation amicably established, with as little delay as possible; and the citizens and subjects of the two powers, for all the purposes of trade and intercourse with the Indians, confined to their respective sides of it.

—Senate Committee on Indian
Affairs, 1829

The Great Plains, still sternly forbidding, still enigmatic, were being forced to yield their secrets by the onslaughts of the Americans. Strong, energetic, brash, and aggressive, the Santa Fé traders and the fur trappers were subduing a land that had resisted subjugation for many years, pushing their way into its remotest corners and banding its surface with well-traveled water routes and familiar trails.

Those wishing to go north and west followed the Missouri River, still treacherous and fickle, too shallow at one time for deep-draft boats, too full at another to make progress against its current easy. Yet it carried the traveler as he expected, first west from St. Louis, then north in modern North Dakota, and from that point, where Peter Cruzatte shot Lewis, it turned west again toward the Three Forks deep in the heart of the Blackfeet's country. Branching off from it was the Yellowstone, a mighty tributary to a mighty river, a match in ca-

priciousness for the Missouri itself, and the route into the Bighorn Mountains and beyond.

Along the waterways skulked uncertain Indian tribes whose professions of friendship could sometimes be valued only according to the size and strength of the group toward whom they were made. Fifty well-armed trappers in a stout-bulwarked keelboat might find those professions as firm as the rock at the heart of a butte; a lonely trapper, leading a mule loaded with a pack of beaver skins, might find them as valueless as a note issued by the Bank of St. Louis when it was operated by the speculative cashier to whom Pilcher had so objected. But the dangers were known by all except the newest tenderfoot.

With neat precision, General Atkinson in his report had described each tribe, its location, and its character. He was somewhat overoptimistic—as perhaps a peace commissioner should have been—about their friendly intentions toward Americans, but he had appraised their characters and their fighting strengths and located their territories. A Congressman from Maine or Virginia who had never strayed more than a hundred miles from the Atlantic Ocean could call for Atkinson's report and become more familiar with the Indians of the Upper Missouri than la Vérendrye had been in almost a lifetime of study.

Few, however, would any longer take Lewis and Clark's route across the continent. In their day, when the origins of the Missouri were still unknown to white men, the great river had seemed the logical course both north and west, but the tangle of mountains at the river's source could be avoided by leaving the Missouri and following the Platte.

A number of men had now done this, and their knowledge was available to all who wanted it. The Platte flowed lazily from the west past the modern town of Casper, Wyoming, and then through the middle of Nebraska until it joined the Missouri at the eastern border of the state. Never the monster that the Missouri could become, it was also too shallow to be a major waterway, so it served as a guide and a source of water, game, and browse in that arid land rather than a means of transportation. Its southern fork, too, was now well known through the exploration of Long and the travels of Ashley, and although the Rockies were not yet an area that most men wished to reach, it provided a route into the heart of the mountains near Denver.

Beyond the point where the North Fork of the Platte turns its course from north to east was South Pass. Unknown to Lewis and Clark, but now familiar to trappers like Jedediah Smith, the young man who worked for Ashley and had proved himself one of the most extraordinary explorers of that extraordinary group, it presented a far better route to the Snake and on down to the Columbia or into what would become Utah than the torturous way followed by Lewis and Clark.

The variety of the routes did not result in a variety of travelers. As both Pike and Long had foreseen, nothing on the Great Plains attracted settlers. The country was too wild, too dry, too filled with Indians, and there was land enough farther east for those who wanted to drive their plows into the soil and see it bring forth man-planted crops. The people who traveled the Platte and the Missouri were all in some manner connected with the fur trade. They were trappers, interpreters, suppliers, or messengers between one band and another, but their ultimate interest was in the packs of skins brought back to St. Louis.

As the trade grew and reached farther and farther west, many of the individuals engaged in it changed. For it was a business fraught with risks. Those who went into the mountains faced the constant danger of Indian attacks, the sudden ambush as they rode along a lonely mountain trail, the daybreak attack on their camps when the morning started with the sound of rifles cracking and the zing of arrows flying toward them and their horses. Only the high profits that a trapper could earn during a successful year and the beckoning of the wilderness that appealed to some kept them in the trade. But there were also those like Henry, who, after being attacked again and again, quietly retired to a gentler life.

Even the men who did not risk their lives but only their fortunes sometimes turned from the speculative fur trade, in which the possible profits were matched only by the possible losses, to other forms of investment. No one who provided the capital for a venture in furs could be certain that he would get anything back at all, for the sinking of a keelboat or the raid of an Indian band might plunge the entries in his books from black to red with alarming suddenness. Ashley had taken both risks, physical and financial, and although he made money, a few years of the trade were sufficient for him. He had proven that the idea of holding a rendezvous instead of erecting posts would work, and his men had opened up a whole new territory for trapping. That and the money he had earned were reward enough, so in 1826 he sold out to three of his most reliable trappers, William Sublette, Jedediah Smith, and David Jackson.

Astor had done little pioneering on the Missouri River. But although he may not have been in the forefront of the western fur business, he was ready to gobble up those who were. His strengths were severalfold. He had a high degree of native intelligence wherever a dollar was involved. No wolf tracking down a wounded buffalo had a better scent for his bloody victim than Astor had for a possible profit. Sitting in his New York mansion, he could sense a dollar to be made on the Upper Missouri and would generally make it. Perhaps, as Ramsay Crooks had told him, he had been overly cautious in entering the western fur business on his own behalf, but the delay had cost him little. In fact, it may have saved him money, for it permitted him to watch others make such mistakes as Lisa and Pilcher's attempts to enter the Blackfeet's country while he shepherded his funds. Another of his strengths was his ruthlessness. A doting husband and father and faithful to his relatives, he was brutal with everyone else. The manner in which he had handled his Canadian partners in the South West Company revealed the man's duplicity and willingness to sink to any levels or employ any trick to get what he wanted.

His greatest strength, however, was the enormous size of his organization and the enormous amount of capital he had gathered. He could buy goods in Europe at the lowest prices, he could ship them to the United States at the lowest cost, and he could underprice any merchant in St. Louis whenever he wanted. Moreover, he could also afford losses such as no other company was able to sustain. Therefore he could put down the price of what he sold and raise the price he paid for pelts whenever he thought that one of his competitors needed to be hurt. So while the Rocky Mountain Fur Company brought back the wealth that lay beyond South Pass, Astor and his representative Crooks nibbled away at the lesser firms. Pilcher posed no problem. The defeat of Immel and Jones at the hands of the Blackfeet had dealt his company such a blow that he considered leaving St. Louis altogether. Other smaller traders either complied with Astor's plans through one form of commercial agreement or another or held off, making as much money as they could before they were finally plucked.

East of the Rockies the one company that could stand up to the Astor interests was the Columbia Fur Company, in which Kenneth McKenzie had become the dominant figure. Born in Scotland, far from the heart of the fur trade and the American wilderness, McKenzie nevertheless had an aptitude for the business that was unusual and a feel for the Indians and the frontier that made him outstanding among outstanding men. Whereas Astor was a genius at manipulating money, politicians, and partners, McKenzie was a genius at field operations. Although his financial resources fell far short of Astor's, he soon had posts along the Upper Missouri and was unquestionably the master of that area. He was also unusually successful at attracting the business of some of the Indians who ordinarily traded with the British companies to the north, so successful that dark rumors floated in St. Louis that he was somehow still associated with his former associates in Canada. (The rumors, of course, could have been started by Astor or his representatives.) The insinuations—and that was all they were—cut so deep that McKenzie answered them in a public letter printed in the St. Louis *Enquirer,* in which he pointed out that in the North West Company he had never been a partner, only an employee, and that he had applied for

American citizenship almost immediately after his arrival in the United States.

Although he responded to the false charges, he was too tough and too smart to let them distract him from his main purpose—to become rich in the fur trade. Under his skillful guidance, the Columbia Fur Company was able to pay off the debts it had originally incurred and to stand firm in its dealings with Astor. In fact, when Astor inevitably approached McKenzie, with Crooks as usual serving as the intermediary, the terms that McKenzie set were far too high for the American Fur Company to accept.

On the other hand, McKenzie also understood the futility of competing with Astor over the long run. The Columbia Fur Company was doing well, but not well enough to amass the capital necessary to withstand a full-fledged Astor assault. No company in the country could have done that. So approximately a year after Astor turned him down and when the articles forming the Columbia Fur Company's partnership were about to expire, he let Crooks know that he was ready to consider a sale. It was not a difficult one to negotiate. The two companies were not equals, but each had something the other wanted. McKenzie and his partners desired the backing of the American Fur Company and the knowledge that they would not have to face its potentially disastrous competition. Astor and his associates wanted the operation that McKenzie had put together along with most of its personnel.

In 1827 the two came to an agreement. The American Fur Company bought out the Columbia Fur Company, but it also established the Upper Missouri Outfit of its Western Department with McKenzie as its head. And it gave every encouragement to McKenzie to retain the people he already had working for him. For Astor did not want to put McKenzie out of business, as he did with so many of his competitors. He wanted McKenzie in his employ, and when he succeeded in this, he had formed a virtual monopoly of the Missouri River trade. For all practical purposes, there were now only two fur companies in the West: Astor's on the Great Plains and the Rocky Mountain Fur Company under its new ownership.

Although the trappers were making fortunes, too many of them were being killed by Indians. Ashley had withdrawn from the business, but he still kept himself informed about what was going on. (No man in St. Louis with political hopes could afford not to.) In 1829, responding to questions from Benton, he said that eight men had recently been slain by Indians and that four were missing, presumably killed. These deaths had not occurred in one massive confrontation between the Americans and the Indians, which would have allowed the trappers to pinpoint both the reason for their casualties and the identity of their specific enemies, but in a slow and harrowing war of attrition in which individual Indian bands picked off individual Americans. Such attacks, the Americans believed, were incited by the British. This obsession had been one of the causes of the War of 1812, and certainly during that conflict the British had done nothing to discourage any Indians who wanted to raid the Americans. Now even though the war was over, the belief was still deep-rooted in the frontiersmen's minds.

Ashley, for example, thought it highly suspicious when Samuel Tulloch, an American trader, left the camp of Peter Skene Ogden, a representative of the Hudson's Bay Company, and was attacked by Indians. Three Americans died in that fight, and Tulloch lost forty-four horses and about $4,000 worth of furs. Yet, according to Ashley, he was within twenty miles of the Hudson's Bay Company's camp. Senator Benton, never one to be left out of an issue affecting the West, thundered out that a Santa Fé caravan had been attacked and robbed by Indians whose guns were of British manufacture and a type that both the Hudson's Bay Company and the former North West Company used in their trade. Cooler heads might point out that American traders, too, often sold British goods, since the Indians showed a preference for them. But cooler heads were not popular in the West of the late 1820s.

Another thing that concerned the Westerners was the joint occupancy of Oregon. This contested land was rich in furs, and the Hudson's Bay Company's profits were high. Ashley reported that over a three-year period about a hundred American trappers had taken furs worth $180,000. Yet Ogden's outfit alone, according to what he had heard, with only sixty men had taken skins worth $600,000, all of them south of the 49th parallel. In Ashley's opinion, regardless of the boundary commission's decision, these men were poachers, taking the best of the fur crop away from the Americans to whom it rightfully belonged. As Ashley put it, and many other traders would have done so, too, the British "would be compelled to withdraw from the country in October, 1828, when the privileges granted them by the treaty of 1818 would expire." The use of the word "privileges" was not an accident. To many Americans, the agreement to share Oregon jointly had not been a way out of a diplomatic impasse but a temporary and gracious concession to Great Britain.

One more concern of the traders was the necessity of relying on British goods. In a report that William Clark helped prepare, the writers pointed out that "the Indians are peculiar in their habits; and, contrary to the opinion generally entertained, they are good judges of the articles offered to them. The trade is not that system of fraud which many suppose . . . and the Indian easily knows the value of the furs in his possession; he also knows the quality of the goods offered to him, and experience has taught him which are best adapted to his wants." Since the manufacturing industry in the United States was not nearly as advanced as Great Britain's, American trade items were generally of poorer quality, and the Indians knew it. But the federal government's tariff on imports meant that American traders had to pay more than the British for the articles they exchanged for furs.

The American traders wanted the relaxation of duties on their imports, better protection from the Indians, and the British removed from Oregon. John Jacob Astor added his lamenting voice to the others, and when he wished to, no one could sound poorer. "I believe I am safe when I say," he wrote, "that all our Indian traders, for these twenty years past, with very few exceptions, have been losing time and property in the trade. . . . When I engaged in it, twenty years ago, I was promised by the administration the protection of the government—and, in fact, more; but I regret to say, hitherto nothing has been done."

Having pictured himself as a public-minded and long-suffering citizen, interested solely in the nation's welfare and wholly scrupulous in all his dealings, Astor launched into a description of the Hudson's Bay Company that in reality was a good self-portrait. "The Hudson's Bay people come on our frontiers, and by means of selling goods cheap, and giving spirituous liquors, they draw our Indian trade for hundreds of miles from us to them." Unless the government took steps to help the Americans, he continued, ". . . we must give up the trade with the Indians, which I am authorized to say, had by great exertions and expenses, been put, and is at present, on a respectable footing—much more so than it has ever been."

Since he completely controlled the American Fur Company, bought its trade items, transported them, and sold its furs—all at a fee—he extracted a profit from almost everything it did. As a result, it was completely unnecessary for him to have it formally declare a dividend, and in his role of pathetic victim of his government's ingratitude, he made a point of this. "The American Fur company," he wrote, "have for years past, and now do employ a capital of a million or more of dollars. They have not yet been able to declare a dividend—they require the protection of government, which I hope will no longer be withheld, and to the obtainment of which I take the liberty to call on you for your good aid." Then with a note of piety he added, "I ask it on account of the many young and enterprising men engaged in the trade."

So the trappers and traders continued to move back and forth across the Great Plains, following the lines of the Missouri and Platte rivers, cursing in the several languages they knew, enduring hardships, poling their keelboats, riding their horses, setting their traps, trading with some Indians and fighting with others, and sometimes finding their fortunes or sometimes losing their lives.

Although their immediate impact might be temporary and fleeting, their influence on the long-term development of the nation was profound. They had opened the area, had kept it open, and would never be satisfied until the Oregon question was settled—in favor of the United States. Furthermore, they were profoundly affecting the picture that all Americans had of themselves and were already becoming a legend. James Fenimore Cooper, who had never been to the Great Plains but who was as sensitive to popular moods as any writer of his day, published *The Prairie* in 1827. In it Natty Bumppo, now about ninety years old by every calculation except the author's, left the woods and went west.

" 'Too late! too late,' exclaimed the trapper [Natty Bumppo], 'for the creatur's are in open view; and a bloody band of accursed Siouxes they are . . . they are going down the swell towards the encampment,' he continued in his former guarded tone, 'no, they halt in the bottom, and are clustering together like deer in council, and we are not yet done with the reptiles.' "

Thus wrote Cooper, and in doing so, he helped initiate an American tradition.

The two routes that led across the northern half of the Great Plains carried only one type of traffic, the fur traders and trappers. That to the south—the road to Santa Fé—carried not only trappers who, using Taos as their headquarters, worked the mountains, but also the traders who dealt with the people of Santa Fé and other Mexican settlements and composed the major part of the southern traffic. Because of the advantages that Storrs had so clearly outlined in his report to Benton, the Americans were able to do a brisk business, and more and more men entered the commerce. So Congress, taking cognizance of the growing west-

ern vote and the power of Benton in the Senate, appropriated funds for surveying the road as Storrs had suggested.

George C. Sibley, who had operated a government-sponsored trading post, was one of the three commissioners. As a guide, he employed Stephen Cooper, the nephew of Benjamin Cooper, whom James had met coming out from Franklin, Missouri. He knew the road that the traders were already following.

In addition to conducting the survey, Sibley and the other commissioners were also to make treaties with the Indians through whose lands the road went, buying from them free passage and a promise not to molest the caravans. The first of the councils was held with the Osages on the banks of the Neosho River in Kansas, where the heavily treed bottomland provided ample wood for campfires and the gentle bluffs gave protection from the weather. When the Osages assembled, they readily ceded the rights Sibley wanted in return for $800 in trade goods. To them, this was nothing but an unexpected windfall, for they could not see that the agreement changed anything. The only grumbling was done by a few warriors who disliked the way the leaders divided the gifts. Because of the meeting, Sibley called the spot Council Grove and had one of his men carve the name in large characters on the trunk of a tree.

After making a similar treaty with the Arkansa Indians, the expedition came to the Mexican boundary and halted, for the commissioners had not heard whether the Mexican government would permit them to enter. After a long delay and still without knowing the response of the Mexican government, Sibley went on by himself, and the other two commissioners returned to Missouri, thinking that the presence of one unauthorized official would be less distasteful to the Mexicans than three. During the following summer, Mexico City finally gave Sibley permission to survey, but not to mark, the road, and he did so on his way back to the United States. In 1827 he set out again. The survey had now been corrected, and he marked the part of the road that ran through American territory.

The results hardly justified three years of work. Even where Sibley placed marks, they soon vanished, washed away by rains, destroyed by Indians, or trampled by buffaloes. Since early travelers had noted the difficulty of crossing over the Cimarron, the harsh land that must be traversed, and the absence of water, the survey went farther up the Arkansas before turning to the Cimarron. But this was a long route and led those who followed it around three sides of a triangle. Thus it was generally ignored. The surveyed road also went to Taos, because that was the nearest New Mexican city. But the heart of the trade was at Santa Fé, and that is the city toward which subsequent caravans headed, survey or no survey.

Regardless of all this, the survey might have added greatly to the knowledge of those making the trip to New Mexico, for the man in charge of the technical work was careful in performing his duties, taking his measurements exactly and keeping all the necessary notes. But having gone to the expense of the survey, the federal government never got around to publishing it. Therefore it was not generally available to those who might have found it useful.

Senator Benton, however, had done what his constituents wanted: he had had the survey made. But he could not get them military protection. Although not familiar with the area personally, General Atkinson studied the question closely. As he saw it, the logical place for a fort, if one were to be established, was at the Big Bend of the Arkansas River, which he calculated was about halfway "and the only place where water, and a scanty supply of fuel can be obtained." But the usefulness of such a fort seemed to him limited. "If the post should be contemplated as only a point to rest the caravans, I presume one company would be sufficient for that object; but if it should be intended that the caravans shall be protected on their journey, a garrison of four or five companies will be necessary, with horses to mount a hundred men." From what he had heard, many of the caravans consisted of thirty to forty Americans; and when they did, the Indians apparently did not bother them. This being the case, he continued, ". . . when we take into view the limited number of troops scattered along our extensive frontier, and which appear necessary for the protection of our frontier settlements, I could hardly recommend that any of them should be withdrawn from that service to establish the contemplated post."

As a public figure dependent to a considerable extent on the goodwill of those he served, Atkinson was not willing to take final responsibility for denying military protection to the Santa Fé traders; and almost as an afterthought, he added, "I nevertheless feel sensibly the claim which that enterprising class of our citizens, who trade to Santa Fee [*sic*], have upon our government for protection, but the means of affording it is for higher authority to determine."

What haunted Atkinson, in addition to the strains already put on his small command, was the outcome of the government's future plan to move all the Eastern Indians to the West and form on the Great Plains an enormous reservation. This was an idea that Jefferson had entertained and should the federal government decide to increase the Indian population of the Great Plains with emigrants from the East, the army would have more than it could handle.

Even without the military protection they would have liked, the traders still carried their goods over the Santa Fé Trail. Originally they had started at Boone's Lick and Franklin, Missouri, taking advantage of the westward course of the Missouri to carry them and their goods some distance on their way. As the route became better known, the starting point shifted farther west to Independence, Missouri, where the river makes its big bend toward the north and nothing further was to be gained by following its course. This, in turn, gave way to Council Grove in modern Kansas, where Sibley had met with the Osage Indians. For as the country grew more settled, there was less and less danger in reaching this spot, nestled under a bluff at the edge of the Neosho River. Here were water and timber, two items the traders would see little of on their long, dusty journey toward the gold at the foot of New Mexico's rainbow in Santa Fé. So common were wagon trains lumbering in from the east and the west that a tree served as a post office where those who wished to could leave letters for relatives, friends, and associates whom they expected to pass that way.

Because the land was gracious, the traders could comfortably wait there until enough of them had assembled, either by prearrangement or accident, to provide sufficient men to defy the Indians. Having then agreed to travel together, their next step was to elect a captain, for they realized that some sort of discipline would be necessary during the coming weeks.

As Alexander Wetmore, who was elected to such a position when he traded with Santa Fé in 1828, remarked, the officers were not regarded seriously and were "invested with such authority as may be voluntarily conceded from day to day, or such as they may have address to enforce. This is greater, or less, as the dangers increase or diminish."

At night the wagons were thrown into a circle or square, forming a small, temporary fortification overshadowed by the great dome of black sky above it and a fire in the center to provide light and warmth for its transient inhabitants. Aware of the constant dangers of Indian attack, the captain or one of his lieutenants appointed the guards. Since military order did not prevail, the sentries, according to Wetmore, would "watch or sleep, as their interest or love of repose may predominate."

Mules and horses generally provided the transportation, and when the traders had agreed on their companions and had selected their officers, the day came when the train moved out, and the woods of Council Grove rang with the curses of the muleteers as they lined up their teams and set them on the road. (Those driving oxen and horses had less recourse to swearing; mules, on the other hand, had to be talked to, and the muleteer's vocabulary was as important to him as his whip and his reins.)

Although the Great Plains were flat and treeless, a few landmarks stood above their surface and helped assure the traveler that he had not missed his way. One of these was Pawnee Rock at the Great Bend of the Arkansas near the modern town of Larned, Kansas. Although not high by most standards, it was higher than anything near it, and those who climbed to the top could see in every direction the plains rolling off into the distance. Since the rock that formed its core was relatively soft and susceptible to scratching with a penknife, it became a sort of registry on which those who passed could place their initials or names, so that others could learn who had gone by. For the traders, while they competed hotly once they were in New Mexico, shared in a large brotherhood while they were on the road. The threat of Indian attacks, the storms that sometimes stopped their caravans, the stampedes that occasionally sent their livestock racing over the plains, the shortage of water, and the other dangers and hardships formed the blood oath of a loyal fraternity. And when they had created their nightly fortress out of their wagons, they might discuss the origins of the rock's name, how the Comanches and Pawnees had fought a great battle there and how the Comanches, admiring the bravery of their enemies, had ever after called the rock by their name.

A choice of several fords led across the Arkansas. Ordinarily the current presented no hazards except in June when the river could become a swirling torrent, capable of sweeping the mules off their feet and the wagons downstream. As with many streams on the Great Plains, dangerous quicksands lurked along its banks and streambed. These had to be avoided at all costs, for a wagon wheel lurching onto their unstable surfaces might turn an otherwise profitable trip into a disaster.

With the Arkansas behind them, the drivers and outriders braced themselves for the next stage of the journey, a trek that could last two or three days without water. Once in a while the caravans would be lucky, and heralded by swarms of mosquitoes, ponds would lie in their way. But most often what little water was available for man and livestock had to be carried in their already heavily loaded wagons.

To make this stretch of the trip even more harrowing, just when no delay could be afforded because of the lack of water, the trail itself was likely to disappear. In the hard arid ground the wheels of previous caravans had failed to leave their usual marks. The guides therefore had to grope their way across this desolate area and hope that neither their instinct nor their sense of direction failed them. (One year, however, unusually heavy rains fell, the soil became soft, and the wagon wheels bit into it. From that time on, the marks remained, and at least one hazard was removed.)

Once the valley of the Cimarron was reached, the most difficult and longest part of the trip was over. Some hills resembling rabbit's ears rose from the ground and served much the same purpose as Pawnee Rock, comforting the traders by showing them they were making progress toward their goal and were still on the trail. Round Mound and Wagon Mound, two more protuberances above the flatness of the Great Plains, also reassured them and told them that their long trip was nearing an end.

The New Mexican town of San Miguel, where James had noted that the inhabitants made so little use of their natural resources, next greeted them, and they knew they were back in civilization again and had only about fifty more miles to go. At this point the traders and their employees began thinking of the pleasures that lay ahead, the coins that would pour into their leather purses as the Mexicans bargained for the goods they had carried so far, the smiles of the Mexican girls, who welcomed the influx of robust, free-spending, although sometimes uncouth, strangers, and the amenities of dry cover, warm fires, and plentiful water that they had been so long without.

The only unpleasantness was paying the custom duties on their imports. Ever since the trade had begun, the Americans had resented these imposts, considering them unjust and suspecting that they even might be illegal under Mexican law. They protested to their congressmen, including Senator Benton, but the collector was always there, demanding the price of entry into the lucrative market. The price was paid, of course. The profits were high enough to cover it, but, lamented the traders, they would have been so much higher if the federal government would only act.

That was the trouble, the frontiersmen assured each other. The federal government would not act.

The question of Oregon was one good example. Men like Ashley and Pilcher, fur traders who looked beyond the confines of the Louisiana Purchase, considered Oregon as belonging to the United States and the British as enjoying privileges extended to them by diplomats who had never set a trap, never fired at a raiding Blackfoot, and did not know what it was like to see their companions cut down by Indian guns. Yet when the old agreement was due to expire, instead of asserting American rights, throwing the British out, and cutting them off from the Blackfeet warriors, the politicians simply renewed it for another ten years, thus postponing American occupancy of what was justly America's.

John Quincy Adams sat in the White House, a man of the old Northeast, which had long since graduated from and forgotten—except in its historical societies—its frontier stage. He was a person of aristocratic leanings who loved his country dearly, served it well and loyally, but was unable to voice the thoughts of the common man or even really to speak to him. During his administration, the War Department, through General Atkinson, could announce that the traders were capable of taking care of themselves on the Santa Fé Trail, leaving the question of permanent posts and military escorts "for higher authority to determine." It could recommend against the establishment of a serviceable fort on the Upper Missouri as being too expensive, while the Treasury Department protected eastern manufacturers by collecting the duties that fur traders eventually had to pay.

The West had regained both its spirits and its land since the end of the War of 1812, but it felt neglected by the government. Even the voice of Senator Benton could not attract the help and recognition it wanted. Yet in 1828 it had a sense that this might change. Andrew Jackson, who had shown the Creeks a thing or two and who had properly battered the British at New Orleans, was running for President, and there was little question which way the West would vote. At last there was a man of their own, a frontiersman like themselves. If enough other people in the country liked him, he might replace that dour New Englander as the nation's leader. The election was one in which the West had great interest and whose results it awaited with bated breath.

Chapter 17

On to Santa Fé

War seems to be the element of the prairie Indians, notwithstanding but few possess much intrinsic bravery. . . . They rarely attack an enemy with a decided advantage; for the prospect of losing even a single warrior will often deter them from undertaking the most flattering venture. It is true that, in addition to their timidity, they are restrained by the fact that the loss of a man often casts a gloom upon the most brilliant victory, and throws a whole clan into mourning.

—Josiah Gregg, 1844

In the presidential campaign of 1828, the adherents of neither side felt bound by the limits of decency or truth. The political issues between the two candidates were obscure, but personal vilification was rampant. The pro-Jackson forces accused Adams of having purchased gaming equipment for the White House at public expense whereas he had paid out of his own purse for the billiard table and chessmen that provided the basis for the charge; and the letters spelling "corrupt bargain," referring to Adams's appointment of Henry Clay as Secretary of State, were picked out of the type case again and again by newspaper compositors as they set the copy submitted to them by their editors.

Jackson's supporters, on the other hand, had repeatedly to hear their candidate criticized for having court-martialed and executed several militiamen and for the frontier brawls in which he had engaged. Worst of all were the accusations thrown at his long-loved, long-suffering wife, Rachael, who was portrayed as an adulteress unfit to stain the threshold of the White House with the imprint of her foot.

Such feverish emotionalism reflected the underlying mood of the country. Rapid growth in both population and geography and a greater emphasis on industrialization were undermining the former simplicity of its social structure. Consequently many felt themselves cut off from the roots of authority and neglected by the government whose purpose they supposed was to serve them. What they wanted was to exert greater influence. So the campaign became one not of issues or even personalities, but rather of section against section, class against class.

The West, of course, was on the side of Jackson, whom they regarded as one of their own. Even Clay's loyalty to John Quincy Adams could not hold their votes for the New Englander. The South, mistakenly thinking Jackson was more of a states' righter than he was, also voted for him, as did Pennsylvania and most of New York. The result was an overwhelming victory at the polls and in the Electoral College.

His followers were jubilant, his opponents somber. Daniel Webster, long familiar with politics, wondered where the future of the country lay. John Marshall, who had battled with Jefferson on constitutional questions, delivered the presidential oath with the shuddering thought that his lifetime work in the judiciary would prove wasted.

Guests invited to the inaugural reception at the White House were shocked by the conduct of the horde that followed Jackson back from the ceremony at the Capitol; the mob was delighted at its ability to force itself past the White House doors and into the rooms that had so long been occupied by the privileged. They had already filled every hotel and rooming house in the city, overflowed into Georgetown, and had nearly caused a whiskey shortage in the District of Columbia. Now the press of their bodies in the sedate halls and salons of the White House crushed the furniture and created chaos until the attendants lured them outside by placing tubs of punch on the lawn.

Regardless of the nation's upset decorum, a new figure in the White House meant a new ear to listen to the West's troubles. And troubles had struck the Santa Fé Trail in 1828 while the Adams-Jackson campaign was being waged. Two friends, who were returning to Missouri, had ridden a short distance ahead of the main body of their caravan. When they came to a small stream, they dismounted, drank the fresh water, and then foolishly fell asleep. Indians came upon them and shot them both with their own guns, killing one and seriously wounding the other.

When the caravan reached them, the men loaded the two bodies onto the wagons and then, frightened in spite of the calming words of some of the more experienced traders, pushed forward as fast as they could to escape the unseen Indians. The wounded man, however, was past help, and after they had traveled about forty miles, he died.

The caravan paused to bury the two bodies, doing them such honors as they could in the faraway Cimarron Valley. Just as they were concluding, about six or seven Indians appeared, probably innocent victims of their own unfortunate timing, for otherwise they would not have dared approach the irate white men. Without pausing to ask questions or to determine the identity of these new arrivals, the men of the caravan grabbed their rifles and began firing just as senselessly as the Indians who had earlier killed the two white men.

Seeing the rifles raised, the Indians turned their horses and began a frantic dash away from the bullets aimed in their direction. But one of them turned too late. A few minutes earlier he had hoped for a present of tobacco. Now his horse fell beneath him, struck by the bullets. Before he could rise to his feet and escape, the white men's guns were all leveled at him, and death came instantly.

Revenge begot revenge. Two white men had died. Now an Indian had been killed, and the score to be settled on each side was steadily rising. When the Comanches learned of the death of their warrior, they pursued the caravan. As usual the traders had readily accepted pesos in payment for their goods (Mexican currency in parts of Missouri had now become more common than American), and when pesos were not available, they had taken horses and mules. Having had a profitable trip, they had acquired about a thousand head. Near the Arkansas the Comanches succeeded in stampeding the animals and made off with almost all of them.

Later in the year a second group of traders left Santa Fé to return to Missouri. Composed of about twenty men, the caravan had a hundred and fifty horses and mules, four wagons, and a large amount of silver coin. Nothing eventful occurred until they were just about to go into camp at the Upper Cimarron Springs. As they came to the top of a hill that separated them from the place where they expected to spend the night, they saw a large Comanche encampment across the trail. Because of the terrain, they could not turn back, nor could they go around it. Holding their rifles in readiness, they decided to bluff their way through.

The chief of the band, however, came forward and greeted them cordially in Spanish, inviting them to spend the night and assuring them that the young men would guard their livestock. The traders knew this invitation was a trap, so they refused and started driving their livestock and wagons through the camp to the other side. As the caravan was on the verge of escaping, the Indians grabbed the bridle reins of the last three men and started to fire at them. Two of them got away, but one was killed almost instantly.

Fighting a rearguard action, the caravan was able to go about a half-mile before darkness forced them to make camp. They corralled their wagons and staked their bell mare nearby. Whenever the Indians' shooting would permit them, they would slip out and ring the bell, thus holding their herd together during the night.

"The next day," recalled one of the members, "we made but five miles; it was a continuous fight, and a very difficult matter to prevent their capturing us. This annoyance was kept up for four days; they would surround us, and then let up as if taking time to renew their strength, to suddenly charge upon us again, and they thus continued to harass us until we were almost exhausted from loss of sleep."

When the caravan emerged from the valley of the Cimarron, they thought they were safe, but the Comanches suddenly charged them again, stampeding all their livestock. During the fighting the Americans killed one Indian, which caused the Comanches to withdraw temporarily. Taking advantage of this respite, the Americans frantically corralled their wagons again and built breastworks with their saddles and harnesses. Soon the Indians were back, and the battle lasted until two hours after dark. Then the moon followed the sun over the horizon, and night put an end to the day's fighting.

"Darkness was now upon us," continued the participant. "There were two alternatives before us; should we resolve to die where we were, or attempt to escape in the black hours of the night? Our little band looked the matter squarely in the face, and, after a council of war had been held, we determined to escape, if possible."

Obviously they could not take the wagons, since they had lost their livestock. So they abandoned them and much of their coin, carrying the remainder with them as they slipped away from their makeshift fort into the night. Their way led to the east, but to avoid the Indians, they turned north, traveling all night, the next day, and into the next night before resting. Exhausted and hungry—like Cabeza de Vaca, they had subsisted on prickly pear cacti—they decided they could carry their coins no farther and buried them on an island in the Arkansas River. Since they were now out of the normal range of the Comanches, they shot a buffalo and an antelope. But after three weeks more of walking, they began to wonder if they would ever reach Missouri.

At this point they decided the five strongest men should go ahead and try to get help at Independence. "I shall never forget the terrible suffering we endured," one of them later wrote. "We had no blankets, and it was getting late in the fall. Some of us were entirely barefooted, and our feet so sore that we left stains of blood at every step. Deafness, too, seized upon us so intensely, occasioned by our weak condition, that we could not hear the report of a gun fired at a distance of only a few feet."

For eleven days the diet for all five men consisted of one turkey, one coon, a crow, and occasionally some elm bark and wild grapes. But they finally reached a frontier shanty about fifteen miles from Independence. The people of Independence were shocked at the sight of the survivors and several men immediately went in search of the others, who were now scattered along the trail. "Not more than two of the unfortunate party were together," one of the traders wrote. "The human rescuers seemingly brought back nothing but living skeletons wrapped in rags . . ."

With reason these attacks caused concern among those who thought of going to Santa Fé in the spring of 1829, for they disproved the old assump-

tion that a sufficiently large number of traders in one caravan would deter the Indians. Although the government had previously remained relatively indifferent to the wants of the frontier, the election of Jackson had changed its attitude. When a congressional bill to provide a military escort for the next caravan died in committee, the President personally requested the War Department to take action even though additional funds were not available. Brevet Major Bennet Riley with four companies of the Sixth Infantry—about two hundred men—was ordered to provide a military escort to the Mexican border.

As an economy measure, the army assigned infantry to the task instead of cavalry, which would have been more effective against the mounted Indians of the Great Plains. Furthermore, it provided oxen in place of a full complement of mules and horses to carry the companies' baggage. This, too, saved money, because the oxen were cheaper and could be eated as their loads were used up. (Part of their cost could be charged to the budget for food.) But the suitability of oxen to the Great Plains was still unknown, and many believed they would have to travel at a far slower pace than the caravan. From the point of view of the traders, all this was bad enough, but even worse was the limited scope of Riley's mission. He was to take them to the American-Mexican boundary but no farther. Yet the Indians whom they most feared lived on the other side of the line.

Nevertheless, enough traders finally gathered to make the trip possible. As usual they elected a captain, choosing Charles Bent, an experienced fur trader for the thankless job. The second-in-command was David Waldo, another man with a level head and an understanding of the problems they might face. Each of these was accompanied by a brother, both of them named William.

The first part of the journey passed uneventfully except for the men's surprise at the performance of the oxen, which proved capable of keeping up with the horses and mules and perhaps even better adapted to the hardships of plains travel. More than one trader decided he himself would use oxen in the future. At Chouteau's Island, where the Upper Ford of the Arkansas River was located, the traders did their best to persuade Riley to remain with them all the way to Santa Fé. Understandably he refused to jeopardize his army career by flagrantly violating his orders.

On July 10 the traders left the United States and Riley. Before departing they persuaded him to write a letter to the New Mexican authorities suggesting they provide an escort through their own territory. Riley also agreed to wait for the caravan's return until almost the middle of October.

After safely fording the river, the caravan went into camp and on the following day, July 11, 1829, started the part of the journey that would take them through Mexican territory. In spite of the fears they had voiced, the men were derisive of the discipline needed to ensure their protection from attack; and Charles Bent, familiar with the hopelessness of trying to enforce what was unenforceable, resigned himself to the slackness that inevitably occurred.

Turning south, the wagons entered a small ravine that opened out into a sandy basin, which in turn led to another narrow defile. Charles Bent had assigned three men to serve as an advance guard. They rode across the basin and, seeing nothing to alarm them, dismounted and lazily waited for the others to catch up.

William Bent was riding by himself on the flank when he suddenly saw a band of Indians come over a rise. There was no question of their intention, for they were riding hard and brandishing their guns and bows. Bent fired a single shot in their direction and then, without waiting to reload, spurred his mule back toward the caravan.

Hearing him shout a warning, two men who were nearby dashed in his direction. The sight of two more white men appearing so quickly made the Indians pause in their onward rush, but William Bent did not stop. He had seen more Indians on the trail ahead attacking the dismounted advance guard. Those three men, abruptly shaken from their torpor, leapt into their saddles, but one was riding a mule which, in this moment of danger, failed him. Instead of racing back to safety, it moved so slowly that the Indians shot and killed its rider, then stripped and beheaded him.

The drivers now regretted the derisive attitude they had taken toward Bent's instructions, for instead of being bunched together in a defensible formation, they had allowed the wagons to straggle out over a long line. What they most needed was a brief respite during which they could pull the wagons together.

Charles Bent rushed forward to buy the time for them. William joined him, and the two brothers, brandishing their rifles and aiming here and then there, but never firing the two single shots that would have left them both unarmed, slowly retreated back to the wagons. Their determined resistance and the threatening manner in which they pointed their guns, first at this advancing Indian

and then at that one, made the Indians slow their attack. None of them wished to be the victims of the bullets that would permit their fellow warriors to overrun the two white men.

Someone thought of an abandoned cannon they had salvaged earlier from along the trail, but it was so carefully packed away they could not get it out in time to fire it at the Indians' first charge. When they finally freed and loaded it, its loud retort startled the Indians, who were accustomed only to hand-held guns. Once more they paused, and the combination of delays caused by the Bents and the cannon gave the drivers time to pull their wagons into a circle. The livestock were placed inside, where they could not be driven off, and the men quickly dug rifle pits that would provide them some cover while they returned the Indians' fire.

So far Bent's actions had all been defensive. In the unfortunate position in which the Indians had surprised him, he could have done little else, particularly since he did not have enough men to launch a counterattack. But once he had secured the animals and wagons, he began to think of Riley's troops, who were still only a few miles away. Diplomatic protocol would not prevent Riley from crossing the border and coming to their aid since they were under actual attack. But the problem was to get word to him.

Nine men volunteered to go on the dangerous mission. Because the Indians were circling the beleaguered men in their customary fashion, a breakthrough would be difficult, but by using the cannon and concentrating his men's fire, Bent was able to create an opening through which the riders were able to pass. Flogging their horses to their utmost speed, they raced to Riley's camp on the other side of the Arkansas.

Night fell as the traders still peered from their rifle pits and from behind their wagons, searching for Indians. Their foolish bravado and insolent disregard of instructions had now vanished, and they listened to their leaders and fought as a unit. Discouraged by the traders' resistance, the Indians broke off the attack, intending to resume it when the sun again splashed its light across the Great Plains.

The moon remained high while Major Riley found his way through the sandhills in which the caravan had been ambushed and then conveniently dropped below the horizon as he reached the traders, so he could take up his position without being seen by the Indians. But the next morning his bugler, failing to understand the situation, blew reveille, thus announcing to the Comanches that the soldiers had arrived. With this dramatic change in odds, the Indians faded away.

As he looked over the terrain in which the caravan had been ambushed, Riley realized that it was extremely unfavorable for defense. The sandhills provided good cover for the Indians, and the narrow defiles through which the wagons would have to pass gave them little space in which to maneuver. So he agreed to accompany them until they came to more open country and then left to return to the United States.

Sobered by their recent experience, the men behaved more cautiously and were more respectful of Charles Bent's instructions. Shortly they were met by about a hundred Mexican buffalo hunters, who had heard that several thousand Indians had gone on the warpath. Fearful, they asked to travel with the Americans.

This unforeseen reinforcement was not entirely welcome. The Mexicans were undisciplined and poorly armed, but Bent could not refuse them. Yet it was the Mexicans, riding in advance, who discovered the ambush the Indians had prepared at the Rabbit Ear Mountains. In the fighting they lost one of their men.

Once safely at Santa Fé, the traders did a brisk business, perhaps because there were fewer of them than usual, and soon they were ready to return to Missouri. An inspector general in the Mexican army, Colonel José Antonio Viscarra, was in Santa Fé; and when he heard of the many difficulties that the caravan had experienced, he volunteered to escort it back. Nothing could have heartened the Americans more, and Bent eagerly accepted the generous offer.

The addition of some Spanish civilians, the Mexican soldiers, and their employees increased the total to almost three hundred persons, a body sufficiently large to discourage most Indian attacks. When they reached the Cimarron, however, a group of Indians did approach them, but they had tied an arrow to a spear, thus making a cross, the sign of peace that dated as far back as Coronado's invasion of the Río Grande Valley. They said they wanted to camp with the caravan for the night.

The traders would have nothing to do with such a proposal; Viscarra, less suspicious, agreed to let them provided they surrendered all their arms. This condition did not deter the Indians, but they said they would not give them up unless Viscarra sent the Americans some distance off. To all appearances, they trusted the Mexicans but not the traders.

As soon as the Americans were out of sight and while they were still talking to the Mexicans, the Indians opened fire on them. Their primary target was Viscarra himself, and he would have been killed if a Pueblo Indian accompanying him had not stepped forward and taken the bullet in his own body. The sound of the shots reached Bent and the traders, and they rushed back to help their escort.

The subsequent fighting was brutal. The Indians' small supply of ammunition gave out, but this did not stir any feelings of mercy in the hearts of the Americans. To them, this attack was one more example of Indian treachery, and they were determined to administer a lesson that would not be quickly forgotten. They with their Mexican allies ran down as many Indians as they could and scalped them, sometimes when they were still alive. The brother of the slain Pueblo Indian stabbed and killed the Indian who had tried to shoot Viscarra; and the Americans, to add to the gruesomeness of the affair, skinned some of the dead Indians and in at least one case tacked the skin on the outside of a wagon. Drying and shriveling in the sun, it warned others what might befall them if they fought an American caravan.

During the weeks that he had waited for the return of the traders, Riley had been suffering from Indian harassment, losing several men. He had told the traders he would wait until October 10 at the latest, and when they had not arrived by that date, he started for Missouri. Fortunately they arrived at the Arkansas shortly after and, finding that he had departed, sent messengers to him.

Riley turned back, and on October 12, 1829, Viscarra crossed the Arkansas to be received with military honors by Riley and his now ragged four companies. That evening in the wilderness the men of both nations celebrated. The mainstay of the meal was bread and buffalo meat, but the Americans also had in reserve a little whiskey and salt pork, and the Mexicans had a few onions. These delicacies made it a notable occasion.

The assemblage on the banks of the Arkansas amounted to about five hundred persons, a medley of nationalities and classes. The Spanish civilians were there with their women. Some of the Mexicans were cultivated, educated men; many of their soldiers were coarse, ill-bred, and poorly trained. With them were numerous Indians drawn from the Pueblo tribes. Among the Americans were the traders—a few of them important men of business—and their employees, who were often drawn from the roughest elements of the frontier. Some of the military were college graduates; others were underpaid ruffians who could find nothing better to do. And in addition to Spanish, English, and Indian dialects, many of the men, since this was a fur-trapping society, spoke French as their mother tongue. The strange group needed only a tower to be another Babel.

Returning Riley's hospitality, Viscarra later invited some of the Americans to dine with him and served them ham, cakes, and wine at a table set with silver eating utensils. Yet the same evening in the same camp the Pueblo Indians mourned their dead and celebrated their victory with wild songs and a display of the scalps they had taken. Then the two groups parted, each headed in the direction it called home.

By using oxen on the Great Plains, Riley had created a revolution in transportation. Less expensive than mules or horses, easier to handle because they were less skittery, simpler to graze and water, and useful for food, oxen provided a means of moving goods and people across the plains that was within the means of more persons. But while he was marching up and down the banks of the Arkansas waiting for the caravan's return, an even greater revolution in transportation was taking place at Carbondale in eastern Pennsylvania. The Delaware and Hudson Company had laid inclined tracks between its mines and the canal that led to the Hudson River in New York. Gravity carried the cars down to the water's edge, where the coal was loaded onto the barges. On August 8, 1829, just a few days after Riley had beaten off an Indian raid on his livestock, the company prepared to run a locomotive over these tracks. The engineer built up the pressure of steam and released the brakes, and the engine moved forward. Its turning wheels were the first to run in the United States. That same year two other railroads were under construction, the Baltimore and Ohio and a line running between Charleston and Hamburg, South Carolina. In slightly more than a decade, the United States had moved from pirogues and keelboats to steamboats and from wagons to locomotives.

These technological changes did not immediately alter life on the Great Plains, but steamboats were beginning to ply the waters of the Lower Missouri in a way that the *Western Engineer* had been unable to. Between St. Louis and Independence travelers and shippers could use the regular packet that was instituted that year, and Kenneth McKenzie, who remained in charge of the Upper Missouri business of the American Fur Company, was thinking about using a steamboat to replace the more primitive forms of transportation on which the company still relied.

When Astor had purchased the Columbia Fur Company with the thought of obtaining McKen-zie's services, he had acted wisely. With his customary vigor, McKenzie had secured a firm grip on the trade of the Upper Missouri and was beginning to reconstruct a fort at the mouth of the Yellowstone, where Clark had waited for Lewis to reappear from his trip up the Marias. Although Clark had been driven away by the mosquitoes, the site was no worse at the wrong season of the year than any other, and McKenzie saw that it was strategically located for control of the traffic of the two great rivers. Fort Union—he changed its name from Fort Lynn—was to be the most elaborate one owned by the American Fur Company and, he was sure, would soon justify its cost. He also envisioned linking it to St. Louis by steamboat, although some of the other stockholders in the company were not certain this would be practical.

Yet in spite of all that McKenzie and his other partners had accomplished, Astor still had not obtained the monopoly of the fur trade that he wanted. The Rocky Mountain Fur Company remained the dominant factor to the west of the Great Plains. Farther west in Oregon the Hudson's Bay Company still retained its unique position. Dr. John McLoughlin was the agent in charge there, but neither he—even if he had wished to—nor anyone else could make the Blackfeet discontinue their hostile attitude toward the majority of American trappers. They had been enemies ever since their encounter with Lewis, and their bands, as well as those of several other tribes, posed a threat to anyone traveling through the mountains.

In March, 1832, for example, a group of eight trappers decided to travel south through the mountains of Santa Fé to purchase some horses, trapping as they went. When they returned to their camp after a short absence, they found that the Indians had robbed them of everything but one blanket apiece. That night they made a counterattack on the Indians' village.

Quietly they crawled on their hands and knees toward one of the fires they could see and were within eight or ten paces of it, when a large dog suddenly started barking and growling. The sleeping Indians woke instantly; and the trappers, realizing that they had lost the advantage of surprise, began retreating to the top of a small hill, determined to put up a hard fight. The Indians quickly encircled them, and for about an hour both sides shot at each other in the moonlight without inflicting many casualties. Then the Indians, realizing that the trappers were resolute in their defense, opened up the side of the circle away from their camp and let the white men escape.

"The scenes of this night," wrote one of the

trappers later, "will ever be indelibly impressed upon my memory. After traveling five or six miles we came to a deep ravine or hollow—we carefully descended the precipice to the flat below, where we encamped for the night; but from fright, fatigue, cold and hunger, I could not sleep, and lay contemplating on the striking contrast between a night in the villages of Pennsylvania and one in the Rocky Mountains. In the latter, the plough-boy's whistle, the gambols of the children on the green, the lowing of the herds, and the deep tones of the evening bell, are unheard; not a sound strikes upon the ear, except perchance the distant howling of some wild beast, or war-whoop of the uncultivated savage . . ."

In March, 1832, when the trapper was thinking of—and regretting—his peaceful life as a boy in western Pennsylvania, a group of young men were meeting every Saturday in Massachusetts and wishing that more excitement filled theirs. The leading spirit was Hall J. Kelley, a former schoolteacher. A man of many interests, he had helped found in Boston the Young Men's Education Society and, not to show prejudice in favor of one sex only, the Penitent Female Refuge Society. When he was not teaching or helping penitent females, he did surveying and engineering, which led him to become involved in a Massachusetts textile mill. Having inherited some money from his father, he invested it all in the mill and lost it. But he was not one to give way to discouragement, and instead of returning to teaching, he moved on to an even more glorious idea—the settlement of Oregon by Americans.

He had been reading about that distant country ever since the publication of Biddle's edited account of the expedition of Lewis and Clark, and the marvels of what they had seen danced in front of his eyes. He had petitioned Congress for help in carrying out his idea, but a government that could not afford to protect its traders and trappers was not interested in Kelley's projects. So he formed a company, which he incorporated in 1831 and called the "American Society for encouraging the settlement of the Oregon territory."

Among those who listened to Kelley's imaginative romanticizing was a Massachusetts ice merchant, Nathaniel Wyeth. Although a practical man of business, the thought of the West fired his spirit; and setting aside all difficulties, he pictured himself as heading a profitable settlement in Oregon, whose inhabitants would both trap and farm and find an outlet for their products in China and elsewhere overseas. Without the hampering limitation of facts, Wyeth was able to talk some twenty young men into joining his project. Among them

was his brother, a doctor, and his nephew, as well as a gunsmith, a blacksmith, two carpenters, two fishermen, and farmers and laborers. Lest they enter the wilderness unprepared, Wyeth had them meet at his house every Saturday night during the winter of 1831–1832 to discuss possible contingencies and ways of handling them.

Like others before him from Lewis to Long, Wyeth gave considerable thought to a new means of transportation and devised an amphibious wagon that could be converted into a boat by removing its wheels and tongue. Pleased with this invention, he had three of them built. His design was so carefully thought out that he even foresaw the problems that might be caused by the caulking. Since this could be melted by the sun, he eliminated it entirely, trusting to the fine joints used in the wagons' construction to keep out the water.

He also adopted a uniform for the group's use, a coarse woolen jacket, pantaloons, striped cotton shirt, and cowhide boots. Each man was also equipped with a firearm, most of them rifles, a bayonet, a clasped knife, and an ax. This was to be no ragamuffin band of adventurers but a neatly dressed corps. To add to his men's training, Wyeth had them all camp ten days on an island in Boston harbor—all, that is, except Kelley, whom he had dropped from the rolls as being too impractical. Following this experience, they went by boat to Baltimore, where they loaded themselves and their three wagons on board the cars of the newly constructed Baltimore and Ohio Railroad, which carried them the full length of its track—slightly more than sixty miles—toward the Allegheny Mountains.

At St. Louis Wyeth and the members of his company began for the first time to understand the difficulties they faced. In Boston they had imagined themselves successful fur trappers and traders; in St. Louis they learned about the American and Rocky Mountain Fur companies and realized they would have little chance of competing against such experienced giants. In Boston they had camped on an island surrounded by the friendly water traffic passing in and out of the harbor; in St. Louis they learned about the Blackfeet and realized that their ten-day camping trip had little bearing on the reality of the plains and mountains. In Boston their amphibious wagons seemed like clever inventions; in St. Louis they saw the Missouri and understood how useless they would be and sold them for half what they had cost.

Their self-confidence was subsiding, but none of them yet wished to turn back, so they went by steamboat to Independence, the starting point for their trek across the Great Plains. There two of the party changed their minds and decided they preferred the familiar Charles River to the unknown Platte. They also met William Sublette, one of the principals in the Rocky Mountain Fur Company, who was leading an expedition of more than sixty trappers to the mountains. Not fearing any competition from this band of New England novices, Sublette kindly invited them to join him and also advised them to purchase two yoke of oxen and some sheep, since they could not always count on living off the country.

Before they reached the Platte, three more members of Wyeth's party had seen enough of the West, and they, too, headed for home. Quickly the remainder learned the soundness of Sublette's advice to buy the oxen and sheep, for even with those animals they ran out of meat before they were able to shoot their first buffalo. Like so many others, they were appalled at the country and their own lack of preparedness. "The Missouri Territory," one of them later wrote, "is a vast wilderness, consisting of immense plains, destitute of wood and water, except on the edges of streams that are found near the turbid La Platte. This river owes its source to the Rocky mountains, and runs pretty much through the territory, without enlivening or fructifying this desert. Some opinion may be formed of it by saying that for the space of six hundred miles, we may be said to have been deprived of the benefits of two of the elements, *fire* and *water*. Here were, to be sure, buffaloes, but after we had killed them we had no wood or vegetables of any kind wherewith to kindle a fire for cooking. We were absolutely compelled to dry the dung of buffalo as the best article we could procure for cooking our coarse beef. That grumbling, discontent, and dejection should spring up amongst us, was what no one can be surprised at learning. . . . Every one who goes to sea may lay his account for coming to short allowance, from violent storms, head winds, damaged vessel, and the like; but for a band of New-England men to come to short allowance upon land, with guns, powder, and shot was a new idea to our Oregon adventurers, who had not prepared for it in the article of hard bread, or flour, or potatoes, or that snug and wholesome article, *salt fish*, . . . so convenient to carry."

Not only did they suffer from shortages of meat, but the water of the Platte, which was their source of drinking water, disagreed with them. As a result several of the men, including Wyeth's brother, the physician, came down with diarrhea. Still with the help of Sublette, they continued along the Platte, taking its South Fork for a short distance and then crossing over to the North Fork.

By the time they reached the Laramie Mountains, several of the men were so weak they slipped from the horses and mules they were riding, too feeble and unsteady to hold on. Yet they could not leave the sick behind, for there would have been no way for them to catch up. Furthermore, although they had met no Indians, they had seen signs of them.

That year the Blackfeet were in no better mood than before, as Thomas Fitzpatrick, a noted trader and a principal in the Rocky Mountain Fur Company, could attest. In 1832, while riding alone and scouting out the land, he stumbled on a band of them, who chased him, stole his horse, and did their best to kill him.

Although he escaped by hiding among some rocks, he then had to make his way on foot and dared travel only at night. "When found," wrote one of those with the group that first encountered him, "he was completely exhausted, and so much wasted in flesh, and deformed in dress, that, under other circumstances, he would not have been recognized. The poor man was reduced to a skeleton, and was almost senseless. When his deliverers spoke of taking him to camp, he scarcely seemed to comprehend their meaning."

The rendezvous that year was held at Pierre's Hole in present-day eastern Idaho just over the Wyoming border. A grassy valley, it was about thirty miles long and took its name from the Pierre (now Teton) River. This, of course, was Sublette's destination, and when they arrived there, they found about two hundred trappers and five hundred Indians, many of them Flatheads, already assembled.

While Sublette conducted his business, Wyeth's group camped a few miles away, glad of the opportunity to rest for a while, but also concerned about the future. Even though they believed the worst of the journey was over, some of them doubted whether they wanted to continue to Oregon; and when he called the roll several of them announced their intention of returning east.

Just after the rendezvous broke up, a number of trappers encountered a band of Blackfeet, and fighting almost immediately broke out. Reinforced by additional trappers who came racing to the scene, the Americans charged forward, but unknown to them, the Indians had built a breastwork of cottonwood behind which they took refuge. A withering fire brought down five Americans, eight Flathead Indians, and ten Nez Percés, as well as wounding many more. This broke up the charge and made the Americans retreat and reconsider their plans.

They then decided to invest the Blackfeet's fortification. One of the Americans who tried to steal up close to it with two other white men and two Indians later described his experience. "We advanced closer and closer," he wrote, "crawling upon our hands and knees, with the intention of giving them *a select* shot; and when within twenty yards of their breastwork, one of our Indians was shot dead. At this we lay still for some time, but Smith's foot [Smith was one of the Americans], happening to shake the weeds as he was laying on his belly, was shot through. I advanced a little further, but finding the balls to pass too quick and close, concluded to retreat.

"When I turned," he continued, "I found that my companions had deserted me. In passing by, Smith asked me to carry him out . . . After getting him on my back, still crawling on my hands and knees, I came across Kean [the other American who was with him], lying near where the first Indian fell, who was also mortally wounded and died soon after."

In spite of heavy casualties like this, the fighting continued until late afternoon. By then the Americans had completely surrounded the breastwork and were close to it. As soon as the sun went down, they intended to set fire to it and drive the Blackfeet into the open where they could be killed.

"Having made all these preparations, which were to put an end to all further molestations on the part of the Blackfeet," continued the same participant, "our whole scheme and contemplated victory was frustrated by a most ingenious and well executed device of the enemy. A few minutes before the torch was to be applied, our captives commenced the most tremendous yells and shouts of triumph, and menaces of defiance, which seemed to move heaven and earth. Quick as thought a report spread through all quarters, that the plain was covered with Blackfeet Indians coming to reinforce the besieged. So complete was the consternation in our ranks, created by this stratagem, that in five minutes afterwards, there was not a single . . . man . . . within a hundred yards of the fort. Every man thought only of his own security, and ran for life without ever looking around, which would at once have convinced him of his folly."

Enraged at their own gullibility, the Americans counted their casualties. They had lost thirty-two of their people, most of them Indians; and since it was now dark, they decided to break off the fighting and return to the rendezvous.

The next day they came back to the battlefield ready to fight again. But the Blackfeet, knowing they were outnumbered, had fled, leaving behind a considerable number of horses, including Fitzpat-

rick's. Although driven away temporarily, their fighting force had not been crippled by the battle, and they were ready to pounce again on any bands of trappers they might meet. In fact, within a few days five men who left the rendezvous in a group found themselves facing the Blackfeet again. Two were killed outright, and another was mortally wounded.

To those of Wyeth's party who had decided to return home, the battle only confirmed what they had already begun to think: life on the Great Plains and in the mountains was hard, dangerous, and only for a select company of men.

The trip back to St. Louis for those returning east was relatively uneventful. The travelers were stopped by a band of Blackfeet, but the Indians apparently had not heard of the battle at Pierre's Hole, for they merely demanded some tobacco and let the group go on. (Since Sublette had about $80,000 worth of furs with him, he was especially anxious to avoid a fight.)

Once back in Massachusetts, John Wyeth, Nathaniel's nephew, wrote an account of the trip, hoping to warn others not to be as gullible as he had been. ". . . this extravagant and fallacious account [Kelley's] of the Oregon was read and believed by some people not destitute of a general information of things, nor unused to reading; but there were circles of people, chiefly among young farmers and journeymen mechanics, who were so thoroughly imbued with these extravagant notions of making a fortune by only going over land to the other side of the globe, to the Pacific Ocean, that a person who expressed a doubt of it was in danger of being either affronted, or at least, accused of being moved by envious feelings. After a score of people had been enlisted in this Oregon expedition, they met together to feed each other's hopes and visionary notions, which were wrought up to a high degree of extravagance, so that it was hardly safe to advise or give an opinion adverse to the scheme."

In conclusion Wyeth said, "Reader: The book you have in your hands is not written for your amusement merely, or to fill up an idle hour, but for your instruction—particularly to warn young farmers and mechanics not to leave a certainty for an uncertainty, and straggle away over a sixth part of the globe in search of what they leave behind them at home." But the warning was to no avail. With the optimism of a young and hopeful people, thousands were beginning to think about Oregon and whether they could not improve their lot by moving there.

Chapter 18

Art and Business

It has been, heretofore, very erroneously represented to the world, that the scenery on this river [the Missouri] was monotonous, and wanting in picturesque beauty. This intelligence is surely incorrect, and that because it has been brought perhaps, by men who are not the best judges in the world, of Nature's beautiful works; and if they were, they always pass them by, in pain or desperate distress, in toil and trembling fear for the safety of their furs and peltries, and for their lives, which are at the mercy of the yelling savages who inhabit this delightful country.

One thousand miles or more of the upper part of the river, was, to my eye, like fairyland. . . .

—George Catlin, 1832

In spite of John Wyeth's well-founded misgivings about his uncle's attempt to settle in Oregon, Nathaniel Wyeth's trip across the Great Plains completed the pattern of development that would dominate the area for the next decades. Changes would come, but they would be modifications of what had already occurred, not fundamental differences in what had been done before.

Slightly less than thirty years had elapsed since the Louisiana Purchase, but the Great Plains were not the same place through which Lewis and Clark had traveled. Now traders' forts were common along the Missouri and other rivers, and most of the important trans-plains routes were well known; the road to Santa Fé, which in Pedro Vial's day was familiar to only a few adventurers like himself, was well traveled, and the ruts of wagon wheels marked its course for others to follow. Several ways of reaching Oregon had been explored, and at least one of them had been found practical, probably even for wagons, although no one had as yet taken wheeled vehicles over South Pass.

Nathaniel Wyeth's journey, no matter how badly conceived, added a new purpose for crossing the Great Plains. He and his party had made the

journey with the intention of remaining on the West Coast as permanent settlers, not transient trappers and traders. Always in the back of the Americans' minds was the concept that made them so different from the Spanish, French, and British: the idea that the land would be permanently settled and become a part, not a colony, of the mother country. It was this, perhaps more than anything else, that made them so tenacious in their hold on the land.

Of course, during those bitter days of the War of 1812, they had been pushed back and back until it almost looked as though the Great Plains would revert to the Indians, the British, and the French-Canadians; but the war had ended, and the Americans had been sufficiently resolute to regain what they had lost. But in their forward rush, they might have looked backward and been grateful to those who had come before them, especially the French and the Spanish. French trappers and traders and persons of French descent still played active roles in the fur business, and French names had been planted on the landscape—St. Louis, St. Charles, Cache la Poudre Canyon. French culture, however, was being displaced by the Americans'. Yet

215

it was the early Frenchmen who gave Americans the techniques that first enabled them to penetrate and take possession of this land. If it had not been for men like la Vérendrye, who developed the means of unlocking the wilderness, the Americans might well have been checked at the edge of the Great Plains for many years.

The Americans looked down on the Mexicans, regarding them as a retarded nation, unable to utilize what they had. Yet they might have given them and the Spanish their due, too. Coronado and others, marching across the Great Plains in splendiferous uniforms with burnished armor, would have seemed ridiculous to a hard-bitten St. Louis boatman, and the trails they had opened were long since overgrown with prairie grass. But they had left their mark on every square foot of the Great Plains, for the herds of wild horses now roving them had come originally from Spain. When the fur traders of the Rocky Mountain Company abandoned keelboats and took to pack horses, which were largely of Spanish stock, they were able to ascend the Platte, and mules and horses largely of Spanish descent also pulled the wagon trains to Santa Fé.

As Long had noted on his expedition to the mountains, the Great Plains were now rich in horses, and horses were playing an increasing role in the area's development, not only as a method of transportation across the arid lands, but, too, as a basis for trade in themselves. And as Pike had seen on his trip through Mexico, it was the Spanish who had developed the methods to utilize that profusion of livestock. Herders by tradition, they and their descendants knew how to *lasso* the *broncos*.

The Spanish, too, had left names on the landscape—San Miguel, Río Grande, El Paso—but, also like the French, their contribution to the Americans' advance had been greater than adding to their nomenclature. The Americans could be proud—and perhaps even a little astonished—at what they had accomplished in those relatively few years, but they were advancing from a base provided by others.

Although John Wyeth found disillusionment on the Great Plains, other Americans, more adapted to the frontier life, were discovering fulfillment in the stern, austere land. Kenneth McKenzie, in charge of the American Fur Company's Upper Missouri Outfit, ruled like a lord at Fort Union at the mouth of the Yellowstone. Each season massive piles of furs moved in and out of his storeroom. He also had the good fortune to be visited by an old trapper named Jacob Berger, who had worked for the Hudson's Bay Company and knew the Blackfeet well. McKenzie suggested that he join the American Fur Company and attempt to secure the Blackfeet's trade. Berger agreed to try, and succeeded in persuading a band of Blackfeet to visit Fort Union. With an unusual lucky chance and a brilliant diplomatic stroke, McKenzie accomplished in a short time what Lisa had never succeeded in doing—gaining access to the beaver-rich northern Rockies.

That same year he had received delivery of the *Yellow Stone*, the steamboat he had persuaded the company to order, but low water brought it to a halt just short of the modern city of Pierre, South Dakota. Those who had opposed its purchase unkindly remarked that the money had been thrown away, but since the company now owned the vessel, it instructed the crew to try again in 1832, leaving earlier in the spring to take full advantage of the high water.

When in March that year the *Yellow Stone* pulled away from St. Louis, it was heavily laden with supplies and equipment belonging to the American Fur Company as well as many of its employees and contractors, who were riding upstream. Among them were also a few persons who had no direct connection with the fur trade. One of these was a former Pennsylvania attorney, George Catlin. As a boy he had lived on his father's farm in the Susquehanna Valley—his mother had been captured by the Indians during the Wyoming Massacre—and had then gone to law school at Litchfield, Connecticut. But Blackstone appealed less to him than art, and he shortly abandoned the law for a career as a portrait painter.

Because of his technical skill and his pleasing personality, he could easily have made a living as a society painter, but he had another ambition: to paint the Indians of North America. First he traveled among such eastern tribes as the Senecas, Oneidas, and Tuscaroras, and then in 1830, with letters of introduction in his pocket, left for St. Louis. There he met William Clark, who took an immediate liking to him and also approved of his project, and Pierre Chouteau, who was now one of the principal figures in the American Fur Company, invited Catlin to ascend the Missouri on the *Yellow Stone* in 1832.

Also on board the *Yellow Stone* were several Indians, who were in the charge of Major John F. Sanford, an Indian agent. These were warriors who had made another ceremonial trip to Washington to see the President. One of these was an Assiniboin chief named the Pigeon's Egg Head.

To him, the trip to Washington had been a glorious adventure, and as the steamboat left St. Louis, he stood at the front of the upper deck, where everyone could see him in the resplendent dress he had acquired. Around his neck hung a blue ribbon. Attached to this was a silver medal that shone against the dark of his full-dress uniform, the coat of which was decorated with gold lace. At his side was a sword, and on his shoulders tasseled epaulets. Covering his head was a top hat of beaver with a long red feather mounted in the band. In his left hand he carried a furled umbrella and in his right an unfolded fan. Pleased though he was with the white men's presents, he was a travesty of the mingling of two cultures, a man who had been gulled into accepting the worst of one and making a mockery of his own.

At every Indian village the crew fired the twelve-pound cannon with which the boat was equipped, followed in rapid succession by its three four-pound swivel guns. The blast of these weapons, so much louder than anything the Indians had heard before, struck fear among them, as it was intended they do. The American Fur Company, the guns said, was the mightiest force on the Upper Missouri.

Like most Missouri River boats, the *Yellow Stone* frequently went aground; and about two hundred miles below Fort Pierre, the company's post near modern South Dakota's capital, the water became so clogged with shallow sandbars that the crew were uncertain whether they could proceed farther upstream. While the others, hoping that the water would rise, waited on board, Catlin and about twenty men went on foot to the fort. There he was pleased to find that more than six hundred lodges of Sioux were camped nearby. Immediately he set about painting pictures of the Indians, although the medicine men warned that death and ill fortune would be the fate of anyone who permitted himself to be depicted in this way.

In one case, a picture of Catlin's did result directly in a brief, but bloody war between two bands. Catlin's sitter was a member of the Hunkpapa Sioux, one of the small divisions described by Atkinson in the report he filed after his mission up the Missouri. Catlin was painting the man in profile when another Sioux, looking at the portrait, remarked that the sitter was only half a man, since Catlin was painting only half his face. This rude comment brought a quick reply, and when the session was over, both men went for their guns. The sitter was killed by a ball that by coincidence tore away the side of his face that Catlin had not painted, a circumstance that seemed to fulfill the medicine men's dire prophecies.

Fighting broke out between the bands to which the two warriors belonged; the men at the fort closed the gates and loaded their guns; and since the Missouri had flooded again, enabling the *Yellow Stone* to reach the fort, the traders put Catlin on board and urged the pilot to get him out of there as quickly as possible.

Their fears for his safety were well justified, for they afterward learned that the Indians had decided that Catlin should die because of the trouble he had caused. This death sentence was lifted only when the sitter's band finally succeeded in tracking down and killing the murderer. But that one painting cost at least three lives.

Because of the delay caused by the period of low water, the *Yellow Stone* now pushed ahead as fast as possible toward Fort Union, but it stopped at the village of the Pigeon's Egg Head to permit him to disembark in all his regalia. While the men on the boat watched, he went ashore with his umbrella in one hand and a keg of whiskey in the other. For a long time he stood in silence while the people of the village looked at him in equal quiet, although they knew perfectly well who he was. Then they acknowledged his presence, and he theirs.

The aftermath of his trip to Washington was unfortunate, as Catlin later learned. Gradually he let himself be persuaded to tell what he had seen, but the Indians regarded his tales as so exaggerated that they considered him a degenerate liar, and he fell into disgrace among his own people. Even his wife lost respect for him and cut up his fancy uniform to make clothes for herself. Finally he had little left other than his memories and his umbrella, which he used to take with him even when he was buffalo hunting.

On June 17, 1832, the *Yellow Stone* reached Fort Union, proving that the use of steamboats on the Missouri River was after all feasible. So the American Fur Company ordered another one, and from that time on, at least one boat made the journey to Fort Union each year, carrying the post's supplies and often loaded as well with cargo being delivered for the government. The day of the boatmen with their cordelles, poles, and unbelievable capacity for work was coming to an end, pushed into the past by the boilers and pistons of the *Yellow Stone*.

Fort Union, Catlin discovered, was a substantial post, not one of those that fur traders sometimes erected only to abandon shortly afterward. More than two hundred feet square, its palisade was made of twenty-foot pickets. At two corners stood stone bastions, which were thirty feet high and armed with cannons. Inside were numerous buildings, including McKenzie's two-story residence, which had stone fireplaces and glass windows. Although he had no coffee, bread, or butter to serve his guests, he did possess a plentiful stock of meat and even served wine regularly at dinner. More exciting from Catlin's point of view, a large number of Indians came there to trade, including Crees, Assiniboins, Crows, and Blackfeet. Several of these tribes were hostile to each other, but McKenzie had been able to establish—and enforce reasonably well—the rule that they must not fight each other near the fort.

McKenzie gave Catlin a room in one of the bastions as a studio. Describing his working conditions, Catlin wrote that he "was seated on the cool breech of a twelve-pounder, and had my easel before me, and Crows and Blackfeet, and Assiniboins, whom I was tracing upon the canvas. . . . My painting-room has become so great a lounge, and I so great a 'medicine-man,' that all other amusements are left, and all other topics of conversation and gossip are postponed for future consideration. The chiefs have had to place 'soldiers' (as they are called) at my door, with spears in hand to protect me from the throng, who would otherwise press upon me; and none but the worthies are allowed to come into my medicine apartments, and none to be painted, except such as are decided by the chiefs to be worthy of so high an honor."

When the men at the fort went on a buffalo hunt, Catlin went, too and he wrote, "I dashed along through the thundering mass, as they swept over the plain, scarcely able to tell whether I was on a buffalo's back or my horse—hit, and hooked, and jostled about, till at length I found myself alongside my game, when I gave him a shot, as I passed him.

"I found," he wrote, "that my shot had entered him a little too far forward, breaking one of his shoulders, and lodging in his breast, and from his very great weight it was impossible for him to make much advance upon me. As I rode up within a few paces of him, he would bristle up with fury enough in his *looks* alone, almost to annihilate me . . . and making one lunge at me, would fall upon his neck and nose, so that I found the sagacity of my horse alone enough to keep me out of reach of danger. . . ." Catlin was an artist first and a hunter only second, for at that moment, as he later wrote, "I drew from pocket my sketch-book, laid my gun across my lap, and commenced taking his likeness. He stood stiffened up, and swelling with awful vengeance, which was sublime for a picture, but which he could not vent upon me. I rode around him and sketched him in numerous attitudes, sometimes he would lie down, and I would then sketch him; then throw my cap at him, and rousing him on his legs, rally a new expression, and sketch him again."

After a month of intense activity, Catlin started downstream in a pirogue with two company employees who had earned leave and were returning to St. Louis. At the Mandans' villages, he paused for a while to paint more pictures, using a room in the American Fur Company's fort as a studio. By then he had become so well liked by the tribe that they permitted him to watch many of their ceremonies, including one dance in which warriors drove skewers into their bodies. The skewers were then attached by cords to a high pole. By pulling on the cords, the dancers' attendants raised them from the ground and left them hanging. Such self-mutilation was common among many of the Plains Indians, and the scars were marks that the warriors bore proudly.

After leaving the Mandans, Catlin discovered he was being pursued by a band of them. One of the women he had painted had become desperately ill, and the Indians thought the picture was to blame. Reluctantly he gave it up, but its surrender did not effect a cure. Ever after the Mandans blamed the woman's subsequent death on Catlin.

When the pirogue finally touched the riverbank at St. Louis, Catlin began unloading the luggage he had brought those many miles down the river. It contained the most comprehensive study that anyone had ever made of the Indians of the Upper Missouri.

When Ashley and Henry replaced keelboats with pack animals and trading posts with the rendezvous, they greatly reduced the amount of capital that an individual needed to enter the fur trade. A small number of men with enough money to buy supplies and horses or mules could enter the mountains on their own, trap and go to the rendezvous. Obviously they would have difficulty competing with the large companies and their danger from Indians would be greater because of the smaller size of their parties, but the new mode of trading opened an opportunity for a few independent traders such as Captain Benjamin Louis Eulalie de Bonneville. Son of a French immigrant and a graduate of West Point, Bonneville had been assigned to the frontier, where he heard of the quick wealth some men earned in the fur business, wealth exceeding anything an army captain could expect. The temptation was too great to be resisted, and he took a leave of absence from the military and raised enough money, principally in New York, to organize a trading expedition of his own.

He intended to follow the general strategy initiated by Ashley and Henry, but he also planned to make one important change in their method of transportation: to replace pack animals with wagons. He saw several advantages. Draft animals hitched to wagons were less easy to stampede and therefore more difficult for Indians to steal. In the morning they would only have to be harnessed, and in the evening, unharnessed. This was easier and less time consuming than loading packs. The wagons could also serve as a temporary fort during an Indian attack the way they did on the road to Santa Fé. This in itself was an important advantage, particularly on the treeless, flat plains, where cover was almost always scarce. Furthermore, the traders could carry more goods and equipment with fewer animals, an important consideration for a man lacking the backing of a large company. The disadvantage was getting the wagons across the steep-sided ravines that the streams often cut into the surface of the Great Plains. Pack animals could clamber down and up the banks; draft animals with their loads could not. But Bonneville believed that this disadvantage was outweighed by the many benefits.

On May 1, 1832, Bonneville left Fort Osage with slightly more than a hundred men, most of whom were experienced in the business. His goods and supplies were in twenty wagons, drawn by oxen, mules, or horses and divided into two columns that formed the center of the train with men riding in the van, rear, and flanks.

His course took him west, following the Kansas River. Ashley had already taken a wheeled cannon along the Platte, and the Rocky Mountain Fur Company had used wagons two years before when going to the rendezvous in the Wind River Valley, but the sight of wagons was still so rare that the Kansa Indians were astonished by them. Coming from a culture that had been unfamiliar with the wheel until the arrival of the Europeans, they were astonished at the ease with which Bonneville's expedition carried its belongings.

From the Kansas River, the captain led his train north to the Platte, reaching its banks near present-day Grand Island, Nebraska. There he turned west, following the sluggish river across the flat country through which it flows and making the gradual climb toward the base of the mountains. The great sky arched above him and the marching column seemed tiny in the enormous landscape through which it traveled. On every side the land spread out in the distance, and only an occasional tree near a water course or a small rise interrupted the vast panorama.

At the Forks of the Platte, Ashley, taking the advice of the Pawnees, had gone south; Bonneville, knowing that the North Platte went more directly toward his destination, preferred that route.

After two days of travel, he located a possible ford across the South Platte and instructed his men to remove the wheels from the wagons, the bottoms of which he then covered with buffalo hides and caulked with tallow and ashes. Having thus converted them into crude boats, three men got in each while the others, wading in the river, helped push them over to the opposite bank, where the men reassembled them and started north.

The impression of continual flatness was broken later on when they saw some thirty miles ahead of them a column rising to the sky. Near it were the bluffs that formed the ridge of the river valley, but it stood apart from them, a tall spire based on a conical hill with an overall height of about five hundred feet. This was Chimney Rock, one of the famous landmarks of the Great Plains and a sight that many travelers noted in their journals and memoirs.

Composed of the clay common in the area, interspersed with volcanic ash and sandstone, it had withstood the eroding effect of the waters and winds of centuries that had washed away the surrounding land and left this geological marvel. The appearance of Chimney Rock in the distance, in the dry air always farther off than it appeared to be except to the initiated, was a welcome sign that the traveler was making progress in his trip across the plains.

Farther on, Bonneville's party came to another break in the flatness, a tangle of rising land known as Scotts Bluff. Already the tale of Hiram Scott, the man after whom this formation had been named, had been obscured by legend. A fur trapper, he had become ill on the way home, and his companions, believing he was on the point of death and finding their resources strained by caring for him, left him to die at that strange and eerie spot. In itself that would not have been cause for celebrity. Many fur traders died under similarly horrible circumstances. But Scott had not been as close to death as his companions had thought. Subsequent travelers discovered his purported skeleton—here the legends differed—some said on the other side of the Platte from where he had been left, others sixty miles away. The vision of the lonely man, gaunt and weak, staggering blindly over the plains stirred the travelers' imaginations and formed the subject of many campfire discussions.

From Scotts Bluff, Bonneville continued west past the mouth of the Laramie River, a point well known to the fur traders and opposite the site of present-day Laramie, Wyoming. His teams heaving against the drag on the wagon tongues, the wheels still turning over the dirt, sod, and stones, Bonneville pushed toward the west, the ground rising beneath him until he crossed the Continental Divide at South Pass. From there he turned to the headwaters of the Green River, which he had selected as the place to build a trading fort.

Enthusiastic and expansive, Bonneville was a failure as a fur trader. But he had taken the first wagons over the Continental Divide north of New Mexico, and if that had not brought him fortune, it did earn him fame.

Having survived the critical year of 1829, when the nerves and resolution of the traders were weak, the Santa Fé trade continued to be active. For a select group of men, capable of buying wisely in the United States, making the trip across the wilderness, and selling wisely in New Mexico, the business offered good profits. But it was not work for those who minded the hot sun, the flooding rains, the dust raised by the feet of the animals, the ever-present threat of an Indian raid, and the rough-and-ready companionship of frontiersmen. Bankers who disliked getting their hands dirty and trustees of family estates, whose law offices and counting houses were removed from the rabble, thought it better to invest in railroads and mortgages than in such a risky trade carried on by ruffians.

In spite of the battle with the Indians, Charles Bent remained in the business; but his younger brother, William, did not. He wanted even more adventure, so in the fall of 1829 he went to Taos, the center in New Mexico for the American trappers. There he fell in with a group of men as high-spirited as himself, who decided to do some fur trading on their own account. Pooling their resources, they built a small palisade on the Arkansas and waited for customers. The first Indians to appear were a party of Cheyennes, who proved friendly and interested in the goods that Bent and his partners had to offer. In fact, two of them decided to stay on after the others left.

Shortly afterward another band of Indians arrived, this time a group of Comanches. Since they and the Cheyennes were enemies, Bent's guests were in danger. Quickly Bent hid the two Indians within his small enclosure, but the Comanches noticed their footprints. Bent was in a difficult position. If he revealed the whereabouts of the two Cheyennes, they would most certainly be killed. If he did not, and the Comanches discovered them, not only would the Cheyennes die but probably the white men, too. He decided to protect them and, lying, told the Comanches that all the Cheyennes had gone off together. Thus he saved their lives.

Young and restless, William Bent next attempted to trap along the Gila River but, learning that beavers were scarce and the Apaches fierce, he resumed his venture on the Arkansas.

His protection of the two Cheyennes had created a lasting friendship between him and that tribe, making them customers that no other trader could have lured away. Yet he was not entirely content. All his goods came from Santa Fé, which was a secondary market, and he had to bring them over the mountains by pack train. At some point he talked to his brother, Charles, who had formed a partnership with another man, Ceran St. Vrain. Charles immediately saw the advantages that William had gained. The two major fur companies operated either farther north or west, and so William had established himself in one of the few places the giants had not reached. Furthermore, his relations with the Cheyennes were such that even Astor would have had difficulty dislodging him. But he needed more capital, and therefore Charles and St. Vrain took him into their partnership.

Their next step was to build a real fort, one in which large quantities of goods could be stored and which would be impregnable against attack. A Cheyenne chief, Yellow Wolf, who had become a friend of William, told them to stay near the buffalo country, for their post would then be available to most of the tribes that roamed the southern plains. They therefore selected a site on the Arkansas about twelve miles west of the mouth of the Purgatory River.

Since little wood was available, they hired workmen to build it of adobe bricks. This was not to be one of those temporary posts that had dotted the Great Plains, serving their owners for only a few years, but one that would match McKenzie's Fort Union in size and importance.

About 1833 the two brothers and Ceran St. Vrain could admire their finished building. A main gate, guarded by two heavy wooden doors, opened into a large plaza, which was roughly a hundred feet long and eighty wide. Completely surrounding it was series of buildings that contained living quarters, trading rooms, storerooms, a dining room, a council room where the partners could treat with the Indians, blacksmith's and carpenter's shops, and a kitchen. Also within the walls was a corral for the livestock, where they could be protected from Indian raiders, a wagon house, and, most important, a well. If anyone, Indian or White, tried to lay siege to the establishment, the defenders would be independent of an outside source of water. At two corners of the fort stood bastions for its defense, and, as a fitting touch, the establishment even included an upstairs billiard room, where the partners could entertain an occasional visitor from Santa Fé or Missouri. The sharp click of the balls as they bounced off the cushions and struck each other was a strange contrast to the moan of the wind, sweeping across the flat wilderness that surrounded the fort.

Bent, St. Vrain and Company was based on a three-cornered trade, more complex than those of most companies. Charles continued to handle the St. Louis end of the business, buying American goods and selling the pelts and livestock they might have received in Santa Fé. St. Vrain remained in New Mexico, even taking out Mexican citizenship so that he and the partners would have less trouble with the authorities. William made his headquarters at Bent's Fort, as their new building was named. (It was also called Williams's Fort, but that name was not generally used.) If his Indian customers wanted Navajo blankets, as they often did, William had a supply that had been brought from Santa Fé. If they wanted guns or beads, he had some that had come from St. Louis. No one in the Southwest could better fill their needs, for he offered them the goods produced by two cultures. As for St. Louis and New Mexico, Bent, St. Vrain and Company could buy and sell at those centers, too.

Their wagons rolled along the Santa Fé Trail in both directions, some of them taking the Cimarron Cutoff, which was the more direct route between Missouri and New Mexico. Others, however, took what was known as the Mountain Branch, passing the fort and going in the direction of present-day Trinidad, Colorado, and over Raton Pass into New Mexico, a longer but somewhat safer route, since it avoided the area where the Comanches were most likely to roam. It also brought the wagons by the fort, where they stopped to deliver goods to William and pick up the skins he had purchased from the Indians.

The empire over which the two brothers and St. Vrain reigned was enormous. On the west, it reached into the Rocky Mountains, on the east, deep into the modern state of Kansas. From the south came Indians who lived in Texas to trade at the fort; from the north, Indians who lived in Wyoming. Because of their wisdom in dealing with the various tribes, no one, not even the government, overlooked their advice in Indian matters. And because of their business sense, no one could enter the commerce of the Southwest without taking them into account. Truly theirs was the kingdom and power. As for the glory, they were too busy to worry about it.

Chapter 19

A Prince and Other Travelers

The vast tracts of the interior of North-Western America are, in general, little known, and the government of the United States may be justly reproached for not having done more to explore them. Some few scientific expeditions, among which the two under Major Long produced the most satisfactory results for natural history, though on a limited scale, were set on foot by the government . . . The observations of the manners of the aborigines is undoubtedly that which must chiefly interest the foreign traveller in those countries, especially as the Anglo-Americans look down on them with a certain feeling of hatred.
—Maximilian, Prince of Wied, 1843

Along the Missouri River, no ambiguity surrounded the word "company." It meant only one organization: the American Fur Company. Little happened without its concurrence, as one trader learned when he tried to enter McKenzie's fief without permission. Three of his men were seized on the grounds that they had previously left the company before the expiration of their contracts; his supply of liquor was confiscated; and he found himself facing a group of armed men, who had supplemented their guns with a cannon that they planned to use if he did not turn back.

On the other hand, as Catlin had learned, the company's partners and representatives could be extremely gracious to those who were not its competitors. So when Maximilian, Prince of Wied, came to St. Louis in 1833 and expressed a wish to go up the Missouri, he quickly discovered that he would need the company's assistance and that Pierre Chouteau, Jr., the St. Louis partner, and Kenneth McKenzie, who happened to be in town, were both delightful and agreeable men. The company now had two steamboats operating on the river, the original *Yellow Stone* and the *Assiniboine*; and they invited him and Carl Bodmer, a Swiss art-

ist who was accompanying him, to ride to Fort Union on the *Yellow Stone* with McKenzie.

As the steamboats chugged up the river, McKenzie had much on his mind. The Americans' attitude toward the Indians was ambivalent and swung between extremes. Sometimes it took the form of repressive measures and more troops; at others it became humanitarian and concerned. At the moment it was in the second phase, and Congress had passed legislation that severely restricted the amount of liquor that could be imported into the Indians' country. Liquor had always been a problem in the fur business, for the Indians loved it and would do almost anything to get a drink, even the watered-down drinks that the economical traders served. Once started, they would dispose of their furs at almost any price in order to get more, so liquor offered the cheapest means of buying pelts. In the long run, it demoralized the Indians, which was bad for business; in the short run, however, no trader could compete with another who offered it unless he did so, too.

That was McKenzie's problem. The traders who carried their goods inland by pack train or wagon could more easily evade the government's inspections than those who went up the river as he did. This placed him at a serious disadvantage, and McKenzie, along with other officials of the American Fur Company, had exerted all their influence to have the law repealed, but for once had failed in getting what they wanted. McKenzie had then seen a way around the law. He carried a stock of whiskey, which the soldiers might seize. But he also had hidden away in the cargo of his two boats the parts for making a still. The wording of the law specifically prohibited the importation of liquor but said nothing about distilling it in the Indians' country. If he were caught, McKenzie intended to use this fine distinction as a defense.

Major Riley, who had rescued the Santa Fé caravan, was in command at Cantonment (later Fort) Leavenworth, located on bluffs overlooking the river in present-day Kansas. He was a career officer, thorough in the performance of his duties and unafraid of the American Fur Company as long as he was carrying out his orders. His men went over the two steamboats carefully, uncovered the company's stock of liquor, and even haggled with Maximilian over the amount of alcohol he could take for preserving the specimens he hoped to collect. But they did not find the parts for the still.

After leaving Leavenworth, the *Yellow Stone* steamed by the spot where Lewis and Clark had buried Sergeant Floyd—Maximilian carefully noted the fact—and passed the Black Snake Hills, site of today's St. Joseph, Missouri. Many changes had occurred since the two captains had led their small expedition up the river. Fewer buffaloes roamed its banks, the Omahas were depleted by smallpox and the attacks of the Sioux, but the Arikaras remained the same. A pirogue coming down the river contained several of the company's employees, and they told McKenzie that the Arikaras had recently killed three white men.

At Fort Pierre, located near the present-day capital of South Dakota, Maximilian was impressed by the size of the establishment, manned as it was by more than a hundred employees and stocked with goods valued at $80,000. Outside the fort was a village of Yankton Sioux tipis, one of which belonged to the old interpreter Dorion, who had become something of a public figure. While Maximilian took notes, Bodmer drew pictures, and then the boat was on its way again.

At Fort Clark, a trading post near the Mandans, Maximilian found that Charbonneau, Sacajawea's husband, was still living with the Hidatsas. When one of the Indians became angry with Maximilian, because he would not sell his compass, Charbon-

neau came to the prince's rescue; and the crude, untutored frontiersman saved the polished European nobleman from possible unpleasantness.

On June 22 the *Yellow Stone* ran into serious difficulties. "About ten o'clock," Maximilian wrote, "we had an alarm of fire on board: the upper deck had been set on fire by the iron pipe of the chimney of the great cabin. We immediately lay to, and, by breaking up the deck, the danger was soon over, which, however, was not inconsiderable, as we had many barrels of powder on board.

"We had scarcely got over this trouble," he continued, "when another arose: the current of the swollen river was so strong, that we contended against it to no purpose, in order to turn a certain point of land, while, at the same time, the high west wind was against us, and both together threw the vessel back three times on the south coast. The first shock was so violent, that the lower deck gallery was broken to pieces. Our second attempt succeeded no better; part of the paddle-box was broken, and carried away by the current. We were now obliged to land forty men to tow the vessel . . ."

In spite of these mishaps, the travelers safely reached Fort Union, where McKenzie, as he had done with Catlin, played the gracious host. Maximilian, however, was alarmed by what was happening to the buffaloes. "It is difficult," he wrote, "to obtain an exact estimate of the consumption of this animal, which is yearly decreasing and being driven further inland. In a recent year, the Fur Company sent 42,000 of these hides down the river, which were sold, in the United States, at four dollars a-piece. Fort Union alone consumes about 600 to 800 buffaloes annually, and others in proportion. The numerous Indian tribes subsist almost entirely on these animals, sell their skins after retaining a sufficient supply for their clothing, tents, &c., and the agents of the Company recklessly shoot down these noble animals for their own pleasure, not making the least use of them, except taking out the tongue." No species, as Maximilian knew, could withstand this sort of slaughter forever.

For about two weeks, Maximilian and Bodmer enjoyed the hospitality of Fort Union, eating well, having such luxuries as wine, and watching the arrival and departure of the Indian bands that came to trade. Then by keelboat they went upriver to Fort McKenzie near the mouth of the Marias River. Here where Lewis and Clark had puzzled over which water course to follow, Maximilian and Bodmer found conditions quite different than at

Fort Union. Located at the limits of the American Fur Compay's empire and designed to handle the Blackfeet's trade, the post itself was more primitive and the Indians around it less peaceful in their attitude toward the Americans.

Even with the help of the remarkable Jacob Berger, who had negotiated the agreement between the company and the Blackfeet, David Mitchell, the man in charge, had difficulty keeping peace among the Indians who came to the fort. On several occasions while Maximilian was there, fighting broke out among them. In one case, a Blood Indian killed the nephew of a Blackfeet chief, an act that demanded revenge. In another, about six hundred Crees and Assiniboins attacked a small Blackfeet encampment near the fort.

"When the first information of the vicinity of the enemies was received from a Blackfoot, who had escaped," Maximilian later wrote, "the *engagés* immediately repaired to their posts on the roofs of the buildings, and the fort was seen to be surrounded on every side by the enemy, who had approached very near. They had cut up the tents of the Blackfeet with knives, discharged their guns and arrows at them, and killed or wounded many of the inmates, roused from their sleep by this unexpected attack. Four women and several children lay dead near the fort, and many others were wounded. The men, about thirty in number, had partly fired their guns at the enemy, and then fled to the gates of the fort, where they were admitted. They immediately hastened to the roofs, and began a well-supported fire on the Assiniboins."

Then came a startling revelation. Undisciplined, the *engagés* had been making money on the side by selling to the Indians the ammunition that had been issued to them for their own use. Thus they were unable to defend themselves until Mitchell broke open new supplies and provided both them and the Blackfeet with powder and bullets.

Like most of the company's posts, Fort McKenzie had blockhouses—or bastions—at each of two corners. These contained cannons, which gave the inmates a tactical advantage over any attackers. Mitchell ordered them fired, but many of the Blackfeet had been swept up in the crowd of the attackers. It was impossible to kill one without killing the other, so the cannon remained silent. Not understanding the reason, the Blackfeet on the roof became angry with Mitchell for apparently not supporting them more vigorously.

Meanwhile he and Berger rushed to the gate to open it for some more of the Blackfeet who had run toward it. One of the Assiniboins shouted to him to step aside, so he could shoot the Blackfeet.

This evidence that the Assiniboins and Crees were not planning to fight the company's employees made Mitchell have second thoughts about engaging in the battle. His men, however, were now too excited to stop firing even when he ordered them to. "A spectator alone of this extraordinary scene," Maximilian wrote, "can form any idea of the confusion and the noise, which was increased by the loud report of the musketry, the moving backwards and forwards of the people carrying powder and ball, and the tumult occasioned by above twenty horses shut up in the fort."

In the face of the Blackfeet's steady fire, the Assiniboins lost some of their earlier enthusiasm for the fight and began to withdraw. When some additional Blackfeet from another encampment came rushing to reinforce those at the fort, the Assiniboins withdrew even farther, and the pursuers became the pursued.

"We who remained in the fort," Maximilian reported, "had the pleasure of viewing a most interesting scene. From the place where the range of hills turns to the Missouri, more and more Blackfeet continued to arrive. They came galloping in groups, from three to twenty together, their horses covered with foam, and they themselves in their finest apparel, with all kinds of ornaments and arms, bows and quivers on their backs, guns in their hands, furnished with their medicines, with feathers on their heads; some had splendid crowns of black and white eagles' feathers, and a large hood of feathers hanging down behind, sitting on fine panther skins lined with red; the upper parts of their bodies naked, with a long strip of wolf's skin thrown over the shoulder, and carrying shields adorned with feathers and pieces of coloured cloth."

But the splendor of their costumes and the support of Mitchell did not give the Blackfeet a taste for prolonged fighting. Mitchell often found himself leading the chase, but when the Assiniboins took a stand behind some trees at the mouth of the Marias River, the Blackfeet failed to dislodge them. For all practical purposes, the battle was over, and the Assiniboins and Crees faded away.

After leaving the rendezvous at Pierre's Hole, Nathaniel Wyeth and those members of his party who had decided to remain with him finally reached the Hudson's Bay Company's post on the Walla Walla River and were hospitably received by the man in charge. From there they went to Fort Vancouver and on to the mouth of the Columbia River. In laying his plans for a settlement, Wyeth had emulated Astor's program for establishing Astoria, for to supplement his overland march, he had chartered a small boat to carry supplies and meet him on the West Coast. When he reached the Pacific, however, he learned that the boat had been wrecked.

Wyeth spent the winter of 1832-1833 at Fort Vancouver and early in February set out with an employee of the Hudson's Bay Company on the overland trip back to the East. On the way he stopped at the rendezvous, where he talked with Milton Sublette, who was representing the Rocky Mountain Fur Company and who asked him to bring out a supply of goods the following season. In view of his previous experience a commitment on Wyeth's part might have seemed rash, but he had great confidence in himself, including his ability to persuade his Boston associates to provide more capital.

In August, 1833, while Maximilian was at Fort McKenzie, Wyeth reached Fort Union. As usual McKenzie played the genial host, escorting Wyeth and his companions around the fort, entertaining them, feeding them well, and boasting about the success of his new still, which was now pouring forth a plentiful supply of trade whiskey. With his typical ingenuity, McKenzie was buying corn from some of the agricultural tribes down the river, and he was also encouraging his various posts to raise crops of the grain for him. As long as he could obtain enough corn, no other trading company would have more liquor than he, and so the still was making farmers out of the frontiersmen.

Before leaving Fort Union, Wyeth made some purchases from the post's stores, but when he came to pay for them, the prices McKenzie demanded startled him. As a host, McKenzie was gracious and open-handed, but he saw no reason for supplying his competition with goods at anything but the highest rates, and he certainly was not going to let them have any of his precious whiskey. Furthermore, he knew that William Sublette and Robert Campbell, principals in the Rocky Mountain Fur Company, were planning to invade the Upper Missouri. Wyeth, however, did not see the situation as McKenzie did. To him, McKenzie was simply trying to take advantage of him, and he left Fort Union angry.

He had gone only a short distance when he met Sublette and Campbell, who intended to build a post near Fort Union right under McKenzie's nose. This was the most direct challenge that had been made to the American Fur Company in many years, and McKenzie was marshaling his forces to combat them.

With the coming of fall, Maximilian and Bod-

mer prepared to go down the river to Fort Clark, the American Fur Company's post that traded with the Mandans. Those Indians had held a fascination for Europeans ever since la Vérendrye had first visited them, and the prince and his artist planned to spend the winter among them. On their way, they passed, of course, the villages of the Hidatsas and discovered that Sublette and Campbell had already erected a post there, too, and their men were busy trying to secure the trade of that tribe. In fact, they had already hired Charbonneau away from the American Fur Company. Both employees and Indians were being freed from the oldtime monopoly and now had a choice of companies with which to do business.

At Fort Clark, Maximilian and Bodmer learned the distressing news that cholera had broken out in St. Louis, and a large number of persons had died. The boats traveling up the river had spread the disease, and at one post, seven out of ten persons had died within a few days. Fortunately it had not spread as far as Fort Clark.

The prevalence of cholera throughout the world was one of the reasons for the momentous decision Astor made that year. The original charter for the American Fur Company gave it a life of twenty-five years. Astor now had to decide whether to arrange for its extension or leave the fur business. At that time the market was not especially good, and on his trips to Europe he had noticed the increasing substitution of silk for beaver in men's hats. Many kinds of furs, including buffalo robes, sold well, but beaver pelts had always been at the heart of the trade. Furthermore, there was a suspicion that cholera was spread by pelts, another factor that would hurt their sale. One of Astor's great commercial strengths had been his ability to foresee the future. Since his own health was poor and his son, William, was more interested in the family's real estate holdings, he offered to sell out to some of his former associates. Ramsay Crooks was among those who took over the Northern Department, and Pierre Chouteau, Jr., was one of those who purchased the Western Department.

These changes did not affect McKenzie's attitude toward Sublette and Campbell. He was prepared to take any steps necessary to crush them, and he told each of his posts on the Upper Missouri that they had a free hand as long as they drove Sublette and Campbell out of business. During their winter at Fort Clark, Maximilian and Bodmer witnessed a vicious price war, as the amount the American Fur Company was willing to pay for a beaver skin finally reached twelve dollars. This was three times the amount paid on the commercial markets or an outright loss of eight dollars a pelt, not counting the costs of transportation and maintaining the posts. No concern except the American Fur Company could sustain this sort of expense for long; and by December, 1833, Maximilian noted, Charbonneau had returned to his former employers, a sign of things to come.

The cold bore down bitterly on the forts and the Indian villages. "The appearance of the prairie at this time," Maximilian wrote, "was very remarkable resembling the sea agitated by a violent storm. The extensive surface of the snow was carried by the wind in a cloud; it was scarcely possible for the eye to bear the cold blast which drove the snow before it, and enveloped us in a dense cloud, above which the sky was clear, and the tops of prairie hills were visible. We were, therefore, the more sensible of the enjoyment of our bright fire, seated about which we passed our time agreeably in various occupations."

With the coming of spring, the time had arrived for Maximilian and Bodmer to continue down the river again, their luggage bulging with pictures and manuscripts, for they had made use of every minute of their trip into the American wilds. Spring was also the time when the men who worked for Sublette and Campbell had to make up their minds whether they wished to go down the river, too, or remain and work for the American Fur Company. McKenzie's tactics had been successful. The posts of Sublette and Campbell had been able to purchase only a few furs and were low on supplies. Nevertheless, Pierre Chouteau, Jr., who was less aggressive than McKenzie, was afraid that their good standing in St. Louis would enable them to raise more capital and continue their effort to break the American Fur Company's monopoly. So he began negotiations to buy them out. Along with a slight payment for the goods and equipment they had on hand, he would agree to stay out of the Rocky Mountains for a year, provided the partners did not try to return to the Upper Missouri. After the mauling that McKenzie had given them, they were glad to accept.

When McKenzie heard what Chouteau had done, he was furious. He did not share Chouteau's concern that the two men could raise the capital to continue the war. He had them on the run, he was sure. Their employees were leaving them, and the Indians were refusing to trade with them. One more season, or even part of a season, and they would be beaten forever.

To add to his disgust, he was in deep trouble over his still. When Wyeth and his companions had left Fort Union angry over the prices McKenzie had charged them, they had bided their time until they reached Cantonment Leavenworth. There they reported to the Indian agent all they had seen and the method by which McKenzie was bypassing the government's prohibition of liquor. The agent, of course, immediately forwarded his report to William Clark in St. Louis, and Clark, in his capacity as Superintendent of Indian Affairs, demanded an explanation from Chouteau.

Although Chouteau had helped order the still, he was all innocence about what McKenzie was doing. The American Fur Company, he explained, had thought that some of the countryside's "wild pears and berries" might be used to make wine, which was not against the law. If McKenzie had exceeded his instructions and had started making whiskey instead, he had done so entirely on his own initiative. He also assured Clark that he would send someone to Fort Union immediately, and if Wyeth's report proved true, he would put a stop to the distilling.

In addition to making his explanation to Clark, Chouteau severely criticized McKenzie for having embarrassed the company. This rebuke irritated McKenzie. He did not mind being a scapegoat if it would help the business, but he did not like Chouteau's holier-than-thou attitude. Nevertheless, he fabricated a story to salvage the company's position.

The still, he explained, really did not belong to the company. A friend of his who lived at Pembina, a settlement to the east on the Red River, had wanted a still but had had no means of transporting it up the Missouri. Merely trying to be helpful, McKenzie had offered to purchase one and bring it up by steamboat. While it had been stored at Fort Union waiting for his friend to collect it, an American happened to come to the post and had asked as a favor to be allowed to assemble it and experiment with some of the local fruits. This request seemed reasonable, and McKenzie granted him permission but, of course, on a purely temporary and experimental bases. The results, he explained, had been satisfactory, and the "wine" was tasty. He hoped Clark would realize that all this had nothing to do with the American Fur Company and that the experiment would cease as soon as his friend was ready to pick up the still.

The story was completely transparent, but there had been a time when the company might have gotten away with it. That day was past. News of McKenzie's still had reached Washington, and the authorities were furious over this flagrant violation of the law. The American Fur Company had turned back competing traders with the threat of a cannon and it had several times been accused of inciting the Indians against its competitors. On top of those offenses it was now openly flouting the federal government itself. Even its good friend, Senator Benton, could not prevent the revocation of its license to trade with the Indians unless the still was dismantled. For once the forces aligned against McKenzie were more than he could handle. He had victoriously battled Indians and competitors, but he could not add to them the company's management and the United States government. In 1834 he broke up his still, came down the river, took a trip to Europe; and although he returned to Fort Union for a short while, he was never again the active figure in the fur trade that he had once been.

George Catlin was not satisfied with his growing portfolio of Indian pictures. Although he had more of them than anyone else in his time, his collection was far from complete, and there were still many tribes he had not seen. So when he learned that the government was sending the First Regiment of Dragoons under the command of Colonel Henry Dodge to visit the Comanches and Wichitas (then known as the Pawnee Picts), he applied to the secretary of war for permission to accompany the expedition.

The dragoons had evolved after Major Riley's earlier experience had demonstrated that infantrymen could not move quickly enough against the Indians. First the army had made an attempt to enlist rangers, mounted militia drawn from the local people, but enthusiasm had not been high, so it had formed the dragoons. These were not trained cavalry, but infantry mounted on horse- or muleback.

The starting point for the expedition was Fort Gibson, located on the Neosho River about three miles above its confluence with the Arkansas, and the scene that greeted Catlin at this post was a curious one. Decades before, Thomas Jefferson had envisioned west of the Mississippi a vast Indian reservation in which many of the Eastern tribes would be relocated, thus relieving the conflict between them and the advancing settlers. Under the supervision of the government the partial—but tragic—exodus had taken place, and around Fort Gibson were many Indians who were as alien to the land as the white men stationed there. Catlin had no particular interest in semi-civilized tribes whose cultures had already felt the white men's influence, but he had to wait for about two months while the expedition assembled and spent the time making more drawings and taking more notes. Henry Leavenworth, whose dilatory tactics against

the Arikaras had so annoyed Pilcher, was now a general and took personal charge of organizing the men. But even with the long delay, he mustered at Fort Gibson only about half the authorized strength of eight hundred dragoons.

Catlin was in high spirits when they finally set out. To make the journey, he had purchased the best horse he could find; and as a companion, he had brought a young man from St. Louis named Joseph Chadwick, whose company he enjoyed and who helped him carry his art supplies. By the time they reached the Red River, however, conditions had drastically changed, for sickness had swept over the soldiers. ". . . [N]early one half the command," Catlin wrote, "and included amongst them, several officers, with General Leavenworth, have been thrown upon their backs, with the prevailing epidemic, a slow and distressing bilious fever. The horses of the regiment are also sick, about an equal proportion, and seemingly suffering with the same disease. They are daily dying, and men are calling sick . . ." Rather than remain rooted in the same place while the disease continued to spread, Leavenworth ordered Dodge to go ahead with those men who were still well. That reduced the expedition's strength to 250, a relatively small number with which to deal with the Comanches.

On the march westward the men saw many wild horses, and Catlin tried to crease one but unfortunately killed it, which he much regretted. One of the hunters who accompanied the expedition, a Frenchman who had lived with the Indians, used a lasso; and Catlin was amazed at the speed with which he caught a horse and broke it so he could start riding it. It had taken the man only an hour, their usual time for a midday halt.

On the fourth day after leaving General Leavenworth, Catlin wrote, ". . . [W]e discovered a large party at several miles distance, sitting on their horses and looking at us. From the glistening blades of their lances, which were blazing as they turned them in the sun, it was at first thought they were Mexican cavalry. . . . On drawing a little nearer, however, and scanning them with our spyglasses they were soon ascertained to be a war-party of Commanches, on the look out for their enemies."

As the soldiers advanced toward them, the Indians, suspicious of these strangers who had entered their country, disappeared and then reappeared on another mound some distance away. After they had repeated this maneuver several times, Dodge ordered the main body to remain behind while he went ahead with only a few of his staff and a white flag. One of the Comanches then rode forward to meet him. By the use of Spanish, which many of the Comanches understood, Dodge was able to explain his mission, and the Comanches agreed to take him and his men to their village.

The visit was entirely friendly (Catlin was amazed at the thousands of horses the Comanches owned), and the Indians provided Dodge with guides to the Wichitas, another tribe with whom he had been ordered to treat. At first the negotiations did not go well, for the Wichitas denied having in their possession an American boy whom they had kidnapped earlier. But at last they released him in return for some Wichita prisoners whom the government had purchased from the Osages, and they also promised not to molest American travelers through their country.

The trip to the Wichitas and back to the Comanches' village took fifteen days, and the men when they returned were destitute and hungry, having had little opportunity to shoot any game. Dodge immediately ordered a move to the north bank of the Canadian River, where, according to the Indians, there were buffalo herds at that time. The necessary six days of travel were a horror. "Many," Catlin wrote, "are now sick and unable to ride, and are carried on litters between two horses. Nearly every tent belonging to the officers has been converted to hospitals for the sick; and the sighs and groaning are heard in all directions.

". . . [S]ometimes for the distance of many miles," he continued, "the only water we could find, was in stagnant pools, lying on the highest ground, in which the buffaloes have been lying and wallowing like hogs in a mud-puddle. We frequently came to these dirty lavers, from which we drove the herds of wallowing buffaloes, into which our poor and almost dying horses, irresistibly ran and plunged their noses, sucking up the dirty and poisonous draught, until, in some instances, they fell dead in their tracks—the men also (and often times amongst the number, the writer of these lines) sprang from their horses, and ladled up and drank to almost fatal excess, the disgusting and tepid draught, and with it filled their canteens, which were slung to their sides, and from which they were sucking the bilious contents during the day."

The heat was torturing, and the browse for the horses poor, but they did find the buffalo herds and were able to get enough meat not only for their immediate needs but to feed them on their way back to Fort Gibson. But their health did not improve. Catlin had to be helped on and off his horse, and finally became so ill that they carried him in an empty baggage wagon along with other sick men.

Yet his lot was better than that of some of the others, for Dodge was forced to leave behind many of his soldiers, some of them unable to move. Even General Leavenworth lost his life. Although he had expected to catch up with Dodge, his sickness, too, became worse, and he died without seeing his command again.

In spite of Dodge's tenacity in carrying out his mission, the expedition had not been a success. He had penetrated into Mexican territory in much the same manner that Malgares had entered the United States, but the effect was inconsequential. He had held councils with several tribes, hoping to cement a friendship between them and the Americans. But given the temporary nature of Indian alliances, his meetings had not ensured the safety of Americans who might happen to pass through that country.

His greatest enemy had proved to be neither the Indians nor the Mexicans, but the land itself, both on the Great Plains and at their edge. American troops apparently could not advance into that territory during the hottest months of the year. Pike and Long had both reported that the southern Great Plains were uninhabitable except by nomadic Indians. Dodge's experience seemed to bear them out.

Although no one except trappers and traders thought of living on the plains, Americans were still intrigued by what they had heard about the mist-shrouded Pacific Northwest, a land rich in sea otters, beavers, and enormous trees that grew in its rain forests. Ever since the first ships had touched that shore, the stories they had heard had stimulated their imaginations, and when several Flathead Indians arrived in St. Louis and asked that the Americans send missionaries among them the appeal was irresistible.

Without stopping to question the Indians' motives or to reason why those on the West Coast should be converted before those in the Rockies, ministers began to speak from their pulpits about the need for saving this almost unknown tribe. The Methodists were the first to act and recruited Jason Lee, a man with previous missionary experience in Canada, and his nephew, Daniel, to work among the Flatheads. Jason was a strong, stocky man, not eloquent or brilliant, but steady, dependable, a good preacher, and well suited for the difficult assignment. As Jason and Daniel toured the Northeast collecting money for their mission, they read in the Boston newspapers about Nathaniel Wyeth's return and his plans to undertake another expedition. Jason hurried to Boston and found Wyeth willing to help in any way he could, answering questions, appearing at public meetings, and inviting the missionaries to join his own expedition across the plains and mountains.

On his return to Boston, Wyeth formed the Columbia River Fishing and Trading Company and, because of his persuasiveness and the contract he held to supply the Rocky Mountain Fur Company, had little difficulty raising enough money to return to the Northwest and again attempt to establish a business there. An educated man with wide interests, he had also come to know Thomas Nuttall, the impetuous scientist who had gone up the Missouri with Hunt and Lisa and had now published his famous book on North American plants. Nuttall, still eager to learn everything he could about American botany, gladly accepted Wyeth's invitation to accompany the expedition and brought with him a young ornithologist, John K. Townsend.

When he arrived back in Independence, Missouri, Wyeth found the town stirring with unrest and suspicion. The Mormons, who had been driven from community to community by the vague fears they always aroused, had moved to the small frontier town and had once more incited hatred of themselves. Finally the population had risen up against them and forced them to take refuge on the other side of the river. But the citizens of Independence were now expecting the members of the sect to counterattack. Consequently many of the people who should have been busy supplying the outward-bound travelers were instead engaged in military maneuvers and parades, for they had formed a militia to protect themselves.

Jason and Daniel Lee, who had finally raised enough money to purchase the supplies they required, were waiting as well as three more young men who had decided to go with them. Milton Sublette, whom Wyeth now knew, was also going to the Rockies, so he and Wyeth joined forces, for there was always strength in numbers when crossing the Great Plains.

As they prepared for the journey, Wyeth and his men were busy "arranging and packing a vast variety of goods for carriage," as Townsend noted in his journal. "In addition to the necessary clothing for the company, arms, ammunition, &c., there are thousands of trinkets of various kinds, beads, paint, bells, rings, and such trumpery for the Indians, as well as objects of trade with them. The bales are usually made to weigh about eighty pounds, of which a horse carries two."

On April 28, 1834, everything was in readiness, and at ten o'clock in the morning the expedition of approximately seventy men with some 250 horses left Independence. As a stranger to this sort of travel, Townsend noted Wyeth and Sublette's ar-rangements with interest. "The party," he wrote, "is divided into messes of eight men, and each mess is allowed a separate tent. The captain of the mess, (who is generally an 'old hand,' i.e. an experienced forester, hunter, or trapper,) receives each morning the rations of pork, flour, &c. for his people, and they choose one of their own body for a cook. . . .

"When we arrive in the evening at a suitable spot for an encampment, Captain W. rides around a space which he considers large enough to accommodate it, and directs where each mess shall pitch its tent. The men immediately unload their horses, and place their bales of goods in the direction indicated, and in such manner, as in case of need, to form a sort of fortification and defense. When all the messes are arranged in this way, the camp forms a hollow square, in the center of which the horses are placed and staked firmly to the ground. The guard," Townsend continued, "consists of from six to eight men, and is relieved three times each night, and so arranged that each gang may serve alternate nights. The captain of a guard (who is generally also the captain of a mess) collects his people at the appointed hour, and posts them around outside the camp in such situations as they may command a view of the environs, and be ready to give the alarm in case of danger.

"The captain cries the hour regularly by a watch, and all's well, every fifteen minutes, and each man of the guard is required to repeat this call in rotation, which if any one should fail to do, it is fair to conclude that he is asleep, and he is then immediately visited and stirred up." Townsend noted that "in case of defection of this kind, our laws adjudge to the delinquent the hard sentence of walking three days."

But he realized the difficulty of imposing such punishment, for he added, "As yet none of our poor fellows have incurred this penalty, and the probability is, that it would not at this time be enforced, as we are yet in a country where little molestation is to be apprehended . . ."

On May 18 they reached the Platte and began to follow its course west, expecting within a few days to reach the normal ranges of the buffalo herds, a sight they anticipated with eagerness. On the afternoon of May 20 they saw some on the other side of the river, but the animals caught their scent and stampeded off into the distance. But "towards evening," Townsend wrote in his journal, "on rising a hill, we were suddenly greeted by a sight which seemed to astonish even the oldest amongst us. The whole plain, as far as the eye could discern, was covered by one enormous mass of buffalo.

Our vision, at the very least computation, would certainly extend ten miles, and in the whole of this great space, including about eight miles in width from the bluffs to the river bank, there was apparently no vista in the incalculable multitude.''

A few days later the herd had completely disappeared, and several hunters went in search of them to get some more meat. Townsend accompanied them and with great difficulty killed a bull, but like a novice he had chosen an animal that was both large and old, a fine trophy perhaps, but not good for eating. "It was now past mid-day," he wrote describing his experience, "the weather was very warm, and the atmosphere was charged with minute particles of sand, which produced a dryness and stiffness of the mouth and tongue, that was exceedingly painful and distressing. Water was now the desideratum, but where was it to be found?''

This was the question so many travelers on the Great Plains faced. "The arid country in which we then were, produced none, and the Platte was twelve or fourteen miles from us, and no buffalo in that direction, so that we could not afford time for such a trifling matter. I found that Mr. Lee [one of the missionaries] was suffering as much as myself, although he had not spoken of it, and I perceived that Richardson [a professional hunter who accompanied the expedition] was masticating a leaden bullet, to excite the salivary glands. Soon afterwards a bull was killed . . .

"We were all suffering from excessive thirst, and so intolerable had it at length become, that Mr. Lee and myself proposed a gallop over to the Platte river, in order to appease it; but Richardson advised us not to go, as he had just thought of a means of relieving us, which he immediately proceeded to put in practice. He tumbled our mangled buffalo over upon his side, and with his knife opened the body, so as to expose to view the great stomach, and still crawling and twisting entrails. The good missionary and myself stood gaping with astonishment, and no little loathing, as we saw our hunter plunge his knife into the distended paunch, from which gushed the green and gelatinous juices, and then insinuate his tin pan into the opening, and by depressing its edge, strain off the water which was mingled with its contents.

"Richardson always valued himself upon his politeness, and the cup was therefore first offered to Mr. Lee and myself, but it is almost needless to say that we declined the proffer, and our features probably expressed the strong disgust which we felt, for our companion laughed heartily before he applied the cup to his own mouth.''

But the deadly thirst lingered on. Richardson,

Townsend went on, later "induced me to taste the blood which was still fluid in the heart, and immediately as it touched my lips, my burning thirst, aggravated by hunger, (for I had eaten nothing that day,) got the better of my abhorrence; I plunged my head into the reeking ventricles, and drank until forced to stop for breath." When he was finally sated, Townsend looked up at Lee and saw no approval on his face. Then the missionary could control himself no longer and burst into laughter. Only then did Townsend realize what a sight he must have presented, his face covered with blood and himself become almost a brute.

"When we arrived at the camp in the evening," he wrote, "and I enjoyed the luxury of a hearty draft of water, the effect upon my stomach was that of a powerful emetic: the blood was violently ejected without nausea, and I felt heartily glad to be rid of the disgusting encumbrance. I never drank blood from that day." But Townsend had learned the desperate lengths to which thirst could drive men on the dry Great Plains.

In fact, much of the trip was a learning process for him. When they crossed the South Fork of the Platte to pick up the North Fork, he began, in common with many other travelers, to discover how much more equipment he had brought with him than he needed or could really afford to carry. Spare waistcoats, shaving boxes, and soap were among some of the items he and Nuttall left by the trail, where, if they were not washed away, some curious Indian would find them and wonder at them. As he tossed these articles out, he gained a new understanding of why the more experienced men dressed themselves in buckskin "without a single article of civilized manufacture about them" and why they let their hair and beards grow long rather than take the trouble to carry razors and shave them.

The weather, as it often did on the Great Plains, became capricious. One morning, Townsend said, " . . . the whole camp was suddenly aroused by the falling of all the tents. A tremendous blast swept as from a funnel over the sandy plain, and in an instant precipitated our frail habitations like webs of gossamer. The men crawled out from under the ruins, rubbing their eyes, and, as usual, muttering imprecations against the country and all that therein was . . . During the whole day a most terrific gale was blowing directly in our faces, clouds of sand were driving and hurtling by us, often with such violence as nearly to stop our progress; and when we halted in the evening, we could scarcely recognize each other's faces beneath their odious mask of dust and dirt.''

Traveling at a pace faster than Townsend and Nuttall would have liked, for it interfered with their studies, the expedition followed the North Platte toward the mountains in the west. Chimney Rock stood like a "kind of obelisk," as Townsend observed, and they entered the rough country around Scotts Bluff, where "the road was very uneven and difficult, winding from amongst innumerable mounds six to eight feet in height, the space between them frequently so narrow as scarcely to admit our horses, and some of the men rode for upwards to a mile kneeling upon their saddles."

At the mouth of the Laramie River, they found that William Sublette and Robert Campbell were still intent on expanding their business, for the two partners were constructing a new post, named Fort William. Located in the heart of productive fur country, it also stood on the principal route between the Missouri and South Pass.

After leaving this outpost of civilization, they went on to the rendezvous, which proved a bitter disappointment to Wyeth. Regardless of its oral contract with Wyeth, the Rocky Mountain Fur Company purchased all its goods from one of its regular suppliers and refused to honor its agreement with him. Deep in the wilderness and far from the jurisdiction of any court, he had no way of forcing the company to live up to its obligation. If he were to get rid of the large supply of trade goods he had brought, he would have to look to his own ingenuity.

On the Snake River in Idaho, he put his men to work building a trading post named Fort Hall, which he stocked with the items the Rocky Mountain Fur Company had refused to buy. While he was there, a Hudson's Bay trader, Alexander McKay, camped nearby with a band of French and Indian trappers. Townsend was greatly impressed by the "order, decorum, and strict subordination which exists among his men, so different from what I have been accustomed to see in parties composed of Americans."

On their last Sunday at Fort Hall, Wyeth and McKay asked Jason Lee to hold a church service. Lee was well liked, for although he sometimes remonstrated with the men over their conduct and language, he did so with such evident goodwill that he did not annoy them. So after selecting a shady spot near the fort, most of Wyeth's party and all of McKay's joined in listening to him. "The people," Townsend wrote, "were remarkably quiet and attentive, and the Indians sat upon the ground like statues. Although not one of them could understand a word that was said, they nevertheless maintained the most strict and decorous silence, kneeling when the preacher kneeled, and rising when he rose, evidently with a view of paying him and us a suitable respect, however much their own notions as to the proper and most acceptable forms of worship might have been opposed to ours.

"A meeting for worship in the Rocky mountains," Townsend concluded, "is almost as unusual as the appearance of a herd of buffalo in the settlements." The church service was not only unusual; it was a portent of the future. The joint occupancy of the Oregon territory by transient fur trappers was possible. But trappers and traders, at least American trappers and traders, did not bring ministers with them. Only settlers did that, and settlers could not live under a divided government.

Chapter 20

Wives and Missionaries

It is more than one hundred and fifty years since white men penetrated far into the forests, their canoes freighted with goods, coasting the shores of the remote lakes, and following up the still more remote rivers, to traffic with the Indians for their furs, not regarding hunger, toils, and dangers. These enterprises have been extended and pursued with avidity, until every Indian nation and tribe have been visited by the trader.

What is the power of that principle which draws these thousands from their country, and their homes and all the ties of kindred? Are the love of gain and the hope of wealth the motives by which courage and daring are roused, and dangers defied? And shall Christianity be a less powerful principle? Has it only furnished twenty or thirty missionaries, whose sole motive is to carry the gospel to the many ten thousand Indians in the widely extended country, over which are ranging nine thousand traders, trappers, and hunters? Are these the only evidences the church of God can give of sincerity in her professions of attachment to Christ, and to the interests of the immortal soul?

—Samuel Parker, 1838

The winter of 1834–1835 held the Great Plains in its bitter grip. Indians and trappers stayed close to their fires, as the winds drifted the snow, and even the buffalo battled the cold, their shaggy coats crusted with ice as they searched for the dried grasses that were the ghosts of the past summer. But for all its sameness, the season that year witnessed a change, small in appearance, great in significance.

On the advice of Dr. John McLoughlin, Jason Lee had selected a site for his mission on the Willamette River and had constructed a mission house for himself, his nephew, and the three young men who had joined them. By February, 1835, he had three small Indian children living with him and was spending an hour every evening teaching them to read and spell English. In the spring he intended to plant twenty acres of land and hoped the mission board would send him a man with a family to take care of the farm. He emphasized the man should

have a family, for he wanted no more bachelors. In fact, he hoped that the fiancée of his nephew, Daniel, could be sent out as soon as possible. Women, he had been told by the Hudson's Bay Company, would add to the mission's effectiveness among the Indians. His serious, sober community, setting up a small school and preparing to plow the earth, might be less grand and impressive than Bent's Fort or Fort Union with their palisades and bastions, but it was a sample of American culture placed in the wilderness and a deeper influence on the future.

Nuttall and Townsend were also on the West Coast, two men as unlike the traders as Lee's mission was unlike a fur company's post. Continuing their scientific investigations, they kept collecting birds and plants and exploring the biological aspects of the land as no one had ever done before. Nathaniel Wyeth and his party were also at work, for his past disappointments had not dimmed his hopes for a permanent settlement and a flourishing business near the Pacific.

Even Hall Kelley, pursuing his misty dreams, had finally arrived at the opposite side of the continent. Ebullient as ever despite Wyeth's defection, he had followed a circuitous route to his promised land. Going west to the Ohio River, he had followed the inland waters to New Orleans, taking passage from there to Mexico. Travel-weary but still tenacious of purpose, he reached California and, falling in with a band of Americans, had persuaded them to accompany him to Oregon.

That winter more Americans were on the West Coast than ever before, and they represented a broad spectrum of American society, from the minister to the scientist, from the promoter to the businessman. In contrast to the British traders and trappers, their numbers were few, but even the blindest must have sensed the trend.

If the nation's expansion was to continue, peace among the Indians, although difficult to obtain, was necessary. As long as they retained their warlike habits, attacking each other and stealing each other's horses, they were likely also to sweep down on small groups of white men on the Great Plains. Universal peace was, therefore, an objective of American Indian policy, peace between Indians and peace between white men and red.

On the northern Great Plains, where the giant fur companies operated their strings of forts, the traders tried with varying degrees of success to maintain order among their customers. The less powerful Bents and St. Vrain could not duplicate this function on the southern Great Plains, so the task of making peace there was given to Colonel Henry Dodge. In 1835 he received orders to march again with three companies of dragoons, totaling approximately 120 men, to the Rocky Mountains and back, demonstrating American military strength and holding councils with the Indians whenever he could.

On May 29, 1835, he left Fort Leavenworth and in the second week of June entered the valley of the Platte, where he met with the Oto Indians, and shortly after that the Omahas, who were at peace with the Otos, arrived. The general format of the councils was about the same as that followed by Lewis and Clark three decades previously—the long speech, the Indians' answers, the distribution of medals, then the presentation of gifts. Although the Indians were now more familiar with the Americans, their understanding of the ceremony had not increased. Skilled at oratory, they often practiced it as an art rather than a means of setting

policy. And in spite of the journeys that some of them had made to Washington, the majority of them still had no sense of the size and strength of the white men's nation. Therefore they accepted the presents and medals, glad for the gifts, but without considering them as anything but an expression of temporary friendship and goodwill.

Continuing up the Platte, Dodge held another council with the Grand Pawnees. Then, after passing Grand Island on the Platte, he came to a village formerly occupied by the Arikaras but now deserted. Wandering through the empty lodges, the soldiers entered one whose owner's finger, cut off at the second joint, hung with a crooked stick from the center pole. This evidence of self-mutilation, a common practice among many of the Plains Indians, bewildered and disgusted the men.

Dodge's interpreter went in search of the Arikaras and on July 5 returned with most of their principal chiefs and many of their warriors. The state of this tribe had deteriorated greatly since they had defeated Ashley's trappers and driven back Nathaniel Pryor. "The Arikaras," said Dodge's report, "are considered the most savage tribe of Indians west of the Mississippi, and have always been characterized by a want of faith in their promises, and an inveterate hostility to the whites, killing all they could meet. They are at war with most of the surrounding nations, and large numbers of them are killed every year. They formerly lived on the Missouri river, but were driven from this country by the Sioux, with whom they have long been at war. They have no land they can call their own; and are wandering about like the Arabs of the desert, killing and robbing almost every one they meet." Their nasty tempers had not changed, but the Sioux were accomplishing what Leavenworth with his dilatory tactics had not.

On a beautiful, cloudless day, Dodge preached peace to them and found them in a conciliatory mood, asking for nothing more than a piece of land. In fact, when the council was over, one of their leaders presented Dodge with an ornamented hunting shirt, a gesture that only a few years previously no Arikara would have made.

After passing the mouth of Cache la Poudre, Dodge crossed over to the Arkansas and on to Bent's Fort, where he held a conference with a large assemblage of Cheyennes, as well as some Arapahoes, Gros Ventres, and a few Blackfeet, who had wandered far from their normal haunts to the north. (The promise of presents always ensured good attendance at the Americans' councils.) When Dodge finished speaking and the Indians replied, he found himself again faced with the perplexing question that plagued so many negotiators. Which of the Indians was the chief of each band? In order to make an appropriate distribution of the presents he had to know, and he also had to know the men with whom the Americans should deal in the future. But as he looked at the rows of watching faces, he could not tell who was important and who was not.

When in desperation he asked the Cheyennes to appoint their own chief, they remained silent. The white men's concept of an absolute leader was completely foreign to them, and they were not sure what Dodge wanted. Finally he turned to one Cheyenne named Little Moon and asked him to appoint the chiefs. When Little Moon picked out some nominees, Dodge questioned the gathering to determine if anyone objected. Since no one did—after all, what did it matter to them?—Dodge made the selection final and gave out his presents and medals.

A few days later he came upon another Cheyenne village and again faced the same problem. When he insisted that they name a chief, according to the expedition's journal, they "pointed to five men sitting together, saying they were the principal men. They appeared reluctant to make the selection from among these five. The colonel then told them they must select some one to receive the presents, and have them distributed. One of the braves was finally led forth, to whom the medal was given, together with the presents, and a letter from Colonel Dodge, stating that he had been made a chief. His name was White-man's chief. They appeared well pleased with their reception and went away highly gratified."

So, too, did Colonel Dodge. He had been given the mission of meeting with as many tribes as possible, persuading them to adopt lives of peace, and reward them for their good behavior. This, he thought, was what he had done, and certainly the Indians had received his words—and presents—with every sign of goodwill. But behind him he left not one "white-man's chief," but many, and his imposition of the Americans' social structure on the Indians was like the rolling of a wagon wheel over rock, making no impression and changing little.

The reports that Jason Lee sent from Oregon excited the public's interest in the welfare of the West Coast Indians, and the American Board of Commissioners for the Foreign Missions, which served both the Presbyterian and Congregational churches, decided it, too, should be active in Oregon. In fact, it had already chosen as its representative a native of Ashfield, Massachusetts, named Samuel Parker. Appointed too late to go out the previous year, he was prepared to make an exploratory trip in 1835. With him he planned to take a physician, Dr. Marcus Whitman, who, although born in New York State, had had experience in some of the frontier communities of Canada.

The two men met by arrangement in St. Louis in the spring, and in many respects they were an odd pair. Parker dressed in a white stock and a tall hat, which he wore on every occasion, while Whitman preferred clothes more suited to the rough life they were to lead. Their dress was symbolic of their characters. Although Whitman heartily disapproved of the trappers' intemperance, he was a husky man, willing to share the work that had to be done. Parker, on the other hand, was reserved and aloof and considered himself above the more menial tasks, perhaps because he was in his middle fifties.

Like most other travelers, they were dependent on the American Fur Company for protection, and as usual, the company quickly agreed to let them accompany the expedition going to the annual rendezvous. Some differences of opinion, however, quickly developed between the two missionaries and the fur traders. Parker and Whitman disliked traveling on Sunday, and since the caravan was at first moving fairly slowly, they stayed in camp over the Sabbath and caught up with it later. This did not make them popular, and spitefully the traders cut the bindings on a raft they had to use to cross a river. Their popularity diminished further when they refused to drink any whiskey with the men and would not even wet their lips with liquor.

At Bellevue, Nebraska, while they waited for the men of the American Fur Company to arrange their packs, they talked at length about the Indians to Joshua Pilcher, who was now an Indian agent. "He appeared," Parker wrote, "to be not only intelligent and candid, but well disposed towards Indian improvement." Before they could leave cholera broke out. As a doctor, Whitman accepted the challenge of this dread disease and worked tirelessly and relatively effectively to get the epidemic under control. As a result, the attitude of the traders toward the missionaries changed markedly. The two men might not like to travel on Sundays or drink whiskey, but in the midst of this crisis Whitman was a useful person to have around.

On June 22 the caravan turned west; and toward evening on July 10, Parker noted that "we had an unusual storm of thunder, hail, rain, and wind. The horses and mules could not be controlled, and turned and fled in all directions. The whole caravan was scattered over the prairie; but when the storm abated, they were again collected without much difficulty, and nothing was lost. If any hostile band of Indians had been about us, it would have been easy for them to have made us prey. But the Lord not only rode upon the storm, but was also near for our defense. The scene was alarming, and yet grand—sublime.''

The Lord's protection, however, did not induce the caravan to stop traveling on Sundays. On the following Sabbath, Parker wrote, ''We are in a land of dangers, but God is our preserver; how desirable it is, that his mercies should be had in grateful remembrance, and that the portion of the time, which he has set apart as holy, should be observed as such. The caravan traveled a part of the day, but were under the necessity of stopping on consequence of rain, which wet their packages [his word for 'packs']. It is worthy of notice that various providences have thus far prevented them from traveling much upon the Sabbath. But this day has been one of confusion and wickedness. In consequence of the men being drenched with rain, whiskey was dealt out freely, to keep them from taking cold. Most of them became much excited, and one . . . stabbed a man, with full intent to have pierced his heart; but the knife, striking a rib, turned aside and only made a deep flesh wound.

''I think,'' Parker continued, ''I know the feelings of David, when he expressed a strong desire after the sanctuary of God, and to dwell in his tabernacle.''

Yet his religious concerns did not blind Parker to the country. He marveled at the buffalo herds and even joined the hunters. (So great was his excitement that in order to have a steadier aim he dismounted to shoot, a dangerous practice.) He was amazed at the speed of the antelopes, which left their swiftest dogs behind after only ten or twenty rods. He made a special side trip to observe Chimney Rock and was interested in the topography of Scotts Bluff. Everything about this new land fascinated him.

At Fort Laramie, Sublette and Campbell's new post, they rested; and the men received their usual ''day of indulgence,'' as it was called, during which they could drink and do what they pleased. In the course of their celebration, one man, according to Parker, ''shot another with the full intention to have killed him. The ball entered the back, and came out at the side. The wounded man exclaimed, 'I am a dead man'; but after a pause, said, 'No, I am not hurt.' The other immediately seized a rifle to finish the work, but was prevented by the bystanders, who wrested it from him and

discharged it into the air.'' The nature of the traders had not changed since the time that Lisa's employee had almost downed him with the swivel gun.

When they reached the rendezvous, Whitman found many calls for his services. James Bridger, one of the earliest and best of Ashley's employees, was bothered by an Indian arrowhead he had been carrying in his back for three years, and Whitman agreed to extract it. The operation was difficult, because the arrowhead had bent when it struck a bone and therefore had a hook at its end. Under the watchful eyes of the Indians and trappers, Whitman cut it out. The success of this operation brought him another patient, a trapper who for two and a half years had had an arrowhead in his shoulder. When Whitman removed this, many of the older men came to him for similar treatment, and he found himself continually busy.

At the rendezvous Parker saw a mountain man pick up a rifle, mount his horse, and challenge anyone to engage him in single combat. Kit Carson, who had run away as a youth and was now a trapper, accepted the challenge and, holding a pistol, rode up to the bully. Both men fired at the same time. Carson's ball entered the bully's hand, while the bully's passed over Carson's head. When Carson reached for his second pistol to finish the job, the bully screamed for mercy, and Carson gave him his life. ''Such scenes,'' Parker commented, ''sometimes from passion, and sometimes from amusement, make, the pastime of their wild and wandering life. They appear to have sought for a place where, as they would say, human nature is not oppressed by the tyranny of religion, and pleasure is not awed by the frown of virtue.''

At the rendezvous Parker and Whitman had an opportunity to talk to the Indians, particularly the Flatheads and Nez Percés, among whom they hoped to work. Since theirs was an exploratory trip only, they decided they now had enough information for Whitman to return east and report to the board, while Parker continued on. Whitman was especially anxious to do this, because he had become engaged before leaving. He knew now that if he married, he could take his bride over the trail. So the two men parted at the Green River, planning to meet again the following year.

The year that Whitman returned home, the seeds of a revolution in armaments were quietly being planted in the United States. In Patterson, New Jersey, Samuel Colt, a young inventor, had begun production of his Colt's revolvers and other firearms.

In the hands of an Indian, a bow and arrow was a formidable weapon. As the early Spaniards had learned, an arrow had great penetrating power and was capable of piercing their armored mail. At least one visitor to Fort Union had been surprised to see an Indian put an arrow completely through the body of an antelope. The principal disadvantage of bows and arrows against the Americans' guns was their shorter range. Expert marksmen in open country could sometimes keep the Indians at a distance, but bows and arrows also had one important superiority to guns: the Indians could shoot much faster, often sending several arrows into the air at once from a single bow. Colt's repeating firearms would give the Americans the same advantage of shooting rapidly.

Whitman as a man of medicine had little interest in such death-dealing devices. On his return his principal concerns were the organization of a new expedition to Oregon and the woman to whom he was engaged, Narcissa. Devoted to each other, they were married in February, 1836; and although the road to Oregon was a long one, her family did not seem to object either to the journey or to the cause she hoped to serve. What worried them was the company of the minister who was to travel with the newlyweds to Oregon.

The Reverend Henry H. Spaulding had grown up in the same town as Narcissa, had attended the same school for a while, and was generally regarded as a rejected suitor. His marriage of several years to another woman and his ordination as a Presbyterian minister did not allay dark suspicions in the minds of Narcissa's family, although they finally gave their blessing to the journey, and the travelers departed for Liberty, Missouri.

The bitter competition in the fur trade had finally persuaded the partners in the Rocky Mountain Fur Company to dissolve their firm, leaving the field to the American Fur Company. With that company's purchase of Fort William, more generally called Fort Laramie, it gained control of the Platte route to the mountains and was the major force in the business except for Bent and St. Vrain. Yet it still retained its old ambivalence—rough with competitors, gracious to others. So Whitman had no difficulty securing permission to accompany its annual expedition to the rendezvous.

Despite the protection of the company, the trip was a difficult one for Narcissa and Spaulding's wife, the first two white women to cross the plains. The dust swirled from under the feet of the livestock, rising into the air and seeping into everything. The wind blew continuously, the sun baked them, and often fresh game was scarce. They had, however, as Narcissa noted in a journal she kept for her mother, "plenty of dried buffalo meat, which we have purchased of the Indians, and dry it is for me. I can scarcely eat it; it appears so filthy; but it will keep us alive, and we ought to be thankful for it." Then in an aside to her sisters, she added, "Girls, do not waste the bread; if you knew how much I should relish even the dryest morsel, you would save every piece carefully."

Yet she responded to the challenge. "Do not think I regret coming," she wrote, "no, far from it. I would not go back for a world. I am contented and happy, notwithstanding I sometimes get very hungry and weary. Have six weeks' steady journey before us. Will the Lord give me the patience to endure it? Feel sometimes as if it was a long time to be traveling. Long for a rest, but must not murmur." In spite of her own discomfort, she could still be concerned for others, and after considering her own state, she wrote, "Feel to pity the poor Indian women, who are continually traveling in this manner during their lives and know no other comfort."

Fort Laramie provided a welcome break in the journey. For the first time since leaving Missouri, Narcissa had a chance to do her washing and rid her clothes of their accumulation of dust and dirt. She even noted the niceties of the post and remarked that it had real chairs with leather bottoms, a decided relief after days in the saddle.

At Fort Hall, which Wyeth had built, she had a chance to do her washing again, but she noticed that the post was neither as well constructed nor as comfortably furnished as Fort Laramie. With the instinct of someone responsible for providing a family's meals, she looked at the garden that supplied the post. "The turnips . . . appeared thrifty," she wrote, "the tops very large and tall, but the roots were small. The peas looked well, but had most of them been gathered by the mice. Saw few onions that were going to seed, which looked quite natural. That was all the garden contained." But she likened the stops at the forts to those rests that were sometimes granted Christian as he made his pilgrim's progress.

Like most emigrants to the West, they had come ill-equipped and overburdened. Whitman finally despaired of getting his wagon all the way to Oregon and abandoned it, taking with him only the wheels. That meant that Narcissa would have to leave the trunk her sister had given her. Being separated from one more object that reminded her of home was difficult. "Dear, Harriet," she wrote in her journal, "the little trunk you gave me has come so far and now must leave it here. Poor little trunk, I am sorry to leave thee. Thou must abide here alone, and no more by thy presence remind me of my dear Harriet. . . . Thus we scatter as we go along."

"It would have been better for us," she added later, "not to have attempted to bring any baggage whatever, only what was necessary to use on the way. It costs so much labor, besides the expense of animals. If I were to make this journey again, I would make quite different preparations." Like Townsend and Nuttall, who had also scattered their belongings as they went, she was learning why the experienced traders and trappers traveled so light and could do with so little. But Nuttall and Townsend were men; she was a woman, and one of the Hudson's Bay Company's men, noticing her sadness at being separated from her trunk, offered to carry it for her. She rejoiced at this kindness.

At last the long weeks spun themselves out, and the party reached Fort Vancouver. As she looked around her, Narcissa noted many things that needed a white woman's touch. The Indian wives of the traders and trappers were not, she remarked, "first rate housekeepers." The beds were wooden bunks filled with about a dozen Indian blankets, but there were also several beds stuffed with the feathers of game fowl. She resolved to make one herself as soon as time permitted, even though she had nothing really suitable for ticking. And when she wrote one of her first letters home, she asked for fruit seeds and added, "Another important article for us house wives, some broom corn seed. We brought a little, but we are afraid it will not do well. They have nothing of the kind here, but use hemlock boughs for broom." Narcissa's broom might not sweep clean the Oregon territory, but it was a symbol of a new and lasting influence.

Except for the fur traders, most Americans thought the Great Plains nothing but an obstacle to reaching the Pacific Coast. Yet each westward party added to their knowledge of the area. And now in addition to their interest in Oregon, they were casting covetous eyes on California. A number of Americans had seen its long coast, high mountains, and rich valleys, and a few had come there to remain. One of these was a man named John Marsh, a graduate of Harvard with a propensity for roaming. He had followed the fur trade to Minnesota, then had gone to Santa Fé, and from there to Los Angeles, a trip that was being made more and more often. California appealed to him

and on the strength of his Harvard diploma, the significance of which no one really understood, he set himself up as a physician, acquired some land, and reinvested his patients' fees in livestock. He was soon a successful, wealthy rancher, and his enthusiastic letters home helped arouse interest in the land south of Oregon.

Neither Nuttall, Townsend, nor Wyeth remained long on the West Coast, but before leaving, Nuttall and Townsend collected many specimens of plants and birds that had never before been identified and that added to their scientific achievements. (John James Audubon, who had watched the *Western Engineer* when Long stopped at Cincinnati, had not been able to get that far west, but he later studied Townsend's specimens and included them in his *Birds of America*.)

Wyeth, able and plucky though he was, was unable to match the scientists' success. On the West Coast he was pursued by one difficulty after another. His supply ship from the East was delayed by lightning. McKay, with whom he had prayed in the wilderness, set up a Hudson's Bay Company post near Fort Hall and soon secured all the trade in the area. In 1836 Wyeth was forced to sell out to his competitors. He then returned to Boston, where he built up a profitable business shipping ice to the West Indies. Although his time in the West was brief, spanning only three years, and although the country defeated him, he had been unlike the others—the explorers, traders, and trappers—who had gone before him. They had followed the lonely trails over the Great Plains with the intention of returning; Wyeth and the people he had taken with him hoped to stay.

Stephen Austin had picked up Moses Austin's work and done it well. In spite of his fight with Joshua Pilcher, he was a level-headed, conscientious man, and he made every effort to live up to the agreement between his father and the Mexican government. The settlers he brought to Texas joined the Catholic Church and promised to abide by Mexican law in return for the grants of land they received. But as the colony grew, differences inevitably developed between the *Norte Americanos* and the citizens and government of their adopted land. Brash, bold, and impatient, they wearied of Mexico's bureaucracy and customs, and the troubling issue of slavery further enlarged the gulf between the two cultures. The American settlers, many of whom were Southern planters, wanted to farm their lands with slaves (there was not the usual labor supply of peons in that area), but the various Mexican governments prohibited the institution.

By 1835 the differences had become so great that armed conflicts had broken out between the Mexicans and the Americans; and in October, when the Mexican dictator, General Antonio López de Santa Anna, dissolved the state constitutions, the Americans knew that Texas would receive no special privileges.

In anger, they took the field with other dissidents against Santa Anna and in December drove out the soldiers stationed at San Antonio. In February, 1836, Santa Anna came to recapture the town. Any possibility of reconciliation vanished in the gunsmoke with which he filled the rooms and corridors of the Alamo, once a peaceful mission and now a human slaughterhouse. Santa Anna's brutal conduct strengthened the Texans' will to fight and brought recruits from the United States to the Texans' army. On March 2, 1836, Texas declared its independence; and at San Jacinto, the Texans under the command of Sam Houston caught Santa Anna off-guard, defeated his army, made the dictator a prisoner, and set their own terms for peace. Shortly after, they ratified their new constitution and elected Sam Houston as president.

Now when the traders crossed the Arkansas and headed toward the Cimarron, they no longer entered Mexican territory. Instead on their way to Santa Fé they passed through lands claimed by the Republic of Texas. The memory of Coronado might still haunt the Llano Estacado, but possession had slipped at least technically from the hands of his descendants into the hands of Americans turned Texans.

The Texans' struggle for independence caught the imagination of the American people. Previously only a relative few had settled in Austin's colony, but they now looked at the former Mexican province as another promised land and began pouring across the border, attracted by liberal offers of acreage and the romanticism with which Texas was surrounded. Jackson as President did not discourage this movement, but he meticulously waited until he had the approval of Congress before recognizing the independence of Texas on his next-to-last day in office in 1837.

That same spring a young Baltimore artist, Alfred Jacob Miller, left his hometown to seek his fortune in New Orleans, where he set up a studio. Shortly after his arrival, he had an unusual visitor, an aristocratic Scotsman named William Drummond Stewart. Adventurous and wealthy, Stewart had become intrigued by the American West and had already visited the Rocky Mountains. He

planned to make one more journey with the American Fur Company that spring and asked Miller to accompany him.

On the trail Stewart, who had served in the British army, proved to be something of a martinet in Miller's opinion. He required the artist to catch his own horse and perform his share of the routine duties around camp. (He did permit him to pay a substitute for guard duty and employ a trapper to set up his tent.) At the same time, he wanted Miller to paint first this and then that scene until finally Miller complained that he could not carry out his employer's instructions with only one pair of hands.

Yet Miller rejoiced in the wild, free spirit of the trappers' lives. He watched the men hunt buffalo, carefully noting every detail as they dashed among the herds. He listened to the old-timers recount their adventures and made paintings of some of their stories. He painted Chimney Rock, too, as well as Scotts Bluff and Fort Laramie, which now belonged to the American Fur Company. Every tribe they met—Arapahoes, Blackfeet, Snakes, and Sioux, among others—formed subjects for Miller's pictures, as did the trappers, their Indian wives, and the activities around camp. He watched wild horses stampede across the Great Plains, taking pleasure in seeing them wheel like cavalry, and also observing how the Indians caught them. He painted pictures of animals like prairie dogs, grizzlies, and elk, which they sometimes hunted as a change from buffalo meat. He painted the caravan at rest and breaking camp, he showed it fording rivers and crossing the Continental Divide, and when he returned at the end of the season, he had a portfolio of sketches and paintings from which he could work for many years. In spite of Stewart's patronage, however, he never during his lifetime obtained the recognition he would have liked. But just as Bodmer and Catlin left a record of the Upper Missouri and Catlin one of the Southwest, Miller gave the country a graphic portrayal of life on the trail to the annual rendezvous.

That spring of 1837, the steamboat, loaded with the traders' goods and the usual government presents for the Indians, started up the Missouri River as it had done every year since McKenzie had persuaded the American Fur Company to buy the *Yellow Stone*. Its decks were crowded with the company's employees, raucous as they always were at the beginning of a new season and shooting off their guns in celebration. Its engines throbbed as the steam from its boilers pushed against the pistons, and its pilot blew the whistle to let the whole of Missouri know that the boat was on its way again. This year, however, the boat's principal cargo was tragedy. For among the people on board at least one was coming down with smallpox.

Before the boat reached Fort Union, several more persons had caught it. Even for whites, some of whom had been vaccinated and some of whom had acquired immunity from previous exposure, smallpox was deadly. But the Indians were much more vulnerable to it. Ever since Dr. James had demonstrated the water-soaked vaccine to the Pawnees, humanitarians had feared the consequences of epidemics among the Indians.

Several days before reaching Fort Union, the boat sent word ahead of the coming danger, and the personnel of the fort urged the Indians to stay away from the boat when it finally pulled against the bank. But the Indians knew it was bringing their treaty presents, and nothing could keep them away.

About the middle of June, the disease broke out in the Mandan villages. Already greatly weakened by previous outbreaks of disease and by the constant attacks of its enemies such as the Sioux, the tribe was now practically extinguished. The Hidatsas and Arikaras were out hunting, so the disease did not reach them until about a month later, but the effects were equally disastrous. Ever since the Americans had first come up the river, the Arikaras had demanded tribute and otherwise harassed them, but now few Arikaras were left to cause them trouble. The Hidatsas suffered equally.

At Fort Union the men set up temporary hospitals but for little purpose. Few Indians who came down with smallpox seemed able to recover from it, and some died within a few hours. The men collected the bodies into piles and, unable to bury so many, threw them into the river.

Soon the disease appeared among the Blackfeet, those Indians who had kept their lands free of the white men for so long. It reached into the Assiniboins, who had no more resistance than any of the others; and it brought death, too, to the Crows. The whole society of the Great Plains changed within a single season. "The warlike spirit," one observer wrote, "which but lately animated the several Indian tribes, and but a few months ago gave reason to apprehend the breaking-out of a sanguinary war, is broken. The mighty warriors are now the prey of the greedy wolves of the prairie, and the few survivors, in mute despair, throw themselves on the pity of the Whites, who, however, can do but little to help them. The vast preparations for the protection of the western frontier are superfluous; another army has undertaken the defence of the white inhabitants of the frontier; and

the funeral torch, that lights the red man to his dreary grave, has become the auspicious star of the advancing settlers, and of the roving trader of the white race." The guns of the traders and of the soldiers who sometimes followed them had done far less injury to the Indians than the disease brought by the steamboat. Few tribes on the northern Great Plains would be the same again.

Although American interest in Oregon continued high, the government had little information about this vast part of the continent except that drawn from informal sources, such as the reports of missionaries and fur traders and the unreliable studies of individuals like Hall J. Kelley. To remedy this deficiency, the secretary of the navy assigned William A. Slacum, a purser, to make an official tour and write up his findings. After visiting the various settlements in early 1837, and making, as he had been instructed to do, an estimate of the number of white men now living in the area, he returned home and filed his report.

"I consider the Willamett as the finest grazing country in the world," he wrote. "Here there are no droughts, as on the pampas of Buenos Ayres, or the plains of California, while the lands abound in richer grasses, both in winter and summer. . . . The river called 'Rougues,' or sometimes Smith's river, abounds with the finest timber west of the Rocky mountains; and it will be fairly estimated that the valleys of the rivers certainly within the limits of the United States [he was excluding the Willamette and Columbia, both in disputed territory] contain at least 14,000,000 acres of land of the first quality, equal to the best lands of Missouri and Illinois."

Although the United States was striving to develop more industry, it was still an essentially agricultural country; and Slacum's extravagant praise of the Willamette Valley and other portions of Oregon was enough to stir the heart of any farmer, particularly one striving to make a living from the rock-studded fields of New England.

Enthusiasm for crossing the Great Plains was kindled further by the appearance of Jason Lee in the East in 1838. After reporting to the Mission Board, Lee made a tour, visiting more than eighty eastern cities to raise money for his work and publicizing the territory.

Lee received the Mission Board's support for enlarging his establishment in Oregon; and when the group that was to return with him gathered in New York, it numbered approximately fifty persons—five additional ministers, a physician, a business agent, carpenters, farmers, others able to carry on the secular work, and four women teachers, as well as the wives of several of the men. Because of the size of the party and the supplies they were taking with them, the Mission Board chartered a ship to take them to the Columbia River.

On the morning of October 9, 1839, in New York harbor, the group assembled on the deck of the *Lausanne,* as their vessel was named, and held a brief religious ceremony. At the conclusion one of the ministers baptized two of the children of the families who were making the trip. The name chosen by the parents of one was "Oregon." Then the ship weighed anchor and departed on its long journey around Cape Horn. Narcissa Whitman and Eliza Spaulding, who had traveled across the vast distance that linked East to West, would not be the only American women on the West Coast.

The trappers went to the Far West in pursuit of furs, the missionaries in pursuit of souls. John A. Sutter was a German Swiss, who had fled his native land to escape debtor's prison and the unpleasantness of his in-laws. After visiting St. Louis and Santa Fé, he went to Oregon, but there he heard about California and decided that it offered even greater opportunities. From the governor of California he received permission to settle in the Sacramento Valley. Within a year—the legal minimum time—he became a Mexican citizen, and the governor gave him a grant of 50,000 acres. Energetic and ambitious, Sutter soon built up a large ranch and farm and became one of the dominant figures in northern California. The presence of Sutter, John Marsh, and others of non-Spanish descent indicated the change that was taking place in the population of the West Coast.

In April, 1839, when the American Fur Company's steamboat started up the river, it carried on board two representatives of the United States Topographical Corps. The senior member and leader of the small expedition was Joseph Nicolas Nicollet, a distinguished French mathematician and scientist who had been driven from his native land as a consequence of some disastrous speculations. Coming to the United States, he had undertaken some private exploration of the Arkansas, Red, and Mississippi rivers. The results he achieved attracted the attention of the secretary of war, Joel R. Poinsett, whose name has become a household word because of a minor accomplishment—introducing into the United States the poinsettia plant.

Nicollet's assistant was John Charles Frémont, a protégé of Poinsett, who had secured for him a commission as second lieutenant in the Topographical Corps. The illegitimate son of a Virginian mother and a French father, Frémont had shown himself to be brilliant, restless, and charming. Without as much formal education as the previous army explorer, Long, he was quicker at learning and more adaptable; and his work under Nicollet was probably the best training he could have had. In 1839 their assignment was to complete a survey of the lands between the northern Mississippi and the Missouri, approaching the area from the west.

Chugging against the current, frequently stopped by changing channels and sawyers and planters, the fur company's steamboat carried them up the river. Nicollet, Frémont, and a German botanist they had employed took turns plotting the river during the daytime. As they made their sketches, they noticed with surprise their difficulty in finding many of the landmarks noted by Lewis and Clark, for the Missouri, like a living creature, was constantly shifting in its streambed and altering its features.

At Fort Pierre, a post that had now received so many visitors, they disembarked and headed in a northeasterly direction, keeping their journals and observations as they went. Because Nicollet was better trained than most of his predecessors, his surveys and reports were the best yet made of the small portion of the Great Plains through which he passed. In addition, he was careful to instruct Frémont, so the young second lieutenant would be capable of making a comparable survey on his own.

In the past the Catholic priests of Spain and France, particularly those who belonged to the Society of Jesus, had roamed the West, crossing its plains and mountains and floating down its rivers. Men like Marquette and Fray Marcos had been in the forefront of the explorers, carrying their crosses into the most remote lands. But the American Catholic Church had not followed their examples, and the Jesuits themselves, suppressed by the Pope and reduced to taking refuge in Russia, had fallen on evil times. On the official restoration of the order, the Jesuits in the United States held only one failing novitiate in Maryland.

A gift of land near St. Louis, however, made possible the opening of a new one. Among those who attended it was a young Belgian, Pierre-Jean De Smet. Cheerful and devout, De Smet had the adventurous soul of his spiritual forebears and, after returning to Europe for several years, gladly accepted an assignment to serve as a missionary among the Potawatomie Indians. Although Lee and Whitman had answered the call of the Northwest Indians, some of the Flatheads and Nez Percés had heard of the "Black-Robes," as they called them, and preferred them to the Protestants. In 1839 they sent a delegation to visit the bishop at St. Louis. He promised to have a priest visit them the following year, and de Smet gladly undertook the assignment.

Joining the men of the American Fur Company, he started west, but after only six days on the trail, he came down with a severe case of malaria. Shaken by alternating bouts of fever and chill, he at times became too weak to sit on his horse and would take temporary refuge in one of the wagons, where he rode jostled by the boxes and barrels it contained.

Yet even in his sickness de Smet brought to the Great Plains an appreciative and poetic eye. Other travelers had been concerned with water shortages, Indian attacks, and the never-ending wind, dust, heat, and cold. Some, such as James when he approached the mountains, or Catlin when he ascended the Missouri, had noticed the region's beauty, but few had the romantic vision of de Smet. "I was often struck with admiration at the sight of the picturesque scenes which we enjoyed all the way up the Platte," de Smet wrote. "Think of the big ponds you have seen in the parks of European noblemen, dotted with little wooded islands; the Platte offers you these by the thousands, and of all shapes. I have seen groups of these islands that one might easily take, from a distance, for fleets under sail, garlanded with verdure and festooned with flowers; and the rapid flow of the river has made them seem to be flying over the water. . . ."

When they came to the buffalo herds, he wrote, "Whole bands were lying amidst flowers on the grass; the scene altogether realized in some sort the ancient tradition of the holy scriptures, speaking of the vast pastoral countries of the Orient, and of the cattle upon a thousand hills. I could not weary of gazing upon this delightful scene, and for two hours I watched these moving masses in the same state of excitement."

He agreed with previous travelers that settlement would be difficult in the arid parts of the Great Plains, but he was struck by Chimney Rock. "It seems," he wrote, "to be the remnant of a lofty mountain which the winds and the storms have been wearing down for ages; a few years more and this great natural curiosity will crumble away and make only a little heap upon the plain; for when it is examined near at hand, an enormous crack appears in its top. In the neighborhood of this wonder, all the hills present a singular aspect; some of them have the appearance of towers, castles, and fortified cities. From a little distance one can hardly persuade himself that art is not mingled in them with the fantasies of nature."

At the rendezvous, held that year on the Green River, de Smet was greeted by a deputation of Northwest Indians, who had come to guide him the rest of the way. About a week more of traveling brought him to Pierre's Hole, where the trappers had battled with the Blackfeet. There he found waiting a large encampment of Flathead and Pend d'Oreille Indians, who had come that far to meet him. They had even brought with them a bell, which they presented to Father de Smet.

There in the mountains the "Black-Robe" performed mass and baptized almost six hundred Indians. (He might have baptized more, but he had promised them he would return the following year and did not want them to think that baptism was easy to obtain.) After spending some time in Pierre's Hole, the whole encampment moved through the Teton Mountains with Father de Smet saying mass every Sunday and fast day. "The altar," he wrote, "was made of willows; my blanket made an altar cloth, and all the lodge was adorned with images and wild flowers; the Indians knelt within a circle of about 200 feet, surrounded by little pines and cedars, set out expressly."

On August 10, 1840, the time had come for de Smet to return to St. Louis and tell the bishop what he had found. The Indians provided him with an escort to guard him through the country of the Blackfeet. With their guidance and protection, he crossed over to the Yellowstone and reached Fort Union, where, in the tradition of McKenzie, he was well treated and given supplies for the downstream trip. De Smet noted with sadness the sorry condition of the Mandans. That once proud tribe had been almost wiped out by the attacks of the Sioux and more particularly by smallpox. They had now united with the Hidatsas, whose numbers were also far fewer than they had been when Lewis and Clark had come up the river. The Arikaras, too, had moved upstream, for they had also suffered from the onslaughts of their enemies and the white men's diseases. Father de Smet was witnessing the extinction of several tribes.

Farther down the river he met a party of Sioux, who were surprised by his long black robe and missionary's cross suspended on his breast. De Smet noted their large population and warlike temperament. Unlike the Mandans and Hidatsas, who were quickly disappearing, the Sioux were flourishing. (Living much of the time in small nomadic bands, they were less susceptible to epidemics.) Rich and prosperous, the white men's guns and horses had made them the most powerful tribe on the Missouri, a terrifying force to their enemies. The men at the Americans' trading posts and the warriors of the Sioux were between them taking possession of the northern Great Plains, and in the process hundreds of years of previous cultures were being swept away.

Chapter 21

The Emigrants Begin

It is not, however, by means of such long and dangerous voyages [by sea] that citizens of the United States are to effect settlements in Northwest America; and it will doubtless be the care of their Government to render smoother and more secure the routes across the continent to those countries, lying entirely within the undisputed limits of the Republic. *In the possession of these routes, the Americans have infinite advantages over the British, and . . . nothing more is required . . . than the establishment of a few posts, at convenient distances apart, on a line between the Missouri and the passes of the Rocky Mountains, which may serve as forts to overawe the savages, and as caravanserais for the repose, and possibly even for the supply, of travelers. When this has been done, the American settlements on the Columbia will soon acquire that degree of extent and stability, which will render migratory all claims on the part of other nations to the possession of those countries.*
—"Memoir, Historical and Political on the Northwest Coast of North America,"
prepared for the Senate Select Committee on Oregon, 1840

Gently the first spring rains fell on the mountains and the Great Plains. When their drops touched the snow, they sometimes congealed and became part of the icy covering, sometimes they melted a little of the snow, leaving pockmarks in its smooth surface, and sent trickles of moisture seeping toward the ground below. The battle of the seasons had begun, but the tilting of the earth on its axis made the outcome inevitable. With each lengthening day, the water became greater, the snow less. In places the brown dirt showed through the tattered snow, and hills and gullies shed their winter camouflages and resumed their summer shapes.

As the water flowed across the Great Plains, it recommenced its endless etching. The Missouri, removing some of autumn's accumulation of silt, dug its channel deeper as its current began to quicken. The Platte, too, often so lazy, started to scour away its banks, and its current lapped at the shores of its cottonwood-covered islands. The water entered the network of ravines around Scotts Bluff, making each a little deeper and steeper, a little more impassable for wagons. When the water carved the landscape, moving earth and stones toward the Mississippi and on to their final lodgement in the Gulf of Mexico, some of it seeped into the ground, wetting the roots of the dormant grasses that covered the Great Plains. The moisture and the warning sun brought them back to life. Green shoots began to rise toward the sky, providing food for all grazing animals, not only buffaloes and antelopes, but horses, mules, and oxen. They could now feed as they traveled, and that meant that men could travel, too.

A group of them was gathering to make the trip across the plains. Father de Smet was charged with taking two priests and three lay brothers to Oregon to establish a mission among the Flatheads. Several trappers wished to return to the mountains but did not care to make the journey alone. Two men were interested in seeing the country and taking a pleasure trip. A Methodist minister, who had his family with him, wanted to join the Lees in Oregon, and a number of people in Missouri thought they could improve their fortunes by moving to California. John Marsh, the Harvard graduate turned "doctor" and rancher, had written to some friends in Missouri, describing his life on the West Coast in glowing terms; and Antoine Robidoux, a fur trapper, had spoken publicly of the advantages of living in California. A number of Missourians, some with wives and children, decided to take the chance that these reports were true and risk the danger of leaving behind everything they knew to venture across the plains and mountains in search of a new and better life.

Of the various groups, de Smet's was the best prepared. He had made the trip before and therefore knew what to expect, and he had raised enough money to hire teamsters and a hunter and purchase four carts and a small wagon. He had also wisely engaged Thomas Fitzpatrick, who had been so active in the Rocky Mountain Fur Company, to serve as guide. As was the custom on the Santa Fé Trail, the prospective settlers, who had not yet organized, got together and drew up their rules. Then they elected one of their members, John Bartleson, captain, and another, John Bidwell, secretary. On one point they all quickly reached agreement. De Smet was in charge of the Catholic missionaries, Bartleson captain of the settlers, but Fitzpatrick, the most knowledgeable man among them, would act as "pilot"—to use Bidwell's word—of them all.

On May 19, 1841, they started off. (Richard Williams, the Methodist minister, would overtake them later. Having the faith of his calling, he believed that his God would protect him while he traveled a few days by himself.) On the twenty-first the oxen that made up part of the train wandered off during the night, causing a late start in the morning. Two days later, as a result of the carelessness of their owners, they again disappeared, and the caravan had to waste further time searching for them. This produced considerable grumbling among some of the members. If they traveled this slowly, they would be spending the winter in the Laramie Mountains and subsisting on their mules. Tempers were not improved when two wagons broke down just a few days later.

One of Williams's daughters was in love with a man who was traveling with them and decided she did not want to wait the long weeks until they reached Oregon to be married. Her family did not object, and Williams himself presided over the ceremony by the trail. The earth was the altar, the domed sky the vault, and the wind moaning over the Great Plains took the place of a choir. At the conclusion, Bidwell noted in his journal that "we now have five families if we include a widow and child."

But the sentimentalism that naturally followed the sight of the father performing his daughter's marriage ceremony in the vast expanse of the plains did not provide unity. The following day the secular members of the caravan held a long discussion. Tough and experienced, de Smet wanted to reach the Northwest before winter and was pushing his men and wagons along. Some of the others, particularly those who had already delayed the travelers by losing their oxen, preferred a more leisurely pace. Perhaps, they suggested, it would be better if the two groups parted. Under the rules they had adopted at the beginning, they held a meeting, everyone expressed his opinion, and they took a vote. Wisely the majority decided that Fitzpatrick's services were too valuable to lose. Since he was attached to de Smet's group, they would go on ahead with the Jesuits.

On the Great Plains, if it was an Indian scare one day (this caravan had been frightened by a band of Cheyennes), it might be weather the next. They had broken camp one morning and were on the trail again when the winds started to blow violently and dark clouds piled up in the sky. Then they saw what Bidwell called a "water spout"—perhaps it was actually a tornado—and it seemed to be coming directly toward them. They made ready to protect their wagons, but it fortunately veered to one side instead of striking them. They had hardly recovered from their fright when the skies pelted them with the largest hailstones they had ever seen. After the storm had passed and the sun had warmed the ground for an hour, Bidwell found several hailstones that were still as large as turkey eggs.

Like all newcomers to the area, the men were impressed by the size of the buffalo herds. But Bidwell was also shocked at the number of bones they found littering the plains on every side. Rightly he predicted that the great herds would become extinct if this sort of slaughter persisted. The herds also caused trouble with the oxen. If the owners were not careful, the oxen would mingle with them during the night; and even if they did not, the tracks of the buffaloes made it difficult to distinguish those of the oxen when they wandered off. So once again they suffered delays because of

The Missouri's shifting course and its springtime floods delayed the use of steamboats on the river. Once proved practical, steamboats became a major means of supplying the fur traders, the army, and the settlements. *National Archives*

After 1849 the wagon trains traveled in small groups but sometimes formed an almost continuous line across the western part of the continent. Thus one group of emigrants was often able to help another when they came to difficult stretches on the trail. *National Archives* these animals, and Bidwell accused the owners of carelessness in watching over them.

Each of the caravans, particularly those like this one that included women, soon became a microcosm, a complete world in itself, cut off from everything else. The group had suffered from an Indian scare, the weather, and the dissension over the speed at which they were traveling, and they had all enjoyed the wedding ceremony and the common bond it provided for a few short hours. Now tragedy overtook them. One of the best liked of the young men pulled his gun from a wagon, taking it by the barrel instead of the stock. The trigger caught on something as he dragged it toward him, the gun went off, and the bullet killed him. (By a bitter irony, his last name was Shotwell.) This time there was no rejoicing when the clergy performed a ceremony, and sadly they placed the body of the man who had ventured into the new world of the West into the grave they had dug.

After passing Chimney Rock, whose strange appearance interested them, they came to Fort Laramie. There they auctioned off the dead man's belongings and rested for a day before starting off again. They were joined there by a few men from the fur company who were going farther west, and in about a week one of them married the widow. This time de Smet performed the service, and the young widow whom Bidwell had earlier counted as a family was now truly a member of one.

When they reached the Oregon-California fork in the trail, some of those who had originally intended to go to California preferred to remain with Fitzpatrick, who knew the way to Oregon and was a certain guide. Theirs was the less harrowing trip. The rest continued with Bidwell and Bartleson toward California; and partly through perseverance and partly through bumbling good luck, they finally found their way over the Sierra Nevadas.

In encouraging settlers, Marsh had been acting for his own benefit, not the benefit of others; and Bidwell soon became annoyed with his miserliness and the high prices he charged for everything he sold them. When he wrote home to his friends in Missouri, he denounced Marsh and advised them to pay no attention to his invitation to come to California. John Sutter, on the other hand, was, in Bidwell's opinion, one of the finest men in California and a true friend of every emigrant, which indeed was true.

Bidwell's journal and his observations on the country were printed in the East and served as a rudimentary guide to others who wanted to make the trip. The trail that had first been found by the fur trappers and had known only their feet had now been followed not just by those seeking furs or even by those taking the Christian faith to the Indians, but by bachelors and families who had no other purpose than to make their homes on the West Coast. Most important were the families, for in the long run it was they who would conquer the Great Plains.

Although the Santa Fé trade had never been able to equal its peak year of 1831, business continued brisk, and a number of men were finding it profitable. To the Republic of Texas, heavily in debt and its economy stagnating, the trade presented a tempting prospect. Furthermore, the terms of Santa Anna's capitulation made many Texans believe that the country's western border was the Río Grande del Norte. If so, Santa Fé lay within its boundaries.

Mirabeau Bonaparte Lamar, the second president of Texas, considered these circumstances and came to the conclusion that the republic should send an expedition to Santa Fé. At the least it could do some business with the New Mexicans. At the most it might be able to assert Texas's jurisdiction. Lamar was not prepared to wage a war with Mexico over this issue—Texas did not have the resources for such an undertaking—but he had heard that many New Mexicans were weary of their central government and would welcome independence. Perhaps the appearance of a group of Texans would lead them peacefully to break their ties with their mother country.

In spite of considerable opposition in the Texas legislature, Lamar went ahead with his plans, instructing Hugh McLeod, inspector general of the army, to head the expedition and sending another officer to New Orleans to purchase supplies. A call for volunteers produced more than three hundred men willing to undertake the venture, and George W. Kendall, founder of the New Orleans newspaper the *Picayune,* decided to go along, too, as he thought the expedition might prove worth writing about.

Assembling near Austin, then a tiny hamlet of about five hundred inhabitants, the men and their officers began preparations for their long journey. They were a motley group, made up of four different categories: the military, the merchants, the three commissioners who were to take over the government if the New Mexicans declared their independence, and several observers such as Kendall.

July's scorching sun found them struggling through the Cross Timbers, which lie partly in

Texas and partly in Oklahoma to the east of the Great Plains. Although McLeod drove the men hard in order to make better time, the Texas Pioneers, as they called themselves, had many problems extricating their wagons from the Cross Timbers and then took a course that led them northwest. By the time they had reached the foot of the caprock that rims the Great Plains in western Texas, they were weary, short of supplies, and desperately searching for the way to Santa Fé.

McLeod had chosen Samuel Howland, who knew the country better than most of his men, to lead a party of three to San Miguel. They were to ascertain the mood of the people and purchase supplies. But they had not returned, and there was no way of knowing whether they had reached New Mexico, had been killed by the Indians, or had died of starvation.

Kendall summed up their predicament. "We were completely lost," he wrote, "and without power of moving forward; our provisions, which had for weeks been scanty, were now almost entirely exhausted; the men were enfeebled by long marches, with only poor beef enough each day to support nature; and in addition we were surrounded by a large and powerful tribe of well-mounted Indians, scouring our vicinity, and always on the look-out to pick off any small party that might be sent out to hunt, or for other purposes. All these reasons considered, it will at once be seen that but two courses offered—one to destroy the wagons, and to retreat hastily towards Texas; the other, to divide the command, and send one party forward with orders not to return until the settlements were reached."

Being certain that the Mexicans would welcome them, if not declare themselves part of Texas, they decided to send an advance party to obtain help for the others. "I will not say the wise course was adopted," Kendall said, "but in answer to any one who may blame the leaders of the expedition for dividing the command, I would remark that few men, under the circumstances, would have advised to the contrary."

To undertake this mission, McLeod selected a hundred men, enough to repulse attacking Indians. In charge was William G. Cooke, one of the civilian commissioners; Captain John S. Sutton, twenty years old and a native of Delaware, was in command of the soldiers, and Kendall, a good newspaperman who wanted the full story, went, too.

Without the wagons they were able to climb up the caprock and emerged on the Llano Estacado, the Staked Plains of Texas that had so frightened Coronado's men. In every direction except to the east, the land lay flat, rimmed only by the sky, but slashed in places by the deep-sided canyons cut by the occasional rivers. These, however, were invisible at any distance. "We were going forward at a rapid pace," Kendall wrote, "the prairies before us presenting no other appearance than a slightly undulating but smooth surface, when suddenly, and without previous sign or warning, we found ourselves upon the very brink of a vast or yawning chasm, or *cañon*, as the Mexicans would call it, some two or three hundred yards across, and probably eight hundred feet in depth! As the front ranks suddenly checked their onward course, and diverged at right angles, the rear sections were utterly at a loss to account for a movement so irregular; they could not see even the edge of the fearful abyss at a distance of fifteen feet from its very brink."

Not being able to find a way down or around it, they finally cooked a supper with some of the spoiled meat they had brought with them and made camp for the night. They had been asleep only about an hour when a storm broke. Kendall and a companion had found shelter in a small sandy gulley, which turned immediately into a running stream, drenching them and soaking their guns and saddles. ". . . [N]ever shall I forget the early part of that awful night," Kendall wrote. "The lightning appeared to be playing about in the chasm far below us, bringing out, in wild relief, its bold craggy sides. Deafening peals of thunder seemed rising from the very bowels of the earth, and then muttered away in the distance, rejoicing, as it were, at their escape from confinement. The yawning abyss appeared to be a workshop for the manufacture of the storm, and there we were at the very doors where the Ruler of the elements sent forth a specimen of his grandest, his sublimest work."

On the following day, after considerable searching, they located a trail used by buffaloes and Indians that led them into the canyon and up the other side; but although it was clearly marked by the imprints of thousands of hooves, they found the going rough. Emerging on the far rim, they rested their horses and then continued their journey. "Not a tree or a bush, and hardly a weed could be seen in any direction," Kendall said. "A green carpeting of short grass, which even at this season was studded with strange flowers and plants, was spread over the vast expanse, with nought else to relieve the eye. People may talk about the solitude of our immense American forests, but there is company even in trees that one misses upon the prairie. There is food for thought too, in the ocean wave, not to be found in the face of these great Western wastes, and nowhere else does one feel the sickly sensation of loneliness with which he is impressed when nothing but a boundless prairie is around him. There he feels as if *in* the world, but not *of* it—there he finds no sign or trace to tell him that there is something beyond, that millions of human beings are living and moving upon the very earth on which he stands.'' About three hundred years in time separated Kendall from the early Spaniards; in space, however, there was no gap between them. As he looked at the endless plains around him, Kendall's feelings were the same as those of the *conquistadores*—amazement, bewilderment, and a sense of man's unimportance.

He learned, too, what the Spaniards had learned: here the scenery was down, not up. Born in New Hampshire, Kendall was accustomed to a horizon bounded by hills and mountains, always irregular and sometimes above him, sometimes below. Here it was always at the same place, and the only variety was in the canyons. These contained separate worlds, visually unrelated to the surrounding plains.

The next day they came to another canyon, even larger than the first. "No one was aware of its existence," Kendall wrote, "until we were immediately upon its brink, when a spectacle, exceeding in grandeur anything we had previously beheld, came suddenly in view. Not a tree or bush, no outline whatever, marked its position of course, and we were all lost in amazement as one by one we left the double-file ranks and rode up to the verge of the yawning abyss.''

Once again they searched for a trail used by buffaloes and Indians; and when they located one, it was so steep that the horses balked at descending it. Selecting a sure-footed mule, they used it as the lead animal, and the others followed, the men behind, driving them.

"We found," Kendall later recalled, "a running stream on reaching the lower level of the chasm, on the opposite side of which was a romantic dell covered with short grass, and a few scattering cotton-woods. . . . As we journeyed along this dell all were again struck with admiration at the strange and fanciful figures made by the washing of the water during the rainy season. In some places, perfect walls, formed of reddish clay, were seen standing, and were they anywhere else it would be impossible to believe that other than the hand of man had formed them. The veins of which these walls were composed were of even thickness, very hard, and ran perpendicularly; and when the softer

sand which had surrounded them was washed away, the veins still remained standing upright, in some places a hundred feet high, and three or four hundred in length. Columns, too, were there, and such was their appearance of architectural order, and so much of chaste grandeur was there about them, that we were lost in wonder and admiration. Sometimes the breastworks, as of forts, would be plainly visible; then, again, the frowning turrets of some castle of the olden time. Cumbrous pillars of some mighty pile, such as is dedicated to religion or royalty, were scattered about; regularity was strangely mingled with disorder and ruin, and nature had done it all.''

On the opposite side the same trail led upwards, and men, horses, and mules ascended it with great difficulty. "By the middle of the afternoon," Kendall continued, "we were all safely across, after passing five or six hours completely shut off from the world. Again we found ourselves upon the level prairie, and on looking back, after proceeding some hundred yards, not a sign of the immense chasm was visible.''

These sights, however impressive, did nothing to alleviate the men's discomfort or direct them on the proper course. With their supplies exhausted and game scarce, they were reduced to eating anything they could find, and the man who killed a snake or a tortoise was envied by his fellows. A single buffalo became the object of a two-day hunt, brought down at last by the use of the expedition's fastest horse and one of Samuel Colt's revolvers. (They had been turned down by the army and navy, but the Republic of Texas had ordered a number.) In the distance they could see mountains, so they knew they were nearing their goal, but they still were not sure of their direction or how far they had yet to go.

After entering New Mexico near present-day Glenrio, they kept pushing toward the west, hungry and increasingly desperate. Once they thought they saw people. While the main party halted, three or four men rode off in their direction with Kendall's handkerchief, no longer white, serving as a flag of truce. On closer inspection they decided that their supposed humans were merely a herd of horses and disconsolately returned to where the others were waiting. Once they came upon a road and were overjoyed, but it soon dwindled to nothing in the sandy prairie.

They picked up the Canadian River northwest of present-day Tucumcari, New Mexico, and followed it as it ran through a valley and a narrow gorge. When they came out on the other side they discovered a camp of ragged Mexicans, who had been trading with the Comanches and the Kiowas. From the Mexicans, the Texans learned that they had taken the wrong course since leaving McLeod and that the journey should have required only four days, not thirteen. This was good news, and before setting out the next morning, Cooke employed several of the Mexicans to return to McLeod and show him the way.

The Mexicans, however, also had disturbing news for the Texas Pioneers. Manuel Armijo, the governor of New Mexico, had aroused the province against the Texans and had already imprisoned the advance party under Howland. Such information might have caused Cooke either to turn back or at least remain where he was, but the reports of the Mexicans were contradictory and seemed uncertain. Therefore he decided to move on as he had originally planned, sending ahead a delegation of several Texans, including Kendall, to announce their arrival.

When the advance party reached the small community of Anton Chico they found the population frightened at their appearance; and that night a Mexican warned Kendall that a group of men was assembling at the next town in order to take the Texans prisoner. He concluded by saying that the plan was to shoot them. Kendall would have believed him except that the man demanded a dollar for his information, which led Kendall to think he had concocted the story in order to extract some money from the party.

Outside the next small town, they were greeted by about a hundred *rurales*—or local militia— under the command of an officer named José Salazar. After addressing them cordially, Salazar asked them if they were not from Texas. When they said they were, he expressed pleasure. Escorting them to the nearest house, he dismounted and his men gathered around as though they wished to hear what their leader said. In the most courteous terms, Salazar asked the Texans to deposit their weapons with him. They could not, he explained, enter the country armed and added that this, of course, was the custom of civilized nations. Kendall, in particular, was reluctant to surrender his guns, but Salazar's manner was pleasant and the travelers were outnumbered twenty to one.

Once they were disarmed, Salazar informed them that he would have to search them. This seemed like an indignity, but they now had no way of resisting. Then Salazar ordered twelve of his soldiers to come forward. It was immediately apparent that they were a firing squad and that Salazar intended to execute his prisoners on the spot. One of the men who spoke Spanish well heard the orders given, and meanwhile the crowd that had

gathered was clearing a space behind the Texans so that no one else would be hit by stray balls.

Death was at hand. While they had struggled across the Great Plains, they had dreamed of reaching New Mexico and safety at last. Instead they were helplessly facing a firing squad. At that critical moment, one of the local landowners spoke up. The Texans, he told Salazar, had come peacefully and expressed a desire to speak to the governor. They should be permitted to do so. Fortunately he was a man of considerable influence in the area, and his opinion prevailed.

Death released its grip, but comfort did not take its place. Salazar forced the men to march on foot to San Miguel. After spending the night there, he made them march toward Santa Fé at a brisk pace. Toward the middle of the afternoon, they met Armijo coming from the capital. Armijo first boasted to them of his own prowess as a warrior and then ordered them to march back to San Miguel on foot, although some of them were now suffering from serious disabilities. At San Miguel they were thrown into prison.

The stories they had heard about the three earlier emissaries being arrested now proved true. In their presence, one of them was brought forward and cruelly executed. (The soldiers' first shots only wounded him.) Next Howland, who had been in charge of the first advance party, was brought out. His hands were tied behind him, and his left ear and cheek had been cut off. Also his left arm had been hacked, probably with a sword. Without letting any of his friends speak to him, the Mexicans forced him to his knees and shot him in the back. Both men, they warned the remaining Texans, had tried to escape.

The Pioneers had been completely misinformed about the people of New Mexico. Instead of welcoming independence or at the least wanting to buy the Texans' goods, Armijo had worked them up into an ugly frame of mind, and he himself was in a mood to show little mercy. Cooke's party, coming along behind, was easily surrounded by a vastly superior force and asked to surrender their guns. Once disarmed, they, too, were quickly made prisoners.

The end of the expedition was near. McLeod, waiting at the foot of the caprock, was in desperate straits. More than once the Kiowas attacked him, his men were demoralized, and he was short of supplies. Often the party talked about beating a retreat to Texas, but before they did so, the messengers arrived from Cooke. They explained that the way to San Miguel, if the expedition followed the right course, was short.

Day after day dragged by as the remaining Pioneers crossed the Llano Estacado and approached the settlements of New Mexico. Not hearing any further word from Cooke, McLeod sent several smaller groups ahead, and they were inevitably captured.

Finally McLeod himself met the Mexican soldiers. Just as they had done with Cooke and the others, they first asked him to have his men give up their arms. McLeod was immediately suspicious, but the alternatives were bleak. Even if he was able to overpower the Mexican detachment, what could he do? He could not fight his way into Santa Fé, and his men could not make the long trip back to Texas. So he and those with him did as the Mexicans asked. Of course, they were also immediately taken prisoner.

Although the Mexicans had never recognized the independence of Texas, they had done little to try to reassert their jurisdiction over it. Therefore the Texas Pioneers should have been considered prisoners of war. The Mexicans, however, regarded them in a different light, and treated them as though they were hardened criminals, chaining them, putting them in the worst jails, and otherwise subjecting them to hardships and indignities. Through the intervention of the United States and Great Britain, some of them were finally able to return to their homes with memories of the horrors of the Llano Estacado—that trackless waste that provided so little water or food—and the filthy Mexican prisons.

After the expedition was over, the southern Great Plains were controlled by Mexico. But in the long run Texas was not the loser. When he was released, Kendall wrote an account of the affair that became a best-seller, and it along with other reports of the expedition's treatment lessened Americans' sympathies for Mexico and increased their warm feelings for the Texans. Although the effects were not immediately apparent, Armijo, by maltreating a weak enemy, had created a strong one.

Texas was in trouble. Heavily burdened by its national debt and with little industry or agriculture, it had now annoyed its southern neighbor in such a way that raids and reprisals were inevitable. Its best hope of salvation lay in annexation by the United States, but the American government, partly for diplomatic reasons and partly because of the internal political problems raised by the possible extension of slavery, refused to negotiate the new republic's admission to the Union.

On the other hand, while Texas had lost any pretension to a boundary as far west as the Río Grande in New Mexico, the United States was strengthening its hold on the North American continent. Its power came, not from the movement of armed troops, but from the number of men and women who listened to descriptions of Oregon and California and wanted to move west.

In May, 1842, approximately 160 of them gathered at Independence, Missouri, to follow in the footsteps of the Bidwell-Bartleson party. These were not experienced mountain men accustomed to the hardships of the wilderness, but a motley group of bachelors and families, half of them women and young children incapable of bearing arms. One was a man named Lansford W. Hastings, who intended not only to keep a journal of the trip, as others had done, but to write a book entitled *The Emigrants' Guide to Oregon and California*. Hall Kelley had told prospective settlers about the benefits of life in the West; Hastings planned to tell them how to get there, what provisions to take, which routes to follow, and what conditions to expect when they reached their destination.

The inexperience of the group became apparent almost immediately. As Hastings later commented, "The harmony of feeling, the sameness of purpose, and the identity of interest, which here existed, seemed to indicate nothing but continued order, harmony and peace, amid all the trying scenes incident to our long and toilsome journey. But we had proceeded only a few days travel, from our native land of order and security, when the 'American character' was fully exhibited. All appeared to be determined to govern, but not to be governed. Here we were, without law, without order, and without restraint; in a state of nature, among the confused, revolving fragments of elementary society!" As Thomas James had noted years before, the American desire for independence resisted the discipline necessary for frontier life. The "captain" of the group suggested, therefore, that they halt and hold a council to draw up a set of laws to govern their conduct.

The first item considered at the meeting was the case of an emigrant who had decided to try to steal an Indian horse. After discussion of the legal niceties, the meeting concluded that the man was not guilty of any offense. It also established a committee to draw up a code of law for the party, but the committee decided that none was necessary. After hearing that recommendation, someone proposed killing all the dogs that were accompanying the party. This resolution passed by only a small majority, and when a few dogs had been slain, the owners of the remainder threatened to do some killing themselves, not of dogs but of humans. Since both sides were determined to have their way and both sides were armed, fighting was on the verge of breaking out. But the "captain" wisely convened another council, "which being done," Hastings said, "the dog decree, as it was called, was almost unanimously abrogated." These disagreements, of course, delayed the progress of the party, which was held up a few more days by sickness that afflicted one of the families. The couple's daughter died from it, and the mother became so ill that her husband decided they would return east.

A few days before the party reached the Forks of the Platte, they came upon their first large buffalo herds and, like all other travelers across the Great Plains, were amazed at their size. Quickly they learned how to hunt the animals and laid in a good supply of fresh meat. But the welcome change in their diet did not change the spirit of dissension that had again arisen. A number of the party had become incensed with their leaders, so they held another election and chose replacements. "This . . . gave," Hastings said, "some dissatisfaction, to a few of the party, especially the disaffected and disappointed office-holders and office-seekers, who now, together with a few others, separated themselves from the main body, and went on a few days in advance, to Fort Laramie. . . ."

There the group, still rent by disagreement, reassembled and laid their future plans. After considerable argument, they decided to go on together, for otherwise the smaller faction would not be able to continue west, their numbers being too few to fight off an Indian attack. But they disagreed on whether to try to sell their wagons at Fort Laramie and buy pack animals or whether to take the wagons on farther. Since their information was uncertain, some made the exchange while others did not. Their best bit of fortune at Fort Laramie was to find that Thomas Fitzpatrick, the well-known mountain man, was willing to guide them part of the way.

Before they reached Oregon they had a number of other mishaps. Several members of the party were captured by Indians, although they were shortly released. One man was killed when another man's gun went off accidentally. "While he survived," Hastings said, "every possible exertion was made to afford him relief, but all to no purpose. . . . The physician now gave up all hopes of his recovery; his voice faltered; death was depicted upon his countenance, and every thing seemed to indicate a speedy return of his immortal spirit, 'to God who gave it,' yet, even now, he was to be heard, urging us all, in the most emphatic language, to be more cautious in the future, and thereby, avoid similar accidents. . . . This was truly a most solemn and awful scene; and these admonitions coming from such a source, and under such circumstances, must have produced an impressive and lasting effect! . . . We now followed to the grave the second corpse of our little company! As we marched along, in solemn procession, the deepest gloom and solemnity was depicted upon every countenance, and pungent and heartfelt grief pervaded every breast! While we were silently and solemnly moving on, under arms, 'to the place of the dead,' the sentinels were to be seen, standing at their designated posts, alternately meditating upon the solemnity of the passing scene, and casting their eyes watchfully around as if to descry the numerous and hostile foe, with whom we were everywhere surrounded, and thus, to avert accumulating danger! At the same time, the young man, who was the unwilling instrument of this, our trying calamity, [the one whose gun had gone off] was also to be seen, walking to and fro, suffering the most extreme mental agony; apparently noticing nothing that was transpiring around; seemingly unconscious of every thing, but his own unhappy existence, and the sad departure of his, and our lamented friend! The ordinary rites, after interment, having been performed at the grave, the company returned in the same solemn manner, to the encampment, where all sat down in silent, mournful mood, contemplating the many trying scenes of the desolate past, and anticipating the dreadful future!"

Before the party reached Oregon, the man who had fired the accidental, but fatal, shot drowned while crossing a river. One man refused to stand sentry duty and, when the other members of the party tried to expel him, threatened to shoot them. The expedition also broke up into factions again over the question of using wagons, but they finally arrived in Oregon.

Inglorious in many respects as their trip had been, they had knowingly proved an important point: that the road to Oregon, first broken by Lewis and Clark and then by the fur traders, was now so familiar that even the incompetent and inexperienced could hope to make the journey. And with the publication of Hastings's book, this became even more true.

The growing number of people emigrating to the West kept the politicians interested in the question of the joint occupancy of Oregon, and Senator Thomas Hart Benton was determined that the issue be settled and the boundary placed no farther south than the 49th parallel. He and Lewis F. Linn, the junior senator from Missouri, secured an allotment of some $30,000 in the budget of the Topographical Corps for a study of the Oregon Trail across the Great Plains as far as the mountains. The trail, of course, was now well known and marked by the feet of the livestock and the wheels of the wagons that had passed over it, but the senators realized that such a study would demonstrate to the emigrants the government's interest in their fate and would also be helpful in locating forts. Although Nicollet was obviously the person to lead the survey, he was seriously ill, and the logical man to take his place was John Charles Frémont, whom he had so carefully trained.

Since his original trip with Nicollet, Frémont had been given a number of additional assignments, some of them designed to keep him away from Benton's daughter, Jessie; for although the two had fallen in love, a junior army officer was hardly a suitable husband for a woman who was captivating Washington society and was the daughter of a distinguished senator. But the separations had not lessened the young couple's love for each other, and they had risked the senator's wrath by marrying secretly. When they told Benton what they had done, he was furious, but rather than lose his daughter, he agreed, albeit reluctantly, to accept Frémont as his son-in-law. This tie was yet another reason for the head of the Topographical Corps to give Frémont the assignment.

By June 10, 1842, approximately a month after Hastings's party had left, Frémont was ready to start. In the tradition of Meriwether Lewis and Nathaniel Wyeth, he had designed his own method of water transportation—an india-rubber boat with airtight compartments that he had ordered built in New York. Other than his purchase of this device, his arrangements were extremely practical. He assembled about twenty men, most of them experienced frontiersmen, a German topographer named Charles Preuss, and, as his hunter, Lucien Maxwell, a member of a noted New Mexican family. Most important of all, he had recently met Kit Carson, who had worked for the Bents and who had challenged the bully at the rendezvous. Carson was not at the time well known except among his fellow frontiersmen, but Frémont quickly recognized his outstanding qualities and offered him the position of guide. Since the fur business was declining, Carson was willing to work for a salary.

At the Forks of the Platte, Frémont divided his party. His primary responsibility was to map the emigrants' route along the North Platte, but as he could do that on his return, he decided to take a few of his men and go up the South Fork and meet the others later at Fort Laramie. Although the center of operations for Bent and St. Vrain continued

to be Bent's Fort on the Arkansas, the enterprising firm had also established a post on the South Platte to take care of their more northern Indian customers. "At the fort," Frémont said, "we found Mr. St. Vrain, who received us with much kindness and hospitality. Maxwell [Frémont's hunter] had spent the last two or three years between this post and the village of Taos; and here he was at home and among his friends. Spaniards frequently come over here in search of employment; and several came in shortly after our arrival. They usually obtain about six dollars a month, generally paid them in goods. They are very useful in camp, in taking care of horses and mules." Because St. Vrain had not received an expected shipment from Taos, he was unable to sell Frémont the supplies he wanted, but he did spare a few pounds of coffee, a couple of horses, and some mules.

About ten miles from the post, Frémont came to the Cache la Poudre River, which Ashley had ascended in the dead of winter when its waters were frozen and its banks and bed encrusted with snow and ice. In summertime it presented an entirely different sight, and Frémont wrote that "this is a very beautiful mountain stream, about one hundred feet wide, flowing with a full swift current over a rocky bed."

Neither Long nor Pike had had the technical training that Frémont received from Nicollet, and they had both called the western part of the Great Plains a desert. Frémont, however, had a different opinion. As he rode through this area, carefully studying its features, he came to the conclusion that "the constituents of the soil in these regions are good, and every day served to strengthen the impression in my mind, confirmed by subsequent observation, that the barren appearance of the country is due almost entirely to the extreme dryness of the climate." With great astuteness, he had uncovered one of the secrets of the western Great Plains. The area was not inherently a desert, as so many had supposed. Its only lack was the water that had been drained from its skies by the western slopes of the Rocky Mountains.

On reaching Fort Laramie, Frémont noted that the man in charge of the fort had with him two clerks and about sixteen *engagés*. "As usual," Frémont noted, "these had found wives among the Indian squaws; and, with the usual accompaniment of children, the place had quite a populous appearance. It is hardly necessary to say that the object of the establishment is trade with the neighboring tribes, who, in the course of the year, generally make two or three visits to the fort. In addition to this, traders, with a small outfit, are constantly among them. The articles of trade consist, on the one side, almost entirely of buffalo-robes; and, on the other, of blankets, calicoes, guns, powder, and lead, with such cheap ornaments as glass-beads, looking-glasses, rings, vermilion for painting, tobacco, and principally, and in spite of the prohibition, of spirits, brought into the country in the form of alcohol and diluted with water before sold."

The fur trade had changed since the early days of the French or even since the time of Lisa and Ashley. Then beaver skins had constituted the heart of the business, for they were light to transport and commanded high prices. Buffalo skins, on the other hand, were bulky and heavy and brought comparatively less money. But the demand for them was sufficiently great to keep the American Fur Company operating even though it no longer made its former profits. The role of liquor in the business, however, had not changed. Just as in McKenzie's time, the company had to compete with small, independent traders who entered the country from Mexico and the United States, eluding the officials and carrying with them only a few kegs of liquor. That was all they needed to woo away the company's customers unless the company was prepared to offer liquor, too.

"The fort," Frémont continued, "had a very cool and clean appearance. The great entrance in which I found the gentlemen assembled, and which was floored, and about fifteen feet long, made a pleasant shaded seat, through which the breeze swept continually; for this country is famous for high winds."

When Frémont's account of his expedition was printed by the government, Senator Linn commented, "This report proves conclusively that the country for several hundred miles from the frontier of Missouri is exceedingly beautiful and fertile; alternate woodland and prairie, and certain portions supplied with water. It also proves that the valley of the Platte River has a very rich soil, affording great faculties for emigrants to the west of the Rocky Mountains."

Times were swiftly changing. The Great Plains had belonged to the Indians, the traders and trappers, and a handful of adventurous missionaries and settlers. But now the mystery that had surrounded them was being stripped away by the government; and knowledge of the route across them, once the possession of only a handful of men, was

available to all. The day of the western emigration had begun.

Jim Bridger had been in the fur business ever since Ashley and Henry had formed the Rocky Mountain Fur Company, and his exploits were known wherever men gathered around a campfire and talked about the early days in the Rocky Mountains. He had roamed through the unknown wilderness, finding rivers, valleys, and mountain peaks that had never before been seen by white men. He had been the first to reach the Great Salt Lake, had become a partner in the company when he was only twenty-six years old, had fought the Indians many times (Marcus Whitman had removed an old arrowhead from his back in 1835), and when the Rocky Mountain Fur Company was dissolved that year, he had gone to work for the American Fur Company. Few people had deeper roots in the trade; few were more reluctant to give it up.

In 1842, however, as Astor had foreseen, silk had replaced beaver fur in the making of hats, and the profits from other types of fur were not sufficient to warrant the large-scale activity that had once characterized the business. Yet as he looked over the situation, Bridger saw new opportunities for an enterprising man. Usually the emigrants moving west brought with them enough cash to pay for goods and services, and by the time they reached western Wyoming they often needed them. The rough terrain and the long climb since leaving the Missouri had worn out their wagons, and the fittings often required repairs. Horses and oxen needed new shoes, and the prospective settlers, in spite of all the advice they had received, generally found themselves short of one article or another. A post at the right point along the trail might do a brisk business with the travelers.

In 1842 he began to construct one near present-day Fort Bridger, Wyoming, on a tributary of the Green River. After crossing the Great Plains, the emigrants could stop at Fort Laramie. About four hundred miles farther on their road and after crossing the South Pass, they could stop for supplies and help at Fort Bridger. Among other services that Bridger offered were those of a blacksmith's shop, and in 1843 he ordered a supply of goods from St. Louis to stock his shelves. When James Bridger stopped trapping furs for a dwindling market and began instead to take care of settlers, one era had ended and another had opened.

Chapter 22

War with Mexico

In further vindication of our rights and defense of our territory, I invoke the prompt action of Congress to recognize the existence of the war, and to place at the disposition of the Executive the means of prosecuting the war with vigor, and thus hastening the restoration of peace. . . .

The most energetic and prompt measures and the immediate appearance in arms of a large and overpowering force are recommended to Congress as the most certain and efficient means of bringing the existing collision with Mexico to a speedy and successful termination.

—James K. Polk, 1846

When the Americans began establishing their first settlements along the edge of the Great Plains, they brought with them what was essentially an Anglo-Saxon culture that had served them well on their westward movement. But it did not help them enter the Great Plains. To accomplish that, they had had to borrow heavily from the French and Spanish, both their techniques and their personnel. When Frémont hired men to go with him on his expedition to South Pass, his rolls were replete with names like Clément Lambert, J. B. L'Espérance, J. B. Lefévre, Basil Lajeunesse, Honoré Ayot, and Louis Menard. At Fort Laramie, when he wanted to hire a man to help handle his livestock, he chose a Mexican and marveled at the speed with which the man turned the most intractable of the mules into a reliable mount. At any gathering of mountain men, Spanish and French were heard almost as frequently as English, and words from those two languages were beginning to enter the Americans' vocabulary.

By the first half of the 1840s, however, the emigrant trains, great lines of wagons carrying the hopeful toward the West, were beginning to introduce something American to life on the Great Plains. In 1832, the year of Frémont's expedition, there had been at the most 160 persons in the west-

ward-bound caravan, a substantial increase in numbers over the previous years, but nothing compared to those in 1843, when approximately six hundred assembled to make the journey. Two of them, Overton Johnson and William H. Winter, like Lansford Hastings, wrote a book as a guide for other emigrants.

For a short distance they followed the Santa Fé Trail, "and again and again," they said, "we passed long trains of Merchant wagons, laden with the products of our Manufactures and other Merchandize, and bearing them afar across the deserts, to be exchanged for the gold and silver of the Provinces of Mexico. This trace is large, and as well beaten as the most important public highways of the United States."

When they had crossed over to the Platte, they found that it is "from one to three miles in width, and the bed of the channel is entirely of quicksand. When we came to it, it was quite full, and the water was everywhere running level with its banks. . . . We found but little wood here, and none except immediately on the River. We were frequently unable to procure it, and were compelled, sometimes, to make a strange substitute in the excrement of the Buffalo, in order to do our cooking." Long before, travelers on the Great

253

Plains had learned that "buffalo chips," if they were dry, made an effective fuel, although subsequent travelers were often repelled at first by the thought of using them.

The emigrants saw Chimney Rock, too, and the hills beyond it, which impressed them much as they had impressed Father de Smet. "A dark cloud arose in the West," the two men wrote, "and the whole region was illumined by the reflected rays of the Sun, which, mellowed by its effect, had lost their dazzling power; and the prospect was softened, until it seemed one vast brilliant picture, wrought with a mysteriously magic touch. Beneath the rising cloud was a vast plain, bounded only by the distant horizon. Here and there, upon its surface, there arose splendid edifices, like beautiful white marble, fashioned in the style of every age and country, canopied by the clouds; yet gilded and flooded by the mellowed light of the midday Sun. It was so beautiful . . . that it could not be lost while it lasted, and though the gathering clouds threatened to drench us with their contents, we continued to gaze until the beautiful illusion passed away."

They passed Scotts Bluff and again retold the story of the fur trader who was deserted by his companions; they paused for a few days at Fort Laramie to rest their livestock and re-equip themselves, and passed on to Bridger's new fort, which had recently been attacked by Sioux. In the middle of November, 1843, the emigrants arrived safely at the Falls of the Willamette River in Oregon, having completed their journey in about five and a half months.

At the falls was a community of about a hundred persons, and "our arrival," Johnson and Winter said, "had a great effect upon the country. The people were beginning to feel lonesome and to fear that it would be long before these far distant lands of Western America would be settled. Property was of doubtful value, and their once high anticipations were fading away. They had heard reports from the Indians, of the approach of a great number of white people; but the reports were disbelieved, and we were our own heralds; for, not until we arrived, were they convinced of our coming. Instantly everything revived; improvements went rapidly on, and the expectations of the people were again excited." Soon more enthusiastic reports would be going eastward to friends and relatives.

The War of 1812 was now long in the past, but many of the differences between the United States and Great Britain remained unsettled. Although the ascension of a more friendly government in England made it possible for Daniel Webster as secretary of state to negotiate several issues, including the boundary line between Canada and Maine and New Hampshire, he had not taken up Oregon. Tyler's attitude toward that question was shown by his statement to Congress in December, 1842. "The Territory of the United States," he said, "commonly called the Oregon Territory . . . , to a portion of which Great Britain lays claim, begins to attract the attention of our fellow-citizens. . . . In advance of acquirement of individual rights to these lands, sound policy dictates that every effort should be resorted to by the two Governments to settle their respective claims. It became manifest at an early hour in the late negotiations that any attempt for the time being satisfactorily to determine those rights would lead to a protracted discussion, which might embrace in its failure other more pressing matters, and the Executive did not regard it as proper to waive all the advantages of an honorable adjustment of other difficulties of great magnitude and importance because this, not so immediately pressing, stood in the way."

Tyler's effort to sidestep the question of Oregon in favor of other issues that he considered more immediate and potentially more explosive was only partially successful. He could stem diplomatic negotiations, but, as the number of emigrants in 1843 clearly showed, he could not stem public interest and enthusiasm. Taking advantage of the current of popular opinion, Benton and Linn pushed through provisions for another exploratory trip, this one to go beyond South Pass and, in effect, cover the whole of what had become the Oregon Trail.

Frémont was again put in charge and in the spring of 1843 began assembling the expedition at Westport, Kansas. Thomas Fitzpatrick, turning increasingly from trading and trapping to guiding, was a member and so was Charles Preuss, the topographer who had served Frémont before. Since he could not appreciably improve on his earlier survey of the Platte route, Frémont decided to strike for the mountains farther south in the hope of finding a passage through them and therefore, as he put it, "a new road to Oregon and California, in a climate more genial." As far as the emigrants' ford on the Kansas River, he followed the trail generally taken by those going west and commented, "Trains of wagons were almost constantly in sight, giving to the road a populous and animated appearance, although the greater portion of the emigrants were collected at the crossing, or already on their march beyond the Kansas River."

Staying for a time on the south side of the Kansas River, Frémont took a more direct route to the South Platte and then to the fort operated by the Bents and St. Vrain, which he reached on the Fourth of July. About ten miles up the South Platte, Frémont came to an individual trading post. Since the trader's Indian business was declining, he had turned to farming. "His post," Frémont wrote, "was beginning to assume the appearance of a comfortable farm: stock, hogs, and cattle, were ranging about on the prairie; there were different kinds of poultry; and there was the wreck of a promising garden in which a considerable variety of vegetables had been in a fluourishing condition, but it had been almost entirely ruined by the recent high waters."

Unlike most other explorers, Frémont was optimistic about the future of farming on parts of the Great Plains. "The soil of all this country," he wrote, "is excellent, admirably adapted to agricultural purposes, and would support a large agricultural and pastoral population. The plain is watered by many streams. Throughout its western half these are shallow with sandy beds, becoming deeper as they reach the richer lands approaching the Missouri River; they generally have bottom lands bordered by bluffs varying from fifty to five hundred feet in height. In all this region the timber is entirely confined to the streams. In the eastern half, where the soil is a deep, rich vegetable mould, retentive of rain and moisture, it is of vigorous growth, and of many different kinds; and throughout the western half it consists entirely of various species of cottonwood, which deserves to be called the tree of the desert—growing in sandy soils, where no other tree will grow; pointing out the existence of water, and furnishing to the traveler fuel, and food for his animals. Add to this that the western border of the plain is occupied by the Sioux, Arapaho, and Cheyenne nations, and the eastern limits of the Pawnees and other half-civilized tribes for whom the intermediate country is a war ground; and a tolerably correct idea can be formed of the appearance and condition of the country." Most people were aware of the rich lands just to the east of the Great Plains, but Frémont reiterated his faith in the agricultural future of the Great Plains themselves.

Following Fountain Creek south, he came to the Arkansas near present-day Pueblo, Colorado, and once more saw proof of the fertility of the land. A group of mountain men—most of them Americans with Mexican wives—had set up a trading and farming center. They owned a fine herd of cattle and were able to sell him a plentiful supply of milk, but little else. For Mexico, already uneasy because of the Texans' attempted expedition to

Santa Fé, were indignant over the recent murder of Antonio José Chavez, one of Santa Fé's leading citizens. Accompanied by a small group of men, he had gone to Missouri with a large amount of cash to purchase goods for resale in New Mexico. On the way a band of border ruffians attacked and robbed him. By itself, his death would have spread consternation in the governing circles of Mexico, but the incident was aggravated by the ruffians' pretending to be agents of Texas. As a consequence the Mexicans had banned all trade with either Texas or the United States, and these mountain men had no other source of goods.

This unfortunate news was offset, however, by the arrival of Kit Carson, whom Frémont sent to Bent's Fort to try to obtain mules while he did some more surveying around the headwaters of the Arkansas. By the time his expedition was reunited at Bent's Fort, he was puzzled. "I had been able," he wrote, "to obtain no certain information in regard to the character of the passes in this portion of the Rocky Mountain ranges, which had always been represented as impractical for carriages, but the exploration of which was incidentally contemplated with the view of finding some convenient point of passage for the road of emigration . . . It is singular that, immediately at the foot of the mountains, I could find no one sufficiently acquainted with them to guide us to the plains at their western base; but," he added, "the race of trappers who formerly lived in their recesses has almost entirely disappeared—dwindled to a few scattered individuals—some one or two of whom are regularly killed in the course of each year by the Indians."

Giving up hope of finding a new route through the mountains, Frémont divided his forces. Some followed the usual trail to Fort Hall, which Nathaniel Wyeth had founded, while he went up Cache la Poudre Canyon in what is now Colorado. Since Ashley had already made this journey, Frémont did not add to the Americans' basic knowledge of the country, but after leaving Fort Hall, his explorations became more extensive. He surveyed the area north of the Great Salt Lake, the valleys of the Snake and Columbia rivers, went south to Sutter's establishment, where the enterprising Swiss was establishing a thriving colony, and then turned east, following the San Joaquin Valley.

Originally the expedition had been expected to take eight months, but Frémont had found so many places to explore that it went on for fourteen, and he did not return to the vicinity of South Pass until June, 1844. His route from there should have led him east, but, as he later wrote, "Southwardly there were objects worthy to be explored . . . We therefore changed our course, and turned up the Valley of the Platte, instead of going down it.''

But Frémont knew that even the longest journey must some time end, so after exploring in the general area of the Rockies that had so entangled Pike, he emerged on the Great Plains at the Arkansas, stopped again at Bent's Fort, and headed east.

All this time Jessie had been waiting for him. He had been able to write her from the lower Columbia River in November, 1843, but that was the last word she had heard from him. As each day passed, her relatives and friends had become more concerned for her. She was still young—not yet twenty-one—and it looked as though the western half of the continent had destroyed her husband. But in August, 1844, he was back in St. Louis again and once more in her arms.

More than forty years had elapsed since Lewis and Clark had first ventured up the Missouri hoping they could find someone among the Indians or trappers who could tell them how to cross the continent. Now hundreds of people knew, not one, but several routes across the Great Plains. Even if they had never made the trip, they could obtain printed reports that described the country, and if they went, they could expect to stop at places like Forts Laramie, Bridger, Hall, and Bent's.

Even the Indians had changed. Many tribes, particularly those that had lived in permanent villages like the Mandans, were either totally extinguished or almost so, wiped out by disease or destroyed by their enemies. The balance of power among them had shifted to those relative newcomers, the Sioux, who now claimed large areas as their own and who were rapidly growing in strength and numbers.

The Indians were no longer surprised at the kinds of goods the traders brought but accepted them as part of their own way of life. To act as traders themselves was no longer possible, because they had been unable to block the white men's advance; and trading posts now operated wherever the white men found it profitable. The Indians could—and did—attack some groups when the opportunity offered, but they were no longer capable of blocking the river as the Arikaras had tried to do.

The greatest change perhaps had occurred in the fur business. The American Fur Company was still a force on the Great Plains (in 1843 Audubon, who had watched Long's expedition during its stay in Cincinnati, went up to Fort Union on a company steamboat, one of the most enjoyable of his many trips), but the rendezvous were over. No longer did the companies and independent traders make the journey into the wilderness with their pack trains of goods but, their methods having come full circle, worked out of fixed trading posts, some small, some large, but many of them catering to emigrants as well as Indians.

Buffalo robes had taken the place of beaver skins as the staple of the business, and the toll on the herds had been enormous. One official of the American Fur Company estimated that his organization was taking about seventy thousand robes a year, the Hudson's Bay Company about ten thousand, and all other companies probably another ten thousand. Commenting on the difficulties of the trade, he said, ''In the northwest the Hudson's Bay Company purchase from the Indians but a very small number—their only market being Canada, to which the cost of transportation nearly equals the produce of the furs; and it is only within a very recent period that they have received buffalo robes in trade; and out of the great number of buffalo annually killed throughout the extensive regions inhabited by the Comanches and other kindred tribes no robes whatever are furnished for trade. During only four months of the year (from November until March) the skins are good for dressing, those obtained in the remaining eight months being valueless to traders; and the hides of the bulls are never taken off or dressed as robes in any season. Probably not more than one-third of the skins are taken from the animals killed, even when they are in good season, the labor of preparing and dressing the robes being very great; and it is seldom that a lodge trades more than twenty skins a year. It is during the summer months, and in the early part of autumn, that the greatest number of buffalo are killed, and yet at this time the skin is never taken for the purpose of trade.'' Therefore the seventy thousand robes represented only a small part of the total slain annually.

The official did not mention the meat wasted in the summer. While he was at Fort Union, John James Audubon went on a buffalo hunt; and although he had a good time, he was appalled. ''What a terrible destruction of life,'' he commented, ''as it were for nothing, or next to it, as the tongues only were brought in, and the flesh of these fine animals was left to beasts and birds of prey, or to rot on the spots where they fell. The prairies are literally *covered* with the skulls of the victims. . . .''

The effect of the killing was becoming apparent. Frémont pointed out that ''the extraordinary abundance of the buffalo on the east side of the Rocky Mountains, and their extraordinary diminution,

With the passage of time, the army's posts became more luxurious. Shown here are the officers' quarters at Fort Larned, Kansas. All the wood used in the construction was, of course, imported from farther east. *Alexander B. Adams*

The slaughter of the buffaloes was a disaster for the Indians who depended on the animals' flesh for food and their skins to make tepees and warm clothing. This view of the Dodge City, Kansas, hide yard indicates the numbers killed and shipped to Eastern markets by American hunters. *National Archives*

will be made clearly evident from the following statement: At any time between the years 1824 and 1836 a traveler might start from any given point, south or north, in the Rocky Mountain range, journeying by the most direct route to the Missouri River; and during the whole distance his road would be always among large bands of buffalo, which would never be out of his view until he arrived almost within sight of the abodes of civilization. At this time [1844]," he continued, "the buffalo occupy but a very limited space, principally along the eastern base of the Rocky Mountains. . . ."

Because buffaloes were the foundation of the Plains Indians' way of life, the decrease in their numbers was causing an upheaval in the Indians' society. "In 1842," Frémont said, "I found the Sioux Indians of the Upper Plains *démontés*, as their French traders expressed it, with the failure of the buffalo; and in the following year large villages from the Upper Missouri came over to the mountains at the heads of the Platte in search of them. The rapidly progressive failure of their principal, and their almost only means of subsistence, has created great alarm among them; and at this time there are only two modes presented to them by which they see a good prospect for escaping starvation: one of these is to rob the settlements along the frontier of the States; and the other is to form a league between the various tribes of the Sioux nation, the Cheyennes and the Arapahoes [these were actually members of the Algonkin family], and make war against the Crow nation, in order to take from them their country, which is now the best buffalo country in the West." The growing shortage of the Plains Indians' most important resource was forcing the disruption of their former relationships.

Great as they were, the changes that had taken place on the plains were smaller than those that had occurred in the settled regions of the United States. In agriculture, two important implements had been invented, both of them essential to America's westward expansion. One was the plow designed by John Deere, an Illinois blacksmith. As the farmers moved into the flat, but fertile, lands east of the Mississippi, they found that their traditional plows were almost useless, for the soil clung to them, and the plowman would have to pause every few steps to remove the dirt by hand. Regardless of the land's fertility, the work of plowing was so difficult that many farmers were prepared to give up. To solve their problem, John Deere designed a plow with a highly polished moldboard and share; and in 1843, when Frémont was preparing for his

long western expedition, John Deere was taking the unusual step of ordering steel from England so he could make his plows in greater volume. (The first American steel produced to his specifications was shipped to him in 1847.)

The other agricultural implement essential to the development of the West was Cyrus McCormick's reaper. Although others had tried to develop a machine to alleviate the labor of harvesting large fields, McCormick's was the first practical reaper. He had gone into commercial production; and the year Frémont left for Oregon, he sold twenty-three of them; the year Frémont returned, fifty.

Other changes were also occurring. The transmission of information across the country was generally slow in spite of the best efforts of the Post Office Department, and letters between the West Coast and the East usually traveled in the luggage of an emigrant or the pocket of some sea captain. But in the spring of 1844, while Frémont was in the Rocky Mountains, Samuel Morse received the famous message from Baltimore, and the telegraph became a practical reality.

The sight of steamboats on American waters was no longer a novelty, but railroads were beginning to carry some of the freight and passengers the steamboat captains had once regarded as solely their own. Gradually they were creeping westward from the East, their equipment better and more standardized, thus making possible longer runs and the transfer of cars and locomotives from one road to another. Some imaginative Americans foresaw the day when a bridge or two might cross the Mississippi and trains would run from the Atlantic to the Pacific.

Perhaps the greatest change that was occurring was in the American spirit. Just before the War of 1812, when the Old Northwest Territory was beginning to fill up, Americans had looked, with thoughts of expansion, across their border into Canada, but the humiliating defeats suffered during the war had dampened the country's martial ardor. In the 1840s the desire for more territory began again to rise. The West wanted Oregon, the South wanted Texas, and there were also those who looked covetously on California. Americans were settling there, too, and Mexico had little real control over the area.

Although Tyler had carefully avoided negotiating the Oregon question with Great Britain, much to the displeasure of men like Benton, he was more than willing to consider the annexation of Texas. Under the Adams-Onís Treaty of 1819, by which the United States had acquired Florida, the government had given up all claim to Texas. During Texas's struggle with Mexico, the United States had remained officially neutral and, in the subsequent years, had rejected Texas's overtures for annexation, much to the annoyance of the young republic. The reasons for the rejections were based, not so much on respect for the Adams-Onís Treaty, as on internal political considerations.

President Tyler, however, saw many reasons for annexation. "The country [Texas] . . . ," he told the Senate, "has been settled principally by persons from the United States . . . who carried with them into the wilderness which they have partially reclaimed the laws, customs, and political institutions of their native land. They are deeply indoctrinated in all the principles of civil liberty, and will bring along with them in the act of reassociation devotion to our Union. . . . The country itself thus obtained is of incalculable value in an agricultural and commercial point of view. To a soil of inexhaustible fertility it unites a genial and healthy climate, and is destined at a day not distant to make large contributions to the commerce of the world. Its territory is separated from the United States in part by an imaginary line . . ."

He spoke of the danger of Texas coming under the influence of another nation (Great Britain was making overtures to it) with a perceptive comment on the structure of the American government: "But one view of the subject remains to be presented. It grows out of the proposed enlargement of our territory. From this, I am free to confess, I see no danger. The federative system is susceptible to the greatest expansion compatible with the ability of the representation of the most distant State or Territory to reach the seat of Government in time to participate in the functions of legislation and to make known the wants of the constituent body."

On June 8, 1844, the Senate voted on the treaty of annexation that Tyler's administration had negotiated. In spite of all Tyler's arguments, the overwhelming issue was slavery. The Senate rejected the treaty by a vote of thirty-five to sixteen.

In the election that year, Henry Clay became the candidate of the Whigs, and James K. Polk the dark-horse candidate of the Democrats. Clay was better known and more popular, but Polk more accurately sensed the mood of the nation. The people wanted to expand. Polk favored annexation of Texas, promised to handle the Oregon question, and made it clear he would like to obtain California, too, if that could be done by honorable means. Clay, on the other hand, vacillated on these issues, and Polk won the election.

The Mexican government then committed a serious error. Although it had not made a concerted effort to recapture Texas and Texas had now been recognized by several governments, it threatened to declare war on the new republic because of its annexation negotiations. Tyler seized this opportunity formally to protest Mexico's action; Mexico replied to the protest in an imperious tone, just the tone to arouse the Americans. Tyler thought he still lacked the two-thirds majority in the Senate needed to ratify the treaty, so on December 18, 1844, he sent a blistering message to both houses of Congress. Calling the menbers' attention to "the extraordinary and offensive language which the Mexican Government has thought to employ in reply" to the American protest, he suggested that both houses pass resolutions approving annexation and closed by recommending to Congress "prompt and immediate action on the subject of annexation. By adopting that measure the United States will be in the exercise of an undoubted right; and if Mexico, not regarding their forbearance, shall aggravate the injustice of her conduct by a declaration of war against them, upon her head will rest the responsibility."

A resolution required only a simple majority in each house, not a two-thirds majority of the Senate. In spite of the outcry that Tyler's strategy evoked, the resolution passed. Just a few days before he left office, James Tyler signed the treaty annexing Texas, and it became the twenty-eighth state.

Clouds of war hung over the deliberations in Washington. Mexico had made it clear that it would fight in the event of annexation, and everyone was now waiting for the formal declaration. Those interested in the West believed that another exploratory expedition was in order, this one to go farther south and examine the Rocky Mountains at the headwaters of the Arkansas and the Río Grande del Norte, and then proceed west over the Sierra Nevada to California, "so as," Frémont put it, "to ascertain the lines of communication through the mountains to the ocean in that latitude. And in arranging this expedition, the eventualities of war were taken into consideration."

In many persons' minds an immediate question was California. "Mexico, at war with the United States," Frémont wrote, "would inevitably favor British protection for California. English citizens were claiming payments for loans and indemnity for losses. Our relations with England were already clouded, and in the event of war with Mexico, if not anticipated by us, an English fleet would certainly take possession of the Bay of San Francisco. . . .

"As affairs resolved themselves," he continued, "California stood out as the chief subject of the impending war; and with Mr. Benton and other governing men at Washington it became a firm resolve to hold it for the United States. . . . This was talked over fully during the time of preparation for the third expedition, and the contingencies anticipated and weighed."

One other military problem, however, had even higher priority—the protection of the emigrants on the trail to Oregon. Their numbers were constantly increasing, but from the time they left Missouri until they reached the West Coast, they had to look entirely to their own arms for defense and could expect no assistance in an emergency except at the trading posts.

Consequently the War Department ordered Colonel Stephen Watts Kearny, commander of the Third Military District, to march with five companies of the First Dragoons from Missouri to South Pass and back. The purpose of the expedition was to impress the Indians and persuade them not to attack the ever larger emigrant trains.

"On the 18th May," Kearny reported, "I left Fort Leavenworth, being in command of 5 companies of my regiment, each 50 strong, well mounted and equipped for any service; each dragoon having his proper arms—a sabre, carbine, and pistol. Two mountain howitzers followed in the rear of the column." From Leavenworth they marched westward until they picked up the Oregon Trail, which took them to the Platte and on to Fort Laramie.

The road was crowded with emigrants, most of them going to Oregon. According to Kearny's estimates, there were about 850 men, 475 women, and around a thousand children. To carry their possessions they had about 460 wagons. With them they had also brought four hundred horses and mules and about seven thousand "cattle," a designation that included oxen. Since Major Riley's experiment when he had escorted the Santa Fé caravan, these animals had become the primary means of carrying goods across the Great Plains. But in a land where grass was always in short supply, any grazing animals in this number created a problem, for so large a herd cropped a wide swathe across the prairie, making it necessary for the emigrants and other travelers to graze their livestock farther and farther away from the trail.

At Fort Laramie, Kearny sent word to the Sioux that he wished to speak with them, and within a few days twelve hundred of them gathered to hear him. "Your great father," Kearny said, "has learned much of his red children, and has sent me with a few *braves* to visit you. I am going to the waters which flow towards the setting sun. I shall return to this place, and then march to the Arkansas, and then home. I am opening a road for the white people, and your great father directs that his red children shall not attempt to close it up. There are many whites now coming on this road, moving to the other side of the mountains; they take with them their women, children, and cattle. They all go to bury their bones there, and never to return."

He then threatened the Indians with punishment if they molested the emigrants, lectured them on the evils of whiskey, which still came into the country, and added, "I have not come among you to bring you presents; but your great father has sent a few things, that you may remember what I have said to you."

The reaction of the Indians was typical. The white men had come with presents to give them. This was simply an unexpected windfall, and they were glad. "If my people will be good to the whites," one of them said, "they will find that the presents they are about to receive will come often. Father does this very well, and pleases me." So with appreciative remarks about the gifts Kearny had brought, they expressed enthusiasm for all he said.

When the council was finished, Kearny ordered his men to hand out the blankets, tobacco, knives, looking glasses, and beads and ordered one of the howitzers fired three times. Most of the Indians had never seen a cannon before and were impressed by this display of the white men's power.

Leaving one company camped near Fort Laramie, Kearny marched with the other four to South Pass. He found that "the country is a sandy, barren desert" and said, "From near Fort Laramie to the South Pass, I do not believe that half a dozen quarter sections of land (of good soil, timber, and water) could be found, which a western farmer would settle upon . . . ."

In his official report he made several recommendations. Benton and others had long talked of a string of forts across the Great Plains to protect the emigrants. Kearny thought that an army post at Fort Laramie would be too difficult to supply. He believed, on the other hand, that a march such as his taken every few years would remind the Indians of the Americans' strength and keep them under control. He also advocated assigning an Indian agent to Bent's Fort, if for no other purpose than to try to stem the flood of whiskey coming in from the south.

He was proud, too, of the speed with which the First Dragoons had traveled, averaging better than twenty-one miles a day. He believed this proved to the Indians that the soldiers could follow them wherever they went, but he was unfamiliar with the manner in which war parties traveled. Carrying almost nothing with them, they could move much faster than that.

Frémont's preparations took longer than Kearny's, and he was not ready to leave until July, 1845. All his previous journeys had been made in peace. This time, however, he was prepared to fight, if necessary, and arrangements were made in the event of war to send him coded instructions.

He assembled a larger force than previously and secured about a dozen extra rifles that he could offer as prizes for marksmanship. "It was getting late in the year," he wrote. "The principal objects of the expedition lay in and beyond the Rocky Mountains, and for these reasons no time could be given to examinations of the prairie region. The line of travel was directed chiefly to pass over such country as would afford good camping-grounds; where water and grass, and abundant wood and abundant game would best contribute to maintain the health of the men and the strength of the animals."

As quickly as he could, he reached Bent's Fort. There he detached Lieutenant J. W. Abert, one other officer, and thirty-three men to survey the Canadian River from its source to its junction with the Arkansas. Abert also was to survey the Purgatory River and the headwaters of the Washita. That his travels would take him into Mexican territory was no longer a matter of consideration. The United States was determined to learn more about the southern Great Plains, for with the annexation of Texas and the possibility of war with Mexico, it was likely that they would come into the possession of the Americans. Then Frémont headed west to California, where he became involved in the intrigues and jealousies that eventually led to his court-martial, his bitter resignation from the army, and the end to his career as an explorer for the government.

Bent's Fort was now well established, and Abert described it in detail in his journal. It "is composed of a series of rooms resembling casemates, and forming a hollow square, the entrance on the east side. A round tower on the left, as you enter, and another diagonally opposite, constitute the flanking arrangements. The outer walls, which are nearly two feet in thickness, intersect in the axes of the towers, thus permitting their faces to be completely enfiladed . . . The coping of the wall [around the cattle yard] is planted with cacti, which bear red and white flowers. Scattered around the fort in different cages we saw some of the birds of this region—the mocking bird . . . mag-

pie, . . . and two of the bald-headed eagle . . ."

Fitzpatrick, who had guided Kearny to South Pass, had remained at Bent's Fort and was willing to serve as Abert's guide. His usefulness proved itself almost at once as he began to teach the men the skills needed on the frontier. "He directed one," Abert noted, "to loosen the noose, which, passing round the mules' nose and neck, held them so closely together as to prevent them eating; another, never to tie his mules in the bushes, for alarmed at every rustle they are constantly looking wildly around, expecting some enemy. These things may appear trifling, but those who have been upon the prairie know well how much depends upon the care and attention bestowed upon the animals."

On August 18 they at last struck their tents and started up the Purgatory. "The nature of the country," Abert said, "at first forced us into an order of travel which we now adopted from choice. It had been our practice to start at daylight, stopping a few hours during the heat of the day, and continuing our journey in the cool of the evening. We now remained in camp until the mules had grazed for an hour or two; then starting, we completed our day's march before ungearing."

Abert's immediate objective was Raton Pass, the longer, but generally safer route to Santa Fé and the one taken by those who passed Bent's Fort. He arrived there toward the end of August and started making the ascent over the mountain spur that juts into the plains. "A splendid view suddenly burst upon us," he wrote, "as we reached the point most elevated in the whole route. . . . Turning into the valley which led down the mountain, we found it at first more open than the one we had ascended the day previous; but it soon became narrower and steeper, so that we had considerable difficulty in getting our wagons over the rough and rock-strewed road. The many fragments of wagons, such as . . . axletrees, proved that those who had preceded us found it no less difficult. . . ."

"We have now finally crossed the Reton ('Retoño') of the Spaniards," Abert noted, "which is the only difficult part of the regular route to Santa Fé by the way of Bent's Fort, which we concluded to be the preferable road at all times, in which opinion we are confirmed by finding it the route most travelled this year. It is, however, 60 miles further; but the beauty of the scenery, the delightful freshness of the snow-cooled water of the mountains, with good grass and timber in abundance, give it greatly the superiority . . ." compared to the long stretches between water on the shorter route.

Abert was now well inside Mexican territory,

but his orders did not forbid him to cross the boundary line. Consequently he kept following the Canadian River even though the stream's tributaries and canyons made the traveling difficult.

While they were trying to get around a ravine that ran into the Canadian, a small black cloud in the east, Abert wrote, "suddenly enlarged and burst upon us with all the fury of a hungry tiger. The storm was terrific. The thunder crashed as if new cañons had been riven. Hail stones as large as musket balls came in profusion, pouring down obliquely, and driven by the force of a strong wind. Many endeavored to shelter themselves from the pitiless pelting by taking refuge under the lee of the wagons, which were scattered about in all directions, for the mules became ungovernable; but finding an attempt to escape from the storm useless, the leaders turned completely round, in order to be sheltered by those behind. My mule was one of the most whimsical in the band, and commenced moving about as if she thought I was pelting her with the hail stones . . . when at length, taxed beyond endurance, she humped her back like an angry cat. Knowing what would follow such a demonstration, I quickly dismounted and took shelter under the lee.

"What a situation! The hail stones had piled up so as to form dams between the tussocks of red grass, and the rain which accompanied them caused the hard ground to be covered ankle-deep in water, while the hail which whitened the prairie was one and a half inch deep. Many of the hail stones did not melt until next morning. . . . The storm was over in less than an hour. We had been looking for water, that we might encamp. Instead of dry ravines, we now found impassable torrents; and, as they bore along in their rapid currents huge fragments of fallen rock, we readily conceived the manner in which the deep channels had been excavated.

"With some difficulty we succeeded in passing one of the shallow streams, and formed our camp on a rock above. As there was a little dry grass in a neighboring valley, we concluded to remain; and by the means of a few moist rags which we sprinkled with powder, and a part of the inside of an old log which had not been wet by the rain, we were soon enabled to light our camp fire . . . and the glad song that arose that evening banished all remembrance of the afternoon's mishap."

Every night when they made camp, Abert explained, "we were always obliged to burn a place in the prairie, in the centre of which the fire is built, some of the people standing by, with blankets ready, to prevent its spreading too far. In this instance the fire got beyond all control; but, fortu-

nately, the wind was blowing from our camp, and by much exertion the fire was kept from spreading in that direction. . . . Soon it reached the trees on the side of the bank, and leaping from bough to bough, quickly despoiled them of their verdant foliage; then, mounting the bluff, was borne rapidly off over the far spreading prairie.

"About 7 o'clock in the evening it had extended to a great distance, and was rapidly advancing in a semicircular form . . . The flames having disturbed the equilibrium of the atmosphere, a counter current soon bore back a heavy black cloud, composed of three lobes, which advanced until directly over our leads, when a severe thunder storm broke upon us, illuminated by vivid flashes of lightning. In the evening we went to the top of the ridge, which skirts our valley, the better to view this grand phenomenon. The sky overhead still shrouded with clouds, which glared with the bright red reflections; the strong black which the night threw around, and the vivid light of the fire, formed a 'chiaro oscuro' which would have charmed a lover of Rembrandt. The crackling of consuming vegetation, and the low murmurings of the whirling eddies of wind which skirted the burning edge, deepened the impression of this scene of grand sublimity."

The next day, as they continued their journey, they marched over the blackened prairie. "We passed," Abert wrote, "within a few feet of the flame without any apprehension. I think that individual risk has been much exaggerated; for, by waiting the near approach of the fire, one might easily spring through and reach the space over which the devastating element had already swept off all that was inflammable. Mr. Fitzpatrick observed that he had never yet seen the fire he could not escape, by dashing quickly through the flames."

Until Abert's mission, knowledge of what is now northeastern New Mexico and northwestern Texas had been largely restricted to the traders who used the Santa Fé Trail—from which they rarely strayed—and the *comancheros*, who were unequipped to write down what they knew. But Abert, with a competent staff and the proper instruments, was able to render a full report of the places he had seen; and since the report was printed, it became available to anyone.

The remainder of his travels took him to the North Fork of the Canadian and eventually to Fort Gibson on the Arkansas, where once again he and his men enjoyed the comforts of civilization. On leaving Fort Gibson, he could see ahead that the road was "literally lined with the wagons of emigrants to Texas, and from this time until we arrived in St. Louis, we continued daily to see hundreds of them.'' The United States was moving west, in both the north and the south.

The nation waited, but Mexico did not declare war. Its government was new and untried, its president a moderate general who had been chosen to replace the recently overthrown dictator, Santa Anna. Although the Mexican ambassador at Washington had lodged a formal protest and demanded his passports, Polk thought there was a chance of settling the differences between the two countries without resorting to arms. In fact, the Mexican foreign minister agreed to receive, not an ambassador, but at least a commissioner to discuss the two countries' problems.

Polk's agent, John Slidell, went to Mexico City with several questions to resolve. The most immediate was the boundary line of Texas. Historically it had been the Nueces River, which enters the Gulf of Mexico just north of Corpus Christi, but the Texans claimed that the terms of Santa Anna's surrender at San Jacinto entitled them to a boundary at the Río Grande, which was considerably farther south.

Polk also wanted to obtain California. The *conquistadores* and priests had early worked up the coast, and they had been followed by settlers, but the Spanish had never been able to establish themselves firmly, and Mexico had done little better. Its hold on the fertile and beautiful land was slight, and the United States feared that Great Britain might seize it.

There were some unsettled claims between the United States and Mexico, several million dollars' worth. These had arisen from various causes, including the summary execution of several Americans whom the Mexican government had suspected of assisting a revolution. Mexico had admitted the claims but, bankrupt as it usually was, had been unable to pay them. Polk, however, was willing to accept land in payment, and in addition to California, he also had his eyes on New Mexico. Although Slidell had been invited to discuss these problems, as soon as word spread in Mexico City that the United States was offering to buy territory, the uproar was great, and a revolution which placed more reactionary elements in power immediately took place.

Meanwhile Polk had ordered General Zachary Taylor to take up a position at Corpus Christi. When Polk learned in January, 1846, of Mexico's refusal to receive Slidell, he ordered Taylor to the Río Grande.

Taylor began building a fort on the Río Grande

and blockaded the river. The Mexican commander on the opposite side attacked him and inflicted several casualties. Without knowing about this, Polk called a meeting of his cabinet on May 9 to discuss sending a war message to Congress. His grounds for such drastic action were, however, weak; but that evening he received news of the attack on Taylor, and his last cause for hesitation vanished. Although it was against his principles to work on the Sabbath, he spent Sunday preparing his message to Congress. What argument could not achieve, the American casualty list did. Within a few days both the House and the Senate overwhelmingly voted for war.

Although the Mexican army outnumbered the American by about five to one (army positions were important patronage), Polk moved aggressively. Taylor was ordered to advance south, Frémont was already in California, naval vessels had previously gone to the West Coast, and Stephen Watts Kearny was ordered to recruit volunteers and lead them and the First Dragoons to New Mexico, capture it, and then proceed to California. It was a bold plan, designed to end the war as quickly as possible and with little bloodshed.

Busy as he was with the Mexican War, Polk did not forget the Oregon question. During his campaign he had insisted on a boundary at 54° 40', but after his election, he had offered a compromise with the British on the 49th parallel. The British ambassador had refused bluntly without even referring the offer to London and demanded that the boundary be set at the Columbia River. Polk reacted by reverting to his previous position.

In 1846 a change of government in London and various considerations, such as England's dependence on the United States as a marketplace, made the British people less willing to fight over the remote corner of Canada. They therefore expressed a willingness to accept the 49th parallel after all. At first Polk was reluctant, but members of his cabinet urged him to accept. Finally he agreed to follow an unusual course. Instead of sending a treaty to the Senate for ratification and thus obtaining its ''consent,'' he submitted it unsigned and asked for its prior ''advice.'' On June 12 the Senate voted to accept the treaty. Polk signed it, and the Senate ratified it on June 18. The long-standing dispute with Great Britain was finally settled.

To Kearny at Fort Leavenworth the Oregon question was of minor importance, for he was having difficulty assembling what would be known as the Army of the West. On June 6, the day that the British ambassador formally proposed a boundary line at the 49th parallel, two companies of dragoons set forth for the Arkansas; and by June 29 Kearny reported that more than fifteen hundred men were on their way in the direction of New Mexico. He himself planned to leave the following day, and two more companies were to follow.

Altogether his command comprised more than sixteen hundred men, among them Lieutenant J. W. Abert of the Topographical Corps. Following them was the Mormon Battalion, recruited entirely from members of that sect. In trouble again with their neighbors, many of them had expressed a desire to move to the West Coast. By enlisting in the army, they received pay while making the move; and the government, in addition to obtaining their services, removed a source of potential internal disturbance.

The adventures of the soldiers were typical of those who traveled the Santa Fé Trail. Sometimes their mules stampeded; they saw rattlesnakes and prairie dogs; the wind blew, and the rains pelted them; they marveled at the great herds of buffaloes and shot many of them; and some of them fell ill, as was inevitable in such a large body. One of these was Kearny himself, who had to be carried in one of the light wagons used by the Topographical Corps, as the heavy, springless wagons used by the traders were too uncomfortable.

Abert also became sick before they reached Bent's Fort, and although they carried him that far, they left him there to recuperate. At the fort Abert talked to Yellow Wolf, a Cheyenne chief, and "a man of considerable influence, of enlarged views, and gifted with more foresight than any other man of his tribe," Abert said. "He frequently talks of the diminishing numbers of his people, and the decrease of the once abundant buffalo. He says that in a few years they will become extinct; and unless the Indians wish to pass away also, they will have to adopt the habits of the white people, using such measures to produce subsistence as will render them independent of the precarious reliance afforded by the game.

"He has proposed to the interpreter at Bent's fort, to give him a number of mules in the proportion of one from every man in the tribe, if he would build them a structure similar to Bent's fort, and instruct them to cultivate the ground, and to raise cattle." With unusual wisdom, as Abert pointed out, "he says that for some time his people would not be content to relinquish the delights of the chase, and then the old men and squaws might remain at home cultivating the grounds, and be safely secured in their fort from the depredations of hostile tribes."

Although Abert appealed for American support

of the Cheyennes, Yellow Wolf's idea died. But he had foreseen the disaster that was approaching for the Plains Indians, and his plan for meeting it was realistic.

All the reports from Santa Fé indicated that Armijo, who was still governor, planned to resist the American advance. Kearny sent emissaries ahead in the hope that he could obtain a peaceful surrender, but to no avail. Consequently he was cautious when he led his men over Raton Pass and into New Mexico and began to advance again over the Great Plains.

About sixteen miles from Las Vegas, New Mexico, a Mexican lieutenant with a small escort met Kearny and advised him that Armijo planned to come to Las Vegas to negotiate with him. Kearny replied that he would be glad to talk with the governor, and the lieutenant rode off.

Las Vegas was a small oasis in the wilderness. "There was," Abert later said, "a large open space in the middle of the town; the streets run north and south, east and west; the houses are built of 'adobes.' The 'azoteas,' or roofs, have just enough inclination to turn the rain, and the walls of the house, which are continued up one foot above the roof, are pierced for this purpose. Through the midst of the town there was a large 'acequia,' or canal, for the purpose of supplying the town with water, and of irrigating the fields." But there was no sign of Armijo.

Somewhat perplexed by his elusive enemy, Kearny took great pains not to offend the inhabitants of Las Vegas. He placed guards to prevent his livestock from getting into their cornfields, and he ordered his men to pay for everything they took. After that he asked the *alcalde* and the two militia captains who were in the village to accompany him to the roof of one of the buildings. From there he addressed the people assembled in the plaza below, promising them that their religious and property rights would be respected but proclaiming the sovereignty of the United States. He then told the three officials standing with him that he would continue them in office provided they swore allegiance to the United States. Reluctantly they took the oath.

Since Armijo failed to appear, Kearny moved on. The route to Santa Fé led through a narrow canyon some miles from Las Vegas, and Kearny was told that six hundred Mexicans were prepared to ambush him there. When he approached the spot, the advance guard drew their sabers in preparation for a fight. "When we arrived, however, at the place where we expected to engage with the enemy," one soldier remarked, "to our great disappointment, the Mexicans had dispersed, and there was no one to oppose our march.'' On further consideration, he added, ''It is perhaps better thus to have gained a bloodless victory by the terror of our arms, than to have purchased it with blood and loss of life.''

Following the trail first taken by the Spaniards hundreds of years before, the Army of the West moved toward Santa Fé through the town of San Miguel, past the Indian pueblo at Pecos, over the mountains, down to the Río Grande, and into the capital city. No army opposed them, for Armijo—frightened, bribed, or perhaps both—had fled the province. Repeating the pattern he had used at Las Vegas, Kearny promised to protect the people in all their rights but compelled their officials to swear allegiance to the United States. He also asserted American sovereignty over the entire province, not just over the old Texas claim to the Río Grande. Then he marched his army west to participate in the capture of California.

When the Army of the West crossed the mountains into the Río Grande Valley, the Mexican War ended for the American Great Plains, but it did not end for the people who were fighting it. California fell to the Americans almost like one of its own ripe plums ready for the picking, but the Mexican government refused to capitulate and come to terms with the United States.

Finally General Winfield Scott landed at Vera Cruz in March, 1847, and began fighting his way toward Mexico City, which he captured in September. The existing Mexican government fell and was replaced with one more moderate and willing to negotiate with the Americans.

By the Treaty of Guadalupe Hidalgo, Mexico ceded California and New Mexico to the United States and recognized the Río Grande as the southern boundary of Texas. Counting Texas, Mexico had lost almost half of its territory. In return the United States paid $15 million and agreed to assume more than $3 million in American claims.

That winter when he addressed Congress, Polk said, ''Occupying, as we do, a more commanding position among nations than at any former period, our duties and responsibilities to ourselves and to posterity are correspondingly increased . . . Within less than four years the annexation of Texas to the Union has been consummated; all conflicting title to the Oregon Territory . . . has been adjusted, and New Mexico and Upper California have been acquired by treaty. The area of these several Territories, . . . over which our exclusive jurisdiction and dominion have been extended, constitute a country more than half as large as all that which was held by the United States before their acquisition. . . . The Mississippi, so lately the frontier of our country, is now only its center.''

Part III 1848-1892

From the Gold Rush
to the End of the Frontier

Chapter 23

Gold!

It was known that mines of the precious metals existed to a considerable extent in California . . . Recent discoveries render it probable that these mines are more extensive and valuable than was anticipated. The accounts of the abundance of gold in that territory are of such an extraordinary character as would scarcely command belief if they were not corroborated by the authentic reports of officials in the public service . . . The effect produced by the discovery of these rich deposits and the success which has attended the labors of those who have resorted to them have produced a surprising change in the state of affairs in California. Labor commands a most exorbitant price, and all other pursuits but that of searching for the precious metals are abandoned. Nearly the whole of the male population of the country have gone to the gold districts. Ships arriving on the coast are deserted by their crews and their voyages suspended for want of sailors. Our commanding officer there entertains apprehensions that soldiers cannot be kept in the public service without a large increase in pay.

—James K. Polk, 1848

The old order had been dying, and at the conclusion of the Mexican War only vestiges of it remained. Some white men still traded with the Indians for furs, and a few still trapped; but the great power of the fur companies was gone and so most of the mountain men who still remained had turned to other pursuits. Bridger, for example, was catering to the emigrant trade, and Fitzpatrick was spending much of his time as a government guide.

The road to Santa Fé was open again, but it no longer passed through alien territory. When the traders crossed the Arkansas, they did not leave the protection of the United States government, and a Major Riley could have followed them all the way to their destination without creating international complications. The Oregon Trail across the Great Plains was so clearly marked that the most innocent tenderfoot, while he might have trouble finding wood and water or handling the Indians, could not conceivably have lost his way. The wagon ruts and heavily grazed prairie marked the route as clearly as the signposts lining the central avenue of a metropolis.

The Americans who pushed westward were not going in the expectation of making a quick fortune and then returning home. In fact, as Kearny had told the Sioux, most of them thought they would never see their homes again and planned "to bury their bones" in some new settlement. But although they were moving to a strange land, it was not a foreign one. True to the spirit of the Northwest Ordinance, enacted so many years ago, they knew that the areas in which they planned to live would soon become part of the United States.

Steps in this direction had already been proposed by Polk. In December, 1848, he told Congress that the new acquisitions "will add more to the strength and wealth of the nation than any which have preceded them since the adoption of the Constitution. But," he immediately added, "to effect these great results not only California, but New Mexico, must be brought under the control of regularly organized governments. The existing condition of California and of that part of New Mexico lying west of the Río Grande and without the limits of Texas imperiously demands that Congress should at its present session organize Territorial governments over them." That, of course, was the first stage toward statehood in the American political system that ensured a single country, not a fatherland with satellites.

At the same time the Great Plains were slowly changing the Americans. The seven thousand oxen that Kearny observed the emigrants driving to Oregon were one indication. Americans had been accustomed to farming and had used oxen to pull the stones from New England fields for years, but they were not notably herdsmen. Yet on the Oregon Trail they depended on oxen as never before, both for food and to move their heavy wagons. The wagons, too, were uniquely American, for the older, more familiar types would not hold up under the hard usage of the plains. So they had been modified—made larger and stronger than traditional American wagons—and became the "prairie schooner." Americans were also turning into a nation of horsemen. They had always used horses, but on the Great Plains, where no forests blocked the way and the distances were so great, horses were becoming a necessity. Even the infantry were placed on horses and became dragoons.

Other changes, less fundamental but also significant, had taken place. The Mormons, who had hoped to entrench themselves at Nauvoo, Illinois, again found themselves hated and resented by their neighbors and moved once more, this time to Winter Quarters, as they called the present site of Omaha, Nebraska. From there Brigham Young led a party of less than two hundred people west over the plains and mountains to the Great Salt Lake. Sick with mountain fever that he had contracted in the Rockies, Young was riding in an improvised bed on one of the wagons, when he came to an overlook. "It is enough," he said. "This is the right place."

The group had brought with them equipment and supplies to start a settlement and immediately laid out a town and began building a wooden fort to protect them from the Indians. That summer, while Winfield Scott was fighting his way to Mexico City, Brigham Young returned east to Winter Quarters to organize another large party for the following year. The great Mormon exodus to Utah had begun.

The Mexican War brought a fortune of sorts to Samuel Colt. Despairing of ever getting enough orders to justify the commercial production of his firearms, he had closed his New Jersey factory. But the war made the War Department less conservative in its choice of weapons, and Colt finally received the government contract he had so long wanted. He entered into an agreement with Eli Whitney, the inventor of the cotton gin, to manufacture his guns. Although the contract was not well drawn, so he did not receive the profit he might have expected, the six-shooter became a part of Western history.

The war years also brought new pressure on Congress to expand the Post Office Department. Letters had been passing between the East and Far West, but on an informal basis. Correspondents had to entrust their mail to individuals who were making the trip or sometimes to persons who were going only partway but who, in turn, would hand the letters on to someone else. Now that the West Coast was part of the United States, such unsystematic methods of communication were no longer acceptable, and Congress began searching for a means of establishing official postal service between the two sections of the country. In solving the problem, the Great Plains and the mountains that lay west of them seemed like an insurmountable barrier, so Congress authorized the construction of steamboats that would take the mail to Panama for transshipment to the Pacific, thus reducing the overland part of the journey from thousands of miles to less than a hundred.

The event that touched off the biggest change, however, occurred so quietly in California that it passed for some time almost unnoticed. Although John Sutter's establishment on the Sacramento River had been started only a few years earlier, it had thrived, largely as a result of his wise and efficient management. It was, however, plagued by one problem: a shortage of wood that bothered his local carpenter, James Wilson Marshall, and some of the emigrants who thought of making their homes there.

To remedy this, Marshall persuaded Sutter to let him build a sawmill about forty-five miles away on the South Fork of the American River. At a place called Coloma, there was a good supply of standing timber and plenty of water; and in August, 1847, Marshall and a crew of men set to work. In January, 1848, Marshall decided to enlarge a sluice that cut through a sandbar. While doing this, he noticed some glittering particles in the sand. Immediately he collected samples and took them to Sutter, who examined them in light of what he knew about metals and what he could learn from an encyclopedia he owned. When he pronounced them gold, Marshall dashed back to Coloma in the middle of the night. Both men had reason, of course, for keeping quiet about the discovery, although they did not yet recognize its magnitude. Sutter permitted the sawmill crew to pan for gold, provided they limited themselves to Sundays, and he arranged to lease some nearby land from the Indians. The news, of course, could not be kept secret, but no one was excited. Tales of gold discoveries made commonplace conversation around campfires. Yet few of the tales had ever proved true.

Samuel Brannan, a Mormon who had led a group to San Francisco, had been investing the Mormon's money in profitable enterprises and building up a commercial empire that included a store at Sutter's Fort. When he noticed that Sutter's employees were increasingly offering gold dust to pay for their purchases, he saw a chance to enlarge his own fortune. Quietly he began buying every article in northern California that a gold seeker might want; and in May, 1848, when he was convinced that he had cornered the market, he started a gold rush. With a bottle of gold dust in one hand, he entered San Francisco and shouted, "Gold from the American River!"

A few remained skeptical, but the majority started for the river—after, of course, buying the equipment that Brannan alone could supply. Since the report, although intended as a fake, turned out to be real, the fever spread. Toward the end of May, the San Francisco *Californian* reported, "The whole country, from San Francisco to Los Angeles, and from the sea shore to the base of the Sierra Nevadas, resounds with the sordid cry of gold, GOLD, GOLD! while the field is left half-planted, the house half-built, and everything neglected but the manufacture of shovels and pick-axes." The same issue also carried an announcement that the paper was suspending publication, because almost its entire staff was going to the goldfields. In one California town when the jailer could find no one willing to guard his prisoners, he took them to the American River with him and set them to work. And the American military commander could not stop desertions from the armed forces, for a lucky soldier might make in a few days more money than he could earn in the army over a period of years.

The New York *Herald* of August 19 carried a notice from a San Franciscan correspondent that said in part, "The gold mine discovered . . . on the south branch of the American fork . . . is only three feet below the surface, in a strata of soft sand rock. From explorations south twelve miles and north five miles, the continuance of this strata is reported, and the mineral said to be equally abundant, and from twelve to eighteen feet in thickness: so that without allowing any golden hopes to puzzle my prophetic vision of the future, I would predict for California a Peruvian harvest of the precious metals, as soon as a sufficiency of miners can be obtained.''

Such a report, however, did not arouse much interest in the East, and although miners came to California from distant places like Hawaii and Peru—perhaps as many as six thousand—few east of the Mississippi made the journey to the goldfields in 1848. Polk, however, needed reason to justify the Mexican War, which, toward its end, had become increasingly unpopular with a large segment of the population; and when he received detailed confirmation from military officers in California of the extent of the find, he incorporated the subject into his annual message. The discovery of gold in California not only provided an opportunity for individuals to make their fortunes, but would also benefit American commerce as a whole.

"If a branch mint," he said, "be established at the great commercial point upon that [West] coast, a vast amount of bullion and specie would flow thither to be recoined, and pass thence to New Orleans, New York and other Atlantic cities. The amount of our constitutional currency at home would be greatly increased, while its circulation abroad would be promoted. It is well known to our merchants trading to China and the west coast of America that great inconvenience and loss are experienced from the fact that our coins are not current at their par value in those countries." The whole nation would prosper from "these mines [that] are more extensive and valuable than was anticipated." The inflammatory words were followed in a few days by the arrival of an army officer in Washington with a tea caddy filled with 230 ounces of gold. This was displayed at the War Department, and the gold rush was on.

The successful conclusion of the Mexican War and the favorable settlement of the Oregon question would in themselves have stimulated the westward migration of the Americans, for they made it possible for those who took up land to secure a firm title. But the emigration that started in 1849 dwarfed anything that would have occurred without Marshall's finding gold and Polk's publicizing it. Gold fever became almost as epidemic among the white men as smallpox had been among the Indians. No class of society was immune to it except perhaps the clergy. Farmers were willing to sell their farms in order to get to the American River, lawyers and doctors to give up their practices and leave their wives. The poor thought they would get rich, the rich thought they would get richer. Some of the gold-seekers were graduates of universities, some could barely write their own names. Some were persons of great honesty, others were crooks and thieves of the lowest sort. Some went for the adventure and thrills, others because they were looking for a means of providing for their families. All they had in common was the desire to see the flash of gold in the bottom of their pans.

Five routes led to California. The least used passed through the Southwest, first to Santa Fé and then along the trail developed by the New Mexicans to the coast. This was difficult and relatively unknown. A second was by ship around Cape Horn. Practical only for those who lived on the East Coast, this voyage could be made in comparative comfort except for the passage around the Horn itself. Hundreds of ships sailed out of ports like Boston and New York crammed with gold-seeking passengers who hoped to find their fortunes. But this route could be taken only by the comparatively well-to-do, for the cost ranged from about $300 up. A third route, one used by those living in Louisiana and other Gulf Coast states, took them by water to Panama; but during the trip across the Isthmus, they risked exposure to disease and possible long delays; and the journey, like the voyage around Cape Horn, was expensive. Another route, also expensive, was to go to Vera Cruz, cross Mexico, and then go by boat to California.

The fifth route—and the most popular—took the traveler across the Great Plains. It was filled with hazards—most people knew of the horrors endured by the Donner Party trapped in the mountain wastes—but it was relatively inexpensive. It was possible to go by railroad and boat from New York to Missouri for less than $50. A net investment of a little more than $50 apiece for a party of four would provide the equipment for going the rest of the way, bringing the total cost to less than $100. Not all those who traveled the Oregon-California Trail were poor, but poor men could rarely use any of the other alternatives.

As in the past, there were a number of starting points, but the three communities that made a business—often a highly profitable one—of equipping emigrants were Westport, Kansas, and Independence and St. Joseph, Missouri. Sometimes the emigrants went alone; sometimes they organized their groups before leaving home. Several citizens of Boston, for example, incorporated the Mount Washington Mining Company in March, 1849. It had approximately fifty members, most of them from Boston or nearby, although two each came from Vermont and New Hampshire.

"Our company," wrote one of the participants, "was composed of men from many different walks in life, among them lawyers, doctors, preachers, teachers, students, merchants, clerks, and mechanics. The larger number of them were in the prime of their manhood, though several students from institutions of learning were but little past their majority." Many of the emigrants, however, went to the starting points as individuals, hoping to attach themselves to some large group for the trip through the wilderness.

Usually they took the steamboat from St. Louis to their point of departure, for boats now ran regularly on the Missouri. Alonzo Delano, an emigrant from Illinois in the spring of 1849, described his traveling companions on the voyage from St. Louis to St. Joseph aboard the *Embassy.* "There was," he wrote, "a great crowd of adventurers on the *Embassy.* Nearly every State in the Union was represented. Every berth was full, and not only every settee and table occupied at night, but the cabin floor was covered by the sleeping emigrants. The decks were covered with wagons, mules, oxen, and mining implements, and the hold was filled with supplies. But this was the condition of every boat—for since the invasion of Rome by the Goths, such a deluge of mortals had not been witnessed, as was now pouring from the States to the various points of departure for the golden shores of California. Visions of sudden and immense wealth were dancing in the imaginations of these anxious seekers of fortunes, and I must confess that I was not entirely free from such dreams . . . I wondered what I would do with all the money that must necessarily come into my pocket!"

But the trip up the Missouri, although safe now from Indians, carried its own hazards, for such concentrations of people quickly spread disease. On the second day out the cry went around the *Embassy,* "The cholera is on board!" "At length," Delano wrote, "calmness gained the ascendancy, and excitement passed away; but the subdued tones of those who had been the most gay, attested the interest which they felt in the melancholy announcement. A young gentleman, belonging to a company from Virginia . . . expired at ten o'clock on the morning after he was taken ill. It was a melancholy spectacle, to see one who had left home with high hopes of success, so prematurely stricken down . . ."

On landing at St. Joseph, Delano learned that the party he intended to join had moved farther up the river "where they would halt until the grass was sufficiently advanced to afford forage for our cattle . . .'' He and his companions could not stay at St. Joseph, "as every public house in town was crowded by emigrants to overflowing," so they camped for the night in their wagons. Before daybreak they heard the cries and moans of one of their men. He, too, had come down with cholera and, in spite of all they could do for him, shortly died.

The Mount Washington Mining Company had the same problems. Going up the Missouri to Independence, two of the boat's crew died of cholera, and before reaching Independence, one of their own members had also died. Outside Independence, they found a grove of oak trees where they went into camp. For more than a month they remained there, while thirteen more members of their party came down with cholera, four of whom died.

If they escaped death from disease before starting across the Great Plains, they had other problems with which to contend. As Reuben Shaw, who was with the Mount Washington Mining Company, remarked, "While some of our men were caring for the sick, others were scouring the country for mules and horses to complete our outfit . . . We found the buying of such animals as was required in that sparsely settled country a difficult task, as the supply near at hand had been exhausted by parties making an earlier start."

Some of the mules they purchased had seen service in the Mexican War; and although they looked in poor shape, having received little care during the winter, they proved serviceable. Others, however, had not been broken. "A number of our mules," Shaw said, "were never thoroughly subdued until reaching the alkali region, by which time they had worn themselves out and became food for coyotes."

Not only were goods and animals scarce, sellers demanded the highest possible prices. Since two of Shaw's companions were still so weak from their recent illness that they could not ride, the company wanted to buy an ambulance. "We therefore purchased," he wrote, "the running-gear of an old spring wagon, which had seen many years of hard service and been thrown aside as worthless, though the owner made it appear very cheap at ten dollars . . ."

Once on their way, the various parties took different routes, depending on their departure points, but they all had a common destination, the valley of the Big Blue River which flows south into the Kansas River. Here the routes converged, and all the parties began taking the Oregon-California Trail proper. They next picked up the Little Blue. Its valley ran northwest toward the Platte, and its headwaters were only an easy day's journey to the larger river. Thus the emigrants, by staying to the road, were sure of a good supply of water.

The increase in emigration had caused the government to take another look at the protection afforded travelers, and the year before it had built a new fort, Kearny, on the Platte River in Nebraska—it replaced another fort of the same name, which had been erected too far from the road—and here the travelers sometimes tried to sell the surplus supplies they had brought. Flour and bacon often went for as little as one cent a pound, and what the men at the post did not buy was thrown away.

Those going west were not making a lonely, isolated trip into the wilderness. Ahead of or behind them they could see the wagons of their own or other parties, the drivers often walking beside the oxen, while women, children, and the weak rode. A start early in the year was not possible, because the travelers had to wait for the grass to spring up high enough to feed their stock, but by May 24, 1849, 1,980 wagons had already rumbled past Fort Kearny, and yet they still kept coming. By May 28, the total had risen to 2,500, two hundred of them in that one day alone; and by the middle of June, it had reached 5,400.

As one of the emigrants who kept a journal said, "Although I speak particularly of our own train, and the events that came under my own eye, the reader should remember that there were probably twenty thousand people on the road west of Missouri, and that our trains did not travel for an hour without seeing many others, and hundreds of men. For days we would travel in company with other trains, which would stop to rest, when we would pass them; and then perhaps we would lay up, and they pass us. Some we would meet again after many days, and others, perhaps, never."

Since the emigrants traveled so close to each other on the road, they often visited back and forth and sometimes would unexpectedly find an old friend in another group. Particularly in the evening, if there was enough grass and water, they would camp near each other. "It was curious," wrote one, "to see the quaint names and devices on some of the wagons; the 'Lone Star,' would be seen rising over a hill; the 'Live Hoosier' rolled along; the 'Wild Yankee,' the 'Rough and Ready,' the 'Enterprise,' the 'Dowdle Family,' were moving with slow and steady pace, with a 'right smart sprinkle' of 'Elephants,' 'Buffaloes,' and 'Gold Hunters,' painted on the canvas of the wagons, together with many other quite amusing devices. Around the camp-fires at night, the sound of a violin, clarionet, banjo, tambourine, or bugle would be frequently heard, merrily chasing off the weariness and toil of the travelers, who sometimes 'tripped the light fantastic toe' with as much hilarity and glee, as if they had been in a luxurious ballroom at home." Yet all was not gaiety, for he continued, ". . . when morning came, and the day's work commenced, too frequently ill-humor began; and the vilest oaths, the most profane language, and frequent quarrels and feuds, took the place of good humor, which not infrequently required all the patience that a quiet man is possessed of to endure."

The causes for bad humor were many, including disease and death. Captain Howard Stansbury of the Topographical Engineers took the trail that year to make a survey of the valley of the Great Salt Lake. On June 1, he wrote, "In the course of the afternoon we passed the travelling-train of a Mr. Allen, consisting of about twenty-five ox-teams, bound for the land of gold. They had been on the spot several days, delayed by sickness. One of the party had died but the day before of cholera, and two more were then down with the same disease." Five days later, he noted that "in the course of the morning, [we] passed the fresh grave of a poor fellow whose last resting-place had been partially disturbed by the wolves. They had burrowed a large hole near the head, which, however, had been subsequently filled up with sticks by some compassionate traveler. It was an affecting object, and no good omen of what might be looked for, should any of us fall by the way in our long and arduous journey."

Only two days later they passed another fresh grave. "It was heaped up with earth," Stansbury said, "and covered longitudinally with heavy split logs, placed there to prevent the depredations of wolves; the whole being surmounted by a wooden cross, with the name of the deceased and the usual significant abbreviation, IHS, carved rudely upon it. We had passed six graves already during the day. Melancholy accompaniments they are . . . and ill-calculated to cheer the weary, drooping wayfarers. . . . Just above us was a wagon with a small party of emigrants. They had lost most of their cattle on the journey; and the father of three of them having died on the road, they in conformity with his dying wishes, were now on their return to the settlements. A short distance beyond these, we found another small company, which had been encamped here for twelve days on account of the illness of one of their comrades. They were also on their return. Had we been going out on a private enterprise," Stansbury added, "discouragements were not wanting as well from the dead as the living."

Not all the graves, however, contained human bodies. Stansbury wrote that he witnessed "an instance of no little ingenuity on the part of some emigrant. Immediately alongside the road was what purported to be a grave, prepared with more than usual care, having a headboard on which was painted the name and age of the deceased, the time of his death, and the part of the country from which he came. I afterward ascertained that this was only a ruse to conceal the fact that the grave, instead of containing the mortal remains of a human being, had been made a safe receptacle for divers casks of brandy, which the owner could carry no further." But, Stansbury added, "he afterward sold his liquor to some traders farther on, who, by his description of the locality found it without difficulty."

Much of the travelers' unhappiness came from their own lack of experience. In spite of the various guidebooks that were being published, few of them were well prepared for the journey. Stansbury met a trader with a train of fur-laden wagons. "He had been forty days on the road," Stansbury noted, "and had met not less than four thousand wagons, averaging four persons to a wagon. This large number of emigrants appeared to him to be getting along rather badly, from their want of experience as to the proper mode of travelling on the prairies, to which cause much of the suffering experienced on those plains is doubtless to be ascribed."

At Fort Kearny he noticed the pack train of a party of New Englanders. They knew nothing about making up their loads, and as a result their mules were in horrible condition with galled backs and sides. Many of the others overloaded their oxen, and some of them made the canvas tops of their wagons so large that it was difficult to drive them against the wind. But the most common error was trying to take too many possessions to their new homes in the West.

Stansbury "passed an old Dutchman, with an immense wagon, drawn by six yoke of oxen, and loaded with household furniture. Behind, followed a covered cart containing the wife, driving herself, and a host of babies—all bound to the land of promise, the distance to which, however, they seemed to have not the most remote idea. To the tail of the cart was attached a large chicken-coop, full of fowls; two milch-cows followed, and next came an old mare, upon the back of which was perched a little, brown-faced, barefooted girl, not more than seven years old, while a small sucking colt brought up the rear.'' The soldiers passed and repassed this man several times, and, Stansbury said, when they last noticed him he was ''engaged in sawing his wagon into two parts, for the purpose of converting it into two carts, and in disposing of everything he could sell or give away, to lighten his load.''

In places the trail was littered with the belongings of emigrants, and Narcissa Whitman would have smiled at the memory of her little trunk in comparison. ''We passed to-day,'' Stansbury remarked at one point, ''the nearly consumed fragments of about a dozen wagons that had been broken up and burned by their owners; and near them was piled up, in one heap, from six to eight hundred weight of bacon, thrown away for want of means to transport it farther. Boxes, bonnets, trunks, wagon-wheels, whole wagon-bodies, cooking utensils, and, in fact, almost every article of household furniture, were found from place to place along the prairie, abandoned for the same reason.''

At another time, he remarked that ''the road has been literally strewn with articles that have been thrown away. Bar-iron and steel, large blacksmith's anvils and bellows, crow-bars, drills, augers, gold-washers, chisels, axes, lead, trunks, spades, ploughs, large grindstones, baking-ovens, cooking-stoves without number, kegs, barrels, harness, clothing, bacon, and beans were found along the road. . . .''

Discipline was as necessary as it had ever been while traveling across the Great Plains and as difficult to enforce. Men sometimes refused to do their assigned chores, quarreled with each other, and occasionally murdered each other during the journey. Most of the groups adopted some sort of self-government to preserve order, the forms and formality varying from party to party.

Some went to impractical extremes. Colonel Joseph S. Watkins, who had been a member of the Virginia legislature for twenty-one years, explained to Delano that his party ''were seventy strong, having a republican and military form of government, a constitution and by-laws, a president and vice-president, a legislature, three judges, and court of appeals, nine sergeants as well as other officers, who, by their laws, were to be exempted from the performance of camp duty by virtue of their dignified stations—leaving it for the plebeans and common soldiers to do the drudgery of camp duty, and of standing guard at night. All this read very well on paper, and quite to the satisfaction of

those who were to do the labor, but reduced to practice, it was not strange that it produced murmuring, which ripened into actual rebellion.''

Watkins petitioned the ''legislature'' to amend the constitution, but after considerable discussion he was called out of order, because he was not a member of that body. Since none of those who were would introduce his proposal, Watkins withdrew from the party, taking with him thirteen other wagons. ''Thus,'' Delano said, ''this sublime government fell to pieces by weight of its own machinery and exclusive privileges.''

The coming of the emigrants had created numerous changes along the road since the day when Ashley had led his pack train up the barely explored Platte. Fort Kearny, of course, was new and erected for their protection; and the government had purchased Fort Laramie from the American Fur Company.

Between Courthouse Rock, one of the landmarks on the trail, and Chimney Rock, emigrants had picked out a ledge to serve as a post office. ''It was full of water-worn fissures,'' Delano wrote, ''and in one cavity we saw a number of letters deposited, for individuals who were behind, and in the rock was cut in capitals, 'Post-Office.' The usual mode of giving intelligence to friends behind, is to write on a bleached buffalo skull, or shoulder-blade. Thousands of these novel communications lay upon the plain, and we frequently got intelligence in this way from acquaintances who preceded us.''

Regular mail across the Great Plains, was, of course, nonexistent, but those persons going east would sometimes offer to carry letters back, usually charging twenty-five cents or more for each one. As many of the communications never reached their destination, the emigrants decided the supposed couriers merely pocketed the money and threw away the mail. Other services, however, were somewhat more honest. At Scotts Bluff an enterprising man, Stansbury remarked, had set up a blacksmith's shop, ''established for the benefits of the emigrants, but especially for that of the owner, who lives in an Indian lodge, and had erected a log shanty by the roadside, in one end of which was the blacksmith's forge, and in the other a grog-shop and sort of grocery. The stock of this establishment consisted principally of such articles as the owner had purchased from the emigrants at a great sacrifice and sold to others at a great profit. Among other things, an excellent double wagon was pointed out to me, which he had purchased for seventy-five cents.

''The blacksmith's shop,'' he continued, ''was

an equally profitable concern; as when the smith was indisposed to work himself, he rented the use of the shop and tools for the modest price of seventy-five cents an hour.'' Even at this price, Stansbury had to wait for two hours before getting two of his horses shod.

Beyond Fort Laramie another enterprising man operated a ferry service over the North Fork of the Platte. ''The ferry-boat,'' Stansbury reported, ''was constructed of seven canoes, dug out from cotton-wood logs, fastened side by side with poles, a couple of hewn logs being secured across their tops, upon which the wheels of the wagons rested. This rude raft was drawn back and forth by means of a rope stretched across the river, and secured at the ends to either bank.'' Although the ferry looked flimsy, it carried the heavily loaded wagons safely across for two dollars each. As Stansbury said, ''The price, considering that for months the ferryman had been encamped here, in a little tent, exposed to assaults of hordes of wandering savages, for the sole purpose of affording this accomodation to travellers, was by no means extravagant.''

Within the confines of the trail the Great Plains had become a white man's world, filled with his belongings and people. At Ash Creek, a tributary of the Platte, Stansbury said, ''The traces of the great tide of emigration that had preceded us were plainly visible in remains of camp-fires, in blazed trees covered with innumerable names carved and written on them; but, more than all, in the total absence of all herbage. It was only by driving our animals to a ravine some distance from the camp, that a sufficiency for their subsistence could be obtained.''

The plains had always been known for their ability to support large herds of grazing animals, but this concentrated use was beyond their capacity; and the passage of the emigrants was creating a temporary desert in a long strip between Missouri and South Pass, temporary only because of the grasses' recuperative powers, but a real desert for part of the season.

The effect on the buffaloes was apparent. When Stansbury's command reached the Platte, his guide told him that ''the last time he had passed this spot, the whole of the immense plain, as far as the eye could see, was black with herds of buffalo. Now, not so much as one is to be seen; they have fled before the advancing tide of emigration. Driven from their ancient and long-loved haunts, these aboriginal herds, confined within still narrowing bounds, seem destined to final extirpation at the hand of man.''

Eight days later he still had not seen a single buffalo, although he met a party of emigrants who had found a small herd of a hundred and had shot one. The following day, Stansbury's hunters killed their first buffalo, but, he said, ''in order to obtain it [they] had to diverge some four or five miles from the road, and to pass back of the bluffs, the instinct or experience of these sagacious animals having rendered them shy of approaching the line of travel. This has not always been the case,'' he continued, ''for it is a well-attested fact, that when the emigration first commenced, travelling trains were frequently detained for hours by immense herds crossing their track, and in such numbers that it was impossible to pass through them. In many instances it was quite difficult to prevent their own loose cattle from mingling with the buffaloes . . .''

Heedless of the change it was creating, the long line of wagons stretched across the Great Plains, at times reaching from one side to the other, a great band laid across the face of the earth. Almost every driver, plodding alongside his oxen, was a dreamer, and his dreams were of a golden future.

Although the majority of emigrants took the Oregon-California Trail, some preferred going to Santa Fé and on to the West Coast. The people of Fort Smith, Arkansas, were particularly interested in developing this route. Because their community could be reached by steamboat up the Arkansas River, they envisioned it becoming the starting point and perhaps turning into a metropolis. In 1848 they began to lobby for the construction of a federal road to New Mexico; and when Congress proved unresponsive, Arkansas's senator appealed to the War Department for an armed escort to accompany the emigrants. He had in mind not only the protection of the travelers, but also publicity for Fort Smith. Since the War Department was interested in learning more about the Canadian River as a supply route to New Mexico, it agreed to provide both the escort and members of the Topographical Corps to conduct a survey.

The officer in command was Captain Randolph B. Marcy, a thirty-seven-year-old graduate of West Point, who had seen service in the Mexican War. Early in April, 1849, he started west and with the help of a Delaware Indian, one of the many that the government had forced to move west, found a wagon route through the tangled Cross Timbers, which had so baffled the members of the Texans' expedition to Santa Fé. As the long line moved westward, the soil became poorer and firewood more difficult to obtain, but the spirits of the company remained high and their confidence in Marcy firm. When an emigrant wife gave birth to twins, the parents named one "Marcy." "For my part," the captain wrote in his journal, "I feel highly complimented; and if I never see the gold regions myself, I shall have the satisfaction of knowing that my name is represented there. I wish the young gentleman a safe journey to California, and much happiness and gold after he gets there."

In the middle of June they reached the Llano Estacado. "It is a region," Marcy wrote, "almost as vast and trackless as the ocean—a land where no man, savage or civilized, permanently abides; it spreads forth into a treeless, desolate waste of uninhabited solitude, which always has been, and must continue, uninhabited forever; even the savages dare not venture to cross it except at two or three places, where they know water can be found."

When the troops and emigrants reached the more rolling country on the other side, they encountered a band of twenty or thirty Comanches, whose chief proclaimed himself a friend of the Americans. "Seizing me," Marcy said, "in his brawny arms (as we were still mounted on our horses) and laying his greasy head upon my shoulder, he gave me a most bruin-like squeeze; after undergoing which I flattered myself that the salutation was completed; but in this I was mistaken, and was doomed to suffer another similar torture, with the savage's head upon my other shoulder, at the same time rubbing his greasy face against mine; all of which he gave me to understand was to be regarded as a most distinguished and signal mark of affection for the American people . . . " It was an embrace, Marcy noted, "which, for the good of the service, I forced myself to submit to."

Marcy reminded the chief of the treaty between the Americans and the Comanches and the Indians' promise not to molest travelers; and after the chief replied that he intended to abide by the agreement, Marcy said, "I made him a present of tobacco and pipes, and some fresh beef, and they departed well pleased."

At Santa Fé, Marcy, who was a New Englander and a Presbyterian, found the fun-loving New Mexicans uncongenial and was glad to be again on his way. Since the best trail from New Mexico to California started south of Santa Fé, Marcy thought he could help future emigrants by finding a more direct route between that point and Fort Smith. Consequently his return trip took him farther south over the Llano Estacado.

As soon as he was back, he set about writing his report, for he was enthusiastic about the route he had followed. A transcontinental railroad, he believed, could run along it to California. Although neither the North nor the South was willing to build a railroad in the other's territory, his trail across the Great Plains became next in importance to the Platte for those who wished to go to California.

The advancing settlements in Texas had irritated the intractable Comanches, and one of their chiefs had visited several surveying parties and warned them to leave. Part of the trouble, the Indian agent believed, came from the rumors spread by renegade Mexicans and Indians near San Antonio, who told the Comanches that the troops that had passed through the land would come back and massacre them. Another problem was the steady flow of whiskey into the area, brought in by itinerant traders. "In the absence," the agent reported to Washington, "of all law regulating intercourse with our wild bands, and the serious difficulties attending the introduction of ardent spirits into their country, I shall be compelled, for self-preservation and the protection of our frontier settlers, to deal with the traders in the most summary manner." Since he did not always have the power to back up his orders, he sometimes resorted to subterfuge. In one case he relieved a group of traders of forty gallons of whiskey by convincing them that he could influence the Indians into killing them if they commenced selling their liquor.

After holding a council with some of the Indians, he wrote the commissioner of Indian affairs, "I would respectfully call the attention of the Commissioner to the great scarcity of provisions at present among the several prairie bands. . . . They will be obliged to turn their attention to agricultural pursuits for a livelihood; as the buffalo and other game have almost entirely disappeared from our prairies." The Indians were not being driven out; they were being starved out.

The Mexican War had reopened the Santa Fé Trail, and once again heavily laden wagons were rolling from Missouri to the former Mexican city, presenting tempting targets to the Indians. The government had established one more fort along the road, Fort Mann, about eight miles from present-day Dodge City, Kansas. Although troops were sometimes stationed there, its primary purpose was to provide service for the quartermaster trains moving between Fort Leavenworth and Santa Fé. A young man who volunteered to work there while the fort was being constructed said, "Six days before our arrival, a small party of Comanches shot and lanced a man fishing in the river, not three hundred yards from the fort, in sight of forty armed men; then, waving the reeking scalp aloft with yells of triumph and derision, they retreated to the plain unharmed. Two days subsequent to the above, fifteen yoke of oxen and forty mules—these latter staked within seventy yards around the fort—were carried off by the Indians . . .''

Skirmishes such as these, which had been prevalent along the Santa Fé Trail for years, forced the men to be constantly alert. The caravans, too, had to be on guard at every moment. When Colonel William Henry Russell, one of Frémont's warmest defenders in his quarrel with Kearny, returned from California with an escort of sixteen experienced men and a train of thirty wagons, he was attacked by a reported four hundred Indians. (Estimates of the numbers in an attacking force were often high.) For about an hour the Indians surrounded the teamsters and soldiers, but since the white men kept up a brisk fire from their secure, although temporary, fortification of quickly corralled wagons, the Indians rode away. On the other hand, the well-known Santa Fé trader, James M. White, made the fatal mistake of riding ahead of the caravan with which he was traveling. The Indians attacked and killed him and kidnapped his wife and daughter.

Farther north, where white men were even more familiar, the Indians had accepted their presence. They no longer tried to close their travel routes, as the Arikaras and others had done in the past. Yet they were glad to steal and plunder when they could. The Topographical Corps under Stansbury woke one morning to find three horses gone. Two parties of scouts went in futile pursuit and discovered signs that the Indians had also stolen two oxen from another party. Occasionally a band, coming across a few hunters, would strip them of their weapons and horses, and Stansbury learned that one party had had to drive back an Indian attack. Much of the Indians' effort, however, was still concentrated on fighting each other. A band of eighty Sioux approached an emigrant party and informed the captain that "the Pawnees had been up during the winter into their territory, and had stolen several ponies, and that they were seeking vengeance and reprisals, and exhibited five or six scalps as a proof of their prowess. They made anxious inquiries for a Pawnee whom they had wounded, but who had escaped.''

Such warfare diverted the Indians' attention

from the greater threat posed by the Americans and took many Indian lives, but even more costly to them were the diseases still brought to the Great Plains by the advancing Americans. Stansbury waded to the other side of the Platte to examine some lodges he had seen from afar. "There were five of them," he wrote, "pitched upon the open prairie, and in them we found the bodies of nine Sioux, laid out upon the ground, wrapped in their robes of buffalo-skin, with their saddles, spears, camp-kettles, and all their accoutrements, piled up around them. Some lodges contained three, others only one body, all of which were more or less in a state of decomposition," dead from cholera.

A day later he camped a short distance from ten more Sioux lodges. They had been driven from the South Fork of the Platte by an outbreak of the disease, and, Stansbury wrote, "had fled to the emigrant-road, in the hope of obtaining medical aid from the whites. As soon as it was dark, the chief and a dozen of the braves of the village came and sat down in a semicircle around the front of my tent, and, by means of an interpreter, informed me that they would be very glad of a little sugar, tea, or biscuit. I gave what we could spare. They told us there was another and larger band encamped about two miles above, many of whom were very sick with the cholera; they themselves had been afflicted with it, but had in large measure recovered, although they were in great dread of its return. As soon as they were told that I had a doctor . . . with me, and received assurances that some medicines would be prepared for them . . . they expressed much delight, and returned to their village, where, soon after, the sound of the drum and the song, expressive of the revival of hope, which had almost departed, resounded from the 'medicine lodge.' '' But casual treatment by the few doctors who happened to be crossing the plains could not effectively check the spreading deaths. Only the deadly process of exposure would give the Indians a degree of immunity.

The long lines of the emigrant trains, moving westward and leaving behind them their piles of castoff belongings, a heavily grazed strip of land, and their diseases, bespoke the future. The Indians might talk of "their land," but they were losing it to the Americans more rapidly than they knew.

Chapter 24

A Treaty and a Battle

I cannot refrain from expressing it as my settled conviction, founded upon personal observation of not only the Sioux, but of the other principal tribes of the plains, that the time has now fully arrived for teaching these barbarians a lesson, which they are as yet very far from having learned; and that is, how to appreciate and respect the power, the justice, the generosity, and magnanimity of the United States.

—Major O. F. Winship, 1854

The nation was in a jubilant mood. The victorious conclusion of the Mexican War, the successful settlement of the Oregon question, the sudden acquisition of vast territories, and the discovery of enormous quantities of gold, all within the space of a few years, were like a hot spark thrown into the dry tinder of the prairie's grass. Roaring flames of nationalism and self-confidence swept the nation, and the boastful words of Polk's 1848 annual message to Congress seemed less flamboyant and more realistic, a somber appraisal of the country and its future.

Yet the brightest sunshine and the most glimmering optimist could not dispel the dark shadow. The slavery issue, quieted by statesmanship and compromise, sprang again to the fore because of the need to organize the new lands. California, in particular, presented an urgent problem. Rich in its own right and attracting thousands of emigrants, its admission as a state was the surest way to provide for its government and bind it closely to the Union, even if this decision tipped the fine balance between free and slave states. Although the Great Plains were relatively unsettled and therefore posed no immediate organizational questions, Utah and New Mexico, because of the size of their populations, demanded consideration at least as territories.

During the hot summer months of 1850, Congress debated in a political atmosphere that was increasingly passionate and partisan. What emerged was the Compromise of 1850. Texas received compensation for surrendering some of the lands it claimed under its agreement with Santa Anna; Utah and New Mexico were organized as territories; and California became a free state. The basic issue troubling the country was not solved, but at least the split did not widen during the critical period when the nation was assimilating its new acquisitions.

Perhaps next in importance to providing forms of governments for these areas was the need to establish better communications between them and the rest of the United States. For no official mail service existed west of the Mississippi and east of the Sierra Nevadas. In 1850 the federal government contracted for mail service from the Missouri River to Salt Lake City. For $19,500 a year, Samuel H. Woodson of Independence agreed to make one trip each way every month, and the Mormons first learned of Utah's having received territorial status from mail that Woodson carried. It was not fast, for the payment did not permit Woodson to establish relay stations along the way. Consequently the same teams were used for the entire trip, and the journey usually took about thirty days. Yet slow as the service was, the government had taken responsibility for it and made it official.

This one line along the Platte and past Fort Laramie did not, however, fill the void, and plenty of opportunity still remained for private enterprise to serve other parts of the country. The wagons were again rolling between Missouri and Santa Fé, and in July, 1850, the Missouri *Commonwealth* noted, "We briefly alluded, some days since, to the Santa Fé line of mail stages, which left this city on its first monthly journey on the 1st instant. The stages are got up in elegant style, and are each arranged to convey eight passengers. The bodies are beautifully painted, and made water-tight, with a view of using them as boats in ferrying streams. The team consists of six mules to each coach. The mail is guarded by eight men, armed as follows: Each man has at his side, fastened in the stage, one of Colt's revolving rifles; in a holster below, one of Colt's long revolvers, and in his belt a small Colt's revolver besides a hunting-knife; so that these eight men are ready, in case of attack, to discharge one hundred and thirty-six shots without having to reload. This is equal to a small army, armed as in the ancient times, and from the looks of this escort, ready as they are, either for offensive or defensive warfare with the savages, we have no fears for the safety of the mails.

"The accommodating contractors' have established a sort of base of refitting at Council Grove, a distance of one hundred and fifty miles from this city, and have sent out a blacksmith, and a number of men to cut and cure hay, with a quantity of animals, grain, and provisions, and we understand they intend to make a sort of travelling station there, and to commence a farm. They also, we believe, intend to make a similar settlement at Walnut Creek next season. Two of their stages will start from here the first of every month."

The need to improve communications led Congress to reconsider the government's policy for disposing of the public land. When the nation had emerged from the Revolution, its finances shaky and its credit poor, it had looked upon its land as a means of paying the military bonuses it owed and of raising cash. Through a series of laws, it had sold much of the public domain east of the Mississippi. As early as 1827, however, Congress had taken another look at this valuable asset and had decided to pay for the construction of a canal with land grants.

In 1850 Stephen A. Douglas of Illinois thought this same principle might be applied to railroads, particularly one that would run from Galena in northern Illinois to Cairo at the southern tip of the state. Enthusiastic supporters of the idea soon began pressing for an even larger project, a railroad that would run all the way to Mobile, Alabama. Opposition immediately arose among the members of Congress who came from the older states to the east, for they could see no benefit to their constituents in a railroad that roughly paralleled the Mississippi River. During the debate Senator Andrew Butler of South Carolina asked Douglas how many comparable requests were under consideration by the Senate Committee on Public Lands. In his response Douglas was slightly dishonest. He admitted there were several but did not reveal the full total, which was twenty-three.

As the debate went on, the Northeast, being the most industrial and commercial section of the country, began to realize that the railroad would also open up new markets for the products and services it could supply. With growing support, Congress finally passed the Chicago and Mobile Act, which provided the company with a hundred-foot right-of-way and the land in even numbered sections lying within six miles of the track. A new method of financing railroad construction had been instituted, the rush for similar grants was on, and investors everywhere began looking at railroads with great interest.

Congress made another significant change in land policy that same year. The early emigrants to Oregon had been in a precarious position during the joint occupancy, because the United States could not guarantee the titles to the land they had taken up. But Congress now decided that those who had traveled to that far-off country—and some who came later—should be rewarded with 320 acres of land on the condition that it was for their own use and that they intended to reside on it. The public domain was no longer merely a source of revenue; it had become an instrument for encouraging public improvements and westward migration.

In spite of the speed with which the Americans were moving to fill up their lands, the Indians of the Great Plains had been remarkably acquiescent about the intrusion into their country. Although the long line of wagons presented a tempting target, they had made no concerted effort to stop its passage, contenting themselves with occasionally stealing some livestock or committing other relatively minor harassments. (In part their forebearance resulted from their inability to understand what the future held.) But the comparative quiet was not completely reassuring to those who knew

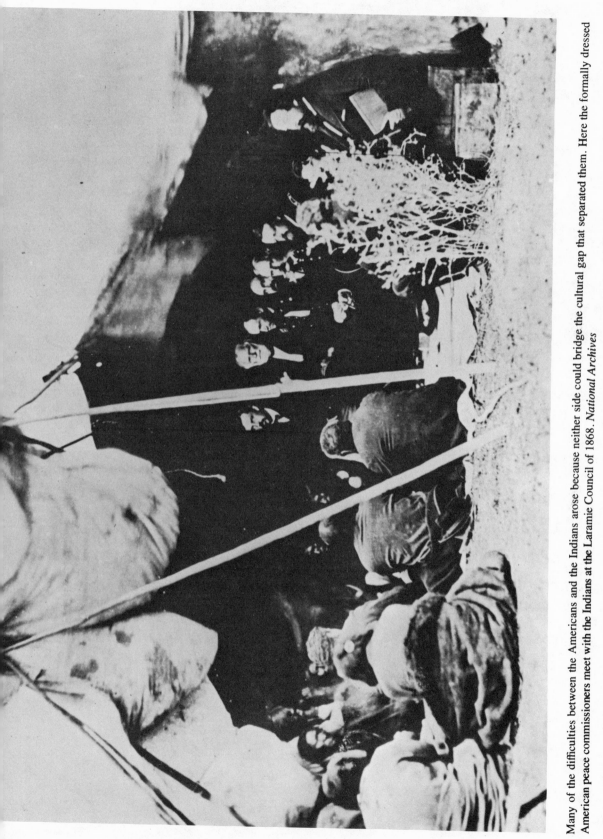

Many of the difficulties between the Americans and the Indians arose because neither side could bridge the cultural gap that separated them. Here the formally dressed American peace commissioners meet with the Indians at the Laramie Council of 1868. *National Archives*

The majority of settlers moving west traveled in wagons, but the Concord stagecoaches provided faster transportation for both mail and passengers. They were especially designed to withstand the rigors of the rough trails, and their grain-fed, carefully selected teams could often outrace attacking Indians. *National Archives*

the Indians well. As a result of their urging, Congress appropriated $100,000 to finance a council to be held with the Indians at Fort Laramie in 1851.

Its purpose was not to purchase land but to obtain a right-of-way through the Indians' territory. As had so often happened in the past, this was largely an attempt to impose an alien concept on the Indians, for they had little idea what a right-of-way could mean. On the other hand, as some of the more able frontiersmen knew, the distribution of presents would engender goodwill and make attacks less likely. The government might think of it as the formal negotiation of a treaty, but these old-timers realized that it was more like the practice of the early fur traders who had paid tribute as they went up the Missouri River.

Fitzpatrick, the former mountain man who had turned government guide, now held the new position of Indian agent for the Upper Platte, and had responsibility for organizing the meeting. Enlisting the services of trappers, traders, government employees, and anyone else who knew the Indians, he began spreading word of the impending council.

One of those who agreed to help him was Father de Smet. In the early summer of 1851, he boarded the steamer *St. Ange* with a companion, Father Christian Hoeken, bound for Fort Union. "We had had a wet spring," he later wrote. "Up to the moment of our departure the rain had been excessive. . . . In ordinary times the sawyers and sand-banks are the principal obstacles to navigation in the western waters; they had now entirely disappeared, and gave the pilot no anxiety. But other dangers had taken their place; the whole face of the waters seemed covered with wrecks; houses, barns, stables, fences of fields and gardens, were borne away in confusion, with thousands of uprooted trees—wood piled on the shore and lumber-yards were all afloat. In the midst of these floating masses, whose dangerous contact we could not always avoid, the *St. Ange* used her whole power of steam to stem an almost irresistible current."

Six days after its departure the *St. Ange,* according to de Smet, resembled "a floating hospital," for cholera had broken out. Father de Smet himself became sick, and his illness prevented him from helping any of the others. But Father Hoeken worked tirelessly, moving between the living and the dead.

After one particularly strenuous day, he returned to his cabin, which was next door to de Smet's. "Between one and two o'clock at night," de Smet wrote, "when all on board were calm and silent, and the sick in their wakefulness heard naught but the sighs and moans of their fellow-sufferers, the voice of Father Hoeken was suddenly heard. He was calling me to his assistance. Awaking from a deep sleep, I recognized his voice, and dragged myself to his pillow. Ah me! I found him ill, and even in extremity. He asked me to hear his confession: I at once acquiesced in his desire. . . . As I was myself in so alarming a state, and fearing that I might be taken away at any moment, and thus share his last abode in this land of pilgrimage and exile, I besought him to hear my confession, if he were yet capable of listening to me. I knelt, bathed in tears, by the dying couch of my brother in Christ—of my faithful friend—of my sole companion in the lonely desert. To him in his agony, I, sick and almost dying, made my confession. Strength forsook him. . . . Father Hoeken, ripe for heaven, surrendered his pure soul into the hands of his Divine Redeemer on the 19th of June, 1851, twelve days after our departure from St. Louis."

Father de Smet was determined not "to leave the body of the pious missionary in the desert," and his plan was "unanimously approved" by the other passengers. Between them, they prepared a heavy, thick coffin, which they lined with tar. Then they buried Father Hoeken in a temporary grave at the edge of the Missouri, and about a month later, when the *St. Ange* returned downstream, its crew stopped long enough to dig up the coffin and carry it back to the Jesuits in Missouri.

As they went up the river they found that smallpox had preceded them and ravaged many bands of Yankton Sioux. "Even during this contagious disease," de Smet noted, "the Indians retained their old custom of giving a last abode to the dead by placing the body, wrapped in a blanket of buffalo-robe, on scaffolds raised eight or ten feet above the plain. They left them thus exposed to the burning heat of a July sun, the most intense of the year. The pestilential exhalations of these corpses infected the air for miles around."

At Fort Pierre the Indians had been suffering from an epidemic of influenza, and they fell into a panic when they heard the rumor that the *St. Ange* had sickness on board. But by this time the epidemic on the boat was over, and they received de Smet gladly. He baptized many of their children as well as the children of the white men who were there. And so he went up the river, spreading the Word of God and news of the coming council.

About the middle of July he reached Fort Union at the mouth of the Yellowstone and began preparing for his overland trip to Fort Laramie. He assembled a band of about thirty persons, most of them Assiniboins, Hidatsas, and Crows, to accompany him and procured two wagons and two carts, probably the first wheeled vehicles to cross that part of the Great Plains.

On his way to Fort Alexander, the American Fur Company's post near the mouth of the Rosebud, one of the Assiniboins demonstrated his great skill at hunting buffaloes, a skill reminiscent of the years when the Indians had no horses. "Alone and on foot," de Smet wrote, "he stealthily approached a large herd of buffalo cows. As soon as he was near enough to them to allow of their hearing him, he began to imitate the cry of a young calf. At once the cows ran toward the place of concealment of the ingenious hunter, and he killed one of them. The troop, alarmed, withdrew hastily and in great disorder. He reloaded his rifle and renewed his cry; the cows stopped, returned as if by enchantment, and he killed a second. The Assiniboin assured us that he could easily have taken more by the same stratagem, but thinking two cows were enough for us, he suffered the rest to go."

After resting at Fort Alexander for a few days while additional supplies arrived by boat from Fort Union, de Smet and his companions again set out along the eastern base of the Bighorn Mountains. On the Powder River he met three young Crows, who gave him directions to Fort Laramie. Although he sensed they might be wrong, he took their advice and entered upon the most difficult part of the trip. Water was scarce, and the terrain rough. One cart broke down completely and had to be abandoned, and one wagon became so battered they had to tie it together with straps of buffalo hide. "The whole region over which we passed," de Smet wrote, "south of the Yellowstone, offers only feeble hopes to civilization. The soil is light, wood scarce, and water wanting during a large portion of the year. It is a country favorable solely to hunters and wandering tribes. All the animals common in the wilderness abound, and during long years to come they will rest undisturbed in their possessions. When all the fertile tracts, yet vacant in the immense Indian territory, shall be occupied, then only will the lands below the Yellowstone attract attention. . .''

When they at last came to the Oregon-California Trail, they found that de Smet's instinct had been right and the Indians' directions wrong, for instead of intercepting the trail at Fort Laramie, they were much farther to the west and close to present-day Casper, Wyoming. But they wasted little time

regretting the wasted miles, because they were so struck by the sight of the road itself. "Our Indian companions," de Smet wrote, "who had never seen but the narrow hunting-paths by which they transport themselves and their lodges, were filled with admiration on seeing this noble highway, which is as smooth as a barn floor swept by the winds, and not a blade of grass can shoot on it on account of the continual passing. They conceived a high idea of the countless White Nation, as they express it. They fancied that all had gone over that road, and that an immense void must exist in the land of the rising sun. Their countenances testified evident incredulity when I told them that their exit was in nowise perceived in the lands of the whites.

"They styled the route the Great Medicine Road of the Whites. The term medicine is applied by them to whatever they find grand, religious, mysterious or incomprehensible. They visited and examined in detail all the foresaken camping-grounds on the way; they brought a great variety of objects to me to have their use and signification explained, they filled their pouches with knives, forks, spoons, basins, coffee-pots and other cooking articles, axes, hammers, etc. With the bits of earthenware which bore any figure or inscription, they fabricated some ornament for their necks and ears. How wonderful will be the accounts given of the Great Medicine Road by our unsophisticated Indians when they go back to their villages, and sit in the midst of an admiring circle of relatives!

"But these relics collected by our savage friends," de Smet continued, "were not the sole vestiges of the great multitude of emigrants who, in search of gold, had crossed this vast plain with a rare courage and unheard-of fatigues and difficulties. The bleached bones of domestic animals disseminated profusely along the route; the rising mound hastily made over the grave of a parent or a friend deceased during the long journey, and the tribute offered to memory in a coarse and rudely-carved inscription on a narrow-strip of board or on a stone, with other graves which offered no such testimonial of affection, furnish ample and melancholy proofs that death had considerably thinned their ranks. By such disasters thousands of emigrants have found themselves suddenly arrested, and been mocked in the flattering hope of wealth and pleasure.

"The countless fragments of conveyances, the heaps of provisions, tools of every kind, and other objects with which the emigrants must have provided themselves at great expense, but which the most impatient, eager to outstrip others in the

Western Eldorado, had forsaken and cast aside, testify to that bold recklessness with which they hazard everything in this enterprise . . ."

Fitzpatrick did his work well, for at Fort Laramie about ten thousand Indians had gathered at the mouth of the river, probably the largest group of people that had ever assembled in one place in the history of the Great Plains. Many of the bands were traditional enemies more accustomed to fighting each other than camping side by side; and although the government had assigned two hundred dragoons to police the meeting, they were too few for effective action, and peace was dependent on the leadership of a few white men and Indians.

Colonel David D. Mitchell was then the United States Superintendent of Indian Affairs for the Central Division. He had been a valuable member of the Upper Missouri Outfit in the triumphant days of McKenzie and had taken personal charge of the council. Although he had had long experience dealing with Indians, he now faced a problem that strained even his skill. The various bands had arrived at Fort Laramie, but not the presents the government intended to give out. Without them, there was no point starting the formal proceedings, but meanwhile the Indians were getting restless, their horses were rapidly eating the last of the forage around the fort, and supplies were giving out.

"Notwithstanding the scarcity of provisions felt in the camp before the wagons came," de Smet said, "the feasts were numerous and well attended. No epoch in Indian annals, probably, shows a greater massacre of the canine race. Among the Indians the flesh of the dog is the most honorable and esteemed of all viands, especially in the absence of buffalo and other animals. On the present occasion it was a last resource. The carnage then may be conceived. I was invited to several of these banquets; a great chief, in particular, wished to give me a special mark of his friendship and respect for me. He had filled his great kettle with little fat dogs, skins and all. He presented me, on a wooden platter, the fattest, well boiled. I found the meat really delicate, and I can vouch that it is preferable to suckling-pig, which it nearly resembles in taste."

Before the presents arrived, the grass around Fort Laramie was completely devoured by the herds of Indian horses. Consequently Mitchell moved the council from the mouth of the Laramie River to Horse Creek, about thirty-five miles farther down the Platte. Here the Indians again set up their lodges and renewed their wait.

Finally on September 8, 1851, Mitchell decided he could delay no longer. At nine o'clock in the morning the soldiers fired their cannon as a signal the council was about to begin; and the Indians assembled, the important leaders sitting in front, the warriors behind them, and the women and children at the outer edge. The treaty, of course, had been prepared beforehand, so Mitchell read it line by line, explaining each of its provisions, while interpreters translated his words into the languages of the tribes that were present. Scrupulously he explained what the United States wanted from the Indians and what it was prepared to give in return; but the terms, of course, were meaningless to most of those who were listening.

They were to refrain from fighting each other, for the United States wished the people of the Great Plains to be at peace. But this request, so simple in terms of a European culture, threatened to undermine the Indians' way of life, which, among most of the tribes, was based on war. That was how they obtained many of their horses and demonstrated their bravery. Without being able to do battle, they could not individually distinguish themselves and create their social structure.

They were to agree among themselves on boundary lines for each tribe and remain within them unless they were hunting. This, too, seemed simple, but the provision was incomprehensible to nomads who were accustomed to going wherever they wanted. Although most tribes had general areas they regarded as their own, the limits were flexible and constantly changing. Ever since the arrival of the white men, the Sioux, for example, had been moving westward, and the Cheyennes who were faithful to Bent had moved south when he erected his fort. Nothing in their philosophy prevented such shifts in population, and the only practical impediment to their movement was the strength of the tribe that might already be established in the land they wanted to occupy. Suddenly to freeze their geographical relationships was asking them to abandon a part of their heritage.

They were to permit the Americans to build roads and forts on the Great Plains, but they had no idea what this meant, for they had no conception of the numbers of white men. The Indians traveling with de Smet had even thought there was no one left in the East and that the great exodus was finished. As for the construction of posts, their experience was largely limited to the few built by the traders, and they could not comprehend the significance of armed garrisons in their midst.

Also each tribe was to assume responsibility for the acts of its individual members. This was almost like requesting them to make the Platte River run backward, for they had no machinery for forcing the will of the majority on the whole membership of the tribe. If a warrior did not care to join his companions on a raid, they had no means of compelling him; on the other hand, if he wanted to go on a raid by himself, they had no means of restraining him. Theirs was a completely individualistic society, and collective responsibility was unknown to them.

Mitchell also faced the problem that had plagued every negotiator with the Plains Indians since the time of Lewis and Clark. To make the treaty effective, one Indian in each tribe had to serve as his people's responsible leader. No wise Indian wished to fill such a position, for no Indian could exercise the necessary authority over his fellows.

Yet the rewards for signing the Americans' paper were great. According to Mitchell, they would receive $50,000 worth of gifts now with additional gifts annually for the next fifty years. And word had come that the wagon train was at last on its way.

For almost a week the Indians debated among themselves, the most respected men taking the lead, and the younger warriors from time to time nodding their assent or signifying their disagreement. Even the question of leadership was finally resolved except among the Sioux. They were the most numerous of the tribes and the one that contained the most subdivisions. Mitchell, however, knew a Brulé Sioux of some standing, a man who had in the past been familiar with many of the fur traders. Brave Bear, as the warrior was named, had no desire to be singled out for the Americans' attention, but he had become convinced that good relations between the white men and his tribe were necessary for the Sioux's survival. Reluctantly he agreed to serve as "the white men's chief," although fortunately the Indians did not give him that derogatory title. Then Mitchell, using his influence among the other Sioux, persuaded them to accept Brave Bear in his new—and practically meaningless—role.

On September 17 the Indians had finished their discussions, and Mitchell believed the time had come to sign the treaty. One by one the leaders came forward and, next to their names at the bottom of the document, affixed their undistinctive X's. The illiterate were approving an agreement they could not read and would not have understood even if they had been able to decipher its letters.

The supply train still had not arrived with the gifts. The grass around Horse Creek resembled that around Fort Laramie. Garbage and filth had piled up in the campgrounds, and the smell became so unbearable that the dragoons, hardy men though they were, made a new camp for themselves some two miles away where the air was fresher.

Finally, on September 20, the wagon train appeared. "The safe arrival of this convoy," de Smet noted, "was an occasion of general joy. Many were in absolute destitution. The next day the wagons were unloaded and the presents suitably arranged. The flag of the United States floated from a tall staff before the tent of the superintendent, and a discharge of cannon announced to the Indians that the division of the presents was about to take place. Without delay, the occupants of the various camps flocked in—men, women and children,—in great confusion, and in their gayest costume, daubed with paints of glaring hues and decorated with all the gewgaws they could boast. They took the respective places assigned to each particular band, thus forming an immense circle, covering several acres of land, and the merchandise was displayed in the centre . . .

"The great chiefs of the different nations were served first, and received suits of clothes. You may easily imagine their singular movements on appearing in public, and the admiration which they excited in their comrades, who were never weary inspecting them. The great chiefs were, for the first time in their lives, pantalooned; each was arrayed in a general's uniform, a gilt-sword hanging at his side. Their long, coarse hair floated above the military costume, and the whole was crowned by the burlesque solemnity of their painted faces."

Then the leaders of each tribe distributed the remainder of the treaty gifts among their own people. Finally the bands began taking down their tipis and dispersing, for the good news had arrived that the buffalo herds were on the South Fork of the Platte, three days away. In a short while they would again have plenty of food.

Mitchell and Fitzpatrick returned to St. Louis with a delegation of Indians from the tribes that had attended the council. From Fort Kearny, Fitzpatrick took them to Westport, Kansas, by a route that brought them through farming country. He hoped they would develop a taste for farm products and therefore be willing to abandon their nomadic life for agriculture. They liked what they ate along the way—potatoes, carrots, melons, apples, and peaches—but following a plow on a hot summer's day across the plains could never replace in their hearts the excitement of a buffalo hunt, nor could the signing of a single incomprehensible document make them change their way of life. With their wagonloads of gifts, Mitchell and Fitzpatrick had purchased time; but they had not, as they hoped, reformed a civilization. Furthermore, they were unaware of the immensity of the problem they had been called upon to solve. For some of the goldseekers had stopped in the Colorado Rockies on their way to California and had panned their streams. A little gold showed up, not enough to deflect them from their journey, but enough so they would not forget it.

The wagon trains continued to roll west, some of their drivers hoping to gain quick fortunes in the goldfields, some hoping to find only a better home than they could farther east. Ezra Meeker, a native of Indiana, was a typical emigrant. When he was married, he and his wife wanted a farm of their own, and so in 1851 they moved to Iowa. But they found Iowa disappointing. The winters were cold, there was little market for their farm products, and civilization in the form of good schools and wagon roads had, in Meeker's opinion, not reached that far. Land was available, at low prices to be sure, but it had to be bought and paid for immediately. On the other hand, he could obtain 320 acres in Oregon free. The temptation was too great to resist, and in 1852 he set out for the West Coast with his wife and his brother.

Once on the trail, Meeker did not try to join one of the organized companies, but he also realized it was unwise to travel alone. "Four wagons, nine men," he recalled years later, "by a tacit agreement traveled together a thousand miles, and separated only when our roads parted, the one to California and the other to Oregon. And yet we were all the while in one great train, never out of the sight or hearing of others. In fact, at times the roads would be so full of wagons that all could not travel in one track, and this fact accounts for the double roadbeds seen in so many places on the trail. One of the party always went ahead to look out for water, grass, and fuel, three requisites for a camping place. The grass along the beaten track was always eaten off close by the loose stock, of which there were great numbers, and so we had frequently to take the cattle long distances. . . .

"People too often brought their own ills upon themselves by their indiscreet action, especially in the loss of their teams. The trip had not progressed far till there came a universal outcry against the heavy loads and unnecessary articles, and soon we began to see abandoned property. First it might be a table or a cupboard or perchance a bedstead or a heavy cast iron cook-stove. Then began to be seen bedding by the wayside, feather beds, blankets, quilts, pillows, everything of the kind that mortal man might want. Not so very long till here and

there an abandoned wagon was to be seen, provisions, stacks of flour, and bacon being the most abundant, all left as common property. Help yourself if you will, no one will interfere, and in fact in some places a sign was posted inviting all to take what they wanted. Hundreds of wagons were left and hundreds of tons of goods. People seem to vie with each other to give away their property, there being no chance to sell, and they disliked to destroy. Long after the mania for getting rid of goods and lightening the load, the abandonment of wagons continued, as the teams became weaker (generally from abuse or lack of care), and the ravages of cholera struck us. It was then that many lost their heads and ruined their teams by furious driving, by lack of care, and by abuse. There came a veritable stampede, a strife for possession of the road, to see who should get ahead. Whole trains with bad blood would strive for mastery of the road, one attempting to pass the other, frequently with drivers on each side of the team to urge the poor, suffering dumb brutes forward."

At one point on the trip, Meeker stopped four days because of his brother's illness. During one of those days, he made an actual count of the wagons that passed and then estimated the number for the other three. The total for the four days was 1,600 wagons, each accompanied by an average of five persons and pulled by six animals. The loose stock, he figured, amounted to about three animals for each one that was working. That added up to about eight thousand people and almost thirty-eight thousand animals. When he reached Independence Rock, he carefully read the inscriptions of those who had gone before and decided that the line of emigrants stretched about three hundred miles ahead of him. From this he calculated that fifty thousand people were moving westward in a column that was about five hundred miles long.

Years later he remembered some of the horrors of the trip. "The dust," he later wrote, "has been spoken of as intolerable. The word hardly expresses the situation; in fact, I cannot say the English language contains the word to define it. Here was a moving mass of humanity and dumb brutes at times mixed in inextricable confusion a hundred feet wide or more. At times two columns of wagons traveling on parallel lines and near each other served as a barrier to prevent loose stock from crossing, but usually there would be an almost inextricable mass of cows, young cattle, horses, and footmen moving along the outskirts. . . . Over all, in calm weather at times the dust would settle so thick that the team of a wagon could not be seen from the wagon; like a London fog, so thick one might almost cut it. Then again, that steady flow of wind up to and through the South Pass would hurl the dust and sand in one's face sometimes with force enough to sting from the impact upon the face and hands.

"Then we had storms that were not of sand and wind alone; storms only a Platte valley in summer or a Puget sound winter might turn out; storms that would wet to the skin in less time than it takes to write this sentence."

Even worse than the dust was the disease. "The scourge of cholera, on the Platte in 1852," he said, "is far beyond my power of description. . . . It did seem that people lost all control of themselves and others. Whole trains would be seen contending for the mastery of the road by day, and the power of endurance tested to the utmost both men and beasts at night. The scourge came from the south . . . ," and in one wagon train forty people died in a twenty-four-hour period. During the four days he waited with his sick brother, Meeker noticed that a neighboring burial place grew from a few graves to fifty-two, and he knew of a family of seven who all died and were buried in a common pit.

Yet the lure of gold (new placers had been discovered in California) and the prospect of free land drove them on, leaving behind them the rutted trail, the ravaged band of overgrazed land, and the lines of graves. Sadness and hope traveled together, and the setting sun was their beacon.

The initial burst of energy that carried the American people across the Great Plains had taken several years to build up, but once unleashed, it was not quickly exhausted. The surge westward continued unabated, and the enthusiasm of the nation for its new lands remained high. But the role of the lonely explorers diminished, to be replaced more and more by government action in various forms. In fact, this change was beginning to affect the Americans' character and their philosophy.

Most of the early development of the East had been underwritten by private capital and carried out by individuals. But as the frontier advanced, this became less and less possible in a country that was not yet wealthy. The fur trade was practically the only business with the profits and the incentive to open up new lands by itself, and even it had sometimes called upon the government for assistance, as Ashley had done when he wished to ascend the Missouri against the wishes of the Arikaras. Now, however, the people increasingly looked to Washington for help in opening up the West, and the government responded.

Fort Laramie and Fort Kearny attested to the importance the government now attached to the safety of the emigrants. Instead of temporary military excursions, such as Atkinson had recommended to protect the fur traders, Washington was now firmly committed to permanent installations, supplemented by heavy investments of money in Indian treaties, exploration, and improvements.

The sources of the Red River, which had eluded both Pike and Long, were still unknown, so Marcy was sent to search for them. In an army expedition in 1852, he finally located them, and one more blank space in America's map was filled in. When the proponents of a southern transcontinental railroad decided that the national boundaries did not include the best route, the government filled in the gap by negotiating with Mexico the Gadsden Purchase of more than forty-five thousand square miles of territory that now constitute the southern portions of Arizona and New Mexico.

Since Texas was still suffering from sporadic Indian raids, particularly by the Kiowas and Comanches, the federal government completed construction of two rings of forts designed to guard the state. About two hundred miles separated the lines, and the strategy was to catch the Indians between them. It was, however, only partially successful. As an additional step toward relieving pressure against Texas and the southern Great Plains, the government negotiated a treaty with the Comanches, Kiowas, and Kiowa-Apaches at Fort Atkinson. By its terms the United States received permission to build roads and posts in their territory, and the Indians promised to refrain from conducting raids in the United States and Mexico. In return, they were to receive $18,000 a year in gifts for ten years.

Texas itself also took a step toward solving its Indian problem. At the urging of the federal government, it contributed some of the public domain it had been permitted to retain toward the establishment of Indian reservations to be selected by the commissioner of Indian affairs. Unfortunately the act passed by the Texas legislature provided for only slightly more than fifty-five thousand acres, too small an amount to solve the problem and only an insignificant portion of the hundred million acres to which the state held title.

Interest was still high in the possibility of a transcontinental railroad. Ever since the passage of the Chicago and Mobile Act in 1850, people had increasingly looked to the government to take a part in railroad construction, so Congress voted an additional appropriation for the Department of War to enable it to survey several routes. The army made five surveys in 1853 (one of which was left incomplete), and the reports were printed for public distribution. Although they were widely read and discussed, the jealousy and suspicion between North and South was still too great to permit further action. The price of dependency on government support was a consensus of opinion, and a transcontinental railroad would have to wait until the question of slavery was somehow resolved.

With so much activity on the Great Plains and so many people of different cultures moving over them, trouble was almost inevitable, and a piece of paper with X's at the bottom could not prevent it. Of particular concern to the soldiers stationed at Fort Laramie were the Miniconjou Sioux. These lived north of the Oglala and Brulé Sioux and, not having participated in the Fort Laramie Treaty and enjoying none of its benefits, did not feel themselves bound by it. They did not come down to the Platte in large numbers but, in Indian fashion, sometimes small bands visited their friends among the other Sioux.

In the summer of 1853 a group of them stole the ferryboat operating on the Platte upstream from Fort Laramie. The commanding officer at the fort, First Lieutenant Richard B. Garnett, ordered a sergeant to retrieve it. When the sergeant crossed the river to approach the Indians' camp, one of the Miniconjous fired at him. Either the Indian was a poor shot, or he was merely playing with the sergeant; in any case, he missed. The sergeant quickly retreated to Fort Laramie and told Garnett what had happened.

By the terms of the treaty and by Indian custom, Garnett should have first asked the Miniconjous to give the ferryboat owner compensation. Only if they refused, did he have the right to use force, for this was a police—not a military—problem. But he regarded the shot aimed at his sergeant as an insult to the army and he ordered Second Lieutenant Hugh Fleming, fresh out of West Point and only a brevet officer, to march against the Miniconjous. Darkness was nearing as he approached their camp; the Miniconjous fled to a ravine; someone fired a shot; and Fleming ordered his men to charge. Fortunately nightfall brought an end to the fighting; but before it did, Fleming had killed three Miniconjous and captured two more.

This might have led to open warfare, but instead of harassing the fort and the emigrants, the leaders of the Miniconjous went to Laramie and asked for gifts to compensate their people for the loss of the warriors. This was the Sioux fashion of ending a quarrel without fighting, but Garnett regarded the Sioux's action as insolent and instead of seizing the chance to restore friendly relations, he scolded the chiefs and refused to give them anything. His attitude infuriated the young warriors, but the older men restrained them. Nevertheless, their resentment spread to the Brulés and Oglalas.

The Indians were further irritated that summer when the Indian agent arrived with the treaty gifts. They had not understood the process by which the Americans made treaties, how the executive branch of the government initiated an agreement and then submitted it to the Senate for ratification. The Indian agent tried to explain this to them when he told them that the Senate had reduced the terms of the payments from fifty to fifteen years. From the Indians' point of view, this was a breach of faith, but they could do little except acquiesce.

In the summer of 1853 they again came to the Platte to receive their presents, but although the gifts had arrived and were stored in the American Fur Company's post some five miles from Fort Laramie, the Indian agent did not appear to distribute them. Fitzpatrick no longer held the position, and the army complained that his replacement was inattentive to his duties.

While the Indians waited, they made their camps on the south side of the river. The Oglalas' started at the American Fur Company's post and stretched downstream for one and a half or two miles. The Brulés' lay just beyond and reached the post of James Bordeaux, an independent trader, married to a Sioux and with long experience in the business. In between the Brulés and the Oglalas was a small camp of Miniconjous containing about fifteen lodges.

As the hot August days wore on, some of the Indians grew restless over the delay and began to run short of supplies. Finally a few of them ran off with two head of cattle belonging to the fort's interpreter, August Lucien, a short-tempered man who was disliked by the Sioux. Fleming, who had led the attack on the Miniconjous the year before, was now in command of the fort, and he sent troops to overtake the thieves. They failed in their mission, however, and Fleming was frustrated by his inability to maintain order within a few miles of the fort.

A few days later, as the emigrants continued up the trail past the Indian camps, a Miniconjou stole an ox. Some witnesses said the ox wandered off by itself into the Indians' camp, others that the Indian approached the emigrant with three arrows, one of which he shot at the man but missed, and another of which he used to kill the ox.

In any case, the emigrant was furious. James

Bordeaux, the trader, was a short, plump man, who often wore a vest and a gold watch chain and impressed some travelers as officious, but he thoroughly understood the Indians and wanted peace, for his business depended on it. So he offered the emigrant ten dollars for the ox, but the man demanded twenty-five. This was too high, so Bordeaux did not raise his offer, and the emigrant went to the fort and complained about his loss.

Brave Bear, the Brulé whom Mitchell had named as chief of all the Sioux at the 1851 council, also went to the fort to report what had happened. He was in an extremely difficult position. As the white men's chief, he was responsible for the actions of all the Sioux, but he had little control over the Oglalas and Brulés and none at all over the Miniconjous. Nevertheless, he offered to help in any way he could and volunteered to try to persuade the Indians to surrender the warrior to the military.

Fleming believed he could not overlook the incident. "This occurred close to the fort," he later explained, "and I was compelled to take notice of it, or give up entirely all protection to those travelling on this route." Accordingly he ordered Brevet Second Lieutenant John L. Grattan to take August Lucien, the interpreter, two noncommissioned officers, and twenty-seven men and arrest the thief. He also permitted Grattan to take two howitzers. In the event the Indians refused to surrender the Miniconjou, he was, according to Fleming, "to act upon his own discretion, and to be careful not to hazard an engagement without certainty of success."

Grattan was glad to receive the assignment. As one eyewitness reported, "He said he would like very well to go, but would not go unless he had orders to bring the offender. He did not think that it would be necessary to fight in order to obtain him; but in the course of this conversation, as well as on several other occasions, he had told me that if it was ever necessary to fight Indians when they were in their village, he would place his artillery some three or four hundred yards from their village, and run the risk of their driving him from his position."

On the way to the American Fur Company's post, Lucien pulled out a small bottle of whiskey and began drinking. By the time they had gone the few miles, he was drunk and excited, for the memory of the cattle he had lost still rankled him. Noticing Lucien's condition, Grattan asked him for a drink, but, when he received the bottle, instead of putting it to his lips, smashed it on the ground. After that he ordered his men to load their guns but

instructed them not to shoot unless he or the sergeant told them to. Then he added, "When I give the order, you may fire as much as you damned please." He also said that he did not expect a shot to go off, but that he "hoped to God they would have a fight." In this bellicose frame of mind and with his drunken interpreter, Grattan and his men reached Bordeaux's trading post.

At Grattan's request, Bordeaux sent for Brave Bear and told the chief that the lieutenant had come to arrest the Miniconjou, who would then be held at the fort until the Indian agent arrived. Brave Bear said he would talk to some of the warriors and soon returned with three other leaders. But they were followed almost immediately by a messenger who brought word that the Miniconjou, who had lost his relatives the year before, probably in the fight with Fleming, would rather die than surrender.

Grattan then made preparations to take the man by force, if necessary, and threatened to move his soldiers to within sixty yards of the lodge where the Miniconjou was now staying. Realizing that a crisis was impending, Bordeaux warned the Indians to get the man quickly. They told him that it was their custom to make a demand four times before acting—four was a magic number among the Sioux—and they hoped that Grattan would do this. Meanwhile Lucien, feeling courageous from the effects of his whiskey and the backing of almost thirty men, was taunting the Sioux. Bordeaux suggested that Grattan order him to remain at the post, but Grattan was apparently unconscious of the trouble Lucien was creating with his wild remarks and jeering insults.

Although Brave Bear said the Indians would not give up the Miniconjou, Grattan decided to march his men into the village. Meanwhile many of the Indians, seeing this band of armed men advancing toward them, hid in a ravine that lay between their camp and the river. Grattan placed his two howitzers in position, lined up his men on either side of them, and began another council with Brave Bear and some of the other leaders. The Miniconjou, however, remained as determined as ever not to give himself up; and the younger warriors, remembering the failure of the Indian agent to distribute the gifts and resentful of the Americans, promised to support him.

Someone sent for Bordeaux. The trader was still anxious to preserve peace between the excited officer and the angry Indians, ". . . but when I got within 150 yards," he later recalled, "I saw that it was too late—the excitement was too great.'' Foreseeing trouble, he returned to his trading post to protect his own belongings as well as he could.

One observer, who watched the Indians' camp from the roof of Bordeaux's house, later said, "The council lasted about three quarters of an hour, and during this time I saw many Indians collecting and mounting their horses near the river, and the women and children were leaving the village. At length I saw the soldiers stand up [they had been resting on the ground] and bring their piece down as if to fire, and at that moment I heard, I thought, the report of Indian guns, followed immediately by that of muskets. The two cannon were fired directly after.''

Whatever his conduct so far, Grattan commited a serious mistake when he ordered his men to shoot as they pleased. Even when they were hunting grizzly bears, Lewis and Clark's expedition had learned that one-half of them should hold their fire, and the fur traders knew this was true, too, when fighting Indians. (The Bents had saved the caravan on the Santa Fé Trail by not firing indiscriminately and thus keeping the Indians at a distance.) But when Grattan's men, who were not armed with repeating guns, fired their muskets and their two howitzers all at once, they left themselves powerless to defend themselves. The Indians, now angry and ready for battle, charged.

"I then saw the limber [the detachable wheeled carriage] of the gun turned and start to leave the camp, followed by the wagon," the observer on the roof continued. "A man was trying to get into the wagon. At the same time the soldiers all commenced to retreat, pursued by the Indians. The limber was overtaken in a quarter of a mile, and the wagon reached the first point of the bluffs which crosses the road, near half a mile, before it was overtaken. The footmen, about eighteen in number—some who had been with the cannon, without arms—reached the road between the two bluffs which cross it, about a mile, where they were all killed by Indians who followed them, and, as I supposed, by those who came from the Oglala camp above. I saw a great many coming from there over the second point of bluffs. Three or four men were killed near the cannon. The interpreter, who was mounted, and a soldier who was on the lieutenant's horse, were overtaken by some Indians who came from near the river below Bordeaux's house, passing close to it, near the wagon where they were killed. The soldiers were loading and firing as they retreated.''

The soldiers were completely routed, and the In-

dians went on the rampage. Bordeaux had finished the few arrangements he was making to protect himself when, as he later said, "a rush was made on the house by a number of Indians, but our friends among them interfered and prevented them doing us any harm. Then a chief, Little Thunder, came and told me that since the Indians had killed all the soldiers at the camp, they were going to kill all at the fort and burn it up. I told him to stop them; that if they did not do any more harm, and did not disturb anybody on the river, I thought their grandfather would forgive them for what they had done. He went out immediately, and with all the other chiefs, harangued the Indians, and did all they could to put down the excitement; but my opinion is, that if the sun had been two hours higher they could not have stopped it.''

The Sioux now started breaking up their camp and moving to the other side of the river, where they felt they would be safer from reprisal. Brave Bear had been mortally wounded—his life was the price he had paid within three years for accepting the white men's designation as a chief—but a few other leaders, including Little Thunder, still tried to restrain the warriors.

"Indians were coming to my house all night begging," Bordeaux recalled; "they said they had been waiting on the agent two months, that their children were starving, and that they were bound to have what they wanted. The chiefs told me to give them what they wanted, because they were just trying to pick a quarrel with me to kill us all, and I gave them whatever they demanded. During the night some of the friendly Indians brought in a wounded soldier, and said if his wounds did not kill him, nobody should hurt him. A few minutes after, a chief came in and advised me to hide him somewhere outside, for fear some of the other Indians would find him there, and make it an excuse for killing us. The man said if I could send some one with him he would prefer to go to the fort, and I sent a white man and two Indians with him, who accompanied him about a mile, and he then said he could go himself.''

When daylight came, the soldier returned to Bordeaux's post to wait another day before trying to get to the fort. He was the sole survivor of Grattan's command, and he died from his wounds.

Their successful slaughter of Grattan and all his men had made the Indians wild. Since the agent still had not arrived, they broke into the American Fur Company post and took the government annuities that were stored there as well as some supplies belonging to the company, while Fleming, helpless to interfere, remained in the fort. "The Indians," he reported in a message to the assistant adjutant general, "are hostile, menacing the fort; but all my men are on duty, and I think we shall be able to keep possession of it. We stand much in need of more troops, and hope they will be sent as soon as possible."

But with their victory over Grattan and their looting of the two trading posts, the Sioux had sated their taste for battle. Instead of attacking the fort, whose strong palisade made it defendable even against great numbers, they gathered up the supplies they had seized, took down their tipis, and began to move north. Some of the wisest white men thought that peace with the Sioux was ended. Even Bordeaux believed he might have to leave the Platte, and some traders told a traveler that "since the day some Sioux had been killed by the troops, they were speaking of nothing else but revenge, and were determined to kill all the soldiers residing on their lands. Their [the traders'] impression was that all this would end in war; that the trade would be ruined—so they preferred leaving the country." A brash second lieutenant and an irresponsible Indian agent had brought their country to the brink of conflict with the largest tribe in the West.

Chapter 25

Slavery, Handcarts, and Oxen

We appeal to the people. We warn you that the dearest interests of freedom and the Union are in imminent peril. Demagogues may tell you that the Union can be maintained only by submitting to the demands of slavery. We tell you that the Union can only be maintained by the full recognition of the just claims of freedom and man. The Union was formed to establish justice and secure the blessings of liberty. When it fails to accomplish these ends it will be worthless, and when it becomes worthless it cannot long endure. . . .

Whatever apologies may be offered for the toleration of slavery in the States, none can be offered for its extension into Territories where it does not exist, and where that extension involves the repeal of ancient law and the violation of solemn compact.

—Salmon P. Chase (and co-signed
by other senators), 1854

Grattan's slaughter came as a shock. It was the most severe defeat ever suffered up to that time by the United States Army on the Great Plains. That the Indians could wipe out an entire command, one supported by artillery, and threaten a major military post seemed almost inconceivable. Years ago, Atkinson had suggested that an occasional army expedition through the country would keep the Indians subdued. Now they had battled and looted within a few miles of a permanent fort, while its garrison was forced to remain inside, helpless to intervene. But the people paid less attention to the incident than they might have because the nation was once again preoccupied by the slavery question.

A principal instigator in the issue's sudden resurfacing was Stephen A. Douglas, the senior senator from Illinois. As a result of the railroad surveys financed by Congress, many people had begun to think that the southern transcontinental route was the most practical, both in terms of its length and the grades encountered. Furthermore, since Texas and California were states and New

Mexico had been organized as a territory, it did not, as the other routes did, run through lands lacking self-government and therefore having no local policing powers.

Douglas was intelligent, resolute, but dominated by self-interest. He was also chairman of the Senate's Committee on Territories, and when a bill was introduced providing for the creation of a Nebraska Territory, Douglas saw many advantages in its passage. As a resident of Illinois and, like many men of that day, a speculator in land, he personally preferred the central railroad route. Passage of the bill would enhance the possibility of its selection.

Senator David R. Atchison of Missouri was a leader in his state among those who favored slavery and the previous year had helped defeat another Nebraska Act. Since the majority of people in Missouri wanted territorial status for the lands on their western border (they thought this would stimulate their own economy and provide additional protection from the Indians), his action had been politically unpopular. Why not, he now argued, seeking a middle way, permit the territory to decide for itself whether it wished to be slave or free? This, he pointed out, had been the procedure followed with California and New Mexico. Douglas accepted this idea, labeled it "popular sovereignty," and used it as a lever to gain the votes of the pro-slavery members of Congress for the establishment of the new territory.

It was a cunning device, for it did not openly flout the Missouri Compromise, although it undermined it as surely as the river undermined its banks each year. But it was not cunning enough and failed in its purpose, for the South, immediately sensing that Douglas was prepared to pay for their votes, raised the price. Instead of accepting Atchison's proposal, they demanded outright repeal of the compromise that had served so well to hold the nation together.

The result was months of stormy debate, but the issue was not clear-cut. Many Northerners who opposed the extension of slavery also wanted the organization of Nebraska as a territory for a variety of reasons: they, too, preferred the central route for a transcontinental railroad, and they believed that the political development of this part of the country would create new markets. The people of Missouri and Iowa were also behind the bill. Regardless of whether the new territory was slave or free, they would no longer be on the frontier. By marshaling these forces and gaining the support of the South, Douglas was able to put the bill through, although this required a council with President Franklin Pierce on a Sunday—and he, like Polk, was reluctant to break the Sabbath. But before the measure passed, Douglas had to accept another change: instead of one territory, there were to be two, Kansas and Nebraska. Kansas Territory was to include part of eastern Colorado, and Nebraska Territory the areas in North and South Dakota west of the Missouri, most of Wyoming, and some of Colorado.

The idea was that Kansas would become slave, Nebraska free, thus preserving the old balance. But the anti-slavery forces were not to be satisfied so easily. Eli Thayer, a free-soiler who lived in Worcester, Massachusetts, did not even wait until the passage of the bill before organizing the Massachusetts Emigrant Aid Society, later replacing the word "Massachusetts" with "New England." Its purpose was to procure lands in Kansas and help emigrants from New England settle them. With typical New England thriftiness, Thayer made his organization a joint stock company and hoped to turn a profit as well as flood Kansas with anti-slavery residents. Although the New England Emigrant Aid Society was not an excellent investment, Thayer and the others who followed his example in helping anti-slavery voters move to Kansas upset the plans of the compromisers by making it uncertain which way Kansas would go.

The wave of emigration that followed the passage of the Kansas-Nebraska Act did not immediately affect the Great Plains themselves. For Americans were not yet prepared to advance in numbers onto the arid Great Plains as long as there still remained fertile lands in the eastern portions of the new territories. Nevertheless, a few adventurous men and women were beginning to take up permanent residence on their western edges, for, as Frémont had noted, the land was fertile. Some of these settlers clustered around a trading post called the Pueblo, which stood in modern Colorado near the point where Pike had camped before his desperate struggle to find a way through the mountains. Dick Wootton, who had followed the Santa Fé Trail and, like many other Westerners at the time, had spent much of his life roaming from one place to another, decided to raise cattle on a large scale and do some farming. He chose a site about twenty miles away from the Pueblo and built his house. Around it he constructed a strong stockade with bastions at two corners, making his home a fort. There he settled down with his wife and four children and became one of the first farmers in Colorado. A hundred yards away an old friend of his, Joseph B. Doyle, also established himself. Two miles away another settler, Charles Ortebees, erected a house, where he lived with his Mexican wife.

Although the danger of Indian attacks seemed remote, in the early part of the winter of 1854–1855, the Utes came down the Arkansas Valley from the mountains and raided some other settlers, driving many of them out. Wootton was worried, especially since Doyle was off trading with the Arapahoes, and he therefore was responsible for Doyle's family, too. But since the attacks seemed to be over just before Christmas, he agreed to go on a hunting trip with some friends. While looking for game, he came upon some elk tracks and among them he saw also the prints of horses. Dismounting, he examined them carefully and came to the conclusion that they had been made by Indian horses. He was for returning home immediately, but his companions had not yet shot any deer and persuaded him to stay out with them one more day. Wootton agreed, but later he caught sight of an Indian's head. "I saw it only for a moment," he recalled, "but I knew just as well what it was as if I had looked at it all day, and I knew that where there was one Indian there were more."

The next morning the hunters started home, and when they passed the Pueblo, an old Mexican came running out to tell them that a large band of horses had crossed the Arkansas River during the night, for he had seen their tracks. Wootton warned him that they were probably ridden by Utes and under no circumstance to let any Indians enter the fort. He also stopped long enough to warn some traders camped on the Arkansas that the Utes were nearby.

On Christmas Day, 1854, Wootton stayed close to his own house and spent much of his time on the roof, keeping a lookout for Indians. About the middle of the afternoon he saw a man riding toward him from the direction of the Pueblo. He was coming as fast as his horse could carry him, and Wootton immediately knew that something had gone wrong at the trading post. The rider said he had seen the Utes entering it and, knowing what the outcome would be, had hurried on.

The Utes next killed the teamsters working for the traders Wootton had warned and burned all their wagons and supplies. They then came toward the place belonging to Charles Ortebees. "He had several men with him," Wootton said, "all of whom were inside his fort and ready to fight, with the exception of one. This one was outside the fort digging a grave for . . . one of the early trappers [who had just been killed] . . . The man who was digging the grave did not see the Indians but he heard them coming, too late for him to gain the fort. He dropped down in the nearly finished grave and the Indians passed along without seeing him."

Instead of attacking Ortebees's dwelling, they split into two parties, and a small group headed toward Wootton's house. Originally he had had four men with him to help him defend his place, but now he had been reinforced by about a dozen more who had come up the river seeking the refuge of his stockade. They made a short sally from the house, being careful not to get too far from it but making the Indians believe that they were strong enough to fight outside the walls. The Utes drew back, gathered up some of Wootton's cattle, and left. Wootton believed they were cautious because they were near the lands of their traditional enemies, the Arapahoes.

Before they recrossed the mountains, the Arapahoes learned of their presence and tracked them down. In the battle that followed, Wootton said, "The Arapahoes gave the Utes a thorough whip-ping . . . but they themselves were the greatest sufferers in the long run. They destroyed the Ute village, tore down their lodges, and carried away their blankets and such other things as they cared for. It turned out that the small pox had broken out among the Utes and the plunder which the Arapahoes carried away being infected, many of them caught the disease and died of it."

As soon as it was safe, Wootton and some other men visited the Pueblo. They found only one old Mexican still alive, and he was mortally wounded. The Indians had approached the fort on Christmas morning and asked to come inside to hold a peace conference with the traders. In spite of Wootton's warning, the traders had admitted them. Although the government tried to prevent hostile Indians from obtaining supplies, many traders were willing to deal with them, in order to buy, in effect, a private peace. As Wootton explained in his own case, "In view of the fact . . . that the authorities seemed at times to be powerless to afford us any protection from hostile Indians, I used to think I had a right to protect myself, even if I had to pursue a course which was not strictly in accordance with the rules laid down to govern us in our intercourse with the Indians."

Seventeen persons had been in the Pueblo when the Utes entered. All were killed except the wounded man with whom Wootton spoke, a Mexican woman, and two children, whom the Indians carried away. The woman was killed before the Utes left for the mountains, and no one ever learned what became of the children.

After that raid, during which thirty or forty people were killed, many of the settlers in that part of what is now Colorado decided to leave. Among them was Wootton's neighbor, Doyle. Wootton, however, remained, dug some irrigation ditches, and did some farming. Later he recalled that he was the first American to do so, although some Mexicans had farmed in Colorado a little earlier.

Established settlers like himself were oases for newly arrived emigrants. After weeks on the trail, the dust blowing in their faces and each sight an unaccustomed one, they came with relief to a building with a touch of home about it. Wootton listened to their tales and watched them rejoice when they saw his fields of wheat, corn, and other crops, which reminded them of their homes. "They would almost always stop with me a day or two to rest and trade," he said, "and at the same time obtain such information as I could give them about the country they had to travel through before reaching the end of their journey."

In one case, a woman, Mrs. George Shaw, arrived at Wootton's. She, her husband, two children, and her mother-in-law had set out from Independence to seek their future in the West. During the journey both the children had become sick and died. Then the Comanches had attacked the train, and George Shaw had been killed fighting them. By the time they reached Wootton's ranch, the widow was completely exhausted with grief. They carried her out of the wagon and into the house, where she said she wished to die, surrounded by the few signs of civilization that it contained. Within hours her wish was granted; and the next morning, which was Sunday, an old Methodist minister, who was traveling with the emigrants, preached a funeral service over her grave, freshly dug beneath a cottonwood on the banks of the Arkansas River. The only survivor of the original family was George Shaw's mother. She had no choice but to continue on into the unknown, trusting the promises of her traveling companions that they would care for her.

Life on the western edge of the Great Plains was harsh, but no more so than on their eastern flanks. Congress had unleashed forces of violence such as the country had rarely known, and unsuspecting emigrants, coming west to seek a new life, found themselves facing death instead, not from the Indians but from their fellow citizens.

The pro-slavery faction and those who called themselves free-soilers were determined to turn Kansas into a battleground for their respective causes. Left to itself, Kansas would probably have been free, for the type of emigrant it attracted and the crops for which it was best suited were not adapted to slavery. But Missouri in particular feared that it might become a sanctuary for runaway slaves, and therefore Missourians intruded into its affairs, crossing the border at election time and casting ballots alongside the territory's own citizens. When the voting for the territorial legislature took place in March, 1855, the total number of ballots cast was so obviously inflated and the irregularities so extreme that the governor, a rather weak appointee of President Pierce, disqualified the returns in six districts. But the struggle was not confined to voting and legal maneuvers. One of the men who had petitioned the governor to take action was seized by a crowd of bullies. They shaved off the hair on one side of his head, tarred and feathered him, and auctioned him only for a cent and a half.

Yet he was fortunate. Night-riders crossed the land, leaving behind them frightened people whose fears were well founded. Brutality was becoming boundless, as emotions soared in self-destructive frenzy. The Congress that had struck the match to the ideological tinder seemed helpless to quench the passions it had aroused, but it decided to take action against the Indians who the year before had threatened the safety of the Oregon-California Trail.

The person chosen to be the instrument of the punishment was Brevet Brigadier General William S. Harney, a veteran of the Seminole and Mexican wars. Tough, able, but somewhat simplistic, Harney marched at the head of about six hundred men from Fort Leavenworth along the Oregon-California Trail toward Fort Laramie.

His coming was a cause of worry for those concerned about the Indians. Most of the Sioux who had participated in the Grattan affair had moved north, where Harney could not reach them. Many of the others had returned to Fort Laramie, made peace with the authorities, and resumed their former ways. These were the ones Harney was most likely to encounter and therefore the ones most likely to get in a fight with him. Consequently the Indian agent asked the Sioux near Fort Laramie to restrict their hunting to the south and advised Harney to leave them alone.

Early that September, a band of Brulés was camped on Blue Creek (then known as Blue Water), a tributary of the North Platte in western Nebraska. Either they did not receive the agent's instructions, or else the hunting was too good to leave. In any case, they remained where they were, just off Harney's line of march. The leader of the band was Little Thunder, who, after the Grattan incident, had done so much to restore order. Without his restraining influence, the aftermath of Grattan's defeat might have been far more serious.

Harney learned about the presence of the band, but not its leadership. "Having no doubt," he later reported, "from the information I had received from the people of the country whom I had previously met on the road, and from the guides accompanying me, of the real character and hostile intentions of the party in question, I at once commenced preparations for attacking it."

At three o'clock in the morning of September 3, he ordered Lieutenant Colonel Philip St. George Cooke to take four companies of mounted troops and move behind the Brulés to cut off their retreat. At four-thirty he himself broke camp and marched directly toward the Indian camp with four companies of infantry with, as he said, "a view of attacking it openly in concert with the surprise contemplated through the cavalry.

"But before reaching it," he continued, "the lodges were struck, and their occupants commenced a rapid retreat up the valley of the Blue Water, precisely in the direction from whence I expected the mounted troops. They halted short of these, however, and a parley ensued between their chief and myself, in which I stated the causes of the dissatisfaction which the government felt towards the Brulés, and closed the interview by telling him that his people had depredated upon and insulted our citizens whilst moving quietly through our country; that they had massacred our troops under most aggravated circumstances, and that now the day of retribution had come; that I did not wish to harm him, personally, as he professed to be a friend of the whites; but that he must either deliver up the young men, whom he acknowledged he could not control, or they must suffer the consequences of their past misconduct, and take the chances of a battle."

Little Thunder was in an impossible position. Among his band were some Sioux who still possessed relics of the Grattan battle as well as some who had letters taken from a mail robbery the previous November. But he could not abruptly surrender them to the American commander. That was not the way of the Sioux. Disconsolately he returned to his camp to warn his people of the impending attack.

As the infantry advanced, some of the Brulés took up a position on the right bank of Blue Creek in a futile attempt to protect their village. But they were greatly outnumbered, and the troops, Harney reported, drove "the savages therefrom into the snare laid for them by the cavalry, which last troops burst upon them so suddenly and so unexpectedly as to cause them to cross, instead of ascending, the valley of the Blue Water, and seek an escape by the only avenue now open to them, through the bluffs of the left bank of that stream."

Fighting desperately for their lives and caught between the two bodies of soldiers, some of the Indians took shelter in a few small caves that lined the creek, trying to hold off their enemy, while the others, unable to flee up the stream because of the cavalry, tried to escape by crossing it.

The Americans showed no mercy, ". . . although they [the Indians] availed themselves of this outlet for escape from complete capture," Harney reported. "[T]hey did not do so without serious molestation, for the infantry not only took

them in flank with their long range rifles, but the cavalry made a most spirited charge upon their opposite or left flank and rear, pursuing them for five or six miles over a very rugged country, killing a large number of them, and completely dispersing the whole party. This brilliant charge of cavalry was supported, as far as practicable, by the whole body of the infantry, who were eager from the first for a fray with the butchers of their comrades of Lieut. Grattan's party."

The battle was soon over, and when the soldiers counted the bodies left on the field, they found they had killed eighty-six Sioux and wounded four. They had also captured about seventy women and children. Their own casualties were light: four dead, seven wounded, and one missing. Many Amerians had called the Grattan affair a "massacre," but the slaughter was slight compared to that carried out by Harney.

From Blue Creek, Harney marched to Fort Laramie. Basically a fair man, he seems to have examined the events of the previous year more carefully, because he became more conciliatory toward the Indians and advised those around Fort Laramie to keep peace with the Americans. As it was now late in the year, he marched from Fort Laramie directly to Fort Pierre.

Having defeated Little Thunder's band of Brulés and penetrated the heart of the Sioux's country, he decided the time had come to try to establish a more enduring peace. His plan received the wholehearted support of the government, and Jefferson Davis, then Secretary of War, wrote him, "The President, ever disposed to treat the Indians with the kindness and forbearance due to a weak and untutored race, when he found it necessary to employ military force against the Sioux to punish their repeated outrages, adopted it as the only measure that could be relied on to stay the hand of violence. As you represent that the several offending bands, broken and dispirited, now implore for peace and throw themselves on the clemency of the government, the President, encouraged to hope that the desired object has been attained, and anxious to spare the further effusion of blood, authorizes you to make a convention or treaty for the restoration of friendly relations with . . . the chiefs and headmen of the respective tribes of the Sioux . . ."

On March 1, 1856, the Sioux assembled at Fort Pierre, and Harney opened the council. His objective was not to acquire territory, but to ensure the safety of the emigrants going west. According to the information he had received, most of the Indian

attacks took place between Fort Leavenworth and
Fort Kearny, which was the country of the Sioux's
traditional enemies, the Pawnees. He suspected,
probably correctly, that many of these attacks were
made by Sioux, who thought the Pawnees would
be blamed for them; and by Pawnees, who thought
they could shift the onus to marauding Sioux. "I
have, therefore, considered it best," Harney reported to Washington, "to keep each nation in its
own country, and hold them responsible for all
deeds committed therein. This course will very
much simplify our relations with these Indians,
and render our control over them more effective."

Harney rightly believed that an essential step toward bringing peace to the Great Plains was to cur-
tail the Indians' wanderings, but he faced the familiar problem caused by their lack of effective
self-government. So he decided to start again
appointing chiefs, but this time give them the
means of enforcing their orders. As he put it in his
report to Jefferson Davis, in the past "certain
chiefs were recognised by the nation, others by the
military, others again by the agents, and the
traders, for their own purposes, have most
unwarrantably given medals and appointed chiefs.
These conflicting interests necessarily weakened
the authority of all these chiefs, and to correct this
evil I most respectfully request that the President
will direct and order that hereafter none other
chiefs of the Sioux but those selected in the late
council, under the conditions there agreed upon,
be recognised by either the War or Interior Departments. This unity of action will greatly tend to promote the influence of the government over these
people."

But his proposal was more intricate than those
offered by earlier negotiators. "That the organization of the Sioux may be more complete," he continued, "I proposed to the chiefs to have a certain
number of soldiers in each band to assist them to
carry out my views. They have each given in the
number which they deemed sufficient for that purpose in each band, and I recommend that these soldiers be regularly named, and receive from the
government a dress or uniform by which they will
be known; and that for the time they may be doing
duty under their chiefs in their villages they will receive their rations. The expense would be trifling,
and their young men would be stimulated and encouraged to seek these positions."

In spite of his brutal attack on Little Thunder's
band and his overoptimism about changing the
Sioux's social structure, Harney was sensitive to
the Indians' needs and aware that they were not
solely at fault for the troubles between them and

the Americans. "The character of the Indians," he
wrote Jefferson Davis, "is undergoing great modifications; the gradual decrease in their supplies of
food, their poverty of means to eke out an existence, with the disease and imposition which has
been put upon them on all sides, have forced upon
the minds of these people the irresistible conclusion that to live hereafter they must work. They
now desire to do so, and have already, in some instances, commenced; but they have not been able
to succeed, and they feel that they are obliged to
depend upon the government for future aid and assistance to enable them to live . . .

"It is not yet too late for us to requite in some
degree this unfortunate race for their many sufferings, consequent to the domain of our people on
the soil of this continent.

"These Indians," he went on, "heretofore
proud, stern, and unyielding, now ask of us that
assistance which all nations have conceded to each
other whenever it has been sought. With proper
management a new era will dawn upon such of the
Indians as yet remain."

The council ended on March 5, and at its conclusion Harney believed he had made constructive
progress toward lasting peace on the Great Plains.
The Sioux had agreed to abide by the constraints
he had placed on them and to adopt the form of
government he had suggested. In return, he had
offered them protection from those Americans who
might come into their lands and had promised to
restore the annuities agreed upon at the Fort Laramie council. For the time being, at least, the emigrants on the trail could travel with a greater sense
of security.

Zealous and determined, the Mormons had been
increasing their numbers by extensive recruiting,
and their missionaries had even gone abroad,
where they enjoyed particularly good success
among the people of the British Isles. To the poor
and unprivileged, they offered a new life in the
Zion of Utah, free from social and economic op-
pression. To further the western movement of their
new converts, they had formed the Perpetual Emigration Fund Company, which, like Eli Thayer's
New England Emigrant Aid Society, was designed, as the Mormons' Thirteenth General Epis-
tle said, "to deliver the honest poor, the pauper, if
you please, from the thraldom of ages, from localities where poverty is a crime and beggary an
offense against the law, where every avenue to rise
in the scale of being to any degree of respectable
joyous existence is forever closed, and place them
in a land where honest labor and industry meet a

suitable reward, where the higher walks of life are open to the humble and poorest.''

The fund was so successful that in 1855, it helped thirteen hundred people reach Utah; but that was a poor year for the Mormons financially. Hordes of grasshoppers descended on their crops, and the rains were few and infrequent. The tithes on which the church existed fell off, and the Perpetual Emigration Fund Company was in such desperate straits that many advised curtailing emigration in 1856. Brigham Young, however, was not of that opinion. Tough and hardy, he announced that "we cannot afford to purchase wagons and teams as in times past. I am consequently thrown back upon my old plan—to make hand-carts, and let the emigration foot it" with their supplies in the carts and with "a cow or two for every ten.

"They can come just as quick," he said, "if not quicker, and much cheaper—can start earlier [because they would not be so dependent on the grass] and escape the prevailing sickness which annually lays so many of our brethren in the dust. A great majority of them walk now, even with the teams which are provided, and have a great deal more care and perplexity than they would have if they came without them . . .

"I think we might as well . . . save this enormous expense of purchasing wagons and teams—indeed we will be obliged to pursue this course, or suspend operations, for aught that I can see at the present." Brigham Young had spoken, and that was the plan adopted.

The emigrants were to take the train to Iowa City, Iowa, where the railroad ended and where they would be met by agents of the church, who had already been busy assembling supplies and equipment. The carts, modeled after those used by porters in the major cities, were generally constructed out of Iowa hickory or oak, with as little metal as possible to save money. Their beds were about six or seven feet long and protruding from the front were two shafts, also six or seven feet long. At their tips, a bar ran from one shaft to another, so a single man—or woman—standing between the traces, could push against it, pulling the cart along, while another person pushed it from behind.

In the cart were the emigrants' supplies and equipment, perhaps four or five hundred pounds of clothing, bedding, cooking utensils, and a tent, enough to provide for a number of people, although only two were assigned to draw each vehicle. In some instances, the Mormons had the time—and the money—to cover the outer surface of the wheels with iron tires, but in many cases

nothing protected the bare wood from the dirt and stones over which the cart passed. The axles presented a particular problem. Few of them were made of metal, and even the wooden ones generally lacked metal skeins on which to rotate. Thus they required constant care and greasing.

The first two companies arrived at Iowa City at approximately the same time, and about twenty individuals were assigned to each tent and placed under the supervision of a tent captain, who was responsible for issuing rations and seeing that everyone did his fair share of the work. Each emigrant was strictly limited to seventeen pounds of luggage, an allowance that some found insufficient. To circumvent this restriction, a few put their extra clothing on their backs. Although they quickly learned that this subterfuge was impractical for people who intended to walk more than a thousand miles, one woman carried a collander and teapot to Utah by tying them to her apron strings.

The first leg of their journey took them to Florence, Nebraska, on the west side of the Missouri just north of present-day Omaha. Until then they had passed through relatively settled country and were able occasionally to augment their supplies from local farmers. From Florence on, as they picked up the Oregon-California Trail, they had to depend on themselves and what they had brought with them.

Their experiences were much the same as those of other westward travelers. A violent thunderstorm sprang up, lightning struck the middle of the handcart train, one of the men was killed, and several others injured. A number of men and women died along the way, the survivors of their families continuing on by themselves. Often food was short and the buffaloes were little used as a source of food, because they did not have horses with which to chase them. The axles of their carts often wore out or grew so sticky the carts were difficult to pull. (Once two men sat up all night, boiling the flesh of a buffalo they had killed, only to find the animal so old that its carcass yielded no grease after the sleepless night's effort.)

In the third company that crossed the Great Plains that year, one man had only one leg, two were blind, another had a single arm, and also among them was a widow with five children. In another family the grandfather became afflicted with severe rheumatism in his hands and legs. Often his relatives had to place him in the cart and push him, along with their supplies and equipment. Under the strain of the trip, some of the members would quarrel with each other, and the church elders would have to restore peace. Some-

times the Indians, surrounding them and demanding tribute, frightened them. Yet they continued to
pull and push their carts across the Great Plains,
often hungry and footsore. (One young girl forgot
her shoes at the Missouri River and walked the
whole distance barefoot.)

Five companies made the trip in 1856, the last
two with great difficulty. They started too late, and
the cold weather caught them after they left Laramie. But the Mormons had found a new way of
making the trip to Zion, and until their settlement
prospered more, they continued to depend on
handcarts to bring thousands of emigrants to Zion.
Much of the country agreed with the correspondent
of the Council Bluffs *Bugle* who in 1856 wrote,
"Having seen several handcart trains . . . we
could not help remark the enthusiasm which animated all classes . . . and the best evidence of
their sincerity is in the fact that they are willing to
endure the fatigues and privations of a journey so
lengthy . . .

"This is enthusiasm—this is heroism indeed.
Though we cannot coincide with them in their belief, it is impossible to restrain our admiration of
their self-sacrificing devotion to the principles of
their faith."

The Mormons might be able to get themselves
and their belongings across the Great Plains by
means of handcarts, but such primitive transportation could not meet the growing demand of a large
part of the West. Goods had to be delivered to the
new markets, such as California and Santa Fé; Indian traders needed to restock their shelves; and
most of all, the government had to supply the posts
it was establishing. As many men were finding, the
business of freighting was both big and profitable.
Henry Wells and William G. Fargo, both from
New York State, formed Wells, Fargo and Company to operate in California. Alexander Majors of
Missouri, who had deserted farming for hauling
goods to Santa Fé, was bidding on government
contracts; and Dick Wootton, giving up his farm in
Colorado, was also trying his hand at the business.

In 1856 he secured a contract for carrying goods
between Kansas City and Fort Union, New Mexico. This was an important post located in the eastern part of the territory and close to both the Cimarron and Mountain branches of the Santa Fé Trail.
Wootton's wagon train was typical of many.
" . . . I had," he later wrote, "thirty-six wagons and to each of these wagons were hitched five
pairs of oxen. This made ten head of cattle to each
wagon, and three hundred and sixty in all. In addi-

tion to these I drove along with the train a pretty
large herd of cattle upon which I could draw to fill
out the team in case any of the oxen were killed or
injured on the way or, as frequently happened, got
sore-footed. Altogether it took over four hundred
cattle to keep up the train, and when the teams
were hitched and stood ready to start we had a
procession nearly a mile long.

"Our wagons were what we called prairie
schooners [modifications of wagons used farther
east]. They were strong, heavy wagons, with long,
high beds, and would carry loads three or four
times as big as can be carried on the ordinary farm
and road wagons. . . It took forty men to manage
the train. There was one driver to each wagon, and
then the wagon-masters, who had a general over-
sight of the train, and the herders, who took charge
of the stock when we went into camp, brought the
number up to forty.

"In addition to the freight wagons we always
had an ambulance [a light wagon] in which we carried some of our provisions, and had room for a
teamster or any one else traveling with the train
who might happen to get sick along the road.
Sometimes we would carry two or three passengers
in the ambulance."

When they made camp at night, the men would
draw the wagons up into two lines with the front
wheel of one wagon touching the rear wheel of the
next. If they thought they were safe from an Indian
attack, they placed the tongues pointing to the outside of the lines. When the oxen were released,
they were free to graze under the supervision of the
men assigned to guard them. If, on the other hand,
an attack threatened, the tongues were left on the
inside. This automatically corralled the oxen when
they were unhitched and prevented the Indians
from stampeding them.

Each morning the wagon train started out at daybreak without waiting to eat breakfast. The order
of the wagons was usually reversed from the day
before, so that those that had been at the rear,
choking on the dust raised by the animals' feet,
would take their positions at the front. About ten
o'clock the train would come to a halt. The teams
were unhitched and permitted to graze and water,
while the men rested and ate. About two or three in
the afternoon, they would again hitch up and start
on their way. In this fashion they generally covered from fifteen to twenty miles each day.

For those with the capital necessary to enter the
business and the skill to get their teams safely
across the Great Plains, the freighting business was
lucrative. In the 1850s, when Wootton entered it,

the freight rate from Kansas City to Fort Union was eight dollars for a hundred pounds. As thirty-six wagons could easily carry 200,000 pounds, the gross revenue for the four-month round trip might be $16,000. The total expenses for wages and provisions usually amounted to $4,000 or $5,000, leaving a profit of more than $10,000 for the journey. On the way back from the West, the wagons, of course, were lightly laden, so men like Wootton would try to buy some furs to take to the eastern markets. In a good year, these would produce enough profit to cover all his expenses.

Yet the work was not easy, nor the responsibility small. The cargo carried in a single wagon train might be valued from $100,000 to $200,000, and the man in charge of the train was personally responsible for its safe arrival at its destination. Only such accidents that could be categorized as acts of God relieved him of his liability. Not only did he have to be alert against Indian attacks, floods, and other external hazards; he also had to beware of mutiny among his own men. For the cargo represented a valuable prize, one that could be easily sold in Oregon or some other place distant from its origin or its intended market.

In 1856 Wootton left Fort Union in New Mexico with about thirty Mexican employees and another thirty Americans, most of them discharged soldiers who were returning home as passengers. Although much of the enmity engendered by the war had been replaced by better feelings between Mexicans and Americans, Wootton nevertheless disliked having quite so many aliens in his crew; but as they were the only men available for the trip, he employed them. As usual, he issued them all arms, because of the possibility of an Indian attack, and, also as usual, he tried to enforce the strict discipline necessary to hold such a company together on the long trip.

As the days rolled into weeks, he began to realize that his Mexican crew was becoming more and more resentful of his leadership and more and more restive under his discipline. Although he tried to avoid an open outbreak, he continued to be strict, thinking it better for the safety of his wagon train to maintain control than to appease his employees by allowing them to become slovenly. All went well until they reached Pawnee Rock, the celebrated landmark on the Santa Fé Trail near the Big Bend of the Arkansas River. As they were getting ready to leave camp in the morning, one of the Mexicans asked for an item from the commissary wagon, and Wootton said he would get it for him in a few minutes. Shortly afterward he walked over

to the spot where the Mexican was standing with his friends. Not suspecting that his relations with the men had reached a crisis, he took with him only his Colt's revolver.

"When I came within a few feet of the group of wagon men," Wootton wrote, "I told the one who had been to see me that I was ready to wait on him. Without giving me any answer he wheeled around, and drawing a butcher knife from his belt advanced toward me, swearing in mixed Spanish and English that he intended to kill me. In an instant I had leveled my pistol at his head and ordered him to throw down his knife. This did not have even the effect of checking his advance, and hoping I shouldn't have to shoot I backed away from him and kept out of his reach until I ran against one of the wagons and could retreat no farther. Then it had to be his life or mine and in a second it was his.

"As soon as my pistol cracked," Wootton said, "the other Mexicans, seeing their mutinous comrade fall, grabbed their guns and before I could place myself in any more advantageous position or seek any kind of shelter they commenced shooting at me. I dared not empty my pistol, because I should then have been entirely at their mercy and should have had no chance of escape. I could do little more than stand there to be shot at . . .

"I don't know how many shots were fired at me, but while I stood there thirteen bullets pierced my clothing, but only one of them grazed the skin. I managed after a little to get behind a tree six or seven inches in diameter and from that shelter I fired one more shot, wounding one of my assailants in the hip. About twenty shots were fired at me after that, but the friendly tree warded off the bullets and I escaped without even a slight wound.

"I think the mutineers must have reached the conclusion that I was bullet-proof," he commented wryly, "for they ceased firing and gave me time to seek a better shelter and to have my rifle and other pistol and knife, along with a supply of amunition, brought to me . . ." Now well armed, Wootton decided that he was safe for the time being, and instead of making more of the affair, took up his place at the head of the wagon train and started again toward the east.

But he was convinced his life was in danger. "The Americans whom I had with me," he said, "had stood as though paralyzed while I was playing target for the Mexicans, and I was satisfied that I could not look to them for any assistance in suppressing future disturbances."

A short distance ahead was a trading post operated by a one-armed American named Bill Allison. In addition to selling to the Indians and to white travelers on the Santa Fé Trail, Allison also did a large business in wolf skins. He would kill a buffalo, fill the carcass with strychnine, and return later to collect the dead wolves that had gorged on the meat. He was a friend of Wootton and a reliable man in a fight, so Wootton rode ahead to his fort and spent the night with him.

The next day he and Wootton, each with four Colt's revolvers stuck in their belts and their rifles in their hands, rode out to greet the approaching train. As the wagons pulled up, Wootton and Allison forced the Mexicans to stop to one side and drop their arms in a pile. Wootton also disarmed the Americans, because, as he said later, "I did not propose to furnish any equipment without being able to command its use in my own defense."

He then stored the guns and ammunition in Allison's fort, leaving weapons only in the hands of a few men he trusted. In doing this, he ran the risk of being defeated if the Indians should attack his train. But that risk, he believed, was slighter than the chance of being assassinated by one of his employees.

The profits in freighting goods across the Great Plains were high, but so were the risks, both financial and personal. It was a business only for the strong and resourceful, those who knew the country and the people who inhabited it. The nation, still not truly a whole, was held together by the feet of the drivers' oxen. As the animals pulled against their heavy burdens, churning the dust into the air and making the wheels of the wagons roll over the face of the Great Plains, they were bridging the geographic gap between the East and West and what might have been a cultural gap as well. When the wife of an army officer stationed at Fort Union sat down to sew a new dress, she used a pattern brought across the Great Plains by oxen. When she read to her children from the Bible, the copy she used had usually come the same way. And when her husband mounted guard or went on patrol, the arms and ammunition that he carried and most of the supplies he used had been transported in those wagon trains. By forcing Major Riley to use oxen when he escorted the Santa Fé traders, the penny-pinching of the War Department had revolutionized the crossing of the plains and had given the nation what it desperately needed—a means of holding itself together.

Chapter 26

Gold Again

And I fervently trust that the fond expectations of these gold-seekers, however chastened, may not be disappointed. For the sake of the weary, dusty, footsore thousands I have passed on my rapid journey from civilized Kansas to this point [Denver], I pray that gold may be found here in boundless extent, and reasonable abundance. Throughout the next six weeks, they will be dropping in here, a hundred or more per day; and I trust that they are not to be sent home disappointed, spirit-broken, penniless. If they must recross the great desert with their slow-moving teams, may they be enabled to do so with lighter hearts and heavier purses.
—Horace Greeley, 1859

Ever since Bent had built his fort on the Arkansas, the Cheyennes had been divided into two groups, those who remained north around the Platte and those who had moved south to be closer to Bent's establishment. In the early spring of 1856, some of the Northern Cheyennes came to the Upper Platte Crossing near the present-day city of Caspar, Wyoming, and had with them four horses reputedly belonging to Americans. The military commander stationed there insisted that the Indians surrender the horses in spite of the Cheyennes' claims that they were strays. He recovered three, but the Indian owner of the fourth refused to give it up.

By taking too firm a stand at the beginning, the military commander, like Grattan, had failed to leave himself a dignified route to retreat and therefore continued to press his demands and finally ordered his men to arrest several of the Indians. One escaped, one was shot while trying to get away, and one was taken prisoner. (He later died while still in the soldiers' custody.) The remaining Cheyennes fled toward the mountains, leaving their tipis and possessions behind. The following night they met an old trapper who was heading for the Upper Platte Crossing, and in revenge for their

losses, they killed him. One horse had cost three lives and the goodwill of a powerful tribe.

Late in the summer of that year a band of Cheyennes went on a raid against the Pawnees. While they were camped on the Platte they saw the mail wagon approaching; and wanting some free tobacco, a young warrior hailed the driver. The driver, misunderstanding the Indians' intentions, drew his pistol and began firing. Some of the younger warriors then shot at him with arrows, and one wounded him in the arm. The older Indians, angered by the foolish behavior of their people, whipped the young men responsible, but the driver dashed to Fort Kearny and told the soldiers what had happened.

The army immediately sent out about forty men. Thinking they had already atoned for the offense, the Cheyennes were not prepared for the army's attack and were routed with the loss of six to ten men. Angry, they retaliated by attacking a Mormon train, killing several people and kidnapping a woman. This success led them to attack again.

Meanwhile another band of Cheyennes came east to raid against the Pawnees. (Harney had been correct when he insisted that fighting among the tribes led to fighting against the Americans.) Unaware of the recent incidents, they accepted the invitation of the commander of Fort Kearny to enter the post. He asked them to identify some arrows his men had picked up; and when they said they were Sioux, he arrested the one Sioux who was traveling with the Cheyennes and attached a ball and chain to his ankle. The Cheyennes pushed the guards aside, the Sioux grabbed the ball in his hands, and they all ran to their horses. In the fracas, one of the Cheyennes was wounded, but they escaped. The soldiers then raided their camp and made off with thirteen horses.

That year the Southern Cheyennes went to Bent's New Fort as usual to receive their annuities (Bent had moved downstream on the Arkansas near present-day Fort Lyon, Colorado), and the Northern Cheyennes apologized to the Indian agent on the Upper Platte for the summer's disturbances. It looked as though peace had been restored between the Cheyennes and the Americans, but the Indians had the long winter months ahead in which to brood over their grievances.

When spring came, a number of them thought they had suffered enough from the Americans to justify their going to war and began haunting the Oregon-California Trail. In at least one instance they attacked the train of an army contractor. Meanwhile the army had ordered Colonel Edwin V. Sumner, stationed at Fort Leavenworth, to take the offensive against them. Sumner, who had been assigned to the dragoons since their first organization in the 1830s, was glad of an opportunity to use his skill. He assigned Major John Sedgwick, a graduate of West Point and an officer who had been decorated during the Mexican War, to proceed up the Arkansas with four companies of cavalry and meet him on the South Platte on July 4. He himself took two companies of cavalry up the Platte to Fort Kearny, where he picked up two companies of dragoons, and then marched toward Fort Laramie.

Except for once finding themselves in the path of a herd of stampeding buffaloes, Sedgwick's command reached the rendezvous without difficulty and without meeting the Cheyennes. Sumner's only problem was the receipt of orders diverting his two companies of dragoons to General Harney's Utah Expedition. (Because of troubles with the Mormons, who had little respect for their federally appointed officials, the government was moving troops into the territory to maintain order.) Continuing his expedition with the two commands rejoined, Sumner at last came upon the Cheyennes on July 29 at the Solomons Fork of the Kansas River. As he grouped his men to do battle, Sumner noticed that "the Indians were all mounted and well armed, many of them had rifles and revolvers, and they stood with remarkable boldness . . ."

Later the Indian agent for the Upper Platte discovered the reason for their daring. "The Cheyennes," he reported to the superintendent of Indian affairs at St. Louis, "before they went into battle with the troops, under the direction of their 'Great Medicine Man,' had selected a spot . . . near a small and beautiful lake, in which they had but to dip their hands, when the victory over the troops would be an easy one, so their medicine man told them, and that they had but to hold up their hands and the balls would roll from the muzzles of the soldiers' guns harmless to their feet. Acting under this delusion, when Colonel Sumner came upon them with his command, he found them drawn up in regular line of battle, well mounted, and moving forward to the music of their war song with as firm a tread as well disciplined troops, expecting no doubt to receive the harmless fire of the soldiers and achieve an easy victory."

Quickly they learned the folly of their overconfidence. ". . . [T]he charm was broken," the Indian agent continued, "when the command was given by Colonel Sumner to charge with sabres, for they broke and fled in the wildest confusion, being completely routed. They lost, killed upon the field, nine of their principal men, and many more must have died from the effects of their wounds, as the bodies of several were found on the route of their flight." Sumner's losses were light, two men killed and nine wounded, including J. E. B. Stuart, then a lieutenant.

Within fourteen miles, Sumner reported, "I came upon their principal town. The people had all fled; there were one hundred and seventy-one lodges standing, and about as many more that had been hastily taken down, and there was a large amount of Indian property of all kinds of great value to them. I had everything destroyed, and continued the pursuit." Finally, as Indians often did when being followed, the Cheyennes scattered in different directions, putting an end to the chase.

Reporting on the effectiveness of Sumner's campaign, the Indian agent commented, "The loss of their [the Cheyennes'] winter supplies, and the destruction of their lodges, is a blow that they will not soon recover from; still they are not yet subdued, have not yet been brought to respect the government, and I trust the government will not be content with the punishment inflicted upon them by

Colonel Sumner, but will continue to follow them up until they shall have been brought to subjection, and been taught that they cannot commit their depredations with impunity. This is necessary for the protection of the immense amount of travel passing over the various roads through their country.'' Sumner's campaign had taught the Cheyennes several things: they could not withstand well-trained troops and howitzers, especially when they were outnumbered. Also they could not wholly trust the Americans.

The Americans were not even trusting each other. Out of Utah came strange stories, some based on fact, some pure fabrications. The Mountain Meadow Massacre, in which more than a hundred emigrants were killed, sent a wave of horror across the country and raised the suspicion that the Mormons had been involved. There were tales, too, of the Danites, the avengers personally responsible to Brigham Young, who rode through the night on their dark missions. More overt was the antagonism between the Mormons and the federal government. (Stephen A. Douglas proposed that Utah be stripped of its territorial status, arguing that its inhabitants were unfit for American citizenship.) Without a single post between Fort Kearny and Fort Laramie, the army was trying to guard the emigrants all the way across the Great Plains and at the same time concentrate much of its strength in Utah.

In Kansas, distrust also existed. Buchanan's victory over Frémont in the presidential campaign (Frémont had abandoned the army for politics) brought a sense of relief to the nation's more conservative elements, for they believed Buchanan would calm the country and avoid crises. But he had hardly been inaugurated before the Supreme Court decided the Dred Scott case, in which a slave had sued for his freedom on the grounds that he had lived on free soil. By sweeping away the last vestiges of the Missouri Compromise and by declaring that Congress had no authority to prohibit slavery, the court's decision inflamed the antislavery forces; their emotions became even more heated and the struggle for Kansas more intense.

Robert J. Walker, a Mississippi Democrat, was appointed governor. Recognizing that more and more Northerners had entered the territory, he lost hope that Kansas would become a slave state but still thought he could hold it for the Democratic Party. Therefore he urged the free-soilers to take part in the convention called to draft a state constitution; but failing to take his advice, they let it fall into the hands of those who wanted slavery. The resulting constitution was similar in most respects to those of other states, but with several important exceptions. In no case could the legislature emancipate the slaves already in Kansas. The constitution also provided that the legislature could not prohibit the immigration of additional slaves nor emancipate those slaves without compensating their owners. This last provision was the only issue on which the electorate was to be allowed to vote. This tactic so enraged the free-soilers that few of them went to the polls.

When the legislature later decided to submit the constitution as a whole to the people, the situation was reversed. The pro-slavery people failed to vote, and the constitution was rejected. Despite Douglas's principle of "popular sovereignty," which had been disregarded, and despite the constitution's rejection at the polls, Buchanan submitted it to Congress for approval as a step toward the admission of Kansas as a state.

Some of the testimony in the ensuing congressional investigation gives a clear picture of how politics were conducted in parts of Kansas Territory. One free-soiler reported that he had asked the election officials at a polling place for permission to keep an independent list of those who voted, but "when the polls were opened they refused to permit a clerk not acting officially to remain inside the room or to keep a record of the votes polled. There was an armed body of men, with guns, clubs, and side arms—say about thirty to fifty men—outside of the room where the election was held, who refused to let any person challenge or keep a tally of votes outside. They would come to the polls swearing that 'no damned abolitionist should challenge any person at the polls,' and using other epithets in like manner; that 'the damned abolitionists should not dictate to them in their election.'"

Another free-soiler and his friends wanted to see what was taking place within a polling place but were crowded back by men carrying clubs. "I did not make any resistance," he said, "as the clubs which they carried I considered an indication of what they intended doing. . . . The clubs carried were about eighteen or twenty inches in length," and he added, "They were too short for walking canes, and were not used as such."

This same observer, a man named J. W. Morris, found a window through which he could look into the polling place and "saw a boy, apparently from fifteen to eighteen years of age, go up and vote, giving his name as Russell. I immediately asked Mr. Franklin (one of the judges) if that boy who gave his name as Russell was twenty-one years of age. He replied, 'Oh, yes, Mr. Russell is twenty-one. It is all right.' Within two minutes the same boy went up and voted again; could not hear what name he gave the second time.

"Another man was led up to the polls and voted, giving his name as Williams; in about ten minutes he went up again and voted, giving the name of Todd. The same person came up the third time and voted again within fifteen minutes; I could not this time hear what name he gave."

Morris continued to watch the election and noted that "some of those who were about the polls also carried bowie knives belted around them. . . . I inquired of J. W. Martin, who is an old resident there, who one person was who voted so many times and voted under the name of Williams and Todd. . . . I believe that that man voted a dozen times at least."

In the Senate, Douglas spoke out boldly against the constitution. Slavery was not the issue, he declared, but the right of the people of Kansas to decide for themselves what they wanted. Nevertheless, the Senate voted to admit Kansas as a state.

In spite of the obvious fraud involved in writing and presenting the constitution, it had its defenders in the House. Alexander H. Stephens spoke out hotly against the free-soilers. "Was it a great wrong or outrage," he asked, "to permit the people of New York, Massachusetts, or other States of the north, as well as the people of the south going into a new Territory, the common property of all, to be as free as they were at their native homes, and in forming new States to enjoy the same rights which their fathers did in the formation of all our present State constitutions and governments? . . . But rather than see this great principle of right, justice and equality carried out, this class of men [the free-soilers] went to the Territory to defeat it at every hazard. Setting themselves up in defiance of the law from the beginning, they now denounce a constitution, made by those who conformed to the law as 'a fraud,' 'a cheat,' and 'a swindle.' But the more *ultra* of the same party elsewhere have long since said much worse things of the Constitution of the United States."

In spite of such rhetoric, the House defeated the bill to admit Kansas as a state. And so in 1858, as controversy raged across the country, the eastern edge of the central Great Plains was denied admission to the Union.

When the postmaster general of the United States reported on the contracts he made for carrying the mail, he gave only a brief description of each one: the route, the name of the contractor, the price, and the date and terms of the contract—only a few words for each. But when the report was printed, the list was so long it filled a good-sized book. Yet there was no contract for a through overland mail service. Letters from the East went to California by one of two means: from western Missouri to Salt Lake City and from Salt Lake City by a separate carrier to Sacramento, or to Panama by steamer, across the Isthmus, and again by steamer up the West Coast.

These arrangements seemed unsatisfactory, however, to some members of Congress who wanted a single direct route across the country. Others pointed out that the government was already spending more than a million dollars a year transporting the mails between the East and the West. The growing division between the North and the South also affected the debate, for what became the course of the mail might well become the path for the railroad. Those who favored a mail line, however, had many arguments on their side—among them the need to attach the West Coast firmly to the Union.

In March, 1857, a bill passed. It provided that the successful contractor should carry the mail in four-horse coaches or spring wagons in which passengers could also ride, and he was encouraged by grants of land to open posts every ten miles. (These, Congress thought, would help protect emigrants crossing the country.) The question of the actual route was left open, for the bill simply said that it was to run to San Francisco from a point on the Mississippi of the contractor's choosing.

Although the postmaster general could not legally select the route, he could pick the contractor, which, as he quickly demonstrated, amounted to the same thing. He rejected all the first bids and made it clear that, being a Southerner, he would favor only a contractor who elected to take a route through the South. He gave the contract to John Butterfield, a principal in Butterfield, Wasson & Co., who knew the express business thoroughly. As a young man, he had been a stage driver. Then he had become a stage owner and finally the proprietor of the principal lines in central New York State. He had also operated a freight line across the Isthmus of Panama, the telegraph line between Buffalo, New York, and New York City, steamships on Lake Ontario and the St. Lawrence, and was a founder of the American Express Company.

He and his associates formed the Overland Mail Company and immediately set about making their preparations, for the contract called for the opening of service within one year. Their task was enormous. The line was to have two terminals in the East: one at St. Louis, where most of the traffic would start, and one at Memphis, because the postmaster general came from Tennessee. These two lines were to join before reaching Fort Smith in Arkansas. The route then more or less followed the course recommended by Randolph Marcy to El Paso, on west through what are now New Mexico and Arizona to California, and up to San Francisco. It resembled, as some pointed out, a giant ox-bow, designed solely to benefit the interests of the South. Of more practical concern to John Butterfield was its length—approximately twenty-eight hundred miles. Within twelve months he had to purchase the coaches and livestock, erect the necessary posts (in the desert this also meant digging wells), and hire the men.

But he met the conditions of the contract. On September 15, 1858, the first transcontinental stagecoaches left San Francisco and Missouri, headed in opposite directions. Less than twenty-four days later, the overland mail arrived in St. Louis and San Francisco. "As the coach dashed through the crowds," reported the San Francisco *Bulletin,* "the hats of the spectators were whirled in the air and the hurrah was repeated from a thousand throats, responsive to which, the driver, the lion of the occasion, doffed his weather-beaten old slouch, and in uncovered dignity, like the victor of an Olympic race, guided his foaming steeds towards the Post Office." And from Washington, President Buchanan telegraphed his congratulations to Butterfield and foresaw that the East and the West would be held together by "a chain of living Americans."

Because of the increasing traffic across the southern Great Plains, the Americans' relations with the Indians in that area became ever more important. By January, 1858, more than a thousand Indians had settled on the two agencies established on Texas's public domain; but, the Indian agent asked, "Is it better to maintain those Indians under control, . . . or shall they again be driven to their former roving and predatory habits, because other Indian bands on our borders are unrestrained and permitted to depredate at pleasure?" For despite all the marching and countermarching and the construction of forts, the army had not yet been able to subdue the Texas Indians.

After reporting that several citizens had been killed, one boy kidnapped, and a large amount of property stolen, the governor of the state asked the general commanding the Department of Texas for help. Explaining that the state had already called

out a hundred men, he said, ". . . but owing to the vast extent of country exposed, and the small-ness of their numbers, they have been found inadequate for its protection. I therefore beg leave respectfully to request that you will cause such mounted force as you may be able to spare from other service to be removed to that frontier . . ."

As the year wore on, the situation did not improve. In September, 1858, the commanding general reported that "indications along the frontier, as well in Texas as outside, augur a general war with the Comanches, Kickapoos, and such other hostile tribes of Indians as they can induce to join them . . . It is said a council of the different tribes has been held this summer, and such was the determination."

Worse yet, the hostile Indians continued to disrupt the lives of the Indians who had agreed to live peacefully on the reservations. The Indian agent in charge of the Comanche agency reported in August that "a notoriously bad Indian," named Satanta, had come to the reservation with some companions. Since they had no business being there, Katemesee, one of the reservation's leading Indians, had asked them to leave, but they had refused, saying they intended to rest there a few days.

Katemesee reported their presence to the Indian agent, who called on Lieutenant Cornelius Van Camp for assistance. "We proceeded to the camp with nineteen men," the agent said, "and found them [Satanta's group] quartered in a house originally occupied by a company of soldiers. Lieutenant Van Camp had the house surrounded and demanded them, but the Indians refused to surrender them; the Indians who had by this time collected armed themselves even to the women and children; the house also contained considerable numbers, all furious, and determined to fight to the death.

"Katemesee and his party only amounted to seven who were willing to assist in the arrest. It being the relief day of Lieutenant Van Camp, and he not having anticipated the prospects of a regular battle; his store of ammunition was entirely exhausted, with the exception of a single round, which utterly forbid the propriety of making a fight against such fearful odds; to have done so would have been madness, and the loss, perhaps, of all his men; he therefore ordered the Indians immediately to leave, and to take with them four or five men from the reserve as far as the Brazos to see that they left the country; this they agreed to, but the escort returned in a short time, leaving the two Indians to go at large, who returned in the evening to Katemesee's gardens, and attempted to kill two Mexicans . . ."

Frustrated and angry, the commanding general, Brevet Major General D. E. Twiggs, demanded an explanation. Van Camp replied that, although greatly outnumbered, he still proposed fighting until he learned from his sergeant about the shortage of ammunition. It was the last day of their tour of duty, and not foreseeing trouble, they had shot up most of their supply. "The small force I had with me," Van Camp said, "would have proved utterly powerless . . . and if it is the intention of the government to assist the agent in maintaining the integrity of the reserve, I am convinced that a much larger force than is stationed here at the present is required for the task."

Trying to cover Texas with too few troops was not the only cause for Twiggs's frustration. For in August he noticed an article in an old issue of the Washington *Star* and wrote the adjutant general's office: "A letter from an officer at Fort Arbuckle, written in August, says he sent out Lieutenant Powell from that post, and a treaty was made with the Comanches, Wichitas, &c. At that time I was fitting out an expedition against those Indians. There ought to be some concert of action. One of us," he concluded, "has made a serious blunder—he in making a treaty, or I in sending a party out after them."

In spite of the shortage of men and confusion over policy, Twiggs was determined to subdue the Comanches and in the fall ordered an expedition against them. Under the command of Brevet Major Earl Van Dorn, four companies of cavalry (to collect that many men, Twiggs had had to strip his other operations dangerously thin) and 125 friendly Indians, who had decided that cooperation with the whites was preferable to continued warfare, made a forced march to a Comanche camp of approximately 120 lodges. On October 1, after battling for an hour and a half, they routed the Indians, burned the village, and captured three hundred head of livestock. In his report Twiggs noted the death of Van Camp, "a young officer of exceeding promise, who fell, pierced to the heart by an arrow, while gallantly charging the enemy in this engagement."

So far in their history the Great Plains had yielded little wealth to any white men except the fur traders, but that business offered few economic opportunities for anyone else on the Great Plains except direct employment. For the traders provided for themselves everything they needed. The advent of the emigrant trains slightly changed this. James Bridger had established Bridger's Fort at least in part to make a living from the passing lines of travelers, and the operator of the ferryboat across the Upper Platte and the owner of the blacksmith's shop at Scotts Bluff had seen a similar opportunity to make a few dollars. Their business, however, was generally small. If anything, the majority of emigrants had too many possessions already.

But although they themselves produced nothing and purchased little on the Great Plains, they brought in their wake a customer with a seemingly insatiable appetite for goods and services and almost limitless resources with which to pay for them—the federal government. With the establishment of permanent posts, such as Forts Laramie and Kearny, the army was no longer self-sufficient beyond the settlements. Each post had to be supplied, and the contracts for military freighting became big business. The posts also required cattle for food, and they were usually brought by civilian drivers. The soldiers, too, opened up a new market, and traders were glad to sell them articles that were not part of their government issue. (One trader went up to Fort Laramie with a wagonload of whiskey.)

The mails were another important source of business. Mail routes were usually laid out in a casual fashion. The proposed legislation was left on a table for the members of Congress to review, and if they did not think their districts were receiving proper attention, they could add whatever routes they saw fit. The bill would be passed and the postmaster general given discretionary authority to open the routes or not. He was a man of tremendous economic power, for, as the opening of Butterfield's route showed, transportation of the mails resulted in the purchase of livestock, construction of buildings, and road improvements.

With the development of Indian reservations another important market grew up. The Indian agency personnel—both military and civilian—had to be supplied, and the annuity gifts had to be freighted in. (Later, when the government began to feed the Indians on beef, this market for meat became enormous.) The government had also undertaken the task of improving the roads. With increasing traffic across the continent, people demanded more than the old trails left by the feet of the travelers and their oxen.

The superintendent of the eastern division of the Fort Kearny, South Pass, and Honey Lake Road, for example, reported in 1858 that he had contracted for a train of provisions to be delivered at Fort Laramie. When he himself arrived at the fort, he continued, "a Mexican train was encountered loaded with flour, kiln-dried meal, and *frijoles*, or Mexican brown beans. The opportunity thus offered of turning to advantage the number of laborers who were destitute and seeking employment along the road . . . was embraced, by the purchase of the freight of this Mexican train. It was bought at prices much lower than the usual rates of the country, and cheaper than I could myself have brought supplies from the States. Fresh oxen and wagons having been purchased for the purpose of moving these provisions to the mountains, the new train was placed in charge of Mr. B. F. Burche . . ." Within a relatively few days at Fort Laramie, he had made several contracts, purchased oxen, wagons, and the Mexicans' food, and provided employment for numerous men. Economic activity on the Great Plains was increasing rapidly, but except for the fur business, the basis of most of it was the federal treasury. The man who was adept at securing government contracts was likely to get wealthy; the man who was not had almost nowhere else to sell either his products or his services.

Although this economic dependency on Washington would continue for many years, in 1858 money that had not originated in either the fur trade or the government began to enter the Great Plains. Among those going to California during the gold rush had been a group of Cherokee Indians from Indian Territory. The Cherokees had been quick to assimilate the ways of white men, and they had originally lived in Georgia, where gold was discovered as early as 1828 and where gold mining had become an important industry. Therefore they were familiar with the process of prospecting. Beginning their journey in Indian Territory, they did not follow the usual trail but went up the Arkansas to Fountain Creek, followed it north, crossed over the South Platte, and on to Fort Laramie.

While they were on the South Platte, some of them panned its waters and discovered a small amount of gold, although not enough to tempt them to discontinue their trip. Others, too, had begun to report signs of the metal in the eastern Rockies, and occasionally notices of these discoveries appeared in the newspapers. But stories of gold and silver had been prevalent since the days of Coronado, and although a few lonely prospectors were always hunting for it, others required fairly conclusive proof of its existence before they left their homes.

Then came the Panic of 1857, which changed the lives of many men. Green Russell, originally of Georgia, had gone twice to the California goldfields and each time had made money, not an enormous fortune but enough to support him comfortably in his home state. But after the panic,

he decided to move to Kansas with his brother, Oliver, and some cousins and take up land. Once there he remembered that the Cherokees had discovered "color," as traces of gold were called, in Colorado and got in touch with John Beck, who had been in the Indians' party. The two agreed to lead a joint expedition of Cherokees and Georgians to Colorado the following spring.

Together they numbered about seventy men well equipped with wagons and livestock, and able to hold off a considerable Indian attack. At Bent's New Fort, they stopped long enough to relax over some whiskey, for which they paid a dollar a pint, and continued toward the mountains; and on June 16, they finally saw the Rockies in the distance. "At first glance," wrote Luke Tierney, one of the members of the expedition, "they appeared like clouds pending from the sky in blue and black shrouds. They were then a distance of one hundred miles from us. In the noonday sun we could distinguish them more clearly. The emotions produced in the mind of the young tourist, sweltering in the mid-summer sun, as he views those snow-capped mountains can be more easily imagined than described."

On reaching the watershed of the South Platte, they stopped long enough at a tributary of Cherry Creek to pan for gold, and one of the men found several particles, but not enough to make them tarry long. Shortly after, they met the members of another gold-searching expedition from Missouri. Since their fear of Indian attacks was greater than their fear of having to share any gold they discovered, they joined forces.

On June 26 they reached Ralston Creek, the spot where the Cherokee party had found gold in 1850, and immediately started prospecting. "On their return to camp," Tierney wrote, "their spirits were very much depressed. For my own part, I felt much encouraged. A few particles of gold had been found during the day; but the prospect fell so far short of their sanguine expectations and feverish hopes, that many began to show evident signs of disappointment and mortification. They no doubt expected to find lumps of gold, like hailstones, all over the surface."

They soon realized that Ralston Creek did not contain enough gold for a commercial operation; the best they could make was twenty-five cents a day. So twelve men separated from the rest and reconnoitered to the north. When they returned unsuccessful, "the company all assembled for consultation," Tierney said. "For a long time all were silent, each meditating on the gloomy prospect, considering whether to return home without further search, or remain and risk further disappointment."

The following day most of the Cherokee and Missouri parties decided they had been chasing a dream and that returning home was the sensible course. Green Russell, however, and most of the men who had come with him decided otherwise. Russell was a dapper man, often dressing carefully even in the wilderness, parting and braiding his long reddish-gold beard into two plaits that he tucked into his shirt. But his appearance belied his resolute determination to find gold. He had succeeded twice in California and hoped to do the same in Colorado. When more of the men lost heart, Green Russell said he planned to stay if two others would stay with him. On hearing him speak, twelve men joined him, making thirteen prospectors out of a group that had at one time contained more than a hundred members.

After saying-goodbye to their homeward-bound associates, they went eight miles up the Platte and that same day found the best placer—or alluvial deposit containing gold—that they had as yet located, one that yielded each man ten dollars for a day's work. A little more than a week later they found an even better placer, one that brought them about twelve to eighteen dollars a day. But they were still not satisfied. This was what they called "drift" gold—ore that had been washed from another spot—and they wanted to locate the lode from which it had come.

With so few men, they did not dare split up into many groups or get far apart, which limited the range of their prospecting; but at length they decided to prospect the area between Cherry Creek, a tributary of the Platte, and the mountains. After eleven exhausting days climbing over crags and panning streams, they found nothing that paid better than ten cents a pan.

After another unsuccessful foray, they returned to the Platte to find that an expedition of gold-seekers from Lawrence, Kansas, had arrived during their absence. Coming west partway on the Santa Fé Trail, they had picked up more recruits, two of them women, Mrs. Robert Middleton and Mrs. James H. Holmes. They and their husbands had planned to go to Utah, but the increasing bitterness between the Mormons and the federal government made prospecting seem preferable. These two were probably the first white women ever to hunt for gold in the Rockies. Mrs. Holmes, in particular, seemed well suited to the adventure. Intelligent and good-looking, she was, in the words of one member of the group, "a regular woman's righter" and complained bitterly when the men would not let her stand guard duty.

Still dissatisfied by the results of their search, the Russell party remained determined to find a lode. "This problem" Tierney wrote, "must be solved, and no doubt will be before another year has passed. Notwithstanding the rich quality and great abundance of drifted gold, which will sufficiently remunerate men of moderate ambition, still the mass of gold seekers will never rest satisfied until they have discovered the source from which all this ore had drifted."

After another reconnaissance trip to the south, they returned to the Platte near the vicinity of modern Denver and to their surprise found even more gold-seekers had arrived. Although none of them had had any greater success than the Russell party, they planned to spend the winter on the South Platte and start prospecting again in the spring. According to Tierney's estimate, there were now about a thousand of them. Some were already at work building log cabins in which to spend the cold months, and they soon laid out two rival communities on either side of Cherry Creek, one of them named Denver, after the governor of Kansas Territory, and the other Auraria, after Green Russell's hometown in Georgia.

As word of the placers spread across the country, more prospectors appeared, and with them came others who hoped to become rich providing the services that a growing town would need, such as a lumber mill and a laundry. Dick Wootton, who had tried his hand at almost every Western trade, had decided at last to return to the East. But before doing so, he made one more trip to the upper waters of the South Fork of the Platte, hoping to find bands of Arapaho and Cheyenne Indians with whom he could trade. Instead he discovered the prospectors and, moving into a log cabin, opened a crude store that proved so successful he ordered more goods and built a two-story building, the only one in town.

"New men kept coming into the camp very rapidly that winter," Wootton later wrote, "and it seemed that about nine-tenths of all those who came were gamblers. They would reach Denver broke, and the first thing to do, of course, was to make a raise. They nearly all came through with ox-teams and they would come to me and leave a good yoke of cattle as security for a loan of twenty-five dollars. On the day following they would bring back thirty dollars or forfeit the cattle. This was a matter of such frequent occurrence that loaning money in this way became a part of my business."

To the men and women who moved to the Great Plains seeking permanent homes, the land often presented a fearsome appearance. Yet by avoiding badlands such as these, they could start prosperous farms and ranches. *Alexander B. Adams*

Most frontier towns were hastily built to meet an immediate need. Deadwood, South Dakota, sprang up in a ravine in the Black Hills in response to the discovery of gold in paying quantities. *National Archives*

Cash was short among the hopeful gold-seekers. When Denver's sponsors were inducing Wootton to remain, they could not offer him money, only land—a hundred and sixty acres of it; and many of the new arrivals were unable to afford even the price of a meal. Wootton found that the hotel he established lost money because of his own unwillingness to turn away hungry, but penniless, men from his dining room.

The town, although it suffered from wide fluctuations in population, continued to grow. The following spring, W. N. Byers founded the *Rocky Mountain News*. Often he was short of the supplies he needed and sometimes printed his journal on foolscap or wrapping paper. At other times he faced the violent anger of his readers, and the editors and printers usually carried guns as they went about their work. In at least one instance two ruffians assaulted the building, shooting out its windows. Byers's employees dropped their pencils and composing sticks, returned the fire, and killed one of the attackers.

As the community grew, it began to attract more and more men who were anxious to make a quick dollar, and whether they obtained it by locating a mine or robbing one of their neighbors made little difference. They caused trouble and danger for the many law-abiding citizens who, finally grown weary of the violence, decided to take justice into their own hands. The first test came when a miner who lived about four or five miles from Denver traveled into town with a companion. On the way he murdered his friend and took from his body a small bag of gold dust. Before he left Denver, some Mexican boys discovered the corpse. The people immediately seized the miner, empaneled a jury, and found him guilty on the basis of his own confession. He was sentenced to be hanged at two o'clock that afternoon.

"An executioner was appointed to carry out the sentence of the court," Wootton wrote, "and at the appointed time three men got into a two-horse wagon and were driven under a cottonwood tree on the bank of Cherry Creek. These three men were the prisoner, the executioner, and a minister who had found his way out from the East along with the great crowd of gold-seekers.

"A rope was placed around the murderer's neck and thrown over a limb of the tree. Then the minister, a good Christian man, kneeled down in the wagon to offer up a prayer and the executioner also got down on his knees." The piety of this scene, however, did not affect the murderer, nor was he moved by the consideration shown for the future of

his soul. "The fellow who was to be hanged," Wootton continued, "didn't follow their example, but stood up until the executioner poked him in the ribs and asked him if he didn't know better than to act like a heathen."

Yet Denver's residents could do little to remove the gray pall of poverty that hung over their community. "A great many of the adventurers who came to Denver while I was there," Wootton wrote, "had a hard time of it. Some came without money and others had so little money when they reached there that it was soon exhausted. There was little or nothing for them to do, and as they could not obtain employment many a deserving man had to go hungry in those days, while others borrowed the wherewithal to secure an occasional meal from sympathetic friends who were more fortunately situated.

"There were hundreds of bitterly disappointed men who seemed to have come to Colorado thinking they could pick up gold nuggets almost anywhere, who found it difficult to pick up a square meal once a week."

When the spring of 1859 began again to make travel easier, more men started for Colorado, thousands of them. Many turned back before they arrived at Denver, discouraged by the news that no one had as yet made a major find, and some of them bitterly denounced the gold rush as a "humbug." Others did not give up the hope that somehow the lode—or lodes—could be located.

A late arrival in Colorado was John G. Gregory, another Georgian, who had been on his way to the Fraser River to search for gold but who had arrived at Fort Laramie too late in the year to cross the mountains. Instead of wasting the winter months, he began to prospect southward along Clear Creek between the Cache la Poudre River, up which Ashley had taken his pack train years before, and Pikes Peak. As he followed the stream, he investigated each tributary that seemed to him promising.

When he came to one, now known as Gregory Gulch, he noticed that the color suddenly increased but faded out above the stream. The conclusion was inescapable. Somewhere in the vicinity was a source of gold. Unfortunately he could not continue his search, for a late snowstorm began to blanket the land and he was running out of food. Returning to his base, he borrowed a "grubstake"—or small loan to keep him going— and recruited two partners, William Ziegler and Wilkes Defrees, to help him.

When they returned to the gulch, he put his two partners to work digging holes in the base of the point that separated the tributary from the creek, while he himself went to the top to investigate the upper surface. As a test, he scraped up a panful of dirt and climbed down to the steam, where he filled the pan with water. With a careful circular motion, he agitated the water in the pan sufficiently to pick up the lighter material in his sample. Then he tilted the pan slightly and let the water flow over the side, carrying the lighter material with it. Repeating the process again, he finally had left only the "drag"—the heavy residue remaining in the bottom of his pan. It contained a half-ounce of gold.

Gregory's heart beat fast with excitement, for this was by far the best find he had made. The next day he searched along the side of the gulch for the lode. When he came to the point where he thought it might be, Defrees started digging a prospect hole and soon uncovered pieces of quartz, which also had the rusty, spongy look of gold-bearing rock. Gregory crushed some of the quartz and again got out his pan. This time the drag contained between one and two ounces of gold. He had at last found what everyone had been looking for—a major lode. On May 10, 1859, he staked out two claims—one being the bonus for his discovery—and the Colorado gold rush was on.

Chapter 27

Speed Across the Plains

Just at that interesting period in our history—when the gold and silver excitement, and other local advantages of the Pacific Coast, had concentrated an enterprising population and business at San Francisco and the adjacent districts—the difficulty of communication with the East was greatly deplored, and the rapid overland mail services became an object of general solicitude. . . . The pony express enterprise continued for about two years, at the end of which time telegraph service between the Atlantic and Pacific oceans was established. Few men remember those days of excitement and interest.

—Alexander Majors, 1893

Many strange things had transpired on the Great Plains since the coming of the first white men. Wagons and stagecoaches had rumbled across their surface, the Mormons had pushed their handcarts from one side of them to the other. But fate reserved a unique experience in transportation for Lieutenant Edward L. Hartz, acting assistant quartermaster for a topographical reconnaissance between the Pecos and Río Grande Rivers in Texas.

When he opened his orders, which had been written a few weeks before Gregory staked his claims, he found that they said: "Sir: Twenty-four camels have been sent to you by Captain Eug. A. McLean, assistant quartermaster, in charge of Conductor Ramsay, and six drivers, for the purpose of transporting military supplies and baggage . . .

"The weight of the burden of the camel is estimated variously, but I believe that it is conceded on all hands that four hundred pounds can be carried by them easily. . . . You may have to pass over declivitous and slippery roads in rainy weather, when the camel, from the peculiar formation of its feet, finds the greatest difficulty in traveling. You will then lighten the burden and transfer the portion of it removed to the mules which I send

with them as adjuncts, as well as to have their efficiency compared with that of the camels, as a means of transportation.

"You will please note the performance of the camels under the state of the roads, and report also their comparative merits with the mules, for the object referred to above." And then the orders admonished the lieutenant, "Let the camel drivers [who had been imported with the animals] be treated kindly."

When the topographical expedition to which Hartz had been assigned started out, he had more trouble with the mules, which had not been broken, than with the camels. "At night," he reported, "the camels constituting each train (there were six trains, of four camels each) were taken charge of by their keepers and made to lie down in a circle, the camels of one train being tied to one picket pin. In this position they would remain quietly until morning, or even until they were released to be herded, evincing no uneasiness and affording no trouble." The mules, on the other hand, "were not only very difficult to manage, but were even dangerous."

After crossing the San Pedro River, the trail ran between the stream banks and the bases of the tablelands along its edge. "Over this trail," Hartz reported, "the camels proceeded quite readily, though their progress was not equal to that of the pack mules. The mules could ascend and descend the declivities and uneven surfaces with facility, while, owing to the bulky packs with which the camels were encumbered, and the aptitude of their saddles to loosen and shift from the oscillating motion of the camel in traveling, necessitating halts to repack every few minutes, the progress of the camels was much slower.

"At present, the source of delay mentioned may be ascribed in part to the high condition of the camels, rendering the humps so full and round that they do not fit into the wedge-shaped cavity in the saddle. The saddles, also, not being yet well set or adjusted to the backs, may be an additional cause."

On the whole, the camels performed satisfactorily, although Hartz explained that "on account of the belligerent feeling entertained by the male camels for each other, the greatest care is necessary to prevent an encounter between them. In consequence of this they cannot be herded with the others, but must be kept picketed by themselves at considerable distances from each other. At one of our camps on the Pecos, while the train was being packed, the keepers in a moment of forgetfulness suffered their male camels to be brought too near together, when they immediately attacked each other with great fury, using their teeth. They were separated as soon as possible, but not before one of them had sustained a severe injury in a hind leg, which will, I think, disable it for some time."

At the end of the journey Hartz was still having difficulty keeping the packs on the camels, but otherwise he found them serviceable and confirmed that they could travel in the arid country with less forage and water than mules.

Gregory was interested in quick profit, not the laborious work of extracting ore from the ground and then refining it. It had taken him less time to locate the lode and stake his two claims than it had taken the quartermaster general of the Department of Texas to write out his orders and get the camels to Hartz. Then he immediately began publicizing what he found, starting a stampede up Cherry Creek, while he sold out for $22,000 and at the same time agreed to hunt for other lodes on behalf of the purchasers for $200 a day. He quickly discovered another branch of the gold-containing quartz dike, and soon three mining camps sprang up in the area, Mountain City, Black Hawk, and Central City.

For the future of Denver, Gregory's strike came just in time. Although prospectors were notoriously optimistic, always expecting that the next week—or month—would bring them a fortune, many had become disheartened by their meager findings. Gregory's strike, however, gave many of them new heart and, as word of it spread, brought additional thousands of hopefuls to Colorado.

The correspondent of the *Missouri Democrat,* published at St. Louis, reported from Denver in early June that "the most convincing evidence of the recovery of this and neighboring place [Auraria] from the general prostration that prevailed in both localities at the time of and three weeks after my arrival, is furnished by the great activity perceptible in every branch of business at the present moment. . . . The increased prosperity of the mercantile business has further caused the opening of three new stores within the last two weeks. One of the establishments recently opened boasts of a stock of goods to the amount of twenty thousand dollars . . ."

William H. Russell, an experienced freighter, and John S. Jones had gone into partnership to operate a freight line known as the Leavenworth and Pike's Peak Express. Although the venture had at first seemed risky because of the uncertainty of finding gold, they were now hauling immense quantities of goods across the Great Plains. As a result, according to the correspondent, "prices have experienced a considerable fall. Sugar can now be bought for 25 cents; coffee for 35; flour for 15 cents per pound, etc., a great difference from the exorbitant price current that prevailed some four weeks ago."

The correspondent also noted that "the erection of various improvements in both towns [Denver and Auraria] has been resumed. Buildings that had been left in a half-finished condition, with the expectation of allowing them to remain in such for all time to come, again reveal a display of the skill of carpenters. The foundations of a number of new structures are being laid in all parts of the towns, and the unsightly log cabins that disgrace the different streets are assuming a more respectable appearance in consequence of the cutting out of window-holes, and the insertion of sashes, with glass—no longer canvass panes."

Yet in spite of the communities' efforts to become respectable, the lure of gold was bringing all sorts of people to Colorado; and the correspondent pointed out that "as shade is the inevitable effect of light, thus the present comparative prosperity of this locality is productive of many phenomena . . . One of these is the opening of a public-

SPEED ACROSS THE PLAINS 311

gambling establishment. In the bar-room of the leading hotel faro banks are kept, and monte and roulette are played from sunup til sundown. The flourishing condition of these institutions furnishes strong testimony in favor of the fact that there is now considerable money in this country.''

Probably the best-known newspaper editor and journalist in the United States at that time was Horace Greeley, who had founded the New York *Tribune*. A rather tall man, he was conspicuously light complexioned. His blue eyes were weak and framed every working hour by glasses, but they noticed much of what was going on in the United States. Greeley was not a desk-bound editor, but a man who liked to see what was happening. He was a lecturer, had served in Congress, had helped found the Republican Party, and was strongly against slavery. He also believed in the westward expansion of his country and decided he should make the trip to California himself and see the land about which he had written so much.

The same week that Gregory made his find, Greeley left New York on the Erie Railroad and began his trip, traveling swiftly until he reached eastern Kansas. There he paused for several days and then, boarding the Pike's Peak and Leavenworth Express for Denver, was soon on the Great Plains. Along the route the company operated small, crude posts, where the drivers could pick up fresh mules and the travelers obtain a meal and where women often played an important role. Of Station Eight, Greeley said, ''There is, of course, no house here, but two small tents and a brush arbor furnish accommodations for six to fifteen persons, as the case may be. A score of mules are picketed about on the rich grass; there is a railpen for the two cows; of our landlady's two sunbrowned children (girls of ten and six respectively), one was born in Missouri, the other at Laramie. I was told that their father was killed by Indians, and that the station-keeper is her second husband.''

Greeley commented favorably on the meal she provided, but added that ''the water was too muddy—the prejudices of education would not permit me to drink it—the spring being submerged by the high water of the brook, which was the only remaining resource. She apologized for making us eat in her narrow tent rather than under her brush arbor, saying that the last time she set the table there the high prairie wind made a clean sweep of tablecloth and all upon it, breaking several of her not abundant dishes.''

The next post, where a woman also lived and worked, was no more civilized. ''Our hostess for the night has two small tents . . . ,'' Greeley said, ''and gave us a capital supper, butter included; but she and her two children alike testify that, in one of the drenching thunderstorms so frequent of late, they might nearly as well have been out on the prairie, and that sleeping under such a visitation is an art only to be acquired by degrees. . . . Their tents were first located on the narrow bottom of the creek; but a rapidly rising flood compelled them, a few nights since, to scramble out, and move them to a higher bench of prairie.''

In spite of the hardships of the journey and the difficulty of writing his dispatches in the bouncing stage or in the crude surroundings of a company post, Greeley enjoyed the journey, and his weak, but quick, eyes noted everything. Like every other traveler, he marveled at the buffalo herds, which, although greatly diminished, were still enormous. He was also fascinated by the wolves that followed the herds and marveled at ''the impudence of these prairie lawyers,'' which usually kept out of rifle range but rarely ran away at their approach. He enjoyed, as many other travelers had done, the prairie dogs, who lived in their ''towns'' along the trail. ''The prairie dog,'' he told his New York readers, ''is the funny fellow of these parts—frisky himself, and a source of merriment to others. He dens in villages or towns, on any dry, grassy ground—usually on the dryest part of the high prairie—and his hole is superficially a very large anthill, with the necessary orifice in its center. On this anthill sits the proprietor—a chunky little fellow, in size between a gray squirrel and a rabbit—say about half a woodchuck. When we approach, he raises the cry of danger—no bark at all, but something between the piping of a frog on a warm spring evening, and the noise made by a very young puppy—then drops into his hole and is silent and invisible.''

As an Easterner, he was unaccustomed to the lack of trees and stones, but he quickly understood what was happening to the land. ''The violent though not frequent rains of this region,'' he reported, ''form sheets of water, which rush down the slopes into the watercourses, which they rapidly swell into torrents, which, meeting no resistance from rocks or roots of trees, are constantly deepening or widening the ravines which run down to the creeks on every side. These gullies or gorges have originally steep, perpendicular banks, over which, in times of heavy rain, sheets of water go tumbling and roaring into the bottom of the ravines, washing down the sodden, semi-liquid banks, and sending them to thicken the waters of the Kansas and the

Missouri. . . . For still the soil is washing away and running off to the Gulf of Mexico; and if this country should ever be cultivated, the progress of this disaster would be materially accelerated." He was unaware of the tremendous holding power of the roots of the prairie grasses, but he accurately foresaw that tilling the soil of the Great Plains would cause tremendous erosion.

As he crossed the continent writing his dispatches, Greeley sent them back to New York, where they appeared in the *Tribune*. Thousands read them. The reports of others such as Long and Frémont, while more detailed and more thorough, never reached Greeley's wide audience.

On his way, Greeley had discouraged further emigrants heading for Colorado by reporting what he heard from those returning east. In his dispatch of May 29, for example, he had told his readers, "Those whom we meet here coming down confirm the worst news we have from the Peak. There is scarcely any gold there . . . Denver and Auraria are nearly deserted; terrible sufferings have been endured on the Plains, and more must be encountered; hundreds would gladly work for their board, but cannot find employment—in short, Pike's Peak is an exploded bubble . . ."

But when he reached Denver and learned of the new discoveries, he reported, "As to gold, Denver is crazy. She has been low in the valley of humiliation, and is suddenly exalted to the summit of glory. The stories of days' works, and rich leads that have been told me today—by grave, intelligent men—are absolutely bewildering. I do not discredit them, but I shall state nothing at second-hand when I may know if I will."

Greeley was stiff and lame from an accident that had taken place only a few days before. He and the other single passenger on the express had been joking together about the steepness of the gullies they so often crossed. The passenger remarked that at least the banks could not be worse than perpendicular; Greeley rejoined that they could, they could also tip to one side. A few minutes later the mules became stubborn, as they started down a steep pitch toward a creek. Down the team plunged, the driver pulling back on the reins. Suddenly the left rein snapped, the team pulled to the right away from the road, and the express rolled over with Greeley still in it. When he emerged, "considerably bewildered and disheveled," he said, "I had a slight cut on my left cheek and a deep gouge from the sharp corner of a seat in my left leg below the knee, with a pretty smart concussion generally . . ." But the soreness he still felt

when he reached Denver did not prevent him from personally going to Gregory's Diggings.

"Six weeks ago," he wrote, "this ravine was a solitude, the favorite haunt of the elk, the deer, and other shy denizens of the profoundest wilderness, seldom invaded by the footsteps of man. . . . This narrow valley is densely wooded, mainly with the inevitable yellow pine . . . Of these pines, log cabins are constructed with extreme facility, and probably one hundred are now being built, while three or four hundred more are in immediate contemplation. . . . As yet, the entire population of the valley—which cannot number less than four thousand, including five white women and seven squaws living with white men—sleep in tents or under booths of pine . . ."

Greeley was torn about the advice he should offer his readers. Gold was there, of that he was certain. He had seen it. But he rightly concluded that conditions in the Rocky Mountains were different from those in California. It was farther from navigable water; crops could not be raised nearby, so food would be expensive; the altitude made it difficult to work the mines more than half the year; and the swift-running streams dispersed the gold so far that mining had to be carried out at the veins, not at placers, which was harder work and more expensive. ". . . I feel certain," he wrote, "that, while some—perhaps many—will realize their dreams of wealth here, a far greater number will expend their scanty means, tax their powers of endurance, and then leave, soured, heartsick, spirit-broken. Twenty thousand people will have rushed into this ravine before the 1st of September, while I do not see how half of them are to find profitable employment here. . . . With the gold just wrested from the earth still glittering in my eyes . . . I adhere to my long-settled conviction that, next to outright and indisputable gambling, the hardest (though sometimes the quickest) way to obtain gold is to mine for it."

During the evening that he was at Gregory's Diggings, fifteen hundred to two thousand miners, probably influenced by the presence of their celebrated visitor, gathered to discuss postal service, mining problems, the possibility of admission as a state, and other political questions. Such meetings were common in mining communities and had a deep effect on the development of the West. As Americans had moved toward the Pacific Coast, they had carried with them Anglo-Saxon customs and culture, but these had been changing as a result of the changing land. Americans had become more dependent on beef for food—no one wanted to drive a herd of pigs across the continent; they used heavier wagons—their lighter ones would not hold up; they rode horseback more—the distances were so great—and used pack animals; they were beginning to lasso their livestock—their old methods did not work on the open range. They also found that their traditional law was not adapted to the problems of their new mines and therefore had to write their own.

The codes they finally adopted were often similar, because the problems were and because many miners moved from camp to camp. Usually the laws limited the amount of land any one man could claim, in some cases to as little as ten feet square. They provided how claims should be registered and marked, and how much the owner had to work them in order to retain possession. These laws all recognized that the resources were limited and therefore provided for their equitable division and use. One man could not grab everything for himself, and he could not let what he claimed lie idle.

The laws also went outside the handling of the minerals themselves and covered the resources necessary to carry on mining, most especially water. (Water was needed to wash away the unwanted materials that surrounded the precious metal.) The older riparian law of the East provided—in broad terms—that the owner of land adjoining a stream could remove as much water as he wanted as long as he did not overuse it by pumping it to some other location or carrying on some extravagant operation that drained the stream. In the drier West, however, this law was too simple. The small pieces of land allotted to miners might not permit a claimant to locate near water but only at some distance away, in which case he would have to build a sluice or a ditch to bring water to his land. By the law of the mining camps, if he was the first to do so, he acquired prior rights to the water from the stream. And those rights would be greater than the rights of a man whose claim later touched on the stream itself. In a dry year, when there was not enough water to go around, those who had used the water first could continue to take what they always had. If there was anything left, those with later rights could use it.

Because of the aridity of much of the West, the shortage of water caused problems in other industries, too; and the law, originally devised in the mining camps, was extended to cover most activities. Since a ranch or farm was worthless without adequate water, the owner had to be certain that he not only controlled water rights, but he also had to know how much he was entitled to and when those

rights had been established. Otherwise he might find himself legally unable to touch the water in the stream that flowed through his land. The laws written by the miners in the camps of Colorado would definitely affect the lives of future settlers.

When Greeley came from the East, the flat land had risen slowly to the foothills of the mountains; but when he suddenly dropped from the mining camps in the heavily-treed, well-watered Rockies onto the plains, he observed them with renewed keenness. "The Plains are nearly destitute of human inhabitants," he wrote. "Aside from the buffalo range—which has been steadily narrowing ever since Daniel Boone made his home in Kentucky, and is now hardly two hundred miles wide—it affords little sustenance and less shelter to man. The antelope are seldom seen in herds—three is the highest number I observed together, while one, or at most two, is a more common spectacle. One to each mile square would be a large estimate for all that exist on the plains. Elk are scarcely seen at all, even where they have hardly ever been hunted or scared. Of deer, there are none, or next to none . . . while a stray buffalo, or two, or three, may linger in some lonely valley for months—for all winter, perhaps—the great herds which blacken the earth for miles in extent cannot afford to do so—they are so immensely numerous and find their safety in traveling so compactly that they must keep moving or starve . . . Take away the buffalo, and the Plains will be desolate far beyond their present desolation; and I cannot but regard with sadness the inevitable and not distant fate of these noble and harmless brutes, already crowded into a breadth of country too narrow for them, and continually hunted, slaughtered, decimated, by the wolf, the Indian, the white man. They could have stood their ground against all in the absence of firearms, but 'villainous saltpeter' [or gunpowder] is too much for them. They are bound to perish; I trust it may be oftener by sudden shot than by slow starvation.

"Wood and water—the prime necessities of the traveler as of the settler—are in adequate though not abundant supply," he wrote, ". . . but at length they gradually fail, and we are in a desert indeed." He could not account for the lack of trees. "The poverty of the soil will not suffice," he wrote, "for these lands, when sufficiently moistened by rain or thawing snowdrifts, produce grass, and are not so sterile as the rocky hills, the pebbly knolls, of New England, which, nevertheless, produce wood rapidly and abundantly. . . . For a time [while he was traveling west], the narrow ravine or lowest intervale of the frequent streams were fairly timbered with cottonwood, and low, sprawling elm, with a very little oak, or white ash at long intervals intermixed; but these grew gradually thinner and feebler until nothing but a few small cottonwoods remained, and these skulking behind bluffs, or in sheltered hollows at intervals of twenty to forty miles.''

He noted the weather of the Great Plains and wrote, ''The fierce drought that usually prevails throughout the summer doubtless contributes to this, but I think the violent and all but constant winds exert a still more disastrous potency. High winds are of frequent, all but daily, occurrence there, within a dozen miles of the great protecting bulwark of the Rocky Mountains; while, from a point fifty miles eastward of this, they sweep over the Plains almost constantly and at times with resistless fury. A driver stated on our way up, with every appearance of sincerity, that he had known instances of tires being blown off from wagon wheels by the tornadoes of the Plains; and, hard to swallow as that may seem, I have other and reliable assurance that when the Missourians' camp on the express road was swept by a hurricane five or six weeks ago, so that, after the wreck, but three decent wagons could be patched up out of their six . . . one of the wheel tires was not only blown off but nearly straightened out!''

For years, the men who lived on the Great Plains or traveled across them had been fur traders and missionaries, followed by those who wanted to take up land in California and Oregon for farms. But particularly with the discovery of gold in California and now in Colorado, the population was suddenly becoming more diverse. Greeley remarked on this. ''The first circumstance that strikes a stranger traversing this wild country,'' he wrote before leaving Denver, ''is the vagrant instincts and habits of the great majority of its denizens—perhaps I should say, of the American people generally, as exhibited here. Among say ten whom you successively meet, there will be natives of New England, New York, Pennsylvania, Virginia or Georgia, Ohio or Indiana, Kentucky or Missouri, France, Germany, and perhaps Ireland.''

He remarked, too, on the diversity of their past occupations: ''The next man you meet driving an ox team, and white as a miller with dust is probably an ex-banker or doctor, a broken merchant or manufacturer from the old states, who has scraped together the candle ends charitably or contemptuously allowed him by his creditors on settlement, and risked them on a last desperate cast of the dice

by coming hither. Ex-editors, ex-printers, ex-clerks, ex-steamboat men, are here in abundance—all on the keen hunt for the gold which only a few will secure. One of the stations at which we slept on our way up—a rough tent with a cheering hope (since blasted) of a log house in the near future—was kept by an ex-lawyer of Cincinnati and his wife, an ex-actress from our New York Bowery—she being cook.

''Omnibus drivers from Broadway repeatedly handled the ribbons [or reins],'' he continued, ''ex-border ruffians from civilized Kansas—some of them of unblessed memory—were encountered on our way, at intervals none too long. All these blended with veteran mountain men, Indians of all grades from the tamest to the wildest, half-breeds, French trappers and *voyageurs* (who have generally two or three Indian wives apiece), and an occasional Negro, compose a medley such as hardly another region can parallel.''

Those in New York who read Greeley's *Tribune* and those in other cities who read the newspapers that reprinted his dispatches had received an accurate picture of the Great Plains and life in the gold mines of Colorado. But on one point he was wrong. On leaving Denver, he went past Boulder, ''a log hamlet of some thirty habitations,'' and skirted along the edge of the mountains toward Fort Laramie, where he planned to catch the stage to California. (He was to return from the West Coast over the Isthmus of Panama.) In his dispatch from Fort Laramie, he wrote about the ''fancied perils'' of his journey and that the ''last portion of my route is at least as perilous as any other, being the only part not traversed by a mail stage or any public conveyance, and lying wholly through a region in which there are not a dozen white settlers, all told, while it is a usual battle ground between hostile tribes of Indians. But,'' he added, ''we were never in any shadow of danger . . .''

Others in the West had reasons for differing with this calm pronouncement on the attitude of the Indians toward the Americans' advance. John Butterfield was one. For operating purposes, he had divided his route into two halves at El Paso. The western half, particularly where it ran through the desert inhabited by the mountain Apaches, was filled with dangers. The eastern half was not much safer. Several hundred Comanches swooped down on the stage one day and forced it to a stop, and while the driver waited helplessly, looked it over carefully, studying each detail of its fittings. When they had satisfied their curiosity, they finally let it go—five hours off schedule.

The coach itself was the least vulnerable part of Butterfield's operation. In addition to the driver, it generally carried armed passengers who were willing to fight for their lives, and its well-fed livestock could usually run faster than the Indians on their ponies. But the men who kept the many stations along the route did not have these advantages. Living in lonely spots with only a few assistants, they also had custody of those tempting prizes—the company's fresh livestock.

The station master whose mules or horses were stolen during the night was unlucky, and so, too, were the passengers on the next stage, who had to continue their journey with tired animals. But he was luckier than the station master who suddenly found himself under attack. One station master in Texas, for example, woke up on an early September morning in 1859 to find arrows and bullets coming through the air. About thirty Indians were outside and with only three assistants and encumbered by a wife and two children, he could not resist their demand for the nine mules that were in the corral. They also killed a bullock and commenced to have a feast outside his door. Fortunately a stage arrived in time to drive them away, but the stage had to go on without the fresh team it had been expecting to receive.

Such depredations along the Texas frontier and the inability of the army to stop them caused a thousand Texans to threaten to take the field themselves. Like many settlers, they suspected—and rightly to some degree—that the reservations formed a focal point for Indian activity. Certainly no agent could completely control the Indians' comings and goings; and in any case, reservation Indians were easier to find and kill than roaming Indians. Fortunately their plan did not materialize, but another group of 250 Texans actually did march against the Comanches' reservation. The cavalry came to the rescue, this time to save not the white men, but the Indians. The agent then moved his charges to an area near Fort Cobb in Indian Territory.

Farther north, the Indian agent for the Upper Platte had been relatively content with the behavior of the Indians supposedly under his control, although he wished he could have discouraged the raiding parties that the various tribes sent against each other. These frequently molested travelers on the Oregon-California Trail, and he suggested the establishment of additional military posts along the road.

On the other hand, the agent for the Upper Arkansas had found that some of his Indians were considering voiding any previous treaties they had made, and he had recommended that they be given a show of force. William Bent, who probably knew the Indians better than anyone else, was also worried. In 1858 he dictated a letter to one of his clerks to be sent to the superintendent of Indian affairs at St. Louis. "The Cheyenne Arappahoe and other Indians of this river," he said, "are now very uneasy and restless about their country, the whites coming into it, making large and extensive settlements and laying off and building Towns all over the best part of their country, on this river also on the South Fork of the Platt and Cherry Creek. This is their principle Hunting Grounds. This movement they do not understand, as they have never been treated with for it. . . .

"The emigration to the Gold Diggins this fall has been very large and they still continue to come. They have all passed unmolested by the Indians, although they have stolen several horses from them already, this they do not think much of, but loosing the favorite Hunting Grounds & their only place to get their summer and fall provisions, that goes rather hard with them . . ."

The punctuation and spelling of Bent's letter may have been unpolished, but his thinking was clear. More than thirty years had passed since he had befriended the Cheyenne who had visited his camp, and during that period his relations with them had been close. A passing observer might believe the Indians' intentions peaceful, their wants satisfied, but Bent knew their language, saw them regularly, and understood what was going on in their minds. Their resentment and hatred were building up, and he recommended that the government offer them a new treaty as quickly as possible.

In the early fall of 1859, a few months after Horace Greeley had left the Great Plains, the Indian agent held another council with the Cheyennes, the Arapahoes, and some of the Sioux. The Indians' complaints were generally what they had been in the past: the intrusion of too many white men and the resulting scarcity of game. After consulting among themselves and with the Indian agent, they agreed to settle down in fixed locations: the Arapahoes on Cache la Poudre; the Cheyennes on the Laramie River; the Oglalas on Horse Creek, where the earlier Laramie Council had been held, and on Deer Creek; and the Brulés, who had been so deeply involved in the attack on Grattan, on the White River. They would try to become farmers and live in cabins, but while they were learning, they would need help.

The Indian agent agreed, and the treaty he proposed gave each of them a reservation and annuities for the purchase of farm implements, seeds, and stock, and provided them with a physician, blacksmith, carpenter, and teachers. But a few weeks later Bent returned from a trip during which he had visited several tribes, and he was not so certain that even on those terms peace could be maintained. Some of the Indians, he believed, sincerely desired good relations with the Americans, but the Comanches in particular, driven north by the attacks made upon them in Texas, were in a hostile, angry mood. With the year's discoveries of lodes in Colorado, he knew that more Americans would be coming into the area, and he foresaw increasing conflicts between them and the Indians. In conclusion he reported that "these numerous and warlike Indians, pressed upon all around by the Texans, by the settlers of the gold region, by the advancing people of Kansas, and from the Platte, are already compressed into a small circle of territory, destitute of food, and itself bisected athwart by the constantly marching line of emigrants. A desperate war of starvation and extinction is therefore imminent and inevitable, unless prompt measures shall prevent it."

In spite of Greeley's reassuring words written at Fort Laramie, the clouds of violence were building up over the Great Plains, thunderheads containing shattering forces. Not only were miners crowding into Colorado, but what seemed like poor gold diggings in Nevada turned out to be fabulously rich in silver and destined to bring more hordes sweeping across the plains.

The violence overtaking the United States was not limited to the West. William Bent had written his report in early October. Two weeks later, John Brown, who had adopted the role of bloody avenger of free-soilers in Kansas, descended on the little town of Harpers Ferry in what is now West Virginia. Accompanied by a small band of armed followers and driven by a mad vision, he hoped to seize the government arsenal and declare a separate nation. The blacks did not come to his support, as he had hoped, and troops under Robert E. Lee quelled the incipient rebellion but not the emotion it raised. Brute force was rapidly replacing words in the great debate between North and South.

Although John Butterfield had conquered most of the problems of the southern route across the continent—the long arid stretches where grass and water were scarce and the areas where the Comanches and Apaches, among the fiercest tribes in North America, roamed—it was apparent that the long "ox-bow" was impractical and that, sooner

or later, the mails should pass over the central route regardless of the Southern sympathies of the postmaster general. Senator William M. Gwin of California was particularly anxious to make the change and began looking for a firm capable of carrying the mails for a time without a subsidy.

The Leavenworth and Pike's Peak Express, which brought goods, mail, and passengers from the East to Denver, had run into financial trouble almost from the very start. Alexander Majors, one of the leading express operators, had foreseen this possibility and had refused to join Russell and Jones in establishing it. Nevertheless, he became willing to merge the line into the bigger firm of Russell, Majors & Waddell, which was one of the largest freighting organizations on the Great Plains. As part of this move, the partners bought out the firm of Hockaday & Liggett, which ran the stage between St. Joseph, Missouri, and Salt Lake City. Hockaday & Liggett, according to Majors in later years, had only "a few stages, light cheap vehicles, and but a few mules, and no stations along the route." But since the two lines paralleled each other for part of the way, Majors thought that by combining them the route could produce a profit.

William H. Russell, one of the partners, was a man of perpetual optimism, less a frontiersman and more a city dweller, and he usually handled the firm's business in Washington. Realizing that Russell, Majors & Waddell already had an interest in the central route, Gwin approached Russell about establishing a pony express to California. As he usually did over a new project, Russell became enthusiastic, but his partners were not, for they did not believe they could make it pay, particularly since Congress was not prepared to offer them a subsidy for the service. Russell pleaded with the two men, saying that once Congress was convinced the mails could be carried over the mountains during the winter months, it would most certainly appropriate funds. Finally Majors and Waddell agreed, partly on the basis of Gwin's promise of a subsidy in the future, partly because they thought the undertaking would give them priority when the central route eventually won out over the postmaster general's route.

Telegraph service ran from the East to St. Joseph, Missouri, so that town became the eastern terminal; and a telegraph line linked San Francisco to Sacramento, California, so they chose Sacramento for the western terminal. Their general plan was to have each rider carry the mail for up to a hundred miles, using four or five horses in the process. To do this, they would need about 190 stations, between four and five hundred horses, and about two hundred new employees, including eighty riders.

In the firm, Russell was the promoter, the Washington lobbyist, and the one who kept in touch with the bankers and other outsiders on whom the firm was dependent. Waddell was the headquarters man, remaining close to the office and attending to the many details that arose while his other partners were away, and Majors was the chief operating partner of the freighting end of the business. To organize the Pony Express, they chose Benjamin F. Finklin, who had been active in the Leavenworth and Pikes Peak Express.

The horses, of course, had to have stamina and be fast, but to experienced dealers in livestock such as Russell, Majors & Waddell, securing them was no great problem. Men, however, were a different question, for they had to meet Majors's own particular standards, standards he had always enforced on his employees even before joining Russell and Waddell. Every man going on the firm's payroll had to sign the following pledge: "While I am in the employ of A. Majors, I agree not to use profane language, not to get drunk, not to gamble, not to treat animals cruelly, and not to do anything else that is incompatible with the conduct of a gentleman. And I agree, if I violate any of the above conditions, to accept my discharge without any pay for my service." Majors also gave each new employee a calf-bound Bible and admonished him to observe the Sabbath whenever practical, paying him the same wages as others paid for a seven-day work week. "I can state with truthfulness," he later recalled, "that never in the history of freighting on the plains did such quiet, gentlemanly, fraternal feelings exist as among the men who were in my employ and governed by these rules."

Richard Burton, the Englishman who had explored the Nile, served in India, and visited the forbidden city of Mecca, went to Salt Lake City in 1860 and rode on the stage line of Russell, Majors & Waddell. He knew about Majors's policy and reported: "Results: I scarcely ever saw a sober driver, as for profanity—the Western equivalent for hard swearing—they would make the blush of shame crimson the cheek of the old Isis bargee [a reference to Egypt]; and, rare exceptions to the rule of the United States, they are not to be deterred from evil talking even by the dread presence of a 'lady.'"

In spite of Burton's critical comments on Majors's personnel policy, the firm was an effective organizer and in slightly more than two months

had hired the men, bought the horses, and built the additional stations it needed to supplement those it already operated for its stage line. The news that the express was going to start galvanized the country, for it would cut by many days the time necessary for letters and news to get from the East to the West.

On April 3 the courier bringing mail from Washington and New York arrived in Missouri. He had missed his connection at Detroit by a few hours, and this had delayed him all the way. But the superintendent of the Hannibal and St. Joseph Railroad, which would carry the mail on the last leg of its journey to the Missouri River, ordered a special train made ready, the track cleared, and one of the best engineers of the line placed at the throttle.

When the train pulled into St. Joseph, a crowd was waiting, the mayor made a speech, and so did Alexander Majors. Meanwhile the mail was placed in the *mochila*, one of the means by which a Pony Express rider could change horses so quickly. (The schedule allowed him two minutes.) It was made of leather and fitted over the saddle, being held in place by the cantle and horn and by the weight of the rider. Its skirts contained four pockets, three for the through mail, one for mail to be left along the way and also for the record on which each station keeper marked the time of arrival. The postage was five dollars a half-ounce, so the editions of the New York *Herald* and *Tribune* that were carried had been printed on special lightweight paper.

As soon as the speeches were finished, the rider leapt into the saddle and spurred his horse—but only as far as the Missouri River, which flows alongside St. Joseph. There he boarded the ferry, which carried him to the other side. Then at last he was on the road, pushing his mount as fast as he could to the first station, dismounting, while the attendant tossed the *mochila* on the already saddled horse that was waiting for him, and dashed off again until he reached his "home" station. There he was able to rest until the eastbound rider appeared, when he would again mount and start the return race over the trail he had previously ridden.

Back and forth over western America, the Pony Express riders made their way, often delivering the mail from St. Joseph to Sacramento in ten days, thus cutting the time of the steamship route over the Isthmus and even the time that John Butterfield had established. Among them they created hundreds of stories, for their lonely lives on the plains and deserts and among the mountains necessarily bred tales. East of the Rockies, they met with relatively little trouble from the Indians, who did not feel it necessary to interrupt this flow of news and business that was helping to hold the nation together. But west of the Rockies, the situation was different, and more than one employee of the Pony Express had to hold off an Indian attack.

But the man who perhaps had the worst of it was Russell, who first promoted the idea. At the time that Russell, Majors & Waddell undertook to establish the Pony Express, the firm was in financial difficulties resulting from the military contracts it held during the time the army was enforcing the law in Utah. The quartermaster had ordered the firm to take some three million pounds of supplies to the troops in Utah, a profitable piece of business except that it came too late in the year. All the firm's men, livestock, and equipment were already on the road, but by the middle of July at great expense the first of the additional wagon trains was on its way. The Mormons, however, had decided to take the offensive and harass the army. They seized several wagon trains, destroying their cargoes and driving off the oxen. Then the army retired to Fort Bridger for the winter. The snow had started covering what forage the Mormons had left unburned, and at Fort Bridger the wagons were converted into sheds to replace in part the buildings the Mormons had razed. The total loss to the firm was almost a half-million dollars.

Russell, Majors & Waddell petitioned Congress for compensation without success. Although they had an enormous operation with several interlocking concerns, the loss left them desperately short of working capital, a fact that was disguised only by their size and reputation. To relieve the pressure on the firm, the secretary of war, John B. Floyd, took a step that was unusual and later ruled illegal: he permitted the firm to issue acceptances against its future earnings on its contracts, which he certified as accepted. Under no circumstaces were these to be cashed, but they could be used as collateral for loans, and Floyd even encouraged some of his banker friends to lend money against them. As a short-term expedient, the maneuver was successful, and Russell was able to raise the much needed cash. But since the firm was only surviving by borrowing against its future earnings, it required a new source of income. That new source failed to appear, for Congress did not vote a subsidy for the Pony Express. Each time a rider swung himself into the saddle and started down the trail with pounding horse hooves, the gap between the company's resources and its need for cash widened. The race was not so much one of meeting the schedule of carrying the mail approximately two

thousand miles in ten days but of finding the money to pay past due bills.

It was a race, too, against the coming of a transcontinental telegraph line. Although Congress had not subsidized the Pony Express, it had passed a bill in June, 1860, authorizing the payment of an amount not to exceed $40,000 a year for ten years to a company prepared to build a telegraph line that would fill the gap between the existing eastern and western lines. Hiram Sibley, president of the Western Union Telegraph Company, became the successful bidder. His associates in Western Union were not as enthusiastic about the plan as he was and feared it might prove too great a strain on the company's resources, so he set about organizing two new companies, the Overland Telegraph Company to build the line from the west and the Pacific Telegraph Company to construct the one from the east. In addition he employed Edward Creighton, an experienced constructor of telegraph lines, to start surveying a route. At the same time, he began building a line from St. Joseph to Fort Kearny, thus shortening the run the Pony Express had to make in carrying the news.

While the Pony Express and Sibley were drawing East and West closer together, the army was attempting to make the land in between safer for the growing numbers of people moving west, many of them going to the new gold fields. Colonel Sumner ordered Major Sedgwick to take the field again, this time against the Kiowas and Comaches, who had refused to make peace. Although he marched through the Indians' lands from the middle of May until almost the middle of August, he had difficulty finding his enemies. One small skirmish near Bent's New Fort was the principal result of his campaigning.

Captain Samuel D. Sturgis, leading six companies of cavalry detached from forts to the south, had slightly better success. After marching for about two months without locating any hostile Indians, he came upon a camp that only the night before the Indians had abandoned, leaving behind them in their haste a large amount of buffalo meat, some hides, and a number of lodge poles. That night, when it became dark, he started north during a violent storm, and the following day overtook the Indians, and fought several skirmishes with them. But the fatigue of his horses forced him to break off his campaign.

Both Sedgwick's and Sturgis's commands were weary from their many days of marching and wished to return home, but the army had other plans for Sedgwick. Washington had finally learned that an occasional foray through the Indians' lands was not sufficient to keep them under control and that the permanent presence of troops was necessary. Consequently it instructed Sedgwick to construct a fort, to be named Wise, on the Arkansas River near Bent's New Fort. Sedgwick protested that he did not have the right equipment, not even the necessary shovels, but the orders remained standing; and on the Arkansas, near its tributary Sand Creek, Sedgwick began construction of the new post, hoping to beat the winter weather. Fortunately the fall that year was dry and warm, and the work proceeded rapidly.

On November 8, 1860, he had finished practically everything except the officers' quarters and was certain that before winter he and his men would be safely and warmly housed. On that day, too, the telegraph key at Fort Kearny, where Sibley had already carried the line from the East, began clicking. The operator took down the first message and handed it to the waiting Pony Express rider, who jumped into his saddle and headed west. Within just six days the message had reached Fort Churchill in Nevada, which was now the eastern end of the telegraph line from the west, and from there it went by telegraph to California. It was the fastest transmission of news from East to West that had ever occurred. That in itself was portentous. But the contents of the message were even more so. Lincoln had been elected President.

Chapter 28

A War and a Railroad

But, supposing the cost of a Pacific railroad to be one hundred and fifty millions of dollars, or even one hundred millions of dollars, how is so large an amount to be procured?

I answer—not wholly by individual subscription, or voluntarily associated enterprise. The amount is too vast; the enterprise too formidable; the returns too remote and uncertain. In the present depression of railroad property and interests, an attempt to raise such a sum for any such purpose, would be madness. One railroad to the Pacific would probably pay; but what assurance could an association of private citizens have that, having devoted their means and energies to the construction of such a road, it would not be rivaled and destroyed by a similar work on some other route? No hundred millions can be obtained for such an undertaking without assurance of government aid.

But neither will it answer to commit the government unqualifiedly to the construction of such a work. Its cost, in the hands of federal functionaries, would be incalculable; it would be an infinite source of jobbing and partisan corruption; it would never be finished; and its net revenues would amount to nothing.

—Horace Greeley, 1859

Lincoln's victory in the four-candidate presidential election did not so much change history as hasten its pace. A majority of the people had finally made their choice of the direction that the country was to take. Although the Republican Party's platform had been temperate—so temperate, in fact, that it displeased many abolitionists—little hope of compromise remained. Even before the voters went to the polls, South Carolina had threatened to secede, and, as soon as the returns were in, put into motion the machinery for making that threat effective.

Over the previous few years so many persons had discussed secession that the debate was exhausted before the crisis came. Men like Sam Houston of Texas could plead for a delay, and Alexander H. Stephens of Georgia, the future vice-president of the Confederacy, might argue that secession would accomplish nothing, but they were talking to the wind. Wisdom and moderation were victims of the day's emotions, and within a few months two governments took the place of one.

While the politicians were making their campaign speeches, Russell was taking desperate steps to save Russell, Majors & Waddell. He had hoped to obtain a contract for the overland mail; that had failed. He had issued all the acceptances the market would accept, and he had insufficient funds to redeem those coming due. If their holders presented them to the Department of War for payment, both the firm and the secretary were in grave trouble. Because rumors of the firm's insolvency were circulating—even its riders complained about the arrears in their pay—unsecured loans were not available. Bankruptcy seemed inevitable.

While he was struggling for funds, Russell met an employee of the commissioner of Indian affairs, Godard Bailey. By marriage, Bailey was distantly related to the secretary of war and listened sympathetically to Russell's description of his plight. At the conclusion, he said that he could not advance the firm money but could lend him some bonds against which he might borrow. Russell, of course, accepted this generous offer and left for New York with $150,000 worth of state bonds. The market was poor. He could raise only $97,000 against the bonds, and his creditors were pressing him even harder.

His only hope was Bailey. Perhaps his benefactor would come to his aid again. Back in Washington, he told Bailey all the details of his position, and Bailey added one detail of his own. The bonds did not belong to him; he had taken them out of an Indian trust fund. Russell may not have originally known the true ownership of the bonds, but he did now, and he willingly accepted almost $400,000 worth of additional bonds. Both men were now heavily committed in their common crime, and nothing but a miraculous infusion of cash into the dying firm would save them. In the latter part of November, 1860—the same month the Pony Express so swiftly carried the message of Lincoln's election to California—Russell received $333,000 more in bonds from Bailey. But disaster was inevitable. The political uncertainties of the year had undermined the market's confidence in state bonds, prices fell, and the lenders wanted even more collateral.

Three days before Christmas, Bailey confessed to what he had done, and the firm of Russell, Majors & Waddell was finished. Bailey and Russell were arrested and placed in jail. Both men were indicted, but neither was ever tried. Bailey failed to appear, thus sacrificing his bail; and Russell, who had voluntarily appeared before a House investigating committee, argued successfully that he could not be prosecuted for any crime about which he had testified.

When Congress reconvened, it again took up the question of an overland stage, and again the South argued against the central route and the North for it. But a bill authorizing subsidized stagecoach service over the central route passed the House and went to the Senate. Russell, always resilient, thought that he and his partners might receive the contract, although they had no capital and little hope of raising any. A Senate amendment provided that the Butterfield operation be transferred to the central route. Senator Gwin, who had induced Russell, Majors & Waddell to undertake the Pony Express, argued unsuccessfully that this was unfair. The counterargument, of course, was that the Butterfield company had pioneered the through

mail and should not now be deprived of the contract.

Remarkable as it may seem, Russell still commanded sufficient influence and respect to insinuate himself into the changed situation. He quickly reorganized the Central Overland California & Pike's Peak Express Company under a new president, but with himself still involved, and secured a subcontract from the Overland Mail Company for the distance between the Missouri and Salt Lake City. The government also required mail delivery to Colorado, and Russell bought out the one possible competitor along that route, securing that subcontract, too. He never realized his dream of heading the through mail service, but he became an important subcontractor.

Before the postal bill was passed, the Confederacy had been formed. To both North and South, California offered a tempting prize. It was important, therefore, for the Union to maintain close communication with the West Coast, so the postal bill included a provision for continuing the Pony Express service between the two ends of the telegraph line. Mark Twain's brother had been appointed Secretary of Nevada, and Mark Twain went with him on the Overland stage that year.

"In a little while," he later wrote, "all interest was taken up in stretching our necks and watching for the 'pony-rider'—the fleet messenger who sped across the continent from St. Joe to Sacramento, carrying letters nineteen hundred miles in eight days! Think of that for perishable horse and human flesh and blood to do! The pony-rider was usually a little bit of a man, brimful of spirit and endurance. No matter what time of the day or night his watch came on, and no matter whether it was winter or summer, raining, snowing, hailing, or sleeting, or whether his 'beat' was a level straight road or a crazy trail over mountain crags and precipices, or whether it led through peaceful regions or regions that swarmed with hostile Indians, he must be always ready to leap into the saddle and be off like the wind! There was no idling-time for a pony-rider on duty. He rode fifty miles without stopping, by daylight, moonlight, starlight, or through the blackness of darkness—just as it happened. He rode a splendid horse that was born for a race [something of an exaggeration, for race horses did not have the necessary stamina] and fed and lodged like a gentleman; kept him at his utmost speed for ten miles, and then, as he came crashing up to the station where stood two men holding fast a fresh, impatient steed, the transfer of rider and mail-bag was made in the twinkling of an eye, and away flew the eager pair and were out of sight before the spectator could get hardly the ghost of a look. Both rider and horse went 'flying light.' The rider's dress was thin, and fitted close; he wore a 'round-about,' and a skullcap, and tucked his pantaloons into his boot-tops like a race-rider. He carried no arms—he carried nothing that was not absolutely necessary . . . The little flat mail-pockets strapped under the rider's thighs would each hold about the bulk of a child's primer. They held many and many an important business chapter and news-paper letter, but these were written on paper as airy and thin as gold-leaf, nearly, and thus bulk and weight were economized. . . .

"We had a consuming desire, from the begin-ning," he continued, "to see a pony-rider, but somehow or other all that passed us and all that met us managed to streak by in the night, and so we heard only a whiz and a hail, and the swift phantom of the desert was gone before we could get our heads out of the windows. But now we were expecting one along every moment, and would see him in broad daylight. Presently the driver exclaims:

" 'HERE HE COMES!'

"Every neck is stretched further, and every eye strained wider. Away across the endless dead level of the prairie a black speck appears against the sky, and it is plain that it moves. Well, I should think so! In a second or two it becomes a horse and rider, rising and falling, rising and falling—sweeping to-ward us nearer and nearer—growing more and more distinct, more and more sharply defined—nearer and still nearer, and the flutter of the hoofs comes faintly to the ear—another instant a whoop and a hurrah from our upper deck, a wave of the rider's hand, but no reply, and man and horse burst past our excited faces, and go swinging away like a belated fragment of a storm!

"So sudden is it all, and so like a flash of unreal fancy, that but for the flake of white foam left quiv-ering and perishing on a mail-sack [aboard the stagecoach] after the vision had flashed by and dis-appeared, we might have doubted whether we had seen any actual horse and man at all, maybe."

When Mark Twain observed it, the Pony Ex-press was already starting to ride into history, its route getting shorter and shorter with the passing weeks, for Sibley was moving ahead with the con-struction of the telegraph. In the spring of 1861, the line from the west had only four hundred miles to go before it reached Salt Lake City, while the line from the east had about eight hundred. In or-der to encourage the two companies to work faster, Sibley arranged that the one reaching Salt Lake City first would receive fifty dollars a day from the other until the lines were joined.

Many persons thought the work could not be completed by July 31, 1862, the date specified in the government's offer of a subsidy, but they had not reckoned on the quality of the contractors. W. H. Stebbins of the Western Union Company had undertaken part of the work. After reaching Fort Kearny, he carried the line to Julesburg, Colorado, by spring. Then he moved on to Salt Lake City, where Brigham Young's support had been enlist-ed, and started building east. Edward Creighton took over at Julesburg, and neither he nor Stebbins had any intention of paying fifty dollars a day to the California company.

Assembling the best equipment he could, in-cluding seventy-five wagons and a herd of beef cat-tle—he was insistent that his men eat well—Creighton began stringing the wire to the north-west. Usually he had about ten men in a line dig-ging the four-foot holes for the poles. When the last man finished, he walked forward to the head of the line, a distance of about a third of a mile, and began digging another. Next two wagons passed down the line and left the wire, insulators, and oth-er material. (Poles, of course, often presented a real problem on the treeless Great Plains and some-times had to be carted from a distance of more than two hundred miles.) Next came four men who set the poles in the ground. They were followed by a gang of four who strung the wire. At the end of the line, they had a transmitter by means of which they could report to the east on their progress and order any additional supplies they needed.

Before the day's work was done, the cook had established camp at the head of the line of workers and begun to prepare supper. A wagon then went back and picked up those farthest away, while the others walked to camp. In the morning the cook made breakfast, and the men returned to their posi-tions of the day before. As they moved forward and passed the cook, he was ready to feed them lunch, and in the evening he once more drove to the head of the line.

Fortunately the Indians did not immediately un-derstand the significance of that string of wire go-ing across the Great Plains. If, for example, a fu-ture Grattan were attacked at Fort Laramie, the commanding officer would not have to send a mounted courier for help; he could send a telegram instead. Along the Platte, troop movements could now be better coordinated, and emigrants could wire home their safe arrival at any of the posts reached by the line. The buffaloes, however, quickly discovered there was no better way to scratch their backs than by rubbing against the tele-graph poles. Sometimes they brought them top-pling down.

323 WAR AND A RAILROAD 323

Pushing his men hard, but feeding them well and keeping them in good spirits, Creighton stretched the wire along the road and completed the line to Salt Lake City four days before the California company, collecting two hundred dollars as a result. On October 24, 1861, the two lines were joined, and messages could then pass between New York and Washington and California in minutes. The Pony Express was dead, but the country had the communications it needed during the troubled days ahead.

The election of Lincoln and the subsequent secession of the Southern states created tragedy; but these events, by eliminating the conflict of the South's interests, gave Washington a new sense of purpose and direction, and Congress began to grapple with issues that had long been submerged by debate. The location of the major transcontinental route was settled, a subject that had taken up much energy over the past years. Kansas was admitted as a state in January, 1861, and then Colorado and Nevada were organized as territories. And in California, the state chartered the Central Pacific Railroad, which had hopes of spanning the country and replacing the stage.

Ever since the first days of the nation, the government had looked on the public lands as a source of revenue; and although a multiplicity of laws had made it possible for the common citizen to settle on them, with few exceptions he ultimately had to pay for what he took. For years there had been a small minority who wished to make settlement on the public lands available to everyone at no payment at all. They held the dream of a society in which every man or woman who wished to work hard enough could become a landowner. As late as 1860, they had tried to introduce such legislation, only to see it emasculated and then vetoed by President Buchanan. But Lincoln had campaigned on a platform of free land; and in 1862 Congress passed, and Lincoln signed, the Homestead Act.

The basic provisions of the law were simple. Any person who was twenty-one years old—or the head of a family—and who was a citizen or had filed a declaration to become a citizen could "enter," as the word goes, 160 acres of land. There were restrictions, of course. He had to pay a few fees; the land must have been surveyed, that is, laid out by the government; and the homesteader had to swear that it was for his own use, not for someone else. He also had to live on it for five years and make improvements.

Much cheating took place under this law and its subsequent amendments. More than one propertied person hired someone else to homestead the land

he wanted and then sell it to him; more than one lied about the required improvements he had made. (Four logs could become an "enclosure"; a doll-sized house a "building.") Much land was closed to the homesteaders; some 125 million acres were eventually allocated to the railroads, another 140 million given to the states, and another 175 million acres of land reserved for the Indians. And, of course, much land had been sold to individuals before the passage of the act. (It was not uncommon to see some of this acreage advertised as being "better" than homestead lands.) But with all its defects, the Homestead Act of 1862 was a remarkable piece of legislation and attested to the generosity of the nation. In no other place in the world could a poor man hope to own 160 acres.

That same year Congress also passed the Morrill Act. Its terms provided that every state, except those in rebellion, should receive thirty thousand acres of the public domain for every senator and representative it had in Congress. The proceeds from the sale of the land were to be used to finance colleges teaching the mechanical and agricultural arts. These skills were rare in the United States, and the growing country needed them. (States that contained no public domain received land script instead.) Like the Homestead Act, the Morrill Act was designed to help those with low or moderate incomes by financing the great land-grant colleges that have contributed so much to the nation.

Congress was not yet through, however. The selection of the central route across the country now made it possible to pass legislation for constructing a railroad with federal help. The railroad, of course, would serve vast areas that needed no service, but it would be a bond between the East and the West. As it was, anyone going from the East Coast to California would need thirty-five days for the journey if he crossed the Isthmus of Panama or 130 days if he went by Cape Horn. (That trip was actually seven hundred miles longer than going from New York to Calcutta by way of the Cape of Good Hope.) The overland stage, of course, was the shortest trip, but that took thirty days and cost two hundred dollars. Moreover, it was uncomfortable and dangerous.

There were to be two railroads, the Central Pacific coming from California, and the Union Pacific, which would cross the Great Plains to meet it. Although the general route would follow the mail, many communities were competing to be the eastern terminus. So the charter provided that the Union Pacific would start in the middle of Nebraska with branches running to several locations on the Missouri, one of them to be built by the Union Pacific, the remainder by other companies.

The Union Pacific was authorized to sell $100 million of stock in shares of $1,000 each and with no one person holding more than two hundred shares. The federal subsidy was to be in two forms. After every forty miles of track was completed, the Department of the Treasury would issue 6 percent bonds to the railroad. These the railroad could either sell or use as collateral for loans, but at the end of thirty years, it was responsible for redeeming them. This was not a gift, but a loan, and as security the government held a first lien on the railroad.

The other federal subsidy was in the form of land. For each mile of track, the company was to receive five odd-numbered sections. This amounted to 6,400 acres a mile. This land it could sell or dispose of in any way it saw fit to help pay the cost of construction. The amount was not overly generous. Much land could be purchased in the United States for less than two dollars an acre, and many of the acres the railroad would receive were worthless unless the coming of the track added to their value. Nobody at that time would pay for land in the middle of the Great Plains unless a town sprang up, and there was nothing except the railroad to make one do so.

Dr. Thomas C. Durant of New York quickly became the leading figure in forming the Union Pacific. A native of Lee, Massachusetts, he had graduated *cum laude* from the Albany College of Medicine but found a physician's practice dull work. He then became a partner in his uncle's firm of Durant, Lathrop and Company of Albany, which exported flour and grain and traded in the foreign commodity markets. Shortly the firm placed him in charge of its New York office.

A tall, lightly-built man with a drooping moustache, Durant was a natural speculator, an able and bold operator on the stock exchange. Becoming interested in railroads, he joined Henry Farnam, the contractor who built the Chicago and Rock Island Railroad, in the Mississippi and Missouri Railroad. This railroad was intended to go to the Missouri, but it got no farther than Iowa City before it became a victim of the Panic of 1857. In the ensuing collapse, Farnam was badly damaged financially; but Durant, reflecting his instinct for self-preservation, was relatively untouched.

He had long been interested in a transcontinental railroad, had lobbied in Congress for one, and while he was involved with the Mississippi and Missouri Railroad had personally helped pay for a survey of part of the valley of the Platte River to determine where an eastern railroad should touch the Missouri in order to pick up future transconti-

nental traffic. By October, 1863, he had been influential in selling the $2 million worth of stock that would permit the Union Pacific to organize. He became vice-president but was the central figure in the company, while John A. Dix, formerly president of the Chicago and Rock Island, became president.

Although the election of Lincoln and the secession of the Southern states affected the Great Plains by permitting the passage of the Homestead Act and the incorporation of the railroad, the area was little involved in the military conflict between the Union and the Confederacy. Except for California, the best prizes for either side were in the East. Nevertheless, the Texans thought they would make a stab across the Great Plains and perhaps secure access to the West Coast.

In 1861 Lieutenant Colonel John R. Baylor marched over the southern tip of the Great Plains and seized Fort Bliss at El Paso, then pushed up into New Mexico along the Río Grande, taking the same route that the Spanish had done when they had arrived from Chihuahua.

Colonel Edward R. S. Canby was in command of the federal troops concentrated at Fort Craig on the Río Grande. After the Battle of Valverde in New Mexico, the way was clear for the Confederates to take Albuquerque and Santa Fé. Realizing that only Fort Union now stood between the Texans and Denver, the people of Colorado recruited a regiment of volunteers under the command of Colonel John P. Slough, whose next ranking officer was Major John M. Chivington. Slough attacked the Confederates at Glorieta Pass in the Sangre de Cristo Mountains, while Chivington fell upon their rear, destroying their wagon train. With heavy casualties and without supplies, they were forced to retreat back to Texas.

During the remainder of the Civil War, the Union Army's greatest problem on the plains was the Indians. As more than one observer had pointed out, only the presence of soldiers assured peace. Now that the army was transferring troops from the West to fight the Confederacy, the Indians had a chance to vent their growing hate of the Americans.

In Minnesota the Santee Sioux, who had not migrated west with the others, had every reason to regret having stayed in their native land. For as soon as Minnesota had become a territory, the settlers there had pressed for more Indian lands. Furthermore, some of the personnel at the agencies were inept, and the annuities were often late. One leader, Inkpaduta, attacked some white men and escaped, and his example stirred up unrest by proving that a Sioux could retaliate against the Americans.

The outbreak came on April 18, 1862. The Indians first broke into one of their agencies and killed a white trader who had insulted them only a short time before. They then went on a rampage, and the few federal troops could not control them. The governor commissioned a former trader, Henry S. Sibley, a colonel and ordered him to take the field. After first relieving Fort Ridgely on the Minnesota River, he caught the Sioux at Wood Lake and defeated them. Although the uprising was over as far as Minnestoa was concerned, some of the Sioux under a leader named Little Crow fled west toward the Great Plains, carrying with them news of the fighting.

Since the Grattan affair, the western Sioux had been reasonably peaceful, but their mood was changing. In his report for 1862, the commissioner of Indian affairs reported that "the defiant and independent attitude they have assumed during the past season towards the whites and especially towards their agent, warns us that not a moment should be lost in making preparations to prevent, and, if need be, resist and punish any hostile demonstration they may make. They have totally repudiated their treaty obligations, and, in my judgment, there is an abundance of reason to apprehend that they will engage in hostilities next spring. Like the southern rebels, these savage secessionists tolerate no opposition in their unfriendly attitude toward the whites."

The peace built by General Harney was beginning to collapse. That spring when some of the Sioux had come to St. Pierre on the Missouri to collect the annuities owed them under the Laramie Treaty, they had expressed grave concern over the inability of the army to protect them. "They stated," the Indian agent told Washington, "that they regretted to see me without a military force to protect them from that portion of their several bands who were hostile to the government, and to them who were friends of the white man and desired to live in friendly relations with this government, and fulfill their treaty stipulations; that Gen. Harney, at Pierre, in 1856, had promised them aid; that they were greatly in the minority; that that portion of their people opposed to the government were more hostile than ever before; that they had, year after year, been promised the fulfillment of this pledge; but since none had come, they must now break off their friendly relations and rejoin their respective bands, as they could hold out no longer; that their lives and property were threatened in case they accepted any more goods from the government; that

the small amount of annuities given them did not give satisfaction; it created discord rather than harmony nor would it justify them to come so far to receive it; that they had been friends to the government and to all white men; had lived up to their pledges made at Laramie in 1851, as far as possible under the circumstances, and still desired to do so, but must henceforth be excused, unless their 'Great Father' would aid them. They requested me to bring no more goods under the Fort Laramie treaty, nor would they receive those present.'' The Indians' fears were not imaginary. When the agent persuaded one leader to accept some goods, his band was shortly after attacked by other Indians and its members driven off in every direction.

The situation had become so tense and dangerous that in spite of the demands of the Civil War, the army decided to launch a campaign against the Sioux. Under the command of General John Pope, Sibley, who had been promoted to general, was to march into what is now North Dakota, and General Alfred Sully was to move up the Missouri. In between them, they should catch the Santees who had fled from Minnesota and any other Indians who were hostile.

Sibley located the Santees between the James River and the Missouri and learned that they were willing to talk about making peace. He did not learn, however, that Inkpaduta, who had earlier killed the white men, had joined them. Therefore there were really two groups. Before the council, one officer rode out to a knoll where he could watch the Indians and Sibley's scouts conferring. A Sioux, probably a member of Inkpaduta's band, shot and killed him, and the battle was on.

"In passing over the summit of the hill [that lay between Sibley's men and the Indians' camp],'' one officer later wrote, "I looked back and saw our whole cavalry force come thundering along, company colors flying with the armor of our men flashing and glittering in the sun, while far back in the rear three or four mounted howitzers and a regiment of infantry were coming up on the double-quick.

"We soon distanced the infantry in our headlong march, passed over the brow of another hill and came in sight of the deserted Indian village . . . while away to the southwest, as far as the eye could see, the prairie was dotted with flying figures. . . . The horses while dragging burdens of three or four hundred pounds were also frequently ridden by the squaws with a child behind and another sitting on top of the pack behind, holding a couple of favorite pups. In this way the caravan . . . dashed along in three parallel lines, while their chiefs and braves rode behind and on either flank, ever ready to defend them from our attack.

"If one of the ponies was unable to keep up and dragged its load the fastenings were cut and the owner would mount the pony and dash away. Thus they were continually dropping their burdens from their overloaded animals until the prairie was dotted over with bundles and packs, which contained a mixed and multiform assortment of the habiliments and trappings and toggery of an Indian's outfit."

The infantry had long since dropped behind, but the cavalry kept up the pursuit. "The fighting force of the Indians," the officer continued, "exceeded that of our cavalry, and as we rode up to open fire on them they spread out in a semi-circle in the rear of their moving train to prevent us from flanking them, causing our line of battle at times to become extended for about a half mile in length. The warriors fought like tigers and in their repeated attempts to check us performed many acts of brave and dauntless intrepidity and rash defiance. Their mode of tactics was to concentrate their forces and come galloping forward in a body, whooping and yelling as if about to make a furious charge, but as we were constantly on the alert and rushed up to prevent them from penetrating our line of battle, they would wheel round, discharge their guns and retreat."

Darkness brought an end to the fighting, and the following day Sibley stayed in camp to rest his men before moving westward again. The Santees had become disgusted with the impetuous warriors of Inkpaduta and broke with him, but he was soon joined by some Western Sioux, including the Hunkpapas, a small band that lived toward the north and whom Atkinson had once reported as being friendly. They tried to attack Sibley, but because his infantry could not keep up with the fast-moving Indians, he fought from a fixed position, using his howitzers to keep the Indians at a distance. Stalemated, the Sioux withdrew toward the Missouri with Sibley again following them. They fought one other small battle in which neither side got the advantage, but during it a young Hunkpapa made off with a saddled army mule. The event was of such importance to him that he entered it in his winter count, the buffalo robe on which Sioux families recorded in pictures the significant events in their lives. His name was Sitting Bull.

Finally the Indians took up a position on one side of the Missouri and the Americans on the other. The Indians could not stop the white men; Sibley could not catch the Indians with his infantry, and he was outnumbered when he tried to use the cavalry alone. All they could do was glower at each other, and finally Sibley marched back to Minnesota.

Sully had been delayed getting his supplies up the Missouri and did not reach present-day North Dakota before Sibley left. So Pope's pincer movement failed. But four troops of Sully's cavalry unexpectedly came upon Inkpaduta's band. Greatly outnumbered, they might have been easily destroyed if the Sioux had not become overconfident. Thinking they had ample time to prepare for battle, they did so in such leisure that Sully arrived before the fighting started. Since the Indians had not broken camp, they had to protect their women and children, and this disadvantage placed them on the defensive. Although they fought hard from the shelter of a nearby ravine to give their dependents a chance to escape, they suffered heavy casualties during the hour-long engagement, and when darkness finally quieted the Americans' guns, Inkpaduta's band was no longer a power among the Sioux. But in the vast area north of the Platte were many other warriors ready, if the Americans should press them, to ignore the Laramie Treaty and the agreement made at Harney's council.

In the bleak days of the Civil War when Congress had chartered the Union Pacific, enthusiasm for railroads had been greater than the means for building them. The times were uncertain, capital in short supply—the war was making enormous demands on the North's resources—and investor confidence low.

Eighteen sixty-three was a much better year on the battlefield. General George C. Meade held firm at Gettysburg, and after a furious fight that lasted three days finally checked General Robert E. Lee's northward advance, breaking the momentum of the Confederacy's offensive. Vicksburg surrendered, giving the Union control of the Mississippi, and General Ulysses S. Grant defeated the South at Chattanooga, driving its soldiers from Tennessee and opening up the route to Georgia. At that point the South had lost its one chance for success—a quick victory. But doggedly it kept its men in the field, determined to fight on against greatly changed odds.

Investor confidence, however, did not return, and capital was still in short supply. Durant and his associates had raised enough money to organize the Union Pacific but not nearly enough to build the road, and the communities along the Missouri were still quarreling over the location of the eastern terminal. (Finally Lincoln, with so many other problems on his mind, had to make the decision himself. He chose Omaha.) Even the Atchison and Topeka Railroad, promoted by local interests to link those two Kansas towns, was having trouble raising money even though the route was short and the terrain relatively easy to cross.

By 1863, the Union Pacific had started grading westward from Omaha about three hundred miles, but not a single rail had been laid. Prospects for a transcontinental railroad looked dim, and the government was growing anxious, because it wanted the road for military purposes. Freighting supplies for the army with oxen was too expensive and slow.

Congress, therefore, reconsidered the original charter and decided to make it more attractive to investors. The new legislation passed in 1864 doubled the land grants and included the mineral rights, which previously had been reserved to the government. It also permitted the railroad to issue first-mortgage bonds and took only a second lien to protect its own bonds. To help the company further, it agreed to issue federal bonds and title to the land grants for every twenty miles of track completed, instead of every forty. This move was intended to cut in half the amount of working capital needed. Congress also reduced the par value on the stock from $1,000 to $100 and removed the limit on the amount any one person could hold. But even this liberalization of the original provisions was not sufficient to attract the funds the company needed.

One basic problem was the requirement that the railroad sell its stock at par. To dispose of $100 million worth at a fixed price with no discount for underwriters and no responsiveness to the market was clearly impossible. The legislation had been intended to prevent the company from throwing its stock on the market, but most investors were unwilling to pay par when they knew that thousands of unsold shares remained in the company's treasury. Yet the government's loans and grants were to be issued after, not before, track had been laid. Thus only through the sale of stock could the company obtain the working capital it needed to get started.

Durant, always a clever manipulator, devised a way around this impasse. Adopting an idea that had been used in building other railroads, he proposed that the men who controlled the Union Pacific should give the construction contracts to a friendly contractor and arrange to pay him in stock. Since he would not be bound by the Union Pacific's charter, he could sell that stock for whatever the market would bring. Obviously he would

have to be paid at a price that would compensate him for the difference between the par value and the market value.

The first contractor they selected to carry out this function was Herbert M. Hoxie of Des Moines, a man of good political connections and little means. (His principal business was operating a ferry across the Missouri.) Since Hoxie clearly had no way to fulfill the contract, Durant formed a partnership with several of his associates, who agreed among themselves to supply $1.6 million in capital—25 percent down—and take over Hoxie's contract. They would then sell the Union Pacific stock that Hoxie was to receive for whatever price they could get and take the profit.

Peter A. Dey, a capable railroad engineer, was in charge of making the surveys, and it was his responsibility to estimate the cost of the construction covered by the contract with Hoxie. He computed it at the rate of $30,000 a mile for the first hundred miles and $27,000 for the next one hundred. On seeing these figures, Durant personally intervened. From the first, he had had little faith in the Union Pacific's ability to earn much revenue. He had seen, however, that vast profits could be made in its construction. Those were the profits that had attracted his attention, and he meant to get his full share of them. Therefore he summarily ordered Dey to change his estimate to $50,000 a mile, a sizable increase and one that ensured large earnings for his partnership. Being an honest man, Dey resigned, but the Hoxie contract went through on the basis of Durant's figures.

Meanwhile Durant had been looking for a corporation he could purchase that would serve as the recipient of the Union Pacific's contracts and selected one known as the Pennsylvania Fiscal Agency. The corporation, although little known, had an extremely broad charter, which was exactly what Durant wanted. It could engage in almost any sort of business and establish branch offices anywhere; and yet it offered Durant and his associates the advantage of limited liability. He purchased it, and then, on the advice of a friend, changed its name to the Credit Mobilier, after a large French company. Although it retained its headquarters in Philadelphia, its principal operations soon centered in its New York office, and Durant quickly arranged to transfer the Hoxie contract from his loose consortium to his newly acquired corporation.

His device circumvented the roadblock that Congress had unintentionally placed in the way of construction, but because the same men controlled the Union Pacific and the Credit Mobilier, it offered an opportunity for costly fraud and exces-

sive profits for a small group of insiders. The Hoxie contract demonstrated that Durant was determined to take advantage of that opportunity.

Shortly after Congress admitted Kansas to the
Union, it organized Colorado as a territory. In
1862 Lincoln appointed John Evans territorial governor. One of Evans's principal interests was the
condition and attitudes of the Indians, and he
quickly became aware that the warring among the
tribes was in itself disruptive. "When I first went
there," he later recalled, "I thought it would be a
very humane and good idea to get those Indians to
quit fighting one another, and I gave them a great
many lectures on the impropriety of these war parties, but I found, after I had done it, that it gave a
great deal of offence to them. One of them said he
had been brought up to war, and to quit fighting
was a thing he could not think of, and he thought it
was an unworthy interference on my part." Evans
had quickly recognized a truth that had eluded
many other white men—that warfare was part of
the Indians' culture. With the coming of guns and
horses, it had become bloodier and more time-consuming, but it and the hunt were still the two reasons for a warrior's being.

Evans also learned that the Indians, just as Bent
had prophesied, were growing angry over the intrusion of the Americans into Colorado. One of the
first he talked to was Little Owl, leader of a band of
Arapahoes. "He said," Evans related, "that the
white people had taken their gold and their lands;
that they wanted their own lands, they did not care
about the gold particularly. I told them that they
had made a treaty at Fort Wise [at a council held in
September, 1860]. He claimed that he was not
there, and a good many of his party said they were
not there . . . He said they would not settle on
the Arkansas."

That winter Little Owl, whom Evans regarded
as a friend of the Americans, died, and in the
spring of 1863, the leader who succeeded him also
talked to the governor and said "that there was a
party of Sioux who had been down with them and
had held a council . . . at Horse creek . . . in
which the question of driving the whites out of the
country and preventing them from settling was the
chief discussion. His claim was that he and a good
portion of his band were opposed to anything of
the kind, but some of them were much in favor of
going to war."

Disturbed by the thousands of Americans coming into the country, Colorado's Indians were in
touch with the Sioux and knew about the uprising
in Minnesota. To add to the fears of the people of

the territory were rumors that the Confederates
were attempting to organize the Indians to the
south and had persuaded them to attack Fort
Larned and Fort Wise. If the Confederates could
gain control of the Arkansas, they might conceivably raid north along the Platte and cut the mail
and telegraph line between the East and California.
Although the alarmists overestimated the ability of
the Indians to coordinate their actions, settlers in
Colorado, Nebraska, and Kansas believed they had
reason to be nervous.

Evans decided to hold a council with the Indians
at the head of the Republican River during the first
week of September, and, he said, "I employed Elbridge Gerry, who has been about twenty-five
years among them and has a Cheyenne wife (and,
by the way, he is a grandson of Elbridge Gerry
who signed the Declaration of Independence, and a
scholar and a man of very good mind)" to find all
the Arapahoes and Cheyennes he could. But the
Indians were no longer interested in treaties. Gerry
reported to Evans that "they did not want anything
more to do with the whites; that they did not want
any more presents, but they wanted their lands,
and would have their lands."

Some who knew the Indians well said the majority were still friendly; others were convinced they
were not. In the spring of 1864, the Cheyennes
were accused by a government contractor of stealing 175 head of cattle. A lieutenant went in pursuit. He caught up with the band, a few shots were
fired, the Indians fled, and he recovered, so he reported, about a hundred head of the cattle.

That spring the Cheyennes also fought a small
engagement with American troops on the South
Platte. They were on their way to attack the Crows
and were reported to have picked up four stray
mules. The effort to recover the mules cost several
lives and added to the mounting tension. By the
end of June, Evans decided that many of the Indians were in a state of war with the Americans and
called upon all interpreters, traders, and agents to
"inform the friendly Indians of the plains that
some members of their tribes have gone to war
with the white people; they steal stock and run it
off, hoping to escape detection and punishment.

"In some instances they have attacked and
killed soldiers and murdered peaceable citizens.
For this the Great Father is angry, and will certainly hunt them out and punish them; but he does not
want to injure those who remain friendly to the
whites. He desires to protect and take care of them.
For this purpose I direct that all friendly Indians
keep away from those who are at war, and go to
places of safety."

After designating the reservations to which the Indians should report, he explained that "the object of this is to prevent friendly Indians from being killed through mistake; none but those who intend to be friendly with the whites must come to these places. The families of those who have gone to war with the whites must be kept away from among the friendly Indians."

Earlier General Twiss, commanding the Department of Texas, had complained about the government's inability to act in concert and that it sometimes made war and peace at the same time. The spring that Evans was putting Colorado on a war footing, the government was holding a peace council not far away at Camp Cottonwood (later Fort McPherson). Located on the South Platte about eight miles above its fork with the North Platte, the post was designed to protect travelers and to control a ford that was much used by the Indians. The council was to be with Sioux, particularly the Oglalas and Brulés, and among those present was the Brulé, Spotted Tail, one of the most respected of the Sioux leaders.

Brigadier General Robert B. Mitchell was in charge of the negotiations for the Americans. A man of fairness, he had come to Kansas as a pro-slavery Democrat but had been so outraged by the excesses of the pro-slavery forces that he had become anti-slavery. He spoke sternly to the Sioux about staying out of the Platte Valley, but the Sioux replied that they would go wherever they wanted. They also asked the Americans to stop surveying a road up the Niobrara, which Mitchell agreed to do, and they wanted the road up the Smoky Hill River closed also. That route was traveled by too many emigrants, and Mitchell said he could not agree to this. Both sides were bluffing, especially the Americans, for Mitchell threatened to fill the Platte Valley with soldiers. With the Civil War still raging, he did not have the men. The council finally broke up with no agreement having been reached.

In Colorado, Evans was preparing to fight; in Nebraska, the government was trying to make peace; farther north, Sully was marching up the Missouri on a punitive expedition. Several Indians ambushed and killed a botanist who was traveling with his expedition. The soldiers went in pursuit, chasing the Indians for about fifteen miles, and finally caught and decapitated them, placing their heads on poles. Word of this treatment quickly spread in the Indian world, infuriating them.

After establishing Fort Rice at the mouth of the Cannonball, Sully moved west into the land toward which Inkpaduta had fled with the remainder of his band the previous year. Inkpaduta had suffered heavily and was not anxious to fight the Americans again, but he had met the Western Sioux, and in numbers there was strength. The Sioux took up a position in the Killdeer Mountains in present-day North Dakota just south of the Little Missouri River. There they had plenty of wood and water, and some deep ravines made access difficult. But in choosing this spot, Inkpaduta, to whom the other Indians had turned since he had already fought the Americans, gave up their greatest advantage, their mobility. Only if Sully became disheartened could this choice for a stand be justified.

Sully was a determined campaigner. He stripped himself of some of his provisions and supplies and made a forced march toward the Indians with about two thousand men. In the center he placed his howitzers, guarded on both flanks by several companies and followed by a strong rearguard. This sort of attack was new to the Indians. The howitzers frightened them, and they could not get at Sully's flanks. Flight seemed the wisest course, so they began fleeing over the mountains onto the plains on the other side. Because of the rough ground, Sully did not dare follow them in the coming darkness, and made camp.

An American woman, Fanny Kelly, had been a captive of the Sioux at the time of the battle. Later she described their retreat. "It was late at night," she said, "when we stopped our pace, when at length we reached the lofty banks of a noble river, but it was some time before they could find a break in the rocky shores which enabled us to reach the water and enjoy the delicious draught, in which luxury the panting horses gladly participated.

"We had traveled far and fast all day long without cessation, through clouds of smoke and dust, parched by a scorching sun. My face was blistered from the burning rays, as I had been compelled to go with my head uncovered, after the fashion of all Indian women. Had not had a drop of water during the whole day.

"Reluctant to leave the long-desired acquisition, they all lay down under the tall willows, close to the stream, and slept the sleep of the weary. The horses lingered near, nipping the tender blades of grass that sparsely bordered the stream."

The next morning the Indians crossed the Little Missouri; and as soon as daylight permitted him to find his way out of the mountains, Sully continued his pursuit in the direction of the Yellowstone. "My feelings, all this time," Mrs. Kelly said, "cannot be described, when I could hear the sound of the big guns, as the Indians term cannon. I felt the soldiers had surely come for me and would overtake us, and my heart bounded with joy at the very thought of deliverance, but sank proportionately, when they came to me, wearing their trophies, reeking scalps, soldiers' uniforms, covered with blood, which told its sad story to my aching heart. One day I might be cheered by a strong hope of approaching relief, then again would have such assurance of my enemy's success as would sink me correspondingly low in despair. For some reason deception seemed to be their peculiar delight; whether they did it to gratify an insatiable thirst for revenge in themselves, or to keep me more reconciled, more willing and patient to abide, was something I could not determine.

"The feelings occasioned by my disappointment in their success can be better imagined than described, but imagination, even in her most extravagant flights, can but barely picture the horrors that met my view during those running flights."

Because Kenneth McKenzie so many years before had introduced steamboats to the Upper Missouri, Sully enjoyed a tactical advantage over the Sioux. He was expecting supplies to reach him by water at the Yellowstone, so he could afford to be extravagant with ammunition and equipment. The Sioux could not. In order to move quickly enough to avoid the army, they had to throw away many of their possessions, knowing that they could not immediately replace them.

At the Yellowstone, Sully broke off his pursuit. His men were tired from their long, fast march, and he was getting farther and farther from his base. After his departure, Mrs. Kelly said that "a scene of terrible mourning over the killed ensued among the women. Their cries are terribly wild and distressing, on such occasions; and the near relations of the deceased indulge in frantic expressions of grief that cannot be described. Sometimes the practice of cutting the flesh is carried to a horrible and barbarous extent. They inflict gashes on their bodies and limbs an inch in length. Some cut off their hair, blacken their faces, and march through the village in procession; torturing their bodies to add vigor to their lamentations.

"Hunger followed on the track of grief; all their food was gone, and there was no game in that portion of the country.

"In our flight they scattered everything, and the country through which we passed for the following two weeks did not yield enough to arrest starvation. The Indians were terribly enraged and threatened me with death almost hourly, and in every form.

"A terrible time ensued, and many dogs, and even horses, died of starvation. Their bodies were eaten immediately; and the slow but constant march was daily kept up, in hope of game and better facilities for fish and fruit."

The casualties inflicted by Sully had not been devastating, but the Sioux, who were usually conquerors in the wars on the Great Plains, were not accustomed to being driven by their enemies. It was probably one of the worst defeats they had suffered since they had moved west, and they had lost practically all of their supplies and many of their lodges. Months would pass before they could recover. But because Sully could not remain in the Indians' territory and had no means of making or enforcing a treaty, the results were only temporary. Nor did the Sioux's defeat have any effect on the situation along the Platte.

There Evans's policy had not been working. In the summer of 1864, the Indians stopped the stage from running for a while, ran off with some government stock, forcing the general in charge to buy more horses for what he called our "dismounted cavalry," attacked settlers on the Little Blue, and became so active the Overland Stage Company asked for army guards to ride on each coach. On August 10, 1864, the commander at Forth Leavenworth reported that he had "telegraphed the commander of Kearny to come down on them [the Indians] if he has force, but forces are scarce in that region. Cannot some of General Sully's command move to Nebraska?" The army could not protect a large area from hit-and-run tactics without sufficient men.

In September, Governor Evans had reached a state of near panic and wrote the secretary of war, "Unless escorts are sent thus [with the wagon trains on certain days] we will inevitably have a famine in addition to this gigantic Indian war. Flour is forty-five dollars a barrel, and the supply growing scarce, with none on the way. Through spies we got knowledge of the plan of about one thousand warriors in camp to strike our frontier settlements, in small bands, simultaneously in the night, for an extent of three hundred miles." Evans had been perceptive in recognizing the role of war in the Indians' life, but he did not understand that the concerted attack he was describing was completely outside their capability.

Some of the Indians, who had been friendly to the Americans, were bewildered by what was taking place. Black Kettle, who led a large band of the Cheyennes, went to Denver with some leaders to talk to the authorities, including Governor Evans, but received little satisfaction. Evans merely told them to go to the military if they needed help. So in the fall of that year they went to Fort Lyon, formerly Fort Wise, downstream from Bent's New Fort. The officer in command was sympathetic to the Indians—so much so that he aroused the displeasure of some of his superiors—and he said they could camp about thirty or forty miles away, where Sand Creek had cut a small ravine.

Shortly afterward he was replaced by Major Scott J. Anthony, who was not nearly so trustful of Indians and objected to their coming so often to the fort. "I talked with them," he later said, "and they proposed to do whatever I said; whatever I said for them to do they would do. I told them that I could not feed them; that I could not give them anything to eat; that there were positive orders forbidding that; and that I could not permit them to come within the limits of the post. At the same time they might remain where they were, and I would treat them as prisoners of war if they remained; that they would have to surrender to me all their arms and turn over to me all stolen property they had taken from the government or citizens. These terms they accepted. They turned over to me some twenty head of stock, mules, and horses, and a few arms, but not a quarter of the arms that report stated they had in their possession. The arms they turned over to me were almost useless. I fed them for some ten days. At the end of that time I told them I could not feed them any more; that they better go out to the buffalo country where they could kill game to subsist upon. I returned their arms to them, and they left the post." Later he spoke in the same terms to a delegation of Cheyennes who came to Fort Lyon, telling them he would not make peace with them but that they could stay at Sand Creek.

"In the meantime," he said, "I was writing to district headquarters constantly, stating to them that there was a band of Indians within forty miles of the post—a small band—while a very large band was about 100 miles from the post. That I was strong enough with the force I had with me to fight the Indians on Sand Creek, but not strong enough to fight the main band. That I should try to keep the Indians quiet until such time as I received re-enforcements; and that as soon as re-enforcements did arrive we should go further and find the main party."

Colonel Chivington, who had helped to deal the decisive blow that stopped the Confederates' advance toward Colorado, was in command of men who had enlisted for a hundred days to fight the Indians. So far, they had seen little action, and their terms were about to expire. His marches brought him to Fort Lyon and, hearing of the Indian camp on Sand Creek, decided to attack it.

He and Anthony began their march on the bitter cold night of November 28, 1864. Snow lay on the ground, and the men, many of them inexperienced soldiers, were in an ugly mood. When they reached Black Kettle's camp the following day, the Cheyennes sent out an envoy to tell the men the band was friendly, and Black Kettle raised an American flag he had been given earlier. But these gestures of friendship meant nothing to the frightened, frustrated soldiers, who had been waiting so long to kill Indians.

Bullets ripped through the lodges; women and children fell; the warriors were completely encircled and outnumbered. In their fury the Americans became savages, shooting indiscriminately at anything that moved and even scalping women. The Indians dug rifle pits in the stream banks and fought for seven hours against a superior force, armed also with howitzers, to give some of their women and children a chance to get away. Since Chivington had issued orders to take no prisoners, even those who wished to could not surrender. It was one of the bloodiest days in Colorado.

The Americans' reaction to the fight was divided. The *Rocky Mountain News* said, "Among the brilliant feats of arms in Indian warfare, the recent campaign of our Colorado volunteers will stand in history with few rivals, and none to exceed it in final results." Others, however, were not so sure. The Indian trader at Fort Lyon said that Chivington had been "determined to have a fight with these Indians . . . All the chiefs who were killed . . . have labored as hard as men could to keep peace between the whites and Indians." In Washington, complaints about Chivington's conduct were so severe that Congress investigated the battle.

Among the Indians the reaction was immediate. Many of them gave up hope of peace with the Americans and began raiding along the Platte. On January 7 they attacked Fort Sedgwick at Julesburg, Colorado, and came up in such numbers that they drove the troops back into the fort and once again temporarily cut the route into Denver. They then swept up their loot and headed north for the winter.

General Mitchell, who had tried to treat with them at Cottonwood Camp, made several unsuccessful forays against them—they were too elusive—and swore that he would rather be in any branch of the army than fight Indians. Finally he sent in word that he would like to be assigned to a warmer place than the central Great Plains or have his resignation accepted. Before leaving the area, he made plans to set fire to the grass between Julesburg and Denver, a distance of about three hundred miles. The morning of January 27, 1865, was the type of day he had been looking for, clear and bright with a strong wind blowing from the northwest. Announcing that he would give the Indians ten thousand square miles of burned prairie, he ordered out the fire details he had stationed along the route. The wind caught the flames, fed them, and tossed them farther. Soon the whole area was raging with a fire that burned through the night, racing across rivers and, according to some reports, in places reaching the Texas Panhandle. Then it died, the black smoke curled from the ravaged land, and the quiet of winter settled over the Great Plains.

Chapter 29

Stalemate

Ordered, first. That at the hour of noon on the 14th day of April, 1865, Brevet Major-General Anderson will raise and plant upon the ruins of Fort Sumter, in Charleston Harbor, the same United States flag which floated over the battlements of that fort during the rebel assault, and which was lowered and saluted by him and the small force of his command when the works were evacuated on the 14th day of April, 1861.

Second. That the flag, when raised, be saluted by one hundred guns from Fort Sumter and by a national salute from every fort and rebel battery that fired upon Fort Sumter.

—Edwin M. Stanton, secretary of war, 1865

Selma, Alabama, was pouring out munitions for the Confederacy; and south of Virginia, men were talking of planting the fields again. The Northern blockade was tight, but the South was becoming self-sufficient in the needs of war. Across Georgia lay the burned track left by Sherman's army, but the Gulf and Atlantic states of the Confederacy were still unsundered. To Jefferson Davis and many others, the war was not lost. But as spring touched the ridges of the Smoky Mountains, turning green their grass and trees, and crept quietly and gently up the Shenandoah Valley, it did not carry with it a sense of renewed hope. Lee's army at Petersburg was in the vise of Grant's, and even an offer to abolish slavery had not induced the powers of Europe to recognize the Confederacy's independence. Morale was low, men and women dispirited, and the gloom of defeat hung heavy over the country below the Potomac.

Finally the moment came. At Appomattox Court House, a tiny hamlet whose place in history has been secured by the gallant conduct of the two opposing generals, Lee surrendered. So simple was the ceremony that Grant wrote the terms with his own hand: officers and men paroled; officers permitted to keep their sidearms; men who own a

horse or mule may take them home to work their farms. Lee signed, swung himself into his saddle, and departed. A cheer of triumph broke out in the Union ranks. Grant ordered it stopped. "The war is over," he said quietly. "The rebels are our countrymen again."

One week later the Department of War issued General Orders, Number 66. "The distressing duty," they said, "has devolved upon the Secretary of War to announce to the armies of the United States that at twenty-two minutes after 7 o'clock on the morning of Saturday, the 15 day of April, 1865, Abraham Lincoln . . . died of a mortal wound inflicted upon him by an assassin."

The magnanimity of the few could not temper the passions unleashed by years of war. Love and hatred rode together across the land, forgiveness and vengeance walked the streets, generosity and greed were frequent companions. The prairie fire of war had scorched men's souls, but soon the green shoots of renewed life pushed to the surface, and the nation began again to devote its attention to the task of its own development.

A continuing problem on the Great Plains was the protection of the emigrants, for they still streamed across the country, additional numbers

333

being drawn by discoveries of gold in Nevada and Montana. Since the Pacific Coast was no longer the single goal and since the settlements to the east were all vying to become the starting point for a road west, Congress in 1865 passed legislation providing for a series of roads. One would run west along the Niobrara River, another along the Cheyenne. They would join at the Powder River and go on to Virginia City, Montana, and Lewiston, Idaho. These routes would shorten the journey west to the goldfields for travelers from the Northeast and would open up a large section of the Great Plains that until now had been visited by few but the fur traders. But before they would be safe for emigrants to use, they would have to be cleared of Indians.

Major General Grenville M. Dodge was in command of the Department of the Missouri and selected Brigadier Patrick E. Connor to take charge of this task. Connor had been born in Ireland on St. Patrick's Day but had gone to school in New York City, where his parents had taken him as a child. After serving with the dragoons on the western frontier and in the Mexican War, he went to California as a civilian during the gold rush. At the outbreak of the Civil War he rejoined the army and was assigned to Utah to guard the overland route. Dodge, dissatisfied with sporadic, ineffectual forays against the Indians, chose Connor to launch a major offensive.

Colonel Nelson Cole was to lead 1,400 men up the Loup Fork to a rendezvous on the Rosebud; Colonel Samuel Walker with about six hundred men was to march from Fort Laramie; General Connor was to accompany the left column, comprising about 475 men and a large wagon train of supplies. He was to go up the North Platte, then north to the Rosebud River, and come downstream to the rendezvous. Connor was in a punitive mood and instructed Cole and Walker, "You will not receive overtures of peace or submission from Indians, but will attack and kill every male Indian over twelve years of age." That was not war, that was genocide, and when copies of the orders reached General John Pope at St. Louis, he was horrified. "These instructions are atrocious," he told Dodge, "and you are in direct violation of my repeated orders. . . . If any such orders as General Connor's are carried out it will be disgraceful to the government, and will cost him his commission, if not worse."

Many delays occurred during Connor's preparations. Contractors failed to ship the necessary supplies, Indians held up some of the wagon trains, and many of the men, now that the war with the South was over, wanted to be mustered out. Finally on July 21 Dodge told Connor, "Get your columns off as soon as possible. We have got these Indian matters now in our hands, and we must settle them." Finally on August 1, 1865, Connor was ready to cross the Platte. This was late in the year for such an important expedition to take the field.

Near present-day Kaycee, Wyoming, on a mesa overlooking the Powder River, he constructed a fort to serve as a base. Then, unencumbered by so many supplies, he began looking for Indians. With him he had a band of about ninety-five Pawnees, who had enlisted as scouts under Frank and Luther North. Traditional enemies of many of the Plains Indians, the Pawnees were delighted to join the Americans in fighting their age-old foes; and when they discovered the trail of some Cheyennes, they raced off and thirty hours later returned to report they had killed more than twenty-five Cheyennes. In spite of their long ride and hard fight, they were in a jubilant mood and began a scalp dance. At first the soldiers were much entertained by the spectacle; but the night wore on, and the dance continued. At last Connor gave the order to stop, so his men could sleep. The next night, the Pawnees started all over again, and Connor finally imposed a ten o'clock curfew.

On August 26, when they were crossing the ridge between the Powder and Tongue Rivers, Jim Bridger, who was serving as their guide, saw columns of smoke in the valley below. Connor looked through his field glasses but could discern nothing, so he gave the order to march on. His confidence in Bridger, however, made him send some of the Pawnees in the direction that the former mountain man had indicated. Two days later, two of the scouts reported they had located a large village, composed largely of Arapahoes with some Cheyennes.

Seizing the opportunity for a surprise attack, Connor marched with about two hundred men and the Pawnee scouts up the Tongue River during the night. He expected to reach the camp by daybreak, but the river valley was filled with underbrush and fallen trees, which greatly slowed his progress. Nevertheless, he kept pushing on after cautioning his men to be as quiet as they could and to stay close to the river bank, so the Indians could not see them. One of the soldiers who was in front later recalled that the trail they were following suddenly led up a steep bank. "I rode up the bank," he said, "and . . . just before me lay a large mesa or table, containing five or six hundred acres of land, all covered with Indian tepees full of Indians. . . .

"Gen. Conner then took the lead . . . and dashed out across the mesa . . . ; every man followed as closely as possible. At the first sight of the general, the ponies covering the tableland in front of us set up a tremendous whinneying and galloped down toward the Indian village, more than a thousand dogs commenced barking, and more than seven hundred Indians made the hills ring with their fearful yelling. . . .

"The whole line then fired a volley from their carbines into the village without halting their horses, and the bugle sounded the charge. Without the sound of the bugle there would have been no halt by the men in the column; not a man but what realized that to charge into the village without a moment's hesitation was our only salvation. We already saw that we were greatly outnumbered, and that only desperate fighting would save our scalps . . . ; in those few moments, less than it takes to tell the story, I was in the village in the midst of a hand to hand fight with warriors and their squaws, for many of the female portion of this band did as brave fighting as their savage lords. . . . The scene was indescribable. There was not much of the military in our movements, each man seemed an army by himself.''

Those Indians that survived the first assault fled up the river with Connor in hot pursuit. His men's horses were tired, and they dropped out one by one until, after ten miles of hard riding, only fourteen were left. At this point, the Indians counterattacked. Connor fell back, picking up stragglers as he did so, until he had returned to the village, which some of the men were destroying.

Only the mountain howitzer kept the Indians at a distance. They "pressed us on every side," the soldier wrote, "sometimes charging up within fifty feet. . . . They seemed to have plenty of ammunition, but did most of their fighting with arrows. . . . Before dark we were reduced to forty men who had any ammunition, and those only a few rounds apiece." But at last, in the darkness, the Indians broke off the battle, and the weary Americans dragged themselves to their camp.

Connor had destroyed about two hundred and fifty lodges and the Indians' winter supplies, killed more than sixty warriors, and captured more than a thousand horses. Yet the Americans suffered casualties, too. Among their wounded, according to the same writer, "was a fine looking soldier with as handsome a face as I ever saw on a man, [who] grabbed me by the shoulder and turned me about that I might assist him in withdrawing an arrow from his mouth. The point of the arrow had passed through his open mouth and lodged in the root of

his tongue. Having no surgeon with us a higher grade than a hospital steward, it was afterwards within a half hour decided that to get the arrow out from his mouth, the tongue must be, and was, cut out.''

While Connor had been marching north to find and chastise the Indians, James A. Sawyers, a contractor who had constructed a number of forts and stockades during the uprising of the Santee Sioux, was moving west along the Niobrara River, laying out the road to Virginia City. He had more than fifty men working directly for him and a military escort of almost 150.

Indians caused no problem during the first part of the trip, and when the infantry's shoes wore out, Sawyers and the commanding officer permitted some of them to go to Fort Laramie for replacements. In fact, they had grown so careless of the Indian danger that the military and the civilians made separate camps at night. But at the Powder River, Sawyers's scouts discovered a village of Cheyennes, and almost simultaneously the Indians discovered the wagon train. Beating a retreat back to the nearest water, the expedition corralled its wagons and prepared for a fight. Soon a stalemate developed. The soldiers could not protect the wagon train when it was moving, and the Indians, shooting from a distance with light loads of powder, were unable to overrun the temporary fortification.

Then they changed their tactics and asked for bacon and other supplies in return for letting the train move on. Charles Bent, the well-known trader, had married a Cheyenne wife, and they had had a son, George. His father sent the boy to an American school and taught him the ways of the Americans, but George had never lost his loyalty to his mother's people and lived torn between two worlds—the white men's and the Indians'. At the time of Chivington's attack, he had been in Black Kettle's camp, and fleeing with those that got away, he resolved to remain with them. He was with the Cheyennes harassing Sawyers's wagon train and was one of the bitterest against the Americans. During the parley, he expressed his feelings by telling Sawyers that the least the Americans could do, if they wanted the Indians' friendship, was to hang Chivington. In his report Sawyers noted that finally "they agreed to let us go on our way. The minority, however, were discontented with this treaty, but were restrained by the majority from fighting.''

After this experience and with memories of the angry words of George Bent, some of the expedition wanted to go directly to Fort Laramie, but the advance scouts brought word that Connor was ahead and that Fort Connor, his base, was not far away, so they continued on in spite of more Indian harassment. So far, neither Sawyers's inadequate road nor Connor's one battle with the Arapahoes had opened up the Powder River country, but Walker and Cole were still in the field.

On leaving Fort Laramie, Walker found both water and forage scarce, and his horses began to weaken. At last he picked up the trail of Colonel Cole and received a dispatch from him saying that, because of the Badlands, he planned to go down the Little Missouri for a few days before crossing over to the Powder. Instead of following Cole, Walker headed directly toward the rendezvous and soon was in a nightmare world. In his journal he noted: "marched this day twenty four (24) miles over the worst country I ever saw, not one particle of vegetation was to be seen the whole earth seemed to be one heap of burnt ashes our horses would sink to their knees at every step. Killed this day ten (10) head of horses to keep them from falling into the hands of the indians. . . ." When he reached the Powder River, he was able to locate Cole, but the scarcity of grass forced the two detachments to camp three miles apart.

Then the Indians attacked Cole and tried to drive off his horses. He went in pursuit and recovered most of his livestock, but he did not dare turn them loose again to graze. Inevitably they grew weaker and weaker. Fortunately for the Americans the Indians did not return; for if they had, they could probably have destroyed both detachments, who were now concentrating solely on trying to rendezvous with Connor.

Inexperienced at frontier campaigning, Cole cursed his predicament and the lack of planning that had produced it. As he said in his official report, "Fatigue and starvation had done its work on both men and animals, in so much they were unfit to pursue with vigor the savage foe that circled around their starving way through this desert whose oases were but inviting delusions, for however pleasing to the wearied eye were the green dresses of the prickly pear and the sage brush, they were bitter mockery to the other senses, for they contained no life-giving essence for man or beast. Certes starving soldiers might well wonder why there was no provisions made for such contingencies; why old Indian fighters had not, with their knowledge, planned a more consistent campaign; created depots here and hunted Indians there; not had a command starving here, unfit to cope with the Indians everywhere around them, and the supplies they needed so much away no one knew where, at least where neither Indians come nor they could compass."

At last, "on the thirteenth of September," Cole's report said, "a courier party of two soldiers and two Pawnee Indians, sent to me with dispatches by General Connor, arrived in my camp. They had left their camp the previous morning and had traveled across to Powder River, and striking my trail near one of my old camping grounds, had followed it up, overtaking my command in the afternoon. They reported the country they had passed over to be positively impassable for trains of any kind. General Connor's dispatch directed me to cross over to Tongue River, where his command was lying, or to push up Powder River to Fort Connor (. . . the existence of which I then for the first time learned) for supplies, leaving it discretionary with me which I should do."

Neither Cole nor Walker had heart for searching further for Connor, so they went directly to Connor's base for supplies and rest. Connor, himself, having finally reunited his command late in the year could not continue his campaign against the Indians, who remained firmly in control of the Powder River country. His offensive had not even diverted them from the Platte. When his quartermaster returned to Leavenworth from Denver after the campaign, the coach he took was the first able to run in three weeks, and the Indians attacked it twice during the trip.

The Homestead Act of 1862 had opened up free land to settlers in the West, and many had responded to the lure of a farm in return for the small filing fees. From that year on until the public domain was finally closed to homesteading in the twentieth century, men and women kept looking for the piece of ground that someday they would like to call their own. But homesteaders did not advance quickly onto the Great Plains. To the east, much land still remained unoccupied even though many acres had been given to the agricultural colleges and the railroads, and it was usually better adapted to farming, because it had more rainfall.

A greater deterrent to homesteading farther west on the Great Plains was the absence of safe, economical public transportation. When Samuel Bowles, the popular editor of the Springfield (Massachusetts) *Republican* went to California in 1865 with Schuyler Colfax, speaker of the House, he found that "long trains of heavily loaded wagons, drawn by mules and oxen, are moving out daily, now; but immense warehouses and large yards are still stored full with massive machinery for working the mines, and goods for feeding and clothing the miners . . . waiting for their turn. The mule trains have been in progress for a month, but the ox-teams have had to wait till now, so that the animals could be fed on the grass *en route.* The Indians made such havoc last year that food for man or beast has been very scarce on the road across the Plains all the winter and spring . . . the necessity of keeping up steady mail and travel communication through this region, and of protecting the immense traffic in provisions, goods and machinery now in progress between the East and far West, enforces upon the government the duty of placing a strong military force all along the various leading roads, and then of sending out troops enough to drive the Indians to the far North and South, and keeping them there, or else of wholly exterminating them.'' Under such circumstances, a 160-acre farm on the edge of the Platte or the Arkansas was not worth even the small filing fees. Aside from the lack of protection from the Indians, the owner would have no way of getting his produce to distant markets.

The problem was the inability of the Union Pacific to get its track laid. Despite the purchase of stock by Oakes and Oliver Ames, two Massachusetts investors with experience in railroads, funds were scarce, and construction was progressing as slowly as a Great Plains stream ever ran during a dry fall. Durant, who had never had confidence in the road itself, was already beginning to sell his stock, although carefully maintaining his interest in the Credit Mobilier. One engine, the *General Sherman,* had been shipped by flatcar to St. Joseph, and then 175 miles up the Missouri River by boat; but when it arrived at Omaha, it had only a mile and a half of track on which to run. Still, it proved useful in carrying supplies and men to the end of the line; and by the close of 1865, forty miles of track had been completed, although the government had not yet issued the bonds that would help the company obtain working capital to build the next forty.

In the spring of 1866, General William Tecumseh Sherman went on a tour of inspection, and he reported from Omaha that he had been "around to the machine and work shops of the Union Pacific railroad, which are certainly on a large scale, exhibiting both the ability and purpose to push their work. The company has on hand here enough iron and ties to build fifty miles of road, and Mr. Durant assured me that he has contracted for enough for one hundred and fifty miles of road. . . . With railroads completed to Forts Kearny and Riley, our military question of supplies is much simplified, and I hope the President and Secretary of War will

continue, as hitherto, to befriend these roads as far as the law allows.''

One reason for Sherman's optimism was General Dodge's decision to resign from the army and accept the position of chief engineer. Before the Civil War he had been a surveyor for the Illinois Central Railroad and later for the Mississippi and Missouri Railroad. (There he had known Peter Dey, the engineer of the Union Pacific who resigned in disgust over the Hoxie contract.) During the war Dodge had distinguished himself as a commander of combat troops until a third wound proved so serious that he was removed from the front lines and made commander of the Department of Missouri. Somewhat vainglorious and with a tendency to exaggerate the importance of his own role, he nevertheless was a highly competent engineer and a man who liked to get things done.

When he arrived in Omaha in the spring of 1866, construction was faltering, and even the laborers were demoralized. Often they refused to do a day's work unless they were paid in advance, so uncertain were they of the railroad's future. Dodge immediately set about reorganizing the operation.

That spring the waters of the Missouri River rose higher than usual, flooding the track and shops and causing more delays, but the most serious damage to the railroad's prospects came with the legislation that Congress passed in July. Originally it had provided for a number of feeder roads that would come from the Missouri and join the Union Pacific relatively close to Omaha. Their purpose was to offer transcontinental service to a number of river towns, thereby giving them access to the major route. Supported by local—and sometimes national—investors, a few of them had been laying track in hope of quickly joining the Union Pacific and reaping large profits both for their supporters and the communities that were their terminals. One of them, the Kansas Pacific, had been chartered to connect with the Union Pacific anywhere east of the 100th meridian. But Congress suddenly upset this provision because of pressure from the people of Denver, who wanted more direct rail service. They persuaded Congress to amend the company's charter and permit it to join the Union Pacific west of Denver. Except for the supply of forts and Indian reservations, little business would originate from the Great Plains in the near future. Now Congress had split that business by licensing a second railroad to run roughly parallel with the first.

Congress dealt the Union Pacific another blow that summer by amending the charter of the Central Pacific, the railroad being built from the West

338 SUNLIGHT AND STORM

Coast. Yielding to the pressure of its supporters, Congress permitted it to come as far east as necessary to meet the Union Pacific instead of stopping 150 miles inside the Nevada border. If a need had existed for finishing the railroads as quickly as possible, this might have been a wise step. As it was, it merely stimulated wasteful competition by creating a mammoth race between the two lines, for the government's payments were based on the mileage of track accepted. From now on the premium was on speed, not quality.

Dodge responded to the challenge. In advance went the surveying parties consisting of engineers, axmen, teamsters, and herders. "When the party was expected to live upon the game of the country," as Dodge later said, "a hunter was added. . . . Each party entering a country occupied by hostile Indians was generally furnished with a military escort of from ten men to a company under a competent officer. . . . Not withstanding this protection, the parties were often attacked, their chief or some of their men killed or wounded, and their stock run off.

"In preliminary surveys on the open country a party would run from 8 to 12 miles of line in a day. On location in an open country 3 or 4 miles would be covered, but in a mountainous country generally not to exceed a mile. All hands worked from daylight to dark, the country being reconnoitered ahead of them by the chief, who indicated the streams to follow, and the controlling points in summits and river crossings. The party of location that followed the preliminary surveys . . . devoted its energies to obtaining a line of the lowest grades and the least curvature that the country would admit." One of Dodge's important contributions toward the location of the railroad was his discovery of Sherman Pass through the Laramie Mountains. This cut seventy miles off the route— and in the race against the Central Pacific, seventy miles was important—and avoided the hazards of snowdrifts at South Pass.

After the route had been laid out, the grading crew went to work, usually taking units of a hundred miles. "The distance," Dodge explained, "was graded in about thirty days on the plains, as a rule, but in the mountains we sometimes had to open our grading several hundred miles ahead of our track in order to complete the grading by the time the track should reach it. All the supplies for this work had to be hauled from the end of the track, and the wagon transportation was enormous."

The logistics of the operation were complex, particularly as the construction picked up speed under Dodge's guidance and the distance from the head of the line became greater. "At one time," Dodge said, "we were using at least 10,000 animals, and most of the time from 8,000 to 10,000 laborers. The bridge gangs always worked from 5 to 20 miles ahead of the track, and it was seldom that the track waited for a bridge. To supply 1 mile of track with material and supplies required about 40 cars, as on the plains everything, rails, ties, bridging, fastenings, all railway supplies, fuel for locomotives and trains, and supplies for men and animals on the entire work, had to be transported from the Missouri River. Therefore, as we moved westward, every hundred miles added vastly to our transportation."

One problem faced by Dodge was the absence of a railhead from the east at Omaha until the winter of 1867. "Till then," Dodge said, "the Missouri River had been the sole route over which supplies could be had. It was available only about three months of the year, and our construction was limited by the quantities of rail and equipment that could be brought to us by boat in that time."

The building of the railroad placed an additional strain on the army's resources, for the strung-out line of men and equipment had to be protected. "Our Indian troubles," Dodge said, "lasted until the tracks joined [those of the Central Pacific] . . . We lost most of our men and stock while building from Fort Kearney to Bitter Creek. At that time every mile of road had to be surveyed, graded, tied, and bridged under military protection. The order to every surveying corps, grading, bridging, and tie outfit was never to run when attacked. All were required to be armed, and I do not know that the order was disobeyed in a single instance, nor did I ever hear that the Indians had driven a party permanently from its work. I remember one occasion when they swooped down on a grading outfit in sight of the temporary fort of the military some 5 miles away, and right in sight of the end of the track. The government commission to examine that section of the completed road had just arrived, and the commissioners witnessed the fight. The graders had their arms stacked on the cut. The Indians leaped from the ravines, and, springing upon the workmen before they could reach their arms, cut loose the stock and caused a panic." But, he added, "we did not fail to benefit from this experience, for, on returning to the East the commission dwelt earnestly on the necessity of our being protected."

One reason for the quick progress of the railroad once its supporters had finally gotten it moving was the work train developed by the contractors, two brothers, Dan and Jack Casement. This train eventually had more than twenty cars and was almost a town in itself. The first car carried supplies such as cables, rope, iron rods, and steel bars as well as a fully equipped blacksmith shop. The next carried feed for the livestock and a saddler's shop. Other cars contained bunks, kitchens, sleeping quarters, and a telegraph office, while the last two carried the most important supply of all—water.

When the rails reached the 100th meridian, Durant issued invitations to all the members of the cabinet, the House, and the Senate, as well as to other notable persons, to ride to the end of the line, hoping in this way to publicize the railroad and attract additional investors. After a ball in Omaha, the guests rode out to the railhead, where about a hundred employees had already set up tents and prepared a variety of entertainment. The guests could watch the men laying track, see a buffalo or antelope hunt, or observe a fake skirmish between Indians hired for the purpose. At the end of the day, the railroad served champagne with dinner, and fireworks burst in the air. The climax was a prairie fire, set far enough off so the guests would not feel endangered by it.

The civilization carried west by the construction train, however, was not usually this elite and polite. By the end of the season the railroad had reached the junction of the North and South Platte, and a town named North Platte sprang up. Gamblers and prostitutes swarmed into it, saloons opened for business, and it soon became the first of the "hells on wheels," as these temporary communities were called. Many of the men working on the road were veterans of the Civil War and therefore accustomed to firearms and killings, and the towns were without adequate law enforcement. No one had a stake in them, and their only purpose was to provide diversions for the workers and money for the railroad's camp followers.

The next such town was Julesburg, which was to be the division terminal for the construction year of 1867. North Platte died instantly, and Julesburg came to life, as the same people flocked into the new community, the gamblers setting up their games, and the prostitutes appearing on the streets, many of them armed with derringers. Observers who had visited the gold camps remarked on the similarities between them and the railroad towns. All of them were magnets for some of the worst of Americans.

In 1866, when Dodge became the Union Pacific's chief engineer, the railroad played no effective role in transportation across the Great Plains, and the wagon trains and the emigrants were still unprotected from the Indians. General Connor's campaign had accomplished little, so the Americans decided to call another peace council at Fort Laramie. As one commissioner observed, "All our treaties have a similar outline, although in some details they differ to suit special localities and particular tribes."

In the case of the Laramie Treaty of 1866, one of the special problems was the route to the Montana goldfields. Most travelers took the Oregon-California Trail to Fort Hall near the Snake River and then turned north; but an enterprising pioneer, John Bozeman, had laid out a much shorter route than went to the east of the Bighorn Mountains. He had hoped to make money conducting emigrants along it, but unfortunately part of it passed through the country in which Connor had campaigned and which was definitely unsafe, particularly since Connor had stirred up the Indians. The peace commissioners hoped to secure a right-of-way along Bozeman's Trail.

When the conference started, it was marked by the presence of two of the most important leaders among the Sioux. Spotted Tail was a Brulé. Once he had made efforts to be friendly with the Americans but had then joined the hostile Indians. He was willing, however, to try once more to make peace. The other important leader was Red Cloud, an Oglala. Recognizing the consequences of the Americans' arrival on the Great Plains, he had tried to resist them. But he was now willing to talk peace, a sign that encouraged the commissioners.

The Americans were so confident the Indians would accept the terms offered that, even before the council began, the army ordered Major Henry B. Carrington to build posts for the protection of travelers using the Bozeman Trail. But when Carrington was camped near Fort Laramie, a friendly chief of the Brulés warned him that many of the warriors had not come to the council and would fight him; and after word of his mission spread among the tribe, the Indians to whom he talked were cold and reserved. Red Cloud was furious. He had come to talk peace but not to let the Americans enter the Powder River country, and he was especially enraged by their preparations to build forts there before the conference was held. Abruptly he left Fort Laramie.

Earlier Carrington had carefully instructed his men never to insult an Indian. But as he sensed the reaction of the Indians at Laramie, he started to prepare for trouble. To headquarters at Omaha, he reported that his supply of ammunition was inadequate, but, he added, "I apprehend no serious difficulty. Patience, forbearance, and common sense in dealing with the Sioux and Cheyennes will do much with all who really desire peace, but it is indispensable that ample supplies of ammunition come promptly.''

At Fort Reno, the fort that Connor had established as a base and had first named after himself, Carrington rested for a few days and then marched to Crazy Woman Creek. Unknown to him, Red Cloud had gathered a band of warriors anxious to fight the Americans, and they had danced the Sun Dance, a sure sign their intentions were serious. While Carrington was searching for an appropriate site for the first fort he intended to build, the Sioux attacked his wagons, ran off some livestock, and killed several soldiers. They also attacked a nearby trader, killing all the white men they could find at his post, and tried to incite the Cheyennes to war. Red Cloud's determination to prevent travel on the Bozeman Trail was becoming more and more apparent.

The location Carrington chose for his post, Fort Philip Kearny, was at the foot of the Bighorn Mountains between Little Piney and Big Piney creeks. It gave him a good supply of water (the corral backed up on the Little Piney), and he could cut all the wood he wanted on Sullivant Ridge a short distance away. The location was well protected from the wind by the higher land surrounding it, but a picket placed on Sullivant Ridge could see up the Bozeman Trail to the north and watch the wood-cutting parties, while another picket on Pilot Hill could see down the trail in the direction of traffic coming from Fort Reno.

The Sioux refrained from attacking the main body of Carrington's force, but they constantly harassed the traffic on the trail, swooping down on a lightly armed wagon train and disappearing, raiding around Fort Reno and running off some livestock, then attacking emigrants and vanishing once more into the wilderness. The council at Laramie, at which the Indians present again pledged peace, meant nothing to the warriors along the Bozeman Trail and only blinded the army to the gravity of Carrington's position.

On July 30 Carrington reported to headquarters at Omaha that the additional ammunition he needed had not come, nor had the supplies he had ordered from Leavenworth. He was also short of officers. "I telegraphed full," he explained, "as there is at Laramie and elsewhere a false security, which results in emigrant trains scattering between posts, involving dangers to themselves and others." Nevertheless, he followed his orders and in addition to Fort Philip Kearny, he built another,

Fort C. F. Smith, on the Bighorn River farther along the trail.

The need for constant vigilance was wearing down the morale of Carrington's men. Jumpy and nervous, they once prepared to attack a band of friendly Cheyennes, who had come to warn them about the Sioux. Only the last-minute discovery of their plans by the guard prevented the soldiers from annihilating some of the few friends they had. One officer, Captain William J. Fetterman, was particularly anxious to come to grips with the elusive enemy. As a contemporary said, he had "recently arrived from recruiting service, with no antecedent experience on the frontier" and yet he "expressed the opinion that a 'single company of Regulars could whip a thousand Indians, and that a full regiment . . . could whip the entire array of hostile tribes.' "

The garrison was most vulnerable when the wood-cutting parties went to Sullivant Ridge. Carrington's pickets watched carefully for Indians, and the fort was close enough to come quickly to the rescue; but on December 6, 1866, Carrington lost several men in an effort to protect the wood-cutting party. He then realized one of the fort's principal weaknesses. Beyond Sullivant Ridge lies another, called Lodge Pole Ridge, which divides the Powder River from the Tongue. Except for the mountains, it was the highest piece of land around, higher even than the stations occupied by the pickets. Since they could not see what lay on the other side, Carrington issued orders that, during an engagement, none of the men were to cross it.

The Indians wanted a major victory, and because they could not attack the stout walls of the fort, they fell back on one of their most common tactics: decoys who, looking weak, would lure the soldiers away from the fort. About ten Indians were chosen for this purpose. Among them was an Oglala Sioux, named Crazy Horse. Unlike most Indians, he was light complexioned and lacked the usual high cheekbones. These physical peculiarities had marked him apart as a boy, and the wise men of the tribe had prophesied future greatness for him. He was determined to live up to that prophecy.

On December 21 the decoys attacked the woodcutters. As usual the picket signaled the fort, and Fetterman asked to lead the rescuers. In a short time he had dispersed the decoys, but instead of returning to the fort, he went to the top of Lodge Pole Ridge. Except for the scurrying figures of the decoys, all appeared quiet below. Here at last was the moment he had wanted, the chance to vent the frustrations of months.

Even the Indians had difficulty finding adequate shelter during the winter months when game was scarce. At this point on Sand Creek in Colorado the Cheyennes under Black Kettle went into winter camp, only to be attacked by Colonel Chivington. The engagement stirred up controversy, some calling it a great victory, others labeling it a massacre. *Alexander B. Adams*

Life at army posts varied between the extremes of boredom and tension, depending on the activity of the Indians. Soldiers stationed at Fort Phil Kearny could see the Boseman Trail to Montana, which entered the notch to the left, and the sentinel posted on Pilot Hill to the right. Unusual activity at either point was a call to action. *Alexander B. Adams*

Over the ridge he went, his men racing behind him. At a medicine ceremony held when they were planning their ruse, the Indians had asked that a hundred Americans be delivered to them. Fetterman was bringing them more than eighty.

When it was too late for the Americans to retreat back up the steep slope, the decoys wheeled around, the other Indians burst from their hiding places, and the pursuers became the pursued. The infantry ducked behind some rocks but could not keep the Indians at a distance and were soon engaged in hand-to-hand fighting against a numerically superior foe. The cavalry retreated up the ridge and also took cover behind some rocks. To their rear was a barren spot, so the Indians could not encircle them, but gradually the attackers moved up the slope, closer and closer, and the Americans could not drive them back. After a brief time, the only sign of life among the Americans was a dog that had followed them. One Indian suggested that it be left unharmed to carry the news to the fort. The others said no, so they killed the dog, too.

At Fort Philip Kearny, Carrington could hear the sound of the shooting, and a relief expedition set out immediately. But by the time they reached the battlefield, nothing remained but the corpses of their former comrades. Already short of men, Carrington was now crippled and needed help. John Phillips, an experienced frontiersman, volunteered to carry a message to Fort Laramie, provided Carrington would let him have the best horse, a simple request in return for such an undertaking.

After dark Carrington himself opened the sally-port gate for Phillips, and the messenger rode off into the darkness.

"There was little repose . . . for any one that dreadful night," wrote one of those who was there. "All ears were expectant of a momentary alarm. Subdued discussion of whether some of the missing ones might not have fallen into the hands of the savages as prisoners . . . continued late into the night, and yet it was somehow borne in upon our minds that all were dead." The weather suddenly turned extremely cold. In the black, bleak night, the only sounds were the calls of the sentries as they paced their rounds. And at North Platte on the Union Pacific, the pianos tinkled merrily in the saloons, and the prostitutes tried to look their most enticing.

Chapter 30

Cowboys and Farmers

The company [the Union Pacific], under date of the 11th of October, report that the road during the present year would probably be extended to a point 537 miles west of Omaha, and that station buildings, engine houses, water stations and the telegraph line to meet the wants of the road had been built. Shops and an engine house have been commenced at Cheyenne. The grading, masonry and bridging in the mountain regions were in active progress. The road has been definitely located 600 miles, and the earthwork will be finished to that point the present year.

—Report of the secretary of
the interior, 1867

Almost everyone had a remedy for the Indian problem. Some of the persons who lived on the frontier believed in exterminating them and loudly applauded the actions of men like Chivington. Others believed the government should separate those that were friendly from those that were hostile and punish the latter. Some thought that all trade in guns and ammunition should be prohibited; others said that if this were done, the Indians would starve. Still others proposed putting all Indians onto reservations and making them stay there and become farmers, although no one was certain how this could actually be done. The military often believed that it was the more sympathetic Indian agents that caused most of the trouble. On the other hand, the commissioner of Indian affairs might report to the secretary of the interior, as he did in 1867, "I enclose a slip from one of these [news] papers, and if it be true that the military has interfered in the way there stated, it accounts fully for most of our Indian troubles, and this strengthens my previous views, that it is owing to the unwarranted interference of the military that we have the numerous conflicts with these people."

None of the proposed solutions seemed to work.

As a result of the many treaties, there were now numerous reservations, but there were few agents who could control the Indians for whom they were responsible. The nomadic habits of most of the important plains tribes made this almost impossible. If the Indians had been willing to become sedentary farmers, the problem would have been different, for it would have been easier for the agents to maintain a roll of the Indians on any one reservation. But few had shown any disposition for farm work.

Selective punishment was practically impossible to carry out, because of the difficulty of learning who had done what and because of the inability of the Indian leaders to control all the members of their own bands. Even Black Kettle, who had professed such strong friendship for the Americans, had in his group young warriors who would occasionally raid and kill. Furthermore, it was difficult to discover which individuals, or even which band, was responsible for a particular act. The Indians struck and then disappeared into the vast wilderness of the Great Plains. Occasionally an expert could identify the participating tribe by the arrows or other paraphernalia they might have left behind but rarely the specific persons who might have been involved.

Extermination would have been costly. Thousands of troops would have had to scour the mountains and plains, for the Indians were elusive and knew every hiding place. More significantly, however, such a policy would have been completely contrary to the American spirit. The Americans might push the Indians hard and settle on their lands, but rarely has a people with such vast military superiority been so tentative in its victories or so generous, taking only what they thought they needed at the moment and trying to provide for the conquered. Chivington's action at Sand Creek, for example, might draw applause from many of the people of Colorado, but elsewhere it caused an uproar and launched a congressional investigation. So each department of government and each individual followed the course it thought best, and often in the process worked at cross-purposes.

One of the army's principal responsibilities on the Great Plains was protecting the travel routes; and these were growing in number, as travelers refused to be restricted to one or two of the older ones. The Platte, of course, was of particular concern because of the Union Pacific, but the road along the Arkansas and the Smoky Hill rivers was also important, for this was the route chosen by the Kansas Pacific.

In the spring of 1867, General Winfield S. Hancock led about fourteen hundred men through the country where the railroad would go with, as was so often the case, inconclusive results. He met with some Cheyennes and then, against the advice of the Indian agent responsible for them, burned their village when they fled during the night. (General George Armstrong Custer and the Seventh Cavalry pursued, but did not overtake them.) He met with Satanta and other important leaders of the Indians on the southern Great Plains, preaching peace and threatening war, yet accomplished little except to impress the Indians that, although his was a strong force, its presence was only temporary.

Yet he accomplished as much as those trying to protect the Bozeman Trail. Phillips had safely reached Fort Laramie, riding about two hundred miles in the bitter cold through Indian lands, and news of Fetterman's disaster flashed across the country. Reinforcements marched out to Fort Philip Kearny, and the Americans braced themselves for the new fights that might occur during the spring and summer.

Like Fort Philip Kearny, Fort C. F. Smith had been well located and well constructed, but it, too, had one weakness. The nearest place to gather hay was about two and a half miles away and out of sight of the fort. Rather than make the five-mile round trip every day, the fort's sutler, who held the contract for cutting the hay, set up a nearby camp, the main feature of which was a corral that held the livestock and could be used as a fort if Indians attacked.

Occasionally Indians appeared. They would let the men cut the hay, but after it was dried and before the men gathered it, they would charge down on the field, send the workers scurrying to safety, and then set fire to it. Although the Americans had to be constantly on the alert, there was plenty of hay, so the attacks did little except cause the men extra work. Some friendly Crows, however, warned that the Sioux were planning a major attack on both forts, with Red Cloud leading the one against Fort Philip Kearny. The Americans did not take this warning seriously.

On August 1 the Sioux arrived at the hayfield in force and drove the Americans—about twenty-five men in all—into their corral. One Indian dashed toward it with a firebrand, hoping to set it ablaze, but a bullet stopped his horse, and another shot killed him. The lieutenant in charge of the escort was also killed almost immediately, but a civilian named D. A. Colvin took charge. He had been a captain in the Civil War and knew how to fight; and under his skillful direction, the Americans held the Indians back.

Giving up hope of overrunning the corral, the Indians next resorted to fire. From a nearby willow grove and bluff, which provided them with cover, they sent flaming arrows flying in the direction of the embattled men. In doing so, they set on fire some hay piled outside the corral. The wind blew the flames toward the Americans, and since the walls of the corral were made partly of willow boughs, they could easily burn. Fortunately the wind reversed itself, and the fire died down. But this attempt had been so nearly successful, the Indians tried several times again, setting torches to the grass in various directions, and again and again charging but never succeeding in destroying the Americans.

Two of the men inside the corral went wild with fear. One wept and refused to fight. Another threatened to commit suicide to avoid capture. But Colvin managed to keep their panic from spreading to the others. Meanwhile no help came from the fort. It was out of sight because of an intervening bluff, but surely the soldiers could hear the shooting.

The hours wore on. During a lull in the fighting,

several men ran to a nearby creek and filled some water buckets. In the afternoon the Indians returned and were even more aggressive than they had been before. Several times they massed together and came riding down on the corral, the hooves of their horses echoing in the warm Wyoming day, but Colvin encouraged his men to hold their fire until the Indians were close. Each time he broke up the charge. Finally the Indians grew discouraged and rode off, leaving the few Americans alone again. Only afterward did they learn why no relief had come from Fort C. F. Smith: The commander had been afraid of repeating Fetterman's mistake.

While the Hayfield Fight, as it later became known, was going on, Red Cloud and Crazy Horse were assembling with other Indians near Fort Philip Kearny. Carrington had been transferred, but the fort's principal weakness remained the same— the need to cut wood. This work was under contract to a civilian, who had built a camp near the site to save traveling back and forth each day. Nearby was the camp of the armed guard. Because the boxes of their wagons were unnecessary for hauling wood to the fort, the men had removed them and used them to construct a corral for their livestock.

The Indians came from several directions at once. Some ran off with the mules, others tried to prevent the fleeing wood-cutters from reaching the fort, while still others concentrated on the men at the corral. A brief charge by the soldiers diverted the Indians just long enough to permit the wood-cutters to reach safety. After that, all the fighting centered around the corral. Bullets and arrows flew through the air, but the stout sides of the wagon boxes provided a good defense. The Indians tried charging the corral without success. Then they attempted to climb up a defile that was near it, but the terrain forced them so close together that an American bullet could pass through one Indian and strike another. Yet still no relief came from the fort. Then suddenly the Indians withdrew. Realizing the severity of the attack, the commander, instead of sending out a hastily assembled group, had organized about a hundred men and equipped them with wagons, ambulances, and a howitzer. This force turned the odds overwhelmingly against the Indians, and the battle was over. Before the beleaguered Americans returned to the fort, they had a good drink of whiskey from the barrel that the commander had sent with the relief party.

Neither the Hayfield Fight nor the Wagon Box Fight, as the one at Fort Philip Kearny was called, had been a victory for the Americans or the Indi-

ans. In both instances, a relatively small group of Americans had held off a much larger body of Indians. On the other hand, the two incidents had proved the seriousness of Red Cloud's threat to close the road. For troops could not hope to protect the Bozeman Trail if they could not even operate freely around their own posts.

That year the government sent yet another peace commission to treat with the Indians. When the commissioners arrived at Omaha, they learned about the two fights but, undiscouraged, went on to Fort Laramie. Many of the Indians with whom they wanted to talk were not there, for they were growing weary of these endless councils, but one Crow said what was in the hearts of many.

"I am hungry and cold," he said. "Look at me, all of you. I have limbs, and a head like you; we all look like one and the same people. I want my people and my children to prosper and grow rich.

"Call your young men back from the Big Horn," he said. "It would please me well. Your young men have gone on the path, and have destroyed the fine timber and green grass, and have burnt up the country. Father, your young men have gone on the road, and have killed my game and my buffalo. They did not kill them to eat; they left them to rot where they fell. Father, were I to go to your country to kill your cattle, what would you say? Would not that be wrong, and cause war? Well, the Sioux offered me hundreds of mules and horses to go with them to war. I did not go. . . .

"I have heard that you have sent messengers for the Sioux like you did to us, but the Sioux tell me that they will not come. They say, you have cheated them once.

"The Sioux said to us, 'Ah! the white fathers have called for you; you are going to see them. Ah! they will treat you as they have treated us. Go and see them, and then come back and tell us what you have heard. The white fathers will beguile your ears with soft words and sweet promises, but they will never keep them. Go on and see them, and they will laugh at you.'

"In spite of these words of the Sioux I have come to see you . . ."

He then related several wrongs and insults he had suffered and concluded by saying, "Father, you talk about farming, and about raising cattle. I don't want to hear it; I was raised on buffalo, and I love it. Since I was born I was raised, like your chiefs, to be strong, to move my camps where necessary, to roam over the prairie at will."

That was an unbridgeable gap between the Americans and the Indians—the desire to "roam over the prairie at will." It was incompatible with the Americans' civilization, for they intended to settle the land, and they could not do so when the Indians went where they wanted and took possession of whatever they happened to need.

Red Cloud did not even bother to attend the council. He had told the Americans that he wanted them to close the Bozeman Trail, and he would not treat with them until they did.

When the Americans of Anglo-Saxon descent had come to America, they had brought cattle with them to use as oxen, to milk, and to eat. Some of these were raised on farms. Others, along the advancing frontiers, were turned loose on unclaimed land to fatten; and later their owners collected them and drove them to market. But herding had never been a truly important business until the Americans reached Texas. There the grass was well suited for cattle and, as some commented, the land was not good for much else. Also the Americans found there the hardy Spanish cattle, which were well adapted to the relatively arid climate.

As the cattle multiplied in the favorable surroundings of Texas, a few men went into the business of herding them and selling them for meat, but the productivity of the Texas range far exceeded the available markets. Since no good transportation led to the East, the big population centers like New York and Boston were closed to the Texas cattle raisers. New Orleans and Mobile were about the only places they could sell their animals, and these cities and their environs did not consume enough meat to make an impression on the rapidly multiplying Texas herds.

The Mexican War created a temporary increase in demand because of the army's needs, and occasionally a daring entrepreneur would drive a herd for some distance. A thousand head, for example, went to Ohio, and another man took cattle from Texas to the Colorado goldfields. But these were the exceptions. In the early stages of the Civil War, some Texas cattle fed the South, and even after the Union gained control of the Mississippi, a few herds were swum across the river below Vicksburg. But the cattle kept breeding so rapidly that in Texas they were hardly worth the trouble of branding.

At the end of the Civil War, according to one cattle shipper, "Many cattlemen entirely neglected their stock, for they were regarded as not worth caring for. Stocks of cattle were, in certain sections, offered at prices ranging from one to two dollars per head, and that often without finding a buyer." One reason the prices were so low was the speed with which a man could build up a herd

without paying out any money at all. Unbranded calves belonged to the owner of their mothers, but mature unbranded cattle belonged to whoever caught them and branded them. By the end of the Civil War Texas contained literally thousands of unbranded cattle.

Also by the end of the war, the price of beef in the North had risen enormously, so the spread between the value of a steer or cow in Texas and at St. Louis or Chicago could be as much as 1,000 percent. This obviously offered an opportunity for a new business, the first major one since the fur trade in which the profits came from the Great Plains themselves.

It was an unusual business, however, and one that differed greatly from stock raising farther east. The cattle had to be allowed to roam freely, because fences were nonexistent. There was no material with which to construct them, and the areas needing enclosure were too great. The native grasses were highly nutritious, but because of the aridity, they were sparse. Therefore in some spots it might take ten to twenty acres to feed a single steer. This meant that the cattle, unlike those on Eastern farms, were wild; and it was not unusual to find a two- or three-year-old that had never seen a man. There were no "bossies" on the Texas range, only animals that were as mean and dangerous as the water buffaloes of India. Also the sparseness of the grass increased the distances that the men working with the herds had to travel. They could not look over their livestock by walking out to the back pasture; they had to travel many miles through rugged country.

Ready at hand, however, were the techniques developed by the Spanish for handling cattle under such conditions, the techniques that had so amazed Pike and other early visitors to the Southwest. The Anglo-Americans were quick to adopt them. They borrowed the Spanish saddle with its high horn for use in roping, the spade bits that could control a wild horse, the *tapederos* or stirrup covers that protected the rider's feet from the brush, the double cinches that kept the saddle from flying off when a steer was roped, and the *riata, lasso,* or plain "rope" as it soon came to be called. They made certain variations. The Mexicans used a *riata* made of braided rawhide and between sixty and seventy feet long. The *riata* was not tied to the saddle but kept loose, and after the rider had roped a steer or cow, he quickly "dallied" the *riata* around the saddle horn and played the animal somewhat as a fisherman plays a fish, giving it rope one moment and tightening it the next, according to the strain. One glance at a vaquero's saddle could show whether he was a working cowboy or merely a gentleman rider. If he had done much roping, his saddle horn would be scarred and burned.

Rawhide *riatas,* however, were expensive to buy and time-consuming to make. Furthermore, they required care, because they could not be allowed to dry out; and they were not strong; hence the need for playing the animal. The Anglo-Americans substituted hemp as being cheaper and stronger. They also reduced the length of the rope to about thirty feet, which made it less clumsy to handle, and tied it permanently to the saddle horn. This simplified the process of roping, but it created an added danger, for the rider, once he had roped an animal, had no way of releasing it. If, for example, an angry steer got to one side of him and his saddle started to slip, he could not get free.

The Anglo-Americans borrowed from the Spanish their means of indicating the ownership of an animal on the unfenced range. This consisted of an ear mark and a brand. The first was cut into the animal's ear. Because the possible variations were limited, it was the least certain means of identifying the owner. Nevertheless, it served a useful purpose, for the brands were difficult to see when the animals were bunched close together, but the ear mark was clearly visible and served for preliminary identification.

The brands were as varied as the imaginations of the men who designed them, and soon a language developed to describe them. A "rocking" letter would be tilted to one side and have a curved line underneath it to make it look like a rocking chair. A "lazy" letter would be on its side. When he drew up his brand, a stockman tried to obtain certain characteristics. For one, he wanted the brand to be as simple as possible and with few lines coming close to each other. (If they did and the animal was branded in wet weather, the mark would tend to smear.) But he did not want it so simple that it could be altered. A single *O,* for example, could be easily converted into any other brand that also contained an *O.* Once the stockman had finally decided on the design, he registered both the brand and the ear mark—the two went together—and thereafter all cattle bearing those marks belonged to him.

He then had his stamp irons made. These had a long handle with the brand wrought in iron at the other end. At round-up time, several of these were kept in a fire, and the man doing the branding would take one from the fire, use it, replace it to heat up again, and take another. This was quick and efficient. But the stamp irons were cumber-

some and usually could be carried only in a wagon, so the ranchers also had another device, the "running iron." This took several forms. Sometimes it was shaped like a fishhook that was about a foot long; at others it was merely a circle of metal that could be held when heated by two sticks of wood. In any case, it was light to carry and could be used to draw any brand. Because of its versatility, it was also used by thieves, but it was the only means by which the cowboy could brand the occasional steer or cow he found that had been missed during the round-up.

The men attracted to the cattle business were of many types—short and tall, irascible and easygoing, but they all had certain qualities in common. A fat cowboy, for example, was a rarity; their lives were too active. And they all had three basic skills: riding, roping, and herding. They dressed simply; the fancy modern Western clothes were largely the products of designers off the range. Many of them carried guns, but few of them were gunmen. Those were the riffraff of the mining, cattle, and railroad towns, looking for a quick dollar at the gaming tables. Several things prevented the cowboys from becoming skillful with their revolvers. One was the restraining influence of the rancher; he could not afford to run an outfit in which his employees were shooting each other. Also, cowboys could not wear the quick-draw holsters that were an essential part of the gunmen's art. For when they were riding or roping, their guns would have been in the air or on the ground more often than they would have been in their holsters.

The cowboys worked long, hard hours, but the work was easier than work in the mines or lumber camps or even on many farms. And they enjoyed great independence. Most of the year they were usually unsupervised. They had their particuar job to do on a particular part of the range, and no one stood over them telling them how and when to do it. Only at round-up time or when they were driving cattle did they have a foreman standing by. The capital for getting into the work was negligible. A cowboy needed to own only a saddle, bridle, saddle blanket, and the clothes on his back. Everything else was supplied by his employer. If he owned his own horse, he could quit anytime he wanted. In the West every visitor to a ranch was entitled by custom to two meals and a night's lodging. So an unemployed cowboy could start riding the "grub line," moving from one ranch to another until he found work. Probably never in the history of the country have men of little means been able to enjoy as much independence as the cowboys enjoyed at the height of cattle days.

For the most part, it was a young man's business, but old age did not frighten these men. Always in the back of their minds they had the thought of a little "spread" of their own someday, and the dream was not illusory. Many a cowboy acquired a few head of cattle and "ran" them in some location of his choosing. Once or twice a year he would drop by to see if they were all right and to brand his calves. In time, if he was lucky, they would multiply, and he would have enough to own his own ranch. Since the range at first was free, he did not have to worry about land; and when it began to be occupied, he took out a homestead. One hundred and sixty acres was not nearly enough for even a small ranch, but if it contained the principal source of water no one else but its owner could use the surrounding land. (Even today many large ranches hold title to a relatively small number of acres. The remainder they lease from the government; because they control the water, the land is valuable only to them.)

Although cowboys quickly caught the imagination of the American people, they were often in trouble with their neighbors. Partly this was because of their behavior when they finally reached town. Young and healthy, their merry-making often took a boisterous turn, but a more important reason was the natural conflict between their business and almost every other enterprise. Cattle raised in the Western style occupied enormous amounts of land, which could not simultaneously be used for anything else. Fences or enclosures blocked the movement of cattle. So did roads or other signs of civilization. Where cattle went, they dug up the ground with their hooves, and they grazed it barren when they were concentrated. Therefore every farmer regarded cattle and cowboys as his natural enemies, and the feeling was reciprocated.

These natural animosities boiled to the surface during the first attempts to drive cattle north from Texas after the Civil War. The farmers did not want cattle trampling their fields, knocking down their fences, and generally destroying their countryside. Also they feared the spread of Spanish fever, a mysterious disease that did not seem to affect the Texas cattle but broke out among other herds wherever Texas cattle had been. The stockmen, of course, branded this fear a fantasy, but it was based on fact. In 1867, the government launched an investigation which "showed that the Texas cattle migration northward, which had been closed during the period of the war, its interruption resulting in total exemption from the Texas cattle disease for precisely the same period, had been

vigorously prosecuted anew on the return of peace, bringing with it the old disease, which raged just in proportion to the extent of the movement of southern droves. Its ravages, in 1866, were mainly confined to Kansas and Missouri . . ." The disease, to which the Texas cattle had developed immunity, was spread by the ticks they carried in their shaggy coats.

The angry reaction of local people to the appearance of herds forced many hardships on the drivers, who were trying to get to a railroad where they could sell their cattle for shipment to St. Louis or Chicago. In 1866, for example, James M. Dougherty, a young Texan, left the state with more than a thousand head, which he planned to take to St. Louis. His story, as told by one of his contemporaries, illustrates the types of problems the Texans encountered.

"Soon after entering the Indian Nation [Oklahoma, then Indian Territory]," the account said, "he found in order to avoid paying an arbitrary tax to the Cherokee Indians, he was compelled to turn his course more eastward, and enter the State of Arkansas near Ft. Smith. Then driving in a northern direction a short distance, he was compelled to turn Northwest on account of the rough, rocky, barren character of the country. Soon after, entering the State of Missouri, he was aroused from the pleasant revery of beautiful prospects and snug fortune easily won, by the appearance of a yelling, armed, organized mob, which ordered him to halt. . . .

"Young Dougherty was told that 'them thar steers couldn't go an inch fudder. No sare.' Dougherty quietly began to reason with them, but it was like preaching morality to an alligator. No sooner did they discover that the drover was a young man and probably little experienced in life, than they immediately surrounded him, and whilst a part of the mob attacked his comrade and shamefully maltreated him, a half dozen coarse brutes dragged the drover from his saddle, disarmed him, tied him fast to a tree with his own picket rope, then proceeded to whip him with hickory withes in the most brutal manner.

"Whilst these outrages were being perpetrated upon the drover and his comrade, a pre-appointed Missourian dashed into the herd of cattle at full speed, flourishing at arm's end a striped blanket, all the while screeching and yelling as only a semi-civilized being can. Of course this had the intended effect. The cattle took great fright at the, to them, unusual demonstrations, and with a whirl and a snort were off at full speed, rushing wildly over everything before them."

Fortunately some of Dougherty's cowboys who were in the rear realized what was happening, turned the herd into a valley, and got it milling in circles. "In a few minutes," the account continued, "the cattle became quiet, and the cowboys turned their heads to the west and hurried them on for a distance of five miles . . . In the mean time, after each one of the Missourians had sated his brutal instincts by whipping their bound victim, they demanded of Dougherty that he would mount his horse and leave the country instantly, not stopping to inquire or look after his herd; but hasten away. . . . Dougherty staggered to where his faithful poney stood, and drawing his lacerated, bleeding body into his saddle, said to his assailants that they outnumbered him and were armed, whilst he was alone and disarmed, and that under these circumstances he would be compelled to do as they directed. . . . After riding a mile or more, his comrade halloed to him from a cluster of under-brush, not far distant, and then rode out to meet him.' . . .

"A few hours after night-fall they beheld a small camp fire and approached cautiously until they were sure they were making no mistake. Once in camp the drover soon had his bruised and lacerated body washed and dressed, as well as could be under the circumstances."

They next drove the herd to the northeast corner of Indian Territory. After Dougherty "had fully recovered from the severe trouncing he had received in Missouri, he started out with a few hundred head of cattle late one evening, and during the night ran the blockade, and after lying in a secluded spot during the day, made good his way to Ft. Scott, Kansas, where he disposed of his cattle without trouble, and secured a buyer who returned . . . with him and purchased the balance of his herd."

Experiences such as Dougherty's were common and did not encourage stockmen to drive cattle north. The solution to the problem came not from Texas, but from central Illinois, where three brothers were in the business of shipping cattle. One of them, Joseph G. McCoy, was particularly intrigued by the money that might be made in Texas cattle and went to Kansas to look over the situation. What he had in mind was selecting a point to which the Texans could bring their herds and from which the animals could be shipped to Chicago.

The Kansas Pacific—also known as the eastern branch of the Union Pacific—now reached as far as Salina, Kansas. After taking a trip on the road, McCoy later said that "Junction City was visited and a proposition made to one of the leading business men to purchase of him a tract of land sufficiently large to build a stock yard and such other facilities as were necessary for cattle shipping, but an exorbitant price was asked, in fact a flat refusal to sell at any price was the final answer of the wide-awake Junctionite." No one wanted Texas cattle around.

Next McCoy called on the president and the members of the executive committee of the Kansas Pacific to ask them for help. The president was interested in anything that would bring traffic to the railroad, but he had so little faith in McCoy's idea that he refused to accept McCoy's invitation to invest the company's money in the facilities.

McCoy then saw the president of the Missouri Pacific. Writing about himself in the third person, he said, "He [McCoy] timidly stated his business in modest terms, and asked what rates of freight would be charged on the stock coming to St. Louis. When he had made his statement and propounded his question, the railroad official, tipping his cigar up at right angles with his nose, and striking the attitude of indescribable greatness, when stooping to notice an infinitesimal object, and with an air bordering on immensity, said:

" 'It occurs to me that you haven't any cattle to ship, and never did have any, and I, sir, have no evidence that you ever will have any, and I think you are talking about rates of freight for speculative purposes, therefore, you get out of this office, and let me not be troubled with any more of your style.' "

Completely taken aback by this reaction, McCoy next visited the general freight agent of the Hannibal and St. Joseph Railroad, the railroad that had brought the first mail to be carried by the Pony Express. Since the road was not making as much money as the Missouri Pacific, he was able quickly to negotiate a favorable contract for shipping cattle from the Missouri River to Quincy and from there to Chicago.

He then returned to the task of finding a community on the Kansas Pacific that would serve as the loading point. Solomon City was as unreceptive as Junction City and regarded the "cattle business with stupid horror." Some inquiries indicated that the people of Salinas were of the same mind. His next choice was Abilene. In 1867, he wrote, it "was a very small, dead place, consisting of about one dozen log huts, low, small, rude affairs, four-fifths of which were covered with dirt for roofing; indeed, but one shingle roof could be seen in the whole city [*sic*]. The business of the burg was conducted in two small rooms, mere log huts, and of course the inevitable saloon also in a log hut was to be found.'' To the people of Abilene, whose future looked otherwise bleak, McCoy's idea seemed a good one, and several of its citizens agreed to subscribe to the expense of building the stockyards.

"Abilene," McCoy said, "was selected because the country was entirely unsettled, well watered, excellent grass, and nearly the entire area of country was adapted to holding cattle. And it was the farthest point east at which a good depot for cattle business could have been made. Although its selection was made by an entire stranger to the country adjoining, and upon his practical judgment only, time has proved that no other so good point can be found in the State for the cattle trade. The advantages and requirements were all in its favor. After the point had been decided upon, the labor of getting material upon the ground began.

"From Hannibal, Missouri, came the pine lumber, and from Lenape, Kansas, came the hard wood, and work began in earnest and with energy. In sixty days from July 1st a shipping yard, that would accommodate three thousand cattle, a large pair of Fairbank's scales, a barn and an office were completed, and a good three story hotel well on the way toward completion.

"When it is remembered that this was accomplished in so short a time, notwithstanding the fact that every particle of material had to be brought from the East, and that, too, over a slow moving railroad, it will be seen that energy and a determined will were at work."

The season was too late to send word to Texas to start herds to Kansas, but McCoy was certain that a few men like Dougherty were already on the trail, hoping to find a way to some market or railroad. So he hired a man who knew the country well and sent him into southern Kansas and Indian Territory to look for drivers and tell them that Abilene provided an outlet for their cattle.

The rider found several, and that year about 35,000 head were shipped from Abilene to Chicago. Those sales made little impression on the herds wandering wild in Texas, but they marked the beginning of the great trail drives. Cattle had suddenly become big business on the Great Plains.

Eighteen sixty-seven was a wet year in Kansas. The Smoky Hill River was flooding its banks, and the grass grew thick, but "too coarse and washy to be good food for cattle or horses." Cholera broke out again and spread among the men driving the

cattle, killing a number of them. The Shawnee and Kaw Indians suffered from it, too, and their bones whitened in the sun at the sites of their campfires. For often their frightened companions simply left them and ran away.

Nevertheless, ten emigrants from Sweden took up land in what is McPherson County, Kansas, near the present-day community of Lindsborg. Vacant land farther east was becoming more difficult to find, so they ventured to the very edge of the Great Plains. They were not far from Abilene, where the cowboys under McCoy's direction were loading cattle onto the cars of the Kansas Pacific Railroad, but their interests were entirely different. The cowboys took pride in their freedom and enjoyed their roving existence. The Swedes at Lindsborg wished to create permanent homes for themselves in the new land and yet retain many of the customs of their own country. Even the name they gave to their community reflected this backward yearning for what they had left behind, and so did the dishes they cooked and the manner in which they decorated their houses.

The year 1867 was extremely wet; the year 1868 was extremely dry. The Smoky Hill River, which only twelve months before had been streaming over its banks, was no longer flowing, and the only water in its bed lay in occasional pools. Farther west, where it was normally more arid, water had become so scarce that the buffaloes moved east by the thousands; and when they came to a pool of water, they often drank it dry. Yet the Swedish families hung on and were joined by others.

The adjustment was often difficult for them. About ten years later, a newspaper editor jokingly wrote about the early days of some of the settlers and their attitude toward buffalo chips, the dried dung they often had to use as fuel. "It was comical to see how gingerly our wives handled these chips at first. They commenced by picking them up between two sticks or a poker. Soon they used a rag, then a corner of their apron. Finally, growing hardened, a wash after handling them was sufficient. And now? Now it is out of the bed into the chips and back again—and not even a dust of the hands!"

The men, too, adjusted. Far from Sweden, their steel plows cut into the virgin land, and their reapers gathered the crops they raised. At the edge of the Smoky Hill River they built a large brick mill, and after the harvest, they drove their loaded wagons to it. While the grain was being processed, they could look through the portholes in the chutes and see the results of their year's work flying by them. Then in the counting room on the first floor, they received their pay.

Drought years and wet years came, but in between were enough good years for Lindsborg to prosper. And its story was the story of the other farming communities that were beginning to creep out into the Great Plains. In the few years that had passed since the end of the Civil War, the nation with a great burst of energy had forged the future of the Great Plains with railroads, ranching, and agriculture.

Chapter 31

Off the Reservations

Personally the men [American volunteers] suffer severely from unaccustomed hardship and exposure; in dangerous climates they die like sheep, half are in hospital, and the other half must nurse them: Nature soon becomes stronger than martial law; under the fatigue of the march they will throw away their rations and military necessaries rather than take the trouble to carry them: improvident and wasteful, their convoys are timid and unmanageable. Mentally they are in many cases men ignoring the common restraints of society, profoundly impressed with insubordination, which displays equality. . . . Their various defects make organisation painfully slow. In camp they amuse themselves with drawing rations, target practice, asking silly questions, electing officers, holding meetings, issuing orders, disobeying orders, "cussing and discussing"; the sentinels will sit down to a quiet euchre after planting their bayonets in the ground, and to all attempts at dislodging them, the reply will be "You go to —— Cap! I'm as good a man as you." . . .

After a reasonable time, say a year, which kills off the weak and sickly, and rubs out the brawler and the mutineer; when men have learned to distinguish the difference between the often Dutch courage of a bowie-knife squabble and the moral fortitude that stands firm in presence of famine or a night attack, then they become regulars. The American—by which I understand a man whose father is born in the United States—is a first-rate soldier, distinguished by his superior intelligence from his compeers in other lands. . . .

—Richard Burton, 1861

Once one of the most remote parts of the country, known only to the mountain men, Wyoming was becoming increasingly populated, and in 1868 Congress organized it as a territory. This action reflected the increasing settlement just to the west of the Great Plains, which, in turn, emphasized the need for making peace with the Indians. So the government asked the peace commissioners who had arrived at Omaha to continue meeting with the various tribes and attempt to work out a solution to the differences between the Americans and the Indians.

Father de Smet, who had never lost his love for the wilderness but had never attained his professional goal of heading a mission among the Sioux, was asked to help. His principal assignment was to enter the Powder River country, where so much fighting had taken place, and persuade the Indians there to send delegates to the commissioners. About four miles from the Powder River, de Smet saw a band approaching. "I at once," he wrote, "had my standard of peace hoisted, with the holy name of Jesus on one side and on the other the image of the holy Virgin Mary, surrounded with gilt stars." The effect of this banner on the Indians was not what de Smet anticipated. "They took it at first sight," he said, "for the hated flag of the United States. At this signal, all the cavalcade halted and appeared to enter into consultation." Four Indians rode forward, inspected the strange flag carefully, and finally assured themselves of de Smet's peaceful intentions. After shaking his hand, they "made signals to all their warriors to advance. They then formed into a single line or phalanx; we did the same, and with the flag at our head we went to meet them. . . . I was touched even to tears at the sight of the reception which these sons of the desert, still in paganism, had prepared for the poor Black-robe."

Affable and sincere, de Smet had little difficulty talking to the Indians, both privately and at a council they called. He even conversed with such leaders as Sitting Bull, who had little interest in peace. He listened to their grievances and learned that word of Chivington's actions at Sand Creek had spread that far north, adding to their distrust and hate. But his evident goodwill overcame their fears, and they agreed to send delegates to meet with the commissioners. So successful was he that "at the close of the council . . . ," he said, "the chiefs begged me most earnestly to leave my great banner of Peace with them as a souvenir of the great day of the council. I gladly acceded to their wish."

Although the wildest of the Sioux had now acquired a picture of the Virgin Mary and although many tribes sent delegates to meet with the Americans, the peace commissioners' work was not entirely successful. For one important Indian was absent—Red Cloud. He would not treat with the Americans until the Bozeman Trail was closed.

The benefits of that route to the emigrants hardly justified the cost of maintaining the necessary forts, so in 1868 the army decided to withdraw from Forts C. F. Smith and Philip Kearny. It sold their contents to a freighting firm for resale in Montana, and in August the wagons arrived to carry the load away. When the last white man had departed, Red Cloud and his warriors put torches to the buildings to make certain they were never occupied again.

In November, long after the peace commissioners had returned east, Red Cloud appeared at Fort Laramie with about 125 warriors. He "affected," according to the major who was in command, "a great deal of dignity and disinterestedness—while other Chiefs arose, advanced and shook hands with the officers with apparent cordiality, he remained seated and sulkily gave the ends of his fingers to the officers who advanced to shake hands with him."

After days of discussing the treaty—the terms of which Red Cloud did not really understand—he agreed to sign it, although he still refused to live on a reservation. Since the two forts had been aban-doned, the major reported, "he rejoices to again take the white man by the hand, as he and their Fathers did years ago, when the country was filled with traders instead of Military Posts." Having spoken those words, Red Cloud placed his *X* along with the others at the bottom of the document, but before he did so, "he washed his hands with the dust of the floor."

Yet conditions on the Great Plains remained much as they had been before. In the fall of 1868, the general commanding the Department of Dakota reported, ". . . the various bands of the Sioux have been almost constantly throughout the year perpetrating acts of hostility, directed chiefly at the mail parties and cattle herds, occasioning a constant activity on the part of the garrison, and often preventing any communication between the posts except by strong parties. The difficulty has been complicated by the visits of bands of half-breeds from the British territory who have supplied the hostile Sioux with whiskey and ammunition. Detachments have been, from time to time, sent out . . . in pursuit of Indians who have committed depredations, but these have usually failed of their object, being parties of infantry called suddenly from fatigue duty and hastily mounted for the purpose."

Conditions along the Arkansas River were even more unsettled. When Major General Philip Sheridan made a tour of inspection in the spring of 1868, he found that "the manner of the Indians, so far as I saw, was insolent and overbearing, and so manifest as to cause me to take all the precautions in my power to protect railroad and other lines of travel in the district of the upper Arkansas."

Nevertheless, "matters went on pretty well" during the early months of summer, although the Cheyennes made a raid against the Kaw Indians and on their return robbed some houses at Council Grove, thoroughly frightening the growing community. As a consequence, the commissioner of Indian affairs ordered their agent to withhold their usual issue of guns and ammunition. "This," Sheridan reported, "incensed the Indians, who told the agent in a very insolent manner, while the teams were hauling the goods [the rest of their annuities] to their camp, that he could haul them back again, as they would have nothing unless they were given their fire-arms and ammunition."

That year the annuities were late in arriving at Fort Larned, which was close to Pawnee Rock on the old Santa Fé Trail. The Kiowas and Comanches, who had gathered to receive them, grew restless and troublesome and began buying illegal whiskey. The soldiers were secure in their fort, but the civilians who had camped or settled nearby were not. Two drunken Indians dashed through a white man's camp, shouting loudly. Frightened, the Americans began shooting and wounded one of them. The Kiowas retaliated by killing a Mexican near Fort Larned. Suddenly their aggressiveness increased with a rush, the way water in the Arkansas did when a raft of logs suddenly broke up. At headquarters General Sherman instructed an aide to list the Indians' attacks from August 10 to October 21. It filled three printed pages, starting with robberies in the Saline Valley and the murder of thirteen settlers on the Solomon River.

Like so many army commanders in the West, Sheridan had too few men to patrol the area for which he was responsible. His total force amounted to about 2,600, evenly divided between cavalry and infantry, the infantry, of course, being practically useless for pursuing the Indians. After asking for reinforcements, he authorized Brevet Colonel George A. Forsyth to employ fifty frontiersmen as scouts. Forsyth's first assignment was to move north of the Kansas Pacific Railroad and determine the direction in which most of the Indian trails were leading. When he had done that, he went to relieve a wagon train that had been attacked near Sheridan City, Kansas. By the time he arrived, the Indians were gone, but he picked up their trail and followed it to the Arickaree Fork of the Republican River, where he made camp for the night.

The next morning before he resumed his pursuit, a small band of Indians swept down on his camp. The scouts quickly drove them off, but could not prevent the loss of seven horses. Then suddenly the whole valley seemed to fill with warriors. Forsyth's position on the riverbank was untenable. Opposite his camp was a small island. Although the water surrounding it was extremely shallow, it was an easier place to defend, so he quickly occupied it and ordered his men to dig trenches in the sand with their knives and hands. They finished this just in time to repulse the Indians' first attack.

Then about three hundred warriors massed and charged them. Armed with Spencer rifles that held seven shots apiece, the Americans fired volley after volley, forcing the Indians to pass on either side of the island rather than overrun it. The Indians suffered heavy losses, but so did the Americans. Forsyth was wounded in both legs—his left shin was shattered; Lieutenant Frederick H. Beecher, his second-in-command, was mortally wounded and suffered hours of agony; the surgeon was also mortally wounded; and so were two of the scouts. Sixteen others were wounded less seriously. His rations had been used up, and all his animals had been killed. Nevertheless, he still had plenty of ammunition and was determined to continue fighting.

In the dark he had his men butcher the dead livestock and dig deeper trenches. Then he asked for volunteers to go to Fort Wallace on the Smoky Hill River for help. Since the fort was about eighty-five miles away, the mission seemed hopeless, but two men volunteered. All the next day the Indians' attack continued, and that night two more volunteers slipped away from the island in the dark but could not get past the Indians. On the third day, since the attack continued, and no relief had arrived, two more men offered to try to get to the fort.

In their rush to the island, the scouts had lost their medical supplies. This and the death of their surgeon made it impossible to care properly for the wounded. Most of them were in severe pain, and maggots were gnawing at Forsyth's legs. The horsemeat they had so carefully saved began to turn rancid on the fourth day. Yet the Indians' attack went on.

The first two scouts who left the island made little progress during the night. Coming across frequent bands of Indians, they constantly had to go into hiding. The second night they covered more mileage but at dawn found they were close to a large Indian village. During the day they lay hidden and escaped the attention of the numerous warriors who rode in and out of the camp, and the following night were on their way again.

Since they saw no Indians, they decided to keep going during the daylight hours. While they were walking in open ground with no cover nearby, they saw a band of Cheyennes approaching. Desperately they looked around them and noticed an old buffalo carcass with enough hide remaining to conceal them. Crawling under it, they kept out of sight as the warriors passed by them. Before it was safe to leave, they heard the familiar sound of a rattlesnake, which had moved in out of the sun. Fortunately one of the scouts was chewing tobacco and long practice had made him an accurate shot. The rattlesnake, unaccustomed to this sort of artillery fire, retired from the field. The two scouts finally reached Fort Wallace, and the commander immediately went to the rescue of Forsyth. (The other two scouts reached the fort later.)

After about a week, the Indians gave up their assault on the entrenched Americans and had left by the time relief arrived to help the scouts back to the fort. The courageous stand of Forsyth and his men against about seven hundred Indians had not materially affected the outcome of the campaign, but the Battle of Beecher's Island, as it became known, was widely heralded wherever men sat around campfires. "The gallantry displayed by this brave little command," Sheridan remarked, "is worthy of the highest commendation, but was only in keeping with the character of the two gallant officers in command of it . . ."

Sheridan had known that his summer campaign could be only a holding action, but he took the offensive with additional troops during the winter. "The objects of the winter's operations," he said, "were to strike the Indians a hard blow and force them on to the reservations set apart for them, and if this could not be accomplished to show the Indian that the winter season would not give him rest, and that he and his villages and stock could be destroyed; that he would have no security, winter or summer, except in obeying the laws of peace and humanity."

The first problem was to distinguish the innocent from the guilty, an almost impossible task. Sherman, who commanded the department, thought the Kiowas, Comanches, and Kiowa-Apaches had not been the real troublemakers during the summer. Those, he believed, had been mostly Cheyennes and Arapahoes. So he ordered Brigadier General W. B. Hazen to hold a council with the Kiowas and Comanches and insist that they go to Fort Cobb in Indian Territory, where they would be protected. As word spread that Sheridan was up to something, more Indians sent delegations to Hazen, and among them was Black Kettle, whom Chivington had attacked at Sand Creek. But he was a spokesman for the Cheyennes and Arapahoes, and Hazen had no authority to treat with him. Sadly he went back to his camp in the valley of the Washita River.

To carry out his campaign, Sheridan established a base of operations, which he called Camp Supply, just to the east of the Great Plains in what is now Oklahoma. There he concentrated his main force. Two smaller columns, as he explained, were to function as "beaters in, and were not expected to accomplish much. The main column, from Camp Supply, was expected to strike the Indians further south."

Sheridan arrived at Camp Supply in November to take personal command. "Hardly had the tents at headquarters been pitched," wrote a newspaper reporter who was with him, "than a violent snowstorm set in, lasting, with but trifling intermission, for three days. At one time, fears were entertained that we were destined to a snow blockade, and thus an end, for some weeks, be put upon active operations. Notwithstanding the storm, Sheridan, with characteristic energy, resolved to send out a column at once, in hopes of striking the savages when he knew their vigilance would naturally relax, and it would be impossible for them to offer any determined resistance. Custer, ever ready to undertake a desperate mission, was to be entrusted with the command; the troops designated for the service were the eleven companies of the 7th cavalry, numbering about seven hundred men."

After three days of marching in the bitter cold, Custer picked up the trail of what seemed to be a war party returning from the north. Leaving his wagons behind, he followed it in the moonlit night over the crusted snow, and it brought him to the valley of the Washita. There below was a large herd of Indian horses and a big village. Dividing his forces into several columns, Custer planned to surround the village at the first sign of dawn.

He was riding toward it in the early morning light when he heard a single rifle shot from the far side of the village and knew that some of his men had been seen. "Quickly turning to the band leader," Custer said, "I directed him to give us Garry Owen. At once the rollicking notes of that familiar marching and fighting air sounded forth through the valley and in a moment reechoed back from the opposite sides by the loud and continued cheers of the men of the other detachments, who, true to their orders, were there and in readiness to pounce upon the Indians the moment the attack began. In this manner the battle of the Washita commenced."

With the band playing gaily, the cavalry swept down on the village, which was taken by surprise. Bullets ripped through the sides of lodges, shredding them. Women and children were killed by the soldiers' fire. As Custer later said, ". . . in a struggle of this character it is impossible at all times to discriminate, particularly when, in a hand-to-hand conflict such as the one the troops were then engaged in the squaws are as dangerous adversaries as the warriors, while the Indian boys between ten and fifteen years of age were found as expert and determined in the use of the pistol and bow and arrow as the older warriors."

Because the Indians put up a strong fight in defense of their families, the battle raged until late afternoon. By that time other bands camped farther down the valley had heard the sounds of gunfire and had assembled in increasing numbers along the valley's rim. Custer was in growing danger of being surrounded. By making a feint in the direction of the other villages, he fooled the Indians into racing down the valley to defend their own families and was able to withdraw safely. Behind him he left the ruined village, the bloody bodies lying on the ground. One of the corpses was Black Kettle's, for it had been his village that Custer had attacked. Hazen's inability to treat with him had cost him his life.

Sheridan was clearly concerned about the reaction in Washington, for in his official report he called Black Kettle "a worn out and worthless old cypher" and included a sworn affidavit from a half-breed that Black Kettle's band had been responsible for much of the previous summer's troubles.

Sheridan then moved his whole force down the Washita toward Fort Cobb, sweeping all the villages before him in the direction of General Hazen, from whom they asked protection. If they were not one of the tribes considered hostile, he let them camp near the post where he could verify their identity. Sheridan next moved the Kiowas, Comanches, and Kiowa-Apaches from Fort Cobb to a new post, Camp Wichita, which is now Fort Sill, Oklahoma. There the soldiers constructed the necessary buildings while the horses rested. Because a promotion took Sheridan back to headquarters, Custer assumed charge of the next phase of the campaign, which started in March, 1869. Its purpose was to subdue the remaining Cheyennes.

Leaving the Washita Mountains behind him and pushing westward into Texas, Custer picked up the trail of a small band that led him directly to the main body of the Cheyennes. His instinct was to attack immediately, but he knew an assault would cost the lives of two white girls whom the Indians held captive. So he restrained himself and entered into a parley with the Cheyennes' leader, Medicine Arrow. In one of their lodges the Indians smoked the pipe with Custer in a ceremony that impressed him by its dignity. Unknown to him, the superstitious Cheyennes, unable to oppose the fifteen hundred soldiers that composed Custer's command, were placing on him an elaborate curse.

While waiting for the curse to take effect, the Cheyennes showed Custer a good campground about three-quarters of a mile from theirs and sent some musicians to entertain and distract him. The alert scouts, however, reported that the Cheyennes were rounding up their horses and preparing to leave. About forty Indians remained in Custer's camp, trying to hold his attention, and Custer determined to seize the chiefs among them as hostages. To protect the lives of the Cheyennes' two prisoners, he would have to do this without bloodshed.

Quietly he instructed about a hundred of his best men to arm themselves and mingle with the Indians. "Indicating in a quiet manner," Custer said, "to some of my men who were nearest to me to be ready to prevent the escape of three or four of the Indians whom I pointed out, I then directed Romeo [the interpreter] to command silence on the part of the Indians and to inform them that I was about to communicate something of great importance to them. This was sufficient to attract their undivided attention. I then rose from my seat near the fire and unbuckling my revolver from my waist asked the Indians to observe that I threw my weapons upon the ground as an evidence that in what I was about to do I did not desire or propose to shed blood unless forced to do so. I then asked the chiefs to look about them and count the armed men whom I had posted among and around them, completely cutting off every avenue of escape. They had attempted, under pretense of a friendly visit to my camp, to deceive me, in order that their village might elude us, but their designs had been frustrated and they were now in our power. . . .

"Upon the first intimation from me regarding the armed men and before I could explain their purpose every Indian who was dismounted sprang instantly to his feet, while those who were mounted gathered the reins of their ponies; all drew their revolvers or strung their bows, and for a few moments it seemed as if nothing could avert a collision, which could only terminate in the annihilation of the Indians and an equal or perhaps greater loss on our part. A singe shot fired, an indiscreet word uttered, would have been the signal to commence."

The soldiers kept calm and grouped themselves, so each Indian faced at least two men, while the interpreter kept repeating Custer's appeals to avoid bloodshed. "Near me," he said, "stood a tall gray-haired chief, who, while entreating his people to be discreet, kept his cocked revolver in his hand ready for use, should the emergency demand it. He was one of the few whom I had determined to hold. Near him stood another, a most powerful and forbidding-looking warrior, who was without firearms, but who was armed with a bow already strung and a quiver full of iron-pointed arrows. His coolness during this scene of danger and excitement was often the subject of remark afterward between the officers whose attention had been drawn to him. He stood apparently unaffected by the excitement about him, but not unmindful of the surrounding danger. Holding his bow in one hand, with the other he continued to draw from his quiver arrow after arrow. Each one he would examine as coolly as if he expected to engage in target practice. First he would cast his eye along the shaft of the arrow, to see if it was perfectly straight and true. Then he would with thumb and finger gently feel the point and edge of the barbed head, returning to the quiver each one whose condition did not satisfy him.

"In this manner he continued until he had selected perhaps half a dozen arrows with which he seemed satisfied, and which he retained in his hand, while his quick eye did not permit a single incident about him to escape unnoticed. The noise of voices and the excitement increased until a movement began on the part of the Indians who were mounted, principally the young men and boys. If the latter could be allowed to escape and the chiefs be retained, the desired object would be gained. Suddenly a rush was made. But for the fact that my men were ordered not to fire, the attempt of the Indians would not have been successful. . . . The result was that all but four broke through the lines and made their escape. The four detained, however, were those desired, being chiefs and warriors of prominence.

"Forming my men about them in such impassable ranks that a glance was sufficient to show how futile all further efforts to escape would prove, I then explained to the four captive Indians that I knew the design under which they had visited our camp; that I also knew that in their village were held as captives two white girls whose release the troops were there to enforce, and to effect their release, as well as to compel the Cheyennes to abandon the war path and return to their reservation, I had seized the four Indians as hostages."

After disarming his prisoners, Custer released one of them and told him to inform the village that they must free their white captives. After several days of unsuccessful negotiations, Custer ordered his men to select a tree and prepare to hang the three remaining hostages. This show of determination brought the freedom of the girls and Medicine Arrow's agreement to come onto the reservation as soon as the band's ponies were fit to travel.

Returning to Fort Hays in Kansas, Custer placed his hostages in the custody of the post's commander, who decided to transfer them from the stockade to the guardhouse. The interpreter failed to translate his instructions, and the hostages thought they were to be executed. Grabbing knives they had hidden in their clothing, they attempted to escape. In the following struggle, all three were killed.

When Congress rechartered the Central Pacific and permitted it to come east until it met the Union Pacific, it started a race between the two railroads,

for the government's loans and subsidies were paid on the basis of the number of miles constructed. Speed was now the only consideration. In 1868 the secretary of the interior reported that the engineer he had sent to inspect the road thought that "as it was the main policy of those acts [the revised charters] to foster and press on the enterprise, the nature of it required a distinction to be drawn, in some particulars, between a provisional and absolute completeness of the work. He held that the standard adopted by the Department [of the Interior] properly recognized the propriety and necessity of an ultimate revision of the road in order to secure that absolute completeness . . ."

The poor construction had become even worse. "The road-bed," the secretary of the interior reported, "was designed to have embankments fourteen feet wide on top, with the usual side slopes, depending on the material excavated, and cuts of not less than sixteen feet in width of bottom. The higher embankments are not brought up to the proper standard, and in some instances the width of the top is less than the length of the ties. . . . Instances also occur where the cuts have not been excavated to the depth designed. The grades are consequently higher than the engineer originally contemplated. . . . Many of the cross-ties must be replaced before the track will sustain the traffic that will be thrown upon it, on the opening of the road. . . .

"The track laying has been done as well as the rapid construction of the road would admit. The commissioners mention as a deficiency that on the curves the rails have not been bent to conform to them. . . . The track has, without exception, been laid on the bare roadway, without the latter having been previously prepared to receive it. As a consequence, except where the embankments were built of gravel or other good material, the track is without ballast, the surfacing having been done by throwing up the necesary material for that purpose from the sides of the embankments themselves."

The finances of the railroad that had now been built across the Great Plains toward Utah were as shaky as its unballasted track. As the secretary of the interior reported, the inspector "states that the cost of the road as shown on the books of the railway company is, of course, equivalent to the contract price per mile. The *actual* [and the italics were his] cost to the contractors forming an association, which embraces most of the larger stockholders of the company, is known only by their private books, to which the government directors have no access." Only the partners in the

Credit Mobilier knew how much of the government aid was going into building the railroad and how much was going into the pockets of the favored few. Unfortunately they were draining off its resources.

The men at the end of the line knew nothing about this, only the hard work and long hours demanded of them by their bosses. Squads of eight "iron men," as they were called, laid the rails, four on each side, dropping into place the thirty-foot pieces of metal, each weighing more than five hundred pounds. The sun scorched them, the wind beat against them, the cold nights froze them, and drinking water was often scarce and bad.

Durant, still the manipulator and pressing for even greater speed in laying track, got into a power struggle with Dodge and sent costs soaring. Still, the men at the end of the track swung the rails into place, and the wilderness air echoed with the sound of their sledges driving in the spikes that held the rails to the ties. Men cursed and swore. During the winter of 1868–1869 blizzards piled the snow twenty feet deep over the track where it crossed the Laramie Plains. For a time two hundred miles of track were out of commission.

Yet the workmen of both companies grew closer and closer and then passed each other. The Union Pacific sent its surveying crews almost as far as the California state line, and the Central Pacific surveyed far into Utah. The tracks began to parallel each other. Since the site of the Central Pacific was slightly higher, its workmen occasionally rolled rocks down on the men laying rails for the Union Pacific. Sometimes the workmen for the Union Pacific would place their blasting powder too far from the surveyed line and laugh as they watched it explode near or in the Central Pacific's right of way. The situation was out of control, and waste was the only result. In April, Grant, who had become President that spring, called in his old friend Dodge and told him that unless the two roads could agree on a site at which to join, Congress would make the decision for them. Under this pressure they agreed on Promontory Point in Utah.

During the early morning of May 10, 1869, the thermometer read slightly below freezing, and a light skim of ice covered the tops of the water pails. The Union Pacific had two trains at the end of its line, and the Central Pacific one until the special train of Leland Stanford, one of the original partners in the Central Pacific and now governor of California, pulled up.

Many prominent people had failed to attend—Grant was prevented by government business;

some of the others by the need to wrestle with the railroads' growing financial problems—but a telegraph operator was ready to flash the news of the junction to the nation, and the nation was waiting to hear. The last two rails were spiked into place, and then the "last tie," made of California laurel and bound with silver, was slipped under them. Someone placed a golden spike into the pre-drilled hole in the tie. Stanford picked up the silver-headed maul, swung, and missed. It was then Durant's turn. He swung and missed. The engineers for the railroad then gently tapped it into place and five days later through service commenced between Omaha and Sacramento.

Even though the roadbeds were poor, the tracks badly laid, and the financial records of the railroads filled with liabilities, the Great Plains would never again be the same. No longer did a traveler go to Missouri and buy a wagon and oxen or even board a stagecoach of the Overland Express. He went to Omaha, got on the train, stopped for supper at Grand Island, Nebraska, and had breakfast at Cheyenne, Wyoming. The sun might bake the cars, the dust pour through the open windows, and the rough railbed rattle his bones, but within four days of leaving Omaha, he was in California. And more railroads were coming. The Kansas Pacific had received permission to join its line to Denver with the Union Pacific at Cheyenne, and the Atchison and Topeka was proceeding westward and building a bridge over the Kaw River. The railroad locomotives, belching smoke, pausing at windmill-driven pumps to get water for their boilers, and pulling lines of passenger, freight, and stock cars, were not only transporting people and goods, they were quickly turning the recent past of the West into legend. The Pony Express had ridden abruptly into history, its riders now phantoms of a bygone era. The stagecoaches, the ox teams that had carried part of a nation across the continent, and the traders like Bent and McKenzie were rapidly joining it on the journey from the present into history.

Edward Judson sensed this, and since it was now a short trip to the Great Plains, he thought he might gather up a little of its remaining romance. So in the summer of 1869 he got off the Union Pacific at North Platte, once the rowdy winter quarters of the railroad gangs. Short, stocky, and moustached, Judson was better known to thousands of readers as Ned Buntline, author of dime novels that sold by the thousands. He wrote stories like *The Black Avenger of the Spanish Main: or,*

The Fiend of Blood, was an inveterate showman, and had led a life almost as implausible as those of his heroes, even taking into account the skillful embroidery with which he adorned each of his own exploits.

After Custer had brought Medicine Arrow's Cheyennes to terms with the capture of the hostages, one important band of Cheyennes under a leader named Tall Bull still remained at large. General Eugene Carr, who had been present when the Indians sacked Julesburg, was in command of the soldiers sent to track down the band. With him he had Major North and his Pawnee scouts, who had fought with Connor; and during the battle in which Tall Bull was defeated, North and the scouts behaved with conspicuous effectiveness. A white officer leading Indian scouts and fighting like an Indian? A white officer so clever that when one of the Cheyennes shot at him he dropped to the ground and told his brother to gallop away with the horse. Just as he had expected, at the sound of the hooves, the Indian peered over the bank where he was hiding to see the effect of his shot. Frank Norton had marked the spot and as soon as his head appeared, killed him. The Indian was Tall Bull himself. Buntline had read the story in the newspapers and recognized it as the raw material of a dime novel.

He had finally located North at Fort McPherson near North Platte, but the major had little use for men like Buntline and no desire to become the hero of a dime novel. Curtly he told Buntline that if he wanted a man to fill the role he would find him in the shade of a wagon that he pointed out. Buntline went over and introduced himself. The young man had been with Carr as a scout, and although he had arrived at the battle late, he was familiar with the details. His personal experience was somewhat limited, but he knew a lot of other stories, too, and he and Buntline got along well. The two men spent much time together during the author's visit to Nebraska.

Shortly after Buntline's return east, the *New York Weekly* announced the start of a new serial: "Buffalo Bill: The King of the Border Men—The Wildest and Truest Story I Ever Wrote" by Ned Buntline. In it, the scout, William Cody—now "Buffalo Bill"—more than took North's place. Not only did he personally kill Tall Bull, he also led the charge into the village and saved the life of a woman whom the Cheyennes had captured. Fifty years ago Cooper had placed his hero Natty Bumppo on the Great Plains. Buntline was bringing the old man up to date and, with Cody's imaginative assistance, helping to create a legend out of what was already fading from reality.

Chapter 32

Indians and Cattletowns

. . . [D]epredations by roving bands of Indians, who, as a general thing, come from some one of the various Indian reservations within the limits of this command, have been exasperatingly frequent. They have attacked our posts, killed and wounded our citizens and carried off their cattle, and, when pursued by our troops, taken refuge within the line of their reservations and coolly boasted of their atrocities. It seems to me that a rigid rule should be made, forbidding their absence from their reservations, and in case they disregarded it, authority should be given the military to follow on the reservation, search out, capture and punish all whom it can be shown have been absent from their agencies, and off the reservations.
— General Philip H. Sheridan, 1873

As Ned Buntline had understood, one order was passing and another was taking its place. The Great Plains over which few had been able to travel without the protection of the American Fur Company or a band of emigrants was disappearing. Wealthier and more sophisticated travelers were being attracted to the West by the convenience of railroad transportation and their own curiosity. Ralph Waldo Emerson, the aristocratic philosopher of Concord, Massachusetts, made the trip across the Great Plains in 1871. General W. Palmer, a leading spirit in the Denver and Rio Grande Railroad, established the Manitou Hotel at Colorado Springs, a resort where women dressed in their finest eastern clothes and men wore fox-hunting coats. When the Grand Duke Alexis of Russia visited the United States and wanted to go on a buffalo hunt, General Sheridan made the arrangements and asked Buffalo Bill to serve as his guide. James Gordon Bennett, publisher of the New York *Herald,* invited Cody to come to New York as his guest and introduced him to social and financial leaders such as August Belmont. Joshua Pilcher would have shaken his head in amazement.

Perhaps even more astonishing was the nation's attitude toward the Yellowstone country. When John Colter, the mountain man, had returned from his lonely journey through the area, few had believed his descriptions of what he had seen. Yet rumors of the strange wonderland lingered on, and in 1869 a group from Montana decided to explore the country and determine the truth. Because they were unable to get a military escort, most of the organizers of the expedition dropped out, but three adventurous men made the trip anyway.

Arming themselves with repeating rifles, Colt's six-shooters, and sheath knives, and carrying provisions to last six weeks, they departed for the Yellowstone in September, 1869. They saw the Falls of the Yellowstone, the Lower Geyser Basin, and other marvels. On their return about a month later, they confirmed the truth of Colter's reports, and one of them wrote a widely read article for the *Western Monthly* of Chicago.

The following year several prominent citizens of Montana Territory organized another expedition under the leadership of General Henry D. Washburn, Surveyor General of the Territory. General Sheridan, on a visit to Helena, became interested and personally arranged for a small military escort of one sergeant and four privates under the command of Lieutenant Gustavus C. Doane. "I think a more confirmed set of sceptics never went out into the wilderness," one civilian member later remarked, "than those who composed our party, and never was a party more completely surprised and captivated with the wonders of nature."

A small sulfur spring was their first sight of thermal activity. Several days later, as they were crossing the eastern slopes of what is now Mount Washburn, they suddenly looked ahead and saw another. "Through the mountain gap formed by the canyon . . . ," Doane wrote, "an object now appeared which drew a simultaneous expression of wonder from every one of the party. A column of steam rising from the dense woods to the height of several hundred feet, became distinctly visible. We had all heard fabulous stories of this region, and were somewhat skeptical of appearances. At first it was pronounced a fire in the woods, but presently some one noticed that the vapor rose in regular puffs, as if expelled with great force. Then conviction was forced upon us. It was indeed a great column of steam, puffing away on the lofty mountain side, escaping with a roaring sound audible at a long distance, even through the heavy forest. A hearty cheer rang out at this discovery, and we pressed onward with renewed enthusiasm."

During the next weeks they saw many of the region's other marvels. They watched the Yellowstone River pour through the narrow cut it had made in the rock and suddenly plummet more than three hundred feet over the cliff that formed its falls. A stream of white, it struck the bottom and created a cauldron of foam and rising spray. The sheer walls of the canyon were spotted here and there with brilliant colors, and the roar of the rushing water broke the wilderness's quiet as they looked in awe. They saw the sparkling waters of Yellowstone Lake with the snow-capped peaks of the Tetons glimmering in the distance. Old Faithful sent its plume of steam into the air, white against the blue sky and slightly bowed by the wind. Then it fell, and only the bubbling of the sulfur at its base gave testimony to the brief miracle. They saw the sulfur springs, boiling hot and their sides painted with bright colors. They saw, too, the outcrops of obsidian looking almost like walls of glass.

Their descriptions of the area caused the U. S. Geological Survey of the Territories to change its plans for 1871 and concentrate on the Yellowstone and the surrounding region. This expedition was under the leadership of Dr. Ferdinand V. Hayden;

and even before his official report had been printed, his enthusiastic comments, along with those of the previous explorers, made some Congressmen consider the possibility of withdrawing the area from the public domain, to prevent its being mined or homesteaded.

To many, the idea was ridiculous. The nation owned millions of acres in the unsettled West, and the country needed people, not areas held in reserve. Yet the House and Senate passed a bill that read: *"Be it enacted by the Senate and House of Representatives of the United States of America in Congress assembled,* That the tract of land in the Territories of Montana and Wyoming, lying near the head-waters of the Yellowstone River . . . is hereby reserved and withdrawn from settlement, occupancy, or sale under the laws of the United States, and dedicated and set apart as a public park of pleasuring-ground for the benefit and enjoyment of the people . . .

"Sec. 2. That said public park shall be under the exclusive control of the Secretary of the Interior, whose duty it shall be, as soon as practical, to make and publish such rules and regulations as he may deem necessary or proper for the care and management of the same."

On March 1, 1872, the President signed the bill, and the Yellowstone became the first national park—not merely in the United States, but in the world. Out of the Great Plains and its people had sprung a unique cultural concept, one that reflected a respect for the values of nature.

Yet many of the basic problems on the plains remained the same. The nation still retained its ambivalent attitude toward the Indians. Most frontiersmen and quite a few in the army were for whipping them into submission. The Indians, it seemed to them, used the reservations only as places to go when they wanted to escape the soldiers or receive their annuities; but whenever they felt like raiding or killing, they easily eluded their agents and rode off on their deadly errands. Others took a more kindly—and perhaps more romantic—view of the Indians' plight, regretting the disruption of their ways and feeling guilty over the absorption of their lands.

On one point almost everyone agreed. The Office of the Commissioner of Indian Affairs was incapable of finding a solution to the Indian problem. There were many reasons for this. Although some agents were high-minded, experienced men, others were political hacks interested only in the pay and who got the contracts. To add to the difficulties, the office had posts as far-flung as the military's but without military discipline and with numerous opportunities for graft.

Coming into office on a wave of popularity and with the renown of having won the war, Grant was able to effect a considerable number of changes during the early part of his administration. One of them was to replace many of the persons who had been working at the agencies. But instead of choosing the new personnel himself, he turned the responsibility over to various religious denominations, assigning each the responsibility for seeing that certain tribes were properly staffed. (The Society of Friends, who had long advocated such a move, was among the most enthusiastic supporters of the plan.)

The same year, Congress authorized the President to appoint nine persons to serve on a Board of Indian Commissioners. They and the secretary of the interior were to control the disbursement of the Indian appropriation, and they were to have authority to inspect the agencies and the records of the Indian office. Yet these changes had little effect. Some of the persons designated by the various sects were incompetent, and the Board of Indian Commissioners, although well meaning, found itself manipulated by some of the clever Indian leaders and lacking real authority over the conduct of Indian affairs.

In the northern Great Plains the Northern Pacific Railroad had sent its survey crews west of the Red River, and the army had provided military escorts to protect them. The Blackfeet, who had so firmly resisted the Americans from the days of Lewis and Clark until finally McKenzie had started to trade with them, were still active. "On frequent occasions," the military commander of Dakota reported, ". . . their war parties had dashed into the settlements, and after killing the inhabitants of such exposed ranches as they could strike before organized opposition could be opposed to them, and burning the houses, had easily made their escape, . . . driving before them all the stock they could collect. In general all efforts to overtake them and recover the stolen stock were fruitless."

Emulating Sheridan's winter campaign of the previous year, the commander of Dakota dispatched four companies of cavalry and some infantry against the Indians in January, 1870. On the Marias River, where Lewis had been nearly killed by them, the soldiers came upon a village of Piegan Blackfeet. They slew 173 and captured a hundred women and children, whom they turned loose again, because they had insufficient rations on which to feed them while bringing them in. "It is to be regretted," the commanding general remarked, "that in the attack on the camp some women and children were accidentally killed . . . As is well known to all acquainted with Indian fighting, a certain proportion of accidental killing will always occur in affairs of this kind, especially when the attack is made in the dim light of the early morning, and when it is a necessary element of success to fire into the lodges at the outset to drive the Indians out to an open contest."

On the southern Great Plains many of the tribes that Custer thought he had subdued were sending out raiding parties again. The commander of Texas reported that in his department the northern and western settlements were suffering. Those on the north were close to the reservations in Indian Territory and, like many other commanders, he suspected the reservation Indians of being less innocent than they appeared. There was, he pointed out, "free and unrestrained intercourse" between the reservation Indians and the marauding bands.

Then he had to contend with the Llano Estacado, still as fearsome as it had been in Coronado's day, a place where a man could get lost even though he could see everywhere around him. Nevertheless, Colonel Ranald Mackenzie of the cavalry had crossed them and discovered a trail leading into New Mexico, which, he thought, might be used by cattle thieves preying on the Texas ranchers. The commanding general also had the problem presented by the Mexican border. "The great cattle ranges of Western Texas," he pointed out, "lie near the Río Grande, which is a mere mark of a boundary without being in the least an obstruction to the thieves. It is only an obstacle to the troops and others that follow them." He was convinced that the cattle thieves were in league with the Indians on the Llano Estacado and supplying them with arms and ammunition. (Only a few years before, cattle had not been worth stealing; with the advent of the railroads they had become so.)

No one really knew how many hostile Indians remained at large. When three commissioners visited the Sioux near Fort Peck in Montana Territory, they found that many of them had refused to abandon their old ways, and the camp of Sitting Bull was one of their rallying points. Some said these hostile Indians numbered seven hundred lodges, some only twenty. One report the commissioners received gave a total of only seven hundred lodges in the whole Powder River country, others claimed there were three thousand Sioux alone, not to mention Arapahoes, Cheyennes, and others. As the commissioners pointed out, they had no means of making an accurate census; but regardless of the estimate used, there were many hostile Indians in the wild land through which Connor had marched his men.

In 1872 Congress decided to take a comprehensive look at the Indian question. Two causes of trouble were immediately apparent. One, of course, was land. The Americans' appetite for territory was insatiable. When they got one road across the country, they always wanted another. Settlers encroached on the reservations, particularly toward the east. The railroads, too, were offenders by force of circumstance. If their route ran through land that had been conceded to the Indians, they took not only their right-of-way but their land grant also. Although the government in such a case would negotiate a new treaty, the Indians still felt wronged.

Congress began to see that serving Indians had become big business. The Upper Missouri Agency alone required almost 2 million pounds of beef cattle a year, more than a 100,000 pounds of bacon, 600,000 pounds of flour, as well as many other provisions. The temptation for the white contractors or agents to cheat was great. Many fine men were attracted to the agencies, but so were many crooks.

In its final report Congress pointed out that it was only natural that the Indians should be "continually apprehensive of the power and bad intentions of the United States Government and people toward them . . ." After all, the report went on, "they should be fearful of the power of a people who have, in so short a time, transplanted them through a continent, turning their hunting-grounds of vast forests and prairies into fruitful fields; their rivers . . . into sources of navigation and travel . . ." and who had used against them the most advanced weapons of warfare. "This doubt and fear . . . " the report explained, "the memory of which is fostered and fed by designing men for personal interests, is one of the fruitful sources of fraudulent and oppressive contracts . . ." Past history had taught the Indians to make concessions whether they wanted to or not.

Congress also looked at the process of treaty-making. This practice had started when the first settlers landed on the continent, and they and the Indians had approached each other as equals. But long ago it should have been abandoned. The reason it had not been was purely political. A treaty required only confirmation by the Senate. That body alone, therefore, had controlled the disposition of Indian lands.

"The secrecy of treaty-making is bad," the House report said, "when one of the parties is not competent to take full care of his interests when making the treaty, and has no power to enforce his rights under the treaty when made.

"Our treaty records abound with amendments arbitrarily made by the Senate of the United States after the treaty was made and signed by the United States commissioners and the Indian officials.

"This is not treaty-making in its purity; it is a mockery on treaty-making."

The report also pointed out that even the government had lost track of its numerous treaties with the Indians. The committee had "taken one step toward harmonizing these treaties by procuring the passage of a bill directing the commissioners whose duties it is to revise the laws to also revise the Indian treaties, so as to set forth the treaties and parts of treaties now in force." In this way, it hoped to bring some sort of order to a complicated situation.

The commissioner of Indian affairs, however, had his own solution to the difficulties with the Indians. "It must be considered," he said, "that the Indians of the plains have, up to a recent date, really believed that they outnumbered the whites. How, indeed, should they have thought otherwise? Most of them had at one time or another, seen as many as five thousand, some as many as ten thousand of their people camped together, one-third fighting men. Of the whites what had they seen? A few ranches miles apart, a few hunters and trappers, a few soldiers. The stories that had been brought to their ears of a country where the whites were like the sand on the sea-shore . . . were received by them as the merest fables invented to amuse or deceive them."

Only when many Indians had come east, he said, would the others begin to recognize the power and resources of the Americans. "As it is cheaper and more humane," he argued, "to bring the savages to a realizing sense of their weakness and the impossibility of long contending with the Government, by giving a few chiefs and braves free rides on our railroads and Broadway omnibuses, than by surprising their camps on winter nights and shooting down men, women, and children together in the snow, it will be well to continue this system, in moderation as to amount of expenditures, and with discretion as to the subjects of it . . . ."

But words had little effect on the brutal life of the Great Plains with its age-old struggles. The Pawnees had been glad to become army scouts under Frank and Luther North and avenge themselves against the Sioux. But in 1873 when they went on their semi-annual buffalo hunt, an assemblage of Oglalas and Brulés fell on them in the valley of the

Republican River near present-day Trenton, Nebraska. The Pawnees were prepared to hunt, not fight, and they had their women and children with them. The engagement, known as the Battle of Massacre Canyon, was devastating to the Pawnees. They fled with the Sioux after them, and only the belated arrival of the cavalry kept the massacre from being complete. After the survivors reached their reservation, they were so broken in spirit that they asked to be sent to Indian Territory.

The Black Hills, looming dark and mysterious over the Great Plains in modern South Dakota, had been retained by the Sioux in the Treaty of 1868. Yet no one knew what was there. Some rumors said the area held valuable mineral deposits, others that it was only a refuge for hostile Indians. In 1874 the army determined to find out.

Although the Indians might not have agreed, the army believed it could legally explore the Black Hills because a clause in the same treaty gave the government the right to send its officials onto reservations. Custer was assigned to lead the expedition, and he started in early July with the band playing "The Girl I Left Behind Me."

He had made arrangements to send back dispatches and mail from the Black Hills, and when he wrote his first report, he told about the beauty and fertility of those mountains. Then he said, "As there are scientists accompanying the expedition who are examining into the mineral resources of this region, the result of whose researches will accompany my detailed report, I omit all present reference to that portion of our explorations until the return of the expedition, except to state, what will appear in any event in the public prints, that gold has been found in paying quantities. I have upon my table forty or fifty small particles of pure gold, in size averaging that of a small pin-head and most of it obtained today from one panful of earth."

The newspapers, of course, made headlines of this exciting news that was later confirmed by Custer in his final report. Whether or not the lands belonged to the Indians made no difference. It never had when gold was concerned.

The commissioner of Indian affairs reported that the Custer expedition had "occasioned great excitement among the whole Sioux people during the summer. They regard it as a palpable infraction of their treaty stipulations, and were filled with the apprehension that it might lead to their exclusion from a country held sacredly their own, and highly prized as their home and last refuge from the encroachment of settlement. The exaggerated ac-

counts of rich mines and agricultural lands given in the dispatches of the commander and correspondents of the expedition intensified the eagerness of the people all along the border to take possession of the country." As they had done in Colorado, the gold-seekers were not waiting until the government had negotiated yet another agreement and cleared the Indian title to the land. By that time, white titles would have been established, and there would be no gold left. So they began to converge on the Black Hills, and further resentment swept through the Sioux.

The fur trade as Ashley and McKenzie had known it was long since dead, its markets dried up, its sources depleted. But in its place had sprung up an enormous business in buffalo hides and meat, made possible by the coming of the railroads. Until then the relatively low value of a buffalo hide compared with its weight and bulk presented a transportation problem. Shipment by ox-drawn wagons was expensive, but the market for the hides could absorb the comparatively lower charges for carload lots. Then, too, the railroads themselves were a market. A few hunters could feed the surveyors and track layers inexpensively, and buffalo meat was a staple in the railroad builders' diet.

When the northern herds became depleted, the professional hunters concentrated on the buffaloes south of the Arkansas River. The Atchison and Topeka Railroad had now joined up with the Santa Fé, and as it began to approach the Arkansas, some of the officers stationed at Fort Dodge and some of the local merchants chartered a company to found Dodge City, Kansas. Like Abilene in its early days, Dodge City had little to offer prospective settlers except railroad service and its proximity to the fort. To survive, it needed an industry, and it found one in the buffalo hunters.

These were a wild lot. Colonel Richard I. Dodge, a graduate of West Point, was assigned to Fort Dodge in the early 1870s, and he described how the railroads "soon swarmed with 'hard cases' from the East, each excited with the prospect of having a buffalo hunt that would pay. By waggon, on horseback, and a-foot, the pot-hunters poured in, and soon the unfortunate buffalo was without a moment's peace or rest. Though hundreds of thousands of skins were sent to market, they scarcely indicated the slaughter that [resulted], from want of skill in shooting, and want of knowledge in preserving the hides of those slain, on the part of these green hunters; one hide sent to market represented three, four, or even five dead buffalo."

The needs of the hunters quickly created local markets, and Dodge commented, "The merchants of the small towns along the railroads were not slow to take advantage of this new opening. They furnished outfits, arms, ammunition, &c., to needy parties, and established great trades, by which many now ride in their carriages."

By the fall of 1872, Dodge City was booming, and the local merchants had "got the [buffalo] trade pretty well into their own hands. Most of the hunting parties were sent out by them, and were organised for even a greater destruction of buffalo, and with more care for the proper preservation of the hides and meat. Central depôts were established in localities where buffalo were plentiful. Parties were sent out from these which every few days brought back their spoil."

This was not hunting in the normal sense; it was organized slaughter, the wanton reaping of a natural harvest with no thought of how it might be replaced. "In the beginning of the hide business," Dodge said, ". . . every man wanted to shoot; no man wanted to do the other work. Buffalo were slaughtered without sense or discretion, and oftentimes left to rot with the hides on. This did not pay, and these self-organised parties soon broke up. When the merchants got the business into their hands they organised parties for work. The most approved party consisted of four men—one shooter, two skinners, and one man to cook, stretch hides, and take care of camp. Where buffalo were very plentiful, the number of skinners was increased. A light waggon, drawn by two horses or mules, takes the outfit into the wilderness and brings into camp the skins taken each day."

The hunter in each group was in charge. Early in the morning he set out wth a large supply of ammunition and gun in hand. His purpose was to kill buffaloes but without frightening the others away, so he worked upwind and carefully used every ravine or knoll for cover. Sometimes he would shoot a single animal, sometimes three or four before they ran off. "Occasionally," Dodge said, "he may find a herd in an exceptionally favorable position. Crawling like a snake along the bottom of a ravine, he may approach unsuspected to within thirty or forty feet of the nearest. Hiding his every movement, the heavy rifle is brought to bear, and a bullet sent into the heart of the nearest buffalo. The animal makes a plunge forward, walks a few steps, and stops with the blood streaming from his nostrils. The other buffalo, startled at the report, rush together but, neither seeing nor smelling danger, stare in uneasy wonder. Attracted by the blood

they collect about the wounded buffalo. Another bullet is now sent in; another buffalo plunges, stops, and bleeds. The others will stare, and, seeming to think the wounded animals responsible for the unusual noise, concentrate their attention on them. Again and again the rifle cracks. Buffalo after buffalo bleeds, totters, and falls. The survivors stare in imbecile amazement.

"The game is so near, and the shooter so well understands his business, that but one shot is necessary for each life. The wounded animal may walk off some distance, but is sure to come down.

"When the shooter has killed or mortally wounded as many as his party can skin, he crawls off as cautiously as he approached, and returns, well-satisfied, to camp."

At the height of the slaughter in the early 1870s, the buffaloes were so plentiful that the only work was in skinning them. As the men tried to keep up with the hunter, ". . . the ordinary process was found to be much too slow for the 'great American buffalo-skinner,' so he devised a plan of his own. An incision was made across the back of the head, just in front of the ears and around the throat. This thick skin, ears included, was started by skinning down some six or eight inches. Connecting incisions were made from the throat down the belly, and from this down each leg to the knee as is usual. A stout rope was fastened about the thick skin on the back of the head, the ears preventing its slipping off when pulled. A strong iron spike about three feet long was then driven through the head of the buffalo into the ground, pinning it fast. The waggon was then brought up, and the other end of the rope made fast to the hind axle. The horses were whipped up, and the skin torn from the carcass at one pull. I have seen a skin taken off in this way in, I think, less than five minutes (though I did not time it by the watch). Sometimes the skin was badly torn, and always, more or less, flesh adhered to it, giving additional work to the stretcher. When, therefore, the careful preparation of each skin began to be of greater importance than time, this process was abandoned, and the skinner returned to his usual greasy, filthy, and legitimate work."

Dodge tried to discover how many buffaloes were killed each year but found it almost impossible. The railroads' records were inadequate, and many dealers, who illegally traded whiskey and guns with the Indians, hid their transactions by renting whole cars instead of shipping their furs as freight. The Indians also killed buffaloes for their own use and for shipping, added to which was the waste. Assembling the figures, Dodge came to the conclusion that in a period of three years about five and a half million buffaloes had been killed.

As the Kansas herds became thinner, the hunters began to press down into the Texas Panhandle. In 1874, when even more hunters started to move south, a Dodge City merchant, Charles Meyers, decided to follow them and thus get ahead of his competitors. He would buy the hides on the spot and ship them back to Kansas in the same wagons that had brought out his trade goods. William Bent had had a subsidiary trading post, called Adobe Walls, on the South Fork of the Canadian River. It had long since been abandoned, but Meyers liked the area and selected a site about a mile away for his own establishment. Soon several stores, a saloon, and a blacksmith's shop were in operation, and the new community became a center for the buffalo hunters in Texas. Although no adobe had been used in its construction, the hunters gave it the name of Adobe Walls after Bent's old post.

In spite of the optimistic belief of Custer and other campaigners that the Indian menace on the southern Great Plains had been ended, the old hatreds and mistrusts were like the embers in a campfire that has not been thoroughly extinguished. The winds that fanned them into flame in 1874 were many: the late delivery of annuity goods, their dislike of life on reservations, and, most of all, the destruction of the buffalo herds. Although the reservation Indians received rations, these were not sufficient for a year's diet and had to be supplemented by buffalo meat. For those not on reservations and therefore without annuities, the herds were their only source of food. With the inroads being made by the professional buffalo hunters, both groups of Indians—hostile and friendly—foresaw starvation.

In the spring of 1874 the Cheyennes in particular were concerned about the encroachments of the buffalo hunters on lands they considered their own, and they were angry over the depredations of white horse thieves who raided their herds and sold the animals in the American settlements. When they learned that a Comanche medicine man named Little Wolf claimed to have a paint that would turn away the Americans' bullets, they grew excited over the possibility of using it and making war against the white men. The excitement spread to the Kiowas, and bands of the tribes held a council. At the urging of Little Wolf, they decided to attack Adobe Walls.

The buffalo hunters and their suppliers realized that the Indians were becoming more and more troublesome, because several parties of hunters were attacked in the field, but they did not anticipate an attack on Adobe Walls itself, until they received word of the Indians' council from the post traders at Fort Supply, Sheridan's former base. From what they knew of the Indians, the traders thought the attack would come on June 27.

The message went only to the men who had established Adobe Walls, and they did not know what to make of it. They had a profitable business going and did not want to disrupt it, so they did not share the intelligence, although all but one of them, Jim Hanrahan, who owned the saloon, conveniently left for Dodge City before the attack might take place.

On the night of June 26, Hanrahan was in a quandary. Not being certain of the accuracy of his information, he hesitated to announce what he knew, for if the attack failed to materialize he would look like a fool. On the other hand, he did not want everyone asleep. Finally he decided on a ruse. About two o'clock in the morning, he fired his pistol and called out that the ridgepole of the saloon had cracked. This woke the two men sleeping there, and soon Hanrahan had the whole community helping him search for a forked pole that would keep the roof in place.

Now that he had Adobe Walls aroused, he had to keep it awake. He offered free drinks, and he also suggested that some of the men prepare for an early start that day, since they were up anyway. He was not completely successful, for a number again curled up in their bedrolls. But when the Indians did attack, some were awake and saw the warriors coming.

The Indians could not match the accuracy of the buffalo hunters with their long-range guns. Again and again they charged, but although Adobe Walls had not been built as a fort, they were driven back. Finally about four o'clock in the afternoon, they left. Little Wolf, the medicine man who had promised an easy victory, had stayed at a distance from the battle. Nevertheless, one of the buffalo hunters shot his horse out from underneath him even though the horse, too, had been covered with the protective magic paint. In later years some of the Indians translated Little Wolf's name into English as Coyote Droppings.

The army responded immediately to the attack on Adobe Walls but faced its usual problem of trying to locate and pin down hostile Indians in a vast expanse of space without sufficient men. Colonel Nelson Miles left with three columns from Fort Dodge and began searching the country south of the Arkansas, touching at Fort Supply and Adobe Walls. Finally he picked up an Indian trail, which he followed as fast as he could, usually marching twenty-five miles a day. "In many places," Miles recalled, "no water was to be discovered in the beds of the streams, and only at long intervals were there found stagnant holes containing some, often impregnated with gypsum. Men rushed in frenzy and drank, only to find their thirst increased rather than slaked. Even coffee made with it was found so bitter that it could not be drunk. The heat was almost unendurable, the thermometer ranging above 110 degrees in the shade daily." His men were so thirsty they sometimes slit their veins and drank their own blood.

As the trail grew fresher, Miles left his wagons behind in order to move more quickly. His men were ascending the caprock that lines the Llano Estacado, when they finally caught up with the Indians. The brief engagement was inconclusive. The Indians, although they could not defeat the troops, made good their escape.

Miles could pursue them no farther. "The Indians being driven out upon the Llano Estacado," he said, "it was impossible to follow further, as our trains were far in the rear of our command, and the trail leading up the precipitous cliffs told the fruitlessness of longer pursuit in the then condition of the troops. It was, therefore, deemed best to call a halt. After a night's rest the command, with infinite labor, followed the trail and climbed out of the valley of the Tulé and for miles out upon the Llano Estacado. It became evident, however, that no pursuit could be successful without supplies, and that before a train could be brought between the ravines and breaks of the valley to the table-land on the right bank of the Red River, the Indians could get beyond pursuit."

The Llano Estacado had baffled those of European descent ever since the first Spaniards had wandered out onto it. Military men had been puzzled by it, the Texas Pioneers had nearly lost their lives there on their way to Santa Fé, and yet to the Indians, it was a refuge. Colonel Ranald Mackenzie of the cavalry, however, had shown that troops could maneuver in that strange, dry land with its deep canyons, and now he was called upon to do so again.

Mackenzie was a slight man of moderate height. He ate little, kept late hours, was fretful and irritable and a poor rider. But he was fair to his men, inspired loyalty in his officers, and was tenacious in pursuit of the enemy. He had received three wounds in the Civil War and a bad arrow wound in his thigh during the Indian wars and could barely ride twenty-five or thirty miles without being in great pain. Yet during one campaign he rode 160 miles in thirty-two hours without a single complaint.

While he was searching for the Indians on the Llano Estacado, a band tried to stampede his horses. His men fought them off successfully and, when daylight came, pursued the last of them. But suddenly the Indians disappeared as completely as though they had left the earth. Every traveler through that country had noted the deep canyons cut through its flat surface by the few rivers. Obviously the Indians must have dropped into one of these. Mackenzie's course led him to the rim of Palo Duro Canyon, that cleft cut by the Prairie Dog Town Fork of the Red River, a hidden refuge with grass, water, trees, and protection from the bitter winter winds that swept the area. Peering into its depths, Mackenzie saw lodge after lodge.

Getting down to the bottom was his first problem, but he finally found a narrow trail used by the Indians and began the descent. So secure did the Indians feel in this spot that they were unaware of his approach until a single Indian saw the troops and gave the alarm. Taken by surprise, the Indians dashed up the canyon while some of Mackenzie's men followed them and others began the systematic destruction of their lodges and supplies and rounded up their horses.

The terrain was unfamiliar to the Americans but well known to the Indians, who, once they had recovered from the initial shock of seeing troops, began to take up positions among the rocks along the canyon walls and on the rim. Some of Mackenzie's officers wanted to charge them, but he restrained them, knowing that the Indians would enjoy an advantage and the result would be a large loss of American life. As soon as the lodges were destroyed, he drove the Indians' ponies up the trail and out of the canyon, placing them in the center of a marching square of men, so the Indians could not recapture them. After he had selected enough to replace the horses he had lost during the campaign and after giving some to his scouts, he ordered the remainder killed. Somewhere between one and two thousand horses were slaughtered.

Mackenzie's losses were negligible; the Indians had lost between fifty or sixty warriors. But worse, they had no shelter, no provisions, and no mounts. Winter was coming, and if they wished to stay alive, they would have to creep back to a reservation.

Although McCoy had had difficulty finding a settlement willing to be a cattle shipping center,

Abilene's success made other communities envious. The farmers generally remained antagonistic, largely because of the Texas fever, but merchants and other businessmen quickly realized that larger profits could be made from the cattle trade than from the slower development of local farming.

The people of Ellsworth, Kansas, believed they had an advantage over Abilene. The state had enacted legislation establishing a quarantine line to the east of which no one could drive Texas cattle. In the case of Abilene, the law had been quietly overlooked, but Abilene's days were numbered should the law be enforced. These circumstances gave Ellsworth an opportunity.

First, it persuaded the Kansas legislature to establish a state highway from Indian Territory to Ellsworth with the special provision that this road would never be subject to the quarantine law. Next, its people approached the Kansas Pacific for help in building the necessary facilities. The railroad now realized that cattle shipments were an answer to the problem that all the new railroads shared. They had no difficulty getting freight traffic heading west, but their cars came back east almost empty. Cattle provided profitable freight on the return journey. The Kansas Pacific also realized that the farms advancing westward would soon begin to surround Abilene, and the day would arrive when no more cattle would move out of that shipping point. In order to retain its share of the business, it was willing to build the necessary sidings to serve the Ellsworth stockyard. The dairy farmers around Ellsworth began to relax their opposition to Texas cattle when they found out that it was possible to buy cattle from the herds at relatively low prices, fatten them over the winter, and sell them in the spring. So by 1871 Ellsworth, too, was shipping cattle and looking forward to becoming a booming center.

The promoters of Wichita, Kansas, were also looking for an industry for their proposed community. Since their location was just north of a free zone established by the quarantine law, Texas herds could legally drive there, particularly if the stockyards were on the southern side of town. The community was handicapped, however by the absence of a railroad. Even the offer of a subsidy—financed by a local bond issue—was insufficient to bring either the Atchison, Topeka and Santa Fe or the Kansas Pacific. But the citizens floated a bond issue anyway and built a spur railroad to the Atchison, Topeka and Santa Fe. By 1872 the railroad was completed, Abilene was finished as a cattle town, and Wichita shipped more cattle than even Ellsworth.

Several other Kansas towns, such as Hays and Newton, also strove to become centers of the once despised business; but when it became evident that farms in due course would encircle Wichita, its most promising successor was Dodge City. Having been an important shipping point for buffalo hides, Dodge had little adjustment to make except for a few physical improvements, such as corrals. The demands of the buffalo hunters were much like those of the men driving cattle. The Santa Fe Railroad, now anxious for a share in the cattle business, paid the cost of constructing a corral, and in 1877 Dodge began to supplant the other cattle centers farther east.

At first, cattle were so hard to sell in Texas that a man willing to drive them north could dictate the terms on which he bought them. As a consequence, he usually had a long period of time in which to pay for them. The only loans he needed when he arrived at the cowtown were to pay off his hands and take care of current expenses while he waited to make a sale; the money he owed for the cattle was not due until he had actually sold them. But as the market grew brisker, the terms became shorter, and the sellers wanted payment as soon as the cattle reached the shipping point. Therefore the man driving the cattle often had to borrow money to cover his debts in Texas while he waited for a buyer. Soon banking became an important business on the Great Plains.

Other types of businesses profited, too. Food sold well, and often the men driving the cattle ordered supplies sent out even before they arrived in town. The clothing merchants also made money from the wants of the cowboys who, with money in their pockets, were willing to spend it on new boots, shirts, and trousers.

Yet the profits to be derived from the cattle themselves were far from certain. A trail driver might arrive at the shipping center only to find prices badly depressed. In that case he might decide to hold them over the winter, which required capital, or ship them to Chicago himself instead of selling them to a dealer. This, too, required capital, for he then had to pay the freight charges out of his own pocket. And when the cattle arrived at Chicago, the price might have fallen even further.

The year 1873 drove this point home. Until then some cattle had been sold to ranchers north and west of Kansas, who provided an important subsidiary market and drained off any surplus. That year, however, these ranchers had all the cattle they needed and were preparing to make their own shipments. The market was already depressed, and this news sent it tumbling further. By fall, according to McCoy, the number of cattle buyers had dropped to one-fourth the number who had been in the market the year before, yet the number of cattle being offered for sale was greater.

Then came the panic that followed the collapse of Jay Cooke's banking house. "Many cattle that were forwarded east," McCoy said, "did not sell for scarce more than freight and charges. A single firm lost one hundred and eighty thousand dollars in three week's shipments. It was common to hear a shipper say, pointing to his cattle, that every horn in sight was losing a five dollar note, or ten dollars per head. Indeed, money was lost as fast and completely as if a bonfire had been made of it, and kept burning for forty days. It is estimated that the panic lost Texan drovers fully two millions of dollars . . . it is beyond the power of the writer to give by pen or word, even a faint description of the great calamity, or tell of its wide spread ruin. Men by the score could be named who were suddenly bankrupted, and it was very rare to meet a cattle driver, trader, or shipper, who had not lost heavily. Many thousands of stock cattle, especially cows and rough thin steers, were sold at from one to one and a quarter cents per pound gross weight, to be 'tanked'; that is, the hide, horns, and hoofs taken off, and the balance of the carcass placed in a tank and rendered, or steamed; the tallow obtained, the balance was thrown away. . . . The year of 1873 was, taken as a whole, one of great disaster to western cattle men, and will be long and vividly remembered by many whose finest hopes, together with their fortunes, were dashed to the earth and broken."

Like the mining camps, the cowtowns attracted America's riffraff, who gathered to prey off the cowboys arriving from weeks on the trail with their back pay in their pockets. In fact, one reason for making the drive was to get to town, a rare experience for many of the hands. Some even went to Chicago as "cow punchers," or "cow pokes," the men who rode the cattle cars and goaded to their feet any cattle that lay down to prevent their being trampled by the others. ("Cow puncher" and "cow poke" soon became synonymous with cowboy.) Gamblers, saloon keepers, dance hall operators, and prostitutes gathered in the cattle towns to offer their various forms of entertainment. A lawless group, many of them were ready to fight among themselves, with the residents, or with the transient cowboys.

The cowboys themselves, with a few exceptions, were more likely to be naïve than quick with the trigger. But they were generally healthy young men, full of high spirits and looking for a good time. They often had a high sense of camaraderie that could easily set them against the town if they thought one of their own had been offended; and many of them were filled with boisterous, youthful humor that lent itself to practical jokes rather than fine turns of wit. They and the professional criminals made a potentially explosive combination.

The attitude of the townspeople was generally ambivalent. The serious merchants and the staid moneylenders preferred a businesslike atmosphere, but they also knew that their customers wanted to have a good time, and if they could not find it in one community, they would take their business to another. So generally the leading citizens settled for a compromise: a certain amount of misbehavior was permitted but not too much.

They all adopted ordinances. In Abilene, section two provided against "disturbing the quiet of the city or of any lawful assembly of persons at any church." Section three provided "against throwing stones or bricks or any missiles across any street or alley of this city . . ." Section four provided against "discharging any firearms or setting off any fire crackers or squibs or throwing any fire balls or making any bon fire in the limits of the city. . ." (The exceptions to this were the 24th and 25th of December, the 1st of January, the 4th of July, and the 26th of February.)

Section seven said: "For leaving any horse, mule, or other beast of burden in the street without being properly hitched to some substantial place or fastening, any sum not exceeding five dollars or for any fast or reckless riding or driving or racing, any sum not exceeding fifty dollars."

Section eight provided against blocking any "sidewalk or passage or any street or alley or any walk . . . with any boxes, barrels, vehicles, or hose . . . or for placing dirt or rubbish therein, or riding or driving over or upon any sidewalk or digging holes in same . . ." while another section stated ". . . that any person conducting himself in a riotous or disorderly manner or resists officers or openly use profane or indecent language or indecently expose his or her person, or commit any nuisance, shall be liable to a fine of not less than ten dollars."

In enforcing such laws as these, the community leaders usually relied on the discretion of the city marshal. He was supposed to maintain order without driving the customers away, an assignment that was often difficult.

The city marshals varied widely in their characters and attitudes. Tom Smith, who served for a time in Abilene, never even carried a gun. Others were quick with their six-shooters and fond of

To the first settlers, the Great Plains seemed strange and ominous, but as they adjusted their ways to the new land, they made homes for themselves and turned what early explorers had called an uninhabitable desert into an integral part of the United States. *Alexander B. Adams*

As the cattle towns attracted more undesirable elements, law enforcement became increasingly important. Pictured here are the "peace commissioners" of Dodge City, Kansas. The second from the right in the front row is Wyatt Earp; the center figure in back is Bat Masterson. *National Archives* boasting about their exploits. Wild Bill Hickock, who also served in Abilene, liked to tell how in a mirror he had seen a man leveling a gun at him. Like a flash, he drew his own gun, fired, and sent the would-be assassin scurrying. He never realized that the dangerous assailant he described was only the frightened son of a local resident who collected bottle tops by going around to the backdoors of the saloons. Years later the son told of his astonishment when the shots began coming his way.

At times the balance between the various elements in the cowtowns was upset. At Ellsworth in 1873, tempers began to rise in direct proportion to the heat and in inverse proportion to the falling cattle prices. Among the permanent residents of the town a feeling sprang up that the cowboys and other transients were having things too much their way. The law enforcement officers became rigid; tension mounted; the Texans began to gang together against the town, and the town against the Texans. Before the year was out, five lives were lost. This record for violent killing was never surpassed in any cowtown.

Yet the cowboys' lives were not filled with just hard work, dance halls, and gambling. They were also developing their own culture, even their own music. At night when the cattle were bedded down either on the trail, during the round-up, or outside a cowtown waiting to be sold, they might be startled by the sudden approach of a rider. So some cowboys spoke to them, and a few sang songs when they were riding herd in the darkness. The cattle did not respond to the music, just to the advance warning of the approaching cowboy. (If they had been musically inclined, the singing of many a cowboy would have sent them on a stampede.) These songs, which were also sung around the campfires, sometimes borrowed their melodies from other folk music, but the words were distinctly the cowboys' own. They varied from the sad to

the gay, and the saddest were often the best. The cowboy might lament his departing love with "from this valley they say you are going, I will miss your sweet face and bright smile. . ." Or he might sing of the man dying in Laredo, who explained that he was "a young cowboy and know I've done wrong." After asking someone to write to his mother, he went on:

> Get me six fellow cowboys to carry my coffin,
> Six fellow cowboys to lay out my pall.
> Throw handfuls of roses all over my coffin,
> Roses to deaden the clods as they fall.

The life of a cowboy in the 1870s was an uncertain existence. He might find buyers waiting at the end of the trail; he might find the market dead and his employer bankrupt. When he came to town the local tradesmen might give him a hearty welcome or, in a sullen mood, set the town marshal to harassing him. He never knew. And as he rode herd outside of town, waiting for the cattle to be sold, he might sing:

> Oh, bury me not on the lone prairie,
> These words came slow and mournfully
> From the pallid lips of a youth who lay
> On his dying bed . . .

Or, in a less sentimental mood, he might make fun of the discomforts of the trail with ". . . it's starting to rain, and my damned old slicker's in the wagon again." Or he would gaily celebrate his own restlessness, humming, "My horses ain't hungry, they won't eat your hay. Old Paint's saddled, and I'm soon on my way."

He liked the sad songs, but the happy ones best expressed his feelings. In spite of the rain and the stampedes, and the unfriendly city marshals, it was a good life and a free life, and he would not have traded it for any other.

Chapter 33

At the Little Bighorn

The deposits of auriferous gravel in the Black Hills may generally be said to be favorably situated for working, and that the gold can be very cheaply extracted, with the expenditure of but comparatively little time or capital in opening the deposits. . . .

At Cheyenne, the railroad is not more than two hundred and fifty miles from the gold-fields; the roads over which the machinery and supplies are transported are excellent, the grades usually easy and the drives not long between water.

The climate of the Black Hills is wonderfully healthy and invigorating; wood, water, and grass are everywhere abundant and of the best quality.

There is gold enough to thoroughly settle and develop the country, and, after the placers are exhausted, stock-raising will be the great business of the inhabitants, who have a world of wealth in the splendid grazing of this region.

—Walter P. Jenny, 1875

Two inventions were beginning to play an important role in the cattle business. Joseph Farwell Glidden of Illinois had produced a piece of barbed wire in 1873. Here at last was the simple solution to a problem that had plagued the Great Plains and the prairie states to the east. For barbed wire made it possible to create enclosures even when fencing material was scarce locally. Other inventors modified or varied Glidden's design, and wire companies were soon in wholesale production.

The erection of a barbed wire fence was easy. A wagon dropped off the rolls of wire at appropriate locations. The cowhands, who definitely did not like this demeaning work, dug the post holes, either with a post hole digger or by what they called the "bar and can" method. (This entailed loosening the soil by pounding it with a heavy bar and then scooping out the dirt with a can.) Holes were dug only for about every fifth post, the other posts serving as spreaders, often not touching the ground. The posts themselves could be any piece of wood that might be handy, a branch of a cotton-wood tree, for example, and it did not have to be straight, since there were no ends that had to meet or joints to be fitted.

Gates presented no problem. The typical "Texas gate," as it was often called, consisted of two taller posts stuck into the ground and wired together at the top to give them stability. (They had to be high enough for a horse and rider to pass under the wire.) A couple of strands of wire were then stapled to shorter posts. This "gate" was firmly attached to the tall posts at one end and loosely wired at the other. By disengaging the loose end, and pulling the wires and spreaders to one side, men or cattle could pass through. If there was no gate, a rider and his horse could get to the other side by pulling a post out of its hole and laying the fence flat on the ground. Often the rider would take off his chaps, the leather leggings that protected him from the brush, and place these over the wires to keep his horse's hooves from becoming entangled. Once over, he put the post back and was on his way.

Soon fencing pliers were developed. These were about seven or eight inches long. Designed to do one specific job, their jaws were shaped so they could be used to extract old staples. One or both sides of the outside of the jaws were flattened, so the tool could be used as a hammer for driving in new staples. The pliers also contained heavy-duty wire cutters. With no difficulty it could be carried on a saddle, and it was the entire toolbox needed by a man setting up a new fence or repairing an old one.

The other important invention was refrigerated freight cars. In 1875 two carloads of refrigerated meat went from Kansas City to New York and another to Boston. No longer did the slaughterhouse have to be near the point where fresh meat was consumed. This obviously affected the packing industry, but it also broadened the market for beef, because it simplified the processing of the meat.

The profits to be made in ranching had attracted many people. One of the best known was a Texan named Charles Goodnight, a broad-shouldered man whose mind moved as quickly as his little body. In a short time he accumulated a large fortune; but in the year of 1873, when prices fell so low, his confidence in the future led him to buy instead of sell, and the results were devastating. In 1875, while he was still struggling to recoup his losses, he met a wealthy young Irishman, John Adair, who had come to Colorado on a visit and had been so delighted with the area that he set himself up in business there. He and his wife wished to invest in cattle, and Charles Goodnight was the type of man they wanted as a partner.

Together they formed the JA Ranch, destined to become one of the biggest. Since Goodnight knew the business better than they, the Adairs let him choose the location. He liked the Texas Panhandle and knew exactly the right place—Palo Duro Canyon, where Coronado had found the Indians and where Ranald Mackenzie had defeated the hostile tribes. Protected from the winds that blew over the plains and therefore from the heavy drifts of snow in winter, it contained water and forage. An added advantage was its steep, forbidding walls. Cattle could wander up and down the canyon, but the caprock in most places served as a natural fence. Goodnight, who was the managing partner, drove approximately seventeen hundred head into the canyon and started the ranch.

This partnership was especially significant, because it was financed not with local capital or even eastern capital, but entirely with European money. Nothing could have given greater testimony to both the size and the attractiveness of the ranching business. Yet only eight years had passed since McCoy had shipped the first cattle out of Abilene.

The discovery of gold had opened up eastern Colorado, and the spreading cattle business was increasing the area's economic importance. As more people moved into the territory, the desire for statehood grew; and in 1875 Colorado was admitted to the Union. Reading about all this activity, Ned Buntline realized that again times were changing. He had made a hero out of Buffalo Bill Cody and launched him on his career as a showman. But the advancing wave of civilization was pushing the Indians aside, and army scouts, cavalry, and embattled warriors were starting to fade into the past. The current glamor lay in the cattle drives, the lawmen walking the streets of the cowtowns, and the cowboys on the range or on the trail. Buntline decided on another trip to see this new side of the West. But always conscious of publicity, he first ordered some special guns from the Colt factory.

Based on the standard .45 six-shooter, these guns had twelve-inch barrels and an over-all length of eighteen inches, monstrous weapons to carry around all day. A walnut stock could be attached to them, to convert them into rifles, and each was engraved with his name and came with a tooled leather holster.

When Buntline went to Kansas, he took them with him and presented a Buntline Special, as he named them, to three prominent lawmen—Wyatt Earp, Bat Masterson, and Bill Tilghman, with, of course, appropriate newspaper publicity. Earp kept his Buntline Special; it fitted his own flamboyant character and he found the oversized gun useful as a club. Tilghman and Masterson, however, took theirs to a gunsmith and had them cut down to a usable length.

Although fortunes were being made—and lost—in cattle, and the business was sufficiently lucrative to attract foreign capital, it did not monopolize the attention of those who wanted to earn quick money on the Great Plains. While others invested in livestock, they thought of the gold that was lying in wait for the lucky in the Black Hills.

Even before Custer's expedition, Charles Collins, editor of the Sioux City (Iowa) *Daily Tribune,* had tried to arouse interest in making an expedition to the area in search of the precious metal. General Harney's announcement that he would prevent any civilians from entering the Black Hills and Collins's failure to recruit more than two other adventurous spirits put an end to his plan. But with Custer's announcement, he tried again, and this time almost thirty volunteers, including a woman, Annie D. Tallent, signed up.

Since the land belonged to the Sioux and therefore was closed to white men, the group pretended that they were emigrating to O'Neill, Nebraska, and painted the name of that small community on the cover of one of their wagons. But they went right by O'Neill and picked up Custer's trail, which they followed to his former campground near Harney Peak. There they constructed a stockade and prepared to spend the winter. In the spring they expected to be the first Americans at the gold fields and have the best chance of claiming the richest areas. But the army, having grown suspicious of their intentions, located them in April, 1875, and evicted them.

That spring, the government sent another expedition into the Black Hills. This was under the leadership of Walter P. Jenney, a professor of geology, who was to make a scientific appraisal of the minerals in the Black Hills. Jenney quickly discovered that the eviction of Collins's party had failed to check the flow of miners into the area. On June 16 at French Creek, he found "about fifteen miners were . . . camped four miles above the stockade [of Collins's party], where they had been at work for several weeks and had staked off claims, built small dams, and were digging ditches preparatory to commencing sluicing on the bars along the banks of the stream. These miners were very enthusiastic in regard to the mineral wealth of the gulch . . ." A little later he remarked that another "party of miners about five miles above the stockade had put in a small sluice . . . Unfortunately, the work on this bar was stopped by the stampede to new discoveries in Spring and Castle Creeks, before it could be thoroughly tested and the richness of the deposit proved to be constant and regular." Hundreds of miners, Jenney reported, were already at work, although the Indians still held title to the land; and with the publication of Jenney's report, the rush was on.

The army made an effort to keep the area clear until a new treaty could be negotiated with the Indians. General George Crook, who had just been transferred from Arizona, was given the assignment of driving the miners away. A modest, unassuming man, but a tenacious and able combat commander, Crook went to the Black Hills but immediately realized his mission was impossible. The use of force against such a large number of American citizens would have created an uproar, for the majority of the country was sympathetic to the miners. Therefore he issued a proclamation inviting the miners to attend a meeting at the site of the Collins party's old stockade. There he asked them to leave the Black Hills but promised they could return to work their claims as soon as the country was legally opened to prospecting. Meanwhile the army would protect the rights they had built up for themselves. The meaning of Crook's words was clear: this was to be only a temporary withdrawal while the government negotiated a new agreement with the Indians. Many of the miners agreed to Crook's proposal, but as soon as they left, others took their place; and the United States attorneys refused to support the army when soldiers arrested some of the encroachers.

Many Indians who had remained away from the reservation were now coming in, but their willingness to report to the agencies reflected the lack of game, not a new docility. In fact, the agent at Standing Rock reported, "The expedition to the Black Hills by the military, and the subsequent invasion of that country by parties in search of the precious metals, caused much dissatisfaction and bad feeling among the Indians. They emphatically expressed their belief that the Government was trifling with their rights in permitting the treaty to be violated, and asked the pertinent question, 'How can the Great Father expect us to observe our obligations under treaty stipulations when he permits his white children to break it by coming into our country to remain without our consent?' The lawless invasion of the Black Hills by white men, in violation of the intercourse laws of the United States and treaty stipulations with the Indians, and the apparent tardiness or inability of the Government in removing them, caused great distrust and lack of confidence among the Indians toward all white men and the white man's Government."

The Americans could see only one solution to the problem: to make another agreement with the Sioux. By the Treaty of 1868, the Americans had agreed to provide the Sioux with "an appropriation for clothing and other beneficial purposes" for a period of thirty years and a subsistence ration of meat and flour for a period of four. This last provision, which had been intended to give the Sioux time to start raising their own food, had now expired; but because the Indians had shown little aptitude at—or enthusiasm for—farming, Congress had each year voted an additional amount of more than a million dollars in order to continue the subsistence ration. It also looked as though the government would have to pay this money out for a number of years to come or let the Indians starve. (Public opinion would not have accepted the wholesale deaths of the Indians.) Since the government had clearly exceeded its treaty obligations and might have to do so for many more years, the commission of 1875 was instructed to use this as a bargaining point in persuading the Sioux to sell the Black Hills.

The council was to have been held at Fort Sully on September 1, 1875, but the Indians were in a sullen mood and refused to travel that far. The commissioners then agreed to meet them at the Red Cloud agency and sent messengers to the northern Indians asking them to attend also. Most of them, Sitting Bull among them, refused to meet the commissioners anywhere, and the Indians from the Spotted Tail agency refused to go to Red Cloud. Finally the council opened at a point between the two agencies, but this argument had taken up almost two weeks.

Despite this inauspicious beginning, the commissioners did their best to persuade the Indians to sell the mining rights to the Black Hills for $400,000 a year or dispose of the land outright for a total purchase price of $6 million. Some of the Indians seemed willing to accept those terms, but their leaders were not. Red Cloud, who had led the fight against the forts on the Bozeman Trail, was especially adamant and demanded a far higher price, which the commission had no authority to offer him.

One day while they were meeting, a single Indian dashed through the assembled crowd and rode toward the commissioners, yelling that he planned to kill them. Before he got far, several others intercepted him and took him away, but the crowd was now truly excited. A number of warriors began galloping back and forth, an act they often performed before going into battle in order to give their horses their second wind. Others began shouting insults and taunts at the commissioners and the small military guard that was supposed to protect them. Then a band of Sioux charged toward the commissioners, but these, it turned out, were warriors upholding the Sioux tradition of protecting persons with whom they were holding council. These warriors acted as a temporary bodyguard, and the crisis was over. But so was the council.

At least half the Indians took down their tipis and moved away. The commissioners tried to treat with those that remained, but finally they gave up and reported, "We do not believe their temper or spirit can or will be changed, until they feel the power as well as the magnanimity of the Government; and inasmuch as Congress is required by existing law to approve of any agreement before it is made binding on either party, the commission are unanimously of the opinion that Congress should

take the initiative and by law settle for itself what shall be done upon the whole subject, and then notify the Sioux Nation of its conclusion. If they assent to the terms proposed, let them be carried out by the Government; if they do not consent the Government should withhold all supplies not required by the treaty of 1868. If the Government will interpose its power and authority, they are not in a condition to resist. This authority should be exercised mildly but firmly, and should be directed mainly to provisions looking to the ultimate civilization of the Indians. They can never be civilized except by the mild exercise, at least, of force in the beginning."

The failure of the commissioners to reach agreement with the Indians did not prevent more goldseekers from entering the Black Hills, and scattered bands of Indians occasionally opposed them. As one army officer noted, ". . . the miners kept going into the Black Hills, and the Indians kept annoying all wagon-trains and small parties found on the roads. There were some killed and others wounded and a number of wagons destroyed, but hostilities did not reach a dangerous state, and were confined almost entirely to the country claimed by the Indians as their own. It was evident, however, to the most obtuse that a very serious state of affairs would develop with the coming of grass in the spring."

That fall of 1875 the commissioner of Indian affairs sent an inspector to the northern Great Plains. He came to the conclusion that some of the Sioux, such as those that followed Sitting Bull, could not be subjugated by the methods that the government was then using. "The true policy, in my judgment," he reported to the commissioner of Indian affairs, "is to send troops against them in the winter, the sooner the better, and whip them into subjection. They richly merit punishment for their incessant warfare, and their numerous murders of white settlers and their families, or white men wherever found unarmed."

Acting on this recommendation, the secretary of the interior ordered all Indians to report to the agencies by January 31, 1876, or face action by the army. This was an unrealistic demand. The winter was unusually severe; the messengers had difficulty reaching the various bands, and many of those who might have wanted to come in would have found it impossible to travel with their women and children through the heavy snow that lay on the ground. Nevertheless, on February 1, 1876, the secretary of the interior notified the secretary of war that the Indians still at large "are hereby turned over to the War Department for such action on the part of the Army as you may deem proper under the circumstances.''

As the secretary of war later admitted, the army underestimated the magnitude of the task of subduing these Indians and thought that a thousand men could force them to the agencies. The task of doing so was given to Crook.

Having heard that some Indians were camped on the Powder River, Crook left the North Platte on March 1, 1976, with ten companies of cavalry and two companies of infantry. The weather was bitter cold. The cook cut the bacon with an ax before dropping it into the frying pan, and the soldiers had to warm their bits in hot water before placing them in the mouths of their mounts. Just at the time that Crook was running out of rations and thinking of turning back, one of his scouts spotted two Indian hunters and thought they might lead the soldiers to the village. Crook had with him an officer, Colonel J. J. Reynolds, who had served in the Department of Texas, been reprimanded, and relieved of his command. As an act of kindness, Crook told him to take all but four companies and go with the scouts. If he found the village, he was to burn the lodges but keep the meat and horses, which would be used to resupply the command. If he did not find the village, they would rendezvous on the Powder River.

Reynolds discovered the village and divided his detachment into three groups for the attack. Two of the groups promptly carried out their orders, but the third was late in appearing. That meant the Indians were able to concentrate their fire on the first attackers. Nevertheless, Reynolds's plan would have succeeded if he had not suddenly lost his nerve and ordered a retreat, leaving his dead behind him and, according to rumor, one man who was only wounded. Crook thought he had given him a chance to redeem himself. Instead Reynolds was deeper in trouble; and having failed to preserve the Indians' supplies or to prevent the recapture of the Indians' horses, he had undermined the whole campaign. As one officer commented, ''There was nothing to do but abandon the expedition, and return to the forts, and reorganize for a summer campaign.''

Crook's experience had demonstrated that a single column pushing into the Indians' territory could not defeat them. A much larger scale offensive was required. So Sherman devised a new plan that combined the Department of the Platte with the Department of Dakota for the purpose of a major campaign. There were to be three columns. The Montana Column, consisting of 450 men under the command of Colonel John Gibbon, would march from a fort near the town of Bozeman, Montana. The Dakota Column, consisting of 925 men and including the Seventh Cavalry under Custer, would be commanded by General Alfred H. Terry. It would march from Fort Abraham Lincoln on the Missouri River in present-day North Dakota. Crook was to come again from the Platte.

Toward the end of May, all three columns were in the field, and Sherman hoped that the Indian wars on the Great Plains would soon be at an end. Each of the columns, he thought, could defeat any band of Sioux it might meet, and between them they could scour the country. No matter which way the Indians attempted to retreat, they would run up against one column or another.

While Sherman was making his preparations, the Indians were making theirs. Those Sioux who were opposed to the Americans began to congregate around the camp where Sitting Bull resided, and it made no difference whether they were Hunkpapas, Brulés, Oglalas, or any other branch of the Sioux nation. If they hated the white men, they were welcome. So, too, were the members of any other tribe—Cheyennes, Blackfeet, Arapahoes—just as long as they shared the desire to drive the Americans from the country.

Sitting Bull was not the leader of the group. In their usual informal manner, the Indians had no single leader. Sitting Bull, broad-shouldered and angry, was an important figure as he walked among the Indians exhorting them to fight; but Crazy Horse, who had defeated Fetterman, was also present, and he was dreaming of fulfilling the medicine men's prophecy that he would be among the great men of the Sioux. Gall, Sitting Bull's rival, was also in the camp, and he saw in the coming battles an opportunity to win a reputation for himself that would last for all time. The number of warriors was in the thousands—probably the largest group of Indians that had ever assembled on the Great Plains for the purpose of waging war; and Sherman's three columns thought there were no more than seven hundred hostile Indians in all.

After reaching the Tongue River, Crook left his wagon train behind, so he could move more rapidly. If he located a village, he planned to attack it, capture its supplies, and then march forward until he met either Gibbon or Terry. If he failed to find a village, he would fall back to his base and hope that the other two columns would drive the Indians in his direction.

By June 16 he had reached the valley of the Rosebud, one of the tributaries of the Yellowstone, and on the morning of June 17 started marching down it. The horses were tired from the previous day's journey, so at eight o'clock Crook ordered a brief rest. Unknown to him, a large group of Sioux and Cheyennes were in the bluffs and hills on either side, and Crazy Horse had worked out a plan of attack that was unusual for Indians. Instead of trying to overrun the Americans with a charge or lure them into the hills with a few decoys, he planned to send decoys from many directions, hoping to entice the Americans into dividing their forces. Hidden among the ridges away from the valley were the majority of the warriors, ready to pounce on the Americans when they gave pursuit. If this plan failed, Crazy Horse intended to lead Crook down the valley. Fallen trees and other debris had created a natural dam, raising the water about ten feet. This small lake would block the Americans' further advance, and since the sides of the ravine were steep at that point, he thought Crook would be unable to escape.

The Americans' Crow scouts were covering the soldiers' flanks, so they were the first to meet the Sioux and Cheyennes. Greatly outnumbered, they quickly retreated to the valley and the protection of the Americans' main force. The soldiers' fire drove the Sioux and Cheyennes back. But when the Americans countercharged, the Indians would retreat only a short distance to one of the many ridges that lined the valley and attack again. Each of these maneuvers extended Crook's line dangerously, and he began to realize he had no idea how many Indians surrounded him.

The Indians were also fighting differently than they usually did. Sitting Bull had gone through the painful ceremony of the Sun Dance just before the battle, and this self-sacrifice had stimulated them. Instead of stopping to count coup as they usually did, they seemed intent only on killing as many Americans as they could. Finding himself hard pressed on both sides, Crook decided to make a feint downstream, where he supposed the Indians' village was. This tactic, which he had learned during his years as an Indian fighter, usually put them on the defensive, as they had to protect their women and children. But in this case he was doing exactly what Crazy Horse wanted, for he was sending his men into the steep-sided ravine blocked by the artificial lake.

At that critical moment, if Crazy Horse had been able to relax his attack, he might have destroyed Crook. But the warriors, sensing victory, pressed hard against Crook's rearguard and forced him to turn back to its defense. Thus Crazy Horse's two plans had failed. He had been unable to draw the Americans far enough into the hills to cut them up

in small groups, and Crook at the last moment had avoided the trap that was Crazy Horse's alternate plan. Disheartened, the Indians withdrew.

Although Crook had held the Indians off, he could hardly claim a victory. A newspaper reporter was with the column, and he wrote, "The General was dissatisfied with the result of the encounter, because the Indians had clearly accomplished their main object of their offensive movement—the safe retreat of their village. Yet he could not justly blame the troops who, both officers and men, did all that could be done under the circumstances. We had driven the Indians about five miles from the point where the fight began, and the General decided to return there in order that we might be nearer water. The troops had nearly used up their rations and had fired about 25,000 rounds of ammunition. . . .

"Our wounded were placed on extemporized travois, or mule litters, and our dead were carried on the backs of horses to our camp of the morning, where they received honorable burial. Nearly all had turned black from the heat, and one soldier . . . had not less than a dozen Indian arrows sticking in his body . . .

"We went into camp at about 4 o'clock and were formed in a circle around our horses and pack train, as on the previous night. The hospital was established under the trees down by the sluggish creek, and there the surgeons exercised their skill with marvelous rapidity . . .

"General Crook decided that evening to retire on his base of supplies—the wagon train—with his wounded, in view of the fact that his rations were almost used up and his ammunition had run pretty low. He was also convinced that all chance of surprising the Sioux camp was over for the present, and perhaps he felt that even if it could be surprised his small force would be unequal to the task of carrying it by storm."

By July 19 Crook was back at his wagon train. He sent a detachment with his wounded to the nearest fort on the Platte and instructed them to bring back more supplies. He then waited for their return and also to hear from Terry. Clearly he was stunned by the experience. A tough, resolute commander, he was accustomed to combat, but this had been different. He had expected to encounter only a few hundred Indians, but had fought many more than that. He had expected to be on the offensive and had found himself on the defensive throughout the entire Battle of the Rosebud. It was an experience he had never had before, and he needed time to recover from it.

When Sitting Bull danced the Sun Dance, he

had seen a vision that promised the Indians a great victory. They had not gained it, for they had not annihilated Crook's command. But however disappointed they might be, they had checked one of Sherman's three columns and forced the retreat of one of the best Indian fighters in the army.

General Terry was beginning to have second thoughts about the campaign. A lawyer by profession, he had joined the army during the Civil War and had proved himself a capable and well-liked commander. Now he was beginning to suspect the truth: that the Indians had gathered in greater numbers than anyone had supposed. First, he ordered Gibbon and the Montana Column to remain a while at Fort Pease. Then, instead of permitting Gibbon to operate on his own, he instructed the colonel to come down the Yellowstone and join forces with him and the Dakota Column. During his march, Gibbon saw Indians on the opposite bank of the river and nearly attacked them, but the difficulty of getting his men to the other side prevented him from carrying out this plan. Nor did the Indians harass him; they were intent on reaching their big camp, for never had excitement run so high among them.

When Terry had brought the two columns together, he intensified his search for the Indians. Although he moved cautiously, he was determined on a fight. When he reached the Tongue River, he sent Custer with part of the Seventh Cavalry up the south bank of the Yellowstone as far as the mouth of the Rosebud, while Major Marcus A. Reno with the remainder of the Seventh was to scout the headwaters of the Tongue and Powder. Custer saw no signs that indicated where the Indians were gathering, but Reno discovered tracks that might have been left by more than three hundred lodges. He followed them far enough to be certain of the direction the Indians were taking and then notified Terry of his discovery. The day Reno decided he knew the location of the Indian village and turned back down the Rosebud was, by a twist of fate, the day that Crook had been trying to fight his way out of the valley. The officers were not far from each other, and if they had joined forces, they might have administered a resounding defeat to the Indians. As it was, they were soon going in opposite directions, Crook back to his supply base and Reno back to the Yellowstone.

On receiving Reno's first report, Terry moved up the Yellowstone to the mouth of the Rosebud. "The particulars [of Reno's discovery] were not fully known," wrote one of the officers with Terry. "The camp was full of rumors; credulity was raised to the highest pitch, and we were filled with anxiety and curiosity until we reached Reno's command [at the Rosebud] and learned the details of their discoveries. They had found a large trail on the Tongue River, and had followed it up the Rosebud about forty miles. The number of lodges in the deserted villages was estimated by the number of campfires remaining to be about three hundred and fifty. The indications were that the trail was about three weeks old. No Indians had been seen nor any recent signs. It is not probable that Reno's movements were known to the Indians . . ."

Custer disagreed with this opinion. In a letter he wrote to his wife, Libby, he was highly critical of Reno for not having followed the trail and engaged the Indians. As it was, he thought that Reno had merely warned them of the Americans' presence.

The steamboat *Far West* had brought supplies for Terry (many years had passed since McKenzie had persuaded the partners in the American Fur Company to use a steamboat on the Upper Missouri), and the vessel was a convenient place to hold a conference. On board Terry discussed his next steps with his officers. He was not afraid of defeat. Although he had been acting cautiously, he did not think the conquest of the Indians would be difficult with the force he had available. What concerned him more was that they might escape. For often when faced with superior numbers, the Indians melted away, breaking up into small groups that were impossible to follow.

The results of Reno's scout indicated that the Indians had moved over to the Little Bighorn. Custer was to take the Seventh Cavalry up the Rosebud until he was above the Indians' presumed location. Then he was to cross the ridge between the two valleys and march back downstream. Meanwhile Gibbon would be leading his column up toward the camp. Terry hoped that the Indians would be caught between the two with no chance to escape.

Custer was delighted with this plan. Ambitious and constantly seeking publicity, he saw an opportunity for glory and threw himself into his preparations. Often he traveled with a considerable number of appurtenances (once his hounds had warned an Indian village of his approach), but this time he stripped his men of their tents, sleeping equipment, and sabers, and he turned down Terry's offer of some Gatling guns. These effective weapons with their revolving barrels could fire quickly, but they were difficult to transport. He did, however, accept some of the best Crow scouts with the Montana Column.

The only incident that marred his departure was the performance of his pack train. Ordinarily the Seventh Cavalry carried its supplies in wagons, but this time Custer decided to use pack animals, because they could move faster. His men were clumsy, and several of the packs fell off. A mild rebuke from Terry embarrassed him further. Yet he and those around him knew what Terry's orders meant. ". . . [I]t is understood," one officer commented, "that if Custer arrives first, he is at liberty to attack at once if he deems prudent. We have little hope of being in at the death, as Custer will undoubtedly exert himself to the utmost to get there first and win all the laurels for himself and his regiment."

That is what Custer had in mind. The first day out, he led his men at a moderate pace, covering about fifteen miles. Then he began to press them to move faster, for he was afraid that Gibbon might get there first. When they picked up the Indians' trail, the Crow scouts were startled by the size of it. It had been made, they said, by far more Indians than anyone had expected. Custer thought they were being timid, although he did agree that perhaps fifteen hundred warriors had passed that way. But that was not too large a camp, he thought, for the Seventh Cavalry to handle.

On the evening of June 24 the trail turned to the west and began to ascend the ridge dividing the valley of the Rosebud from that of the Little Bighorn, and from the freshness of the trail, it was evident that the camp was near. At that point Custer made a critical decision. Months before, when the Cheyennes had invited him to their lodge, they had placed on him the heaviest curse that lay within their power. It had not taken effect in time to prevent him from seizing the three hostages and forcing the band to report to the reservation. But on the ridge above the Little Bighorn, the medicine man's wishes for Custer's fate came true. Instead of obeying the intent of Terry's orders and moving farther upstream before crossing over into the valley, Custer decided to move directly toward the camp, thus assuring that he would reach it before the arrival of Gibbon's column. The glory of conquering it would be his, and his alone.

In order to be in a position to attack in the morning, he marched again after dark, but his pack train gave him trouble once more. Some of the supplies dropped off, and in the morning he sent a detachment back to recover what they could. They found some Indians breaking into a container of hard bread and fired at them. The Indians ran, and when Custer heard of the incident, he was certain his presence had been given away. In this he was mistaken. Either the Indians never told what happened, or, if they did, no one paid any attention to them.

Around noon on June 25 the soldiers reached the top of the divide. Here Custer divided his men into three groups. One under Captain Frederick W. Benteen was to continue farther to the southeast parallel to the river before dropping into the valley. In part, this fulfilled Terry's orders, because the move was designed to keep the Indians from escaping in that direction. The other two groups were under the command of himself and Major Reno and marched side by side toward the valley. A little after two o'clock in the afternoon they came upon an old Sioux campsite and saw about forty warriors, who raced on horseback toward the river. Off in the distance, they noticed a cloud of dust rising in the air, a sure sign they had found the main camp. Custer ordered Reno to pursue the fleeing Indians while he led his own group a little farther downstream opposite the cloud of dust and attacked the village. Shortly after he gave those orders, he saw the village for the first time.

The Little Bighorn ran through the valley so slowly that it had cut several large meanders. The Indians had set up their camp at one of them with the Cheyennes downstream and the Sioux up. There was much visiting back and forth, and plenty of grass for the many horses, and the smoke was rising from the tipis. As Custer looked at the scene below him, he could see that the Indians were preparing to move their women and children, but what struck him most forcibly was the size of the village. The estimates of the Crow scouts had been correct. The American force was entirely inadequate. Immediately he called his bugler and ordered him to race after Benteen and bring him back. Custer needed every available man.

In accord with Custer's orders, Reno raced into the valley in pursuit of the forty warriors they had seen, rapidly forded the Little Bighorn—the Indians' camp was on the other side—and turned toward the lodges. Whenever they were attacked in one of their villages, the Indians' first consideration was the safety of their women and children; and as soon as the Indians had noticed the approaching soldiers, they had started making arrangements to move their dependents. By a curious twist, the speed with which Reno advanced brought the battle to an immediate head. As Gall, the Hunkpapa leader, later recalled, the major's charge forced the Indians to abandon all hope of fleeing with their dependents and forced them to fight.

Reno's weary troops—they had marched late the night before—met the onrush of Indians from the village by forming a skirmish line near the river. But the Indians kept slipping past the line, putting Reno in danger of encirclement. So he dropped back to a grove of cottonwoods. This position was not much better, for although the trees protected the Americans, they also concealed the Indians and made it possible for them to draw closer and closer.

Reno could not remain where he was. The only possible place of refuge was among the gullies that ran down the opposite slope. Yet there were Indians between him and the river, and the slippery banks were about four feet high, difficult for either men or horses to ascend. Nevertheless, he gave the order to retreat. While the men were in the water they were unprotected, of course, from the Indians' bullets and arrows; and the toll was enormous. Reno lost almost thirty killed or wounded out of approximately 140.

Many of those who reached the other side were completely demoralized. For weeks everyone from General Terry down had been telling them how easy it would be to defeat the Indians. Then suddenly they had faced a charge such as they had never imagined. Indians were coming from everywhere; their companions were falling; blood flowed from their own wounds; no recruiting sergeant had ever told them that war was like this.

Some of the Indians, instead of sustaining their attack, rode back to the village to announce their victory. The women came out to strip the dead of their belongings and to mutilate the bodies lying in the sun. Horrible as this was, it offered the soldiers a brief respite in which to seek safety on that treeless slope.

Custer's bugler had reached Benteen, and the captain had raced back. The first Americans he saw were Reno's men, and noticing the state they were in, he threw his soldiers around them, giving them a chance to regroup.

When Custer crossed the gentle slope that lay at the top of the ridge and looked down into the valley below, it was too late to withdraw. Figures were scurrying here and there among the lodges, some of them trying to help the women and children leave, others grabbing for their guns and bows and preparing to fight. In moments, Custer was surrounded by Indians. The Cheyennes were the first to attack him—he had struck the camp at their end—but they soon were reinforced by others. There was no cover for the Americans. As the positions of their bodies afterward testified, some of them tried to retreat up the slope. Discipline was impossible. They broke up into a small group of men here, another there; some became isolated and fought all by themselves. They could not keep the Indians at a distance and soon were engaged in hand-to-hand combat. Adding to the confusion was the dust the soldiers and warriors raised as they grappled with each other. It formed a cloud that could be seen miles away, and the soldiers and

warriors could barely distinguish each other. After the battle the Indians found the bodies of some of their own people with arrows in them. Mercy was absent from the field. The Americans expected none and received none, and the fighting ceased only when there were no more Americans to kill. Custer had ridden toward what he had thought would be glory; on the slope above the Little Bighorn he found hell.

Reno's men could hear the sound of guns in the distance. Captain Thomas B. Weir volunteered to go to Custer's aid, but Reno forbade him. The danger to him and the men he took would be too great. Nevertheless, Weir with several other volunteers went to a point overlooking the battlefield. He could see the dust in the distance and knew where the fighting was taking place, but the appearance of a number of Indians forced him to withdraw. After about an hour, the sound of the shooting died. Reno's men speculated about Custer's fate, and some of them believed he had retreated to safety.

The soldiers could not move from their precarious position on the dusty slope. Nature had stripped it clean of hiding places, and Indians were everywhere. So they dug rifle pits in the dirt, clawing at it with their fingers, jabbing at it with their rifle butts, cursing the day they had enlisted, praying that somehow they would be rescued. Where the dirt was hard and they could not make an impression in it, they used their packs and the dead horses to construct crude breastworks. Some of the horses' bodies were already growing stiff, and the men wrestled with legs that would not bend, necks that were like boards. Down in the valley the campfires of the Indians now twinkled in the darkness, and on the slope the wounded moaned in pain, and the men's hearts beat with fear.

Slowly the sky brightened in the east, a flush of pink against the black night. It brought with it no hope. The sound of a shot shattered the quiet morning, and the fight was on again. The Indians were completely aware of the Americans' helplessness. Like terriers playing with rats around a trader's post, they enjoyed the sport of annihilating their enemies. During the night Reno had arranged his men as best he could. The wounded lay in a small depression under a doctor's care. Five companies formed a semi-circle to the north. Others, placed behind a barricade of dead mules and horses, protected the east, and some soldiers along with the men from the pack train held a rise that pointed toward the south. Benteen and a semicircle of troops covered the flank to the west. Benteen's was the weakest point, and sensing this, the Indians concentrated their fire on him, drawing closer and closer as they did so and massing for a charge.

Benteen saw their plan. Courageously he ordered his men to leap from behind their crude breastworks and charge the Indians first. This sign of aggressiveness so startled the warriors they pulled back, and the pressure on that front was relieved.

But not for long. The Indians returned, drawing nearer and nearer. The Americans could not stop their steady approach. Benteen suggested to Reno that they repeat his previous feint, but with all the men joining in. Shouting as loudly as they could, the Americans leaped forward. The Indians, again startled, drew back. For about eighty-five yards the soldiers pressed onward. Then unable to maintain their advance, they returned to their makeshift fortress; and once again the deadly circle of warriors closed in around them.

The hot July sun beat down upon the ragged group of men. Their throats were thick with dust and thirst. The wounded begged for water. Several men volunteered to make a dash for the river. Four sharpshooters covered them, as they slipped down a small ravine toward the Little Bighorn. The Indians, intent on destroying the remnants of the Seventh Cavalry, did not notice them, and they returned with their canteens and camp kettles filled. The water was tepid, and the few men could carry only a little of it. But each swallow was a blessing, the only blessing the day had brought.

The afternoon wore on. The Indians' attacks became less frequent. Down in the valley Reno and Benteen could see signs that looked as though the Indians were planning to move their village. It might be a trick, the two officers agreed, so they held their men in their position on the slope. But the Indians actually were withdrawing, for they had sighted the approach of Terry and Gibbon. As a last act of defiance, they touched torches to the prairie grass to destroy the forage. The flames rose in the air, smoke curled from the ashes, and then all was quiet.

The commander of Terry's advance was Lieutenant James H. Bradley. As he approached the Little Bighorn, he saw three Indians and thought they might be the Crow scouts Gibbon had loaned to Custer. With smoke signals, he indicated his identity, the scouts recognized him and came to him, wailing dolefully for the dead. From them the Americans learned about the battle.

"Did we doubt the tale?" Bradley later wrote. "I could not; there was an undefined vague something about it, unlooked for though it was, that commanded assent, and the most I could do was hope that in the terror of the three fugitives from the fatal field their account of the disaster was somewhat overdrawn. But that there had been a disaster—a terrible disaster—I felt assured."

Chapter 34

A Great Change

In an agricultural point of view, the vast tract of prairie extending through all these regions, is an important object of consideration. Amongst intelligent Americans, the question of—whether it can or cannot be peopled by civilized man? has often been agitated. Accustomed, as they are, to a profusion of timber, for buildings, fuel, and fences, they are not aware of the small quantity of that article which may be dispensed with, in a country abounding in another substance [buffalo chips] for fuel; nor can they conceive, that fences, and even buildings, may be constructed with the application of a very small portion of timber. Under these impressions, the belief in America is, that the prairie cannot be inhabited by the whites . . . My own opinion is, that it can be cultivated; and that, in process of time, it will not only be peopled and cultivated, but that it will be one of the most beautiful countries in the world.
—John Bradbury, 1817

"Of the movements of General Custer and the five companies under his immediate command," General Terry reported after the battle, "scarcely anything is known from those who witnessed them, for no officer or soldier who accompanied him has yet been found alive. His trail from the point where Reno crossed the stream passes along and in the rear of the crest of the bluffs on the right bank for nearly or quite three miles; then it comes down to the bank of the river, but at once diverges from it as if he had unsuccessfully attempted to cross; then turns upon itself, almost completing a circle, and closes. It is marked by the remains of his officers and men, and the bodies of his horses, some of them strewn along the path; others heaped where halts appear to have been made. There is abundant evidence that a gallant resistance was offered by the troops, but they were beset on all sides by overpowering numbers."

Five companies of cavalry and their commander had been completely wiped out. It was the worst defeat the Americans had suffered in the Indian wars since General Arthur St. Clair's army was routed in 1791. But those soldiers had been ill-equipped and ill-trained. This was the Seventh Cavalry, well known, rated as combat-ready, and commanded by an officer whose exploits were familiar to every newspaper reader. One editor expressed the reaction of many people when, using the largest type he had, he printed as a headline across his front page the single word "HORRIBLE."

For the moment, the army could do little but regroup. The Sioux and Cheyennes had blunted the three-pronged campaign against them, checking Crook at the Rosebud and leaving Terry to count the dead at the Little Bighorn. Yet they could not capitalize on their triumph. The Americans were reeling, but the Indians were unable to throw fresh warriors against them and force the long conflict to a conclusion. They could not even hold the territory they had defended on the Little Bighorn. There was insufficient game and forage to support such a large gathering; so by the time Terry arrived, they were already gone, splitting into smaller bands and disappearing into the wilderness.

As the army recovered from the state of shock into which Custer's defeat had thrown it, its generals reappraised the problem and realized that a column here and a detachment there would never end the war. What was required was incessant warfare, grindstone tactics that would give the Indians no peace, winter or summer, night or day. With the Americans' superiority in numbers, equipment, and supplies, this could be done.

On July 13, 1876, seven companies of the Seventh Infantry reached Crook's camp to reinforce him, and the Fifth Cavalry, commanded by Colonel Wesley Merrit, soon followed. Terry also received reinforcements—the Fifth Infantry commanded by Brevet Major General Nelson A. Miles. The Americans were ready to move again.

Crook had approximately two thousand men under his command, a force large enough to destroy any Indian band he might encounter. Buffalo Bill was serving as a scout, and after Crook had held a staff meeting that Cody attended, John Finerty of the Chicago *Times* interviewed him. "He would not, of course, say anything about what had passed in the General's tent," Finerty wrote, "but I remember that he felt doubtful of striking any Indians with the force we then had.

"'If they want to find Indians,' said he, 'let them send a battalion, which I am willing to guide, and I'll engage we'll have our fill of fighting before reaching the Little Missouri. The hostiles will never face this outfit unless they [the officers] get it in some kind of a hole, and there are plenty of them in this country. Crook ain't going to run into them, though. He served in Arizona too long for that.'"

Cody had pinpointed Crook's problem. Before such a force, the Indians would fade away, avoiding conflict against such odds. But after Custer's dramatic defeat and his own experience in the valley of the Rosebud, Crook did not dare divide his men into smaller units. So he marched down the Tongue River, crossed over to the Rosebud, and, passing the scene of his former battle, met Terry at the Yellowstone. Nothing had been accomplished, and both generals were short of supplies.

The two men agreed on a new plan. Terry, the less experienced Indian fighter, would patrol the Yellowstone to prevent the Indians from fleeing north, perhaps into Canada. When the winter weather forced him to withdraw, he would leave Miles and the Fifth Infantry to continue. Crook would immediately return south and, picking up a trail he had seen earlier, try to press the Indians into submission or a battle.

By making requisitions on every post he could quickly reach, Terry scraped together enough rations to supply Crook for a fifteen-day march, and Crook moved back again into the wilderness. Finerty compared the two generals' methods of operation. "Terry's men," he wrote, "moved with 205 wagons, Sibley and A tents, together with a pack train, while Crook's command had only rations on their mules, and all the clothing they possessed on their frames. Terry's troops applied to Crook's a nickname unfit for ears polite, but which unmistakably referred to the dilapidated condition of the rear portion of their pantaloons. . . . Crook is severe, and I'd rather be with Terry as regards food, shelter, and clean flannel, but he goes for the Indians as one of themselves would do, and has shown that an American army can stand, without much growling or the slightest approach to mutiny, more than any other troops upon this earth."

During the first days of Crook's march, sheets of rain fell on the soldiers. Their bedding and clothing were sodden, the firewood at their campgrounds was so soaked they could barely get it to burn. Yet Crook pushed on. "The horses sank in the mud to their knee-joints," Finerty wrote, "and soldiers' shoes were pulled off in trying to drag their feet through the sticky slime. 'Can hell be much worse than this?' said an officer to me next morning. He was cleaning about twenty pounds of wet clay from his boots with a butcher-knife. His clothes were dripping, his teeth chattering, and his nose a cross between purple and indigo. If looking like the devil could make a man fit for the region he inquired about, that young lieutenant was a most eligible candidate."

Crook picked up an Indian trail and followed it, but although he marched as rapidly as possible and his scouts told him the signs were getting fresher, he had not overtaken the village by September 5. He had now crossed from the Little Missouri to the Heart River and was running out of supplies. Fort Abraham Lincoln, which was located a few miles below present-day Bismarck, North Dakota, was 160 miles away, the Black Hills 200. The remaining food would provide only half-rations for two and a half days. Common sense dictated that Crook march to the nearer of the two posts, but he was worried about the miners in the Black Hills, who were subject to constant Indian attacks. Crook believed it his duty to get there and protect them.

"I interviewed General Crook on the subject," Finerty wrote. "This is what occurred.

"'You are sending a courier, General?'

"'Yes, to Fort Lincoln. He will carry some mail and telegrams for the command,' Crook answered.

"'What do you propose to do now, General?'

"He paused for a moment, and, pulling his pe-

382 SUNLIGHT AND STORM

culiar beard, said very slowly: 'We are five full marches from Fort Abraham Lincoln. We are seven at least from the Black Hills. By going to the Missouri [where Fort Abraham Lincoln was located] we lose two weeks' time. By marching on the Hills we gain so much. I march on the Black Hills tomorrow. Between going to and coming back from Fort Lincoln we should lose more than half our horses.'

" 'How many rations have you left?'

" 'Only two days' and a half half rations, but we must make them last for seven, at least. It must be done. The Indians have gone to the Hills and the agencies. The miners must be protected, and we must punish the Sioux on our way to the south, or leave this campaign entirely unfinished.'

"I looked at him in some amazement, and could not help saying, 'You will march 200 miles in the wilderness, with used-up horses and tired infantry on two and one-half days' half rations!'

" 'I know it looks hard,' was the reply, 'but we've got to do it, and it shall be done. I have sent a telegram for supplies to General Sheridan. The wagons will meet us at Crook City or Deadwood [in the Black Hills]. If not, the settlements must supply our wants. Nobody knows much about this region, but it looks fair. We'll kill some game, too, perhaps, to make up for short rations. Half rations will be issued after to-night. All will be glad of the movement after the march has been made. If necessary,' he added, 'we can eat our horses.'

"This suggestion," Finerty added, "fell upon me like a splash of ice water."

The march was as terrible as Finerty had feared. One day, he wrote, ". . . I observed a small group of soldiers by the side of the trail busily engaged in skinning a dead horse and appropriating steaks from its hinder parts. This was the beginning of our horse rations. The men were too hungry to be longer controlled, and the General wisely ordered that as many horses as would be necessary to feed the men be selected by the officers and slaughtered day by day. It was a tough experiment, but there was no help for it, and anything outside of actual cannibalism was preferable to slowly starving to death." Because of this diet, the journey became known as the Horsemeat March.

A detachment that Crook sent ahead to secure supplies at the Black Hills picked up the trail of a band of Sioux led by a warrior named American Horse. The detachment attacked them and quickly learned that the band was larger than they had thought, but the timely arrival of Crook with the main force turned the Battle of Slim Buttes into an American victory. In spite of certificates of good

behavior from the Indian agent, the Indians had among their possessions a glove that had belonged to one of Custer's officers, a letter addressed to one of his privates, and several horses bearing the brand of the Seventh Cavalry.

Since Custer had penetrated the Black Hills, settlers had been arriving in large numbers, and the first town Crook reached—named Crook City by the miners he had befriended on his first visit— contained about two hundred and fifty houses, either frame or made of logs. The residents turned out to welcome him, and someone fired off a cannon. With the discovery of gold in the vicinity, the community had mushroomed quickly, but by this time it was suffering the problem that constantly afflicted miners—lack of water. The original placers had been near a good supply, but they had been worked out, and the residents were now building a sluice to divert water from another stream to fresh placers.

Since Crook had been ordered to confer with Sheridan at Fort Laramie, he had turned his command over to Merrit and traveled quickly through the Black Hills. His route took him to Montana City and Lower Deadwood, where Finerty was amused by the number of buildings placed at intervals that all bore the same sign, "Saloon." (Finerty was also struck by the number of miners working the streams, for until then he had underrated the rush to the Black Hills.)

Deadwood, although only recently organized as a town, was a comparatively large community. Wedged into a narrow canyon, as many mining towns were, there was still room for several commercial streets to run parallel in the main section, although the houses had to climb up the surrounding hills. Finerty noticed that "it possessed a multitude of variety theaters and a crowd of brazen and bedizened harlots, gambling hells, drinking dives, and other abominations. . . .

"Nuggets and gold dust, quartz and placer mining made up the conversation of those times in what might be called Deadwood society. I was shown specimens of gold in all forms until I felt like a jaundiced patient. Everything I looked at turned yellow, and I thought of Midas and the unpleasant fix that gentleman got himself into when he touched any object." But Finerty noted that the placers, on which individual miners depended, were already becoming exhausted. When they were used up, the people of Deadwood would have to work the quartz mines, and that required capital.

"I visited half a dozen hells," Finerty said, "where I noticed some Chicago toughs, all engaged in the noble art of faro or some other thimble-rigging devilment. In that lively time Deadwood sports killed off a man or two every night. Between them and the Sioux it was a hard matter to keep the population of the place up to the maximum standard. Women . . . acted as dealers at many of the tables and more resembled incarnate fiends than did their vulture-like male associates. I observed that decided brunettes or decided blondes were more engaged in evil works than their negative fellow-women. Most of the miners would prefer playing faro or monte with men, for the women were generally old and unscrupulous hands whose female subtlety made them paramount in all the devices of cheating, and theft. I observed one of them—a brunette, either French or Italian, something of the Latin order anyway—with some attention. She had a once-handsome face which crime had hardened into an expression of cruelty. Her eye glittered like that of a rattlesnake and she raked in the gold dust or chips with hands whose long white fingers, sharp at the ends, reminded one of a harpy's talons.

"Every gambler appeared to play for gold dust. Nobody took greenbacks, and the gold-scales were in constant requisition. They allowed twenty dollars for every ounce of gold . . . Not alone in gaming, but also in commercial transactions was dust used. A miner swaggered up to the bar with five or six others and called for the drinks. They were supplied and he tossed his buckskin wallet to the bartender, who weighed out the requisite amount of dust and handed back the balance. I am inclined to believe that this display of crude bullion was made a good deal for effect, to make people believe that gold was as plentiful in Deadwood as were sands on the seashore."

No matter what the Sioux did now, the Black Hills were lost to them. Even more victories like the Battle of the Little Bighorn would not drive the Americans away from the gold.

Pleased by their victory at the Little Bighorn and with Crook and Terry scouring the wilderness in search of them, many of the Indians were starting to drift back to the security of the reservations for the winter, although, according to information Sheridan received, Crazy Horse and Sitting Bull remained out in the Bighorn country to form the nucleus of new hostile activity in the spring. Therefore Sheridan ordered Crook's command to go to the Red Cloud and Spotted Tail agencies, disarm the Indians, and take away their horses. This would leave them helpless when the weather again turned warm and prevent a recurrence of the 1876 outbreak.

While Crook was confiscating the guns of the reservation Indians, Miles was preparing for his winter campaign and defending his supply trains, which the Indians harassed. He was tracking down these raiders when two Indians came to him with a flag of truce and said that Sitting Bull was willing to talk to him. Miles agreed to meet him, and the two men, one accompanied by six soldiers, the other by six warriors, held a council.

"On first meeting Sitting Bull," Miles said, "I naturally studied his appearance and character. He was a strong, hardy, sturdy looking man of about five feet eleven inches in height, well-built, with strongly-marked features, high cheek bones, prominent nose, straight, thin lips, and strong under jaw, indicating determination and force. He had a wide, large, well-developed head and low forehead. He was a man of few words and cautious in his expressions, evidently thinking twice before speaking. He was very deliberate in his movements and somewhat reserved in his manner. At first he was courteous, but evidently void of any genuine respect for the white race. Although the feeling was disguised, his manner indicated his animosity toward those whom he had to meet. During the conversation his manner was civil and to some extent one of calm repose. He might have been mistaken for a mild, plain-spoken, inoffensive man until I developed the other side of his nature."

Their positions were irreconcilable. Miles insisted that Sitting Bull surrender and go on a reservation; Sitting Bull insisted that Miles and the other Americans leave the country. Finally Miles broke off the talk and returned to his camp.

The Indians were divided in their opinion. Some wanted to fight with the Americans, others thought it would be wise to go on a reservation at least for the winter. As a result, Sitting Bull asked to meet with Miles again the following day, but their second talk was as fruitless as their first. At last Miles issued an ultimatum: Sitting Bull and his band must surrender within fifteen minutes, or the Americans would attack. The Sioux greatly outnumbered the soldiers, but Miles had artillery. For two days he pursued the Indians, who had begun to withdraw. As he later said, "The engagement demonstrated the fact that the Indians could not stand artillery, and that there was no position they could take from which the infantry could not dislodge them." Wearied by Miles's persistent harassment and frightened by the prospect of a winter without supplies, many of the Sioux met with Miles again. They agreed to go on a reservation and let him have five hostages to ensure their fulfillment of these terms, but Sitting Bull and Gall and those loyal to them remained at large.

Earlier Crook had tried to enlist scouts from among the Cheyennes and Sioux who had already surrendered. (He had used Apache scouts successfully when he was fighting in Arizona.) The Indians had been extremely reluctant to serve against their kinsmen; but by the fall of 1876, their attitude was changing. Many of them realized that those still off the reservations were caught between two of the most aggressive generals in the army and could not win. Therefore they were willing to help bring a quick end to the fighting.

Through his new Indian informants, Crook learned the location of the Cheyennes' village led by a chief named Dull Knife. Ranald Mackenzie once again took the offensive. "In the gray twilight of a cold November morning . . . ," one of Crook's officers later wrote, "Mackenzie with the cavalry and Indian scouts burst like a tornado upon the unsuspecting village of the Cheyennes . . . and wiped it from the face of the earth. There were two hundred and five lodges, each of which was a magazine of supplies of all kinds—buffalo and pony meat, valuable robes, ammunition, saddles, and the comforts of civilization—in very appreciable quantities. The roar of the flames exasperated the fugitive Cheyennes to frenzy; they saw their homes disappearing in fire and smoke; they heard the dull thump, thump, of their own medicine drum, which had fallen into the hands of our Shoshones [scouts]; and they listened to the plaintive drone of the sacred flageolets upon which the medicine men of the Pawnees [also scouts] were playing as they rode at the head of their people. Seven hundred and five ponies fell into our hands and were driven off the field; as many more were killed and wounded or slaughtered by the Cheyennes the night after the battle, partly for food and partly to let their half-naked old men and women put their feet and legs in the warm entrails."

Some of the Cheyennes who escaped later crept close to the Americans' camp and were amazed to see how many Indians were now serving as scouts. Even their own people were turning against them. When Dull Knife, his band now destitute in the middle of the winter, turned to Crazy Horse for help, the Sioux received his plea indifferently. If many of his own people were fighting him and his allies would not assist him, Dull Knife reasoned that he might as well surrender, too.

Although the snows piled high in the Yellowstone country that winter, Miles kept up his patrols. On January 7, while marching up the Tongue River, Miles's advance captured a small party consisting of one warrior and several women and children. These happened to be related to some of the prominent Indian leaders, so the Sioux made an effort to free them. Coming down the valley in far greater numbers than the men under Miles's command, they taunted the Americans and looked forward to a victory. Their confidence, however, was unwarranted. Miles had two pieces of artillery, which he had concealed by covering them with canvas and making them look like wagons. "As the fight opened," Miles said, "the canvas covers were ripped off from the pieces of artillery and the two . . . guns exploded shells within their [the Indians'] lines, creating great consternation, and the reechoing of the guns through the valley, while it gave the troops much confidence, undoubtedly multiplied the number of our guns in the estimation of the Indians themselves."

Both sides were hampered by the heavy snow—the American infantry could "charge" only at a slow walk—and the fighting soon broke off. "The backs of those retreating warriors," Miles said, "presented the most delightful picture, as it then seemed to us, that it was ever our fortune to see on the opening of a new year."

After returning to his cantonment, Miles sent one of his scouts and two of the captives he had taken to the hostile village. The Indians were in desperate straits, suffering greatly from the cold while their horses were dying from exposure and starvation. When they learned that Miles had treated his prisoners well and was still willing to hold a council with them, they sent a delegation to visit him.

Winter was always a difficult time for the Indians. Game was scarce, and the meat they shot poor. Their horses grew weak from lack of forage, and snow blindness became a common ailment. Staying alive was a full-time occupation; they could not fight a war, too. After long negotiations one of the leaders told Miles, "We are weak, compared with you and your forces; we are out of ammunition; we cannot make a rifle, a round of ammunition, or a knife; in fact we are at the mercy of those who are taking possession of our country; your terms are harsh and cruel, but we are going to accept them and place ourselves at your mercy."

The victory over Custer had been won under the warm summer sun with the grass green and the ponies fat. The warfare being waged by Crook and Miles was different. To the usual horrors of winter, the two officers were adding a grinding, gloryless war. With Miles's latest success, practically all the Indian leaders except Crazy Horse and Sitting Bull had gone to reservations.

The surrender of the Cheyennes and their willingness to be friends with the Americans was a blow to Crazy Horse. Existence as a hostile Indian was becoming lonelier and lonelier and more dangerous. Spotted Tail and Red Cloud were both related to Crazy Horse; and, according to one observer, when Spotted Tail "counted upon his fingers the hundreds of allies who were coming in to the aid of the whites in the suppression, perhaps the extermination of the Dakotas [Sioux], who had so long lorded it over the population of the Missouri Valley, he saw that it was the part of prudence for all his people to submit to the authority of the General Government and trust to its promises."

The Sioux were beginning to pay the price of their past aggressions. One hundred Pawnees, remembering years of war and their defeat at Massacre Mountain, were ready to take the field with Crook. The Crows, who had long suffered from the depredations of the Sioux, sent two hundred and fifty warriors, who joined the Americans on Christmas morning, 1876. The Shoshones, too—Sacajawea's tribe—were willing to send fighting men against Crazy Horse. White soldiers alone were difficult enough to fight, white soldiers with numerous Indian scouts were certain victors. Spotted Tail and Red Cloud began negotiating with Crazy Horse on behalf of the Americans. Finally in May, 1877, Crazy Horse came to Fort Robinson near present-day Crawford, Nebraska. In the pleasant valley rimmed with light-colored rocks where the fort stood, he surrendered to the Americans.

One of the officers who talked to him said, "I saw before me a man who looked quite young, not over thirty years old, five feet eight inches high, lithe and sinewy, with a scar in the face. The expression of his countenance was one of quiet dignity, but morose, dogged, tenacious, and melancholy. He behaved with stolidity, like a man who realized he had to give in to Fate, but would do so as sullenly as possible. . . . All Indians gave him a high reputation for courage and generosity. In advancing upon an enemy, none of his warriors were allowed to pass him. He had made hundreds of friends by his charity towards the poor, as it was a point of honor with him never to keep anything for himself, excepting weapons of war. I never heard an Indian mention his name save in terms of respect."

In the Battle of the Little Bighorn, according to some of the Indians, Crazy Horse had played a crucial role. Reno's approach had at first caused panic among the women and children and some of the men, but Crazy Horse had grabbed his warclub,

brained one of the soldiers, and rallied the warriors. He had lured Fetterman and the cavalry to their deaths, and he had driven back Crook in the valley of the Rosebud. But his fighting days were over.

The surrender of Crazy Horse left Sitting Bull's band all alone. In the summer of 1877, they crossed the border into Canada, hoping to find a better existence under the Great White Mother, as they called Queen Victoria. Sporadic fighting might again break out between small bands of Indians and the white men just as it sometimes broke out between white men and white men; but with the surrender of Crazy Horse and the retreat of Sitting Bull, general peace had at last come to the Great Plains, and the long years of war were over.

Indians, mountain men, soldiers, and ranchers had all been dominant figures on the Great Plains, exploring its vast expanses, following its rivers, living off its game, and making the land their own. But their dominance was slowly being contested by a quieter type of settler, the farmers who had been slowly creeping into the plains from the east and the west, buying land from the railroads or the states or taking up homesteads. Slowly they were making their power felt, and even the ranchers had to bow to them when they selected their shipping points.

The land did not welcome the farmers warmly. Ever since the beginning, when Cabeza de Vaca had walked across it and Coronado had entered it from the mountains of New Mexico, it had seemed strange, formidable. It had beauty, great beauty, the sky arching above it, the land itself rolling off in every direction. There was room for a man to move about; nothing closed him in. It contained fascinating sights, too—Chimney Rock, its spire rising from the floor of the plains; the magnificent canyon of the Yellowstone River; the buttes on its western edge, soft purple in the evening sun, glaring bright at noontime; the Badlands, where the wind and water had etched the earth with results that made it seem as if they had been guided by a superior sense. But it was not a friendly land.

The farmer who came from the East found himself beset by unfamiliar problems, and they became worse as he moved west. When he took up his 160 acres, he usually learned that they contained little out of which he could build his house, perhaps a few cottonwoods along a streambed, a streambed not necessarily filled with water when he most needed it. Often his first house was a dugout. Finding a suitable bank, he would cut a hole into it and roof it over. (One of these formed

Goodnight's first ranch house in Palo Duro Canyon.) Yet a dugout was not bad if the builder knew what he was doing, and it could be warm in winter. The biggest problem was the roof. Usually he laid logs across the opening and then covered them with wattles and sod or dirt. Being level with the ground, a cow or steer might walk across it. More than one woman, cooking her family's dinner, heard a sound and looked up to see a bovine leg sticking down through her ceiling. Because the roofs were flat, they also had a propensity to leak. Yet there were those who could build a roof that did not. If the family were rich enough, they might even buy window frames to insert in the front wall. Into this crude structure they would carry all the belongings they had brought with them. A family near Buffalo, Wyoming, had a piano in theirs. (The first spring the roof leaked, and they had to cover the instrument to protect it from the water.) They were not usual, but they were not unusual.

As time went on, settlers learned to make sod houses, and as soon as the homesteader had time, he started to construct one. Usually he waited until fall when the grasses were thick and woody. With a breaking plow, especially designed to cut into the virgin sod, he would generally slice out a strip three inches thick. (About an acre of sod sufficed for the average house.) He then cut the slices into blocks, which he laid like bricks with the grass side down. The walls were generally three "bricks" thick, staggered so the joints did not come opposite each other.

There was one important trick to building a satisfactory sod house. The experienced man knew that the walls would settle during the first year or two, crushing his window and door frames unless he took special care to protect them. So he left a gap of six to eight inches above each frame and filled it with paper or old rags. As the walls settled, the gap would gradually close until the house was neat and tight. A sod house, depending on its builder, could be relatively elegant with a kitchen, parlor, and separate bedrooms, and its thick walls also provided excellent insulation both winter and summer.

The next step was, of course, a frame house, but those were expensive. The lumber came from the East to the nearest railroad station, and then the owner hauled it by wagon to the site. Even before he had laid down the first sill, he had made a large investment. So he built a frame house only after he had become successful. Barbed wire solved another of his problems. With it, he could at last build the fences he needed to keep his own livestock in and his neighbor's out.

But the land and the extremes of the climate presented difficulties. He could cut the sod with a plow like John Deere's, but he might not be able to make anything grow. Sometimes it rained far too much, drowning his fields with inches of water; more often it rained too little, and he watched his crops wither and die. Sometimes it snowed too early, and his land was covered with the drifts; sometimes it became warm too late, or the temperature suddenly rose, and the sun blazed with killing heat. The men on the Lewis and Clark expedition had noticed the hordes of grasshoppers that stripped the land along the Yellowstone. Swarms like those swept down on other parts of the Great Plains, and where they passed, nothing green was left. The wind, too, was a problem, that wind that seemed to blow endlessly, moaning around the house, fluttering the curtains, raising the dust. The dust might well be from the farmer's fields, for once the sod was broken, the wind could easily blow the soil away if a cover crop did not grow quickly and lushly.

Another problem was the 160-acre limit that Congress had placed on a homestead. In Massachusetts or Pennsylvania or Ohio that much land made a good-sized farm; on the Great Plains, particularly toward the west, it was not enough. The land was fertile, as Frémont had noted, but because of the scarcity of water, the crops grown on each acre were comparatively small.

Congress became aware of this problem and tried to alleviate it by passing various laws. One was the Timber Culture Act of 1873. A homesteader could enter an additional quarter section by agreeing to plant forty acres of it in trees. The purpose was severalfold: to provide an opportunity for settlers to get additional land and to encourage the growing of trees for building materials. (Some also thought the trees might change the climate, making it moister.)

The year 1873–1874 was a particularly bad one for farmers. Widespread droughts destroyed the crops that summer; in places they looked almost as though they had been touched by fire. What was left after the sun and heat had done its work was consumed by grasshoppers. When winter came, many settlers were destitute. Benevolent societies in the East sent out aid, and the army, when it was not fighting Indians, distributed government supplies among starving settlers.

Yet enthusiasm for moving to the Great Plains, while it fluctuated from year to year, never lapsed. Partly this was because of the railroads. Aside from the federal government, they were the biggest landowners, and they had an interest in seeing the flood of immigrants continue unabated. Sale of their lands provided the railroads with revenue, and so did the traffic created by new settlers. So they advertised their holdings widely, often in the most extravagant terms, not only in the East, but in Europe, too. To numerous European farmers the idea of owning 160 acres was like a dream. So they would come by steerage to New York, make their way to the Great Plains, and take up homesteads. Many regretted it, but many did not. And some brought with them new strains of seeds from the old country and farming techniques that were more adaptable to the plains than those the Americans had been using. The Russians shrugged their shoulders when they saw the response of their American neighbors to the hardships of farming in that dry land. The Great Plains? They were like the steppes, and they felt at home.

In 1877 Congress passed another law to help the farmers, the Desert Land Act. This extended to the Great Plains a provision that the year before had been applied to part of California. Under its terms a man could for a modest sum obtain possession of 640 acres of untimbered land, not containing minerals and not productive of grass. He had, however, to irrigate it. The Mormons had demonstrated what could be accomplished by irrigation, and Congress was anxious to encourage other settlers to do the same. In many places, of course, there was little water, although at one time or another, every expedient was tried, from diverting streams to digging wells. Laws such as the Desert Land Act were often abused, just as the Homestead Act itself had been. A big rancher might employ either one to secure his waterholes and keep small farmers out; speculators slipped by the technicalities and used the acts to amass large blocks of property; but still they encouraged farmers and often actually helped them.

In spite of the difficulties, new settlers kept coming. Ned Buntline paid no attention to them. They were not the stuff of dime novels, but they were riding the wave of the future. The fabric of a stable, settled society, they were less proud, less glamorous than Crazy Horse or Custer or the cowhands riding into Dodge City, but they dug their roots into the soil the way their own crops did, and they were there to stay.

Chapter 35

A New Order

To one hurrying through by steam there was a certain exhilaration in this spacious vacancy [the plains of Nebraska], this greatness of the air, this discovery of the whole arch of heaven, this straight, unbroken, prison-line of the horizon. Yet one could not but reflect on the weariness of those who passed by there in old days, at the foot's pace of oxen, painfully urging their teams, and with no landmark but that unattainable evening sun for which they steered, and which daily fled them by an equal stride. They had nothing, it would seem, to overtake; nothing by which to reckon their advance; no sight for repose or for encouragement; but stage after stage, only the dead green waste under foot, and the mocking, fugitive horizon. But the eye, as I have been told, found differences even here; and at the worst the emigrant came, by perseverance, to the end of his toil. It is the settlers, after all, at whom we have a right to marvel. Our consciousness, by which we live, is itself but the creature of variety. Upon what food does it subsist in such a land? What livelihood can repay a human creature for a life spent in this huge sameness? . . . His eye must embrace at every glance the whole seeming concave of the visible world; it quails before so vast an outlook, it is tortured by distance; yet there is no rest or shelter, till the man runs into his cabin, and can repose his sight upon things near at hand. Hence, I am told, a sickness of the vision peculiar to these empty plains.

Yet perhaps with sunflowers and cicadae, summer and winter, cattle, wife and family, the settler may create a full and various existence.

—Robert Louis Stevenson, 1878

For centuries the Great Plains had resisted the impact of the white man, but change was rushing down on them with the speed of a herd of stampeding horses that no obstacle can deflect. The ox wagons were gone, the Indians were under control; only ghosts followed the Old Santa Fé Trail; corn and potatoes grew in places that never before had supported any crops but the natural grasses of the prairie; steam engines raced down trails that men had followed on foot; but perhaps the greatest change of all was the need for large amounts of capital to engage in most of the businesses of the Great Plains.

Gone were the days when a man of limited means might set himself up as an independent fur trader or buy a few wagons and take some freight to Santa Fé. Now most people were working for someone else. Even the cowboy who dreamed of the day when he might own his own "spread" usually was on someone else's payroll. Except for the individual homesteader and a few small businessmen, many of the decisions that most affected the Great Plains were made not in North Platte or Bismarck or Lyons or Meade, but in Chicago, San Francisco, New York, or even London. Goodnight's partnership with Adair was a portent, and Finerty's prophecy about the mines in the Black Hills was coming true. The individual prospector, pan in hand and leading a burro that carried his pick, bedroll, and other equipment, was still a familiar sight and would be for years to come. But the placers were rapidly being exhausted, and those who were making important money were mining the gold-bearing quartz. This required crushers and men and engineering techniques—resources that the small prospector could not afford.

The arrival in the Black Hills of L.D. Kellogg, a mining engineer, in June, 1877, reflected this change. Kellogg had no pickax, did not own a burro, and was not searching for gold on his own account. He was there respresenting William Randolph Hearst of California and his associates. They were interested in making mining investments in the new fields that were being discovered, and they had employed Kellogg to do the preliminary exploring for them. Kellogg looked at a claim that had been staked out by two brothers from Ohio, Moses and Fred Manuel. He liked it and took an option to purchase it for $70,000. He also took an option on another nearby property and returned to San Francisco.

Hearst and one of his associates then made the trip to the Black Hills themselves. They, too, thought the claims looked good and picked up the two options, paying out $105,000. That, however, was not the end of their investment. Using Kellogg's advice and their own judgment they bought two other claims nearby, and when they left the Black Hills to return to San Francisco, their agents were negotiating several more purchases. This type of operation took money—big money.

The Manuels had named their claim the Homestake, because Moses had said he wanted only enough money to go home and sit down. So the name Hearst chose for the new company he incorporated under the laws of California was the Homestake Mining Company. One of the first steps the new company took was to purchase a stamp mill for crushing the quartz and ship it to Lead, where the claim was located. That took almost $150,000. Shafts went down six hundred feet; tunnels ran out from them. This required equipment, timbers, the means of transporting large amounts of rock, engineers to direct the work, and men to do the digging and drilling. There was no room at the Homestake for small individual enterprise, particularly when the Hearst interests began buying up even more properties nearby. If a prospector wanted to make a living at Lead, he went to work for the Homestake Mining Company.

Although the Homestake became one of the world's greatest producers of gold, its ore was not especially rich. The efficiency of its operation was the foundation underlying its success, and soon other mine owners were emulating it. Mining in the Black Hills had become a corporate undertaking.

Railroads had always been big business, but now there were more of them, and they dominated much of the life of the Great Plains. Many people worked for them directly as locomotive engineers, firemen, tending water stations, repairing tracks, or manning the stations. The railroad provided their livelihoods. Others were dependent on them for transporting the goods they needed or for taking their products to market. In many parts of the Great Plains the decisions of the railroads could spell the difference between success or failure. As the experience of the cattle towns had shown, the question of a spur or even a siding could make or break a community.

The Union Pacific, still suffering the effects of its early fiscal mismanagement, was roaring along the valley of the Platte, carrying goods and passengers at speeds no ox driver could have envisioned. During the year that Hearst became interested in Black Hills gold, the Southern Pacific was laying rails east from California to join the Texas Pacific at El Paso and form another link between East and West.

The following year James Jerome (Jim) Hill, an enthusiastic, hard-working Canadian, took over the St. Paul and Pacific Railroad. It had been a victim of the Panic of 1873, but although its few miles of track had been badly laid and the organization allowed to disintegrate, Hill after careful study thought the road had possibilities. He immediately started building north to Winnipeg to join the Canadian railway system and west across the Great Plains toward Montana and the coast. Hill was an investor, not a speculator, and had the common sense to realize that he needed the best track at the least expense. The key to this was the selection of the route, so he personally laid out much of the line, an unusual occupation for a railroad president. The coming of the Great Northern, as the road later was named, created new jobs, new markets, and opened up new areas in the Great Plains.

The Atchison, Topeka and Santa Fe beat the Denver and Rio Grande to Raton Pass in Colorado (the mountain branch of the Old Santa Fé Trail), which gave it a good route to Albuquerque. In 1881 it connected with the Southern Pacific at Deming, New Mexico, and formed another rail route across the Great Plains by which goods and freight could be moved between East and West. (Later it would run directly to California over its own line.) After a long period of time marked only

390 SUNLIGHT AND STORM

by vicissitudes, even the Northern Pacific was coming to life again.

Many feeder lines were also in operation, and the Great Plains was criss-crossed with roads, leading to a chaotic rate structure. Earlier Horace Greeley had pointed out that private capital would be reluctant to invest in a transcontinental railroad because of possible future competition. (A single transcontinental line, however, would have only crossed the Great Plains, not served them.) His foresight had proved correct. In many markets, the struggle between the railroads for traffic was murderous, pushing down their tariffs in cut-throat price wars. In others, however, they sometimes enjoyed a monopoly and made the most of it. Local shippers in those areas were understandably bitter over the prices charged them.

But the railroads were not owned and operated by Great Plains people. Their capital requirements were too great, and so the most important decisions were usually made in the nation's financial centers, not in the country through which the railroads ran.

Jefferson had envisioned a country of small farmers, independent and owning a tract of land sufficient to support their dependents. This had been one of the goals of the Homestead Act—to keep property out of the possession of large owners and place it in the hands of individual families. To an extent, the act had succeeded, but landowning was also becoming big business. The census of 1880 showed that 16 percent of the farmers in Kansas and 18 percent of those in Nebraska were tenants, not owners. Men of capital were buying up land from the rialroads, the states, and from homesteaders who had obtained title but, discouraged by droughts, grasshoppers, and the harshness of life on the plains, wished to sell out.

Even ranching was becoming big business, financed with Eastern—and eventually with European—money. Goodnight had already drawn on Irish capital; Hubert E. Teschemacher and his Harvard classmate Frederic deBillier used Boston money. In 1879 the two young men formed a cattle company that had its headquarters about forty miles from Cheyenne, Wyoming. A few years later, when the partners decided they needed more capital for their operation, they raised about a quarter of a million dollars in Boston.

They were not alone in attracting distant money to the cattle business. No longer did a small, independent operator buy cattle cheap in Texas and drive them to the railroad. Cattle were becoming expensive, and the ranches were becoming larger. The Cheyenne Club in Cheyenne, Wyoming, re-flected the change. Only a few years before, Cheyenne had been a shanty town on the railroad; a few years before that, merely a place in the wilderness. Yet the Cheyenne Club, which was founded in 1880, was regarded by many visiting Easterners as excellent. Its leather chairs were as good as those of the Union League Club in New York; it served the finest wines; and in a short time it even offered tennis. Easterners felt perfectly at home there, and Owen Wister, who knew the best of Philadelphia's clubs, called it "a pearl."

Bigness and high finance were influencing the life of the Great Plains. Railroad magnates, rancher barons, and large landowners might sit down after dinner on Beacon Hill, Boston, or Murray Hill, New York, and talk with familiarity of the Platte, the Little Missouri, and the Texas Panhandle. They probably had investments there.

Although the changing life of the Great Plains made it possible for the members of the Cheyenne Club to ask the waiter for their favorite wine or cigar and for young Harvard graduates to enter the cattle business, none of this luxury spilled over into the lives of the Indians. Their great days were over, although in 1877, one last flurry of activity occurred.

The Nez Percés, who had befriended Lewis and Clark so many years before and who had wanted a Black-Robe like de Smet as a missionary, had finally broken with the white men. In their desperate attempt to evade the army, they fled east and entered the Great Plains at the northern border of Wyoming. Here they turned north, hoping to reach the security of Canada.

News of their outwitting the soldiers spread through the reservations, and the members of other tribes became restless. Perhaps they had given up too easily and too quickly. Hope began to rise that maybe the Indians were the white men's equals after all when it came to waging war. But the period of excitement was brief. When the secretary of war submitted his report at the end of the year, he remarked succinctly, "After Joseph's defeat by General Howard [Joseph was the leader of the Nez Percés] on the 12th of July, there was no longer any question of other Indians joining the former; and operations subsequently were the pursuit of a mere banditti, who certainly displayed great courage, energy, and enterprise, leading their pursuers many hundreds of miles over a most difficult country, but who were finally compelled to surrender unconditionally to Colonel Miles, Fifth Infantry, after a sharp and sanguinary engagement, on the 30th of September, not far from the British possessions, after all those who had been engaged in the murders of citizens at the commencement of hostilities had been killed.''

Crazy Horse became the indirect victim of the Nez Percés' flight. Both Indians and white men on the northern Great Plains became tense during the period the Nez Percés were at large. Crook had originally been ordered to join the pursuit, but Sheridan changed his mind and wired him to remain at the Red Cloud agency. The surrender of the Nez Percés, he said, was "but a small matter compared with what might happen to the frontier from a disturbance at Red Cloud."

Crazy Horse, still dreaming of the glory that had once been prophesied for him, had grown more and more regretful of his decision to surrender. Rumor said he was planning to leave the agency, and when he refused to come to a council with Crook, the general gave orders to have him arrested. At the guardhouse at Fort Robinson, he drew a knife and tried to escape. In the scuffle that followed he was killed. Thus ended the career of one of the most brilliant and courageous of the Sioux leaders. Commenting on his death, one of Crook's officers said, "Crazy Horse was one of the great soldiers of his day and generation; he never could be the friend of the whites, because he was too bold and warlike in his nature . . . as the grave of Custer marked the high-water mark of Sioux supremacy in the trans-Missouri region, so the grave of Crazy Horse, a plain fence of pine slabs, marked the ebb."

Years ago Bent had split the Cheyennes when he built his fort; and when the government forced the Indians onto reservations, the southern Cheyennes were placed in Indian Territory. Now the government decided to move the northern Cheyennes south, too. Although superficially it seemed logical to bring the two parts of the tribe together and at the same time split up the Indians who had fought at the Little Bighorn, the decision was cruel. As one Cheyenne later said, "We could not forget our native country anyway—where we grew up from childhood, and knew all the hills and valleys and creeks and places we had hunted over; where the climate was cooler, the air purer and healthier, the water sweeter and better, than in the southern country to which we had been sent by the government . . . instead of being better than the land we left, everything was so much worse, we got homesick for our own country again," and the warrior's wife added, ". . . I should never get over my desire to get back north; I should always want to get back where my children were born and died and were buried . . ."

Finally the Cheyennes with Dull Knife leading them left the agency and started to fight their way home, preferring to die in battle than remain in Indian Territory. Their move was a bold one. They had miles to go, miles that were patrolled by many soldiers. In their group were about three hundred people, but only about seventy of them were warriors, the rest being women and children. Several times the army located their whereabouts and tried to stop them. The Cheyennes were willing to fight, but not surrender, and in every skirmish, they were able to break away and continue their desperate journey.

In October, after crossing the Platte, they encountered an army detachment that was too large for them to evade. Dull Knife with a white flag approached the commander and explained that they intended only to go to the Red Cloud agency and that the army should have no concern about them. During the night reinforcements arrived; and in the morning the Cheyennes saw that the soldiers' artillery was pointed into the heart of their camp. For ten days the white men and the Indians argued. Dull Knife insisted on going to the Red Cloud agency; the soldiers insisted that he and his people surrender at Fort Robinson. Since more troops kept arriving, the Cheyennes were soon hopelessly outnumbered and agreed to go to Fort Robinson.

They had understood that as soon as the formalities of the surrender had been completed, they would be allowed to leave for the Red Cloud agency. But once at Fort Robinson, they were told that they would be held there until the government decided their fate. Although they were prisoners, the post comannder allowed them to roam the surrounding hills as long as they reported in each night. This arrangement worked well until one of the Cheyennes slipped away for a few days to visit his wife at the Red Cloud agency. His unexplained absence destroyed the peaceful relations that had existed between the soldiers and the Indians. The post commander demanded that they return immediately to Indian Territory; Dull Knife flatly refused.

The post commander then placed them under guard and cut off their rations. Later a Senate committee declared, "The process of starving and freezing women and children, *in order to compel men into obedience*, is not justifiable in the eyes of civilized men." It was not only uncivilized; it did not work. For a time the Indians survived by eating leftover scraps of food and huddled together to keep warm. When their water was also cut off, they licked the frost from the windowpanes.

On January 9, 1879, still unwilling to return to

392 SUNLIGHT AND STORM

Indian Territory and yet unable to withstand their thirst and hunger, the Cheyennes broke out of the guardhouse. Dull Knife and his son were the first to leap through a window and the others followed close behind. The move was one of desperation, because there was no way to escape detection by the soldiers.

Shots rang out, and the Cheyennes returned the fire with a few guns they had been able to keep hidden. Over the frozen ground they raced, trying to escape the Americans' bullets. Men, women, and children fell, for the soldiers in the darkness could not distinguish between them. Some reached the limits of the post and plunged into the wilderness, but the soldiers were close on their trail. Dull Knife with a few other Indians remained out the longest. They found a cave where they hid, eating sinew and moccasins and a few roots they were able to find. Then they, too, surrendered. Approximately one hundred and fifty Indians had escaped from the guardhouse. More than sixty were killed, twenty returned to Indian Territory, and the remainder were allowed to stay at the Pine Ridge agency.

The government had beaten the Indians into submission, but it had not solved the Indian problem. Part of the trouble lay in the division of responsibility. When the Indians were at peace, they became the wards of the commissioner of Indian affairs. When they were at war or seemed likely to go to war, the Department of the Interior turned them over to the Department of War. Therefore no one department had continuing responsibility for their welfare. Another part of the problem was the cupidity of some of those involved in Indian affairs. Grant's policy of turning to the religious denominations for help had not been successful. The churches chose many good men, but some of their nominations were as poor as those of the politicians.

General Gibbon, who had commanded the Montana Column under Terry, expressed the frustrations of many officers when he said, "As was to be expected, any attempt to place the control of Indian affairs under two departments so radically opposed in principle as the Military and Indian Departments, has resulted in clashing of authority and a state of affairs which is working to the detriment of the Indian. The average Indian agent, intent upon the spiritual welfare of the red man, desirous of elevating his *soul*, and achieving what has never yet been reached in a single generation—making a civilized man of him—but too frequently neglects his *bodily* wants, and while the agent is preparing

him for heaven, as he thinks, is actually making a hell for him upon earth by leaving him unclothed and unfed, whilst but too frequently the price of his clothing and food is put into the agent's pocket. The Army officer, on the other hand, compelled by the system of responsibility under which he has been educated to account strictly for every cent's worth of property he receives from the government, and anxious, by feeding and clothing the Indian, to keep him peaceful, and thus avoid wars in which *he* and not the soul-saving Indian agent takes part, and which are not only tedious and harassing, but without glory, attends first to the Indian's bodily wants, and hence gains credit in the minds of a great many well-meaning people of being not only utterly regardless of his spiritual needs, but entirely opposed to any steps being taken toward advancing him in the scale of civilization."

The government tried various methods of getting the Indian agents under control. One was to assign army officers to inspect the Indians' annuities and witness their distribution; but, Gibbon commented, ". . . few seem to be aware of the fact that from the defective system of responsibility in the Indian Department these inspections form no check whatever upon the operations of the Indian agents, whose accounts seem to pass scrutiny in Washington just as well without these inspections as with them."

Another method was devised by Carl Schurz when he became secretary of the interior. His plan was to send undercover agents onto the reservations, collect evidence of frauds, and try the guilty in court. Resentment flared in the West. The *Press and Dakotaian*, published in Yankton, Dakota Territory, roared in anger, "If the control and management of the Indians were left to the average western man, he would first capture them, i.e., take all their guns, ponies and feathers, then domicile them on the Missouri River at convenient points and keep them well fed. Such a course would stop all Indian wars, cause to cease all raids and other troubles in the Sioux Country and save millions annually to the Government.

"But your scheming sentimentalist will have no such commonsense solution of the Indian question. They want to make little angels of the papooses and big angels of the head chiefs."

With local opinion such as this, few juries would convict the defendants. In addition, the undercover investigators were not always skillful in obtaining their evidence, and few Western juries would believe an Indian who testified against a white man. In Dakota Territory, in spite of the prosecution's pretrial promise to expose a great scandal, everyone charged was acquitted.

Even the best-meaning people could make no headway. Corruption and inefficiency haunted the agencies, and the Indians' own attitudes were damaging to their futures. Understandably proud, they were unwilling to give up their cultures and adopt the white men's ways. Yet to live an Indian's life in a white man's world was clearly impossible, particularly since the land-hungry Americans kept whittling away at the size of the reservations. If settlers who were skilled farmers had difficulty raising enough to support a family on 160 acres, Indians could not be expected to even if they had taken up agriculture. So their existence became one gray day after another; sad memories of the past, hunger, and destitution filled their hours; and when in the morning the sun rose over the rim of the prairie, it brought no hope that this day would be different.

Yet conditions were no better on the Great Plains north of the border, where the Canadian government had promised Sitting Bull it would not molest him as long as neither he nor any members of his band committed any depredations. This was a small price to ask for protection from Miles and Crook and the other American generals who had proved so untiring in their harassment. But the great buffalo herds were no longer roaming the prairie even there, and without buffaloes the Sioux could not continue their old life. Many a night they went to bed hungry or subsisted on the dole of a trader or a government official. Canada would not give them regular rations, for they were American Indians, so the handouts they received were infrequent. Even Sitting Bull, stubborn and resolute as he was, began to question the benefits of this sort of freedom.

Desperately he appealed to the Canadian authorities to give him and his people a reservation, but the answer was no. If he wanted to live on a reservation, the Amercans had one waiting for him. Sadly Sitting Bull and his few remaining followers accepted the inevitable and in 1881 headed south to surrender. Instead of using ponies, as they had in the glorious days of the past, they carried their few belongings in clumsy two-wheeled carts lent them by a trader. They were a sorry sight as they straggled back onto American soil.

"I am thrown away," said Sitting Bull.

One aspect of Western life always startled Easterners on their first visit—the attitude of the people toward guns. Many men in the West did not wear guns, but many did, far more than in other parts of the country. There were reasons for this. One was the vast distances between habitations. If a burglar entered a ranch house during the night, the owner could not lean out the window and shout for help, for no one would be passing along the road outside. A cowboy, working in a lonely line camp (a sort of ranch outpost) and beset by ruffians, could not expect anyone to come to his assistance. It was comforting to have a gun around.

Cowboys sometimes carried them as a protection against being "dragged." Sometimes when a horse threw its rider, the man's foot would slip through the stirrup, and the galloping horse would drag him over the ground. What with rocks and cactus, this could be an experience that might well end in death. The cowboy's high heels usually prevented this—that was one reason for having them—but if it did happen and if the rider had a gun, he could shoot the horse and save his life—provided, of course, that the gun was still in its holster, that he could reach it as he bounced along the ground, and that he shot the horse before some rock knocked him out. There were rattlesnakes, too. If a man saw a rattlesnake and he had a gun, he could always shoot it. Of course, a rattlesnake presents a small target and shooting down at the nearby ground invites a ricochet, which may do more harm to the shooter than the target. A practical man who wants to kill a rattlesnake will use a stick. It is safer and surer, but, of course, less fun.

The best reason for carrying a gun was that Westerners liked guns. The fur traders had always been armed—they had to be—and so did the men on the Santa Fé Trail and those crossing the plains before the army protected travelers. Guns had become part of the Westerner's heritage. He liked the look of them, the blued metal, the well-designed grip. He liked the smell of gun oil, he liked the excuse for having a nicely tooled piece of leather for a holster, and he liked the feeling of manliness and independence his gun gave him. To a Westerner, a gun was like a necktie to a proper Bostonian; he felt uncomfortable without it.

Some merely wore a gun and occasionally used it for target practice; others made a hobby of their weapons. They experimented with the quick-draw holsters professional gunmen used. They tried tie-down holsters, holsters that hung from the belt but were also tied to the user's leg, so they would not rise out of place when he drew. (Quick-draw holsters often had this feature.) They took their guns apart and with a file converted them to hair-trigger guns, which required little pressure on the trigger in order to fire. This kind of gun had two advantages. A split second was saved shooting it, and the aim might be better, because it eliminated the jerking motion that sometimes resulted from a stiff action. It also had the disadvantage of sometimes going off when its owner did not want it to.

Those who liked guns also learned how to "fan" them. The fanning motion consisted of quickly brushing the free hand back over the hammer instead of using the trigger. Someone skilled at this could get off his shots more rapidly than a man who pulled the trigger each time.

The crime rate was not particularly high on the Great Plains except among some of the scum that emigrated to it. Aside from cattle, there was not much to steal in most of the area, and little reason to commit murder. But the prevalence of guns added a new dimension to the problem of law enforcement: when trouble did occur, guns were always handy and, as a consequence, likely to go off.

The peace officer, therefore, had to be prepared to defend himself against pistol fire as well as the usual fists and knives; and while parts of New York City were undoubtedly more dangerous than all of Dodge City, a New York policeman might spend his entire career without hearing a gunshot.

The Dodge City *Times* carried a report on an incident that illustrated how violence could erupt from a bit of horseplay, a practical joke, or what would otherwise have been a minor disturbance. Three or four men from one of the trail herds had come into town, had some drinks, and about three o'clock in the morning prepared to return to their camp. "They buckled on their revolvers, which they were not allowed to wear around town," the paper reported, "and mounted their horses, when all at once one of them conceived the idea that to finish the night's revelry and give the natives due warning of his departure, he must do some shooting, and forthwith he commenced to bang away, one of the bullets whizzing into a dance hall near by, causing no little commotion among the participants in the 'dreamy waltz' and quadrille. Policemen Earp and [James] Masterson made a raid on the shootist who gave them two or three volleys, but fortunately without effect. The policemen returned the fire and followed the herders with the intention of arresting them. The firing then became general, and some rooster who did not exactly understand the situation, perched himself in the window of the dance hall and indulged in a promiscuous shoot all by himself. The herders rode across the bridge followed by the officers. A few yards from the bridge one of the herders fell from his horse from weakness caused by a wound in the arm which he had received during the fracas." The wounded cowboy was taken immediately to a doctor, but he died about a week later.

In a community farther east, the young men would probably have contented themselves with throwing rocks at the streetlights or knocking over the residents' garbage cans. In Dodge City, they fired their guns, and the fire was returned.

Because of the frequent use of guns, the peace officer on the Great Plains was unlike his counterpart farther east. Often he was a man who was sometimes on one side of the law, sometimes on the other. As a small boy long before he became a peace officer, "Wild Bill" Hickock, according to one report, was already accustomed to outwitting the sheriff. His father and a friend were engaged in working for the Underground Railroad and often drove a wagon of slaves north. Partly to disguise what they were doing, the men sometimes took their young sons along. Once they had to get off the road while the sheriff's posse went by, and "Wild Bill" learned how to hold a horse's nose to keep it from whinnying. Although the cause was worthy, he was already a law violator.

He was still a young man when he shot and killed David Tutt in Springfield, Missouri, after a dispute over a card game. The jury acquitted him, but in doing so, according to the local newspaper, went against the facts. For Hickock did not kill Tutt in self-defense or on the spur of the moment. He had taken up a position in the public square and had waited an hour or so for his victim to appear. Hickock was a rough-and-ready man who was accustomed to shooting and that qualified him for a law enforcement position.

William Tilghman, before he became a peace officer, had been arrested several times on charges ranging from attempted train robbery to horse thievery, although each time he was released for lack of evidence. Wyatt Earp, another well-known officer, seems to have avoided brushes with the law as a youth; but around Wichita, it was well known that his sister-in-law was a prostitute.

Perhaps more typical of the Great Plains law enforcement officer was a sheriff in the Oklahoma Panhandle. Chosen by his fellows to maintain order, he was traveling one day and needed shelter and food. Passing the house of a newly arrived settler, he went to it and found it deserted and the door padlocked. Drawing his six-shooter, he blew the lock apart, entered, and took what he needed. Before leaving, he wrote a note to the owner, thanking him for the food and reminding him that in that part of the country honest people did not lock their doors.

Some of the early peace officers were fine men, some were not, and some were in between. But most of them had several qualities in common. They could stand long hours and hard work, they liked the rough society of the cattle country, they generally got along well with their fellow citizens, they were not afraid of a fight, and they knew how to handle a gun. Their period did not last long, for the ranchers soon abandoned the long drives that made the cattle towns where the best-known peace officers flourished. But their guns had blazed a place for themselves in American folklore.

The State of Texas wanted a capitol, not just an ordinary building but one that would compare favorably with the capitol of the United States. Although the state had no money to pay for one, it did have land. Alone, it had been permitted to retain its public domain when it was admitted to the Union. So the legislature established the Capitol Reservation consisting of more than three million acres spread over ten counties in the Panhandle. The idea was to use this land to finance the construction.

In west Texas, however, land was not worth much. A few men like Goodnight had moved onto the Llano Estacado and were raising cattle, but lack of water and railroad transportation and the occasional presence of cattle thieves and other unpleasant characters made the area unattractive to settlers. The law provided that fifty thousand acres be sold to pay for the survey, but when the Capitol Board put this acreage up for bids, it received only two, both of which it rejected. When it tried again, there was only one bidder, who offered fifty-five and a half cents an acre. As this was high for west Texas land at the time, the board snapped at it. The price also indicated that the three million acres remaining in the Capitol Reservation were worth about a million and a half dollars, the estimated cost of constructing the building which the architect had planned.

In the early 1880s, land and cattle were regarded as promising investments by serious financial men, and a group of business leaders in Chicago formed a syndicate that eventually secured the contract to build the capitol in exchange for the land. The partners in the syndicate were all astute, as their many other activities demonstrated, but they were not familiar with that part of the country. Charles Goodnight was at the time buying land from Texas

at twenty cents an acre; and as with most preliminary building estimates, the one Texas had obtained for its capitol was far too low. The completed building cost more than twice the amount originally envisioned. Furthermore, the syndicate never looked at the land before assuming the contract.

One of the partners, A.C. Babcock, arrived in Texas in March, 1883, to examine the syndicate's holdings. He secured the assistance of the state surveyor of the land district that included most of the Capitol Reservation and hired some cowboy helpers and a Mexican cook. The expedition was an incongruous assortment of people. First of all, none of them had been over the land before, not even the surveyor, who had recently moved to Texas from Alabama. The cowboys and the cook, of course, were well accustomed to frontier life; Babcock definitely was not. The others rode horseback; he rode in a wagon. At night they threw their bedrolls on the ground; he slept in a wall tent with a stove to heat it and lay down on a cot. The others ate the regular camp fare and enjoyed it; Babcock had brought a trunk filled with canned items such as boneless chicken, cheese, and crackers. His foresight was fortunate, because when he saw the Mexican cooking over a fire made from buffalo chips, his reaction was the same as that of the pioneering ladies of Kansas.

The land was a shock to him. Wind and water had long ago erased the hoof marks of Coronado's horses, but not much else had changed. It rolled off in every direction toward the horizon, an almost unlimited expanse of space. Although he reported to his partners that it was suited for raising grain "adapted to that climate"—an important qualifier—and for grazing, there was no way to sell it off to settlers, which had been the snydicate's original plan. No farmer would want it, if for no other reason than that he could not get there, much less sell any crops he might be able to raise. The main lines and feeders of the railroads criss-crossed the Great Plains, but this part of Texas was a blank on the railroad guides of the time. There was not even a state wagon road leading through it. With millions of better watered, more accessible acres still available under the Homestead Act, no farmer would be so foolish as to pay for any of the acreage owned by the syndicate. Perhaps in the future, but that future was far distant.

Yet Babcock was not discouraged. Eventually the land would sell, and until the market was ready for it, the syndicate could use it to raise cattle. He had been looking into that business, and the prospects were amazing. Yearlings, he had been told, gained about one to two hundred pounds during the first year they were placed on the Panhandle. The previous year, the calf crop on Goodnight's JA Ranch, he learned, had been 98 percent. In other words, had doubled. Cattle, he discovered, could be purchased for about twenty dollars a head—a big rise over a decade ago, but still not expensive. Even the most conservative investor could see what those figures meant. A hundred and fifty thousand head of cattle would cost three million dollars. If the calf crop were only 90 percent instead of 98, at the end of five years the herd would be worth more than four and a half million dollars. This represented a gross return on investment of about 30 per cent annually, much better than Treasury bonds or railroad stocks. There would be expenses, of course, but they were minimal. It took only a few men to handle a large herd, particularly if the range was fenced to prevent the livestock from-drifting. The brand laws in Texas were strictly enforced; consequently thievery was no problem. Without hesitation the Chicago partners, who had never been on the range, set about establishing the XIT ranch, which became the largest fenced ranch in the world.

Babcock, of course, had been naïve, but he was not alone. When John V. Farwell, one of the original members of the syndicate, founded the Capitol Freehold Land and Investment Company in England to raise British capital for the enterprise, he had no difficulty in persuading the Marquis of Tweeddale, who was governor of the Commercial Bank of Scotland, to serve as chairman of the board, and the other directors were distinguished, conservative businessmen. After all, Babcock's estimated profits were well below those of many other cattle investors. It was perfectly possible that the calf crop would be 100 percent, and if the ranch was located on land adjoining the public domain, there was no carrying charge for the range. It was free. (When the directors of the Capitol Freehold Land and Investment Company met at their London headquarters, they were able to raise a million pounds.)

Even excluding the somewhat unusual case of Charles Goodnight, Farwell was not the first to tap British capital for American ranching. The Prairie Cattle Company, Ltd., was a joint stock company with 200,000 pounds sterling, raised from Edinburgh investors. Its purpose was to buy land along the streams of Colorado and New Mexico, and it had already lived up to its promoters' expectations.

Another visitor to Great Britain ahead of Farwell had been Alexander Swan, a Wyoming rancher.

Representing three ranches with a total investment of almost two million dollars, he went to Edinburgh to raise more capital and founded the Swan Land and Cattle Company, Ltd. The Scots were wary at first, because they were unacquainted with the circumstances pertaining to the public domain so they had difficulty understanding that if a man controlled the sources of water, he also controlled the surrounding range even if he did not own it. Once they understood this and had had a Cheyenne law firm check the company's titles to its water, they began to invest heavily in the new company.

The Matador was another large American ranch that went abroad for financing. The Great Plains had long since become so involved in big business that it had exhausted its own capital resources. Men like Marshal Field, who owned the largest department store in Chicago, and James Gordon Bennett, owner of the New York *Herald*, were investors in Western ranches, but even they could not supply all the money needed. So the cattle business, as did many of the nation's major growing industries, went to the large pools of capital wherever they might be. The day of the little rancher was not over, but the giants had come.

The increasing accessibility of the Great Plains and the influx of Eastern and foreign money in the area both combined to broaden interest in the region and enlarge the types of people it attracted. Charles Russell was a cowhand and beginning to look at his surroundings with an artist's eye and put what he saw on paper. He was not successful commercially until he married and his wife assumed the role of business manager for the family. Then he became one of the great interpreters of the West. Russell was self-taught, but Frederic Remington, who went west for his health in the early 1880s, had studied at the Yale Art School and the Art Students League in New York. He liked the rough-and-tumble life of the West and followed the troops when they pursued the Apaches in the Southwest, but his origins were those of a sophisticated Easterner. So were Owen Wister's. The son of a prominent Philadelphia family, he had traveled abroad, studied music in Paris, and tried working for a conservative Boston brokerage house. But ill-health led him to follow the course taken by other wealthy Easterners and seek the clear, pure air offered by the West. To his new surroundings he brought a sensitive, quickly stimulated imagination, although he himself was not the center of his stories. Yet in *The Virginian* he said all that others had said, and perhaps even more, about this land in which every man stood on his own rights. Russell, Remington, and Wister quickly gained wide audiences throughout the nation, for their mixture of the myth with the truth was what the nation wanted to see and hear.

Other important emigrants to the Great Plains included the Cather family from Virginia. They moved there in 1883, taking with them their young daughter, Willa, who later wrote about the Great Plains. Even though they were sparsely settled even in the last half of the nineteenth century compared to other sections of the country, the Great Plains had their share of chroniclers and artists. There was something about the life, the people, and the land that inspired painters and writers.

Not only were the wealthy investing in Great Plains enterprises, some of them were moving there to live, and the impact was startling. The cowboys around Kaycee, Wyoming, were astonished to see red-coated Englishmen riding to the hounds over the range. An aristocratic British family had bought a ranch, built a large house, and transported their English customs to the American West. It was a little unsettling to the democratic society of the community to find their daughters taking jobs as maids and learning how to polish silver and set a table in the great house, but the girls earned money that way, and cash was sometimes difficult to obtain. The English parents, on the other hand, were concerned that their eligible sons, for whom they had greater social aspirations, might be taken by some of the delightful Wyoming girls and went to considerable effort to keep them apart.

In the North Dakota Badlands, Antoine-Amedee-Marie-Vincent Manca de Vallombrosa, Marquis de Mores, had taken up residence and had built for himself what the local residents called a "château." Actually it was more of a summer "cottage" for the marquis when he was visiting his ranch. In case visitors came, the house contained five hundred pieces of china that had been made to the marquis's design in England. The servant did not stand in the dining room; she remained behind a screen until the marchioness called for her. Being French, the marquis had had his chaps made in France by a French leather worker; and they were a bit too short, because the leather worker did not know what chaps were used for. Babcock, during his tour of the XIT lands, had slept each night on a cot in a heated tent. The marchioness slept in a canopied bed by herself. The marquis had a separate bedroom where he slept, with his valet occupying one corner.

The marquis was not a dilettante. He came from a good French family whose title dated back to the seventeenth century; he spoke fluent English, German, and Italian in addition to his native French; he had gone to St. Cyr, the French military academy, and then to the special academy that trained cavalry officers. He had held a commission in the French army, which he had resigned only out of his boredom with peacetime service, and was a good shot and an excellent hunter. His wife, whom he had met when she was vacationing in Cannes, was the daughter of a New York banker. While working for his father-in-law, de Mores had become impressed with the potential profits in the cattle business.

He was going into it in a big way. He had founded the nearby town of Medora—named after his wife—where he operated a general store, a hotel, and several other establishments, and he was also the majority stockholder in the Northern Pacific Refrigerator Car Company. He had selected the site for his home because it was on the eastern edge of the cattle range, therefore reducing the shipping time to Eastern markets; there was good grass and water, so he could hold the herds until he was ready to put them on the market, and he was interested in doing the butchering at Medora and pioneering the use of refrigerated cars on the Northern Pacific Railroad. A number of influential people were backing him.

Not far off was a young man from New York, Theodore Roosevelt. He had come to North Dakota to hunt buffalo. The animals were now so scarce it took several days before he shot a solitary bull, but he liked the country and bought a ranch before returning east. During the following year his mother and his wife died within a few hours of each other, and he and his friends were edged out at the Republican National Convention. These misfortunes so discouraged him that he decided to abandon politics and enter the cattle business, and in 1884 he bought a second ranch. (He did not, however, hold title to the land, because the Northern Pacific had not yet received its grants, and the area had not been surveyed for homesteading.)

He and the marquis had much in common. They were both well educated, both came from affluent families, both were sophisticated men of the world. But they represented two entirely different—but typical—approaches to Western life. The marquis transplanted his way of existence in France to South Dakota just as the English family outside Kaycee brought their fox-hunting customs to Wyoming. Roosevelt, on the other hand, went native. He loved the life, and he became more Western than most Westerners. The *Bad Lands Cow Boy*, Medora's newspaper, said of him, "Mr. Roosevelt is still . . . hunting and playing cowboy,'' and a few days later observed, ''Theodore Roosevelt, the young New York reformer, made us a very pleasant call Monday in full cow-boy regalia.''

He acted the part continually. When some thugs stole the rowboat he used to cross the Little Missouri, he went after them, and no manhunt in Western history was carried out in better style. When he at last caught up with them and found their camp, they were away; and so Roosevelt and the two men with him waited in hiding until they returned. ''When they were within twenty yards or so,'' he wrote, ''we straightened up from behind the bank, covering them with our cocked rifles, while I shouted to them to hold up their hands—an order that in such a case, in the West, a man is not apt to disregard if he thinks the giver is in earnest. The half-breed obeyed at once, knees trembling as if they had been made of whalebone. Finnigan [the ring leader] hesitated for a second, his eyes fairly wolfish; then, as I walked up within a few paces, covering the center of his chest so as to avoid overshooting, and repeating the command, he saw that he had no show, and, with an oath, let his rifle drop and held his hands up beside his head.''

Roosevelt and his companions had to get their prisoners to town, a journey of several days. They were sitting around their campfire one evening when somebody spoke ''of a man whom we all knew, called 'Calamity,' who had been recently taken by the sheriff on charge of horse-stealing. Calamity had escaped once, but was caught at a disadvantage the next time; nevertheless, when summoned to hold his hands up, he refused, and attempted to draw his own revolver, with the result of having two bullets put through him. Finnigan commented on Calamity as a fool for 'not knowing when a man had the drop on him' and then suddenly turning to me, said, his weather-beaten face flushing darkly: 'If I'd had any show at all, you'd have sure had to fight, Mr. Roosevelt; but there wasn't any use making a break when I'd only have got shot myself, with no chance of harming any one else.' I laughed and nodded, and the subject was dropped.''

Roosevelt was finally able to hire a wagon and driver for himself and the prisoners, and send his two employees back to the ranch. But his adventure was not over. ''It was a most desolate drive. The prairie had been burned the fall before, and was a mere bleak waste of blackened earth, and a cold, rainy mist lasted throughout the two days. The only variety was where the road crossed the shallow headwaters of Knife and Green rivers.

Here the ice was high along the banks, and the wagon had to be taken to pieces to get it over. My three captives were unarmed, but as I was alone with them, except for the driver, of whom I knew nothing, I had to be doubly on my guard, and never let them come close to me.''

At last he reached Dickinson, North Dakota, and turned over to the sheriff the men who had stolen his boat. ''Under the laws of Dakota,'' he wrote, ''I received my fees as a deputy sheriff for making the three arrests . . .'' Ned Buntline could not have done it better. Yet Roosevelt and many others like him believed in what they wrote and said. De Mores, elegant and sauve and trying to make a complicated business succeed, had difficulty understanding this attitude. Yet it was no wonder that Remington, the Yale Art School student, and Roosevelt became friends, and that Remington illustrated the text of Roosevelt's book. They both were romanticists about the Great Plains.

To men like Roosevelt, the Great Plains offered an escape into a romantic world. Although the Northern Pacific roared across the plains only a few miles from his ranch and the Indians were all on reservations, Roosevelt wrote, ''Civilization seems as remote as if we were living in an age long past. The whole existence is patriarchal in character; it is the life of men who live in the open, who tend their herds on horseback, who go armed and ready to guard their lives by their own prowess, whose wants are very simple, and who call no man master. Ranching is an occupation like those of vigorous, primitive pastoral peoples, having little in common with the humdrum, workaday business world of the nineteenth century; and the free ranchman in his manner of life shows more kinship to an Arab sheik than to a sleek city merchant or tradesman.''

They might ''call no man master,'' but unless they were out of a job and riding the grub line, they were probably on the payroll of Theodore Roosevelt of New York, the Marquis de Mores, the Marquis of Tweeddale, John V. Farwell of Chicago, or someone else with the money necessary to get into the cattle business. Myth and reality both could be found on the Great Plains.

If the cowboys were becoming the employees of large corporations, the farmers were becoming the victims of them—or at least of the railroads. In 1883 the Transcontinental Traffic Association was formed. Railroads had become more numerous, and freight had not increased proportionately. The

Love of their homelands often drove the Indians to feats of extraordinary heroism and daring. Dull Knife, the Cheyenne chieftain, led his people on a desperate march from Indian territory (now Oklahoma) to Nebraska, eluding the American army most of the way. *National Archives*

Where the rivers cut deep into the land, they often create badlands such as the walls of this canyon. But the bottomlands might be rich and fertile. On land such as this along the Little Missouri River, Theodore Roosevelt entered the ranching business. *Alexander B. Adams*

association was an attempt by the railroads to get together and fix rates and apportion traffic, a legal act at that time but one that aroused the ire of a certain number of shippers. Fortunately for the users of railroads, the companies had differences between themselves, and the association was never thoroughly effective.

The role of the small entrepreneur on the Great Plains was becoming less and less important. Even the land was slipping away from him. Cattlemen had traditionally hated fences that kept them from moving their herds freely, and in Kansas more than one farmer had seen his fences threatened by angry cowboys. But barbed wire was changing their attitude, and they were beginning to use fences for their own purposes. Outside of Texas, much of the range remained in the possession of the government, and many ranchers, particularly the bigger ones, were beginning to look on it as their own. They smply ran a fence around it and kept everyone else out.

In 1883 the commissioner of public lands reported that "the practice of inclosing public lands by private persons and companies for exclusive use as stock ranges is extensively continued in States and Territories west of the Mississippi River. These ranges sometimes cover several hundred thousand acres. Special agents report that they have ridden many miles through single inclosures, and that the same often contain much fine farming land.

"Summer and winter ranges in different sections of country are frequently controlled in the same manner by the same persons, who cause their cattle to be driven from one to the other, according to the season, keeping the whole of the land under fence and preventing the stock of smaller ranchmen from feeding upon any portion of it.

"Foreign as well as American capital is understood to be largely invested in stock-raising enterprises involving unlawful appropriation of the public lands. Legal settlements by citizens of the country are arbitrarily prohibited, public travel is interrupted, and complaints have been made of the detention of the mails through the existence of these inclosures. Reports have been received of the use of violence to intimidate settlers or expel them from the inclosed lands."

The drought of 1883 brought the issue to a head. When some of the smaller cattlemen tried to move their herds north or south to fresh grass, they found their way blocked by the fences of the larger ranches. Out came the fence cutters, and bullets sometimes flew, as the employees of large ranches defended their enclosures.

This was not the only problem that the commissioner observed. He also pointed out that "a frequent incident to this control of large bodies of land is the acquirement of title by stock owners to the valleys, water-courses, and other especially valuable lands within the inclosures by means of fraudulent or fictitious entries caused to be made under the pre-emption, homestead, and desert-land laws."

In 1885 the abuses were still continuing. The commissioner of public lands said, "Wealthy speculators and powerful syndicates covet the public domain. . . . So thoroughly organized has been the entire system of procuring the survey and making illegal entry of lands that agents and attorneys engaged in this business have been advised of every official proceeding and enabled to present entry applications for the lands at the very moment of the filing of the plats or survey in the local land offices."

As an example, he pointed out that "early the whole of the territory of Wyoming and portions of Montana have been surveyed under the deposit system and the lands on the streams fraudulently taken up under the desert-land act, to the exclusion of future settlers desiring homes in those territories."

In 1886 the chairman of the House Public Lands Committee and a fellow congressman finally made the House aware that the public domain was falling into the hands of speculators, not small individual landowners, and even worse, many of the largest holders were not even Americans. Lord Dunraven had acquired 60,000 acres in Colorado; the Dundee Land Company, which was foreign owned, held 217,000 acres; and another alien had amassed 200,000 acres in Illinois, Missouri, Kansas, and Nebraska, which he was renting out in the fashion of an Irish absentee landlord. Altogether they estimated that 20 million acres in large holdings were owned by aliens and perhaps an additional 10 million acres in smaller parcels.

Yet the big operators on the Great Plains were also beginning to have troubles during the last half of the 1880s. The optimistic projections of the original promoters did not materialize, because their reasoning had been faulty. A drought in 1886 hit the Texas Panhandle. The foreman of the XIT reported to John Farwell that in order to get enough water for one part of the ranch they had first dug a fourteen-mile ditch, then a well by hand to the depth of eighty-five and a half feet. So the men could work in it, they made it eight feet wide, which meant they had handled a large amount of earth. As they still did not have enough water, they drilled the well deeper and pumped the water that filled it with horse-tread power and still did not have enough for their cattle. They were ordering more drilling equipment, he told Farwell.

The Matador, another of the large ranches with heavy foreign investment behind it, reported that prices for cattle were low. (Banks had called their loans as a result of the Panic of 1884, and many ranches had been forced to dump their livestock on the market.) In addition, the "northers" had been bad during the winter, dumping snow on the plains and piling it in drifts. Instead of boasting about their calf crop, they were writing off two and a half percent of their entire herd. Even Roosevelt, for all his enthusiasm, began to learn that there was another side of ranching. The winter of 1886–1887 was one of the most severe on the northern Great Plains in the memory of old-timers. It was estimated that some ranches lost as much as seventy five percent of their herds. Roosevelt was somewhat better off. He thought he might lose only half of his investment and decided this was the time to get out of ranching.

Then Congress had launched an investigation of some of the railroads' practices. Startled by what was revealed, it passed the Interstate Commerce Act. That was a fatal blow to the Transcontinental Traffic Association or any other plan of the roads to manipulate tariffs among themselves.

Although the big cattle outfits were more dramatic, perhaps the most significant change was in the population of the Great Plains. Many farmers were pushing into the area, about fifteen families a day in Wyoming alone. In themselves, they were creating a new force that would work against the big ranches, for although weak individually, they had political power in their numbers. They were also gaining new allies. As the expected earnings of the big ranches failed to materialize, they began to lay off men. The unemployed cowboys who once rode for the Matador or the XIT or the Swan Land and Cattle Company were now thrown on their own, and they fell back on what they had planned to be the safeguard of their old age. They took up homesteads. For the first time since the beginning of the large cattle drives, the farmers and the cowboys were beginning to have something in common.

Chapter 36

The Heritage Lives

There had been silence over in the corner; but now the man Trampas spoke again.

"And ten," said he, sliding out some chips from before him. Very strange it was to hear him, how he contrived to make those words a personal taunt. The Virginian was looking at his cards. He might have been deaf.

"And twenty," said the next player, easily.

The next threw his cards down.

It was now the Virginian's turn to bet, or leave the game, and he did not speak at once. Therefore Trampas spoke. "Your bet, you son-of-a_____."

The Virginian's pistol came out, and his hand lay on the table, holding it unaimed. And with a voice as gentle as ever, the voice that sounded almost like a caress, but drawling a very little more than usual so that there was almost a space between each word, he issued his orders to the man Trampas: —

"When you call me that, smile!" And he looked at Trampas across the table.

—Owen Wister, 1902

The Great Plains lay under the burning sun of the last half of the 1880s. Rising above the horizon in the mornings, it glowed like coals. Even the usually cool moment of dawn, when the world gradually awoke, was shattered by its heat. By noon its rays had sought out every drop of moisture, and the leaves of grass and plants began to shrivel. Rivers shrank to streams, streams became trickles, and trickles disappeared altogether. Untired, it resumed its work the next day as though angry with the world beneath it. The surface of the earth cracked, fields turned to dust, and the range faded to brown.

In winter the "northers" were like a pack of half-starved wolves, snarling, hateful, and vicious. They drove the falling snow at an angle that carried it under the bushes and into the barns and houses; and when it finally rested on the ground, they picked it up again, tossed it in the air and re-created the storm; whether it was actually snowing or not,

it seemed as though it were. The dry ground, hot to the touch in summer, was cold as a dead man's hand. The white bones of the buffaloes scattered over the prairie were joined by the fresher bones of cattle. The Great Plains became a graveyard of dreams.

Yet the settlers kept coming. The emigrant trains, cheap and overcrowded, pulled into the stations with a roar, disgorged their bewildered passengers, and roared into the distance again to return with more. Those standing by the now empty track picked up their belongings, so hastily tossed to the ground, for the locomotive was impatient and would not wait. Hope and fear alternated in their hearts, as they asked directions from the nearest stranger.

Some were rich; most were poor, their shabby cardboard suitcases cracked and dirty from the journey, their hands already calloused. This was the promised land to which they had come from

Poland, Austria, Russia, Scotland, Ireland, Sweden, the fetid slums of New York, or the now barren fields of the East and South that could no longer support them. The parched land sneered at them as if calling them fools before they had set foot upon it, much less turned its sod. A quarter-section of this man-eating waste was theirs if they could break and tame it, bend it to their will the way a cowboy tamed a quick-hooved, snapping bronc.

The spirit of the struggle was much the same, a battle between civilization and the forces of nature. The biggest difference was in time. The leather squeaked as the cowboy swung into the saddle; a glorious explosion of energy; hooves struck the earth, fanned the air; the horse "sun-fished" and "crow-footed"—the riders had names for their motions—trying to toss the human from its back; dust circled above the corral. But neither man nor beast could keep it up for long. Either the man lay crumpled on the ground, or the horse, panting and sweaty, accepted the burden.

The settler's struggle was like the slow, upward rise of the plains toward the mountains, grinding, life-consuming, dramatic in its whole perhaps, but not in its parts. He pitched his tent, he excavated his dugout. His wife tried to convert the shelter to a home. The dusty wind smeared the calico curtains she might have hung over an opening, it penetrated the hiding places where she kept her treasured possessions, pictures of her family, an old copy of *Godey's Lady's Book*, a china cream pitcher that had survived the journey—things that reminded her of whence she came. She helped him dig the soil, she prayed with him for rain, she watched him curse when the rain did not come, his angry face turned to the empty sky, his fists clutched tight in desperation. In the winter she helped him push open the door against the snow banked against it and kept the fire against his return, eking out the slender supply of fuel. She saw him against the white surface of the plains and thought he had never looked so small, tiny and frail compared to the great sky and land; once she had thought him so big and strong.

The Great Plains defeated many of them. They broke their backs against the earth; they broke their spirits against the loneliness. The moaning wind was like a constant funeral lament, the sky like a pall. Their crops shriveled in the sun, and so did they. Despair sat with them at the supper table. Hopelessness stood by their bed waiting for them to rise in the morning. If they stayed long enough to complete their homestead, they often sold it. If they did not stay long, they had nothing when they left.

Some had the spirit for the Great Plains. The man forced the land to yield to his will. He broke up its sod and harrowed its surface and made it bring forth corn and wheat and potatoes; he built a sod house and turned the dugout into a storage area. She brushed the dirt floor as though it were parquet, tended the chickens they had acquired, and, if they were lucky, milked the cow. The land strengthened their children. Once tamed, its energy seemed to enter the souls of its tamers. The sons grew heavy muscled, able to do a man's work when they were only boys, bronzed-faced from the sun, their spirits like the wide sky above them. The girls knew the cleanliness of open air, the smell of laundry hung fresh in the sun, the sense of the family's common toil; and if they could not always do a man's work, they did it in an emergency.

As time passed, the woman looked around her. Pictures hung on the wall; the cream pitcher had been unpacked and stood on the shelf along with a few other pieces, bought one at a time, generally by mail order. In the front yard the fruit trees she had planted showed signs of bearing; and what was in her heart was more than happiness, it was like the gentle fall of life-giving rain, like a beam of sunlight playing on a green leaf. If she went east—now they had the money—to visit her family, she worried that she might not be in style and they would think her a country bumpkin. Then laughing at her foolishness, she went back to her chores, humming to herself, as she did the endless jobs that made a home of their dwelling. He heard her and was glad and thanked the sky and earth.

In 1886 homestead entries reached their all-time high, soaring more than twenty percent above the previous year; and although they fell in 1887, they continued for the rest of the decade to run substantially over the number in the 1870s. One reason was a growing understanding of how to farm on the Great Plains and a realization that it was wheat country. As early as 1839 the Methodist missionaries among the Shawnee Indians had planted a hundred acres of wheat, probably the first planted in that future state. By 1850 several farms had tried it as a crop, but corn remained the staple.

The Russian Mennonites were the most successful at growing wheat. They used a strain called Turkey Red, brought by their parents when they came to the United States. It made excellent bread, but many millers complained that it was too hard to grind. Usually, therefore, the Mennonites ground it themselves.

The Kansas Pacific Railroad was interested in finding ways of growing wheat, both because of the freight it would produce and the farmland that would be purchased. By experimentation, one of its agents and T.C. Henry of Abilene learned that many winter wheats could be grown in most of Kansas without irrigation, and in 1873 Henry contracted for five hundred acres sown with Early Red May and Little Red May. In spite of a drought and swarms of grasshoppers, the crop did well, and in the season of 1877-1878, he had ten thousand acres under contract.

In Dakota Territory farmers were also having success with wheat. The first half of the 1880s brought good growing weather, and tales of the quick wealth to be gained from Great Plains farming — tales that were trumpeted by the railroads and others with land to sell — brought new crowds of emigrants. Farming was important enough to call for research, and the land-grant colleges, financed at first by the Morrill Act, were developing new farming techniques and spreading the knowledge.

Those who might most have benefited were the Indians. Even though the Americans kept reducing the size of their reservations, they still had land, but they had no wish to become farmers. When Sitting Bull surrendered, the agent at Standing Rock, James McLaughlin, had twelve acres plowed for him and his band. "I sent two white employees to instruct them," McLaughlin said, "staking off a separate piece of ground for each family. Sitting Bull worked with the others, using a hoe, but rather awkwardly, and in two days they had their fields planted." But little came of the effort. Neither Sitting Bull nor most of the other Indians cared much about farming. Instead they looked back with nostalgia on the old days when the Sioux had roamed the plains on their horses, chasing the buffaloes, fighting their enemies, and demanding tribute from the traders' boats going up the Missouri. They would have preferred to go back to those glorious times—not forward into the future.

At a conference held at Standing Rock in 1883, the subject of farming again came up, for it seemed the only way to make the Indians independent. Senator Henry L. Dawes was chairman, and he asked a Sioux named Red Fish, "Have you any land of your own that you are trying to raise crops on?"

"Yes, sir."

"What have you got growing on your land?"

Proudly Red Fish replied, "I plant every kind of crop that will give me nourishment."

"Can you tell us how many acres you have under cultivation?"

"I have one acre planted," Red Fish said and changed the subject.

Later Dawes came back to it. "Would you like to have 160 acres of land all to yourself, just like a white man?"

"No, I would not," Red Fish replied.

Dawes finally asked if he was healthy and could work. At first Red Fish made no reply. Then he said, "I am not able to work as your people work."

Before he had finished, an Indian in the uniform of a police sergeant told Red Fish to sit down, that he "looked and talked like a man who had been drinking whiskey." But that was not so. Red Fish was saying what was in the hearts of the Sioux and most other plains tribes. Strong and sturdy, they were physically equipped to be farmers, but not emotionally. They had been raised as nomadic hunters, a life at which they were superb, and they could not in a single generation become sedentary agriculturists.

Yet no one could find another answer to their problem. Even if they had horses and guns, they could not revert to their old life. Much of the country was covered with farms and ranches, and, most important, the buffaloes were gone. Off the reservation, they would have starved to death. Yet on the reservation, most of them were unhappy, drifting from one day to another, purposeless and resentful, living on the dole of their conquerors. In 1876 the government had agreed to help feed the families that worked, at the same time reserving the right to withhold rations from those who did not. This policy might have proved successful in some countries, but not in the United States. The electorate would have been as furious over starving Indians as Congress had been with the post commander at Fort Robinson when he tried that tactic on the Cheyennes. "The process of starving and freezing women and children, *in order to compel men into obedience*, is not justifiable in the eyes of civilized men," Congress had said. That opinion was still valid and shared by the public.

Yet the expense of supporting the Indians was great. At another conference held at Standing Rock in 1888, one of the commissioners said, "How much money do you suppose the Government has taken from the people and spent for you since 1868—in the last twenty years? I told you . . . where this money comes from. It does not grow on trees, nor do they pick it up off the ground. The white people have to work for it and put it into the Treasury. I have asked you how much do you suppose the Great Father has had to pay for you since 1868? It does not come far from a million and a half dollars a year. Up to this time as much as $30,000,000 has been spent by the Great Father upon the great Sioux Nation since 1868."

The purpose of the council was to persuade the Sioux to enter into yet another agreement with the Americans. They still possessed an enormous reservation, but they could not live on it without American aid unless they farmed it. And that many of them would not do. Meanwhile white settlers wanted to have it opened and put to use. The new plan was to give each Indian family an allotment of land from the reservation. Hopefully they would farm it and become self-supporting. To protect them from rapacious white men, the deed would be held in trust for twenty-five years. Since they could not borrow against it, the property could not be taken from them by foreclosure. The remaining lands were to be opened to settlement at a price of fifty cents an acre. The receipts were to be placed in a trust fund for the benefit of the Indians.

One of the commissioners pleaded with them. "I want to tell the young men that are here . . . that after a while these old men, like myself, will pass away, and it will not be long either. Our shadows are growing long as we go down the hill toward the setting sun, and it will not be long before these young men will have to take the front seats that are occupied by the old men now. I want to ask these young men this morning if they want to live always as they have in the past. Don't you want . . . to learn how to read and understand all that is going on in the world? Don't you want to have good, warm, comfortable homes in the winter for your families? Don't you want to have all the comforts of life that the white men have? If you say you do, I tell you that you cannot get them by standing still in the fix you are now in. You have got to move on in the line of improvement."

Of course, the Indians wanted all the comforts of life that the white men had, but they did not understand the need for working as the white men did in order to gain them. The Treaty of 1868 had stipulated the number of signatures that must be obtained for a new agreement to be binding on the Sioux. The commission could not obtain the requisite number.

But change was not to be held back forever. Settlers were rushing into Dakota Territory; statehood was imminent; the lands reserved for the Sioux stood mostly idle; no state would tolerate such a void in its midst. New commissioners returned with another offer. Each family was to get 320 acres instead of 160, and the remaining lands would be sold for a price of $1.25 an acre the first three years, then at seventy-five cents an acre for the next two, and then for fifty cents. (The best lands supposedly would go first.)

The Sioux did not like this offer either, but even

their best friends advised them to accept it. It was not likely they would get a better one, and they might get one that was worse. Reluctantly the Indians placed their X's on the paper. In 1889 Montana and North and South Dakota became states. When he signed them, the President shuffled the papers of the two Dakotas, so neither could later claim admission before the other. And the same year, Oklahoma was opened to settlement. The Comanches, Kiowas, and other tribes of the southern Great Plains were faring no better than those of the north.

The changed status of their lands did not improve the status of the Sioux. They were not farmers, and ownership of their allotments did not encourage them to turn to agriculture. Disgruntled and demoralized, they drifted through their days, much as they had done before, their dreams centered on the past, their present monotonous, dull, and pitiable.

Ever since the white men had first known them, the Great Plains had been a place of violence. Their rivers in the springtime became roaring, dangerous monsters, filled with sawyers and planters ready to sink white men's boats. Their storms amazed every traveler, who had not seen hailstones that large, snow that deep, or winds that strong. Their Indians were fierce, brilliant fighters, defying civilians and soldiers alike until they were ground to pieces by superior numbers and equipment. Although white men had now traveled over every part of the Great Plains, grazed and plowed their soil, built cities on their surface, and sent trains running across them, the Great Plains had not spent their violent spirit, and the Indians had not lost all hope.

On January 1, 1889, the moon crossed the face of the sun, part of Utah became dark during the daytime, and a Paiute medicine man named Wovoka fell into a trance, during which he claimed to have seen a vision. The white men's Christ had returned to earth, and because they had killed him, the white men disappeared. The buffaloes returned, and the Indians were again supreme in the land. Word of this vision spread among the tribes. Clutching at this straw of hope, many of them traveled to see Wovoka, and the medicine man, glad for notoriety, began to develop a sect and a tenet: those who danced as he prescribed would see this new world before its scheduled arrival in 1891.

An army officer sent to observe the ceremony reported, "This dance is not a war dance but a religious one. The Indians, men, women and children, dance in a ring, call on Jesus to come, to hasten his coming, and say that they are ready. They expect him to remove the white man, bring back the buffalo, and raise the dead Indians . . . they believe that Christ will come, but he is traveling slowly with all the dead Indians and buffalo. They expect him to be here in April or May of next year [1891]. When he gets here the white people will disappear from this reservation and from the United States. This removal is to be effected by Jesus alone, and the Indians are not to assist but look on.'' Nevertheless, many white men attributed more serious meaning to what was called the Ghost Dance and thought it might portend an uprising. Worried citizens discussed it, each contributing to, not calming, the anxiety of the other. Tension mounted, suspicion deepened, concerned reports flooded Washington, and those who tried to quiet the fearful found few listeners.

Among the Indians, Wovoka's dance did not find universal acceptance. Some danced it faithfully and regularly, hoping that at last the injustices of the world would be turned right, that the Indians would be restored to their former lives. Others were completely indifferent, having no faith in such a vision. Their medicine men had failed too often in the past.

Those who most actively accepted Wovoka's preaching were, of course, the most discontented and unhappiest of the Indians, the ones whom the white men regarded as potential troublemakers. This added to the white men's fears. It seemed to them that the Ghost Dance was kerosene dumped on the fire of the Indians' latent hatred. They expected the flames to burst up at any moment.

Sitting Bull naturally espoused the ceremony and became one of its faithful practitioners. Living in a remote part of the Standing Rock agency, regretting the days when he had danced the Sun Dance, hoping that somehow time would run backward and return him to the Little Bighorn and the glorious hour of Custer's defeat, he found comfort in leading his small band of followers through the ceremony and chanting the song:

> Father, I come;
> Mother, I come;
> Brother, I come
> Father, give us back our arrows

Over and over they repeated the monotonous words sung to a monotonous tune, men and women, joined by their children, their heads moving from side to side, their bodies swaying. Each of them was dressed in a special shirt painted with figures representing birds, bows and arrows, the sun, moon, and stars. They circled, pausing to pick up handfuls of dust, which they threw over their heads. Working themselves up emotionally, several would drop unconscious to the ground. At one point, according to an observer, ''they raised their eyes to heaven, their hands clasped high above their heads, and stood straight and perfectly still, invoking the power of the Great Spirit to allow them to see and talk with their people who had died.'' That was all they wanted—to drift in a trance back into the past.

Originally McLaughlin did not take Sitting Bull's involvement seriously, but later he became more concerned. ''Sitting Bull,'' he reported, ''is high priest and leading apostle of this latest Indian absurdity. In a word, he is the chief mischief maker at this agency, and if he were not here this craze so general among the Indians would never have gotten a foothold at this agency. . . . He had announced that those who signed the Agreement ratifying the Act of March 2nd, 1889, opening the Sioux reservation [the last agreement made with the Sioux], will be compelled to accept a small corner to be set apart and subdivided into small tracts for them to settle upon, where they will be obliged to remain and support themselves, but those who have refused to ratify the Act, or, who have ratified but will now oppose surveys and refuse to accept allotments, will have all the unoccupied portions of the reservation to hold in common and continue to enjoy their old Indian ways. . . .''

After he had made several vain attempts to persuade Sitting Bull to abandon the dance, McLaughlin recommended that he be arrested and confined at a military post away from the reservation. He did not want to take such action immediately, however, but preferred to wait until the cold weather set in. Part of his reasoning was based on the effect of winter on the Sioux. Traditionally that was a quiet period for them when they huddled beside their fires. Much less excitement would occur over the arrest if the authorities waited.

But fate ran against McLaughlin and those who favored calm. Appointments to the Indian agencies were regarded as political patronage to be given to the faithful, and a recent change of administration had brought new, inexperienced men onto the reservations. One of them was Daniel F. Royer, a former member of the territorial legislature and now agent at Pine Ridge. Nervous and frightened by the rumors he heard and disturbed by the weird ceremony, he telegraphed the acting commissioner of Indian affairs that he could not control his agency and needed the help of troops.

As usual the army was again given responsibility for the Indians now that it looked as though there would be trouble. Miles, who had fought so hard through the long winter campaign against them, was in command. He had seen enough Indian action to know that it would be explosive to throw his troops against them, but he did think the leaders should be arrested, and he was especially concerned about Sitting Bull. After all, he had parleyed with the man several times and learned not to trust him. By happenstance Miles saw Buffalo Bill and asked the former scout to make the arrest; and Cody, always glad for publicity, rushed to Standing Rock. McLaughlin's hand was forced. He could no longer wait for the cold weather.

Confident that his Indian police could carry out the assignment more effectively than the flamboyant Cody, with one strategem and another he held Cody at the agency sufficiently long to have his orders rescinded. Then he sent Lieutenant Henry Bull Head of the Standing Rock police to bring the old leader in.

Sitting Bull had two cabins a few rods apart. At daybreak on December 25, 1890, approximately forty Indian police surrounded and entered the two cabins. Sitting Bull offered no resistance when they explained their mission, but then he asked for time to get dressed, time for one of his wives to get some clothes from the other cabin, time to have his favorite horse saddled. Meanwhile word spread through the small settlement where he lived, and his followers began to assemble. Angry, they refused to leave at the policemen's request. Tempers flared. A gun went off. The bullet struck Lieutenant Bull Head in the right side. Bull Head fired a shot and hit Sitting Bull. Two more shots rang out, one of them inflicting another, mortal wound on Sitting Bull.

General fighting then broke out. The Indian police were well enough armed and well enough trained to hold off the Indians until the cavalry rescued them. But the hero of the Little Bighorn was dead.

News of Sitting Bull's death spread quickly among the already excited Indians. The appearance of troops, brought about by Royer's call for help, had already disturbed them. Some had fled to the Badlands, where they hid, waiting for the trouble to pass over. On Sitting Bull's death, more Indians became panic-stricken and fled to join the others who had rushed away. The army had the task of rounding them up and bringing them back.

One of the leaders at the Pine Ridge agency was Big Foot, a Sioux known for his peaceful relations with the white men. Nevertheless, Colonel E. V.

Sumner was assigned to keep an eye on his village. Big Foot visited the officer's camp and assured him that there would be no trouble; but when Sumner learned that some of Sitting Bull's followers, having fled the Standing Rock agency in terror, might be coming to Big Foot, he ordered Big Foot and his entire band to report immediately at the agency. The Sioux's arguments that it would be difficult to move the women and children were to no avail. Sumner insisted, and Big Foot went back to his village to study a way out of his quandary.

All might have gone well except for the appearance of some of the Indians from Standing Rock and the presence of a white man, a friend of Big Foot, whom Sumner had sent to persuade him to move to the agency town. The newly arrived Indians told of the horrors of Sitting Bull's death, undoubtedly emphasizing every incident and adding some created in their own imaginations; the white man foolishly tried to frighten the Indians into obeying Sumner's orders. As a result, the band fell into a panic and, during the night, tried to slip away to the Badlands.

Escape was impossible, for the reservation swarmed with soldiers. Before the next day was over, Big Foot and his village were stopped by four companies of the Seventh Cavalry, which Custer had commanded. To the question whether he wanted to fight or surrender, Big Foot replied that he would surrender. There was nothing else he could do.

That night soldiers and Indians camped near Wounded Knee Creek. The general commanding the operation on the reservation sent four more companies of the Seventh Cavalry, some scouts, and a Hotchkiss battery as reinforcements. The arrival of additional soldiers made the Indians more fearful than ever, and the soldiers, who had been marching around but seeing no action, were on edge.

The following morning the colonel commanding the Seventh Cavalry decided to disarm the village. He told the warriors to collect their weapons and stack them in front of Big Foot's lodge. When the first twenty men appeared, they brought with them only two guns. Since the Sioux were apparently not going to obey him, the colonel told the soldiers to move up and search the lodges. They were quick and brutal, pushing the Indians aside, and tearing open their bags and bundles; the Sioux screamed and protested. Those who could hid knives or guns under their blankets.

No calming voice made itself heard, no officer called for restraint. A young warrior approached the growing stack of rifles with his own in his hand, ready to place it on the pile. Two soldiers tried to grab it from him. A medicine man had been boasting that when he threw up a handful of dust, the white men would be blinded. At that moment he did toss dust in the air. A shot sounded; a soldier fell. The Americans began firing. With the few guns they still had, the Sioux fired back and those who has no firearms drew their knives or used their warclubs. The Hotchkiss guns went off; the village became a burning, bloody wreck. The Indians fought hard and killed a number of Americans. The Americans in the confusion that Wounded Knee had become killed some of their own.

When the Indians attempted to retreat, the soldiers pursued them. They had become maniacs out of control and shot at anything that moved. Since the sound of the shooting could be heard for some distance, the Indians who had remained on the reservation began to gather. Although they had been friends of the white men and had not fled, they could not bear to see their fellow tribesmen killed this way. They became menacing, and because the Seventh Cavalry was soon outnumbered, it withdrew.

The casualty list was high. Thirty-one white men were killed and thirty-three wounded, numbers of them by their own companions at arms who had fired into the village. One hundred and forty-four Indian bodies were recovered, sixty of them women or young children. No one knows how many died of wounds or exposure after the struggle.

The pathetic resistance of Big Foot's ragged band was the last Sioux "outbreak," as some of the frontiersmen would have called it. For both sides, it was a sorry end.

Three problems haunted the big ranches: rustlers, range, and water. Even the best-designed brand could be altered in some fashion and the cattle driven elsewhere. When calves were separated from their mothers by a skillful rustler, no one could tell in a year to whom they had originally belonged. (Possession of a cow with two calves made the owner suspect). Generally speaking, alert, loyal cowhands, however, could keep rustling to a minimum.

Range and water were different. The public domain supposedly belonged to everyone until some settler took up 160 acres and made it his own. If that 160 acres happened to include a spring or the best part of a stream, it might be the only source of water for miles around. In that case, the surrounding range was useless to anyone but the home-

steader. Although the big ranchers knew how to circumvent the Homestead Act and other land laws, there was a limit to how much land even they could take title to. Thus they hated homesteaders, for these were the people who could put them out of business.

In Wyoming the Cheyenne Club was not only comparable to the finest in the East, it was also a center of power. Most of the big ranchers belonged, as did most of the important politicians; and when Wyoming became a state, they all worked together to take control. Between them they ran the governorship, the Wyoming Livestock Association, and the Wyoming Livestock Commission, which had the authority to seize cattle suspected of having been stolen. The proceeds from the sale of these animals supported the association; and its considerable authority made it an awesome power.

In Johnson County, however, the big ranchers had less of a hold. The range there was excellent, and many of the cowboys who were laid off as cattle prices fell went there to homestead and start their own ranches. Undoubtedly many of them took some of the big ranchers' cattle for a beginning, but more important, they were taking up the best water. If something was not done about it, the big ranchers would find themselves driven from some of the best grazing in the state. But the local cowboys had elected their own sheriff.

The first step was to use the Wyoming Livestock Commission. Many of the cattle shipped by the homesteading cowboys of Johnson County were seized by the commission and sold. The way the law was written, the cowboys had little means of regaining their stock, for the burden of proof lay on them, not the commission. So they began to make up for their losses by rustling in a big way.

Finally some of the members of the Wyoming Livestock Association came up with an idea: to invade Johnson County with their own employees and put to death the men they suspected of being "rustlers" even if the word meant only that they had homesteaded in places that blocked the range for the big operators. They recruited thugs in Texas and Colorado, bought horses, equipped the men, and hired a special train to carry their army to Casper, about 125 miles from Buffalo, the center of Johnson County, where they began the march toward their objective.

The invasion started on schedule, and the cattlemen killed their first "rustler," an obscure cowboy named Nate Champion, but they had not reckoned on the strong communal loyalty of the people of Johnson County and their fierce determination as fighters. Soon the invaders were barricaded at a ranch around which swarmed numbers of small owners. Just as they were preparing to batter down the building with a battering-ram of their devising, the garrison from the nearby post arrived and enforced a truce. (The garrison had been noticeably inactive when the Wyoming Livestock Association was ahead in the struggle).

None of the the conspirators suffered the criminal consequence of their act, but the cowboys of Johnson County had written a new phase of Great Plains history. For the invasion marked the high point of the large ranchers' arrogant behavior. In the face of the wide publicity attending the Johnson County War, as it came to be called, they were forced by public opinion to become more moderate in their ways. They still retained power, but from then on the large livestock owner was no longer king. Just like the railroads, he had gone a step too far. The Great Plains was changing once more, and the common man was coming back into his own.

The sound of the last gun, echoing against the foothills of the Little Bighorns during the Johnson County War, was like the tolling midnight bell that marks the passing of a year. It saluted the old and heralded the new.

The free range, as the stockmen had called it, was gone. In a few places the concept might linger on a while longer in pockets of antiquarianism, but the public domain had been returned to the people from whom it had come. Years before at the Constitutional Convention they had decided that the open spaces to the west—the west then being east of the Mississippi—belonged to the whole nation. It would never be the select province of the few, whether the few were states or individuals, and further, that it would be incorporated into the country. The United States, which had fought so hard and long to throw off its own colonial status, would have no colonies itself.

Unity and union were to be its watchwords. Men had died on the sorrowful, heart-rending battlefields on behalf of that cause in its simplest form, but the idea was not limited to the sectionalism of North against South. The concept covered every geographic area of the land and every class; this was not intended to be a nation divided against itself in any way, but a single people living in a single land.

The Swedes, the Poles, the Germans, the Russians, and the others who had come to take up land on the Great Plains knew this. It was one of the reasons they had made the long voyage by steerage and the long journey by oxcart and later by train.

No country in Europe could offer them this. The Indians, still shocked by Wounded Knee and justly resentful, did not share this feeling. For they were not emigrants. What was now the American land had once been theirs, and it had been taken from them, often by bloody means. The bones of their warriors lay longside the trails the white men had trod. Yet they, too, had opportunities ahead of them. They had forgotten the guns and horses the white men had brought them, how their standard of living had suddenly changed, that the glorious days they remembered—and now regretted—had been made possible by what the white men had brought. And they overlooked in their bitterness the generosity of the Americans. Few conquerors had ever said to their victims, Come and be one with us on equal terms. For the road to citizenship—to sharing in the whole—was open to them. As they sat huddled in their tipis, their eyes blinded with tears for their dead, they could not see the future rising before them. Perhaps someday they would.

The Great Plains had been a hard anvil on which to hammer the edge of a nation's spirit. Many a time they had seemed too vast, too stern, too forbidding ever to be conquered, but like the Indians who had once roamed freely over them, they had finally surrendered to vast numbers and undiscouragable enthusiasm. Every part of them was now known. A rancher just possibly might ride his horse across a piece of land that had never known a white man's presence, but the chances were slight.

To effect the conquest, the people had had to turn increasingly to their government for help, more so than in most other parts of the country. They had called on the army to protect them, the Indian agents to control the tribes, the Congress to help them build railroads, and they had lived for long periods not off the products of the land, but off the government contracts they secured. Yet there was nothing wrong with this. The Great Plains would not succumb to individuals; it took the resources of the whole nation to subdue them. As long as the individuals remembered this, it could do no harm. But if they forgot it or, remembering, applied the concept to less worthy causes, they themselves would be the losers. For the independence of the individual, the willingness to embark alone on a dangerous trail, had taken the fur traders into the unknown, had guided the first cattle up from Texas, had uncovered the gold and silver of Colorado and the Black Hills. It was the essential ingredient, the cap on the cartridge that made the rest work.

Change, once it had started, once it broke

through the seemingly impenetrable barriers of centuries, had come quickly, almost too quickly for the people and the land to absorb it. Then it slowed and broke from a gallop to a walk. Already, yesterday had become history, and in 1893 Frederick Jackson Turner stood before a meeting of the American Historical Association held in Chicago and read his famous paper, "The Significance of the Frontier in American History." He had noted a remark in the census of 1890 that the frontier of settlement no longer existed and therefore would have no further place in the reports.

"This brief official statement," he told his audience, "marks the closing of a great historic movement. Up to our day American history has been in a large degree the history of the colonization of the Great West." American civilization, he pointed out, had not advanced on a single course. The frontier had constantly forced it to return to primitive conditions and begin over again. "This perennial rebirth," he said, "this fluidity of American life, this expansion westward with its new opportunities, its continuous touch with the simplicity of primitive society, furnish the forces dominating the American character."

The final frontier had been on the Great Plains. Compared to Oregon and California, with their rich soils, well-watered lands, and timbered slopes, the Great Plains had been unwelcoming and resisting. They had stretched out the battle to the last, and those who had shared in it would never forget.

In 1897 homestead entries fell to a low. The best quarter-sections had been taken up, although a few were left for the knowing to find and take. The open ranges were gone, the furs depleted, the Indians on reservations. Yet the dreams remained alive, not only in the hearts of the old, but also the young. Cooper and Buntline had put their fingers on something that had become an integral part of the nation's tradition and spirit.

In 1898 the battleship *Maine* sank in Havana Harbor, and the country went to war. Theodore Roosevelt, always wanting to be in the center of things and flamboyant as usual, formed the Rough Riders, and nothing in the fighting so captured the Americans' imagination. A few of the socialites he knew in New York joined up, and so did some of the cowboys he had known on the Great Plains. When they went through the South to go into train-

ing, crowds gathered at the railroad stations to cheer them. It had been a long time since Southerners had cheered federal troops. In their common experience on the Great Plains—and their pride in it—North and South could at last find a meeting place.

The war was not what many would have wished it to be. Remington was there and complained bitterly. This was not like the Indian wars that had been the subject of so many of his pictures. How could he make interesting the wheels and machinery of the battleship to which he was assigned? And the Rough Riders never performed the way Roosevelt had envisioned them doing.

Yet when the war was over, Remington painted a picture of Roosevelt charging up San Juan Hill. It made no difference that the hill was not actually San Juan, but another one, or that the Rough Riders did not charge, they had to crawl up it. This is what the people wanted, and they did not care whether it was Nat Bumppo or Theodore Roosevelt. And since Roosevelt was running for President, and Bumppo was not, they elected him.

Somewhere in space, somewhere in that twilight of every man's imagination, the Virginian's pistol came out, and his hand laid it on the table, holding it unaimed. His voice was as gentle as ever, the drawling came slowly, and he looked at Trampas.

"When you call me that, *smile!*" he said.

The thunderheads rose on the horizon, dark and ominous. The lightning flashed, the rain fell, splattering against the rocks and soil. The water ran along the trails that Ashley and Pilcher had followed and made puddles on the site of the old Mandan villages; it poured down Sand Creek where Black Kettle had camped, it filled the gold-bearing streams of the Black Hills. The Little Bighorn rose as it received the floods of its tributaries and swept past the foot of the ridge where Custer had first seen the Indians' camp. The rain fell on the fields that now covered the trails that had once led to Abilene and Dodge, and the routes that Pike and Frémont had followed, and bathed the Great Plains with life-giving moisture.

Then the clouds broke apart, their violence spent. The sun freed itself from the darkness that had enveloped it and shone in the clear sky, hot and red and never changing.

Acknowledgments

No book is written by a single person; here are some of those who helped me write this one:

W. Eugene Hollon, professor of history at the University of Toledo, who maintains the old tradition of scholarship by generously sharing his knowledge with the less informed. I never leave his company without knowing something that I did not know before.

Jack Haley, assistant curator of Western Americana at the University of Oklahoma, one of those rare individuals who is a practitioner of the life that he studies and a warm-hearted dispenser of the knowledge he possesses.

Archibald Hanna, who presides over the Western Americana collection in the Beinecke Library at Yale University, and who always finds time to help track down an obscure item or the answer to an obscure question.

Howard Roberts Lamar, professor of history at Yale University, whose extraordinary interest in making dissenting opinions known marks him apart and who has shared with me his store of knowledge and made available to me the opportunity to exchange views with some of his graduate students.

Anyone who writes about American history must be indebted—directly or indirectly—to that remarkable organization, the National Archives and Records Service. Its personnel seem tireless in their willingness to help, whether the search involves a manuscript or a photograph. Of the many individuals who worked with me there, I would particularly like to thank Robert M. Kvasnicka.

Among others who have been of assistance to me are Mrs. Carol Parke, who is in charge of the Government Document Room at the Sterling Library, Yale University, and whose gracious assent to my innumerable requests earns her a special place in my list of creditors; Mrs. Virginia S. Neuschel of the United States Geological Survey, who helped me with a technical definition of the Great Plains as well as tracing for me how that definition has changed at various periods in the study of American topography; and Mrs. Elsie Lloyd and Mrs. Amy Chubb of Kaycee, Wyoming, who showed me places in the Hole-in-the-Wall country and the surrounding area that I would never have found by myself.

In addition, I would like especially to thank the following and certain individuals on their staffs. Some of these organizations obviously have more important collections than others, but small, local museums often provide a vivid picture of the life of ordinary people and the special problems of their own locales. For this reason they are sources for material not to be found in other ways.

Abilene Room of the Abilene Public Library, Abilene, Kansas (Mrs. Robert Acre); Adams Memorial Museum, Deadwood, South Dakota; The Alamo and the library of the Daughters of the Republic of Texas, San Antonio, Texas (Mrs. Grace White); Arrow Rock State Historical Site, Arrow Rock, Missouri; Bent's Old Fort Historical Site, La Junta, Colorado; Black Kettle Museum, Cheyenne, Oklahoma; Bloom House, Trinidad, Colorado; Bradford Brinton

411

Memorial Ranch, Big Horn, Wyoming; and the Chimney Rock National Historic Site on the Oregon Trail, Nebraska.

And the Colorado Historical Society Museum and Library, Denver, Colorado; Council Grove Museum on the Kaw Indians, Council Grove, Kansas; Custer's Battlefield National Monument on the Crow Agency, Montana; Dickson County Historical Society Museum, Abilene, Kansas (Miss Irene Dobson); Fort Bufford Museum at the confluence of the Missouri and Yellowstone, near the Montana-North Dakota line; Fort Davis Historical Site, Texas; Fort Lancaster, Texas; Fort Laramie National Historic Site, Wyoming; Fort Lincoln Museum, Mandan, North Dakota; Fort Lyon, Colorado (now an army hospital but still retaining some sense of the past); Fort Robinson, Crawford, Nebraska (whose director was unusually helpful to me); Fort Sumner Historic Site, New Mexico (Jack Rigney); Fort Union Museum at the Fort Union National Monument, New Mexico; Fort Union at the confluence of the Missouri and Yellowstone rivers (near Fort Bufford); Jim Gatchell Memorial Museum, Buffalo, Wyoming; Kansas Heritage Center, Dodge City, Kansas (Mrs. Jane Robinson); Indian Village (Department of Anthropology, University of Oklahoma), Anadarko, Oklahoma; LeNoble House, Abilene, Kansas (Mrs. Kirt Kessinger); Museum of the Fur Trade, Chadron, Nebraska (Mrs. Charles E. Hanson, Jr.); and the Museum of the Sioux Indians, St. Francis, South Dakota.

Nebraska State Historical Museum, Lincoln, Nebraska (Donald Snoddy); Northern Plains Soil and Water Research Center, Sidney, Montana (Ardell Halvorson); Old Baca House and Pioneer Museum, Trinidad, Colorado; Old Mill Museum, Lindsborg, Kansas; Overland Trail Museum, Sterling, Colorado; Palo Duro Canyon Museum, Canyon, Texas; Panhandle-Plains Historical Museum, Canyon, Texas (Miss Claire R. Kuehn); Rice County Museum, Lyons, Kansas; San José Mission State and National Historic Site, San Antonio, Texas; Southern Plains Indian Museum and Crafts Center (United States Department of the Interior), Anadarko, Oklahoma; St. Joseph and Pony Express Stables Museum, St. Joseph, Missouri (whose director, Richard Nolf, is a longtime friend); Theodore Roosevelt National Memorial Park, Medora, North Dakota; University of Colorado Library, Boulder, Colorado; and West of the Pecos Museum, Pecos, Texas.

All those interested in the Great Plains also owe a debt to Walter Prescott Webb for his pioneering work.

Although they have not supplied me with information, several persons have assisted me with this book in other ways: Burke Meehan, Rowayton, Connecticut; Sylvia Carman, South Norwalk, Connecticut, who has brought to the typing of these many pages unusual dedication; and my old friend, Louise Horton, Wilton, Connecticut, who has read this and many other of my manuscripts in their roughest form and helped me with her suggestions.

If the writing of a book as comprehensive as this requires patience on the part of the author, perhaps it requires even more on the part of the editor. William Targ of G. P. Putnam's Sons has, as always, been generous with his time and wise and gentle in his counsel.

My gratitude also extends to those in the long-ago past who first taught me how to saddle a horse and throw a rope and whose stories around the fire in the evening stirred my imagination and love for the West.

And if there are others that I have forgotten, may I be forgiven for the frailty of a human memory.

Appendix A

Defining the Great Plains

The Great Plains form a part of the immense region known as the Interior Plains, which lies between the Appalachians to the east and the Rocky Mountains to the west. This part of the United States has the common characteristic of flatness, but little else. In the east, their general altitude ranges from 500 to 1,000 feet, but in the west, they rise to between 500 and 5,500. They also differ widely in climate. In the east, they are well watered with many streams and plentiful rainfall, but toward the west, they become progressively drier until water becomes a principal factor in dictating the location of settlements and what livelihoods the inhabitants shall pursue.

Because of these variations, the Interior Plains can be divided into two physical divisions: the General Stable Region (or Central Lowland) to the east and the Great Plains to the west. (John Wesley Powell, the explorer and noted geographer of the West, divided the eastern portion into two regions: the Prairie Plains and the Lake Plains.)

Technically the Great Plains are described by the United States Geological Survey in these words:

The Great Plains together with the *Central Stable Region* form the *Interior Plains* of the United States. The two plains areas are separated from each other on the basis of aridity and elevation. The eastern boundary of the Great Plains is defined approximately by the 2,000 foot contour line (elevation), the 100th meridian, and the 20-inch rainfall line and by an irregular east-facing escarpment extending from North Dakota to southern Texas. The elevation increases gradually westward to about 5,500 feet at the western boundary, the Rocky Mountains. The Great Plains are underlain by almost flat-lying sedimentary rocks intruded by a few igneous bodies that form several mountain ranges (the Black Hills of South Dakota and smaller mountains in Montana). In keeping with the definition of a plain, the Great Plains is a region of generally uniform slope of low relief, dissected by shallow river valleys.

In Canada they continue northward parallel to the Rocky Mountains gradually dropping in elevation along the MacKenzie River until they reach sealevel and form the Arctic coastal plain of northwestern Canada and northern Alaska. In Mexico, the Plains terminate between the Gulf Coastal Plain and the folded ranges of the Sierra Madre Oriental.

On a map, this roughly includes: the major portion of west Texas, the Oklahoma Panhandle, the western half of Kansas, most of Nebraska, and those parts of North and South Dakota that lie west of a line that generally follows the curves of the Missouri River but anywhere from thirty to a hundred miles east of it. In the west, the Great Plains include: approximately the eastern third of New Mexico, the eastern half of Colorado, eastern Wyoming (the Great Plains occupy only a small part of the southwestern corner, but they curve west in the northern part of that state), and the larger part of Montana.

But the Great Plains are more than a physiographic province. They are also a state of mind, and this is more difficult to define, because it crosses physiographic boundaries. This book, therefore, includes areas that technically do not fall within the Great Plains but lie at their borders. For in spirit, many of these areas also belong to the Great Plains region.

Appendix B

States of the Great Plains

Note: The date given for territorial status is as an organized territory.

NAME	ORGANIZED AS A TERRITORY	ADMITTED TO UNION
Colorado	Feb. 28, 1861	Aug. 1, 1876
Dakota	March 2, 1861	———
Kansas	May 30, 1854[a]	Jan. 29, 1861
Montana	1864	Nov. 8, 1889
Nebraska	May 30, 1854[a]	March 1, 1867
New Mexico	Sept. 9, 1850[b]	Jan. 6, 1912
North Dakota	———	Nov. 2, 1889[c]
South Dakota	———	Nov. 2, 1889[c]
Oklahoma	May 2, 1890[d]	Nov. 16, 1907[e]
Texas	Declared its independence, March 2, 1836; recognized by the United States, March 3, 1837	Dec. 29, 1845[f]
Wyoming	July 25, 1868	July 10, 1890

(a) Created by the controversial Kansas-Nebraska Act.

(b) Texas originally claimed as far west as the Río Grande. In 1861 part of New Mexico became part of the Territory of Colorado. In 1863, New Mexico was separated from Arizona.

(c) North and South Dakota can both claim to be either the 39th or 40th state, because President Harrison is reputed to have deliberately shuffled the proclamations before signing them.

(d) Officially designated as Indian Territory (but not organized) in 1834; first opened to white

415

settlement with the "run" of April 22, 1889. (The most famous "run" was to the Cherokee Outlet, 1893.) The western portion, which had been opened to white settlement, was the portion organized as a territory.

(e) Both the western and eastern portions of the former Indian Territory were combined.

(f) Texas seceded and joined the Confederacy on February 1, 1861. It freed all slaves on June 19, 1865, and was readmitted to the Union on March 30, 1870.

Notes

The notes to a book of such broad scope as this present something of a problem, because they could easily become overburdensome and occupy a whole volume of their own.

After considering several possibilities, I finally decided to place them at the back, where they would not interrupt the reader as he went through the text, and at the same time put them in essay form, so they could be read as a whole. Although the temptation to do otherwise was great, I have not—and I repeat the word "not"—listed every source consulted. What I have attempted to do is list only those that are most easily available and

that provide generally accurate coverage of the subject matter. These references should enable a reader to pursue a subject further. I have also cut the notes severely, eliminating much detail that would be primarily of interest only to a specialist. Those who wish more detail may write me in care of my publisher, and I will make every effort to answer their questions.

This approach, I realize, will not meet with favor on every hand, but, as Herbert Bayard Swope once wrote, "I cannot give you the formula for success, but I can give you the formula for failure—which is to try to please everybody."

Chapter 1
The Castaways' Remarkable Journey

No self-respecting attorney would go into court armed only with the type of evidence that supports the details of Núnez Cabeza de Vaca's journey. After their safe arrival in New Spain, the travelers submitted a report to the *audencia*, but at best, this could not have been extremely accurate. They had been absent from 1528 to 1536, and they did not have with them a single sheet of paper on which they could take notes. Under such circumstances, few persons could give an account that was accurate in details.

And we do not even have the original of this re-

port. It has disappeared, and all that remains is a transcript prepared and sent to Spain by the Spanish historian Oviedo. And he said he had done some editing. A jurist would consider this evidence as hearsay.

The other evidence is the *Relación* of Cabeza de Vaca himself, but this was not published until 1542, long after the event; and, of course, it, too, was written without the benefit of notes. Consequently no one can state with any real certainty the exact route the men followed until their arrival in New Spain and their first meeting with their fellow countrymen. But the direction in which they moved and the topography of the land would have combined to bring them across the foot of the Great Plains.

Numerous scholars have attempted to trace their trail with some precision, and several of their efforts are listed in the bibliography. Those readers who like detective stories might particularly enjoy Cleve Hallenbeck's book on the subject.

It is incorrect to shorten the last name of Núñez Cabeza de Vaca. Núñez was his last name, and Cabeza de Vaca was the ancestral name he adopted. But to those unaccustomed to Spanish names, it sounds awkward, especially when repeated several times within a few pages, as of necessity it must be. So I have taken the liberty of dropping the Núñez in the hope this will be more pleasant to the reader's eyes and ears.

The quotations are from Smith's translation and are as follows: chapter heading, p. 11; the description of bows and arrows, p. 39; their arrival at the coast, p. 45; God's helping the Indians to heed the advice not to harm them, p. 75; digging roots, p. 85; life among the Indians before their escape, p. 111; the help they received from God, p. 120; the description of the country's wealth, pp. 176–177; the pillaged land, p. 174; and the hospitality of Melchior Díaz, p. 190.

Chapter 2
Death of a Dream

Although de Soto turned back before actually reaching the Great Plains, he should be included in a book about them because he established Spain's claim to their eastern approach. Bourne's volumes were especially helpful to me in writing this short account. There are, of course, other editions of the accounts he includes.

Fray Marcos presents an interesting subject. Of course, we have only his word for it (see the listing under Niza in the bibliography for the edition of his account that I used) that he saw the first of the Seven Cities of Cíbola, and he is vague in his description of both the circumstances and the city itself. After prudently deciding it was better not to risk his life by entering it, he claimed he observed it from a distance. But since he had no glass of any kind, that distance could not have been great. So then, where were the Indians? They had been told of Fray Marcos's coming and were aroused. How did he get that close without their seeing him? It seems to me that there is a better than fifty-fifty chance he never saw it at all.

"Tiene muy hermoso parescer de pueblo, el mejor que en estas partes yo he visto; son las casas por la manera que los indios me dixeron, todas de piedra con sus sobrados y azuteas [apteas] . . . ," he wrote and then continued, "La población es mayor que la cibdad [ciudad] de Mexico . . . Diciendo yo á los principales, que tenia conmigo, cuán bien me parescia Cíbola, me dixeron que era la menor de las siete cibadades, y que Totonteac es much mayor y mejor que todas las

siete cibdades y que es de tantas casas y gente, que no tiene cabo."

This can be translated: "The town appeared to me to be very handsome, the best I have seen in this part of the country; the houses, as the Indians had told me, were all of stone and had second stories [more literally, attics] and terraces . . . The population [or the town] is greater than the city of Mexico . . . Telling the leaders who were with me how Cíbola appeared to me, they said that it was the least of the seven cities and that Totonteac is much larger and finer than all the seven cities, and it has so many houses and people that it has no outer boundary."

Aside from saying that the city was on a plain, which he did earlier in the *Relación*, Marcos de Niza merely confirms what the Indians have told him, adding no details. It is reasonable to suspect that after the shock of meeting Estavanico's followers, he decided to go no farther.

Coronado is an appealing person, partly because he was sincerely interested in not maltreating the Indians even if he was determined to conquer them and partly because of the personal tragedy the expedition produced for him. His story has been told a number of times, but perhaps the most valuable single volume is Winship's. Bolton's book on Coronado is good.

The severity of the hailstorm startled the Spaniards, as well it might have. The Great Plains are noted for their storms, and the reader might be interested in *Severe Local Storm Occurrences:*

1955–1967, prepared by the United States Weather Bureau. The data it contains underline this point. This is an area where the weather can leap from one extreme to another.

Nor should the reader be surprised at the frequency with which individual Spaniards got lost. It was—and still is—easy to do in many parts of the plains. I have likened them to the ocean, and in places getting lost on the Great Plains is as simple as getting lost on the sea.

Wissler's is a good book for any reader who wants to get a general idea of the various Indian cultures and their differences, such as those that existed between the plains Indians and the Pueblos. As regards the relations of the white men and the Indians in what is now the Southwest of the United States, Spicer's book is most helpful.

A good description of the buffaloes will be found in Cahalane's excellent and enjoyable book. Even today buffaloes have a potentially important food value. By developing a breed of cattle that contains a large strain of buffalo, one rancher has produced a beef animal that can fatten on grass in-stead of the expensive feed usually provided. This could greatly reduce the cost of meat in this country. But when asked why he did not simply raise buffaloes, the rancher replied they were dangerous to work with horses. Apparently his experience was the same as that of the early Spaniards who tried to round up buffaloes on the Great Plains.

The quotations in this chapter are as follows (the page references are to Winship): the chapter heading is from Coronado's letter to the king, 10/20/1541, p. 369; Estavanico's conduct, Casteñeda, p. 190; the fight at the Zuñi pueblo, Coronado to Mendoza, 8/3/1540, p. 325; the soldier describing Coronado's discouragement over Cíbola, Coronado to Mendoza, p. 328; the buffalo herds, *Relación del Suceso*, p. 356; ease of getting lost on the plains, *Relación Postrera de Sívola*, p. 349; Coronado on the flatness of the plains, Coronado to the king, p. 367; the hailstorm, Casteñeda, pp. 240–241; the Quivirans, Coronado to the king, p. 368; and Coronado's search for anything of value, Coronado to the king, p. 368.

Chapter 3
The Struggle for an Empire

The first part of this chapter is so general in nature that it seems unnecessary to cite the many available sources. A reader who wants more information about the early explorers and the expansion of the Spanish empire in North America may find helpful Bolton's *The Colonization of North America: 1492–1783* and Chapman's book on colonial Hispanic America. For the history of the Spanish in what is now the American Southwest, I would recommend Hollon's excellent book, *The Southwest: Old and New*.

For the account of the Rodríguez expedition I have relied on the various depositions made by Gallegos, Bustamante, and others. These will be found in Bolton's book. The Spanish penchant for recording information was extraordinary. So although they were often operating far from civilization, they left behind them an enormous amount of data about their activities.

For the account of Espejo's expedition, I have relied largely on his own report and on his letters to the viceroy and the king. (See Bolton's book.) This is also true of the accounts of Bustamante and Barrado of the Rodríguez expedition. Gallegos's account is included in Hammond's "The Rodríguez Expedition to New Mexico."

Oñate's letter to the viceroy and other documents describing his attempt to found a colony in New Mexico are also contained in Bolton's book. In addition, reference should also be made to Hammond's "Don Juan de Oñate and the Founding of New Mexico."

The French were not as given to formal record-keeping as the Spanish, but they fortunately left much written material behind them. Of great importance are the *Jesuit Relations* edited by Thwaites. These provided a basis for my brief account of the journey of Joliet and Marquette down the Mississippi. Two secondary sources of considerable value in understanding this journey and also the background of French relations with the Indians are Bishop's and Donnelly's books, as well as those of Parkman.

La Salle's efforts to establish bases on the Mississippi are described by both Tonty and Joutel, those two loyal followers who supported him when others were faithless. These are basic contemporary accounts. Margy, of course, did a path-finding job in collecting many pertinent documents that round out the story. Parkman's *La Salle and the Discovery of the Great West* stands up well after all the years since it was written, and it is good reading, too. Those who would like a more modern, and somewhat shorter, secondary account might prefer Osler's book.

Some have questioned whether la Salle hoped to establish his settlement at the mouth of the Mississippi or at some other location, for he was familiar with the lack of adequate building sites along the lower banks of the river. On the other hand, he knew that control of the Mississippi meant control of the interior country, and that was the stake for which he was playing.

Of course, one of the basic books on the Canadian fur trade is Innis's classic. As I have tried to bring out in the text, the demands of the fur trade had a profound influence on the French and the British when they were dealing with the Indians and resulted in an entirely different approach to that used by the Spanish.

Incidentally, Tonty's name is often spelled with an *i* instead of a *y*. That is the original spelling of this remarkable Italian's name, but when he became for all intents and purposes a Frenchman, he used a *y*. Being an admirer of the man, I have followed his own usage.

The quotation at the beginning of the chapter is from Parkman's *La Salle and the Discovery of the Great West*, p. 308, and describes la Salle's proclamation at the mouth of the Mississippi in which he made France's claim to the entire watershed of that great river.

Chapter 4
Exploring an Unknown World

La Salle played a significant role in the history of the Great Plains, for he established France's legal claim to the area and also whetted the interest of other Frenchmen in exploring it. His was the vision that saw they might fall under the French flag, and they almost did. Unfortunately there is not sufficient space to tell in detail the story of the survivors of his ill-fated enterprise. Their journey back was an extraordinary espisode in the history of exploration. Three of them later wrote accounts. One is short; one is somewhat suspect; the one most generally regarded as reliable is Joutel's.

Henry Kelsey was one of those faithful servants every organization needs. But at his death he had not earned enough to make his widow financially independent, and several times she had to petition the company for funds. Kelsey wrote accounts of his own trips. Further information about him is contained in the company's records. Many of the pertinent portions are reproduced in Innis and in the introduction to *The Kelsey Papers* edited by Doughty and Martin. The point that his inducement to explore was an increase in salary is shown in the company's letter of May 21, 1691, quoted on p. xxv of the latter, and the company's evaluation of his journey is in its letter of June 17, 1693, which appears on the same page.

Bolton in *The Colonization of North America*

gives a good general picture of what was taking place in the struggle between France and Spain. So does Hollon in his excellent book on the Southwest. Parkman's *A Half Century of Conflict* is also well worth reading. More detailed accounts are given in Nasatir's *Before Lewis and Clark* and in the book written by him and Loomis.

The quotation from la Vérendrye that starts the section given over to his journey is taken from the "Continuation of the Report of the Sieur de la Vérendrye touching upon the discovery of the Western Sea. Annexed to the letter of M. de Beauharnois of October 10, 1730." It appears on pp. 43–46 of Burpee's edition of de la Vérendrye's papers. In part, the translation is my own from the French.

The basic source of information about the journey made by la Vérendrye is his journal from July 20, 1738 to May, 1739. This appears on pp. 290–360 in Burpee's edition.

The state of North Dakota now maintains a state park and museum at the mouth of the Heart River. The site is historic, because it was also the location of several army posts, including Fort Abraham Lincoln, where Custer was stationed when he was assigned to accompany Terry on the campaign that resulted in his death. The fort itself has long since gone, but the area on which it stood has been preserved free of buildings. The state has also constructed replicas of the Mandan lodges, which form part of the museum's exhibits.

The opening quotation by Henry Kelsey comes from his rhymed account of his trip to the plains in 1690. It appears on page two of his papers as edited by Doughty and Martin.

Chapter 5
Changes in Ownership

The la Vérendryes were typical of the best of the French traders—aggressive, farsighted, and capable—but they became victims of the French colonial system. Forced to finance their own explorations, they could not give full rein to their adventurous spirits and had to spend much of their time haggling with their creditors, an effort that drained much of their energy.

One of the la Vérendrye brothers, known as the "Chevalier," kept a journal of their trip. Although the names of all the sons are known, it is somewhat difficult to establish his identity. This journal is reproduced in the volume of la Vérendrye papers edited by Burpee.

Over the years scholars have differed in the precise route the brothers followed from the time of leaving the Mandan villages until their arrival back on the Missouri. One reason is the difficulty of making positive identifications of the Indian tribes they visited. Especially after the coming of horses, many of the Plains Indians became somewhat alike, and more detailed observations than the Chevalier supplied are needed for identification. Some historians have held that the mountains they saw were the Bighorns; others, that they were the Black Hills. But it seems certain that they did travel in Montana, Wyoming, and both the Dakotas.

On the Great Plains the period between the explorations of the la Vérendrye family and the French and Indian War was one largely of isolated, uncoordinated expeditions, as Britain, France, and Spain feinted for control of the area. Nasatir's own text in *Before Lewis and Clark* gives a good general picture of what was taking place, as does his associate, Loomis, in *Pedro Vial and the Roads to Santa Fe*. For the effects of French competition on the Hudson's Bay Company, see Innis, pp. 138–139. Innis shows clearly how effectively the French were cutting off the best of the trade. One of the more interesting of the British traders at this time was Anthony Hendry, another of those persons who was willing to venture into the unknown.

Laclède, who founded St. Louis and exercised such great influence on the future of the fur trade, was destined to be thwarted in reaping the benefits of his work. He became entangled in debt and, after spending two years in New Orleans trying to straighten out his affairs, died in 1778 on his way back to St. Louis. Even his name did not carry on, because his wife, Marie Thérèse Chouteau, had deserted her husband. Under French law, her children had to bear her husband's, not Laclède's, name.

The resolution creating the public domain that was adopted by the Continental Congress was a fundamental step in the development of the United States. So, too, was the legislation of 1785, establishing the rectangular survey, and the Northwest Ordinance, in 1787.

The smaller states, that originally insisted on the creation of the public domain, were certainly wise, because their fears of being dominated by those with western claims would most certainly have been realized. New York deserves a special citation for being the first to surrender its western claims. The reader who wishes to pursue the subject further will find that a comprehensive history is contained in Gates's book, written for the Public Land Law Review Commission and published in 1968. Two other interesting books are Rohrbough's and Robbins's. A study of the Texas lands, which, of course, were handled differently, will be found in Bishop's book.

The Land Ordinance of 1785 is also covered in these books, as it is an integral part of the story.

The period between the end of the American Revolution and the signing of Jay's Treaty is a fascinating one. Although Great Britain had lost the war, it acted almost as though it had not. Yet it also knew that the friendship of the new country might prove extremely valuable. Consequently it took an ambivalent attitude toward its former colony. Bemis's book is an important contribution to an understanding of those perilous years, and I have drawn on it for my discussion of their effect on the Great Plains.

Pedro Vial is an interesting figure. He comes to us out of the shadows of history, his notable accomplishments having been performed when he was a relatively old man and his earlier life remaining obscured by rumor. His story, as well as that of other explorers, is told in Loomis's book about him. Loomis has also included the records kept by him and others on his trips, thus providing an on-the-spot picture of what took place. It was unfortunate for the Spanish that they lacked the economic and military strength to capitalize on what he did.

Loomis, pp. 380–388, discusses a remarkable map that Vial drew, which indicates that his knowledge of the Great Plains and their adjoining territories was more extensive than either the French or the Spanish realized. Apparently he did an unusual amount of traveling before he became a government explorer. It is unfortunate we do not know more about his earlier days.

The establishment of the Missouri Company and the development of the fur trade in Louisiana while the territory was under the Spanish is well covered by Nasatir in *Before Lewis and Clark*. The introduction gives a narrative account of what was taking place and, of course, he includes the texts of many of the pertinent documents. His article "The Formation of the Missouri Company" also adds to the picture.

Alexander Mackenzie's two expeditions, carried out with no fanfare, were historic. Particularly interesting is the absence of any serious mishaps to his men or to the Indians whom he met.

Since his later life had little effect on the Great Plains, it has no place in this book. I wish I could report that everything went well for him, but it did not. He was knighted and became an even more important figure in the fur business. Yet like so many men of vision, he suffered frustration after frustration and found his ideas and plans were unacceptable to lesser men. Finally he left Canada

and returned to Great Britain, where he lived the rest of his days. Unfortunately by then he had lost some of his fortune.

Later in this chapter mention is made of the special translation of his journal prepared for Bernadotte. The story was told by Bernadotte to one of Mackenzie's relatives in 1824. An account of it appears on p. 35 of Lamb's edition of Mackenzie's journals and letters.

Both Quaife's and Lamb's editions of Mackenzie's journals were most helpful. Lamb's has the advantage of also including some of Mackenzie's letters, which throw further light on his many activities as well as on his trials.

The Missouri Company's choice of Trudeau as its representative is puzzling. The men behind the company were some of the most seriously business-minded people in the town, and they wanted the company to be a success. Yet they selected Trudeau to carry on their difficult enterprise, although he apparently lacked most of the necessary qualifications. Many of the documents pertaining to Mackay's service to the company are contained in Nasatir's *Before Lewis and Clark*.

An interesting study could be made of the reasons for the Spaniards' general inability to adapt to the needs of the fur trade. Names like d'Église and Trudeau and Mackay and Evans keep cropping up even when Louisiana belonged to Spain. The French, of course, pioneered the trade, but the British were quick to catch on to how it was done. With few exceptions, the Spanish were not able to do the same. Something about their cultural heritage or their training seemed to prevent them.

One brief discussion of the Louisiana Purchase the reader may like is Bailey's. Several of the pertinent documents will be found in Bartlett, including Jefferson's assessment of the situation, which appears on p. 104.

The quotation that heads the chapter appears on p. 109 of Bartlett's collection of documents relating to American diplomacy.

Chapter 6
The Two Captains

Jefferson's doubts about the constitutionality of the Louisiana Purchase were deep. Like many another person in his day, he feared the expansion of the federal government's power. Yet he faced a practical dilemma. Could the nation afford to let this great opportunity slip by? He finally decided no. In justification of his action, he proposed a philosophy that, in effect, stated that necessity must at times take precedence over the law. This was a dangerous attitude, but Jefferson had no desire to become a dictator and applied his new philosophy only to the Louisiana Purchase, an act that has benefited all Americans. Any reader who would like to learn a little more about this aspect of his thinking might enjoy reading Koch, pp. 236–246.

Like Thoreau's *Walden,* Lewis and Clark's journals may constitute one of America's best known—and least read—books. In part this resulted from the unfortunate circumstances surrounding their eventual publication.

Lewis had fully intended to take the journals and records kept by him and Clark as well as those written by other members of the expedition and create out of them a narrative of the journey. His untimely death (whether by suicide or murder, no one knows) prevented him from carrying out his plan.

Since Clark showed no disposition to undertake the task—he was less intellectual than Lewis—the papers were entrusted to Nicholas Biddle, the Philadelphia financier and scholar. In addition to the two captains' journals, he also used the journals of Sergeants John Orday and Patrick Gass. He also consulted Clark; and George Shannon, one of the enlisted men, was assigned to work with him, putting his recollections at Biddle's disposal. The War of 1812 interrupted Biddle's work, and he turned it over to Paul Allen, a Philadelphia journalist. By that time, however, Biddle had accomplished most of what had to be done. But as a consequence of all these delays, the published narrative did not appear until almost eight years after the captains' return, an unfortunate circumstance that undoubtedly dampened its reception.

Clark had hoped to realize some profit from the publication of this remarkable book, but through the failure of the publisher, he received only the plates and the copyright.

In 1893 Elliott Coues, a doctor with the army and later secretary and naturalist of the United States Geological Survey, edited a new edition with a new biographical introduction and other additional material. In 1904 and 1905 Reuben Gold Thwaites, the American historian who produced many volumes of carefully edited source material, brought out the *Original Journals of the Lewis and Clark Expedition.*

Except to those deeply interested in the journey, the more scholarly editions of the narrative and journals may make for rather difficult reading,

since the journals were long and, having been written in the field, filled with misspellings, poor punctuation, and other obstacles. An abridged edition that still provides a good feeling of the explorers' ordeals and emotions is DeVoto's. The United States National Park Service has produced a volume, *Lewis and Clark,* which contains a narrative account of the journey, background information on the participants, and descriptions of many of the sites they visited as they are today. It is also accompanied by excellent maps.

Separate from their journals the captains also kept records of the flora, fauna, and geology of the country through which they passed as well as notes on the Indian dialects. On Lewis's death Clark contracted with Benjamin Smith Barton, a professor of the College of Philadelphia (later the University of Pennsylvania), to prepare a formal account of the natural history observed during the course of the expedition. Biddle, therefore, passed over this aspect of their journey. Barton died in 1815, and nothing of Lewis and Clark's work, including their notes, could be found among his papers. As Coues later observed, the captains were thus deprived of much of the honor that should have been theirs for new scientific discoveries.

The early means of navigation on the western Rivers and the traffic that plied their waters is a fascinating field in itself. Those who would like to pursue further the operation of keelboats and other such vessels would certainly enjoy Baldwin's book.

The bullboats used by the Indians on the Missouri combined practicality and simplicity to an unusual degree, but they were not unique to that area. Similar boats were used in such diverse places as ancient Britain and Tibet. A description of them with pictures appears in Lowie, pp. 45–46.

The quotation at the head of the chapter is from Jefferson's letter of instructions to Lewis, the full text of which is printed in Coues and DeVoto. The originals of the other quotations can be located by their dates.

In connection with the expedition, the word "interpreter" has two senses. One is the usual meaning; the other is as the name of a special rating that permitted the captains to hire experienced frontiersmen at a higher salary than that paid to privates. Their usefulness could be as hunters, for example, rather than literally as interpreters.

Chapter 7
Winter on the Plains

The notes to Chapter 6 discuss the various editions of the journals that were written during the Lewis and Clark expedition. These are also major references in this chapter.

The sojourn of the Americans among the Hidatsas and the Mandans is well described in their own accounts. We also have the journals of Larocque and Charles MacKenzie, both of which appear in Masson. These give a slightly different picture. For example, they contain an account of the Hidatsas' complaints about the niggardliness of the Americans' gifts. As might be expected of men who were accustomed to traveling with small parties in the wilderness, they were somewhat scornful of the size of the Americans' expedition, although they were grateful to Lewis for repairing a compass and they appreciated having a blacksmith nearby.

The thought of Pedro Vial, the old renegade gunsmith, appeals to me, but for this book his purposes have been accomplished, and there seemed little point in taking the reader on this last of his trips for the Spanish. He was, as I have indicated in the text, too late to be effective. The game was now in other hands and played a different way. Those wanting a full account of his trip will find it in Loomis.

The quotations at the beginning of the chapter are from successive days in Clark's journal as winter began to close around Fort Mandan.

Chapter 8
A Journey West

The references for this chapter are the same as those set forth in the notes for Chapter 6.

The Hidatsas had told Lewis and Clark that the River that Scolds All Others was the best route to the Rocky Mountains. This was the continuation of the Missouri. The Falls of the Missouri, alas, are no longer the sight that Lewis witnessed, for engineers have since harnessed their waters.

The quotation at the head of the chapter is from Lewis's journal entry of April 7, 1805. The misspellings are his own, but I thought I would not spoil their charm by interjecting *sic*'s.

Chapter 9
The Way Home

Both Coues and Thwaites edited Pike's journal. So has Donald Jackson, who being later, of course, had available to him more information than the other two. In following Pike's travels, I have followed his journal as edited by Jackson. Because the sources are evident from the dates, I have not made specific references to page numbers.

Those who wonder at the complaints of Lewis and Clark about mosquitoes and the influence of these insects on the men should remember that they were frightful in their attacks. Here are some extracts from the journal of that experienced fur trader Alexander Henry: "Monday, July 7th, 1806 . . . the mosquitoes were intolerable. The women closed the opening of the cabins, and made a smudge inside; it only made matters worse by choking us with bitter smoke. If we covered our heads, we were suffocated with heat; if we remained uncovered, we were choked with smoke and mosquitoes. I, therefore, thought it best to get out of doors, but was then in danger of being trampled to death by the horses, which surrounded the cabins to enjoy the smudge. . . . July 8th . . . The mosquitoes continued so troublesome that it was only with difficulty that we could keep our horses from throwing themselves down and rolling in the water, to get rid of those cursed insects. . . . We passed a very uncomfortable night, hot and sultry, with clouds of mosquitoes which so annoyed us that we took no supper. It was impossible to sit anywhere out of the smudge, although nearly suffocated by it, and while lying down we were in continual danger of horses treading on us, as the night was dark, the poor animals could not eat, and were continually crowding in the smoke. July 9th . . . the mosquitoes tormenting us as usual. Our horses, which had little rest last night, were almost ungovernable, tearing up the grass, throwing their fore feet over their heads to drive away the insects, and biting their sides till our legs were in danger of their teeth. In a word the poor tortured and enraged beasts often attempted to throw themseves down and roll in the water. We also suffered intolerably, being almost prevented from taking breath."

Mosquitoes sometimes rated next to warring In-

dians, floods, and blizzards as a hazard in plains travel.

The Hidatsas' poor opinion of the Lewis and Clark expedition is detailed in Henry Thompson's *Journal*, which is included with Alexander Henry's. He was on the Upper Missouri in 1806 before Lewis and Clark returned.

Whatever Lewis and Clark's accomplishments may not have been, the psychological effect of having once crossed the continent was great. History is replete with examples of the second, third, and fourth quickly following the first. Think of the number of persons who climbed Mount Everest in a relatively few years after the first ascent. Lewis and Clark removed the mystery from the continental crossing in a way that Mackenzie's epic journey did not.

The quotation comparing the two ventures is contained in Jackson's edition, pp. 401–402, and is also quoted in Lamb, p. 52. The quotation at the head of the chapter is from Lewis's unfinished "Essay on an Indian Policy" and appears in Coues's edition Vol. III, p. 1217.

Chapter 10
The Traders Follow

Wilkinson's feelings toward Lisa are made clear in his instructions to Pike to block his westward movement toward Santa Fé. These are quoted in Douglas. Lisa's plan, as outlined by Wilkinson, was perfectly in keeping with his daring, imaginative outlook. In this project, he was associated with Clamorgan. Although Lisa subsequently dropped out, Clamorgan in 1807 made a trip to Santa Fé and Chihuahua in an effort to secure trading privileges.

Wilkinson was a man who could complicate the simplest act and therefore left a tangled trail behind him. For a brief, but clear, analysis of his performance in 1806, when he suddenly turned state's evidence, see Hollon's *The Lost Pathfinder*, pp. 90–100.

Pike's unsuccessful effort to capture the mustangs was a historic event, because it was probably the first American attempt at what later became an American institution—a round-up on the Great Plains. Earlier in the text, I noted that the grass in the dry areas of the Great Plains was especially nu-

tritious, so the reader may wonder why Pike had trouble keeping his horses well fed. The answer is relative simple: because of the Indians, he could not permit them to range sufficiently widely when they were grazing. The grass is good, but the animals have to cover a large area to get enough of it.

Pike neither climbed Pikes Peak nor named it after himself. In his journal he referred to it simply as the Grand Peak. During Long's later expedition, Dr. Edwin James and some companions became the first persons known to reach the top. (They believed—and probably correctly—that no Indian had made the ascent.) Long named the mountain James' Peak. John C. Frémont, when he explored the Rockies some years later, referred to it as Pike's Peak and so marked it on his maps. The mountain, therefore, acquired two names. During the Colorado gold rush of 1859, common usage and the slogan "Pike's Peak or bust" gave permanency to the one as against the other. Since then, as we do with most possessive names, we have dropped the apostrophe.

Although the altitude of Pikes Peak—14,110 feet—is surpassed by many other mountains, it stands close to the plains and higher than the mountains immediately surrounding it so it can be seen from miles away. This prominence made it a landmark for all those that traveled that way.

Once Pike crossed the mountains and entered the San Luis Valley, he was, of course, far from the Great Plains. His actions during his enforced stay under the Spanish flag had little bearing on the history of the more eastern area. Therefore I have not treated them in the detail I would have wished.

Pike's comments on the Great Plains appear in his "Dissertation on Louisiana," which was an appendix to Part II of the 1810 edition of his journal. (It is reprinted in Jackson's edition.) Their significance lies in the debate that followed for many years as to whether the western Great Plains constituted the Great American Desert or whether the area was habitable by normal European standards. In a measure, both sides were right. Time showed that much of the land could be cultivated, although not in the fashion most Europeans normally did, but the area was—and still is—plagued by lack of water.

Incidental note: most Americans pronounce the name of the Arkansas River just as they pronounce the name of the state. In Kansas, however, it is generally called the Ar-KAN-sas River.

Two good accounts of Lisa's trips are contained in Oglesby and Douglas, the first being perhaps fuller, the second containing the text of more of the supporting documents.

The assessment of the problems of the private fur traders as opposed to those faced by the leaders of official expeditions can be found in Brackenridge, p. 90.

Although the story of Colter's escape is somewhat reminiscent of other tales, there seems little reason to doubt it, and it is a classic. The version I have followed is Bradbury's, who repeated it as he got it first-hand from Colter.

The page numbers for the quotations from Pike's *Journal* are self-evident from the dates when they were made. Drouillard's reaction to the killing of Bissonet appears in Oglesby, pp. 5–6. Lewis's quotation at the head of the chapter is from Lewis's unfinished "Essay on an Indian Policy," and can be found in Coues's edition, Vol III, p. 1219.

Chapter 11
The Lure of Riches

Douglas gives a good picture of the 1809 expedition that Lisa led, and Oglesby goes into even more detail. James, of course, provides a first-hand account, although his views of what happened were not at all sympathetic to Lisa.

Experts differ on the total number of men who accompanied him. Oglesby's calculations support James's estimate of 350. Others believe that that figure is considerably too high. In any case, it is safe to say that the expedition was the largest up to then to set forth from St. Louis, and it certainly represented a great change from the previous smaller efforts of other traders.

John Bradbury, who visited Lisa's fort in 1811, wrote a description of it in his journal, p. 143. Although it may have been added to by the time he arrived, it is probable that it was originally much as he described it. Menard and Lewis expressed their opinions about the company's future in letters to Chouteau and Meriwether Lewis. (Reuben Lewis had no way of knowing about his brother's tragic

death.) These are reproduced in both Oglesby's book and Hiram Chittenden's *The American Fur Trade.*

Both Astor and Lisa were rugged capitalists in the truest sense of those two words. Each was solely interested in profits; each was willing to do battle with his competition whenever necessary; each had little sympathy for those he could defeat commercially. But there was nevertheless a vast difference between them in their attitude toward government. Lisa had little use for it. Astor, on the contrary, regarded government as a potentially valuable ally and was careful always to maintain good political connections. Government was the means whereby he could obtain a monopoly for his own interests or other special privileges, such as making and receiving shipments from abroad when the Embargo and Non-Intercourse Acts prevented others from doing so.

Astor's various ventures—and intrigues—are far too complicated even to summarize in this book, fascinating as they are. So I have had to restrict myself to those that affected the Great Plains and even then have not been able to treat them in detail. Those readers who wish to examine them more closely should find Terrell's book helpful. Washington Irving's *Astoria* contains the story of that venture. Since Irving was on friendly terms with Astor, his book is weighted in Astor's favor.

The trips of Hunt and Lisa up the Missouri were well documented, because both Bradbury and Brackenridge kept journals that were later published.

I particularly included Bradbury's and Brackenridge's remarks about the Arikaras' chiefs. In spite of the Americans' love of democratic institutions, they had difficulty in understanding that many of the Indian tribes were even more democratic in the selection of their officers. As it is almost always easier to conduct diplomatic negotiations with easily identifiable, powerful rulers, the Americans kept looking for them even though they were usually nonexistent. The Indians' system for preventing the accumulation of power and wealth by the holders of public office was an aspect of their form of government that the white men might have adopted with great benefit.

The quotations in this chapter are as follows: James's remarks about Manuel Lisa appear on pp. 28 and 30 of his book; his description of his frightful trip from the Little Missouri to the Yellowstone on pp. 38–39; his feet inside his moccasins, p. 40; Drouillard's reply to the warning about trapping alone is quoted in James, p. 82; Astor's instructions to Thorn appear in Irving's *Astoria,* p. 44; Brackenridge's comments on Lisa are on pp. 199–200 of his book; his descriptions of the Arikaras' leaders is on p. 254; and Bradbury's comment on the same subject appears on p. 166.

The quotation from Ross, refering to Astor's Pacific Coast venture and appearing at the head of the chapter, is from pp. 5–6 of his book. Ross went to Astoria on the *Tonquin.*

Chapter 12
The Frontier Retreats

It is not possible in the text of this book to go into much detail about the intellectuals who accompanied Hunt and Lisa except to stress, as I hope I have done, the growing intellectual interest in the American West.

The delay in Bradbury's return to England was caused by the War of 1812. Frederick Pursh, the noted botanist, was the person who had first access to his collections. Nuttall, who had been collecting on behalf of William Barton of Philadelphia, went to England and then could not get back to the United States because of the war. While he was there, Pursh looked at Nuttall's collection, too; but when Nuttall's book came out, he had the satisfaction of knowing that he had added many species that were unknown to Pursh. A good summary of what took place is contained in Pennell.

The story of Astor's loss of Astoria is covered in Irving's book, which I mentioned in the notes to Chapter 11. Astor's quotation about the loss of Astoria is from Irving, p. 365. His quotation at the head of the chapter is from a petition he sent to Congress in 1812, asking that the President be given discretionary power in regulating the Indian trade. It is reprinted on p. 377 of Irving's *Astoria.*

Chapter 13
The Slow Return

Notes to preceding chapters have included some of the references to Astor and Lisa that have been used in the preparation of this one, too. Sunder's book covers Joshua Pilcher, and some of his letters and reports are extant. Another book of considerable interest to those wishing to explore the subject further is Hiram Chittenden's classic.

The principal source for following Long's expedition is, of course, James's book, in which he detailed the expedition's progress. Captain Bell also kept a journal, which was not available to James when he was writing but to which references were made by another contemporary scholar. It then disappeared completely. About a hundred years later it reappeared among the possessions of a family living in California. It had been acquired by one of their ancestors, although no one knew how, and brought by him from New York State. (Bell died in Henrietta, New York, which may account for his apparent connection with the family.) In any case, on learning of the document's importance, the family graciously gave it to the Department of History of Stanford University, which deposited it with the university library. Such finds and such generosity are both uncommon.

David Meriwether, who was with the sutler who supplied the military branch of the Yellowstone Expedition, is my authority for my statement that the Indians were not fooled by the appearance of the *Western Engineer.* He describes their reaction on p. 43. Snake or no snake, they did regard the vessel with awe, however, for they had never before seen a steamboat. The mechanical failures of

the vessel cannot all be attributed to Long's inability as a designer. Steamboats were new, and the Missouri offered particular problems of its own. They later came to play an important part in the commerce on that river, but Long was ahead of his time.

The quotations describing the trip are taken from Edwin James and are as follows: In Volume I, Long's orders appear on p. 424; the description of the thunderstorm, p. 431; the description of the scenery along the Platte, p. 454; and the description of the Rockies as they were first seen by the travelers, p. 489 (I particularly wanted to include this, because it is a classic, catching the sight well); in Volume II, the initial attempts to climb the outer ridges appear on p. 2; the view from Pikes Peak, p. 30; the sharing of the tent, p. 83; the day of August 3, pp. 93–94; and their disappointment at finding themselves back on the Arkansas, p. 167.

Long's evaluation of the region was included in his report to Calhoun on January 20, 1821. The text can be found in James's book, Vol. II, p. 361.

The quotation at the head of the chapter is from Washington Irving's *Astoria* and appears on p. 17.

Chapter 14
The Road and the River

As the reader has seen, the development of the American trade with Santa Fé was hardly accidental. For many years men had been dreaming of an East-West trade, but the difficulties of the journey, the hostility of the Indians, and the isolationist policy of the Spanish government greatly delayed it. Once the Mexicans relaxed that policy, Americans were lured into the business by the thought of the gold and silver they believed abounded in New Mexico. That the area was not as rich as some Americans originally supposed did not prevent the trade's growth.

As the trade grew more important, it encouraged expansion into the Southwest. Among the accounts of the original pioneers in this traffic are the journals of William Becknell and Jacob Fowler. Thomas James also included the story of his own expedition in his book. Several Americans had reached Santa Fé prior to these. One was James Pursley, whom Pike met while he was in the city. But for one reason or another they made little appreciable contribution to the future trade, and

their trips were outside the mainstream of events. Because of their almost accidental nature, I have not discussed them in the text.

For those wanting an overview of the Santa Fé Trail and the trade that built it, Josiah Gregg's two books are, of course, classics. Inman's brings the subject more up to date. Those wanting a briefer and more contemporary account I would refer to Vestal's book.

After the battle with the Arikaras, Ashley blamed his defeat on the failure of his men to obey his orders. For this he has been roundly criticized by at least one eminent historian on two grounds: one, he could have dropped farther down the river where the Indians could not have attacked him from behind the cover of their village, or two, he could have enforced his orders by threatening to shoot any man who disobeyed him. The second suggestion carries little weight, for he was not a military commander. If Ashley had made such a threat, he might have been shot himself. His real problem was the horses, because they required the presence of men on shore, and that made him vulnerable.

Leavenworth's role in the attack on the Arikara villages has been the subject of considerable controversy. On his behalf it should be noted that he suffered from several handicaps, not the least of which was his undertaking the campaign without being able to consult his superiors.

On the other hand, a stronger officer might have realized that the Sioux would not remain allies unless the action was quick and that the two fur companies had a common interest in keeping the Missouri open. He would also have recognized that Pilcher and Henry were the two who best understood the Indians' temperament. If he had placed greater confidence in them, the outcome would probably have been more decisive.

Because the engagement was so controversial and a matter of national importance, it caused considerable congressional concern. Senate Executive Document No. 1, 18th Congress, 1st Session, contains the basic story. Those wanting more summarized accounts will find them in Chittenden, Dale, Sunder, and Denig. The latter, written by a fur trader, emphasizes the effect on the Sioux.

The quotations in this chapter are as follows: James's description of their uneasy night appears on p. 130 of his book; the subsequent Indian council, p. 131; and the meeting with Cordaro, p. 135; Pilcher's comments about Leavenworth are quoted in Chittenden, *The American Fur Trade*, Vol. II, p. 600; his comment about the loss of Immell and Jones is in a letter by O'Fallon, the Indian agent, and is included in 18th Congress, 1st Session, Senate Executive Document No. 1.

The quotation from Monroe at the head of the chapter comes from his Seventh Annual Report and can be found in Richardson.

Chapter 15
New Goals in the West

As history is more like a river than a ladder, its points of change are not clearly defined. An event here, an event there, like tiny side eddies, may portend a quickening of the current ahead, but who can say where the rapids themselves start or end, who can draw a straight line across the river to mark the spots? In the midst of the rapids, the change is apparent. No one can mistake their turbulence for the quiet pools that may lie above or below. So it is with much of history; the change is apparent, but not the point when the change began. As I have tried to emphasize in the beginning of this chapter, it is impossible to state the exact time when the Indians of the Great Plains lost their usefulness to the Americans; their uselessness had commenced before the burning of the Arikaras' villages; their usefulness continued after it. But it seems to me that Pilcher's act dramatized what was happening, although if others choose some different point of reference during this general period, I would not disagree.

In some respects Thomas James was an obnoxious man, complaining and vainglorious, as those who read the last few pages of his book will see. But his trip to the Comanches was important, not only because he was one of the few Americans who traded with them, but because he was a witness to the change in their culture. Their handling of the wild horses presaged the coming of the great ranches for which in time the plains would become famous. The skills and techniques used were not natively American but an inheritance from Spain and adopted by Indians before they were adopted by Americans.

The general references for the story of the further development of the fur trade on the Upper Missouri and farther west in the Rockies are Terrell for Astor's American Fur Company, Sunder for Pilcher, and Dale and Morgan for Ashley's activities. Morgan is especially valuable, since he includes most of the pertinent original documents such as reports, letters, and newspaper items. With a slight amount of background, his book will make the period come alive for the reader and give him far more detail than a general book can do.

Senator Benton's Committee on Indian Affairs conducted the study of the need for a fort on the Upper Missouri. Its presentation of the material it collected is contained in 18th Congress, 1st Session, Senate Executive Document No. 56. It should be noted, of course, that Indian affairs then fell under the War Department, a natural outcome of the years of conflict. It was not until 1832 that the Office of Commissioner of Indian Affairs was established in the War Department and not until 1849 that the Office of Indian Affairs was established and placed in the newly created Department of the Interior.

Storrs's report was printed as 18th Congress, 1st Session, Senate Executive Document No. 7. Storrs's views carried weight with Benton, and they also reveal an interesting grasp of conditions in New Mexico. With the benefit of the wider view that comes with the years, it is easy to see how the Spanish system was self-defeating.

The principal source for Ashley's unusual trip is his narrative and journal. The narrative, which covers a longer period of time than the journal, was in the form of an official report to General Atkinson. Unfortunately the original has been lost, but two copies remained. The journal is included in Dale's book. Morgan has also included a large part of it and added the journal. Those wishing to understand Ashley's accomplishment can refer to one or the other or preferably both. Jim Beckwourth, a mulatto who later became famous in the fur trade, also wrote an account. Beckwourth had a human proclivity, completely understandable, for playing up his own heroic role in events, and his account is more colorful than Ashley's. Yet it adds another dimension to the story. Elinor Wilson's book is a sympathetic account of his life.

Atkinson's official report appears in 19th Congress, 1st Session, House Executive Document No. 117. It is especially interesting because of his description of the state of the various tribes in 1825.

It is impossible within the text of this book to do more than give the significance of the exploits of Ashley and his men in the area beyond the Great Plains. But they would make a book in themselves. Both Dale's and Morgan's books will give the reader an understanding of their accomplishments and also insight into some exciting adventures.

The year 1825 also marked the crossing of the plains by James Ohio Pattie, who later wrote one of the classics of early Western America. Unfortunately, since a large part of it deals with his trapping adventures after he reached Taos and not his journey over the area covered by this book, I have had to omit it from the text but still recommend it to those interested in that aspect of frontier life.

The quotations in this chapter are as follows: James's account of the Comanches catching wild horses, pp. 241–242 of his book; Pilcher's comments on the need for a fort, 18th Congress, 1st Session, Senate Executive Document No. 56, p. 16; Storrs's comments on the Mexican economy and the Santa Fé trade are included in his report, 18th Congress, 1st Session, Senate Document No. 7, p. 10; the attitude of the Mexicans toward the Americans, p. 7; Atkinson's comments on the Arikaras and the Hunkpapas appear on p. 10 of 19th Congress, 1st Session, House Executive Document No. 117, and his comments on a fort at the Three Forks on p. 14.

The quotation at the head of the chapter is among the answers Pilcher gave to questions put to him by the Senate Committee on Indian Affairs. It appears on p. 12 of 18th Congress, 1st Session, Senate Executive Document No. 56.

Chapter 16
Questions of Protection

In describing the condition of the fur trade in the last half of the 1820s, I have drawn heavily on 20th Congress, 2nd Session, Senate Executive Document No. 67. This was a study made by the Senate Committee on Indian Affairs. It is comprehensive from the point of view of the American traders, although of course it does not express the points of view of either the British or the Indians.

In the notes for preceding chapters, I have discussed general sources of information about the Santa Fé Trail. These again include Josiah Gregg's classics, Inman, and Vestal's more recent and popular book. Hiram Chittenden's *Fur Trade of the American West* also contains a considerable amount of information about the trail, because it was used so much by the Taos trappers, who entered the fur country from the south. This is also true of the numerous government reports on the fur trade. The two could not be separated.

Sibley's *Journal,* as edited by Kate Gregg, contains much information both about the survey and the trail.

Wetmore's comments, as well as a journal he kept during an 1828 trip, can be found in 22nd

Congress, 1st Session, Senate Executive Document No. 90.

Other sources of primary information used in writing this chapter are 20th Congress, 2nd Session, Senate Executive Document No. 27, and 19th Congress, 1st Session, House Executive Document No. 117.

The quotations in this chapter are as follows: Ashley's comments on the joint occupancy of Oregon appear in 20th Congress, 2nd Session, Senate Executive Document No. 67, p. 14 (two statements of his were included in the committee's report); Clark on Indian trade articles, p. 10; and As-tor's remarks, p. 17; the quotation from Cooper's *The Prairie* is on pp. 33–35; Atkinson's comments on escorts for the traders appear in 19th Congress, 1st Session, House Executive Document No. 117; and Wetmore's comments on captains and guards in 22nd Corfgress, 1st Session, Senate Executive Doument No. 90, p. 31.

The quotation from the Senate Committee on Indian Affairs that appears at the head of the chapter is one of the committee's recommendations in its report contained in 20th Congress, 2nd Session, Senate Executive Document No. 67.

Chapter 17
On to Santa Fé

Although the word "the" is used with the Santa Fé Trail, I hope that I have made it clear in the text that there was not one single route between Missouri and the New Mexican capital. The point of departure, as I have tried to indicate, constantly shifted in a westward direction, so quite a number of communities can—and do—call themselves the start of the trail.

In general the caravans picked up the Arkansas at its Big Bend in south-central Kansas. They then went to present-day Larned, Kansas, at which point two routes were open to them to Fort Dodge. Later on, two more choices awaited them. One, the Lower Crossing, took them in a southwesterly direction to the Cimarron River; the other took them to the Upper Crossing. The route again led southwest to Watrous, New Mexico.

At the Upper Crossing yet another choice faced the caravans, for they could continue westward along the Arkansas to La Junta, Colorado, then on to Trinidad, Colorado, and over Raton Pass to Raton, New Mexico, and to Watrous. This route was longer but less subject to Indian attack.

After Fort Union was built, caravans on all the routes could take the slight detour to its site before reaching Watrous. From Watrous all the caravans generally used the same route through Las Vegas, New Mexico, over Glorietta Pass and up to Santa Fé. Sometimes, however, they would cross the mountains farther north and go to Taos before Santa Fé. The government discouraged this route by not making Taos a port of entry.

The route that led from the Lower and Upper Crossings of the Arkansas was known as the Cimarron Cutoff, because it represented one side of a triangle. Highways today follow most of these routes, testimony to the practical choices made by the early traders.

The principal sources of information about the 1829 caravan are contained in Inman, who quotes some old newspaper interviews of Waldo and Cooke, who participated in the trip, and 21st Congress, 1st Session, Senate Executive Document No. 46, which contains Riley's report. Young has done an excellent job of pulling all the material together, including contemporary newspaper comments and other such items.

The trapper lamenting his boyhood life in Pennsylvania was Zenas Leonard, who came from Clearfield County. He went west in 1831 and subsequently wrote an account of his experiences. Although I have left him in Wyoming, he went as far as California.

John Wyeth's account of the Wyeth expedition is the principal source of information about that trip, although National Wyeth has left us a journal.

Leonard and Wyeth both wrote accounts of the battle between the trappers and the Indians, and so did Washington Irving, who interviewed some of the participants. Although differing in some details, the general features of the various accounts are the same. The Blackfeet did build a "fort," as Leonard called it, and it was effective, and the casualties were high. It was much more of a pitched battle than usually took place with the Indians.

The quotations in this chapter are as follows: the

fight with the Comanches are from Inman, pp. 70 and 71, the weakened condition of the survivors, p. 72; and their arrival at Independence, p. 74; the description of the trapper thinking about Pennsylvania appears in Leonard, p. 10; the description of the Great Plains by a member of Wyeth's expedition is in John Wyeth, pp. 50–55; the description of Fitzpatrick's condition when he was rescued appears in Leonard, p. 17, the battle with the Blackfeet, p. 22, and the retreat from the breastwork, p. 23; John Wyeth's warnings to others appear on pp. 79–80 and 105 of his book.

The quotation at the head of the chapter is from Gregg's *Commerce of the Prairies,* p. 413.

Chapter 18
Art and Business

Catlin's contribution to American ethnology was extraordinary, and without his pictures and detailed notes much that is known about the Indians of the Great Plains would have been lost. Most of his collection is now in the Smithsonian Institution, where he had hoped it would be. Unfortunately this did not occur until after his death. In spite of his importance, he did not exert an immediate effect on the development of the Great Plains, for the information that he brought back, remarkable as it was, did not particularly help traders, trappers, or settlers.

His own writings are the best account of his adventures among the Indians. McCracken's biography with its many illustrations will give the reader a balanced view of his long, and quite unhappy, life.

It has been pointed out that Bonneville might have been ignored by history if Washington Irving had not taken his notes, diaries, and unfinished manuscript and created *The Adventures of Captain Bonneville,* an interesting, well-written account of his adventures and the fur trade. Nevertheless, he demonstrated the feasibility of taking wagons over what was to become the Oregon Trail.

The Bents were men of action, not of letters, and therefore did not themselves write up accounts of their own lives. But some of their letters remain (the Beinecke Library at Yale has some), and because of the wide scope of their activities, there are numerous references to them in the contemporary accounts of others. To anyone who wants a general overview of their enterprise, I would recommend Lavender's book.

As the reader will learn later, there eventually were two forts, Bent's Old Fort and Bent's New Fort. The latter was eventually acquired by the military and became Fort Lyon. The former, the building of which is discussed in this chapter, was later razed by William Bent himself. Its site is now a national historic site, where careful archaeological work is being done. This has revealed much about the fort itself and the life that was led there.

Catlin's description of his studio at Fort Union is from his book, *Letters and Notes on the North American Indians,* Vol. I, p. 42, and his description of drawing the wounded buffalo is from same volume, pp. 26–27.

The quotation from Catlin at the head of the chapter comes from his *Letters and Notes,* Vol. I, p. 18. Although the edition I have used was published in 1842, I have given the quotation the date 1832. The material was originally a newspaper article that Catlin sent back to New York, so I have used the date of its first appearance.

Chapter 19
A Prince and Other Travelers

The contrast between Maximilian and Catlin is interesting. Maximilian had considerably more in the way of funds, and he also had his own artist, so that he could concentrate on taking notes and writing while Bodmer concentrated on the artwork.

The best general account of the fur trade during this period is Chittenden's, and he gives a considerable amount of detail about McKenzie and his still, including some of the words that passed between him and Chouteau. Terrell's book gives a good picture of Astor during this period and the various factors that led him to sell out.

The official record of Dodge's trip through the Southwest in 1834 is contained in 23rd Congress, 2nd Session, Senate Executive Document No. 1, pp. 73–93. Catlin also wrote a description of it in the letters that he sent east and that were later reprinted in book form.

On his second journey across the continent, Wyeth had a more sympathetic chronicler. Townsend liked and respected him as his nephew had not. But the difference may have resulted as much from the circumstances as from the characters of the two writers. Wyeth was clearly a quick learner and· an adaptable man, and on his second trip his leadership was probably just as different as the two accounts make it appear.

Jason Lee wrote many letters back home to his friends, associates, and superiors. These were often printed in the religious journals of the time in an effort to arouse support for his mission. The texts of many of them are given in Bronson's book.

The quotations in this chapter are as follows: Maximilian's description of the fire and accident on the *Yellow Stone* appears on p. 183 of his book; his comments on the buffaloes, p. 191; his description of the fight with the Assiniboins, pp. 273, 274–275; winter on the plains, p. 429; Catlin's description of the sick soldiers, Vol. II, p. 49 of his book; meeting the Comanches, Vol. II, p. 55; the sick troops changing camp in search of buffaloes, Vol. II, pp. 76–77; Townsend's description of the trade goods, p. 137 of his journal; method of making camp, pp. 143–144; the effects of thirst, pp. 169–172; the dress of the mountain men, p. 176; the windstorm, pp. 176–177; Chimney Rock and Scotts Bluff, pp. 178–179; McKay's party, p. 226, and the religious service p. 228.

The quotation from Maximilian of Wied at the head of the chapter appears on pp. vi–vii of his book.

Chapter 20
Wives and Missionaries

The state of Jason Lee's mission and his plans for the coming spring appear in a letter dated February 6, 1835, that is on p. 7 of Bronson's book, and Powell has collected Kelley's pertinent writings both before and after his trip to Oregon.

Dodge's expedition was another of the many American attempts to bring peace and order to the Great Plains without fully understanding the problem. The journal kept during Dodge's trip appears in 24th Congress, 1st Session, House Executive Document No. 181.

Parker kept a journal during the trip to Oregon that he later included in his book. This gives a refreshing picture of the Great Plains. I find Parker an interesting person. His religious intensity brought him to the brink—if not over the brink—of prudery. Yet he still retained enthusiasm and a healthy curiosity. And he certainly had courage at his age to start an entirely new way of life far from everything he knew. Two general books also provide good background concerning the mission, Cannon's and Nard Jones's.

On her trip west, Narcissa kept a journal in the form of a letter to her mother, which she sent home after she reached Vancouver. The circumstances of the journey were such, of course, that she did not keep it regularly, nor does it contain any sign that she intended it to be a record of a historic occasion. The copy that I used was a typewritten transcript in the possession of the Beinecke Library at Yale. From the same source I have drawn Narcissa's reference to the broom seed. This was contained in another letter written about the time the journal was concluded. As the total is so short, I have not indicated page numbers.

In themselves the activities of the artists on the Great Plains were not immediately important, but we owe them much for the record they have left us. Miller's life, except for his trip with Stewart, was not particularly eventful. The best description of his journey is contained in the notes he kept, many of which appear in *The West of Alfred Jacob Miller*.

Slacum's report is contained in 25th Congress, 2nd Session, Senate Executive Document No. 24.

Frémont's recollections of his journey are contained in his *Memoirs*. A good account of his life is Nevins's.

For Father de Smet's trip I have drawn on Chittenden's edition of his life and letters. His travels were among the more remarkable of the many remarkable journeys that were taken during the opening of the trans-Mississippi West. Apparently no distance was too long, no route too dangerous to prevent him from attempting to spread the Catholic doctrine among the Indians.

The quotation describing the outbreak of smallpox comes from Lloyd's introduction to his translation of Maximilian's book, p. ix. It is contained in a report that he reprinted. The excerpt from Slacum's report appears in 25th Congress, 2nd Session, Senate Executive Document No. 24; the description of the Arikaras' condition and Dodge's naming the Cheyenne chief appear on p. 14 and p.

29 respectively of 24th Congress, 1st Session, House Executive Document No. 181; Parker's description of Pilcher appears on p. 44 of his book; the storm, p. 56; traveling on the Sabbath, pp. 56–57; the fight at Fort Laramie, pp. 68–70; and Carson's fight, p. 84; those from Narcissa Whitman's journal are discussed elsewhere in these notes; de Smet's description of the Platte is from pp. 203–204 of Chittenden's edition of his *Life and Letters*, the buffalo herds, p. 206; and Chimney Rock p. 209.

The quotation at the head of the chapter is from Samuel Parker's book and appears on pp. 189–190. Although the copy I have had available was printed in 1846, I have used the earlier date of the original copyright as more reflective of its applicability.

Chapter 21
The Emigrants Begin

Bidwell's journal contains an account of their trip to California. De Smet's book also deals with the same journey, but he does not give as much detail.

The story of the Texas Pioneers is a strange one, although the failure of the Texans to evaluate properly the information they received when they talked with the first Mexicans they met is understandable. Having come so far, they had passed the point of no return. The Llano Estacado and its canyons were a terrible barrier between them and home, and even if they had retreated, they probably would not have reached Texas safely.

Fortunately we have several accounts of the trip. Kendall and Falconer each give considerable detail, and Kendall, being a professional writer, was especially successful at capturing the feel of the land. Loomis has done a good job of recounting the story and analyzing it.

The Hastings trip was important largely because of its success in spite of its amateurish approach to the journey and also because of the book that Hastings later published. This was widely read and greatly encouraged emigration. Almost anybody, it seemed, could get to Oregon or California. (It should also be noted that it was Hastings's advice that later led the fated Donner Party astray, for he recommended to them a route that he did not personally know.)

Frémont's story is told in the four-volume edition of his journals edited by Jackson and Spence and also in his own *Memoirs of My Life*. Nevins's biography of him gives a good—and somewhat briefer—picture of his career. Nevins has also edited a shorter edition of his travel narratives.

Hiram Chittenden in *The American Fur Trade of the Far West* quotes Bridger's letter to St. Louis, p. 475, in which he ordered supplies and told about his new business, although he implied that the fort was built in 1843 instead of 1842.

The quotations in this chapter are as follows: Kendall's description of the Kiowas' attack appears in his book, Vol. I, p. 221–22; the decision to divide the command, pp. 225–226; the canyon, p. 236; the storm, p. 237; the loneliness of the plains, pp. 240–241; the second canyon, pp. 244–245; Hastings's description of the dissentions among the emigrants appears on pp. 6, 7, and 9 of his book; the death of the wounded emigrant on p. 10; Frémont's description of the fur traders who tried to descend the Platte is on pp. 84–85 of his *Memoirs;* his description of Bent and St. Vrain's fort, p. 102; comment on the aridity of the Great Plains, p. 104; descriptions of Fort Laramie, pp. 111–112 and 113; and Linn's comments on the significance of Frémont's report were made when he was introducing a resolution to have the report printed and appear on p. 164 of Frémont's *Memoirs*.

The quotation about the routes to Oregon, which appears at the head of the chapter, is from a report prepared for the Senate Select Committee on Oregon and printed as 26th Congress, 1st Session, Senate Executive Document No. 174, p. 199.

Chapter 22
War with Mexico

The significance of the 1843 emigration was its startling increase over 1842, an increase of about 200 percent in a single year. This was enough to attract the politicians' attention and set in motion the steps necessary to make the journey safer and to end the joint occupation. The account by Johnson and Winter tells of their trip in some detail.

The principal references for following Frémont's expedition of 1843–1845 have been cited in the notes for the preceding chapter. His accomplishment lay not so much in being the "pathfinder," but in presenting the information he gained in a form that others could use.

Frémont and Audubon were not the only ones to be startled by the massacre of the buffaloes. As the reader may recall, I pointed out that Meriwether Lewis was amazed at the wanton slaughter by Indians. There is no question that the impact of the white hunters on the massive herds was devastating, but the Indians were also wasteful. Audubon's *Missouri River Journals* (a part of *Audubon and His Journals*), from which his quotation is taken, provide an excellent picture of the fur trade on the Upper Missouri during its final days. I go into further detail about his trip in my biography, *John James Audubon*.

Kearny's march is reported in 29th Congress, 1st Session, House Document No. 2, pp. 210–217. This contains his official report and extracts from a journal. Those wishing to read a sympathetic biography of Kearny might enjoy Clarke's.

Abert's journal of his 1845 expedition in the Southwest appears in 31st Congress, 1st Session Senate Executive Document No. 64. (This is supplemented by Isaac Cooper's account.) What makes his journal particularly interesting is his position as one of the first trained men to investigate and report on the area. Previous travelers had been there only on business.

The Mexican War had a direct and important bearing on the history of the Great Plains. Yet the war itself was mostly fought elsewhere. Therefore I have not dealt with it in much detail. Many of the documents pertaining to the annexation negotiations are contained in 28th Congress, 1st Session, House Document No. 271.

Kearny's march with the Army of the West is described in a number of journals. Among them are the journal of John T. Hughes, and the record kept by Edwards, both contained in 30th Congress, 1st Session, Senate Executive Document No. 23.

The quotations in this chapter are as follows: Johnson and Winter on the Santa Fé Trail, pp. 9–10 of their book; the hills near Chimney Rock, p. 17; the reaction of the people in Oregon to their arrival, pp. 39–40; Tyler's views on the Oregon question were expressed in his second annual message, December 6, 1842; Frémont on his reason for taking a more southern route west comes from his *Memoirs*, p. 170; his description of the emigrant trains, p. 170; the farm, p. 176; the soil of the Great Plains, pp. 180–181; his inability to find a new route through the Rockies, p. 187; his reason for taking an indirect route home, p. 398; the comments of the American Fur Company official on buffalo hunting are quoted on pp. 219–220 of Frémont's *Memoirs;* Audubon's comment appears in Vol. II of *Audubon and His Journals*, p. 107; Frémont's remarks on the diminution of the buffaloes appears on p. 219 of his *Memoirs;* the effect on the Indians, p. 220; Tyler's comments on Texas are contained in his message to the Senate, April 22, 1844; his recommendation to pass a resolution annexing Texas in his message of December 18, 1844; Frémont's comments on the purpose of the third expedition appear on p. 422 of his *Memoirs;* his description of the California question on p. 403; and the start of the expedition, p. 425; 29th Congress, 1st Session, House Executive Document No. 2, contains Kearny's description of the start of his expedition to South Pass, p. 210; his speech to the Indians, p. 211; his evaluation of the land between Fort Laramie and South Pass, p. 212; Abert's description of Bent's Fort is on p. 2 of his journal, which appears in 29th Congress, 1st Session, Senate Executive Document No. 438; his description of Fitzpatrick's usefulness, p. 6; their method of travel, p. 13; his comments on Raton Pass, pp. 17–18; his description of the hailstorm, pp. 24–25; the prairie fire, p. 31; the emigrants to Texas, pp. 74–75; Abert's discussion with Yellow Wolf is contained in 30th Congress, 1st Session, Senate Executive Document No. 23, p. 6; his description of Las Vegas, p. 28; the failure of the Mexicans to appear outside Las Vegas comes from Hughes's account that appears in Connelley, p. 191; the quotation from Polk at the end of the chapter comes from his annual message of December 5, 1848.

The quotation from Polk that appears at the head of the chapter is from his message to Congress, May 11, 1846.

Chapter 23
Gold!

Polk's annual message of 1848 mirrored the nation's mood in that year. With its enormous territorial acquisitions, it was moving into a new era, and the prospects looked bright.

A good general account of the actual discovery of gold will be found in Bean. Even Marshall and Sutter were not at first aware of the importance of the find, for otherwise they would have dropped everything else to concentrate on the placers.

The western emigration of the gold rush was a mass exodus of people, thousands of them all at once. Among that many people, a number were bound to recognize that the experience was historic and keep journals either for publication or for their own families. Some were published in their writers' lifetimes, some were published later, and some are still in manuscript form. Among those that I have particularly drawn on for this account are: Gibson, Stansbury, Delano, and Geiger; and Bryarly, Gould, and Staples as presented by Hannon, Shaw, and Manley.

Although relatively uneventful and unspectacular, Marcy's expedition to Santa Fé cannot be ignored, because it established an important east-west route that was used by many emigrants and later by John Butterfield's Overland Express. Marcy's journal appears in 31st Congress, 1st Session, Senate Executive Document No. 64. For those who would like to know more about Marcy, I would recommend his own *Thirty Years of Army Life on the Border* or Hollon's readable biography. Other accounts of army exploration of western Texas in 1849 are contained in the journals of Lieutenant Francis T. Bryam and Second Lieutenant N. Michler and the report of Second Lieutenant William F. Smith, which appear in the same Senate document as Marcy's journal.

A description of the Indian problems along the Texas frontier in 1847 is contained in the reports of the Indian agent, which appear in 30th Congress, 1st Session, Senate Executive Document No. 1. They also express his frustration at trying to enforce order over a large area with inadequate means. Garrard has left a good description of Fort Mann while it was being built and of the Indians' harassment as well as the attack on Russell's train. The death of the White family is described in Kit Carson's *Autobiography*, pp. 131–134. Inman also tells the story in *The Old Santa Fé Trail*, but he is confused about both the year and the circumstances.

The quotations in this chapter are as follows: Polk's recommendation of territorial status for California and New Mexico appears in his annual message of December 5, 1848; the statement of the San Francisco *Californian* on the effects of the gold rush is reprinted in Bean, p. 112; the report of the New York *Herald*, Brewerton, p. 15; the quotations from Polk are from his annual message of December 5, 1848; Shaw on the composition of the White Mountain Mining Company, p. 13 of his book; Delano on the steamboat, p. 15 of his; cholera on the boat, pp. 15–16; St. Joseph, p. 17; Shaw tells of purchasing mules, p. 18; the quality of the mules, p. 19; buying the spring wagon, p. 21; Delano on the numbers of wagons, p. 95; the wagons at night, pp. 71–72; Stansbury on deaths, pp. 15–16, 18–19, and 21; the grave with brandy, p. 71; the fur trader's remarks on inexperience, p. 18; the farmer and all his equipment, pp. 24–25; the burned wagons and other litter, p. 55; the collection of castoff articles, p. 63; Delano on the complicated government, p. 85; the "post office," p. 70; Stansbury on the blacksmith's shop at Scotts Bluff, p. 52; the ferry, pp. 60–61; the shortage of grass, p. 41, on the shortage of buffaloes, pp. 29

and 33–34; the emigrants naming the child Marcy appears in his journal, 31st Congress, 1st Session, Senate Executive Document No. 64, p. 182; his description of the Llano Estacado, p. 185; the Comanche's embrace, p. 187; his council with the Comanches, p. 189; the reports on conditions among the Texas Indians appear in 30th Congress, 1st Session, Senate Executive Document No. 1, pp. 902 and 905; the attacks on Fort Mann are in Garrard, pp. 255–256; the Sioux fighting the Pawnees appears in Delano, p. 49; and the Sioux and cholera, Stansbury, pp. 43 and 44–45.

The quotation from James K. Polk at the head of the chapter comes from his annual message of December 5, 1848.

Chapter 24
A Treaty and a Battle

The discussion of the Compromise of 1850 is greatly oversimplified, for a number of other problems, such as the fugitive slave laws in the District of Columbia, were also included. But the immediate effect of the compromise on the Great Plains was primarily the establishment of New Mexico as a territory and the settlement of the boundary dispute between New Mexico and Texas.

The early part of Hafen's book, *The Overland Mail*, gives a good overall picture of the overland mails in their early days. Inman tells about the stage service on the Santa Fé Trail. Gates, pp. 357–359, contains a discussion of the Chicago and Mobile Act.

Descriptions of the council held at Fort Laramie in 1851 can be found in the Report of the Indian Commissioner for that year and in Hyde's *Spotted Tail's Folk*, pp. 34–48, Nadeau, pp. 61–82, Grinnell's *The Fighting Cheyennes*, pp. 100–101, and in Chittenden's edition of de Smet, pp. 675–691. The treaty is referred to as the Horse Creek Treaty, the Fitzpatrick Treaty, or more commonly the Fort Laramie Treaty, although it was not actually signed there.

The description of the Oregon-California Trail in 1852 in this chapter is based on Ezra Meeker's account.

Grattan's defeat demonstrated that trained men, even when they were armed with howitzers, could not necessarily hold off a large number of determined Indians. As a consequence, the army investigated the affair thoroughly and the pertinent material was assembled in 33rd Congress, 2nd Session, House Document No. 63, which contains the statements of a number of persons who either saw the fighting or later talked to those who had. The absence of any American survivors helps to obscure the truth, but the accounts agree on most of the essential facts.

Other writers who have presented narrative accounts are Grinnell in *The Fighting Cheyennes*, pp. 104–108; Hyde in *Spotted Tail's Folk*, pp. 48–54, and Nadeau, pp. 83–110.

James Bordeaux (the name appears both with and without an *x*) is to me an appealing figure. Sometimes accused of being pompous, he nevertheless understood the Indians on the Platte better than almost anyone else around Fort Laramie. An interesting account of his life is contained in Hanson's article. Hanson was also instrumental in reconstructing a post that Bordeaux operated near Chadron, Nebraska, that is now open to the public.

In referring to the second trading post near Fort Laramie, I have called it the American Fur Company's post for simplicity's sake, just as many of Grattan's contemporaries did. The reader will remember, however, that the American Fur Company had sold out to Pierre Chouteau, Jr. & Company.

The quotations in this chapter are as follows: the Missouri *Commonwealth* on stage service to Santa Fé, Inman, p. 146; de Smet on the flooding Missouri, pp. 639–640 of Chittenden's edition of his book; Father Hoeken's death, pp. 641–642; the Sioux graves, p. 649; the Assiniboins hunting buffaloes, p. 658; description of the Oregon-California Trail, pp. 671–673; hospitality of the Indians at the council, p. 682; the distribution of the treaty presents, pp. 682–683; Meeker's general description of the wagon trains, pp. 61–64 of his account; the dust, pp. 70–72; and cholera, p. 80. The quotations concerning the Grattan Affair are from the statements included in 33rd Congress, 2nd Session, House Executive Document No. 63.

Fleming's reason for sending Grattan appear on p. 14; Fleming's orders, p. 20; Grattan's attitude, p. 23; Grattan's remarks to his men, p. 20; Bordeaux's comments on the excitement, p. 25; the observer's account of the battle, p. 21; Bordeaux's account of the night following the battle, pp. 25–26; Fleming's request for aid, p. 2; and the trader's opinion of the future, p. 16.

The quotation by Major Winship at the head of the chapter comes from 33rd Congress, 2nd Session, House Document No. 63, p. 7. He was serving as assistant adjutant general and was investigating the Grattan affair.

Brave Bear's name was obviously difficult to translate, because it appears in several forms, including Bear that Scatters.

Chapter 25
Slaves, Handcarts, and Oxen

The Kansas-Nebraska Act was, of course, one of the great national issues of the 1850s. I have treated it rather briefly, because, as I have pointed out in the text, its immediate effect was on the eastern areas of the new territories, not on the Great Plains.

For the account of life in eastern Colorado in the middle of the 1850s I have relied heavily on Dick Wootton (as told by Conard), who was one of the first to attempt to settle there permanently. I have also relied on his account of the destruction of the trading post at Pueblo. The significance of that event lay in its discouraging effect on would-be settlers in the area.

The incident of the man who was auctioned appears in Thomas D. Clark, p. 167. This was frontier humor at its worst and, it seems to me, illustrates the crude violence that prevailed in Kansas at that time.

Harney's report of his battle with Little Thunder appears in 34th Congress, 1st Session, Senate Executive Document No. 1, pp. 49–51. His report on the council at Fort Pierre and Jefferson Davis's instructions are contained in 34th Congress, 1st Session, House Executive Document No. 130.

The Mormons' use of handcarts to reach Utah is an amazing incident in the nation's history. Some writers have pointed out that walking the whole distance was not new, because the drivers of ox teams walked beside their animals. But that was different, because the drivers did not have to carry any part of the load, and the rest of the family could ride. Hafen's *Handcarts to Zion* not only provides the background for these journeys but also includes quite a number of the journals kept during them as well as rosters of the companies.

For a description of overland freighting, I have obviously relied on Wootton's reminiscences. As I have pointed out in the text, his experiences were typical of those of many men in the business.

The quotations in this chapter are as follows: Wootton's description of seeing the Indian's head, Conard, p. 284; the man hiding in the grave, p. 288; smallpox among the Utes, p. 289; illegal trade with hostile Indians, p. 292; emigrants arriving in Colorado, p. 297; Harney's comments on his battle with Little Thunder, 34th Congress, 1st Session, Senate Executive Document No. 1, pp. 49–50; Jefferson Davis's instructions to Harney appear in 34th Congress, 1st Session, House Executive Document No. 130, p. 4; Harney's comment on the Indians' form of government, p. 3; Harney's remarks on the Indians' condition, p. 2; the description of the Perpetual Emigration Fund Company appeared in the *Millennial Star*, January 26, 1856, and is reprinted in Hafen, *Handcarts to Zion*, pp. 34–35; Brigham Young's statement on the need to use handcarts, the *Millennial Star*, December 22, 1855, quoted in Hafen, pp. 29–30; the Council Bluffs *Bugle* on the faith of the emigrants, August 26, 1856, quoted in Hafen, p. 95; Wootton's description of a wagon train appears on pp. 305–306 of Conard's book; his description of the Mexican mutineers, pp. 323–324, 327.

The quotation from Chase at the head of the chapter is from a paper he helped prepare and distributed widely in an effort to defeat the Kansas-Nebraska Act. The full text can be found in Richard Hofstadter's *Great Issues in American History*, Vol. I, pp. 355–359.

Chapter 26
Gold Again

A principal source of information about the campaign against the Cheyennes is Hafen's *Relations with the Plains Indians, 1857–1861*. He has included the text of most of the official reports and correspondence as well as several journals of men who accompanied the expedition. Grinnell, in *The Fighting Cheyennes*, pp.112–123, also describes the expedition. He broadens the perspective through his discussion of the reaction of the Cheyennes, and is the authority for the statement that the Cheyennes whipped the men who asked the mail driver for tobacco. Other accounts, of course, are the Report of the Secretary of War and the Report of the Commissioner of Indian Affairs for 1857. Another that is available is Lowe's *Five Years a Dragoon*.

The Kansas constitution was a widely debated issue in its day and one that brought out the worst in many people. Most general history books deal with it rather briefly, but the reader who wishes to learn something about it in detail will find many aspects of it discussed in 35th Congress, 1st Session, House Executive Report No. 377, a lengthy study carried out by a select committee of fifteen members. In addition to the postmaster general's reports, there are a number of other sources for those wishing to follow the story of the overland mail service. Hafen's *The Overland Mail* is one of the best. The Bannings' book is also interesting, particularly Captain William Banning's comments on driving a stage, which he had done.

In describing the Indian problems on the southern Great Plains during 1858, I have omitted many incidents. As many of these were unrelated and scattered, weaving them into a cohesive picture would take up much space, but I have tried to point out the army's problems in attempting to patrol so vast an area against warlike tribes without enough men. The reader who might wish to explore the story further will be interested in the report of the Department of Texas in 35th Congress, 2nd Session, House Executive Document No. 2.

The economic dependence of the Great Plains on the federal government is quite at variance with the individualistic spirit of its inhabitants. Yet there was no way they could have provided for themselves. For a report on road-building activities, see 35th Congress, 2nd Session, House Executive Document No. 108.

There are a number of good accounts of the ear-

ly search for gold in Colorado. Spencer, who is a descendant of the Russells, tells the story well, and had, of course, access to family memories. She is the source for the story of how Green Russell both dressed and braided his beard. Hafen's *Pike's Peak Gold Rush Guidebooks* contains much excellent material, including Luke Tierney's guidebook in which he relates the experiences of the Russell Party, as well as other contemporary accounts. A more general book on mining is Young's. It gives the history of the Colorado exploration as well as those that took place in other parts of the West and contains interesting information about mining techniques. Dorset's book makes enjoyable reading for the general reader and covers Colorado's gold mining days in lively style. Of course, much of the actual mining eventually took place in the mountains to the west of the Great Plains. The remarks about Mrs. Holmes were contained in a letter written by one of the men and later published in the Lawrence (Kansas) *Republican* of July 15, 1858, and reprinted in part by Hafen as a footnote to p. 62.

The quotations in this chapter are as follows: Sumner's comments on the Indians' appearance at the time of the battle appear in his report contained in the Report of the Secretary of War in 35th Congress, 1st Session, Senate Executive Document No. 2, pp. 96–97, which is also reproduced in Hafen, *Relations with the Indians of the Plains*, pp. 26–28; the Indian agent's account of the reason why the Cheyennes were so calm and the aftermath of the attack appear in the Report of the Commissioner of Indian Affairs, 1857, pp. 141–148, and also in Hafen, pp. 32–43 (the quotation can be found on pp. 41–42); the descriptions of the voting in Kansas appear in 35th Congress, 1st Session, House Executive Report No. 377, pp. 247, 244–45; Stephens's comments on the free-soilers are in the same document, p. 13; the description of the arrival of the coach at San Francisco is from the San Francisco *Bulletin*, October 16, 1858, and is reprinted in Hafen, *The Overland Mail*, pp. 94–95; the Indian agent's comments on the reservation Indians, 35th Congress, 2nd Session, House Executive Document No. 2, p. 252; the governor of Texas's request for help, p. 249; the possibility of a general war, p. 263; the visit of Satanta to the reservation, p. 264; Van Camp's explanation of his conduct, p. 265; Twiggs's letter, p. 267;

Twiggs's comments on Van Camp's death, p. 277; the road superintendent's description of his business activities is in 35th Congress, 2nd Session, House Executive Document No. 108, p. 47; Tierney's description of the Rockies is from his guidebook, which Hafen has reprinted in full in his *Pike's Peak Gold Rush Guidebooks,* where the description appears on p. 102; the gold at Ralston Creek, p. 107; the prospectors' consultation, p.

108; their determination to find the source of the gold, pp. 118–119; Wootton on the need to lend money appears on pp. 358–359 of Conard's book; the execution, pp. 363–364; and the poverty of many of the emigrants, pp. 367–368.

The quotation from Horace Greeley that appears at the head of the chapter will be found on p. 96 of his *An Overland Journey.*

Chapter 27
Speed Across the Plains

The army's experiment with camels had little effect on the Great Plains, because the Civil War was soon occupying the military's attention with more serious matters; but it has become such an integral part of our folklore that I have included it. The story is told in 36th Congress, 1st Session, Senate Executive Document No. 2, pp. 422–441.

The influence of mining on the Great Plains, although indirect, was important. The discovery of gold in California stimulated the Western migration; and the mines in Colorado, although off the plains proper, had an even greater influence, because they directly contributed to the growth of Colorado cities such as Denver, Auraria, and Golden on the western edge of the Great Plains. Those wanting more information I would refer to the notes for the preceding chapter.

Horace Greeley's description of the Great Plains and mines is important. He was an accurate and experienced observer. Probably his writing did more than almost anyone else's to make the general public aware of what that part of the country was really like. It may be of passing interest that I used to know one of his daughters well and spent many happy hours in her house. I once owned a pair of handsome gold cuff links that she gave me, which I have since passed on to another member of my family. Such gentle ladies as she do not often come our way.

The impact on this country of the miners' improvised laws is an interesting subject. A classic study is Shinn's.

For Butterfield's problems along the southern route, I would again refer an interested reader to the Bannings' book; 36th Congress, 1st Session, Senate Executive Document No. 2, pp. 639–699, deals with the Texans' attack on the reservation.

Hafen's *Relations with the Indians of the Plains* contains the pertinent documents concerning Indian activity on the central Great Plains.

Although the Pony Express lasted only a short time and was a financial disaster for its promoters, it captured the imagination of Americans. Majors's account is interesting, particularly because of his position in the firm. Two other good books are the Settles' and Bloss's. Other sources of information are the congressional documents dealing with mail contracts during the period and the House's report on Russell's financial dealings. Visitors to St. Joseph, Missouri—a delightful, interesting city perched on the edge of the Missouri River—should not overlook the Pony Express Museum. The stables have been restored, and one can almost hear the sound of hoofbeats.

The pertinent documents covering the campaigns of 1860 against the Kiowas and Comanches are contained in Hafen's *Relations with the Indians of the Plains.*

The quotations in this chapter are as follows: the orders concerning the camels appear in 36th Congress, 1st Session, Senate Executive Document No. 2, pp. 422–423; the docility of the camels and the shifting of their saddles, both on p. 425; the belligerent attitude of the mules, p. 431; Horace Greeley on Station Eight of the express, p. 63 of *An Overland Journey;* the next station, pp. 64–65; the prairie dogs, p. 78; water erosion, pp. 79–80; discouraging reports on gold, p. 70; his changing opinion on the abundance of gold, p.97; the accident, p. 87; the village at Gregory's Diggings, pp. 103–104; the chances of making a fortune, p. 105; his description of the people in the West, pp. 131–132; the lack of danger in western travel, p. 153; Bent's remarks on the Indians in 1858 appear in a letter he wrote to the superintendent of Indian affairs contained in the National Archives and reprinted in Hafen, *Relations with the Indians of the Plains,* pp. 173–174; his comments in 1859 after the treaty are in a similar report contained in the Annual Report of the commissioner of Indian affairs for that year, pp. 137–139, and reprinted in Hafen, pp. 183–187; Majors on Hockaday and Liggett, his *Seventy Years on the Frontier,* p. 165; the pledge his employees had to sign, p. 73; his description of the results he obtained, pp. 72–73; Burton's comments on the results of Majors's personnel policies, his *City of the Saints,* p. 8.

The quotation from Majors that appears at the head of the chapter is from *Seventy Years on the Frontier,* pp. 173–175.

Chapter 28
A War and a Railroad

References on the Pony Express appear in the notes to Chapter 27. The degree of Russell's guilt in accepting the bonds was never determined. He denied at first that he knew that Bailey had illegally appropriated them, although Bailey told him when he took the second lot. At that point he was over his head and grabbed at the only chance of survival, legal or illegal. Bailey's motives are not at all clear. Mark Twain's description of the rider is extremely well known, and it deserves to be. A great American writer was describing a great, romantic sight in American history.

The Pony Express was a commercial failure, the telegraph a commercial success. The one became one of the most romantic episodes in our history, the other proceeded so efficiently that it left behind it far fewer tales. A good short account of the stringing of the line is in Dick, pp. 301–311.

For an interesting treatment of the Morrill and Homestead acts, I would suggest the reader look at Gates's book. Both of these acts had a profound effect on the development of the nation, and they opened doors of opportunity to all.

Because railroads were once so important economically in this country and also because they caught the people's imagination as few other industries have done, many books have been written about them. General accounts of the establishment of the Union Pacific and Central Pacific railroads can be found in Oscar Lewis, Howard, Stover, Riegel, and Ames. In writing his book, Ames, of course, had the purpose of vindicating his forebears but, despite the temptation of prejudice, has done an exhaustive job. He also has the advantage of practical experience in finance, which gives him first-hand familiarity with some of the problems faced by the organizers of the Union Pacific.

The Credit Mobilier eventually became the subject of an intense investigation by the House during the Third Session of the Forty-Second Congress. The reports it issued are numbers 77, 78, 81, and 82. Gates ably discusses the subject of railroad land grants.

Robinson contains a good account of Sibley's campaign and reprints the recollections of one of the participants, which first appeared in 1889. Sitting Bull's part in the fighting is confirmed by his winter count, which later fell into the hands of white men.

Grinnell's *The Fighting Cheyennes* covers much of the build-up of war in Colorado. His sympathies are mostly with the Indians. The subject is also covered in the Report of the Joint Committee on the Conduct of the War, 38th Congress, 2nd Session (serial 1214), and in the Report of the Special Joint Commiteee on the Condition of the Indian Tribes, 39th Congress, 2nd Session. Ware, pp. 104–118, gives a vivid picture of the meeting at Camp Cottonwood.

Robinson also discusses Sully's campaign to the Yellowstone. (Both Buck and Riggs were themselves present at some of the earlier events in Minnesota.) Mrs. Kelly's story is an extremely interesting one and well worth reading. It is especially important, because it tells what was going on among the Indians at the time. (Obviously, in time she was rescued.)

The references mentioned earlier in the notes to this chapter also cover the Sand Creek incident and its outcome. Ware tells the story of the attack on Fort Sedgwick and the firing of the prairie. Sand Creek was a controversial affair with the pro-Chivington and anti-Chivington forces in fierce opposition: and even today it arouses strong emotions among some persons. I can recall one woman recently who became practically neurotic when the subject was brought up. (On the other hand, the whole Indian question had her confused, because she wanted to picture Geronimo on his raids crazed with whiskey, disregarding the fact that whiskey was rarely available to him.) Indians are still an emotional topic. Although I find Chivington's conduct unjustifiable, I can understand that it was the outcome of the fear and panic into which many had fallen.

Mark Twain's description of the Pony Express appears in Vol. I, pp. 52–54, of *Roughing It;* the remarks of the Commissioner of Indian Affairs on the Western Sioux and the report of the agent at St. Pierre appear in 37th Congress, 3rd Session, Message of the President of the United States, Vol. II, pp. 71–72; the cavalry officer's description of the battle first appeared in the *Monthly South Dakotian,* October, 1899, and is reprinted in Robinson, pp. 219–320; John Evans on the attitude of the Indians toward going to war with the Americans, p. 44, of the Report of the Joint Special Committee

on the Condition of the Indian Tribes, 39th Congress, 2nd Session, Senate Report No. 156; his conversation with Little Owl and Little Owl's successor, p. 45; Gerry's attempt at holding a council, p. 46; Evans's proclamation to the Indians, Report of the Joint Committee on the Conduct of the War, 38th Congress, 2nd Session, p. 61; Mrs. Kelly's description of the battle, pp. 99–103, in her account; the plight of the Indians, pp. 106–107; the general's request for more men to guard the Platte appears in Report of the Joint Committee on the Conduct of the War, 38th Congress, 2nd Session, p. 63; Evans's plea to the Secretary of War, p. 66; Anthony's discussion with the Indians at Sand Creek, p. 8; the *Rocky Mountain News's* comments on the Sand Creek fight, p. 56; and the trader's comments, p. 15.

The quotation from Horace Greeley appearing at the head of the chapter is on p. 324 of his *An Overland Journey.*

Chapter 29
Stalemate

The best single source on Connor's campaign and on Sawyers's expedition is Hafen's *Powder River Campaigns and Sawyers's Expedition: 1865.* In it he has collected the official reports as well as some of the personal journals of the men who participated. The story they tell is one of the difficulty of maneuvering against an elusive enemy in unfamiliar country. Particularly with Cole and Walker, the struggle was not so much with the Indians as with the land itself. Those interested in pursuing the whole federal road-building program further will find W. T. Jackson's book helpful.

Some general sources for the construction of the railroad have been given in the note to Chapter 28. Although Dodge came in for censure when it was discovered that he, too, owned a few shares of the Credit Mobilier, he was a competent engineer, and his employment by the Union Pacific marked a turning point in that railroad's history. His first-hand story *How We Built the Union Pacific Railway* was first issued as a congressional document and since then has been reprinted separately. It is one of the classics of railroading, but the reader should remember that it was written some time after the event and therefore contains a few minor er-

rors and also that Dodge occasionally makes himself appear more important than he was, a human and forgivable failing.

There are a number of sources for the events that took place at Fort Philip Kearny. Perhaps the most important is 50th Congress, 1st Session, Senate Executive Document No. 33. This contains Carrington's own defense, and many of the papers that related directly to the fort and the troubles there. Frances Carrington, who was then married to another officer, also left an account. (The army encouraged officers to take their wives to frontier posts.) Grinnell in *The Fighting Cheyennes* gives the story as he heard it from the Indians, as does Mari Sandoz in *Crazy Horse.*

General Orders No. 66 appears in Richardson, Vol. VI, pp. 286–287; Connor's orders and Pope's reaction to them are reprinted in Hafen's *Powder River Campaign,* pp. 36, 42, 43; Dodge's message urging Connor to hurry, p. 39; the soldier's description of the battle with the Arapahoes originally appeared in the *Transactions of the Nebraska State Historical Society,* 1887, and is reprinted in Hafen, pp. 129–134; Sawyers's report is contained in 39th Congress, 1st Session, House Executive

Document No. 58, and is reprinted in Hafen. Sawyers's complaints about the inadequacy of the escort appear on p. 228, and the outcome of his parley with the Indians, p. 255; Walker's and Cole's reports are also reprinted in Hafen: Walker's description of the Badlands, p. 94; Cole's complaints and his description of his men, p. 82; the arrival of the Pawnee scouts, p. 83; Bowles's description of travel across the Great Plains appears on pp. 5 and 11 of his account; Sherman's report on the Union Pacific Railroad is in 39th Congress, 2nd Session, House Executive Document No. 23 (serial 1288), p. 2; Dodge's description of the construction of the road appears in his account, pp. 13–15; the quotation concerning the similarity of the treaties is from the report of the Northwestern Treaty Commission, 39th Congress, 2nd Session, House Executive Document No. 1 (serial 1284), p. 171; Carrington's message to Omaha about the need for more ammunition is in 50th Congress, 1st Session, Senate Executive Document No. 33, p. 6; his message about false security, p. 13; and the description of the mood in the fort after the battle, Frances Carrington, p. 150.

Stanton's orders, which appear at the head of the chapter, can be found in Richardson, Vol. VI, p. 283.

Chapter 30
Cowboys and Farmers

As I have tried to point out in the text, there was no simple solution to the Indian problem, although may simplistic ones were offered. Hancock's expedition along the Arkansas River is reported in 41st Congress, 2nd Session, House Report No. 240 (serial 1425), pp. 78–92. Its importance was not that it accomplished something but rather that it accomplished practically nothing and could not have. Expeditions such as his were exercise except as a temporary show of force.

Although the Wagon Box and Hayfield Fights involved relatively few Americans, they are favorite incidents among those who like stories about the West, largely because the Americans fought so bravely and so well. Good descriptions of them appear in *Great Western Indian Fights*, written by the Potomac Corral of the Westerns.

One interesting feature of the 1867 peace conference was the presence of Henry Stanley, the noted journalist who later went to Africa to locate David Livingstone.

In discussing the early days of the Texas cattle business, I chose McCoy, particularly, because of his importance as the person who finally found a way of making the business practical and of taking advantage of the vast herds in Texas. The drives themselves have been so thoroughly treated in so many books that I have not dealt with them in detail. Actually they occupied only a small part of the average cowhand's time, occurring as they did only once a year; and of course, only a small number of cowboys went with them. Instead I have tried to point up some aspects of the cowboys' life that do not generally receive so much attention.

Violence among cowboys has been grossly exaggerated. They were not violent men, although they did occasionally shoot out the lights and engage in other youthful pranks. It was General Crook, I believe, who pointed out that while fighting the Apaches, cowboys played no role of consequence. The work of tracking down human beings was just outside their capabilities. Hollon's excellent *Frontier Violence* reinforced my own thinking and led me to do some statistical work of a preliminary sort, taking into account that this was a young male population, among which the crime rate is usually the highest. The cowboy society comes off well on this basis.

For my description of the cowboys, I have not cited particular sources, since these observations are largely drawn from personal experience as well as the reading of years.

My choice of Lindsborg as a typical farming community is based on its having preserved much of its past, so its origin is clear. It is also a nice spot, and I like it, which perhaps in itself is reason enough. What I wanted was a specific community that would represent the many that were beginning to be established on the edge of the Great Plains.

The statement of the Commissioner of Indian Affairs will be found in 40th Congress, 1st Session, Senate Executive Document No. 13 (serial 1308) in the report entitled Indian Hostilities, p. 10; the speech of the Crow at the 1867 Laramie conference, Stanley, Vol. I, pp. 268–270; the condition of the Texas cattle herds at the close of the Civil War, McCoy, p. 20; the results of the 1867 investigation into Spanish fever, "Diseases of Cattle in the United States," 41st Congress, 2nd Session, House Document unnumbered (serial 4430), p. 179; description of Dougherty's experiences, McCoy, pp. 24–27; his dealings with the Missouri Pacific, p. 43; his description of Abilene, p. 44;

and his reasons for choosing Abilene, p. 50. The quotation about buffalo chips is from a Meade County, Kansas, newspaper in 1879 and is included among the exhibits of the Lindsborg, Kansas, Historical Society.

The quotation from the secretary of the interior appears in 40th Congress, 2nd session, House Executive Document No. 1 (serial 1326), p. 10.

Chapter 31
Off the Reservations

For de Smet's visit to the Indians I have drawn on his own account, as edited by Chittenden. I have not dealt in detail with the peace council, for it was much like the others, with neither side really understanding the other. Major Dye, the commander at Fort Laramie, had a difficult assignment. When he heard that Red Cloud was coming, he wired for instructions, but the telegraph line was down—perhaps a pole had been knocked over by an itchy buffalo. The account of the signing appears in the report he made, which is in the National Archives, LR Upper Platte Agency, W1184–1868.

Fortieth Congress, 3rd Session, House Executive Document No. 1, pp. 1–21, gives the account of Sheridan's attempt to put down the Indians' uprising. Grinnell tells the story more from the Indians' point of view in the *Fighting Cheyennes,* pp. 277–297. Miles discusses it in *Personal Recollections,* pp. 145–150. Custer in *My Life on the Plains* tells of his own role in it. Leckie has written a clear account, pp. 63–87, that would be helpful to any reader wishing more detail. Keim's report is, of course, excellent. He personally observed much of the action or talked with those who had.

Custer in *My Life on the Plains* gives a vivid description of the battle at the Washita and his subsequent campaigning, although he greatly overestimates the numbers of Indians involved in the battle. I have omitted details about the fight because it took place east of the Great Plains. It needs to be mentioned, however, because it affected the Americans' relations with the Cheyennes.

The notes to preceding chapters contain some of the references to the railroads and their progress.

Ames, pp. 338–339, has a good description of who was and was not at the joining of the lines and why. In tracing the progress of railroads, the reports of the secretary of the interior are especially helpful, for he was required to inspect all those receiving government assistance and inform Congress of their progress.

The quotations in this chapter are as follows: de Smet describing his meeting with the Sioux, p. 910 of his account; his leaving the flag, p. 917; Red Cloud's signing the treaty is described in a report in the National Archives, Dye to Ruggles, November 20, 1868, LR Upper Platte Agency, W1184–1868; the commander of the Department of Dakota on the Sioux, 40th Congress, 3rd Session, House Executive Document No. 1 (serial 1367), p. 34; Sheridan on the attitude of the Indians, p. 10; the reaction of the Cheyennes to withholding their ammunition, p. 11; on the courage of Forsyth's men, p. 18; Sheridan's objectives during his winter campaign, 41st Congress, 2nd Session, House Executive Document No. 1 (serial 1412), p. 42; Sheridan's arrival at Camp Supply, Keim, p. 102; the charge into the valley of the Washita, Custer, *My Life on the Plains,* pp. 334–335; his capture of the Indian hostages, pp. 567–571; the comments of the secretary of the interior on the condition of the Union Pacific will be found in 40th Congress, 3rd Session, House Executive Document No. 1 (serial 1366), pp. VII, IX, XII.

The quotation at the head of the chapter appears in Richard Burton's *The City of the Saints,* pp. 376-377.

Chapter 32
Indians and Cattletowns

The establishment of Yellowstone National Park was an extremely important social act, for it was the first time that a nation as a whole had set up a park for the use of the people as a whole. There are numerous sources of information about the origin of Yellowstone. One of the most familiar is Chittenden, *The Yellowstone National Park.*

Miliitary conditions on the southern Great Plains are described in 42nd Congress, 3rd Session, House Executive Document No. 1 (serial 1558), pp. 54–60.

Congress's investigation into the status of Indian affairs is contained in "Investigation of Indian Frauds," 43rd Congress, 3rd Session, House Report No. 98 (serial 1578). This represented a serious attempt on the part of Congress to reassess the whole Indian question.

Much material on Custer's expedition to the Black Hills is contained in his report, which was printed as 43rd Congress, 2nd Session, Senate Executive Document No. 32. The Beinecke Library at Yale contains some additional dispatches from Custer. Elizabeth Custer in *Boots and Saddles* reprinted some of Custer's letters, and Maguire contains the journal of an officer on the expedition. Donald Jackson's book is a good study of the expedition.

There are numerous descriptions of the professional buffalo hunters, who massacred the great herds without restraint or regard for the future. Dodge made a study of them in his *The Plains of the Great West,* pp. 119–144. He also estimated the number that were killed in the 1870s. In defense of the buffalo hunters, perhaps it should be noted that as Texas ranching became more profitable, there would have inevitably been a conflict between buffaloes and cattle for the range. Undoubtedly the cattle, being worth more, would have won out, for their owners would have cleared the range of buffaloes.

The fighting on the southern Great Plains in 1874 is covered in 43rd Congress, 2nd Session, House Executive Document No. 1. (serial 1635), pp. 40–44. Miles deals with it in *Personal Recollections,* pp. 156–181, and Grinnell discusses it in *The Fighting Cheyennes,* pp. 319–327. One of the best summaries of the fights at Adobe Walls and Palo Duro Canyon is contained in the Potomac Corral's book. That also includes a description of Ronald Mackenzie by one of his friends. Miller

and Snell, pp. 197–200, reprint some of the original newspaper accounts of the battle of Adobe Walls.

The development of the cowtowns was an interesting phenomenon, and the competition between them was intense. Considering that they collected a good deal of the scum of the nation, it is surprising that the crime rate was not higher. Aside from contemporary accounts, there are a number of excellent books on the subject. Among others, I would recommend Dykstra, Miller and Snell, Drago on the cattle trails and also Streeter. Hollon, Jordon, and Shirley are all interesting on the question of law enforcement.

To Mrs. Acre of Abilene, Kansas, I am indebted for the story about Hickock. Her father was the small boy.

Several of the towns, such as Abilene, Wichita, and Dodge City, have reconstructed their old towns. The individual exhibits vary in quality. Some are extremely interesting, some are just fun (but what is wrong with that?), and some are . . . In any case, I think most people happening to be near any of those towns would find them worth visiting.

The quotations in this chapter are as follows: the skeptical attitude of the explorers of the Yellowstone is quoted in Chittenden, *The Yellowstone National Park,* p. 69; Doane's report, quoted in Chittenden, p. 70; the text of the act establishing the Yellowstone National Park appears in 42nd Congress, 2nd Session, House Report unnumbered, Geological Survey of the Territories (serial 1520), pp. 164–165; the references to the winter campaign against the Blackfeet will be found in 41st Congress, 3rd Session, House Executive Document No. 1 (serial 1446); the comments on military conditions in Texas, 42nd Congress, 3rd Session, House Executive Document No. 1 (serial 1558), p. 55; the discussion of Indian treaties, 42nd Congress, 3rd Session, House Report No. 98 (serial 1578), pp. 6, 7; the Indian Commissioner on delegations going to Washington, 42nd Congress, 3rd session, House Executive Document No. 1 (serial 1560), pp. 486–487; Custer's report of finding gold in 43rd Congress, 2nd Session, Senate Executive Document No. 32, which contains many of the dispatches Custer sent as well as a report of the expedition; the comments of the Commissioner of Indian Affairs on the expedition,

43rd Congress, 1st Session, House Executive Report No. 1 (serial 1639), pp. 316–317; the description of the professional buffalo hunters, Dodge, *The Plains of the Great West,* pp. 134–138; Miles's description of the Indians' flight to the Llano Estacado, *Personal Recollections,* pp. 166–167, 170; McCoy on the cattle market of 1873, his account, p. 151; the excerpts of the ordinances of Abilene are from those displayed by the Abilene Historical Society; and the quotations

from the songs are from memory. There were many versions of each one, so the reader's may not be the same as mine. Some, too, were particularly adapted to an almost endless addition of new verses. One of these was "The Chisholm Trail," a few lines of which appear in the text.

The quotation from Sheridan at the head of the chapter appears in 43rd Congress, 1st Session, House Executive Document No. 1 (serial 1597), p. 42.

Chapter 33
At the Little Bighorn

Any reader wishing to pursue further the subjects mentioned in the first part of this chapter will find most of them well treated in the books recommended in Chapter 32 in relation to the cattle trade.

Jenney's report is contained in 44th Congress, 1st Session, Senate Executive Document No. 51. Its importance was twofold: it confirmed the reports that the Black Hills were filled with miners, and it also confirmed Custer's reports that gold was plentiful. After it appeared, there could be no holding back the prospectors.

The attitudes of the Indians in 1875 and the unsuccessful attempt of the commissioners to negotiate a new agreement with the Sioux are described in the Annual Report of the Commissioner of Indian Affairs for 1875. Giroud, who had been captured earlier by the Sioux, was one of the messengers sent to persuade those living in the north to come to the council. He gives an interesting picture of his meeting with Sitting Bull, pp. 75–85, which I have had to omit from the text.

Because of its importance and its startling outcome, the campaign waged by the army in 1876 produced a considerable amount of source material. In addition to the usual official reports, the Battle of the Rosebud was covered by John Finerty, a reporter for the Chicago *Times.* He later wrote up his experience in *War-Path and Bivouac.* Another writer with Crook was John Bourke, an officer who served under him and who also wrote up his experience. Both men were naturally biased in favor of Crook. Yet their accounts seem fair and accurate. Another was Captain King, who later became a successful writer of Western tales.

Few events in Western American history have

received as much attention as the defeat of Custer. Graham's book includes a bibliography of some six hundred items, and that is not complete. The official account of the campaign that year will be found in 44th Congress, 2nd Session, House Executive Document No. 1 (serial 1742), pp. 27–29. Elizabeth Custer in *Boots and Saddles* tells of the departure of the Seventh Calvalry. Bradley was with the Montana Column and was the first white American to learn about Custer's defeat. (That part of his account is particularly moving.) Utley's book is excellent, and includes the photographs of the terrain on which he has marked the routes followed by the troops. This is expecially helpful to one who has not visited the battlefield. There are also the proceedings at Reno's court-martial later on. A copy of these was made available to me at the Beinecke Library at Yale. An excellent—and more easily available—volume is Graham's *The Custer Myth.* This contains many of the pertinent documents, including some of the Indian accounts.

The quotations from Jenney's report concerning the miners are in 44th Congress, 1st Session, Senate Executive Document No. 51, pp. 11,13; the report of the agent at Standing Rock on the Indians' reaction to the Black Hills, Annual Report of the commissioner of Indian affairs for 1875, pp. 244–245; the conclusions of the peace commissioners are contained in their report, pp. 184–205 of the Annual Report of the commissioner of Indian affairs for 1875; the army officer's comments on the situation at the close of 1875 are contained in Bourke, p. 244; the recommendation of the inspector appears in 44th Congress, 1st Session, Senate Executive Document No. 81; the officer's comments on the outcome of Reynolds's battle,

Bourke, p. 281; the newspaper reporter on the Battle of the Rosebud, Finerty, pp. 141–146; the reaction of the men to Reno's report appeared in an account by General Edward Godfrey that first appeared in the *Century Magazine* in 1892 and is reprinted in Graham, pp. 129–130; the officer's comments on Custer's intentions, Bradley, p. 143; and Bradley's reaction to the news from the scouts, p. 154.

The quotation from Jenney's report that appears at the head of the chapter is from his report, 44th Congress, 1st Session, Senate Executive Document No. 51, p. 56.

Chapter 34
A Great Change

In addition to the official accounts of Crook's campaign, Bourke and Finerty have left more colorful ones with human detail that makes them come alive. King's book is also good.

Crook had behind him an excellent record as an Indian fighter, but his experience at the Rosebud seems to have momentarily shocked him. When he finally recovered himself, he again did the sort of campaigning for which he was so well known, traveling light, pushing his men to the utmost, and giving the Indians no rest.

Bourke's account continues to supplement the official accounts for the remainder of the 1876–1877 campaign as does Miles's *Personal Recollections*. Both men included details that did not find their way into the official reports.

Fort Robinson was the center of much of this activity, and it was there that Crazy Horse surrendered—and shortly afterward was killed. The State of Nebraska has restored it and, I think, done it well.

The end of the major Indian fighting on the Great Plains came, as I hope I have made the reader understand, in the same way that T. S. Eliot's world ends. There was no great battle with both sides in opposing lines. It was a war of attrition, one band at a time until suddenly it was over.

The subject of farming on the Great Plains would make a long book in itself, and the United States Department of Agriculture and many state agricultural stations are still trying to find answers to the particular problems that the area poses.

Dugouts can still be found on the Great Plains, some of them serving as temporary shelters, some reconstructed for historical purposes. One of the latter is in Palo Duro Canyon. To Mrs. Elsie Lloyd and Mrs. Amy Chubb of Kaycee, Wyoming, I am indebted for the story of the piano in the dugout. It was their father and mother's.

Welsch's monograph on sod houses is excellent. When he was writing it, he was surprised to find how many were still in use. A number of sod houses have also been constructed as museum exhibits. There is one, for example, in the historical society at Canyon, Texas. They are worth seeing.

Fite, pp. 55–74, treats the problems of the farmers in the 1870s. Even when life was hard, however, it was often better than what the immigrants had left behind.

The quotations in this chapter are as follows: Terry's report on Custer, 44th Congress, 2nd Session, House Executive Document No. 1, p. 31; Cody's assessment of Crook's problem, Finerty, p. 235; the comparison of Crook and Terry, p. 272; the description of the lieutenant, p. 267; Crook's decision to march to the Black Hills, pp. 275–276; the soldiers eating horsemeat, pp. 278–279; the town of Deadwood, pp. 319, 320, 322–324; Miles's description of Sitting Bull, Miles's *Personal Recollections*, p. 226; on artillery and the Indians, p. 228; Ranald Mackenzie's attack on Dull Knife's village, Bourke, pp. 392–393; Miles describing his artillery, *Personal Recollections*, pp. 297–298; Miles on the Indians' retreat, p. 238; the Sioux's speech to Miles, p. 243; Spotted Tail's willingness to help Crook, Bourke, p. 394; and the description of Crazy Horse, pp. 414–415.

The quotation from Bradbury appears on p. 272 of his book.

Chapter 35
A New Order

A colorful description of the Homestake Mine can be found in Casey, pp. 213–219, as well as in most books about the Black Hills. Better yet is a visit to the mine. Guides take visitors around the above-ground works, an experience, and the historical society has much information about the mine and the community. Lead (pronounced Leed) is in itself worth seeing. A typical mining community, it is wedged into the surrounding ravines.

Since the management and financing of the railroads occurred mostly off the plains, the space in the text devoted to them is necessarily small. For those who wish to explore this fascinating subject in greater detail I would recommend the references listed in earlier notes.

The reader who is interested in eastern and foreign investment in cattle and land will find Gressley's book excellent. White's is a fascinating study of the interrelationship between East and West and the influence of one on the other.

Although the flight of the Nez Percés was a fascinating part of Indian history and brought them to the Great Plains, I have not treated the subject in detail for it had little effect on the area except for the temporary restlessness it caused on the reservations. General Howard's report of their surrender can be found in 45th Congress, 2nd Session, House Executive Document No. 1 (serial 1794), starting on p. 119. A good account of the whole story is in Josephy's *Patriot Chiefs*.

The events at the Red Cloud agency leading to the death of Crazy Horse are discussed in Bourke, pp. 413–423. The accounts of his death are somewhat confused, because the action took place so quickly the witnesses were not sure. He may have been stabbed by a soldier; he may have been accidentally killed by one of the Indians.

Congress was a helpless giant in trying to cope with many of the nation's problems, including the Indians. The report on Dull Knife, including interviews with many of the persons involved, appears in 46th Congress, 2nd Session, Senate Report No. 28.

A good account of the military's attitude toward the Indian problem will be found in Gibbon's comments that appear in 45th Congress, 3rd Session, House Executive Document No. 1 (serial 1842), p. 69; Lamar's excellent book on Dakota, pp. 182–189, contains an interesting account of the investigations in Dakota into the Indian frauds and the resulting trials.

Sitting Bull's life in Canada is covered by Black. Additional details of his surrender are given in Allison and in Wade. Those readers who are interested in the war with the Sioux might enjoy my book *Sitting Bull,* in which I treat the subject in more detail.

For the section on guns and the Westerner's attitude toward them, I have relied on personal experience and observation. Books on gunfighters abound, and I like them and always have, even if they sometimes contain more glamor than truth. As an excellent reference book, I would recommend Miller and Snell. The authors have gone over all the contemporary accounts they could find and have brought them together for each of the outstanding figures. The picture that emerges is probably an extremely accurate one. Earlier when I was discussing violence, I mentioned several outstanding books on the subject, including Hollon's. The reader may wish to refer back to them.

Hickock's experience with the Underground Railroad is contained in a letter dated August 24, 1852, from Milton D. Harper, which is in the collection of the Adams Museum (no relation) in Deadwood, South Dakota. Harper's father was the other small boy. For other background of Tilghman, Earp, and Hickock, I have drawn on Miller and Snell.

For the part of this chapter dealing with the XIT ranch, I have used Haley's book as a reference. I have also consulted the XIT papers at the Panhandle-Plains Museum in Canyon, Texas, and a long association with some of the Farwell family has perhaps helped. Mothershead gives a good account of the Swan Company. An invaluable aid to any student of the big ranches is the Western Range Cattle Industry Study prepared by the Library of Congress. This consists of microfilm copies of the records of many ranches.

The description of the British establishment near Kaycee is from conversations with people who remember it. The description of the house of de Mores is from personal observation. Goplen's study tells about his activities. In addition to Roosevelt's own writing about his life in the West, Mattison's publications cover it well. The area is now a national park.

The reports of the commissioner of public lands for the first half of the 1880s tell the story of how the land was slipping away from the small individuals. Gates, pp. 482–483, tells the story succinctly.

The quotations in this chapter are as follows: the Secretary of War on the Nez Percés, 45th Congress, 2nd Session, House Executive Document No. 1 (serial 1794), p. 118; the officer on Crazy Horse, Bourke, p. 423; the Cheyennes' feelings about Indian Territory, 46th Congress, 2nd Session, Senate Report No. 28, p. XIX; the opinion of the congressional committee on using starvation as a weapon of compulsion, p. XVIII; Gibbon's comments on the Indian problem, 45th Congress, 3rd Session, Executive Document No. 1 (serial 1842), p. 69; The *Press and Dakotaian* on Shurz's investigation, March 29, 1878, quoted in Lamar, p. 183; Sitting Bull's remark on returning to the United States is in Black, p. 189; the Dodge City

Times's description of the shooting, the issue of July 27, 1878, quoted in Mller and Snell, p. 87; the newspaper descriptions of Roosevelt appeared in the *Bad Lands Cow Boy*, June 19 and 26, 1884, quoted in Mattison (*Roosevelt's Dakota Ranches*), p. 4; Roosevelt on the boat thieves, *Ranch Life and Hunting Trail,* pp. 120, 125, 127, 128; on the life of a rancher, p. 6; the quotations from the Commissioner of Public Lands in 1883 can be found in 47th Congress, 2nd Session, House Miscellaneous Document No. 45, Part 4 (serial 2158); his comments for the year 1885, 49th Congress, lst Session, House Executive Document No. 1 (serial 2378), pp. 167, 168.

The quotation from Stevenson at the head of the chapter is from *Across the Plains,* an account of a journey he made on an emigrant train. The date given is the year he made the trip, not the date of publication.

Chapter 36
The Heritage Lives

The story of the farmers on the Great Plains is a stirring one, although much of it belongs to the period that follows this book. Two contrasting descriptions are contained in Sandoz's *Old Jules* and in Jackson's *The Buffalo Wallow*—one dour, one happy.

Gates, p. 402, gives a record of the number of emigrants and the number of homesteads taken up. Several factors affected the intensity of homesteading at one time: among them, the availability of land and economic conditions in other parts of the country. Although the large "bonanza farms"—as they were called—had already developed east of the Great Plains, the large farms that we now associate with the area edged their way west at a later period. For information about early wheat farming, I am indebted, among other sources, to the Kansas Wheat Commission.

The council of 1883 is reported in 48th Congress, 1st Session, Senate Executive Document No. 283 (serial 2174). The Americans saw the pursuit of agriculture as a solution to the Indians' economic problems; the Indians did not want to abandon their old way of life; and the result was an impasse. The council of 1888 is reported in 50th Congress, 2nd Session, Senate Document No. 17

(serial 2610). Once again the Americans were trying to persuade the Indians that if they wished to survive in the white men's world, they must adopt some of the white men's ways.

One of the most important single sources for the Ghost Dance and the Battle of Wounded Knee (if battle it can be called) is the "Wounded Knee Box" in the National Archives. Here the staff of that remarkable institution has collected most of the pertinent papers concerning the two events. These include a report from an army officer sent out to observe the Ghost Dance at first hand, several reports of the Indian agent in charge of the Standing Rock agency, where Sitting Bull lived, and other documents of a like nature. They describe in detail the events leading up to Sitting Bull's death. The struggle at Wounded Knee Creek is covered in the Report of the Secretary of War for the year 1890. Those wishing to pursue the subject further may find both Miller's and Utley's books of interest, the one on the Ghost Dance and the other on the final struggle of the Sioux.

The Johnson County War can best be understood by visiting the country and the specific sites, supplemented by a reading of Smith's excellent book.

450 SUNLIGHT AND STORM

The quotations in this chapter are as follows: McLaughlin on Sitting Bull's effort at farming, the Annual Report of the commissioner of Indian affairs, 1883, p. 49; the exchange between Dawes and Red Fish, 48th Congress, 1st Session, Senate Executive Document 283 (serial 2174), p. 68; the two quotations from the 1888 conference, 50th Congress, 2nd Session, Senate Executive Document No. 17 (serial 2610), pp. 82, 89–90; the army officer's observations on the significance of the Ghost Dance are in a letter written by Major Wirt Davis in the Wounded Knee collection at the National Archives; the song and the description of the Ghost Dance, 52nd Congress, 1st Session, House Executive Document No. 1 (serial 2834), p. 53; McLaughlin's comments on Sitting Bull appear in his report of October 17, 1890, in the Wounded Knee collection; and Turner on the frontier appears in his essay.

The quotation from Owen Wister at the head of the chapter is from pp. 28–29 of *The Virginian*.

Selected Bibliography

When my editor and I began to realize the length to which the bibliography for this book was running, we were reminded of the French trapper who found that he had caught five beavers but that a male and female grizzly were also standing nearby. As he retreated into the bushes, he muttered to himself, *"De trop, de trop."*

As a consequence, I have limited the bibliography only to specific references cited in the notes and that are not fully identified there. This has, for example, meant the elimination of all manuscript collections as well as many fine works on the Great Plains that I have found useful and would like to have listed as well as all government documents (certain especially pertinent ones are identified in the notes.)

It has also meant eliminating many cross-references—for example, from author to translator. In most instances, only one of several possibilities has been retained.

I do, however, repeat the invitation that I made at the beginning of the notes. If anyone has a special question and will write me in care of my publisher, I will make every effort to answer.

ALLISON, E. H. *The Surrender of Sitting Bull.* Dayton, Ohio: The Walker Litho. and Printing Co., 1891.

AMES, CHARLES EDGAR. *Pioneering the Union Pacific: A Reappraisal of the Builders of the Railroad.* New York: Appleton-Century-Crofts, 1969.

AUDUBON, JOHN JAMES. *Audubon and His Journals.* Edited by Maria Audubon. 2 vols. New York: Dover Publications, 1960.

BAILEY, THOMAS A. *A Diplomatic History of the American People.* New York: Appleton-Century-Crofts, 1958.

BALDWIN, LELAND D. *The Keelboat Age on Western Waters.* Pittsburgh, Penn.: University of Pittsburgh Press, 1941.

BANNING, WILLIAM. *Six Horses.* With George Hugh Banning. New York: The Century Company, 1930.

BARTLETT, RUHL J., editor. *The Record of American Diplomacy: Documents and Reading in the History of American Foreign Relations.* New York: Alfred A. Knopf, 1954.

BEAN, WALTER. *California: An Interpretative History.* New York: McGraw-Hill Book Company, 1968.

BECKNELL, WILLIAM: "Journals of Capt. Becknell." *Missouri Historical Review.* Vol. IV, No. 2 (January, 1910), pp. 68–84.

BELL, JOHN R. *The Journal of Captain John R. Bell.* Edited and with introductions by Harlin M. Fuller and LeRoy R. Hafen. Glendale, Calif.: The Arthur H. Clark Company, 1957.

BEMIS, SANUEL FLAGG: Jay's Treaty: *A Study in Commerce and Diplomacy.* New Haven: Yale University Press, 1962.

BIDWELL, JOHN: *Echoes of the Past about California.* Edited by Milo Milton Quaife. Chicago: R. R. Donnelly & Sons, 1928. *A Journey to California.* With an introduction by Hebert Ingram Priestly. San Francisco: J. H. Nash, printer, 1937.

BISHOP, CURTIS. *Lots of Land.* Austin, Tex.: The Steck Company, 1949.

BISHOP, MORRIS. *Champlain: The Life of Fortitude.* New York: Alfred A. Knopf, 1948.

BLACK, NORMAN FERGS. *History of Saskatchewan and the Old North West.* Regina, Saskatchewan: North West Historical Company, 1913.

BLOSS, ROY S. *Pony Express—The Great Gamble.* Berkeley, Calif.: Howell-North, 1959.

BOLTON, HERBERT EUGENE and MARSHALL, THOMAS MAITLAND. *The Colonization of North America: 1492–1783.* New York: The Macmillan Company, 1956.

BOLTON, HERBERT E. *Coronado on the Turquoise Trail: Knight of Pueblos and Plains.* Albuquerque, N.M.: University of New Mexico Press, 1949.

———, editor. *Spanish Exploration in the Southwest: 1542–1706.* In addition to accounts of the Cabrillo-Ferrelo and Vizcaino Expedition, it contains these accounts concerning the Rodríguez Expedition: Pedro de Bustamante and Hernando Barrado's *Declarations* and the narrative of Escalante and Barrado. For the Espejo Expedition, it contains the account of Espejo and his letters to the viceroy and the king. For the Oñate Expedition, it contains the letter Juan Oñate wrote the viceroy in March, 1599 and other documents. New York: C. Scribner's Sons, 1916.

BOURKE, JOHN G. *On the Border with Crook.* Glorieta, N.M.: Rio Grande Press, 1969.

BOURNE, EDWARD GAYLOR, editor. *Narratives of the Career of Hernando de Soto.* This includes *The Conquest of Florida* as told by a Gentleman of Elvas, a *Relación* by Luys Hernandez de Biedma, both translated by Buckingham Smith, and an account of de Soto's expedition based on the diary of Rodrigo Ranjel, translated from Oviedo's *Historia General y Natural de las Indias.* It also contains an introduction by Bourne. 2 vols. New York: A. S. Barnes and Company, 1904.

BOWLES, SAMUEL. *Our New West: Records of Travel between the Mississippi River and the Pacific Ocean.* Hartford, Conn.: Hartford Publishing Co., 1869.

BRACKENRIDGE, HENRY MARIE. *Views of Louisiana, Together with a Journal of a Voyage up the Missouri River in 1811.* Chicago: Quadrangle Books, 1962.

BRADBURY, JOHN. *Travels in the Interior of America.* Ann Arbor, Mich.: University Microfilms, 1966.

BRADLEY, JAMES H. *The March of the Montana Column: A Prelude to the Custer Disaster.* Edited by Edgar I. Stewart. Norman, Okla.: University of Oklahoma Press, 1961.

BREWERTON, GEORGE DOUGLAS. *Overland with Kit Carson.* New York: Coward-McCann, 1930. With an introduction by Stallo Vinton.

BRONSON, CORNELIUS. *Jason Lee: Prophet of the New Oregon.* New York: The Macmillan Company, 1932.

BUCK, DANIEL. *Indian Outbreaks.* Minneapolis, Minn.: Ross & Haines, 1965.

BURTON, RICHARD F. *The City of the Saints and Across the Rocky Mountains to California.* Edited with an introduction by Fawn M. Brodie. New York: Alfred A. Knopf, 1963.

CAHALANE, VICTOR H. *Mammals of Northern America.* New York: The Macmillan Company, 1954.

CANNON, MILES. *Waiilatpu; Its Rise and Fall; 1836–1847; A Story of Pioneer Days in the Pacific Northwest.* Boise, Idaho: Capital News Job Rooms, 1915.

CARRINGTON, FRANCES C. *Army Life on the Plains.* Philadelphia: J. B. Lippincott Company, 1911.

CARSON, KIT. *Kit Carson's Autobiography.* Edited by Milo Milton Quaife. Lincoln, Neb.: University of Nebraska Press, 1967.

CASEY, ROBERT J. *The Black Hills and Their Incredible Characters.* Indianapolis: Bobbs-Merrill, 1949.

CATLIN, GEORGE. *Letters and Notes on the Manners, Customs, and Condition of the North American Indians.* 2 vols. New York: Wiley and Putnam, 1842.

CHAPMAN, CHARLES EDWARD. *Colonial Hispanic America: A History.* New York: The Macmillan Company, 1938.

CHITTENDEN, HIRAM MARTIN. *The American Fur Trade of the Far West.* With introduction and notes by Stallo Vinton and sketch of the author by Dr. Edmond S. Meany. 2 vols. New York: The Press of the Pioneers, 1935.

———, and RICHARDSON, ALFRED TALBOT. *Life, Letters and Travels of Father Pierre-Jean De Smet, S. J. 1801–1873.* 4 vols. New York: Francis P. Harper, 1905.

———. *The Yellowstone National Park.* Edited and with an introduction by Richard A. Bartlett. Norman, Okla.: University of Oklahoma Press, 1964.

CLARK, THOMAS D. *Frontier America: The Story of the Westward Movement.* New York: Charles Scribner's Sons, 1969.

CLARKE, DWIGHT L. *Stephen Watts Kearny: Soldier of the West.* Norman, Okla.: University of Oklahoma Press, 1961.

CONARD, HOWARD LOUIS. *Unclie Dick Wootton: The Pioneer Frontiersman of the Rocky Mountain Region.* Edited by Milo Milton Quaife. Chicago: The Lakeside Press, 1957.

CONNELLEY, WILLIAM ELSEY. *Doniphan's Expedition and the Conquest of New Mexico and California.* This also contains the original publication by John T. Hughes. Topeka, Kans.: published by the author, 1907.

COOPER, ISAAC (pseud., François des Montaignes). *The Plains, Being No Less Than a Collection of Veracious Memoranda Taken During the Expedition of Exploration in the Year 1845.* Edited and with an introduction by Nancy Alpert Mower. Norman, Okla.: University of Oklahoma Press, 1972.

COOPER, JAMES FENIMORE. *The Prairie: A Tale.* New York: Rinehart & Co., 1950.

CUSTER, ELIZABETH B. *Boots and Saddles or: Life in Dakota with General Custer.* Williamstown, Mass.: Corner House Publishers, 1969.

CUSTER, GEORGE A. *My Life on the Plains.* Edited with an introduction by Milo Milton Quaife. Lincoln, Neb.: University of Nebraska Press, 1966.

DALE, HARRISON CLIFFORD, editor. *The Ashley-Smith Exploration and the Discovery of a Central Route to the Pacific, 1822–1829 and the Original Journals.* Glendale, Calif.: Arthur H. Clark Company, 1941.

DELANO, ALONZO. *Life on the Plains and among the Diggings.* Ann Arbor, Mich.: University Microfilms, 1966.

DE LA VÉRENDRYE, PIERRE GAULTIER DE VARENNES. *Journal and Letters.* Edited with introduction and notes by Lawrence J. Burpee. Toronto: The Champlain Society, 1927.

DENIG, EDWIN THOMPSON. *Five Indian Tribes of the Upper Missouri: Sioux, Arickaras, Assinibones, Crees, Crows.* Edited and with an introduction by John C. Ewers. Norman, Okla.: University of Oklahoma Press, 1961.

DICK, EVERETT. *Vanguards of the Frontier: A Social History of the Northern Plains and Rocky Mountains from the Fur Traders to the Sod Busters.* Lincoln, Neb.: University of Nebraska Press, 1965.

DODGE, GRENVILLE M. *How We Built the Union Pacific Railway.* Ann Arbor, Mich.: University Microfilms, 1966.

DODGE, RICHARD IRVING. *The Plains of the Great West.* New York: Archer House, 1959.

―――. *Thirty-Three Years Among Our Wild Indians.* New York: Archer House, 1959.

DONNELLY, JOSEPH P. *Jacques Marquette, S.J.: 1637–1675.* Chicago: Loyola University Press, 1968.

DORSET, PHYLLIS FLANDERS. *The New El Dorado.* New York: The Macmillan Company, 1970.

DOUGLAS, WALTER B. *Manuel Lisa.* With hitherto unpublished material annotated and edited by Abraham P. Nasatir. New York: Argosy-Antiquarian Ltd., 1964.

DRAGO, HARRY SINCLAIR. *Great American Cattle Trails.* New York: Bramhall House, 1965.

DYKSTRA, ROBERT R. *The Cattletowns.* New York: Atheneum, 1970.

EDWARDS, FRANK S. *A Campaign in New Mexico.* Ann Arbor, Mich.: University Microfilms, 1966.

FALCONER, THOMAS. *Letters and Notes on the Texan Santa Fe Expedition, 1841–1842.* Edited by F. W. Hodge. New York: Dauber & Pine Bookshops, 1930.

FINERTY, JOHN F. *War-Path and Bivouac: The Big Horn and Yellowstone Expedition.* Edited by Milo Milton Quaife. Lincoln, Neb.: University of Nebraska Press, 1970.

FITE, GILBERT C. *The Farmers' Frontier, 1865–1900.* New York: Holt, Rinehart, and Winston, 1966.

FOWLER, JACOB. *The Journal of Jacob Fowler.* Edited with notes by Elliott Coues. New York. F. B. Harper, 1898.

FRÉMONT, JOHN CHARLES. *Memoirs of my life with a sketch of the life of Senator Benton by Jessie Benton Frémont.* Chicago: Belford, Clarke & Company, 1887.

―――. *Report of the Exploring Expedition of the Rocky Mountains.* Ann Arbor, Mich.: University Microfilms, 1966.

GARRARD, LEWIS H. *Wah-To-Yah and the Taos Trail.* With an introduction by A. B. Guthrie, Jr. Norman, Okla.: University of Oklahoma Press, 1955.

GATES, PAUL W. *History of Public Land Law.* With a chapter by Robert W. Swenson. Washington, D.C.: U.S. Government Printing Office 1968.

GEIGER, VINCENT and BRYARLY, WAKEMAN. *Trail to California: The Overland Journal of Vincent Geiger and Wakeman Bryarly.* Edited with an introduction by David Morris Porter. New Haven: Yale University Press, 1945.

GIBSON, J. W. (WATT). *Recollections of a Pioneer*. Reprinted by Practical Personal Planning, Inc. Originally printed by Nelson-Hanne Co., St. Joseph, Mo., 1912.

GOPLEN, ARNOLD O. "The Career of the Marquis de Mores in the Bad Lands of North Dakota." *North Dakota History*. Vol. 13, No.'s 1 and 2. January–April, 1946.

GRAHAM, WILLIAM ALEXANDER. *The Custer Myth: A Source Book of Custeriana*. Harrisburg, Penn.: The Stackpole Company, 1953.

GREGG, JOSIAH. *Commerce of the Prairies*. Edited by Max L. Moorhead. Norman, Okla.: University of Oklahoma Press, 1954.

_____. *Diary and Letters*. Norman, Okla.: University of Oklahoma Press, 1941.

GREGG, KATE L. *The Road to Santa Fé*. Albuquerque, N.M.: University of New Mexico Press, 1952.

GREELEY, HORACE. *An Overland Journey from New York to San Francisco in the Summer of 1859*. Edited, and with notes and introduction by Charles T. Duncan. New York: Alfred A. Knopf, 1964.

GRESSLEY, GENE M. *Bankers and Cattlemen*. Lincoln, Nᴇʙ.. University of Nebraska Press, 1966.

GRINNELL, GEORGE BIRD. *The Fighting Cheyennes*. Norman, Okla.: University of Oklahoma Press, 1956.

GROUARD, FRANK. *Life and Adventures of Frank Grouard*. Edited by Joe DeBarthe. Norman, Okla.: University of Oklahoma Press, 1958.

HAFEN, LEROY R. *The Overland Mail: 1849–1869: Promoter of Settlement, Precursor of Railroads*. Glendale, Calif.: Arthur H. Clark Company, 1926.

_____, editor. *Pike's Peak Gold Rush Guidebooks of 1859*. Glendale, Calif.: Arthur H. Clark Company, 1941.

_____ and HAFEN, ANN W. *Handcarts to Zion, the Story of a Unique Western Migration: 1856–1860*. Glendale, Calif.: Arthur H. Clark Company, 1960.

_____ and HAFEN, ANN W. *Powder River Campaigns and Sawyer's Expedition of 1865*. Glendale, Calif.: Arthur H. Clark Company, 1961.

_____ and HAFEN, ANN W., editors. *Relations with the Indians of the Plains, 1857–1861: A Documentary Account of the Military Campaigns and Negotiations of Indian Agents*. Glendale, Calif.: Arthur H. Clark Company, 1959.

HALEY, J. EVETS. *The XIT Ranch of Texas and the Early Days of the Llano Estacado*. Norman, Okla.: University of Oklahoma Press, 1953.

HALLENBECK, CLEVE. *Álvar Núñez Cabeza de Vaca: The Journey and Route of the First Europeans to Cross the Continent of North America: 1534–1536*. Glendale, Calif.: Arthur H. Clark Company, 1939.

HAMMOND, GEORGE P. "Don Juan de Oñate and the Founding of New Mexico." Historical Society of New Mexico. *Publications in History,* Vol. II, October 1927, pp. 1–228.

_____ and REY, AGAPITO. "The Rodríguez Expedition to New Mexico, 1581–1582. This contains the *Relación* of Hernán Gallegos. *The New Mexico Historical Review*, Vol. II, No. 3, July 1927, pp. 239–268; and No. 4, October 1927, pp. 334–362.

HANNON, JESSIE GOULD. *The Boston-Newton Company Venture: From Massachusetts to California in 1849*. Lincoln, Neb.: University of Nebraska Press, 1969.

HANSON, CHARLES E., JR. "James Bordeaux." *The Museum of the Fur Trade Quarterly,* Vol. 2, No. 1. Spring 1966.

HASTINGS, LANSFORD W. *The Emigrants' Guide to Oregon and California.* New York: Da Capo Press, 1969.

HENRY, ALEXANDER and THOMPSON, DAVID. *The Manuscript Journals of Alexander Henry and David Thompson.* Edited by Elliott Coues. 3 vols. New York: Francis P. Harper, 1897.

HOFSTADTER, RICHARD, editor. *Great Issues in American History.* 2 vols. New York: Vintage Books, Inc., 1958.

HOLLON, W. EUGENE. *Beyond the Cross Timbers: The Travels of Randolph B. Marcy.* Norman, Okla.: University of Oklahoma Press, 1955.

_____. *Frontier Violence: Another Look.* New York: Oxford University Press, 1974.

_____. *The Lost Pathfinder: Zebulon Montgomery Pike.* Norman, Okla.: University of Oklahoma Press, 1949.

_____. *The Southwest: Old and New.* New York: Alfred A. Knopf, 1967.

HOWARD, ROBERT WEST. *The Great Iron Trail: The Story of the First Trans-Continental Railroad.* New York: Bonanza Books, 1962.

HYDE, GEORGE E. *Spotted Tail's Folk: A History of the Brulé Sioux.* Norman, Okla.: University of Oklahoma Press, 1961.

INMAN, HENRY. *The Old Santa Fé Trail; the Story of a Great Highway.* Minneapolis, Minn.: Ross & Haines, 1966.

INNIS, HAROLD A. *The Fur Trade in Canada.* With a foreword by Robin W. Winks. New Haven: Yale University Press, 1962.

IRVING, WASHINGTON. *Astoria or Anecdotes of an Enterprise Beyond the Rocky Mountains.* New York: John W. Lovell Company, no date.

_____ *Bonneville.* New York: Thomas Y. Crowell, no date.

JACKSON, CHARLES TENNEY. *The Buffalo Wallow: A Prairie Boyhood.* Indianapolis: Bobbs-Merrill, 1953.

JACKSON, DONALD. *Custer's Gold: The United States Cavalry Expedition of 1874.* New Haven: Yale University Press, 1966.

JACKSON, W. TURRENTINE. *Wagon Roads West: A Study of Federal Road Surveys and Construction in the Trans-Mississippi West, 1846–1869.* With a foreword by William H. Goetzmann. New Haven: Yale University Press, 1952.

JAMES, EDWIN. *Account of an Expedition from Pittsburgh to the Rocky Mountains.* Ann Arbor, Mich.: University Microfilms, 1966.

JAMES, THOMAS. *Three Years Among the Indians and Mexicans.* Edited, with an introduction by Milo Milton Quaife. New York: Citadel Press, 1966.

JOHNSON, OVERTON and WINTER, WILLIAM H. *Route Across the Rocky Mountains.* Ann Arbor, Mich.: University Microfilms, 1966.

JONES, NARD. *The Great Command: The Story of Marcus and Narcissa Whitman and the Oregon Country Pioneers.* Boston: Little, Brown and Company, 1959.

JORDON, PHILIP D. *Frontier Law and Order.* Lincoln, Neb.: University of Nebraska Press, 1970.

JOSEPHY, ALVIN M., JR. *The Patriot Chiefs*. New York: Viking Press, 1961.

JOUTEL, HENRI. *Joutel's Journal of La Salle's Last Voyage*. A facsimile of the 1714 edition. New York: Burt Franklin, no date.

KEIM, DEB. RANDOLPH. *Sheridan's Troopers on the Borders: A Winter Campaign on the Plains*. New York: George Routledge and Sons, 1885.

KELLY, FANNY. *Narrative of My Captivity Among the Sioux Indians*. Chicago: R. R. Donnelly & Sons, 1891.

KELSEY, HENRY. *The Kelsey Papers*. With an introduction by Arthur G. Doughty and Chester Martin. Ottawa: The Public Archives of Canada and The Public Record Office of Northern Ireland, 1929.

KENDALL, GEORGE W. *Across the Great Southwestern Prairies*. 2 vols. Ann Arbor, Mich.: University Microfilms, 1966.

KING, CHARLES. *Campaigning with Crook*. New York: Harper & Brothers, 1890.

KOCH, ADRIENNE. *Jefferson and Madison: The Great Collaboration*. New York: Oxford University Press, 1964.

LAMAR, HOWARD ROBERTS. *Dakota Territory, 1861–1889: A Study of Frontier Politics*. New Haven: Yale University Press, 1956.

LAVENDER, DAVID. *Bent's Fort*. Garden City, N.Y.: Doubleday & Company, 1954.

LECKIE, WILLIAM H. *The Military Conquest of the Southern Plains*. Norman, Okla.: University of Oklahoma Press, 1963.

LEONARD, ZENAS. *Narrative of the Adventures of Zenas Leonard*. Ann Arbor, Mich.: University Microfilms, 1966.

LEWIS, MERIWETHER and CLARK, WILLIAM. *History of the Expedition under the Command of Lewis and Clark*. Edited by Elliott Coues. 4 vols. New York: Francis P. Harper, 1893.

_____. *The Journals of Lewis and Clark*. Edited by Bernard De Voto. Boston: Houghton Mifflin Company, 1953.

_____. *The Original Journals of Lewis and Clark*. Edited by Reuben Gold Thwaites. New York: Dodd, Mead & Company, 1904–1905.

LEWIS, OSCAR. *The Big Four: The Story of Huntington, Stanford, Hopkins, and Crocker, and the Building of the Central Pacific*. New York: Alfred A. Knopf, 1966.

LOOMIS, NOEL M. *The Texan-Santa Fe Pioneers*. Norman, Okla.: University of Oklahoma Press, 1958.

_____ and Nasatir, Abraham. *Pedro Vial and the Roads to Santa Fé*. Norman, Okla.: University of Oklahoma Press, 1967.

LOWE, PERCIVAL G. *Five Years a Dragoon ('49 to '54) and Other Adventures on the Great Plains*. With an introduction and notes by Don Russell. Norman, Okla.: University of Oklahoma Press, 1965.

LOWIE, ROBERT H. *Indians of the Plains*. New York: McGraw-Hill Book Company, 1954.

MACKENZIE, ALEXANDER. *The Journals and Letters of Sir Alexander Mackenzie*. Edited by W. Kaye Lamb. Cambridge, England: Hakluyt Society, 1970.

_____. *Alexander Mackenzie's Voyage to the Pacific Ocean in 1793*. Historical introduction and footnotes by Milo Milton Quaife. New York: Citadel Press, 1967.

McCoy, Joseph G. *Historic Sketches of the Cattle Trade of the West and Southwest*. Ann Arbor, Mich.: University Microfilms, 1966.

McCracken, Harold. *George Catlin and the Old Frontier*. New York: Bonanza Books, no date.

Maguire, H. N. *New Map and Guide to Dakota and the Black Hills*. Chicago: Rand, McNally & Co., no date.

Majors, Alexander. *Seventy Years on the Frontier: Alexander Majors' Memoirs of a Lifetime on the Border*. With a preface by "Buffalo Bill" (General W. F. Cody). Denver. Colo.: The Western Miner and Financier Publishers, 1893.

Manley, William Lewis. *Death Valley in '49*. With a foreword by John Stephen McGroarty. New York: Wallace Hebberd, 1929.

Marcy, Randolph B. *Thirty Years of Army Life on the Border*. With an introduction by Edward W. Wallace. Philadelphia: J. B. Lippincott Company, 1963.

Margry, Pierre, editor. *Découvertes et Etablissements des Français dans l'Ouest et dans le Sud de l'Amérique Septentriole: 1614–1754*. 5 vols. Paris. D. Jouast, 1879–1888.

Masson, L. R. *Les Bourgeois de la Compagnie du Nord-Ouest*. 2 vols. Quebec. L'Imprimerie Générale A. Coté et Cie. 1889.

Mattison, Ray H. "Life at Roosevelt's Elkhorn Ranch: The Letters of William W. and Mary Sewall." *North Dakota Historical Society Quarterly*, Vol. 27, Nos. 3 and 4, 1960.

————. *Roosevelt's Dakota Ranches*. Bismarck, N.D.: Bismarck *Tribune*, no date.

————. "Roosevelt's Elkhorn Ranch." *North Dakota Historical Society Quarterly*, Vol. 27, No. 2, Spring 1960.

Maximilian, Prince of Wied. *Travels in the Interior of North America*. Translated by H. Evans Lloyd. London: Ackermann and Co., 1843.

Meeker, Ezra. *The Ox Team or the Old Oregon Trail*. Omaha, Neb.: published by the author, 1906.

Meriwether, David. *My Life in the Mountains and on the Plains: The Newly Discovery Autobiography*. Edited and with an introduction by Robert A. Griffen. Norman, Okla.: University of Oklahoma Press, 1965.

Miles, Nelson A. *Personal Recollections*. Introduction by Robert M. Utley. New York: Da Capo Press, 1969.

Miller, Alfred Jacob. *The West of Alfred Jacob Miller (1837) from the Notes and Water Colors in the Walters Art Gallery*. With an account of the artist by Marvin C. Ross. Norman, Okla.: University of Oklahoma Press, 1951.

Miller, David Humphreys. *Ghost Dance*. New York: Duell, Sloan and Pearce, 1959.

Miller, Nyle H. and Snell, Joseph W. *Great Gunfighters of the Kansas Cowtowns: 1867–1886*. Lincoln, Neb.: University of Nebraska Press, 1971.

Morgan, Dale L., editor. *The West of William Ashley*. Denver, Colo.: The Old West Publishing Company, 1964.

Mothershead, Harmon Ross. *The Swan Land and Cattle Company, Ltd*. Norman, Okla.: University of Oklahoma Press, 1971.

Nadeau, Remi. *Fort Laramie and the Sioux Indians*. Englewood Cliffs, N.J.: Prentice-Hall, 1967.

NASATIR, ABRAHAM P., editor. *Before Lewis and Clark: Documents Illustrating the History of the Missouri: 1785–1804.* 2 vols. St. Louis, Mo.: St. Louis Historical Documents Foundation, 1952.

_____. "The Formation of the Missouri Company." *The Missouri Historical Review,* Vol. XXV, No. 1, October 1930, pp. 3–15.

NEVINS, ALLAN. *Frémont: Pathfinder of the West.* New York: Longman's, Green and Co., 1955.

NIZA, MARCOS DE. "Discovery of the Seven Cities of Cibola." Translated by Percy M. Baldwin. Historical Society of New Mexico. *Publications in History.* Vol. 1. November, 1926.

NUNEZ CABEZA DE VACA, ALVAR. *Relation of Núñez Cabaza de Vaca.* Translated by Buckingham Smith. Ann Arbor, Mich.: University Microfilms, Inc., 1966.

OGLESBY, RICHARD EDWARD. *Manuel Lisa and the Opening of the Missouri Fur Trade.* Norman, Okla.: University of Oklahoma Press, 1963.

PARKER, SAMUEL. *Journal of an Exploring Tour Beyond the Rocky Mountains.* Auburn, N.Y.: J. C. Derby & Co., 1846.

PARKMAN, FRANCIS. *A Half Century of Conflict.* Boston: Little, Brown, and Company, 1902.

_____. *La Salle and the Discovery of the Great West.* Boston: Little, Brown, and Company, 1902.

_____. *Pioneers of France in the New World.* 2 vols. Boston: Little, Brown, and Company, 1902.

PATTIE, JAMES OHIO. *The Personal Narrative of James O. Pattie of Kentucky.* Ann Arbor, Mich.: University Microfilms, 1966.

PENNELL, FRANCIS W. "Travels and Scientific Collections of Thomas Nuttall." *Bartonia: Proceedings of the Philadelphia Botanical Club.* Philadelphia, Penna. No. 18. 1936.

PIKE, ZEBULON MONTGOMERY. *The Journals of Zebulon Montgomery Pike With Letters and Related Documents.* Edited and annotated by Donald Jackson. 2 vols. Norman, Okla.: University of Oklahoma Press, 1966.

_____. *The Expeditions of Zebulon Montgomery Pike.* Edited by Elliott Lones. New York, F. P. Hayes, 1895.

POTOMAC CORRAL OF THE WESTERNERS, MEMBERS OF. *Great Western Indian Fights.* Lincoln, Neb.: University of Nebraska Press, 1960.

POWELL, FRED WILBUR, editor. *Hall J. Kelley on Oregon.* Princeton, N.J.: Princeton University Press, 1932.

RICHARDSON, JAMES D., editor. *A Compilation of the Messages and Papers of the Presidents: 1789–1897.* 2 vols. Washington, D.C.: published by Authority of Congress, 1899.

RIEGEL, ROBERT EDGAR. *The Story of the Western Railroads.* Lincoln, Neb.: University of Nebraska Press, 1964.

RIGGS, STEPHEN R. *Mary and I: Forty Years with the Sioux.* Minneapolis, Minn.: Ross & Haines, 1969.

ROBBINS, ROY M. *Our Landed Heritage: The Public Domain: 1776–1936.* Lincoln, Neb.: University of Nebraska Press, 1962.

ROBINSON, DOANE. *A History of the Dakota or Sioux Indians.* Minneapolis, Minn.: Ross & Haines, 1967.

ROHRBOUGH, MALCOLM. *The Land Office Business: The Settlement and Administration of the American Public Lands, 1789–1837*. New York: Oxford University Press, 1968.

ROOSEVELT, THEODORE. *Ranch Life and the Hunting Trail*. New York: Winchester Press, 1969.

ROSS, ALEXANDER. *Adventurers of the First Settlers on the Columbia River*. Ann Arbor, Mich.: University Microfilms, 1966.

SANDOZ, MARI. *Crazy Horse: The Strange Man of the Oglalas*. Lincoln, Neb.: University of Nebraska Press, 1942.

――――. *Old Jules*. Boston: Little, Brown, and Company, 1935.

SETTLE, RAYMOND W. and SETTLE, MARY LUND. *Saddles and Spurs: The Pony Express Saga*. New York: Bonanza Books, 1955.

SHAW, REUBEN COLE. *Across the Plains in '49*. Edited, with an introduction by Milo Milton Quaife. New York: Citadel Press, 1966.

SHINN, CHARLES HOWARD. *Mining Camps: A Study in American Frontier Government*. New York: Harper & Row, 1965.

SHIRLEY, GLENN. *Law West of Fort Smith: A History of Frontier Justice in the Indian Territory, 1834–1896*. Lincoln, Neb.: University of Nebraska Press, 1968.

SMITH, HELENA HUNTINGTON. *The War on Powder River*. New York: McGraw-Hill Book Company, 1966.

SPENCER, ELMA DILL RUSSELL. *Green Russell and Gold*. Austin, Tex.: University of Texas, 1966.

SPICER, EDWARD H. *Cycles of Conquest*. Tucson, Ariz.: University of Arizona Press, 1962.

STANLEY, HENRY W. *My Early Adventures and Travels*. 2 vols. New York: Charles Scribner's Sons, 1895.

STANSBURY, HOWARD. *An Expedition to the Valley of the Great Salt Lake*. Ann Arbor, Mich.: University Microfilms, 1966.

STEVENSON, ROBERT LOUIS. *Across the Plains*. New York: Charles Scribner's Sons, 1918.

STOVER, JOHN F. *The Life and Decline of the American Railroad*. New York: Oxford University Press, 1970.

STREETER, FLOYD B. *Prairie Trails and Cow Towns*. New York: Devin-Adair Company, 1963.

SUNDER, JOHN E. *Joshua Pilcher: Fur Trader and Indian Agent*. Norman, Okla.: University of Oklahoma Press, 1968.

TERRELL, JOHN UPTON. *Furs by Astor*. New York: William Morrow & Company, 1963.

THOMPSON, DAVID. *David Thompson's Narrative*. Edited and with an introduction by Richard Glover. Toronto: The Champlain Society, 1962.

THWAITES, REUBEN GOLD. *Travels and Explorations of the Jesuit Missionaries in New France*. 73 vols. Cleveland: The Burrows Brothers Company, 1901.

TONTY, HENRY DE. *Relation of Henri de Tonty Concerning the Explorations of LaSalle from 1678 to 1683*. The original text and a translation by Melville B. Anderson. Chicago: The Caxton Club, 1898.

TOWNSEND, JOHN KIRK. *Narratives of a Journey Across the Rocky Mountains to the Columbia River.* Fairfield, Wash.: Ye Galleon Press, 1970.

TURNER, FREDERICK JACKSON. "The Significance of the Frontier in American History." Ann Arbor, Mich.: University Microfilms, 1966.

TWAIN, MARK. *Roughing It.* 2 vols. New York: P. F. Collier & Son Company, 1913.

U.S. NATIONAL PARK SERVICE. *Lewis and Clark: Historic Places Associated with their Transcontinental Expedition (1804–1806).* Prepared by Roy E. Appleman. Washington, D.C.: U.S. Government Printing Office, 1975.

UTLEY, ROBERT M. *Custer Battlefield National Monument, Montana.* Washington, D.C.: National Park Service, 1969.

_____. *The Last Days of the Sioux Nation.* New Haven: Yale University Press, 1965.

VESTAL, STANLEY. *The Old Santa Fe Trail.* Boston: Houghton Mifflin Company, 1939.

WADE, F. C. "The Surrender of Sitting Bull." *The Canadian Magazine,* Toronto, Vol. XXIV, No. 4, February 1905.

WARE, EUGENE F. *The Indian War of 1864.* New York: St. Martin's Press, 1960.

WELSCH, ROGER L. "The Nebraska Soddy." *Nebraska History,* Vol. 48, No. 4, Winter 1967.

WHITE G. EDWARD. *The Eastern Establishment and the Western Experience: The West of Frederic Remington, Theodore Roosevelt, and Owen Wister.* New Haven: Yale University Press, 1968.

WHITMAN, NARCISSA. *Journal* and letter dated October 24, 1836. Typewritten transcript. Bienecke Library, Yale University.

WILSON, ELINOR. *Jim Beckwourth: Black Mountain Man and War Chief of the Crows.* Norman, Okla.: University of Oklahoma Press, 1972.

WINSHIP, GEORGE PARKER. *The Coronado Expedition: 1540–1542.* This volume also contains the Spanish texts and translation of Casteñeda's account and the *Relación Postrera de Sivola* and translations of letters from Mendoza to the king and Coronado to Mendoza and the king, the *Traslado de las Nuevas, the Relación del Suceso,* the narrative of Jaramillo, the report of Alvarado, and testimony concerning those who went on the expedition. Chicago: Rio Grande Press, 1964.

WISSLER, CLARK. *Indians of the United States.* Garden City, N.Y.: Doubleday & Co., 1968.

WISTER, OWEN. *The Virginian.* New York: Grosset & Dunlap, 1904.

WYETH, JOHN B. *Oregon; or a Short History of a Long Journey.* Fairfield, Wash.: Ye Galleon Press, 1970.

WYETH, NATHANIEL J. *The Journals of Captain Nathaniel J. Wyeth with the Wyeth Monograph on the Pacific Northwest Indians Appended.* Fairfield, Wash.: Ye Galleon Press, 1969.

YOUNG, OTIS E. *The First Military Escort on the Santa Fé Trail.* Glendale, Calif.: Arthur H. Clark Company, 1952.

YOUNG, OTIS E., JR. *Western Mining.* With the technical assistance of Robert Lenon. Norman, Okla.: University of Oklahoma Press, 1970.

Index

Index

Page numbers in italics refer to the Chronology.

Battles, fights, and skirmishes, when identifiable by a name, will be found under BATTLES.

All specific Indian tribes, such as Crows and Cheyennes, will be found under INDIAN TRIBES.

Mammals, such as buffaloes and oxen, will be found under MAMMALS.

Other major headings under which subsidiary topics are listed are: AGRICULTURE, FORTS, GREAT PLAINS, INDIANS, PUBLIC DOMAIN, RAILROADS, TREATIES, and UNITED STATES DIPLOMACY.

Babcock, A. C., 395–96
Bad Lands Cow Boy (Medora, North Dakota), 397–98
Badlands: *See* South Dakota and North Dakota Badlands.
Bad River, 106
Bailey, Godard, 320–21
Baird, James, 163, 179
Barbed wire, *26, 28,* 370–71, 399
Barron, James, 140
Bartleson, John, 244, 245
BATTLES: Not all fights with the Indians were dignified by the word "battle." Those fights or skirmishes not listed here may be found under the site or the participants.
  Adobe Walls, *26,* 365
  Alamo, 238
  Bleecher's Island, *26,* 353–54
  Blue Creek, *24,* 292–93
  Hayfield, *25,* 343–44
  Lake Champlain, 168
  Little Bighorn, *27,* 376–80
  Massacre Canyon, 363, 385
  Palo Duro Canyon, *27,* 366
  Pierre's Hole, *20,* 213–14
  Rosebud, *27,* 375–76
  San Jacinto, 238
  Sand Creek, *25, 331*
  Slim Buttes, *27,* 382
  Solomons Fork of the Arkansas, 300
  Valverde, 324
  Wagon Box, *25,* 344
  Washita, 354,55
  Wounded Knee, *28,* 406–7
Baylor, John B., 324
Beans: *See* AGRICULTURE, Early farming.
Bear, the, 185
Beaverhead Mountains, 123
Becknell, William, *18,* 182–83
Beecher, Frederick H., 353
Bell, John R., 174–75
Bella Coola River, 89
Belle Fontaine, Missouri, 125
Bellevue, Nebraska, 234
Bennet, James Gordon, 359, 396
Benoit, Francis Marie, 99
Bent, Charles, *20,* 208, 209, 210, 220–21, 335
Bent, George, 335
Bent, St. Vrain and Company, 221, 251, 255
Bent, William, *20,* 208, 209, 220–21, 315, 365
Benteen, Frederick E., 377, 378
Benton, Thomas Hart, *19,* 203, 250, 251, 254, 259; report on forts and Santa Fé trade, 193–94, 201, 227
Bent's Old and New Forts: See FORTS.
Berger, Jacob, *19,* 216, 224

Berthold, B. and Berthold & Chouteau, 169, 178, 183
Bidwell, John, and Bidwell-Bartleson Party, *21,* 244–45
Bienville, Jean le Moyne, Sieur de, 71
Big Belt Mountains, 123
Big Blackfoot River, 129
Big Blue River, 271
Big Foot, *28,* 406
Big Piney Creek, 340
Big Star, 180, 181
Bighorn Mountains, 80, 280, 339, 340
Bighorn River, *17,* 93, 128, 142, 178
Bigotes, 48, 49, 50
Bijou, Louis, 163, 164
Biloxi, Mississippi, 71
Bismarck, North Dakota, 76
Bissonet, Antoine, 141, 144–45
Bitterroot Mountains and River, 123, 127, 129
Black Buffalo, 106
Black Hawk, Colorado, 310
Black Hills: 363, 388–89; negotiations for purchase, 372–73
Black Hills gold rush, *27,* 363, 371–372, 373, 382–83
Black Kettle, 330–31, 335, 354, 355
Black Snake Hills, 223
Blackfoot River, 127
Bluewater Creek: *See* Blue Creek, Battle of.
Bodmer, Charles, *20,* 222–23, 225–26
Bonilla, Leyva de, expedition of, 59
Bonneville, Benjamin Louis Eulalie de, 218–20
Boone's Lick, Missouri, 182, 203
Bordeaux, James, 285–88
Bouché, 141, 142, 143
Boulder, Colorado, 314
BOUNDARY DISPUTES:
  with Great Britain:
    northern Great Plains, 170
    Maine, 254
    Oregon, *18,* 170, 201, 254, 262
  with Mexico: *See also* Texas, Republic of. *22,* 264
  with Spain: 126, 139, 171
Bourgmont, Etienne Veniard de, *13,* 73–74
Bowles, Samuel, 336–37
Bows and arrows: *See* INDIANS, GENERAL.
Bozeman, John, and Bozeman Trail, *25, 26,* 339–41, 343–44, 345, 352
Bozeman, Montana, 374
Brackenridge, Henry Marie, 155, 156, 157, 158, 159
Bradbury, John, 154, 157, 158, 159
Bradley, James H., 379
Brands, 346
Brannan, Samuel, 269
Brave Bear, 281, 286, 287
Bridger, Jim, *20,* 192, 235, 252, 324
Buchanan, James, 301, 302, 323